A NOTE FROM THE AUTHOR

Congratulations on your decision to take the AP U.S. History exam! Whether or not you're completing a yearlong AP U.S. History course, this book can help you prepare for the exam. No matter how deep your understanding of history is, it will take more than knowledge to earn a high score on this exam. Students who perform well on the AP exam not only possess a solid understanding of the chronology and events of history, but also effectively apply and analyze the content knowledge through the various tasks on the exam itself.

In addition to offering a chronological content review of the most tested, up-to-date material on the AP exam, this review guide also features tips on how best to process the events, eras, and scope of U.S. history. You will learn how to dissect multiple-choice questions and quickly eliminate distractors to find the best answers. You will find different methods on how to process and outline information in your readings to write detailed and effective Document-Based Question and Free-Response Question essays. Finally, Kaplan has drafted a sample study schedule to keep you on track, whether you bought this guide in September—or two weeks before the exam!

Over 300 practice multiple-choice questions and over 20 sample essay questions give you the opportunity to see where your strengths and weaknesses lie and to practice the test-taking skills you learn in early chapters.

Good luck using this guide on your adventure in study and review!

Krista Dornbush

RELATED TITLES

AP Biology

AP Calculus AB & BC

AP Chemistry

AP English Language & Composition

AP English Literature & Composition

AP Environmental Science

AP European History

AP Human Geography

AP Macroeconomics/Microeconomics

AP Physics B & C

AP Psychology

AP Statistics

AP U.S. Government & Politics

AP World History

ACT Strategies, Practice & Review

ACT Premier

8 Practice Tests for the ACT

ACT English, Reading & Writing Prep

ACT Math & Science Prep

SAT Strategies, Practice & Review

SAT Premier

SAT Total Prep

8 Practice Tests for the SAT

Evidence-Based Reading, Writing, and Essay Workbook for the SAT

Math Workbook for the SAT

SAT Subject Test: Biology E/M

SAT Subject Test: Chemistry

SAT Subject Test: Literature

SAT Subject Test: Mathematics Level 1

SAT Subject Test: Mathematics Level 2

SAT Subject Test: Physics

SAT Subject Test: U.S. History

SAT Subject Test: World History

AP® U.S. HISTORY

2017–2018

Krista Dornbush

KAPLAN

PUBLISHING

New York

This publication is designed to provide accurate and authoritative information in regard to the subject matter covered. It is sold with the understanding that the publisher is not engaged in rendering legal, accounting, or other professional service. If legal advice or other expert assistance is required, the services of a competent professional should be sought.

© 2017 by Kaplan, Inc.

Published by Kaplan Publishing, a division of Kaplan, Inc.
750 Third Avenue
New York, NY 10017

Printed in the United States of America

10 9 8 7 6 5 4 3 2 1

ISBN 13: 978-1-5062-2468-8

TABLE OF CONTENTS

PART ONE: THE BASICS

PART TWO: DIAGNOSTIC TEST

PART THREE: AP U.S. HISTORY REVIEW

UNIT 1: 1491–1607

UNIT 2: 1607–1754

PART FOUR: PRACTICE TESTS

ABOUT THE AUTHORS

Krista Dornbush teaches AP U.S. History at Marina High School in Huntington Beach, California. Ms. Dornbush has been teaching AP U.S. History since 1995. She serves as a College Board consultant and national leader for AP U.S. History and Pre-AP® workshops. She has also worked as a Faculty Consultant and Table Leader for the Educational Testing Service reading of the AP U.S. History exam since 1998. In addition to authoring this book, Ms. Dornbush has penned a workshop for teachers offered by the College Board in regard to reading in the social studies.

Paul Faeh has taught at Hinsdale South High School in Darien, IL, since 2007, where he teaches AP U.S. History and AP European History. He has been a reader, table reader, and/or exam leader for the AP U.S. History exam since 2001, and also serves as a consultant for the College Board.

Clint Whitfield taught AP United States History at Mosley High School in Lynn Haven, Florida for 6 years. He is currently an administrator and History Fair Coordinator for Bay District Schools. He has been an AP U.S. History exam reader for 3 years. He is the author of two published articles in Journal of the West, "Nelson A. Miles: The Man Who Ended the Plains Indian Wars" and "Red Cloud: Last Defender of the Sioux."

Amy Graiser is an alumna of Brown University, where she graduated in 2005 with a MAT in Social Studies/History and is a 2004 alumna of the University of Georgia with an A.B. in Political Science. She has a wealth of experience serving as a College Board reader for AP U.S. History and as an educator teaching AP U.S. History and AP U.S. Government. Ms. Graiser currently teaches Social Studies for Fulton County Schools in Atlanta, Georgia.

Carl Schulkin taught AP U.S. History and Holocaust Studies at The Pembroke Hill School from 1974 until his retirement in 2009. He served as an AP Reader for U.S. History for ten years between 1990 and 2006. He has been an AP consultant for U.S. History since 1991 and co-leader of the AP Summer Institute in U.S. History at the College of Wooster since 2007.

Susan Pingel initiated the AP U.S. History program at Skaneateles High School in Skaneateles, NY in 1985, where she has taught since 1979. Since 1988, she has served as a AP U.S. History reader, table leader, and College Board AP U.S. History and Pre- AP consultant for workshops and summer institutes.

John Struck has taught AP U.S. History for 28 years, the last 20 at the Thomas Jefferson High School for Science and Technology in Fairfax County, VA. He has been a reader for the APUSH exam since 1999.

William Baird Hudgins Jr. is a career educator at The Pine School in Hobe Sound, Florida with over forty years of experience teaching history, government and economics. He earned his doctorate from The University of Georgia and is an A.P. U.S. History Reader as well as a published author.

KAPLAN PANEL OF AP EXPERTS

Congratulations—you have chosen Kaplan to help you get a top score on your AP exam.

Kaplan understands your goals and what you're up against—achieving college credit and conquering a tough test—while participating in everything else that high school has to offer.

You expect realistic practice, authoritative advice, and accurate, up-to-the-minute information on the test. And that's exactly what you'll find in this book, as well as every other in the AP series. To help you (and us!) reach these goals, we have sought out leaders in the AP community. Allow us to introduce our experts.

AP U.S. HISTORY EXPERTS

Gwen Cash is a Lead Consultant for the College Board and has served on the AP Advisory Council and the conference planning committee in the Southwest region. She also helped to write the AP Social Studies Vertical Teams guide. Ms. Cash holds a BA and an MD from The University of Texas at Austin, and she teaches on-level and AP U.S. History courses at Clear Creek High School in League City, Texas.

Anthony "Tony" Jones has taught AP courses for the past 11 years, including AP U.S. History, AP European History, and AP World History. He has taught at Houston County High in Warner Robins, Georgia, and Rutland High School in Macon, Georgia. He is a member of the World History Association and the National Council for Social Studies. He is a Table Leader and Reader for the AP World History exam. Additionally, he has been a presenter on integrating technology into the social studies and AP classroom at several conferences.

Steven Mercado has taught AP U.S. History and AP European History at Chaffey High School in Ontario, California, for the past 13 years. He has also served as a Reader for the AP U.S. History exam and as a Reader and Table Leader for the AP European History exam.

Part One

THE BASICS

CHAPTER 1: INSIDE THE AP U.S. HISTORY EXAM

INTRODUCTION

Congratulations on your decision to take the Advanced Placement exam in United States history! The test is a big one—its content measures your knowledge of U.S. history from pre-Columbian societies to the present. After taking a college-level class, you will certainly have a large base of historical knowledge heading into the exam. However, the AP exam asks you to take what you've learned one step further and apply that knowledge in complex and analytic situations to show evidence of college-level learning.

This guide offers not only a full review of U.S. history but, more importantly, specific skills and strategies successful students use to score higher on the AP exam. In the following chapters, you will encounter reading strategies for your day-to-day assignments, writing strategies for the Document-Based, Short-Answer, and Long Essay Questions (DBQs, SAQs, and LEQs), and analytical skills for both documents and multiple-choice questions. Rote memorization of facts, dates, and events alone does not ensure success. While a solid foundation of historical knowledge is critical to your learning, application of that knowledge earns top scores. Keep the skills and strategies you learn in this guide in mind as you take the Diagnostic Test in Part Two to assess where you stand before tackling the course reviews.

The course reviews are the meat of this guide. These units and chapters are arranged chronologically to correlate with your classroom textbook and the College Board's course description guide for the new AP exam. We have made sure to give you a solid review of the most-tested vocabulary, people, places, and concepts on the AP test. Each part contains review questions and detailed explanations of test items to help you determine whether you need further study of an era of history or if you can move on to the next one.

Finally, Part Three offers four full-length practice tests that closely mirror the actual AP exam, with test-like DBQs and FRQs and detailed answer explanations.

Are you ready for your adventure through the study and mastery of everything AP U.S. History? Good luck!

OVERVIEW OF THE TEST STRUCTURE

The AP Test Development Committee designs the AP U.S. History exam yearly as an opportunity for you to demonstrate mastery of skills typically found in introductory college U.S. History classes.

The exam, divided into two sections, is three hours and fifteen minutes long. Section I is 1 hour and 45 minutes long and consists of 55 multiple-choice questions and four short-answer questions. Section II is 1 hour and 30 minutes long and consists of one document-based question (DBQ) and one long essay question (LEQ).

Section	Number of Questions	Time
I	Part A: 55 Multiple-choice questions – 40%	55 minutes
	Part B: 4 Short-answer questions – 20%	50 minutes
II	Part A: Document-based question – 25%	55 minutes
	Part B: Long essay question – 15%	35 minutes
	Total:	3 hours and 15 minutes

Section I, Part A: Multiple-Choice Questions

The 55 multiple-choice questions will be divided into sets of two to five questions based on a primary or secondary source, historian's argument, or historical problem. These questions assess your ability to understand and interpret the stimulus material as well as your knowledge of the historical issue being tested. Even if a set of questions is based on a specific portion of U.S. history, the individual questions may require you to thematically link the stimulus to other eras.

Section I, Part B: Short-Answer Questions

These four questions, timed at 10 to 12 minutes each, will concern a theme in U.S. history. At least two of the questions will provide you with a choice so you can exhibit your strengths by having you use historical and critical thinking to react to a primary source, a historian's argument, secondary sources (e.g., data or maps), or general suggestions about U.S. history. All four of these questions will require you to pinpoint and explore examples of historical evidence related to the source or question. Because these questions are short-answer questions, you do not need to develop and support a thesis statement.

Section II, Part A: Document-Based Question

The document-based question (DBQ) allows you to demonstrate your ability to examine and integrate data and appraise verbal, quantitative, or visual evidence. Like the long essay, the DBQ is evaluated based on your ability to devise a thesis statement and back it up with applicable evidence. The documents this essay is based on can vary in length and format. Question content can contain charts, graphs, cartoons, and pictures, in addition to written materials. You are expected to be able to connect the given documents with a historical period or theme while honing in on significant periods and issues. Therefore, it is essential to demonstrate your familiarity with historical themes, rather than just the events and people important to the question's focus, to earn the highest scores.

SECTION II, PART B: LONG ESSAY QUESTION

In this section, you will have a choice of two similar long essay questions to showcase the extent of your knowledge. The long essay questions gauge your ability to use historical thinking to explicate and assess events significant in the scheme of U.S. history. This essay necessitates a central thesis or argument that you support by evaluating specific and relevant historical evidence.

BREAKDOWN OF COVERED MATERIAL

Multiple-choice questions will test your ability to think critically about various kinds of historical evidence, focusing on applying interpretive skills to historical evidence rather than factual recall. Short-answer questions ask you to connect problems or sources from different historical periods. Rather than testing your ability to develop a thesis, these questions gauge your ability to exercise historical thinking.

The DBQ and LEQ will ask you to explain change over time, to analyze cause and effect, to compare one time period to another, or to explain specific developments and changes in a category or categories. To do well on this section, you must have a good understanding of historical analysis and the broader themes of U.S. history. While these two essays remain largely unchanged from the previous version of the AP U.S. History exam, the DBQ will contain only five to seven texts taken from not only secondary but also primary sources.

HOW THE EXAM IS SCORED

All AP exams are rated on a scale of 1 to 5, with 5 being the highest:

5 Extremely well qualified

4 Well qualified

3 Qualified

2 Possibly qualified

1 No recommendation

Scores are based on the number of questions answered correctly. **There is no penalty for incorrect answers.** No points are awarded for unanswered questions. Therefore, you should answer every question, even if you need to guess.

Section I	60%
Multiple-choice questions	40%
Short-answer questions	20%
Section II	**40%**
Document-based question	25%
Long essay question	15%

REGISTRATION AND FEES

You can register for the AP U.S. History exam by contacting your guidance counselor or AP Coordinator. If your school doesn't administer the exam, contact the Advanced Placement Program for a listing of schools in your area that do. At the time of this printing, the fee for each AP exam is $93 within the United States, and $123 at schools and testing centers outside of the United States. For those qualified with acute financial need, the College Board offers a $31 credit. In addition, most states offer exam subsidies to cover all or part of the remaining cost for eligible students. To learn about other sources of financial aid, contact your AP coordinator.

For more information on all things AP, contact the Advanced Placement Program:

Phone: (888) 225-5427 or (212) 632-1780
Email: apstudents@info.collegeboard.org
Website: https://apstudent.collegeboard.org/home

WHAT TO BRING

Testing conditions vary from site to site. However, there are several key items that all students should bring on Test Day.

- Several sharpened No. 2 pencils with erasers. We suggest that you also bring along a separate eraser. White erasers work very well in erasing pencil from scan sheets.

- Several black or dark blue ballpoint ink pens. We suggest that you not use erasable ink or liquid ink pens. They can smear or run, affecting legibility.

- Your school code

- A watch that does not make noise. Some testing sites do not have clocks visible.

- Your Social Security number for identification purposes

- A photo ID

Some items are prohibited or best left at home. These are items not to bring.

- Books, correcting fluid, dictionaries, highlighters, or notes

- Scratch paper

- Computers (unless you are a student with a disability and have been approved to bring a computer)

- Watches that beep or have an alarm

- Portable listening devices, such as MP3 players, CD players, and radios

- Cameras

- Cellular phones or personal digital assistants (PDAs)

- Clothing with subject-related information

ADDITIONAL RESOURCES

The College Board website at **apcentral.collegeboard.com/apc/public/courses/index.html** is the best resource for additional information regarding AP courses, exams, and services. We suggest you visit often throughout the school year to access information regarding updates and test dates and to answer any questions you may have along the way.

CHAPTER 2: STRATEGIES FOR SUCCESS: IT'S NOT ALWAYS HOW MUCH YOU KNOW

READING STRATEGIES FOR THE AP U.S. HISTORY EXAM

Students new to AP history courses often struggle with the sheer amount of reading required to learn the material. Some instructors break the reading up into chunks of 10 to 15 pages a night, while others may assign an entire chapter in one sitting. Depending on your school schedule, the text you use, and the assignments your instructor gives, you must develop a system for completing your reading. Because this is an area of difficulty for many AP students, we will provide you with some active reading strategies that you can build into your daily schedule.

No matter whether you have 10 pages to read every other day or an entire chapter to read in a week, it is critical that you actively engage with your textbook. In AP U.S. History, it is not acceptable to read passively. By this, we mean that you must interact with your text by taking notes, asking questions, and summarizing. It is also not enough for most students to read the material once and only once. You must build time into your schedule for "rehearsal" of the material you have read—you must review your reading at a time well removed from your first read. This may be the next day, or in two days, or in a week, depending on your schedule. Remember: cramming material in the weeks before the exam will not improve your chances of scoring well. Only consistent and deliberate study of your material throughout the year will pay off.

Before we begin discussing specific strategies for daily reading, take a moment to reflect on how you read assigned material.

- ***Where* do you read?** Is it quiet? Noisy? Light? Dark? Comfortable? Do you have the necessary study aids close at hand (pencils, note paper, highlighters, dictionary)? If you read in the gym while waiting for basketball practice to start, chances are that your environment is noisy, dark, and uncomfortable and study aids will not be readily available.

This is not the best place to complete your reading for your AP class. Similarly, if you read late at night in bed, you may find yourself falling asleep before you finish the assignment, only to find yourself rushing to read right before class. We suggest that you complete your reading assignment in a quiet, comfortable, well-lit place in which you have study aids readily available.

- *When* do you read? Immediately after school? After work/practice/rehearsals? Late at night in bed? You should try to complete your reading assignment as close to the end of your school day as possible. This way, the material you discussed in class will be fresh in your mind, and you can apply it to the material in your text.

- *How* do you read? Do you take notes as you read? Do you simply recopy the text? If assigned questions to answer with the reading, do you simply search for the answers and avoid actually reading the chapter? How you read is the most critical to your comprehension and learning. Let's take a look at some ways you can build active reading strategies into your daily homework routine.

Umbrella Questions

Have you ever wondered how your instructors or test developers come up with exam questions? We'll let you in on a secret: Predicting multiple-choice or essay questions is as easy as opening your textbook. History texts are written in a very predictable formula. At the beginning of every chapter, you will find a short summary or introduction. Some authors like to "tease" you with an interesting fact or entertain you with flowery language. Other authors prefer to offer you chapter objectives or a glimpse of what will be covered in the pages that follow. In either case, the authors of your text provide you with clues to the important concepts that will be discussed within the text. Next comes the body of the chapter. Have you ever noticed that there are clever headings for each section of text? Again, the authors are providing you insight into the importance of the arguments that will follow. Finally, to wrap things into a neat package, the authors will provide you with either a chapter summary or a conclusion. Can you connect the summary or conclusion with the objectives, chapter introduction, and section headings?

If you answered yes to these questions, then you have already discovered the magic of the textbook formula. Let's look at a reading strategy that utilizes the textbook formula to assist you in comprehending your reading assignments.

THE HIGHLIGHT REEL

Highlight key phrases! Your life will be much easier when you need to go back and review text later. If you can't highlight in your textbook, try sticky notes.

Turn the objectives, headings, and conclusion into questions before you read the chapter. For example, if your textbook has a heading for a section called "The Impact of *Dred Scott*," your question initially might be "What was the impact of *Dred Scott*?" Write this question down in your notes before you read the text itself. Do the same for every other heading. Now, read each section that covers each question you have created. Is your question exactly answered by the text you have just read? For our previous example, we may read the section and decide that "What was the impact of *Dred Scott*?" is not specific enough to cover the important discussion in the section. We may decide to change our question to "What impact did the *Dred Scott* decision have on sectional tension?" depending on the text. This question can be answered with more depth and analysis than our previous question. Simply identifying what the impact is won't be enough for the AP exam, however. By connecting the *Dred Scott* case to a greater historical theme, you will begin making the associations that will score you points on the exam. While you can easily pick out the broader historical themes in your textbook by looking at chapter titles, it's the specific analysis that leads to mastery.

The next step is to answer the questions you have created for each section of text. If you have trouble answering your own questions, you may need to revise the questions or reread the section. Your last step is to predict a possible essay question that might come from each section. Then, write an overarching umbrella question that ties all your questions together to cover the entire chapter or era. Try to use academic terms to construct your question like the the AP U.S. History sample prompts you will find throughout this book. Can you answer this question by using the evidence you have collected from the answers to all of your smaller umbrella questions? Now you have a study guide for your assigned reading that contains questions for each portion of the text, answers to those questions, and a broad, overarching question similar to an AP essay question.

PERSIA CHART

On almost every AP U.S. History exam, essay prompts will require you to understand various categories historians utilize to analyze events. It is beneficial for you to practice recognizing these categories as you read your text and primary source documents. Here is a method that you can use as you read to categorize the textual information presented in assigned reading.

PERSIA is an acronym that is easy to remember and use. **P** equals Political, **E** equals Economic, **R** equals Religion, **S** equals Social, **I** equals Intellectual, and **A** equals Arts. Historians may use categories like these to analyze or break down the components of an era of U.S. history. As you complete PERSIA charts covering significant time periods, you will have tools to assist you in identifying significant connections between categories and how a certain category may dominate a particular time period. Imagine the power these PERSIA charts will have when you are ready to review for your AP exam! You will have organized the significant aspects of each major era by the very categories you must know to construct an effective essay.

Let's look at a list of key words and questions that you can use to help you complete a PERSIA chart for any era or chapter in your textbook.

P = POLITICAL

You may choose to include the following items: presidents/major leaders, judicial rulings, legislation, major movements, revolutions, rebellions, foreign policy, taxes, and tariffs.

You should be able to answer the following types of questions after you have charted this section:

- How did the U.S. government react to events during this era?
- How did leadership change in the country during this era?
- Why did the government's foreign policy stance change?

E = ECONOMIC

Taxes, tariffs, recessions, depressions, panics, inflation, currency issues, scarcity, gross national product (GNP), and gross domestic product (GDP) are a few possible terms that you can look for to identify economic issues in your reading.

Consider questions such as these:

- How did the government react to economic conditions during the time period?
- Were the economic decisions of the ruling party helpful to the country's overall economic health?
- Did foreign policy play a role in the economic decisions of the country?

R = RELIGIOUS

As you search for examples for religion, keep in mind that you must consider the influence of religion on a given time period, event, or group of people.

Use questions such as these to guide your thinking:

- How did religion play a role in the development of government/society/culture during this era?
- How did religious divisions affect the arrival of a certain event?
- Can you list major religious leaders who influenced the United States during this time?

S = SOCIAL

Here you will want to look for instances of how an event has altered the way people in a culture interact with one another. You will want to keep your eyes open for race, gender, or ethnic relationships and how they have either changed or remained the same in the face of a historical event.

Consider these questions:

- How was the social structure altered during this era?

- Did your reading reveal any social or cultural norms?

- Can you list specific examples from your reading that reveal the social aspects of the culture/country at this time in history?

I = Intellectual

In this category, you are searching for achievements in many different areas. Literature, science, technology, academia, and schools of thought are just a few of the possible items you could look for. You may also consider ideologies during a time period, such as the philosophies of the Enlightenment, to fall under the category of "Intellectual."

These questions may be of assistance:

- How did advances in technology change life for Americans during this time period?

- From what series of events did this school of thought emerge, and how did it impact American society?

- How does the literature of this time period reflect the events that surrounded its creation?

A = Arts

The last section of the list can be one of the most challenging for AP U.S. History students. Most textbooks have very little discussion of art but rather use art to illustrate specific points throughout. Often, the AP exam will ask questions regarding the impact of an artistic movement on a given period.

Questions to consider are these:

- How did this artist portray events, people, or feelings of this era?

- Why did artists feel the need to produce pieces such as the ones in this section?

- How was the art received outside of the art community?

- Was there patronage of the art? In other words, was the art commissioned by a benefactor?

As you read a chapter or section of a chapter, fill in the areas of the PERSIA list as you read. Write down information you believe is significant or important to the era you are studying. Ask yourself, "Has the author or my instructor repeated this information in the text or in class?" If so, chances are that the repeated information is important enough for you to write down.

BE C-R-E-A-T-I-V-E

Throughout the year, create acronyms or other mnemonic devices to jog your memory. For example, SADTWITS can help you remember the American Revolution:

S = Sugar Act
A = Admiralty Courts
D = Declaratory Act
T = Townshend Acts
W = Writs of Assistance
I = Intolerable Acts
T = Tea Act
S = Stamp Act

CHAIN OUTLINES

Many students learn to take notes in a traditional outline format. We need to take this standard outline format and pump some historical skills into it! Try to think like a historian. How would a historian approach the material in your text? A historian would look for patterns, links, and causation. Therefore, your outline should reflect these patterns, links, and causes. We will call this new outline our "Chain Outline." Think of the material you read in your text as a big metal chain with smaller chains attached. Sometimes the smaller chains connect, creating links between larger links within the chain. Let's use the example of the early years of the Civil Rights Movement in the 1950s as our topic for the following Chain Outline.

As you can see from our chain, we have been able to see patterns, links, and causes that show us much more than if we had simply placed these items in a traditional outline. You can take this a step further and add specific details about these events in the margins of your paper. You may even be able to predict possible exam questions by looking at the major themes that run through a section or chapter. There are only so many ways exams can ask about major historical themes!

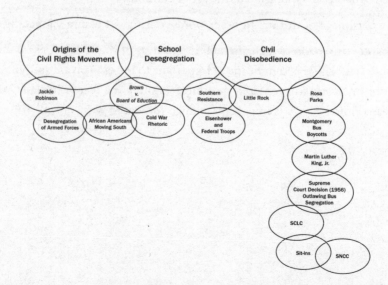

HOW TO APPROACH THE MULTIPLE-CHOICE QUESTIONS

PROCESS OF ELIMINATION

The multiple-choice questions on the AP U.S. History exam are complex, with answer choice distractors designed to keep you on your toes. It is important for you to develop a system to eliminate distractors so you can quickly arrive at the correct answer and move on.

Make yourself comfortable with the style of questions that will be presented on the AP exam by practicing with examples from this guide. Practice eliminating at least two of the four answer choices for any multiple-choice question. Two of the three distractors will be so obtuse that you should, as you broaden your history knowledge, be able to eliminate them right away. The third will be somewhat close—it may just cover the same era as the correct answer. That leaves you with two enticing possibilities to decide between. Remember, you need the best right answer, so look carefully for any clues in the two remaining answer choices. Does either contain words such as *all*, *most*, or *none*? If the answer is yes, chances are that this answer is not correct. The AP exam does not like to make grand, overarching statements. Check the time period of the question and match it up with the remaining answer choices. Can you eliminate one of your answers because it is outside the time frame of the question? At this point, even if you have no means of elimination, it is in your best interest to guess—you've narrowed your chance of getting the right answer down to 50 percent.

TIME MANAGEMENT

With any timed exam, it is in your best interest to practice taking the test under the same time restrictions. You have 55 minutes to complete all 55 questions. And remember, you may not go back to complete Section I once these 55 minutes are over, even if you have time left over in other sections of the exam. Thus, it is critical that you practice so you can develop the ability to work effectively under time constraints.

Use the sample test items in Part Three of this book to practice taking the exam under time constraints. Keep a watch with a second hand or a silent timer next to you as you answer test questions. The first time through, log in approximately how much time it took you to complete the entire test. Then figure out how much time elapsed per test item. Take careful note of the types of questions that took you more time and when during the test you felt the need to slow down. Careful analysis of your test-taking methods at an early point allows you to determine where in the actual AP exam you will encounter difficulty. You can use this information to focus your study.

NO PENALTY SCORING

You may recall from Chapter 1 that Section I of the exam is no longer penalty scored. Incorrect responses are not deducted from your score, so you will benefit from guessing. Every correct answer adds to your score. No points are awarded for unanswered questions. Therefore, you should answer every question, even if you have to guess.

However, you should practice this simple method to help alleviate the need for guessing. When you work on a timed practice exam or as you sit for the actual AP exam, work straight through all of the multiple-choice questions and answer those questions that you can with no hesitation. Skip the difficult questions that bog you down or leave you confused. Then, on the next pass, answer those questions that you can narrow down to two answer choices. Now, you are left only with the questions you need time to think over. Spend the remainder of your testing period answering these questions. If you absolutely cannot come up with an answer, guess. Do not leave any questions blank.

One final point to keep in mind: On most multiple-choice exams, students are encouraged to "go with their gut" when answering questions. On the AP U.S. History exam, this can be dangerous! Remember that distractors are designed to catch you off guard and make you think you have chosen the correct answer. Read all questions and answer choices completely and carefully! Many question stems will have the words "all of the following EXCEPT." Questions like these give test takers the most trouble, because many do not take the time to read the question completely. The distractors for these questions are particularly tricky if you haven't read the question thoroughly.

If you have prepared thoroughly, then have confidence! If you can make an educated guess on a test item, using your knowledge of U.S. history, chances are that you will make the correct choice.

HOW TO APPROACH THE SHORT-ANSWER QUESTIONS

On the AP U.S. History exam, you have 50 minutes to answer four short-answer questions, each of which will have two to three parts. Aim to spend about 10-12 minutes on each question, depending on how many parts it contains.

Use the first minute to identify the two to three parts of the question. Then, before you begin writing your answer, create a plan to guide you through what examples you will be using for each part of each short-answer question. Your responses to each part should be between three and six sentences long.

You will have plenty of opportunities to practice writing responses to short-answer questions in this book, not only in the Practice Tests but also in the end-of-unit reviews.

HOW TO APPROACH THE LONG ESSAY QUESTION

The long essay question on the AP U.S. History exam is designed to test your ability to apply knowledge of history in a complex, analytic manner. In other words, you are expected to treat history and historical questions as a historian would. This process is called historiography—the skills and strategies historians use to analyze and interpret historical evidence to reach a conclusion. Thus, when writing an effective essay, you must be able to write a strong and clearly developed thesis and supply a substantial amount of relevant evidence to support your thesis.

Success on the long essay section of the exam starts with breaking down the task of essay writing into specific steps. As part of your yearlong preparation for taking the AP U.S. History exam, you should be writing at least two essays (one DBQ and one LEQ) each month.

STICK TO THE SUBJECT

In your essay, giving historical information before or after the time period in the essay topic will not get you any extra points.

STEP 1: DISSECT THE QUESTION

Always keep in mind that the AP U.S. History exam is written to be challenging and rigorous. Thus, the questions will require you to identify specific and important information prior to constructing a response. When given an essay prompt, first take some of your time to slow down and understand exactly what the question is asking you to do. The key here is to understand how to answer all parts of the question. Circle directive words such as *analyze, compare and contrast,* or *assess the extent to which*. Commonly, prompts will ask you to validate or refute a statement or to explain the impact of one event on another or the degree of impact. List these directives as pieces of the puzzle that you will attempt to put together with your history knowledge.

THERE'S NO *U* IN HISTORY

Don't include personal opinions in the essay. The reader is looking for your grasp of the history itself and your ability to write about it.

STEP 2: FORMULATE A THESIS

A major area of concern each year for the Chief Readers of the AP exams is that students do not take the time to understand all parts of the question and plan their responses. We have already dissected the question; now it is time to plan a thesis. The thesis is your way of telling the reader why he or she should care about reading your essay. If you have a weak thesis, the reader will not be convinced that you understand the question. He or she will not trust that you have the depth of knowledge necessary to answer the question! Therefore, you must have a thesis that takes a stand, answers the entire question, and shows the reader the path you will take in your essay answer. It is not enough to merely restate the question as your thesis. One of the most important things to do is to take a position. Don't be afraid of taking a strong stand for or against a prompt as long as you can provide proper and relevant evidence to support your assertions.

Think of your thesis as the "road map" to your essay. It will provide the reader with the stops along the way to the final destination—the conclusion. Only through a thorough study of U.S. history can you construct a strong thesis.

THINK AHEAD

During the planning time, make a short outline of all the outside information you're planning to use in your essay; you will have the info handy while you're writing.

WRITING TIP

When composing your essay, start with your most important information; if you run out of time when you're writing, your key points are already in the essay.

STEP 3: PLAN YOUR EVIDENCE

Now that you have a "road map," you need to brainstorm all of the relevant evidence you can recall that relates to the question. There are several ways to do this. Some students prefer to use a cluster strategy; that is, they place the main thoughts in bubbles and then scatter supporting evidence around the main bubbles. Other students prefer to list facts and evidence in a bulleted list. Some like to create an outline of relevant information. Whatever you prefer, this is a step you *cannot* skip! Students who do not take the time to plan their evidence often find themselves scratching out irrelevant information during the exam, thus wasting valuable time. Also, you must learn to brainstorm efficiently—you should use only about five minutes to complete the first three steps of essay writing. Use abbreviations, pictures, or other cues that are efficient for you.

Once you have a list, you can move to the next (and most important) step—writing!

STEP 4: WRITE YOUR ESSAY

As you practice writing essays using the strategies in this chapter, you will have the luxury of taking time to write topic sentences, list evidence, and construct "mini conclusions" for each prompt. However, on the AP exam, time is of the essence! You have 35 minutes to construct a coherent essay response for the LEQ and about 55 minutes for the DBQ. If you practice the prewriting strategies from the previously outlined steps 1 through 3, you will find it easy to write a developed paper in a short time.

There is no "standard" number of paragraphs you must have. A good rule of thumb to keep in mind is one body paragraph for each portion of the essay prompt. Some AP U.S. History exam questions will be structured to fit a five-paragraph essay, while others may need more and others less. You will not be penalized for writing a strong four-paragraph response. Likewise, you will not be rewarded for constructing a weak six-paragraph response. AP readers look for quality, not quantity.

Your first paragraph should always introduce your essay. Your thesis from step 2 is only part of your introduction. The first paragraph of your essay should include your thesis and any other organizational cues you can give your reader. Ask yourself, "Could a complete stranger understand where my essay is going from just my first paragraph?" If your answer is no, then you must rework the introduction. Do not spend time creating a "hook" or flashy statement for your first sentence. Do not use rhetorical questions. AP Faculty Consultants are reading for the items that are listed on the scoring guide. You will notice that creativity in language and structure is not a listed item. However, a well-written and developed argument is a desired item.

Your body paragraphs should follow the "road map" you set in your introduction and thesis. Don't stray from your plan, or you will find yourself straying from the question. You have taken the time to plan, so follow it! Do not merely list facts and events in a "laundry list" fashion. You must have some element of analysis between each set of evidence you provide. Using transition words such as *however*, *therefore*, and *thus* to show a shift in thought can make creating analytic sentences quick and easy. You should practice stringing facts and thoughts together using these "qualifying transitions" in your sentences.

KNOW THE LINGO

Whenever possible, use historical terms or phrases instead of general ones. For example, instead of saying that the South established laws against an owner freeing slaves, say that the South established laws against *manumission*. This shows the reader that you really know your stuff.

Beware of telling a story rather than answering the question. Readers are looking for analysis, not a revised version of your textbook. Do not attempt to shower the reader with extra factoids and showy language. Say what you need to say cleanly and simply. Readers will be impressed with your ability to write clearly and concisely in a way that showcases your historical knowledge, rather than your ability to write creatively. Because this is a formal essay, you should avoid using personal pronouns such as *you*, *I*, or *we*. Avoid the use of terms that could be "loaded" unless you intend on explaining them to the reader. For instance, you would not want to use the term *liberal* to describe Thomas Jefferson unless you were prepared to explain your use of the word *liberal* in the historical context. Do not use slang in any part of your essay. Also, because your essay is about history and thus is about the past, write your essay in the past tense. Do not write about Franklin D. Roosevelt as if he were still alive today.

You should end each body paragraph with a "mini conclusion" that ties the paragraph back to the thesis. It can serve as a transition sentence into the next paragraph or stand alone. In either case, the reader should be able to tell easily that you are shifting gears into another part of the essay.

Lastly, write your conclusion. Many students have learned that they should simply restate their thesis in the conclusion; these students may recopy what they wrote in the introduction word for word. This is incorrect. Yes, you should restate your thesis, but in a new way. Instead of rewriting it word for word, explain why your thesis is significant to the question. Do not introduce new evidence in your conclusion. The conclusion should tie all the "mini conclusion" sentences together and leave the reader with a sense of completion. If for some reason you are running out of time when you reach the conclusion, you may leave it off without incurring a specific penalty on the scoring guide. However, if you practice writing timed essays, you will learn the proper timing it takes to write a complete essay, conclusion included.

HOW TO APPROACH THE DOCUMENT-BASED QUESTION

You can follow the previous guidelines for the DBQ with some important additions. The DBQ requires the use of a "substantial number" of documents and "substantial and relevant" outside information. There is no prescribed number to make up "substantial," but we recommend using half of the documents plus one. So if there are eight documents for a DBQ, use five documents minimum in your response. It is better to use all of the documents than to use the minimum. Likewise, there is no magic formula for "substantial" outside information. A good goal to keep in mind is to use at least three pieces of outside information per body paragraph. Therefore, in a standard five-paragraph response, an essay would have nine pieces of outside information.

The DBQ requires you to analyze the documents in addition to bringing outside information to bear on the question. This is a difficult task, and you have only 15 minutes to plan before you begin writing. Don't panic! Use the same strategies given above for the LEQ for document analysis. Yes, we realize it is a big task for you to complete the strategies for each and every document on the AP exam as we have them outlined in this guide. However, the more you practice using these strategies, the better you will become at quickly finding significance in the documents.

BE A DBQ REBEL

For DBQ questions, you don't have to write a thesis that agrees with the test's thesis. You can also take a "middle-ground" approach.

DOCUMENT ANALYSIS

Many students new to AP may struggle with the reading and analysis of primary source documents. Because the DBQ response on the AP U.S. History exam makes up 25 percent of your overall score, it is important to practice this skill throughout the year. Primary sources are documents that are contemporary to the time period in which they were written. In other words, a letter written by Abigail Adams to her husband John Adams would be considered contemporary to the late 18th century and, thus, a primary source document from this time period. An example of a secondary source would be a textbook offering its interpretation of the same letter from Abigail Adams to John Adams. On the AP exam, you will be required to read, dissect, and analyze primary sources quickly and efficiently. Let's look at a method to practice document analysis that you can learn to adapt for the AP U.S. History exam.

USE YOUR OWN WORDS

When using documents, avoid quoting directly from the document. Your job is to paraphrase the information in the document and—most importantly—to use the source to support your own ideas.

Here is an example of a possible primary source document that could appear on the AP U.S. History exam:

DOCUMENT B

"A house divided against itself cannot stand. . . . I do not expect the Union to be dissolved; I do not expect the house to fall; but I do expect it will cease to be divided. It will become all one thing, or all the other . . . "

Abraham Lincoln, speech, 1858

First, we must consider what a historian would do when asked to analyze a primary source document. Are key features evident on the document, right there on the page? Our first step will be to scan the document for clues. Look at dates, authors, and possible indications of where this document came from. We can see that this document was produced in 1858 and was written by Abraham Lincoln.

Our next step will be to catalog all of the possible outside information we may have about the dates, author, and place of the document. Regarding this document, we know that Abraham Lincoln was vying for the Republican nomination to run for president in 1858. Thus, we can show that this document is important because it illustrates that Lincoln was gravely concerned about the preservation of the Union well before secession and when he was concerned with winning the presidency.

PRACTICE MAKES PERFECT

Mastering how to format the DBQ is half the battle. The more you practice writing DBQs, the more prepared you'll be to write one under pressure on Test Day.

Next we will write down any inferences we may make regarding the document. These may be specific ideas that would further explain why this document would be important to a historian studying this period. For our sample document, we can infer that this speech would be important in the study of the coming of the Civil War. Lincoln was almost acting as a "fortune-teller" by eerily predicting the troubles that lay ahead for the nation. A historian would be interested in discovering exactly how Lincoln was able to have that kind of foresight and how it prepared him to be president in such a turbulent time.

CITATION TIP

When citing a document, you don't have to cite it as "Lincoln's speech of 1858." Save yourself some time and refer to it as "Document 1."

Last, we will tie it all together. Create a thesis statement for this document by using your inferences, outside information, and important facts you have already listed. A thesis statement for our sample document may look something like this:

By 1858, the Republican Party had been formed due to the divisions caused by the passage of the Kansas-Nebraska Act. Senator Abraham Lincoln delivered his prophetic "House Divided" speech to warn his fellow Republicans of the dangers that lay ahead for the strength of the Union.

A simple way to remember this strategy is to call it SCIT. *S* equals scan, *C* equals catalog, *I* equals infer, and *T* equals tie it together. You can practice and complete this strategy for all of the documents on your AP exam in the 15 minutes of mandatory reading time before you begin constructing your DBQ response.

STRESS MANAGEMENT

You can beat anxiety the same way you can beat the AP U.S. History exam—by knowing what to expect beforehand and developing strategies to deal with it.

SOURCES OF STRESS

In the space provided, write down your sources of test-related stress. The idea is to pin down any sources of anxiety so you can deal with them one by one. We have provided common examples— feel free to use them and any others you think of.

- I always freeze up on tests.
- I'm nervous about the DBQ.
- I need a good/great score to get into my first-choice college.
- My older brother/sister/best friend/girlfriend/boyfriend did really well. I must match their scores or do better.
- My parents, who are paying for school, will be quite disappointed if I don't do well.
- I'm afraid of losing my focus and concentration.
- I'm afraid I'm not spending enough time preparing.
- I study like crazy, but nothing seems to stick in my mind.
- I always run out of time and get panicky.
- The simple act of thinking, for me, is like wading through refrigerated honey.
- I have too many AP exams in one week.

MY SOURCES OF STRESS

_____

_____

_____

_____

_____

_____

Read through the list. Cross out things or add things. Now rewrite the list in order of most disturbing to least disturbing.

MY SOURCES OF STRESS, IN ORDER

_____

_____

_____

_____

_____

Chances are, the top of the list is a fairly accurate description of exactly how you react to test anxiety, both physically and mentally. The later items usually describe your fears (disappointing mom and dad, looking bad, etc.). Taking care of the major items from the top of the list should go a long way toward relieving overall test anxiety. That's what we'll do next.

STRENGTHS AND WEAKNESSES

Take 60 seconds to list the areas of U.S. history that you are good at. They can be general, such as "colonialism," or specific, such as "foreign policy in the 1930s." Put down as many as you can think of and, if possible, time yourself. Write for the entire time; don't stop writing until you've reached the one-minute stopping point. Go!

STRONG TEST SUBJECTS

_____

_____

_____

_____

_____

Now take one minute to list areas of the test you struggle with or simply do not understand. Again, keep it to one minute and continue writing until you reach the cutoff. Go!

TROUBLESOME TEST SUBJECTS

_____

_____

_____

_____

_____

Taking stock of your assets and liabilities lets you know the areas you don't have to worry about and the ones that will demand extra attention and effort. It helps a lot to find out where you need to spend extra effort. We mostly fear what we don't know and are probably afraid to face. You can't help feeling more confident when you know you're actively strengthening your chances of earning a higher overall score.

Now, go back to the "good" list and expand on it for two minutes. Take the general items on that first list and make them more specific; take the specific items and expand them into more general conclusions. Naturally, if anything new comes to mind, jot it down. Focus all of your attention and effort on your strengths. Don't underestimate yourself or your abilities. Give yourself full credit. At the same time, don't list strengths you don't really have.

Expanding from general to specific might go as follows: if you listed "politics" as a broad topic you feel strong in, you would then narrow your focus to include areas of this subject about which you are particularly knowledgeable. Your areas of strength might include specific presidencies, legislative acts, Supreme Court decisions, etc. Whatever you know well goes on your "good" list. All right, check your starting time. Go!

STRONG TEST SUBJECTS: AN EXPANDED LIST

_____

_____

_____

_____

_____

_____

_____

_____

After you've stopped, check your time. Did you find yourself going beyond the two minutes allotted? Did you write down more things than you thought you knew? Is it possible you know more than you've given yourself credit for? Could that mean you've found a number of areas in which you feel strong?

You just took an active step toward helping yourself. Enjoy your increased feelings of confidence and use them when you take the AP U.S. History exam.

RELAAAAAAAX

Another way to relieve stress is through progressive relaxation. For example, when you're sitting at your desk, clench your fists tightly for about five seconds, then unclench them slowly and feel the tension disappear.

HOW TO DEAL WITH STRESS

VISUALIZE

This next group of activities is a follow-up to the strong and troublesome test item lists you completed. Sit in a comfortable chair in a quiet setting. If you wear glasses, take them off. Close your eyes and breathe in a deep, satisfying breath of air. Really fill your lungs until your rib cage is fully expanded and you can't take in any more. Then, exhale the air completely. Imagine you're blowing out a candle with your last little puff of air. Do this two or three more times, filling your lungs to their maximum and emptying them totally. Keep your eyes closed, comfortably but not tightly. Let your body sink deeper into the chair as you become even more comfortable.

With your eyes shut, you can notice something very interesting. You're no longer dealing with the worrisome stuff going on in the world outside of you. Now you can concentrate on what happens inside you. The more you recognize your own physical reactions to stress and anxiety, the more you can do about them. You may not realize it, but you've begun to regain a sense of being in control.

Let images begin to form on TV screens on the back of your eyelids. Allow the images to come easily and naturally; don't force them. Visualize a relaxing situation. It might be in a special place you've visited before or one you've read about. It can be a fictional location that you create in your imagination, but a real-life memory of a place or situation you know is usually better. Make it as detailed as possible and notice as much as you can.

Stay focused on the images as you sink farther into your chair. Breathe easily and naturally. You might have the sensations of any stress or tension draining from your muscles and flowing downward, out your feet and away from you.

Take a moment to check how you're feeling. Notice how comfortable you've become. Imagine how much easier it would be if you could take the test feeling this relaxed and in this state of ease. You've coupled the images of your special place with sensations of comfort and relaxation. You've also found a way to become relaxed simply by visualizing your own safe, special place.

Close your eyes and start remembering a real-life situation in which you did well on a test. If you can't come up with one, remember a situation in which you did something that you were really proud of—a genuine accomplishment. Make the memory as detailed as possible. Think about the sights, the sounds, the smells, even the tastes associated with this remembered experience. Remember how confident you felt as you accomplished your goal. Now start thinking about the AP U.S. History exam. Keep your thoughts and feelings in line with that prior, successful experience. Don't make comparisons between them. Just imagine taking the upcoming test with the same feelings of confidence and relaxed control.

This exercise is a great way to bring the test down to earth. You should practice this exercise often, especially when you feel burned out on test preparation. The more you practice it, the more effective the exercise will be for you.

JOG YOUR MEMORY

When you study, put extra emphasis on first-semester material. History from the second semester is usually easier to remember, because you learned it more recently.

COUNTDOWN TO THE TEST

Studying for the AP U.S. History exam can seem daunting because of the sheer volume of material covered in a yearlong course. Whether you have taken the course over a semester or over two years, the exam measures your knowledge and skills in exactly the same way. As we have said, it is only through the thorough study over the course of the year that you will earn a high score on the AP exam. This guide is an excellent addition to the class notes, reading notes, and practice essays you have accumulated throughout the year. This guide is not intended to replace your assigned readings, a textbook, or your instructor. You can, however, use this guide to assist you in studying throughout the year or closer to your exam.

Some students prefer to review what they learned last in class and work their way back to the beginning of the course as they study. This is perfectly acceptable. However, other students prefer to begin their studies with the material that is most distant—material learned at the beginning of the course. Again, this is a perfectly logical way to attack the material. Other students choose to skip around and study only those sections of the course with which they had difficulty. Whatever approach you decide to take, make sure it best suits your needs and helps you feel prepared and secure in your abilities in AP U.S. History.

There is one method we advise against. We do not recommend cramming material into your brain in the weeks before the AP exam. Students who score well on the exam are students who have carefully studied U.S. history and have both a breadth and depth of understanding of the material and how to think historically. Take your time. Allow yourself the opportunity to practice your material often by starting your review early.

Regardless of where you will take your AP U.S. History test, everyone preparing for the AP exam has a Friday morning in early May earmarked as Test Day. For some, the purchase of this guide occurred in September. For others, mid-April. Yet in some cases it may already be May! Whatever your situation, we have provided study calendars below that you can use to set some goals.

MONTHLY STUDY CALENDAR

August/ September	Wow! You're ahead of the game and have already thought about studying for the AP exam—you're off to a great start! Go through the reading calendar provided by your instructor and connect each chapter of this guide to the material you will be learning about in class. By the end of September, you should have completed your study and review of all chapters in this guide in **Unit 1**.
October	By the end of this month, you should have completed the chapters in this guide that are featured in **Unit 2**.
November	Funny how fast time flies! Be sure to make special arrangements for family holidays and gatherings that may change your study time. By the end of this month, you should be through **Unit 3** and well into **Unit 4**.

December	This month's about the Civil War! Make sure you've completed **Unit 5** by New Year's Eve!
January	During this month, you should devise a plan to review all of the material you have covered during the Fall semester. Don't let final exams get you down. Use this time as an opportunity to revisit the content you covered in September! Additionally, you should be through **Unit 6**!
February	Don't let time slip away! This month takes you from the 19th century to the mid-20th century in **Unit 7**.
March	You're in the home stretch! In March, you should cover **Unit 8** and the first part of **Unit 9**. You should also go back through the material you covered during the first part of the Spring semester to get a head start on your review.
April	Can you believe that the exam is only a month away? Complete the guide in the first two weeks of April and concentrate on reviewing the entire guide during the last two weeks, concentrating on areas where you can improve the most.
May	The exam is in a few days. Relax, but don't let up. Keep going over your trouble spots and practice writing. Good luck!

THE QUARTER STUDY CALENDAR

Quarter One	By Thanksgiving, you should be partially through **Unit 4**.
Quarter Two	By your semester finals, you will need to have studied through **Unit 6**.
Quarter Three	This can be a stressful period—the bulk of your review and study to occurs here. You should have all the material through **Unit 8** read by the end of this quarter.
Quarter Four	You do not have much time in this quarter before the exam so you need to finish the guide and start reviewing all materials from the beginning. Remember to concentrate on the areas with the most room for improvement.

LOOK TOWARD THE FUTURE

When reviewing your notes and books for your regular tests during the school year, highlight those areas in your notes that you think you have forgotten (or never fully understood). That way, when the AP exam rolls around, you'll be able to revisit those notes and fix up your weak spots.

The "I have a month" Study Calendar

We will presume that you purchased this guide sometime between the end of March and the beginning of April. With only a month or so before the exam, you don't have time to lose!

We recommend that you make a goal of covering eight chapters of this guide every week, with one day dedicated to reviewing those chapters before moving on. Be sure to concentrate on the material and chapters where you experienced difficulties over the course of the school year.

Three Days Before the Test

It's almost over. Eat an energy bar, drink some soda—do whatever it takes to keep going (but don't overdose on sugar and caffeine). Here are Kaplan's strategies for the three days leading up to the test.

Take a full-length practice test under timed conditions. Use the techniques and strategies you've learned in this book. Approach the test strategically, actively, and confidently.

WARNING: Do *not* take a full-length practice test if you have fewer than 48 hours left before the test. Doing so will probably exhaust you and hurt your score on the actual test. You wouldn't run a marathon the day before the real thing.

Two Days Before the Test

Go over the results of your practice test. Don't worry too much about your score or about whether you got a specific question right or wrong. The practice test doesn't count. But do examine your performance on specific questions with an eye to how you might get through each one faster and better on the test to come.

The Night Before the Test

DO NOT STUDY. Get together the supplies you will bring to the test center.

Know exactly where you're going, exactly how you're getting there, and exactly how long it takes to get there. It's probably a good idea to visit your test center sometime before the day of the test so that you know what to expect—what the rooms are like, how the desks are set up, and so on.

Relax the night before the test. Do the relaxation and visualization techniques. Read a good book, take a long hot shower, watch some bad television. Get a good night's sleep. Go to bed early and leave yourself extra time in the morning.

THE MORNING OF THE TEST

First, wake up. After that . . .

- Eat breakfast. Make it something substantial but not anything too heavy or greasy.

- Don't drink a lot of coffee if you're not used to it. Bathroom breaks cut into your time, and too much caffeine is a bad idea.

- Dress in layers so that you can adjust to the temperature of the test room.

- Read something. Warm up your brain with a newspaper or a magazine. You shouldn't let the exam be the first thing you read that day.

- Be sure to get there early. Allow yourself extra time for traffic, mass transit delays, and/or detours.

TIME TIP

Pay close attention to how much time you have for each section. Move quickly at the beginning and keep checking your progress periodically.

DURING THE TEST

Don't be shaken. If you find your confidence slipping, remind yourself how well you've prepared. You know the structure of the test; you know the instructions; you've had practice with—and have learned strategies for—every question type.

If something goes really wrong, don't panic. If the test booklet is defective—two pages are stuck together or the ink has run—raise your hand and tell the proctor you need a new book. If you accidentally misgrid your answer page or put the answers in the wrong section, raise your hand and tell the proctor. He or she might be able to arrange for you to regrid your test after it's over, when it won't cost you any time.

AFTER THE TEST

You might walk out of the AP exam thinking that you blew it. This is a normal reaction. Lots of people—even the highest scorers—feel that way. You tend to remember the questions that stumped you, not the ones that you knew.

We're positive that you will have performed well and scored your best on the exam because you followed the Kaplan strategies outlined in this section. Be confident in your preparation and celebrate the fact that the AP test is soon to be a distant memory.

Now, continue on to Part Two of this guide, where you can take a Diagnostic Test to determine where you stand right now. This short test will give you an idea of the format of the actual exam, and it will demonstrate the scope of topics covered. After the Diagnostic Test, you'll find answers with detailed explanations. Be sure to read these explanations carefully, even when you got the question right, as you can pick up bits of knowledge from them. Use your score to learn which topics you need to review more carefully. Of course, all the strategies in the world can't save you if you haven't built up a solid knowledge base of U.S. history. The chapters following the Diagnostic Test will help you review the primary concepts and facts that you can expect to encounter on the AP exam.

Part Two

DIAGNOSTIC TEST

AP U.S. HISTORY DIAGNOSTIC TEST

To best use this guide, you must understand where your strengths and weaknesses in U.S. history lie. If you are looking at this guide at the beginning of your school year, the questions in the Diagnostic Test may seem difficult. If you are taking this Diagnostic Test at the end of your school year, your results on this test may assist you in developing a study plan before the AP U.S. History exam. In either case, it is important that you pay very close attention to areas of this test on which you score poorly. These results may indicate that you must study a particular section of this guide a bit more closely than areas in which you scored well. We will provide you with more information regarding how you can use your score on this Diagnostic Test at the end of this section.

Let's go ahead and begin your Diagnostic Test. Find a quiet room with no distractions, get a No. 2 pencil and a silent timepiece, and take the entire test from start to finish. Explanations of all test items are provided at the end of this test. Try not to look at them now. Take this test without any other materials to obtain a true measure of your abilities.

Good luck!

DIAGNOSTIC TEST ANSWER GRID

For updates on how the exam is scored, visit the College Board AP Student website at https://apstudent.collegeboard.org/home.

The breakdown of sections on the exam is as follows:

SCORING BREAKDOWN

Section	Question Type	Number of Questions	Timing	Percentage of Total Exam Score
I	Part A: Multiple-choice questions	55 questions	55 minutes	40%
	Part B: Short-answer questions	4 questions	50 minutes	20%
II	Part A: Document-based question	1 question	55 minutes	25%
	Part B: Long essay question	1 question	35 minutes	15%

1. Ⓐ Ⓑ Ⓒ Ⓓ
2. Ⓐ Ⓑ Ⓒ Ⓓ
3. Ⓐ Ⓑ Ⓒ Ⓓ
4. Ⓐ Ⓑ Ⓒ Ⓓ
5. Ⓐ Ⓑ Ⓒ Ⓓ
6. Ⓐ Ⓑ Ⓒ Ⓓ
7. Ⓐ Ⓑ Ⓒ Ⓓ
8. Ⓐ Ⓑ Ⓒ Ⓓ
9. Ⓐ Ⓑ Ⓒ Ⓓ
10. Ⓐ Ⓑ Ⓒ Ⓓ
11. Ⓐ Ⓑ Ⓒ Ⓓ
12. Ⓐ Ⓑ Ⓒ Ⓓ
13. Ⓐ Ⓑ Ⓒ Ⓓ
14. Ⓐ Ⓑ Ⓒ Ⓓ

15. Ⓐ Ⓑ Ⓒ Ⓓ
16. Ⓐ Ⓑ Ⓒ Ⓓ
17. Ⓐ Ⓑ Ⓒ Ⓓ
18. Ⓐ Ⓑ Ⓒ Ⓓ
19. Ⓐ Ⓑ Ⓒ Ⓓ
20. Ⓐ Ⓑ Ⓒ Ⓓ
21. Ⓐ Ⓑ Ⓒ Ⓓ
22. Ⓐ Ⓑ Ⓒ Ⓓ
23. Ⓐ Ⓑ Ⓒ Ⓓ
24. Ⓐ Ⓑ Ⓒ Ⓓ
25. Ⓐ Ⓑ Ⓒ Ⓓ
26. Ⓐ Ⓑ Ⓒ Ⓓ
27. Ⓐ Ⓑ Ⓒ Ⓓ
28. Ⓐ Ⓑ Ⓒ Ⓓ

29. Ⓐ Ⓑ Ⓒ Ⓓ
30. Ⓐ Ⓑ Ⓒ Ⓓ
31. Ⓐ Ⓑ Ⓒ Ⓓ
32. Ⓐ Ⓑ Ⓒ Ⓓ
33. Ⓐ Ⓑ Ⓒ Ⓓ
34. Ⓐ Ⓑ Ⓒ Ⓓ
35. Ⓐ Ⓑ Ⓒ Ⓓ
36. Ⓐ Ⓑ Ⓒ Ⓓ
37. Ⓐ Ⓑ Ⓒ Ⓓ
38. Ⓐ Ⓑ Ⓒ Ⓓ
39. Ⓐ Ⓑ Ⓒ Ⓓ
40. Ⓐ Ⓑ Ⓒ Ⓓ
41. Ⓐ Ⓑ Ⓒ Ⓓ
42. Ⓐ Ⓑ Ⓒ Ⓓ

43. Ⓐ Ⓑ Ⓒ Ⓓ
44. Ⓐ Ⓑ Ⓒ Ⓓ
45. Ⓐ Ⓑ Ⓒ Ⓓ
46. Ⓐ Ⓑ Ⓒ Ⓓ
47. Ⓐ Ⓑ Ⓒ Ⓓ
48. Ⓐ Ⓑ Ⓒ Ⓓ
49. Ⓐ Ⓑ Ⓒ Ⓓ
50. Ⓐ Ⓑ Ⓒ Ⓓ
51. Ⓐ Ⓑ Ⓒ Ⓓ
52. Ⓐ Ⓑ Ⓒ Ⓓ
53. Ⓐ Ⓑ Ⓒ Ⓓ
54. Ⓐ Ⓑ Ⓒ Ⓓ
55. Ⓐ Ⓑ Ⓒ Ⓓ

DIAGNOSTIC TEST

Section I

Part A: Multiple-Choice Questions

Time: 55 Minutes
55 Questions

Directions: Choose the best answer choice for the questions below.

Questions 1–3 refer to the following image.

Buffalo Hunt under the Wolf-skin Mask, 1832–1833, George Catlin

1. Based on the above painting the group depicted most likely would come from

    (A) the Cahokia Nation located around the Mississippi River

    (B) the Seminole Nation located in the southeastern region of the modern United States

    (C) the American Great Plains west of the Mississippi River and east of the Rocky Mountains

    (D) the Navajo Nation located in the southwestern region of the modern United States

GO ON TO THE NEXT PAGE

2. Which of the following best explains how the environment of the Great Plains Indians would have been impacted by 16th-century European contact?

(A) The introduction of grain crops made the Plains Indians more sedentary.

(B) The introduction of the horse allowed the Plains Indians to hunt buffalo more efficiently.

(C) The development of trade with the Spanish for weapons allowed the Plains Indians to expand their territory, taking land from their traditional enemies.

(D) Transportation technology brought by the Spaniards allowed the Plains Indians to develop a more advanced trade system.

3. Before encountering the Europeans in the late 15th century, American Indian nations on the Atlantic coast developed what type of settlements?

(A) The eastern Indians tended to be nomadic, following the growing season of the various crops they depended upon for survival.

(B) The different Indian nations developed trade agreements to provide necessary resources for all on the Atlantic coast.

(C) The northeast Indian nations' economic systems tended to be based on hunting and gathering, and they were sedentary.

(D) The settlements were small and relatively unorganized; small family groups depended on each other for survival through a combination of nomadic hunting practices and the development of agriculture.

Questions 4–6 refer to the following passage.

"But Virginia and Maryland attracted few aristocrats or gentry, except as occasional governors who soon returned home. Instead, hard-driving merchants and planters of middling origins created the greatest fortunes and claimed the highest offices. As a rule, their education and manners lagged far behind their acquisition of land, servants, and political influence. That lag encouraged grumbling and disobedience by laboring people who refused deference to officials wanting in the gentility and high birth demanded by political tradition."

—Excerpted from *American Colonies: The Settling of North America* by Alan Taylor, Penguin Books, 2001

4. Which of the following best describes Alan Taylor's analysis of early American colonial settlement?

(A) The development of a republican form of government

(B) The evolution of a hierarchical social structure

(C) The progression of economic development in the middle Atlantic colonies

(D) The integration of a system of economics and politics in the English colonies

5. Which of the following 19th-century political groups would agree with the analysis offered by Alan Taylor in regard to themselves?

(A) Jeffersonian Republicans

(B) 1830s/1840s Whigs

(C) Jacksonian Democrats

(D) Know-Nothings

GO ON TO THE NEXT PAGE

6. Which of the following regionally based economic systems started to develop in the late 17th century?

   (A) A society based on yeoman farming

   (B) An agricultural economy based on indentured servitude

   (C) An economy based on cereal grain crops

   (D) A plantation system based on involuntary bondage

Questions 7–9 refer to the following image.

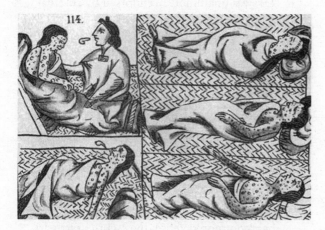

Courtesy of the UCLA Center for Medieval and Renaissance Studies and James Lockhart

7. The previous illustration best depicts which of the following outcomes from the early Atlantic World?

   (A) Interaction of Africans and Europeans resulted in the deaths of thousands due to bubonic plague.

   (B) Thousands of Europeans died of disease as a result of interactions with Native Americans.

   (C) Increased exploitation of local resources led to starvation among various Native American groups.

   (D) Increased interactions between Europeans and Native Americans led to the deaths of millions by diseases such as smallpox.

8. At the establishment of the Atlantic World, one major impact of the events portrayed in the illustration was

   (A) the development of indentured servitude, bringing cheap labor into the tobacco plantations in British North America

   (B) the widespread practice of kidnapping American Indians to use as forced labor

   (C) the increased importation of people from Africa to use as slave labor

   (D) the call for more immigration to the New World by the European colonizers

9. Which of the following 19th-century events is most similar to the incidents depicted in the previous illustration?

   (A) Forced migration of American Indians to the Indian Territory

   (B) The government policy of forced settlement of American Indians on reservations

   (C) Purposely exposing American Indians to disease in treaty settlements

   (D) Indiscriminate killing of unarmed American Indians on reservations

Questions 10–13 refer to the following passage.

"To these grievous acts and measures Americans cannot submit, but in hopes that their fellow subjects in Great Britain will, on a revision of them, restore us to that state in which both countries found happiness and prosperity, we have for the present only resolved to pursue the following peaceable measures:

1. To enter into a non-importation, non-consumption, and non-exportation agreement or association.

2. To prepare an address to the people of Great Britain, and a memorial to the inhabitants of British America, and

GO ON TO THE NEXT PAGE ⟶

3. To prepare a loyal address to his Majesty, agreeable to resolutions already entered into."

—Excerpted from the demands of the *Declaration of Rights and Grievances* of 1774 (passed by the First Continental Congress)

10. According to the previous excerpt, which of the following was being violated in the eyes of the British North American colonists?

(A) Their right to free trade

(B) The colonial rights of speech and to be able to petition the government

(C) Their rights as Englishmen

(D) Their right to more self-government as colonies

11. The main idea expressed in the excerpt was also expressed in which of the following?

(A) The debate over the nullification of the Tariff in 1832–1833

(B) The demands made by Federalists in Hartford (1814)

(C) The debate over the admission of Missouri as a state in 1819–1820

(D) The ideals expressed at the Constitutional Convention in 1787

12. Which of the following was an immediate response to the demands expressed by the First Continental Congress?

(A) A demand for independence by a majority of Americans

(B) A demand by the colonists for a Parliament-sanctioned inter-colonial congress

(C) King George III ignored the demands of the Americans

(D) The creation of a Continental Army

13. Unlike previous attempts to unify British North American colonies (the Dominion of New England, the Albany Plan), the *Declaration of Rights and Grievances* was different in that it

(A) placed all blame for the issues faced by the colonists on the King

(B) threatened a foundation of the British economy by cutting off exports to England

(C) was the idea of Parliament to create the Congress

(D) was unanimously endorsed by colonial leaders

Questions 14–16 refer to the following passage.

"II. Each state retains its sovereignty, freedom, and independence, and every power, jurisdiction, and right, which is not by this Confederation expressly delegated to the United States, in Congress assembled.

III. The said States hereby severally enter into a firm league of friendship with each other, for their common defense, the security of their liberties, and their mutual and general welfare, binding themselves to assist each other, against all force offered to, or attacks made upon them, or any of them, on account of religion, sovereignty, trade, or any other pretense whatever."

—Excerpted from the Articles of Confederation: Articles II and III, 1781

GO ON TO THE NEXT PAGE ⟩

14. The major theories expressed in the previous Articles were used in justifying which of the following concepts a few years after the ratification of the Constitution?

(A) The idea that states had the right to declare federal laws unconstitutional, as in the case of the Alien and Sedition Acts

(B) The rejection of a federal excise tax passed by the federal government

(C) The desire for certain states to declare war on a foreign country without the consent of the federal government

(D) The expectations of different states to make their own treaties with American Indian nations

15. Which of the following statements is most accurate for the 18th century after the ratification of the U.S. Constitution?

(A) American overseas trade grew without foreign interference.

(B) Agreements were made between the United States and foreign countries regarding borders between the United States and European North American colonies.

(C) The United States found it easier to make treaties with European powers.

(D) Threats of war between European nations and the United States ended.

16. Which of the following policies influenced the founding fathers' desire to create a government that encouraged the structure outlined in the Articles of Confederation?

(A) Reinstatement of the Navigation Acts that placed economic restrictions on the American colonists

(B) The rejection of the Albany Plan of Union as proposed at the outbreak of the French and Indian War

(C) The passage of the Townsend Act by the British Parliament

(D) The adoption of the Olive Branch petition

Questions 17–20 refer to the following image.

O Grab Me! **Political cartoon (c. 1807)**

17. The cartoon refers to which historical event?

(A) The boycott by Americans of British goods in events leading to the American Revolution

(B) The smuggling of contraband into America during the French and Indian War

(C) The reaction of New England to the passage of a "no trade" law

(D) American reaction to the writs of assistance

18. Which of the following best describes the sectional strains that resulted from events such as those illustrated in the cartoon?

(A) Immediate demands for secession from the Union were made by Southern states unless economic restrictions on trade were not lifted.

(B) Threats to establish an independent western republic were made over free trade issues.

(C) A meeting of representatives from the five New England states demanded several changes to the U.S. Constitution and an immediate halt to a war.

(D) Several northeastern states began to consider secession and join the Canadian confederation.

GO ON TO THE NEXT PAGE

19. Which of the following best describes the change in American politics between 1798 and 1816?

    (A) The members of the Democrat-Republican Party became stalwarts of free trade, changing from their initial position of strict trade regulation.

    (B) The Federalist Party supported the concepts of states' rights versus a strong central government.

    (C) The Whig Party emerged as a plausible third-party choice.

    (D) The Federalists advocated an expansionist philosophy, hoping to spread their political ideas westward.

20. The main issues represented in this political cartoon could be applied to which 20th-century social issue?

    (A) Immigration quotas from the 1920s
    (B) School segregation issues in the 1950s
    (C) The formation of NAFTA in the 1990s
    (D) Poll taxes in the 1960s

Questions 21 and 22 refer to the following image.

Original illustration from *A History of Wonderful Inventions* (New York: Harper, n.d.) (Merrimack Valley Textile Museum)

21. The task in the illustration most likely took place in which of the following areas of the United States during the early part of the 19th century?

    (A) In the Deep South near the cotton mills
    (B) In the Midwest in the new factories built by industrialists
    (C) In New England in the new textile mills built near small rivers
    (D) In North Carolina in the cotton mills

22. Which of the following most accurately describes the reasons for lower wages and poorer working conditions as the 19th century progressed in the workplace, as illustrated?

    (A) The end of gradual emancipation in the North, which allowed thousands of unskilled workers to look for jobs at lower salaries

    (B) The influx of immigrants from Europe who were willing to work for lower salaries

    (C) The collapse of the agricultural system in parts of New England and the Middle Atlantic leading to a flood of workers looking for jobs at low pay in factories

    (D) The arrival in New England of Chinese immigrants who were willing to work for cheap wages

GO ON TO THE NEXT PAGE

Question 23 refers to the following passage.

"One of the girls stood on a pump and gave vent to the feelings of her companions in a neat speech, declaring that it was their duty to resist all attempts at cutting down the wages. This was the first time a woman had spoken in public in Lowell, and the event caused surprise and consternation among her audience."

—Harriet H. Robinson, "Early Factory Labor in New England," in Massachusetts Bureau of Statistics of Labor, Fourteenth Annual Report (Boston: Wright & Potter, 1883), pp. 380–82, 387–88, 391–92

23. According to the above quotation, which of the following statements most accurately reflects early 19th-century labor?

(A) Labor unions in the United States were growing in popularity and strength.

(B) The traditional role of women in America was changing dramatically, as they were now working in factories.

(C) The idea of the cult of domesticity was growing more popular in the North, paving the way for women to work in factories.

(D) Republican Motherhood was changing in that a woman who worked in a factory was setting a good example on how to build a strong democratic society for her children.

Questions 24–26 refer to the following image.

24. Which of the following was the most significant "pull factor" in the decision of Freedmen (former slaves) to "go to Kansas?"

(A) Government legislation that made Kansas a haven for Freedmen

(B) The rumor that Freedmen would receive free land and money to begin a new life

(C) Industrialization and the promise of jobs enticing many Freedmen to migrate

(D) The fear that if they did not go, they would be sent to Africa

25. A historical event similar to that encouraged by the previous flyer is

(A) the Middle Passage of the 17th and 18th centuries

(B) the Great Migration of Puritans in the early 17th century

(C) the Great Migration of African Americans in the early 20th century

(D) the migration along the Trail of Tears in the 19th century

GO ON TO THE NEXT PAGE

26. Events like those encouraged by the flyer shown most often led to which of the following?

(A) Equal economic opportunity for African Americans with whites

(B) Social acceptance for African Americans by whites

(C) Racial tensions in cities as African Americans migrated from the South

(D) The desire by African Americans to emigrate to Africa

Questions 27–30 refer to the following passage.

"I am naturally anti-slavery. If slavery is not wrong, nothing is wrong . . . And yet I have never understood that the Presidency conferred upon me an unrestricted right to act officially upon this judgment and feeling . . . . I did understand however, that my oath to preserve the constitution to the best of my ability, imposed upon me the duty of preserving, by every indispensable means, that government—that nation—of which that constitution was the organic law . . . . I was, in my best judgment, driven to the alternative of either surrendering the Union, and with it, the Constitution, or of laying strong hand upon the colored element . . . . it shows a gain of quite a hundred and thirty thousand soldiers, seamen, and laborers. These are palpable facts, about which, as facts, there can be no cavilling."

—Letter from Abraham Lincoln to Albert G. Hodges, April 4, 1864, outlining his reasoning behind the Emancipation Proclamation

27. Abraham Lincoln's intended impact on the Civil War in issuing the Emancipation Proclamation was to

(A) give more authority to the army and navy in fighting the war

(B) change the focus of the war to that of giving the executive branch more authority

(C) add ending slavery in the United States to reunifying the country as the purpose of the war

(D) begin a peaceful restoration of the Union

28. Lincoln's pronouncement of the Emancipation Proclamation led directly to which of the following?

(A) The amendment outlawing involuntary servitude

(B) The beginning of Radical Republican Reconstruction

(C) The start of the Back to Africa Movement by the American Colonization Society

(D) The confiscation of plantations in the South to be redistributed to former slaves

29. Which of the following reactions was similar to the immediate reaction by many Northerners after the issuance of the Emancipation Proclamation?

(A) National reaction to the Sedition Acts of 1917 and 1918

(B) National reaction to the Immigration Acts of 1921, 1924, and 1929

(C) Western reaction to the ruling of *Korematsu v. U.S.* in 1944

(D) Southern reaction to the ruling of *Brown v. Board of Education* in 1954

GO ON TO THE NEXT PAGE

30. In regard to American identity, Abraham Lincoln's action most closely resembles which of the following?

 (A) The Progressive movement's support for child labor laws

 (B) The Share Our Wealth plan proposed by Huey Long during the Great Depression

 (C) The passage of civil rights legislation in the 1960s

 (D) The American Protection Association's opinion on immigration in the 1890s

Questions 31–33 refer to the following image.

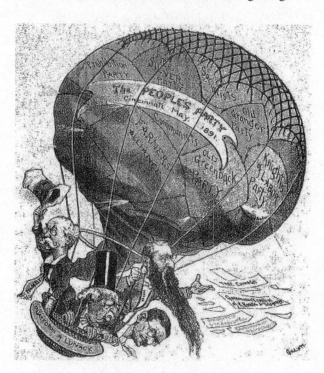

A Party of Patches, *Judge Magazine* (c. 1891)

31. The illustrator of the cartoon was making which of the following statements about the Populist (or People's) Party?

 (A) The party had new ideas for the American people.

 (B) The leadership was able and charismatic.

 (C) The party lacked originality and direction.

 (D) The party was very popular with the American voter.

32. Which of the following political movements could be considered a source of principles for the Populist Party?

 (A) Jeffersonian democracy

 (B) Antebellum reform movements

 (C) The nativist movement

 (D) Radical Republicanism

33. Which of the groups from the late 19th century would have supported the Populist Party?

 (A) Industrialists

 (B) Factory workers

 (C) Agrarian workers

 (D) Middle-class city inhabitants

Questions 34–38 refer to the following passage.

"FINANCE.—We demand a national currency, safe, sound, and flexible issued by the general government only, a full legal tender for all debts, public and private, and that without the use of banking corporations; a just, equitable, and efficient means of distribution direct to the people, at a tax not to exceed 2 per cent, per annum . . . ,

1. We demand free and unlimited coinage of silver and gold at the present legal ratio of 16 to 1.

2. We demand that the amount of circulating medium be speedily increased to not less than $50 per capita.

3. We demand a graduated income tax . . .

TRANSPORTATION.—Transportation being a means of exchange and a public necessity, the government should own and operate the railroads in the interest of the people. The telegraph and telephone, like the post-office system, being a necessity for the transmission of news, should be owned and operated by the government . . . "

—Populist Party Platform, 1892

GO ON TO THE NEXT PAGE ⟩

34. A major reason for demands made by the Populist Movement was

(A) unfair federal income tax rates harmed the American farmer

(B) the railroads and other agriculture-oriented businesses took advantage of the farmer

(C) socialism was very popular among the European immigrants settling in the Midwest

(D) devastation from the Civil War still hurt agricultural productivity

35. Which of the following ideas of the 20th century most closely resembles the sentiment expressed in the excerpt?

(A) Government regulation of the economy during World War I

(B) The amendment that required direct election of U.S. senators

(C) Federal involvement in civil rights legislation during the Truman administration

(D) The creation of federal regulations over the banking industry during the New Deal

36. The excerpt from the Populist Party platform of 1892 reflects which of the following realities in the late 19th century?

(A) The rapid growth of big business went unregulated.

(B) Americans migrated from rural areas to the city.

(C) Massive immigration from Europe created a large number of people willing to work for low wages.

(D) There was an increased concern about the growth of poverty in America.

37. The Populists' ideas about the problems the United States faced were most similar to those of which of the following American political groups?

(A) The Reagan Democrats

(B) The Jacksonian Democrats

(C) The New Dealers

(D) The Know Nothings

38. Which of the following actions by the federal government was most influenced by the Populist Party platform?

(A) Passage of immigration quotas

(B) The breakup of monopolies like the telephone corporation

(C) Government control of the communications industry

(D) Passage of the income tax and direct election of senators amendments

GO ON TO THE NEXT PAGE

Questions 39–42 refer to the following image.

AFRICAN AMERICAN MIGRATION NORTHWARD, 1910–1920

39. What was the major motivation for the migration depicted in the map shown?

(A) An economic depression in the South

(B) A promise of high-paying, skilled jobs in Northern factories

(C) A political and social refuge from the violence and lynching in the South

(D) The promise of industrial jobs with good pay and more political freedom

40. The migration depicted in the map is most similar to which of the following events?

(A) The Exodusters going to Kansas in the 1870s and 1880s

(B) The migration of runaway slaves on the Underground Railroad

(C) The Back to Africa movement led by Black Nationalists in the 1920s

(D) The California Gold Rush in the 1840s

41. Which of the following events expresses a continuation of the impact of the migration illustrated in the map?

(A) The development of the rust belt in the northeast during the 1950s

(B) Continued racial tension culminating in inner-city riots in the 1960s

(C) Supreme Court decisions that reinforced "separate but equal" in the 1950s

(D) Expanded economic opportunities for African Americans in the 1960s

42. Which of the following sociopolitical leaders and their associated institution of the African-American community emerged during the time of the Great Migration?

(A) Booker T. Washington and the Tuskegee Institute

(B) W.E.B. DuBois and the Niagara Movement

(C) Marcus Garvey and the United Negro Improvement Association

(D) Wendell P. Dabney and *The Union*

GO ON TO THE NEXT PAGE ▶

Questions 43–45 refer to the following passage.

"Our society will never be great until our cities are great . . . where . . . we begin to build the Great Society is in our countryside. We have always prided ourselves on being . . . America the beautiful. Today that beauty is in danger. The water we drink, the food we eat, the very air that we breathe, are threatened . . . A third place to build the Great Society is in the classrooms of America . . . . Our society will not be great until every young mind is set free to scan the farthest reaches of thought and imagination. We are still far from that goal . . ."

—President Lyndon Baines Johnson, Great Society speech (Commencement address to the University of Michigan), May 22, 1964

43. Which of the following movements most likely inspired the ideals set forth in President Johnson's Great Society speech?

(A) The New Frontier
(B) The Fair Deal
(C) The New Deal
(D) The Progressive Era

44. Which of the following events from the late 20th century/early 21st century represents a continuation of the ideals expressed in the above speech?

(A) Passage of the Gramm-Rudman-Hollings Act, which required a balanced federal budget
(B) Establishment of the Job Creation and Wage Enhancement Act, which created incentives for small businesses
(C) Passage of the National Community and Service Trust Act, which created the AmeriCorps Program
(D) Adoption of the Local Government Law Enforcement Block Grants Act, which gave local police jurisdictions more local control over funding as needed

45. The Great Society added which of the following to reforms originally addressed in the New Deal?

(A) Deregulation of business and industry
(B) Economic equality
(C) Universal health care
(D) Civil rights and civil liberties

Questions 46–48 refer to the following passage.

" . . . we find ourselves in a position of impotency because of the traitorous actions of those who have been treated so well by this Nation. It has not been the less fortunate . . . but rather those who have had all the benefits that the wealthiest Nation on earth has had to offer . . .

I have here in my hand a list of 205 . . . a list of names that were made known to the Secretary of State as being members of the Communist Party and who nevertheless are still working and shaping policy in the State Department . . ."

—Joseph McCarthy, Enemies from Within speech, February 9, 1950, Wheeling, WV

46. Which of the following best describes what Joseph McCarthy believed to be the most significant issue of the 1950s?

(A) The State Department has too much authority in the government.
(B) The less fortunate and minority groups were missing out on the benefits of the wealthiest nation on earth.
(C) Known communists had infiltrated the government and were directing American foreign policy.
(D) Despite America's affluence, there was a danger of the country falling to communism.

GO ON TO THE NEXT PAGE ⟶

47. Which of the following 21st century issues represents a continuation of the political problems that were relevant in the 1950s?

    (A) Fear of economic recession
    (B) Potential loss of individual civil liberties
    (C) Fear of loss of a free press
    (D) Fear of invasion

48. Which of the following contributed most directly to the fears espoused by Joseph McCarthy in the previous speech?

    (A) The Cuban Missile Crisis
    (B) The fall of China to communism
    (C) The creation of the North Atlantic Treaty Organization
    (D) The conclusion of the Vietnam conflict

Questions 49 and 50 refer to the following passage.

"On September the 11th, enemies of freedom committed an act of war against our country. Americans have known wars but not at the center of a great city on a peaceful morning. Americans have known surprise attacks—but never before on thousands of civilians.

Americans are asking: Who attacked our country? The evidence we have gathered all points to a collection of loosely affiliated terrorist organizations known as al Qaeda . . . . its goal is remaking the world—and imposing its radical beliefs on people everywhere."

—George W. Bush, Address to Congress and the American people following the Sept. 11, 2001, attacks, September 20, 2001

49. Which of the following was a significant outcome of the previous speech?

    (A) Multilateral economic sanctions against countries harboring members of al Qaeda
    (B) Strict United Nations sanctions against Iran
    (C) Multilateral military intervention in the Middle East
    (D) The establishment of internment camps for suspected domestic terrorists in the United States

50. Which of the following constitutional issues became an early 21st-century issue as a result of the events referenced in the previous excerpt?

    (A) Curbing of freedom of the press
    (B) Extra-constitutional authority granted to the president
    (C) Suspension of habeas corpus by the president of the United States
    (D) Fear of a loss of civil liberties by American citizens

GO ON TO THE NEXT PAGE

Questions 51–55 refer to the following cartoon.

One of the "Southern Chivalry" after reading the Southern account of the terror stricken North.

After reading Presd't Lincoln's Message, calling for $400,000,000 and 400,000 men.

51. It can be inferred that the cartoon above reflects what prominent event in American history?

(A) The French and Indian War
(B) The Revolutionary War
(C) The War of 1812
(D) The Civil War

52. Which of the following best describes the perspective of the cartoon's artist?

(A) The artist was a member of the Confederate government.
(B) The artist was a member of the Union government.
(C) The artist was a Northerner.
(D) The artist was a Southerner.

53. Based on the image and its title, which of the following best describes the sentiments of the cartoon above?

(A) sarcastic
(B) friendly
(C) serious
(D) hateful

54. Which of the following people would be most likely to support the perspective of the cartoon?

(A) Robert E. Lee
(B) Jefferson F. Davis
(C) George B. McClellan
(D) Judah P. Benjamin

55. Based on the ideas expressed in the cartoon above, which of the following conclusions might be drawn?

(A) The North and the South both feared the effects of war.
(B) The North was fearful of the Confederate Army.
(C) The South was fearful of the Union Army.
(D) The North and South both feared Lincoln.

IF YOU FINISH BEFORE TIME IS CALLED, YOU MAY CHECK YOUR WORK ON THIS SECTION ONLY. DO NOT TURN TO ANY OTHER SECTION IN THE TEST.

STOP

Part B: Short-Answer Questions

Time: 50 Minutes
4 Questions

1. Two major periods of American expansion occurred during the 19th century: The first began at the start of the century, and the second lasted from 1890 through the early part of the 20th century.

   Answer parts A, B, and C.

   (A) Briefly explain ONE significant similarity in the motivations behind American expansion during the two time periods.

   (B) Briefly explain ONE significant similarity in the effects of the two periods of expansion.

   (C) In a concise statement, explain how the debate over expansion impacted American politics.

2. The following short-answer question is based on the two following excerpts:

   "The incorporation of a bank, and the powers assumed by this bill, have not, in my opinion, been delegated to the United States, by the Constitution.

   1. They are not among the powers specially enumerated: for these are: 1st a power to lay taxes for the purpose of paying the debts of the United States; but no debt is paid by this bill, nor any tax laid. Were it a bill to raise money, its origination in the Senate would condemn it by the Constitution.

   2. "To borrow money." But this bill neither borrows money nor ensures the borrowing it. The proprietors of the bank will be just as free as any other money holders, to lend or not to lend their money to the public . . . "

   —Thomas Jefferson, *Opinion on the Constitutionality of a National Bank,* 1791

   "The circumstance that the powers of sovereignty are in this country divided between the National and State governments, does not afford the distinction required . . . To deny that the government of the United States has sovereign power, as to its declared purposes and trusts, because its power does not extend to all cases would be equally to deny that the State governments have sovereign power in any case, because their power does not extend to every case. The tenth section of the first article of the Constitution exhibits a long list of very important things which they may not do. And thus the United States would furnish the singular spectacle of a political society without sovereignty, or of a people governed, without government."

   —Alexander Hamilton, *Opinion as to the Constitutionality of the Bank of the United States,* 1791

   Based on the information in the two excerpts from the debate on the Constitutionality of the U.S. Bank, answer the following:

   (A) Briefly explain the main point of Thomas Jefferson's argument.

   (B) Briefly explain the main point of Alexander Hamilton's argument.

   (C) Briefly discuss how the basis of ONE of the two arguments impacted the emerging political debate on the authority of the federal government.

GO ON TO THE NEXT PAGE

3. The following short-answer question is based upon the political cartoon by Thomas Nast, which appeared in *Harper's Weekly*, October 24, 1874:

Based on the information in the cartoon and your knowledge of the United States between 1865 and 1890, answer the following questions:

(A) Based on the historical time period, what point is the author trying to convey?

(B) Identify and explain ONE specific piece of evidence that supports your statement in Part A. Keep in mind the time period in which the picture was illustrated.

(C) Identify and explain ONE specific piece of evidence that demonstrates a post-Reconstruction Southern response to the piece of evidence in Part B.

4. For this short-answer question answer all three of the following parts:

(A) Briefly explain ONE area of reform from the 1830s and 1840s.

(B) Briefly explain ONE area of reform from the Progressive Era.

(C) Briefly explain ONE historical factor that accounts for the continuity or change in reform movements between the two time periods listed in part A and part B.

IF YOU FINISH BEFORE TIME IS CALLED, YOU MAY CHECK YOUR WORK ON THIS SECTION ONLY. DO NOT TURN TO ANY OTHER SECTION IN THE TEST. STOP

Section II

Part A: Document-Based Question

Time: 55 Minutes
1 Question

Directions: Question 1 is based on the accompanying documents. The documents have been edited for the purpose of this exercise. You are advised to spend 15 minutes planning and 40 minutes writing your answer. Write your responses on the lined pages that follow the questions.

1. Analyze the development of labor unions and their response to industrialization in the late 19th century and how industrialization impacted workers' lives from 1865 to 1900.

DOCUMENT 1

"When monopolies become stronger than the law, when legislatures become the servants of monopolies, when corporations can successfully bid defiance to public good and trample on individual rights, it is time for the people to come together to erect defenses for personal rights and public safety."

From an editorial in the *National Labor Tribune*, April 24, 1875

DOCUMENT 2

Child Workers in a Spinning Factory c. 1880

GO ON TO THE NEXT PAGE

DOCUMENT 3

I. To bring within the folds of organization every department of productive industry, making knowledge a standpoint for action, and industrial and moral worth, not wealth, the true standard of individual and national greatness.

II. To secure to the toilers a proper share of the wealth that they create; more of the leisure that rightfully belongs to them; more societary advantages; more of the benefits, privileges and emoluments of the world; in a word, all those rights and privileges necessary to make them capable of enjoying, appreciating, defending and perpetuating the blessings of good government.

III. To arrive at the true condition of the producing masses in their educational, moral and financial condition, by demanding from the various governments the establishment of Bureaus of Labor Statistics.

Preamble to the Constitution of the Knights of Labor, adopted 3 January 1878

DOCUMENT 4

Ohio—the mining troubles in Hocking Valley—scene in the town of Buchtel—the striking miners' reception of "Blackleg" workmen when returning from their work escorted by a detachment of Pinkerton's detectives

GO ON TO THE NEXT PAGE

DOCUMENT 5

Eight Hours

We mean to make things over,
We are tired of toil for naught
With but bare enough to live upon
And ne'er an hour for thought.
We want to feel the sunshine
And we want to smell the flow'rs
We are sure that God has willed it
And we mean to have eight hours;
We're summoning our forces
From the shipyard, shop and mill
Eight hours for work, eight hours for rest
Eight hours for what we will;
Eight hours for work, eight hours for rest
Eight hours for what we will.

Labor song of the 1880s

DOCUMENT 6

"You may not know that the labor movement as represented by the trades unions stands for right, for justice, for liberty. You may not imagine that the issuance of an injunction depriving men of a legal as well as a natural right to protect themselves, their wives, and little ones must fail of its purpose. Repression or oppression never yet succeeded in crushing the truth or redressing a wrong.

. . . let me assure you that labor will organize and more compactly than ever and upon practical lines; and despite relentless antagonism, achieve for humanity a nobler manhood, a more beautiful womanhood, and a happier childhood."

From Samuel Gompers, "The Laborer's Right to Life," printed in *American Federationist*, September 1894

GO ON TO THE NEXT PAGE

DOCUMENT 7

Attention Workingmen!

GREAT

MASS-MEETING

TO-NIGHT, at 7.30 o'clock,

AT THE

HAYMARKET, Randolph St., Bet. Desplaines and Halsted.

Good Speakers will be present to denounce the latest atrocious act of the police, the shooting of our fellow-workmen yesterday afternoon.

Workingmen Arm Yourselves and Appear in Full Force!

THE EXECUTIVE COMMITTEE.

Achtung, Arbeiter!

Große

Maſſen-Verſammlung

Heute Abend, ½8 Uhr, auf dem

Heumarkt, Randolph-Straße, zwiſchen Desplaines- u. Halſted-Str.

☞ Gute Redner werden den neueſten Schurkenſtreich der Polizei, indem ſie geſtern Nachmittag unſere Brüder erſchoß, geißeln.

☞ Arbeiter, bewaffnet Euch und erſcheint maſſenhaft!

Das Executiv-Comite.

IF YOU FINISH BEFORE TIME IS CALLED, YOU MAY CHECK YOUR WORK ON THIS SECTION ONLY. DO NOT TURN TO ANY OTHER SECTION IN THE TEST.

STOP

Part B: Long Essay Question

Time: 35 Minutes
1 Question

Directions: Choose ONE question from this part. You are advised to spend 5 minutes planning and 30 minutes writing your answer.

1. Analyze how political values and reform that emerged from the Second Great Awakening created political and social change in the United States during the antebellum years.

2. Analyze how political values and reform emerged in American society after World War II and how these values created political and social change in the United States during the postwar period.

IF YOU FINISH BEFORE TIME IS CALLED, YOU MAY CHECK YOUR WORK ON THIS SECTION ONLY. DO NOT TURN TO ANY OTHER SECTION IN THE TEST.

STOP

DIAGNOSTIC TEST: ANSWER KEY

1.	C	15.	C	29.	D	43.	C
2.	B	16.	A	30.	C	44.	C
3.	C	17.	C	31.	C	45.	D
4.	A	18.	C	32.	B	46.	C
5.	C	19.	B	33.	C	47.	B
6.	D	20.	B	34.	B	48.	B
7.	D	21.	C	35.	D	49.	C
8.	C	22.	B	36.	A	50.	D
9.	A	23.	B	37.	C	51.	D
10.	C	24.	B	38.	D	52.	C
11.	A	25.	C	39.	D	53.	A
12.	C	26.	C	40.	A	54.	C
13.	B	27.	C	41.	B	55.	A
14.	A	28.	A	42.	B		

ANSWERS AND EXPLANATIONS

SECTION I

PART A: MULTIPLE-CHOICE ANSWERS

1. C

The American Indian nations of the Great Plains depended upon the buffalo hunt for survival. They were nomadic groups that followed their food supply.

2. B

The horse was introduced (by accident) to the Plains Indians as runaway horses from Spanish exploration parties eventually made their way into the North American Plains. The Great Plains Indians learned to tame the wild horses and utilize them in the buffalo hunt. This greatly aided the Indians in that it took less time to hunt buffalo, giving Indians more time to develop Indian culture.

3. C

The Indian nations of what became the northeastern United States were highly organized and were sedentary as they had developed a productive agricultural system, plus they supplemented their diet with fish and other local animal life.

4. A

The idea expressed in this excerpt best describes how a republican form of government began to develop in the British North American colonies.

5. C

Jacksonian Democrats believed themselves to be the representative of the "common man"—political leadership should be based on hard work and ability, not through being well-born and wealthy.

6. D

Beginning in the mid-17th century, a slave-based plantation system developed as well as a representative form of government in the colonies (and then state) of Maryland.

7. D

Because Native Americans did not have any natural resistance to smallpox and other diseases indigenous to Europeans, it is estimated millions died due to infection by the European explorers.

8. C

At first, Europeans tried to use local Native Americans as slaves. But as thousands died because of infectious disease, the Europeans (first the Portuguese, then the Spanish) began to import slave labor from Africa. Africans survived longer from infectious disease than the Native Americans. However, the intense labor often led to a relatively short life expectancy once the slaves arrived in the New World.

9. A

The Europeans settled and interacted with the native population in the Western Hemisphere, resulting in the unintended deaths of perhaps millions of natives. The forced migration of American Indians during the 1830s to "Indian Territory" (now Oklahoma) resulted in the unintended deaths of thousands of American Indians. The American government never did anything to try to stop the deaths or forced migration.

10. C

The *Declaration of Rights and Grievances* was written by the First Continental Congress in reaction to the Intolerable Acts, which colonists believed violated their rights as Englishmen. At this point in 1774, the vast majority of colonists was still very loyal to the King and had no interest in declaring independence.

11. A

The debate over nullification of the Tariff of 1832 in South Carolina was similar in that South Carolinians believed that their rights were being violated under the Compact Theory, which gave a state the right to nullify a federal law or secede from the Union.

12. C

As sovereign over the empire, King George did not respond to the *Declaration of Rights and Grievances*. It went against his ideals to address the demands of a colonial people.

13. B

Based on the demands of the First Continental Congress, the Americans promised not to import British goods, purchase or use British goods, or export goods to England to be processed in their factories. This would have harmed the English economy to an extent.

14. A

The Articles of Confederation granted the 13 original states a lot of autonomy. After the ratification of the U.S. Constitution, several states believed that the way the new document was worded still granted the various states a lot of autonomy when it came to federal law—this was illustrated in 1798 by the publication of the Kentucky and Virginia Resolutions, which indicated that states had the authority to declare unjust federal law unconstitutional.

15. C

Before the ratification of the Constitution, the United States found it difficult to sign a treaty with a European power, as evidenced by the failure of the Spanish to come to an agreement in the Jay-Gardoqui Treaty. However, in the 1790s, the United States signed two important treaties—one with Great Britain (Jay's Treaty) and one with Spain (Pinckney Treaty).

16. A

The reinstatement of the Navigation Acts after the French and Indian War was harmful to the American economy in the years 1763 to 1775, partially as the colonists learned how to master smuggling. Americans, from their perspective, were forced to trade through Britain only. This reinforcement of these restrictive acts attempted to cut off the lucrative trade America had with the Dutch and the French Caribbean colonies.

17. C

New England merchants protested the passage of the Embargo Act of 1807 because the New England economy greatly depended upon trade, especially with Great Britain. The Jefferson administration had passed the law to force Britain to stop the practice of impressment against American merchant ships and sailors. This law failed.

18. C

The result of the events begun by the Embargo of 1807, which eventually prompted American involvement in the War of 1812, led to the Hartford Convention in December 1814. The five New England states met and discussed several issues (even entertaining the idea of secession) and ultimately issued several demands, which included never-ratified amendments to the U.S. Constitution and an immediate demand to withdrawal from the war with Great Britain (which had ended by the time the demands of the Hartford Convention were made public).

19. B

In its Hartford Convention statement, the Federalist Party, initially a political party that supported the concept of a strong central government (in the 1790s), alluded to the concepts of the Kentucky and Virginia Resolutions of 1798 (authored by Democrat-Republicans, who advocated states' rights). The party feared that a strong central government led by the Democrat-Republicans would marginalize the influence of the Federalists.

20. B

School segregation was a major civil rights issue in the 1950s. States believed they had the right to determine where children attended school and what groups attended which schools. In the South, it was believed to be a states' rights issue to provide "separate but equal" education for African-American and white children. The Supreme Court case, *Brown v. Board of Education of Topeka, Kansas,* determined otherwise.

21. C

The illustration is a portrayal of a typical worker at the Lowell Mills, established in the 1820s in Lowell, Massachusetts. The factory workers were young females from the surrounding farm areas. Since agriculture was gradually moving toward the Midwest, women took jobs in factories until they got married.

22. B

In the late 1830s and through the 1840s, immigrants, mainly from Ireland and the German states, began to flee their homeland for various reasons. Arriving in America, many (especially the Irish) settled in New England and were willing to take any job for a low salary. This created competition with the Lowell Girls, who were paid relatively well and had safe working conditions (except at the time of their strike in 1836).

23. B

The traditional role of the woman who worked in the home by the side of her husband and as the primary caretaker of the children was changing, beginning in New England, where women were working in factories until they were married. Also, women became active in labor issues—to the point of going on strike in 1834 and 1836 in Lowell, Massachusetts.

24. B

Rumors ran rampant across the South during Reconstruction. Freedmen were attracted to Kansas because of the promise that they would receive several acres of land and $500 to begin a new life.

The conditions of life in the post–Civil War South were not good for the former slaves.

25. C

In the years surrounding World War I, thousands of African Americans migrated from the South (primarily rural areas) to northern cities to work in the factories that were looking for cheap labor. The African-American population in cities such as Chicago, Detroit, and Philadelphia increased dramatically at this time.

26. C

During times of African-American migration in the United States, increased tension developed between the migrants and the white population in northern cities. African Americans were more likely to work for lower wages in the factories than white Americans, and white Americans believed that their jobs were in danger.

27. C

Lincoln's initial goal in fighting the Civil War was to restore the Union. The pronouncement of the Emancipation Proclamation added ending slavery to that goal, although Lincoln initially freed the slaves only in the states that were in rebellion against the United States.

28. A

The Thirteenth Amendment to the U.S. Constitution was ratified in December 1865, ending involuntary servitude forever in the United States.

29. D

The ruling of *Brown v. Board of Education* in 1954 was met with severe reaction in the South, although the Supreme Court used the basis of the Fourteenth Amendment's Equal Protection Clause. Similarly, the Emancipation Proclamation was met with a negative reaction in the North during the Civil War, as many Northerners were willing to fight to preserve the Union but not to free the slaves.

30.   C

The Emancipation Proclamation of 1863 was a first step in the process of African Americans gaining an identity as fully equal American citizens. A culminating movement in this quest came in the 1960s when a series of civil rights acts were passed by Congress that further codified the identity of African Americans as legal equals.

31.   C

The artist was criticizing the lack of credible leadership by using four political and labor leaders from the late 19th century who received a lot of criticism from the mainstream press and politicians (Terence V. Powderly, head of the failing Knights of Labor; Ignatius Donnelly, a Minnesota politician known for starting many third-party movements; Jerry "Sockless" Simpson, Kansas member of the U.S. House of Representatives; and William Peffer, Kansas, U.S. senator). The platform of the party seemed to come from a combination of previously failed third parties.

32.   B

The antebellum reform movements were centered on the idea of creating a more democratic society, either through more public education, more rights for women, or the end of slavery. The concepts shared by these movements were very similar to the ideas of the Populist Party, as they supported popular election of U.S. senators and provided more power to the people through referendum, recall, and initiative.

33.   C

Agrarian workers, or farmers, would have supported the Populist Party. The core of Populists was represented by the Grange and the Farmer's Alliances from the 1870s and 1880s.

34.   B

Railroads and other "middlemen" charged farmers higher rates than they did other groups and businesses, as they knew farmers depended very much on their service to get crops to market before they spoiled. This angered farmers and caused them to form organizations such as the Grange, Farmer's Alliances, and the Populist Party to fight this abuse.

35.   D

During the New Deal, Congress passed several pieces of legislation to regulate the economy. The Federal Deposit Insurance Corporation and other laws were passed to permanently regulate the banking industry.

36.   A

The rapid growth of unregulated big business, especially the railroad industry and large monopolies, led to businesses' ability to take advantage of consumers through high prices and sometimes unsafe products.

37.   C

The New Dealers of the 1930s believed that *laissez-faire* American capitalism needed to be regulated so that another economic disaster such at the Great Depression would not happen again.

38.   D

In 1913, two of the demands of the Populists (and later, the Progressives) were met. The Sixteenth Amendment to the U.S. Constitution called for a graduated income tax, and the Seventeenth Amendment required that all U.S. senators be elected by the people of the state they would represent.

39.   D

Because of the outbreak of the Great War (World War I), many African Americans moved northward to take jobs in the factories that were gearing up for the war effort. Racial tension and riots broke out across the North in reaction to whites' fear that they would be replaced by people who would work for lower wages.

40.   A

Freedmen from the South were attracted to Kansas with the (false) promise of free land and work animals. They were called Exodusters because their mass migration was much like that described in Exodus in the Bible.

41.   B

The perceived lack of social, political, and economic opportunities for African Americans in the 1960s led to several race riots, most notably in Detroit. The frustration of inner city African Americans led to an explosion of anger in the mid-1960s.

42.   B

W. E. B. DuBois emerged as a new, and somewhat controversial, leader of the African-American community in the early 20th century. He was the first African American to graduate from Harvard and the first to earn a PhD from Harvard. He founded the Niagara Movement (the forerunner to the National Association for the Advancement of Colored People) in 1905. The movement was a national organization that supported political, civil, and social equality for African Americans.

43.   C

Historians have identified Lyndon Johnson's Great Society as the continuation or attempt at completion of ideas established during the New Deal by the Franklin Roosevelt administration.

44.   C

AmeriCorps is a federal program in which adults are engaged in service to their community through nonprofit organizations. It was created by the Clinton administration and is modeled after VISTA (Volunteers in Service to America) and the Peace Corps.

45.   D

The Great Society brought civil rights and civil liberties to the forefront of the social issues that America was facing during the 1960s. The Civil Rights Acts of 1964 and 1965 were the centerpiece laws passed by Congress in order to codify and reinforce the provisions of the Fourteenth and Fifteenth Amendments to the Constitution.

46.   C

According to Joseph McCarthy, the State Department had 205 known communists serving under the Secretary of State. These communists,

who had all the benefits of privileged upbringings and superior educations, were influencing American foreign policy in a time when a Cold War was underway between the democratic United States and its allies and the communist Soviet Union and its allies. The fear led to the belief that more nations in Europe and Asia would fall to communism if the United States did not take a strong position against communism at home and abroad.

47.   B

The loss of basic civil liberties—free speech and freedom of expression, for example—was a fear during the Red Scare of the 1950s and post–9/11 America, especially after the passage of the Patriot Act in 2001. There was a fear that the government would spy on select groups of American people and keep records of what people read and with whom they associated.

48.   B

In 1949, when China "fell" to communism, a lot of people in the government questioned, "Who lost China?" The fact that an ally of the United States from World War II became a communist state within four years after the end of the war puzzled a lot of Americans and created a fear that communism was spreading quickly. Senator McCarthy was able to exploit this fear in his bid for re-election to the U.S. Senate.

49.   C

The speech given by President George W. Bush was tantamount to a declaration of war against terrorism. The United States led a coalition of Western allies to invade Afghanistan and defeat the Taliban-led government—a government that was harboring the infamous terrorist organization al Qaeda.

50.   D

Americans feared a loss of civil liberties in the wake of the September 11, 2001, attacks and the impending "war on terror" as Congress passed the Patriot Act, which granted the government the ability to monitor Americans more closely.

51. D

Answer D is the best answer. The date of the cartoon is 1861, when the Civil War began. In addition, the captions within the cartoon make reference to the South and the North and to Lincoln, who was president during the Civil War.

52. C

Answer C is the best answer. The perspective of the cartoon's artist is best described as that of a Northerner who depicts the Southern gentlemen as happy upon hearing about the "terror stricken" North, but shocked and horrified upon hearing that Lincoln planned to call for added funds and troops.

53. A

Answer choice A is the best answer. The cartoon is sarcastic, poking fun at a Southerner's reaction to troop build up. The artist underscores the sarcasm by referring in the first caption to chivalry, a long-standing part of traditional Southern life.

54. C

Answer C is the best answer. As general of the Union Army, McClellan would be most likely to support the critical perspective of the cartoon. Robert E. Lee, Jefferson F. Davis, and Judah P. Benjamin all were key Confederate figures whose perspectives would be quite the opposite.

55. A

Answer A is the best answer. One can draw the logical conclusion from the caption information provided that both the North and South experienced fear as the Civil War accelerated.

PART B: SHORT-QUESTION RESPONSES

1. (A) In the 19th century, the United States developed a policy of expansion, predominantly across the North American continent, that both grew and diversified the American economy. This policy gave American businesses more access to raw materials and created more markets for American-made goods.

    (B) The acquisition of the vast landholdings included in the Louisiana Purchase encouraged agricultural expansion throughout the 19th century. By 1900, the United States also took control of the sugar and pineapple industries in Hawaii and secured a deep-water base in the Philippines. Subsequently, the Chinese market in Eastern Asia opened to American trade.

    (C) The territorial expansion of the United States in the first half of the 19th century led to political disputes. The question of slavery in these newly acquired lands (the Louisiana Purchase and others) served as one catalyst of the Civil War. As the century progressed, overseas expansion caused continued national debate on the validity of economic motivation for U.S. foreign policy.

2. (A) Thomas Jefferson argued that the authority to create a National Bank is not enumerated in the Constitution; therefore, it is unconstitutional to create such an entity.

    (B) Alexander Hamilton's argument is based on the idea that there is a list of "very important things" that the federal government cannot do, but the creation of a National Bank is not among those items. Therefore, the National Bank was indeed constitutional.

    (C) Hamilton's argument demonstrated that the Constitution does not have to explicitly call for something like a National Bank for that entity to exist within the legal structure of the United States. The framers of the U.S. Constitution had no concept of what would happen in the United States, both how quickly the country would expand and the technological development that would occur. The idea that the Constitution had to adapt to different time periods was very significant.

Jefferson wanted to limit the scope of the federal government to the rules explicitly called for so that the government could not take on any extra-constitutional powers or authority that would create a situation like the time before the American Revolution. Jefferson had the dream of an agrarian republic with minimal interference of a federal government. However, even Jefferson had to depart from his philosophy when faced with the opportunity to purchase Louisiana from France in 1803.

3. (A) The political cartoonist is stating that with the end of Reconstruction, it was the intent of white Southerners to return the South to the way it was before the Civil War. White supremacist societies worked to make sure that the rights won by the Freedmen (former slaves) through federal law and the Constitution as an outcome of the Civil War and Reconstruction would all be eliminated in the South.

(B) With the birth of the white leagues and the Ku Klux Klan after the Civil War, the Freedmen were forced to live in fear. Many Freedmen were intimidated as they tried to gain job skills, improve their living conditions, or attempt to vote.

(C) Laws restricting Freedmen from voting by means of literacy tests, poll taxes, or general intimidation by militant white groups prevented many African Americans from registering to vote or casting a ballot.

4. (A) The idea of abolition saw a rise in popularity during the 1830s and 1840s. Leaders such as William Lloyd Garrison and Frederick Douglass led the fight for emancipation of the slaves held in the South. The ultimate goal was to gain social equality and eventually citizenship for former slaves.

(B) During the Progressive Era, women worked hard to try to attain full suffrage. By the turn of the 20th century, women had the right to vote in many states but could still not vote for president. The National and American Women's Suffrage Association was able to claim victory in 1919 when the 19th Amendment, giving women the right to vote in all elections, was added to the Constitution.

(C) A major focus of the reform movements of the two time periods in the early 19th century was the expansion of democracy. To give slaves personal freedom and then citizenship and to give women the right to vote were major steps toward a more complete democracy.

SECTION II

PART A: DBQ SAMPLE RESPONSE

While labor unions existed before the Civil War, they were very limited in scope. With new factories built for the war effort now producing goods for peacetime, thousands of workers were employed in the second and most productive industrial revolution in the United States. However, unsafe working conditions and low wages hurt the poorly educated blue-collar workers. As the nation became more mechanized, these laborers found themselves competing for fewer jobs with an ever-increasing European immigrant labor force. The inconsistency of the American economy also hurt the factory worker. Labor unions made promises to help the displaced American workers with higher salaries, shorter working hours, and safer work conditions.

By the time factories were in full peacetime production, workers found themselves being replaced by labor-saving devices and, at times, a worsening economy caused those still on the job to take a cut in salary. Workers reacted by following an emerging union movement. The call to join unions was heard by thousands who feared that the small but powerful combination of big business and Washington politics would limit their economic livelihood and rights (Doc. 1). The first major union to emerge in the United States, the Knights of Labor, promised workers a larger share of the wealth they created and more leisure time (Doc. 3). To accomplish these goals, workers would need the "blessings of good government" and, according to many unions, the government at this time was not good.

The realities of the 1870s and 1880s hurt the welfare of the working man. The Panic of 1873 brought layoffs and closed business. By 1877 railroad workers were faced with a pay cut. This reduction in salary, while expenses remained the same, was too much for the workers to bear, and the Great Railway Strike of 1877 spread from Baltimore to St. Louis during the summer of that year. Ultimately the workers lost their battle as President Rutherford B. Hayes called in the military to fight strikers and protect the railroad companies. Private detectives, the Pinkertons, were often hired by large businesses to break up major labor strikes by protecting "scab" workers who took the place of union members. In the case of the Homestead Steel Strike in 1892, detectives even took part in a gun battle with striking workers (Doc. 4). Union workers also had to face the reality of child labor in the 19th century as children could be hired for lower salaries and forced to work more than adult men (Doc. 2). Labor unions fought against child labor because, if for no other reason, workers wanted the next generation of Americans to gain a good education and not have to spend their entire life in dangerous factory work.

Inspired by charismatic leaders and rallies, unions did not give up their fight as the latter part of the century passed. One of the major events in the labor movement occurred in Chicago in 1886 at Haymarket Square (Doc. 7). Protesting treatment during a strike, workers rallied to support the union. However, some participants at the rally were considered anarchists who advocated an overthrow of unjust government and the ownership class. A riot followed. Ultimately the Haymarket Affair brought an end to the Knights of Labor, who were wrongfully blamed for the rally and its outcome.

Replacing the Knights was the American Federation of Labor, led by Samuel Gompers, who argued that "the trades unions stand for right, for justice, for liberty (Doc. 6)." The A.F. of L. was less politically motivated than previous unions and was known more for advocating better wages and shorter working hours for union members. The union argued that these changes should be made through the political process in place. There was no outcry within the union to change the American political system as there had been in the Knights of Labor. This stance was more acceptable to many Americans, although unions were still not popular or successful until the early 20th century.

Overall, 19th-century industrialization impacted workers' lives in many ways. Lower wages, longer hours and the replacement of workers with children or machines were viewed by laboring citizens as a step backward. Workers in a consistent manner throughout the time period maintained their focus on a fledgling union movement that promised to right the wrongs of the ownership class and get the workers part of the wealth they helped to create.

Overall, this essay is very strong, well-rounded and balanced. The supporting evidence is superior, all but one of the documents is explicitly utilized—which is acceptable—and there is ample "outside" factual information. The information from the documents and from outside of the documents is woven together to make a very clear argument that supports the thesis.

The thesis for this essay would receive the 1 point credit (out of 1 possible point), and the inclusion of document, outside information, and analysis would earn the 4 points possible. The contextualization of this is excellent, earning the 1 point possible, and the synthesis of the information would also earn the 1 possible point, giving this essay a 7 out of 7 possible points on the DBQ rubric.

PART B: LONG ESSAY SAMPLE RESPONSES

SAMPLE RESPONSE 1

Beginning in the mid-1820s, more Americans were able to participate in the democratic process as the states began to eliminate both property and religious restrictions as requirements for voting. At the same time, the Second Great Awakening inspired some individuals and groups with the idea of creating utopian societies in America. This philosophy, coupled with increased popular voting participation, led to a distinctive dramatic change in the political landscape of the United States. Therefore, prompted by the expansion of democracy during the Jacksonian Era and inspired by the Second Great Awakening, several reform movements took hold during the antebellum period that resulted in political and social change.

The antebellum period witnessed the evolution of the abolition reform movement. Though the abolitionist movement began in the North, it impacted the South as well. The abolitionists' vision of a better world was one without the institution of slavery; however, there was a wide spectrum of abolitionists. Radicals such as William Lloyd Garrison insisted on immediate, uncompensated emancipation. Others, like the Free Soilers, wanted slavery to end by prohibiting its expansion into the newly acquired western territories. The political and social impact of this movement created a vast divide in the United States as the North increasingly became more in favor of ending the institution of slavery and the South becoming more entrenched in its defense of the "peculiar institution."

Closely linked to the abolitionist movement was the growing women's rights movement of the 1840s. Many women's activists who earlier had fought for the emancipation of slaves also campaigned for women's equality: the right to own property, equality in the family, and a right to an education. When several American women attempted to attend the World Anti-Slavery Convention in London, they were refused admission. These women returned to the United States and organized the Seneca Falls Convention. Led by Elizabeth Cady Stanton and Lucretia Mott, dozens of women and men wrote the democratically charged *Declaration of Rights and Grievances* based on the Declaration of Independence. Underscoring the concepts of liberty and equality under the law found in Jefferson's Declaration of Independence, both the women's rights and the abolitionist movements benefited significantly.

To build a more democratic society and expand the ideals of a better nation, the idea of compulsory public education came to the forefront during this era. Horace Mann of Massachusetts and Thaddeus Stevens of Pennsylvania were two leaders in the movement to require public education for all children. Some reformers and politicians believed that if America had a more educated society, then Americans would be more informed and a more democratic nation would emerge. The ideals inherent in the struggle for women's rights and the abolition of slavery were also characteristic of the efforts toward state-supported public education. The reformist literature of the period highlighted the common goals of all three efforts and helped to enlighten and inspire a more concerned American public.

Because of the ideals that emerged from the Jacksonian Democracy and the Second Great Awakening the structure of American politics and society began to change. More Americans were taking part in the democratic process and becoming active in movements that would create change in America. However, within a few years these movements would come to a temporary halt due to the oncoming Civil War.

This analysis does an excellent job tying together three distinctive but interrelated reform movements from the antebellum era: abolitionist reform, women's rights, and public education movements. All three movements were focused on the ideas of democracy and freedom. The amount of factual evidence is good, but could be stronger with the mention of a few more examples like The Liberator and (later) Uncle Tom's Cabin when discussing literature.

Overall, the essay demonstrates good synthesis by demonstrating that all three reform movements had commonalities and were related in some way. Also, the essay clearly organizes the reform movements within the time period.

Based on the draft of the Long Essay Question rubric, this essay would receive a 7.

Sample Response 2

In the years following World War II, the United States went through distinctive and dramatic social and political changes. Reflecting on the wartime experience, Americans began to question a lot of the political and social principles that had existed in the pre-war years, especially those that were based on racial segregation and women's domestic roles.

During World War II, African Americans and whites still served in segregated units that mirrored a segregated society; however, the idea of integrating the military started to emerge. Due to the high number of volunteers and draftees, it became difficult to train everyone without having racially integrated camps. Factories, short of laborers, hired many minorities to fill positions left open by men who went to fight in the war; it did not matter who was working, as long as Americans were working together to win the war. It became apparent to Americans that the United States had been separating different social groups much like the Germans did in the years leading to the war. Within five years after the conclusion of World War II, the U.S. military was integrated. The idea of integrating the military soon influenced life in the United States. African Americans began to protest segregation in society through events such as the Montgomery bus boycott and through the lawsuit that eventually led to the *Brown v. Board of Education* Supreme Court decision. In turn, this led to school integration and a reversal of *Plessy v. Ferguson*, the "separate but equal" theory that emerged in the 1890s. American society was evolving.

Throughout the development of the United States as a nation, women customarily took on the roles of mother, wife, and caretaker. During World War II, these roles dramatically changed as women worked in factories and took on traditionally male jobs. During the war, "Rosie the Riveter" became an American icon that changed the traditional role of women in America. Supported by the equally iconic "we can do it" posters, women worked in factories producing materiel for the war effort. After the war was over and the soldiers returned home, many women remained working as their husbands went to school on the GI Bill. By the 1950s, many homes were becoming two-income homes, families began to move to the new suburbs, and American family life changed dramatically.

In the two decades following the war, other minority groups began to emerge and agitate for their equal rights. In the western states, Mexican Americans pushed for more rights, especially in agriculture with the formation of the United Farm Workers under the leadership of Cesar Chavez. American Indians formed the American Indian movement in an attempt to retain their identity and gain more civil rights. In the late 1960s, the gay rights movement began with the Stonewall riots in New York City, as gay men were angered at being harassed by the local police. These movements, as well as others, all grew out of the civil rights movements inspired by a new era of democratic thought that emerged from the outcome of World War II.

Inspired by events that changed the face of America during World War II, a dramatic political and social change took place that granted more rights to minority groups that had not had full rights. Thus, the United States began to fulfill the political and social ideals on which it had been founded.

This is a strong essay that clearly has a thesis that illustrates an understanding of the question and of the time period. The thesis is supported with several specific facts, although fewer are required for the long essay question. This essay weaves in a lot of evidence without making it seem like a laundry-list type of essay.

The analysis is clear and demonstrates a synthesis of the various changes that occurred in the postwar years. This essay satisfies all of the requirements of the prompt and clearly demonstrates the writer's complete understanding of the time period in relation to the topic. Unique concepts/ideas of the time period are evident throughout the essay, clearly demonstrating the skill of periodization.

Based on the draft of the Long Essay Question rubric, this essay would receive a 7.

HOW TO MAKE THIS BOOK WORK FOR YOU BASED ON THE RESULT OF YOUR DIAGNOSTIC TEST

First, you should know that only one-half of the composite score for the AP U.S. History exam will be from multiple-choice questions. The essays are equally important and potentially easier to master with preparation. No matter what your results on the Diagnostic Test, you should review the essay exam format and expectations carefully.

How you interpret your diagnostic score depends on your situation. How soon is the exam? If you took the Diagnostic Test in the fall or winter, you are likely to score lower than if you took the test in early May. Analyze the types of questions that you missed. The Diagnostic has questions that span from the American Revolution, to World War I, to the Cold War, and many eras in between. Take note of the time periods that you find difficult to recall when taking the test.

This book reviews all eras of AP U.S. History that the AP exam will cover. The review chapters are broken down into five chronological units, each spanning an era of U.S. history. Look over the chapters that comprise these units, paying special attention to your weaknesses. Each review chapter is followed by more practice multiple-choice questions to sharpen your understanding.

Part Three of this book provides more testing practice: four complete exams with 55 multiple-choice questions, 4 short-answer questions and two essays. You will be ready to take these full exams after the bulk of your review. Set a time and a place for taking these full practice exams under test-like conditions without interruptions or distractions.

AP U.S. HISTORY REVIEW

CHAPTER 3: NATIVE POPULATIONS BEFORE EUROPEAN ARRIVAL

OVERVIEW OF NATIVE POPULATIONS

Prior to the arrival of the first Europeans in North America, millions of Native Americans lived in scattered and diverse settlements across the continent. By 1492, at least 375 distinct languages were spoken and societies were structured in many ways. Some tribes were nomadic and could be easily moved to follow food sources or weather patterns, while others were more permanent. Prominent crops included maize (corn), squash, and beans that were supplemented by perfected techniques of farming, hunting, and fishing. There was, however, no livestock, so farming was limited because they were unable to plow fields or use natural fertilizer. Wheeled vehicles were nonexistent because of the lack of domestic animals like oxen and horses to pull them. Native Americans had no metal tools or machines or gunpowder prior to European arrival in the Americas. Unlike the Europeans who had developed systems of maritime navigation, Indians had only large canoes and rafts, which were unable to safely cross open waters like the Atlantic and Pacific oceans, therefore curtailing any expansionist goals.

Even though land was the economic basis of their primarily hunting and farming societies, native populations did not view land as an economic commodity that could be turned into a profit. Village leaders allocated plots of land to separate families for seasonal use and while these families owned the *right* to use the land assigned to them, they did not actually *own* the land itself. Many tribes would claim specific areas for hunting but anyone could use unclaimed land. Unlike their European visitors, indigenous American populations were not dedicated to accumulating riches or material possessions; however, social status with a kinship group or tribe held significance.

Political power structures and religious beliefs varied by tribe but this did not deter the existence of extensive trading routes and communication networks within the present boundaries of the United States. Despite trading and communicating, different tribes were often at war with one another to obtain goods, seize captives, or seek revenge for the deaths of family or tribe members. Conversely, they did frequently conduct diplomacy and make peace despite the lack of a centralized authority until the 15th century when five Iroquois tribes formed the Great League of Peace. The Great League of Peace annually convened as the Great Council with representatives from the five groups aiming to coordinate behavior toward outsiders. Despite this assembly, each tribe maintained its own separate political system and set of religious beliefs, chiefly because Native Americans did not think of themselves as a single, allied people; rather, this idea was invented by European explorers and colonists and only later adopted by the descendants of the native populations themselves.

RELIGION

Native American tribes were widespread throughout what is now the United States and the location of each tribe dictated how they responded to local resources. Because different tribes had to adapt to different locales, tribes became culturally distinguished, which led to tribe-specific rituals, social structures, and tactics for survival. Shamans, medicine men, and other religious leaders were thought to have unusual skills in summoning supernatural spirits and were highly esteemed in their respective tribes. While tenets of religion or spirituality varied among tribes, there were some commonalities. Most Native American cultures had **cosmologies**—origin parables passed on from each generation to the next through the oral tradition. Also, most indigenous Americans worshipped an omnipotent, omniscient Creator or "Master Spirit," a presence that could not only assume different forms but also appear as both male and female. Native American religions supported the idea of afterlife and the immortality of the soul.

In contrast with European religion, however, Native American spirituality did not set forth a distinction between the supernatural and the natural; rather, Indians believed the "material" and the "spiritual" to occupy the same plane. The indigenous North American peoples believed in **animism**, which dictated the spiritual realm pervaded all elements of the natural world and that every being—from rock to animal—had a unique spirit. Human beings lived inside this vast network of the material and spiritual and their interactions with all non-human beings was viewed as social. Europeans believed that the religions they encountered among America's native populations to be heresy and that the native worshippers needed to be converted to the "true" religion of Christianity.

GENDER ROLES

Many Native American tribes were **matrilineal** in that tribal rights and responsibilities and social station were determined by the bloodline of the mother as opposed to the father. Both genders, however, had a voice when it came to decision-making. Because men were frequently away on the hunt, women took responsibility not only for household duties but also for farming. Europeans believed hunting and fishing to be leisure activities and therefore thought of Native American men as weak and not a strong source of support for the family. The fact that women worked in the fields also upset Europeans—they found this to be work meant for slaves and that these gender roles were barbaric and unchristian.

CHAPTER 4: EUROPEAN EXPANSION AND THE COLUMBIAN EXCHANGE

OVERVIEW OF EUROPEAN EXPANSION

The European exploration of the Americas was a byproduct of the search for a sea route to the East: India, China, and the East Indies islands, from which Europeans could import tea, porcelain, silk, spices, and the other luxury goods that acted as the core of international trade during the early modern era.

Christopher Columbus arrived in the Bahamas in October 1492. Shortly after, he discovered the islands of Hispaniola and Cuba. It was not until Amerigo Vespucci's trips along the South American coast from 1499 to 1502 that Europeans realized a continent they had had no knowledge of had been encountered.

THE COLUMBIAN EXCHANGE

Columbus's arrival in the Bahamas in 1492 prompted the transmission and interchange of plants, animals, diseases, culture, human populations (i.e., slaves), and technology among Europe, Africa, and the Americas; this interchange greatly benefitted Europeans while simultaneously bringing catastrophe to Native American populations and cultures.

DESTROYED BY DISEASE

Wherever European colonists and explorers settled, native populations succumbed to dismaying and unparalleled epidemics. Regardless of location, the preliminary exposure to European diseases such as smallpox, typhus, cholera, and measles, afflicted almost every Indian. Within one decade of initial contact, fatalities wiped out nearly 50 percent of the precontact population—even minor childhood illnesses such as chicken pox killed natives, regardless of age. In some tribes, there were so few survivors that those who remained lost their autonomous identity and joined a neighboring tribe or converted to Christianity and assimilated into the newfound European societies. Native Americans had no immunity to the pathogens Europeans brought to the New World and the exchange of such diseases was incredibly one-sided; while European infectious diseases ransacked native populations in one of the most rapid-fire population massacres in human history, Europeans were relatively untouched by the few previously unencountered pathogens found in the Americas, largely due to the fact that the Western hemisphere was home to fewer and less contagious diseases.

Despite their differing religious beliefs, both native and European invaders believed these epidemics to be indicative of some vehement mystic disturbance. Christian colonists asserted that the diseases overtaking the native populations were the work of their God, who was punishing those they encountered who defied the colonists' attempts to convert them to Christianity. The natives, on the other hand, blamed their disease on witchcraft practiced by the colonists. Despite these rationales, colonizers never intentionally disseminated disease fostered in the Old World.

Three factors contributed to the virulence of the diseases the Europeans introduced to the New World. Trade and invasions far from the homeland were more common in Europe and Asia, allowing the trade and transformation of numerous ailments. There were also multiple urban cities scattered throughout the Old World where people lived in permanent and dense concentrations which, in addition to producing and accumulating more waste, bred microbes carried by vermin (e.g., houseflies, rats, roaches, worms) that thrive in filth. Lastly, European, Asian, and African populations lived among large quantities of domesticated animals like cattle, goats, horses, pigs, and sheep. These mammals share infinitesimal parasites with humans, prompting the incubation of new, deadly diseases as the viruses that enter a continuous interspecies exchange. Past experience of the Old World populations rendered them immune, but when these pathogens were carried over to the New World in the blood, breath, lice, and sweat of the colonists, the Indians did not have the same immunological endurance.

The intense damage wreaked on the Native American populations not only inhibited their ability to repel European encroachment but also prevented the invaders from exploiting the Indians for labor as planned; to make up for the lost labor source, colonists turned to West Africa from where they began importing slaves as early as 1518.

ECOLOGICAL CHANGES

Because the colonists wanted to continue farming the European way in the New World, they imported domesticated farm animals such as cattle, honeybees, horses, mules, pigs, and sheep as well as domesticated plants like barley, grapevines, grasses, oats, rye, and wheat.

Along with these purposeful imports, colonizers also unintentionally brought weeds that clashed with the edible indigenous plants of the Americas. While weeds did exist in the New World prior to invasion, they were not as fast-growing or hardy as those imported from Europe.

For colonists, there was more land than there was labor to develop and harvest it, so they took to building fences around their rather small, claimed crop fields. They would then allow their livestock (i.e., pigs and cattle) free reign of the surrounding unclaimed wilderness where the animals scrounged for wild plants, damaging the natural environment that sustained native populations. The unsupervised livestock also directly trespassed Indian crop fields where they ate the natives' crops. Indians would slaughter and eat these trespassers, which the colonists protested before demanding compensation for their killed livestock. Upon the natives' refusal, colonizers often overreacted by invading and setting fire to Native American villages.

While the natives had carefully altered their natural environment through hunting, fishing, forest-burning, field-clearing, and using plants for nutritional or medicinal purposes, the Europeans dramatically reshaped American nature: they destroyed forests to obtain lumber and establish farms. The subsequent farming activities such as plowing and grazing by livestock caused the natural, enriched soil to dry up and corrode.

SPANISH EXPLORATION

The **Treaty of Tordesillas**, signed between Spain and Portugal in 1494, decided how Christopher Columbus's discoveries of the New World would be divided. Because the treaty ensured Spain's claims in the Americas, Isabella and Ferdinand were quick to fund and send explorers to gain riches and "civilize" native populations in present day Mexico, Peru, and the West Indies.

The Spanish expected the indigenous peoples they encountered to relinquish their own beliefs and traditions and turn to Catholicism. Spain asserted that its main concern in colonizing the New World was to rescue the Indians from hedonism. Rather than wanting to vanquish or remove natives, the Spanish colonizers wanted to convert them into docile, Christian subjects of the Spanish monarchy.

Men such as Vasco Nunez de Balboa, Juan Ponce de León, Ferdinand Magellan, and Hernán Cortés expanded the treasures of Spain with land, gold, and silver. Spanish conquistadores enslaved Native American populations using the *encomienda*, a labor system in which Spaniards were given land by the Crown and were obligated to care for their Native American slaves.

In 1550, the *encomienda* system was replaced with the *repartimiento* system, which governed that those living in Indian villages were legally free and deserving of compensation for the amount of requisite annual labor they completed. This system rendered Indian slavery nonexistent: They were allowed land, received compensation, and could not be bought and sold. However, the natives were still abused by Spanish authority. By the end of the 16th century, the work force in the Spanish empire was forced wage labor by the indigenous populations as well as intermittent slave labor by Africans on the West Indian islands and parts of the Mainland.

The promise of finding new sources of gold prompted Spanish explorers to venture north into territory that now forms part of the United States and colonize the first region within the boundaries of modern America: Florida.

Spain's objective in colonizing Florida was to create a military base that could defend their overseas empire from pirates who threatened to pillage the Spanish fleet sailing from Cuba to Europe with gold and silver found in Mexico and Peru. In addition to prevent pirates' plunder of their fortune, the Spanish also colonized Florida in hopes of preventing intrusions of other European kingdoms, specifically France.

In addition to colonizing Florida, Spain sponsored explorations into what is now the Southwestern United States. These incursions were generally considered failures because they did not yield discoveries of gold or sources of labor. It was not until 1598 that Juan de Oñate led a group of 400 colonists, missionaries, and soldiers to establish a permanent settlement north of Mexico.

FRENCH AND DUTCH EXPLORATION

New Netherland and New France were initially economic endeavors that never saw huge populations of European migrants.

FRENCH EXPANSION

France was the first of Spain's European rival nations to set sail for the New World. The original French goal was to find gold and discover a Northwest passage from the Atlantic Ocean to the Pacific Ocean. Arriving in North America around 1524 and focusing mostly on what is now Canada and the upper northeastern United States, for the majority of the 16th century, only adventurers, fishermen, and pirates aiming to plunder Spanish vessels (and eventually fur traders) sailed along and explored America's eastern coast. French explorers such as Jacques Cartier and Samuel de Champlain cultivated a friendly business relationship with Native Americans, dealing mostly in beaver pelts. These vast trade networks spanned the upper Northeast down the Mississippi River to current-day New Orleans. Unfortunately, the French also brought diseases, guns, and alcohol to the Native American populations. Warfare between tribes worsened as the French traded among warring groups and gave guns as presents. The French did attempt to found settlements in Newfoundland and Nova Scotia, but these ventures were thwarted by insufficient financing and organization as well as impedance by the native populations.

DUTCH EXPANSION

Those living in the Netherlands during the 17th century had two freedoms that no other European nation's population enjoyed: freedom of the press and widespread religious toleration. Amsterdam, the Dutch capital, acted as an asylum for European Protestants who were persecuted in their homelands. Approximately half a million Europeans migrated to the Netherlands during the 17th century and many of these immigrants helped settle the Dutch colonies in the New World.

ENGLISH EXPLORATION

In 1585, **Sir Walter Raleigh** sent approximately 100 male colonists to **Roanoke**, a minuscule island off the North Carolina coast, which was then considered to be part of Virginia. This island was surrounded by perilous sandbanks that protected the inhabitants from Spanish discovery and attack; however, the very same natural defenses made it difficult for the English ships to deliver supplies or load commodities. In addition, the soil was sandy and arid, which made it difficult for farming and harvesting crops.

Two years after the initial settlement, Raleigh and his colleagues sent another 94 colonists, including 17 women and nine children, to Roanoke. These were the first English families to arrive in the New World.

In the August of 1590, after venturing to the Caribbean to plunder the Spanish colonies, Raleigh and his men returned to Roanoke only to find it empty of its inhabitants. There were no signs of attack by either the natives or the Spanish. The only clue was the word "Croatan," the name of a nearby island, carved into a tree.

In 1604, the **Treaty of London** ended the intermittent and never officially declared 19-year Anglo-Spanish War. This peace treaty minimized, but did not vanquish, the possibility of Spanish attack on England's New World colonies. Two years later, the **Virginia Company** was incorporated by its investors in London and King James granted a charter to colonize and govern Virginia. The Virginia Company, its employ, and English colonists arrived in Chesapeake Bay on April 26, 1607.

CHAPTER 5: CHANGING WORLDVIEWS FOR AMERICAN INDIANS, AFRICANS, AND EUROPEANS

AMERICAN INDIAN VIEWS

Native Americans thought of themselves as more intelligent and resourceful than the European colonists. While native populations were able to distinguish helpful and harmful resources in both the woods and water, Europeans were unable to do so, rendering the native interpretation of them as inexperienced and lazy. While the Indians were impressed at the metal and cloth goods Europeans brought with them to the New World, the natives perceived that Europeans had exhausted there intelligence in manufacturing these goods out of dead matter, insensitive to living nature.

EUROPEAN VIEWS

Europeans had extreme views on the native populations of the Americas: They perceived Indians as either "noble savages" who welcomed them or as vicious and uncivilized brutes who fought them. The barbaric descriptions were based on the Indians' differing religion, land use, and gender relations, which many Europeans perceived as "backwards." Aside from their perception of Indians as "other" because they were nonwhite, Europeans believed that Native American clothing, architecture, weapons, and lack of technology were primitive. The fact that Indians did not keep written records led the Europeans, who viewed literacy as a sign of education, intelligence, and social status, to believe that the native populations were illiterate and therefore below them. While many Europeans initially believed the native populations they encountered in the New World to be representative of freedom, they soon concluded that Indians had no sense of "freedom" because these native societies to exclude recognized laws or governments.

AFRICAN SLAVERY

Even before Europeans began exploring Africa, slavery existed there. However, it was not unusual for African slaves to obtain freedom. African slavery across the Atlantic began in the Spanish colonies in Cuba and Hispaniola. After Native American populations were destroyed by European invasion, the colonists turned to Africa for laborers and the number of Africans sold into slavery multiplied.

UNIT 1: REVIEW QUESTIONS

Multiple-Choice Questions

Directions: Choose the best answer choice for the following questions.

Questions 1 and 2 refer to the following image.

Algonquin Village c. 1585 in modern day North Carolina
Source: U.S. National Archives and Records Administration

1. Based on the Algonquin Village portrayed in the drawing, which of the following statements is correct?

    (A) The Algonquins were a warrior people, based on the defenses established in their village.

    (B) The Algonquins were nomadic and moved constantly throughout the year.

    (C) The Algonquins had an organized community structure.

    (D) The Algonquins had a highly developed trade system.

2. Based on the Algonquin settlement portrayed in the previous illustration and the nature of eastern North American Indian nations, which of the following statements is most accurate?

   (A) The community depended on trade with other Indian nations for their survival.

   (B) The Algonquins depended on conquering their enemies for the economic goods and food they produced.

   (C) The people of the eastern woodlands were hunter-gatherers and agriculturally oriented.

   (D) The Algonquins believed in human sacrifice to appease their gods.

Questions 3–5 refer to the following quote.

"At the time the first Europeans arrived, the Indians of the Great Plains between the Rocky Mountains and the forested areas bordering on the Mississippi lived partly by corn culture but mostly by the buffalo on foot with bow and arrow. Although Europeans regarded all Indians as nomads (a convenient excuse for denying them the land they occupied), only the Plains Indian really were nomadic. Even they did not become so until about A.D. 1550, when they began to break wild mustangs, offspring of European horses turned loose by the Spaniards."

— *The Oxford History of the American People* by Samuel Eliot Morison Oxford University Press, New York City, 1965

3. Based on the previous excerpt, which of the following had the greatest impact on the lives of the Great Plains Indians?

   (A) The introduction of corn as a staple crop

   (B) The understanding of the concept of land ownership as enforced by the Europeans

   (C) The development of the vast trade network with Europeans

   (D) The use of horses by the Great Plains Indians after the animal was introduced to North America by the Spanish

4. According to the excerpt, the Europeans justified which of the following using the livelihood of the Great Plains Indians as evidence?

   (A) All-out warfare to eradicate the native population

   (B) The creation of an extensive trade network

   (C) European land policy based on the concept that American Indians did not own land

   (D) The creation of the *encomienda* system to Christianize the Plains Indians

5. Based on the previous excerpt, which of the following statements is correct?

   (A) Despite being a nomadic people, the Great Plains Indians had a developed social structure.

   (B) The Great Plains Indians lived in small, democratically run communities.

   (C) Although nomadic, the Great Plains Indians generally remained in two seasonal locations.

   (D) The Great Plains Indians depended upon the river systems for trade.

Questions 6–8 refer to the following quote.

"Developed between A.D. 900 and 1100, Cahokia and its immediate suburbs covered about six square miles and had a population of at least ten thousand (some estimates run as high as forty thousand). Even at the smallest calculation, Cahokia ranked as the greatest Indian community north of Mexico. At its peak, Cahokia contained about one hundred earthen temple and burial mounds as well as hundreds of thatched houses for commoners. The city was surrounded by a stockade, a wall of large posts two miles in circumference with a watchtower every seventy feet."

—From *American Colonies* by Alan Taylor, Penguin Books, 2001

6. Based on the excerpt, which of the following is true about Cahokia?

(A) The Cahokians were a nomadic people.

(B) The culture of Cahokia was not as advanced as other Indian nations in North America.

(C) The social structure of Cahokia was based on an egalitarian philosophy.

(D) Cahokia had developed a complex society.

7. The Cahokia were most like which of the following Native American nations?

(A) The Cahokia were much like the Great Plains Indians, following their food source, the bison.

(B) The Cahokia were much like other American Indian nations on the eastern seaboard.

(C) The Cahokia relied on local crops and self-sufficiency for survival.

(D) The religious beliefs of the Cahokia people were much like the Aztecs in central Mexico.

8. Which of the following statements about pre-Columbian American Indians is true?

(A) American Indian nations coexisted peacefully on the North American continent.

(B) American Indians were predominantly nomadic.

(C) The lifestyle of each American Indian community was greatly influenced by the environment in which it lived.

(D) Pre-Columbian American Indians did not have a monetary system to enhance trade.

Short-Answer Questions

1. "The King to our *oidores, alcaldes mayors* of the Audiencia of the province of Nueva Garcia:

    Juan de la Peña, in the name of the council of justice and government of the city of Guadalajara, has made a report to me saying that because the Indian inhabitants of the province are not gathered into towns where they may have political government, much harm is done and many difficulties arise in their conversion and indoctrination, and they are not taught to live under the control and ordered system conducive to their salvation and welfare. For, scattered as they are over the mountains and deserts, the religious are unable to go everywhere to visit them; moreover, the Indians began to flee for the purpose of preventing interference with their manner and custom of life, and of securing better opportunities to assault, rob, and kill both Spaniards and peaceful Indians on the highways as they had repeatedly done."

    —Original source: Royal Order issued by the King of Spain on May 26, 1570

    For this question, address all three parts:

    (A) Briefly explain the major concern regarding the native population expressed by the King of Spain.

    (B) Briefly explain the misunderstanding the Spanish had regarding the native population.

    (C) Briefly describe one specific event that illustrates an attempt to "civilize" the Indians on the part of the Spanish.

2.

    For this question, address all three parts:

    (A) Briefly describe the labor system portrayed in the picture.

    (B) Briefly explain how the scene impacted the Atlantic World.

    (C) Cite one specific event and briefly explain the development of the labor system mentioned in Part A.

Document-Based Question

Directions: Question 1 is based on the accompanying documents. The documents have been edited for the purpose of this exercise. You are advised to spend 15 minutes planning and 40 minutes writing your answer. Write your responses on the lined pages that follow the questions.

1. Early encounters between American Indians and European colonists led to a variety of relationships between the different cultures—historians call this a "collision of cultures."

   Explain how this "collision of cultures" and the exchange of commodities between the American Indians and Europeans influenced the origins and patterns of development of North American societies in the colonial period.

   Limit your answer to the time period from 1495 to 1650.

DOCUMENT 1

"It appears that . . . [the Indians] had been suddenly pounced upon and bound before they had learnt or understood anything about Pope or Church, or any one of the many things said in the Requirement; and that after being put in chains some one read the Requisition without knowing their language and without any interpreter, without either reader or Indians understanding what was read. And after this had been explained to them by some one understanding their language, they had no chance to reply, being immediately carried away prisoners, the Spaniards not failing to use the stick on those who did not go fast enough."

—Description of scholar Gonzalo Fernandez de Oviedo, c. 1514

DOCUMENT 2

"I will be no man's tributary. I am greater than any prince upon earth. Your emperor may be a great prince; I do not doubt it, when I see that he has sent his subjects so far across the waters and I am willing to hold him as a brother. As for this Pope of whom you speak, he must be crazy to talk of giving away countries which do not belong to him. For my faith, I will not change it. Your own God, as you say, was put to death by the very men whom he created. But mine, my God still lives in the heavens, and looks down on his children."

Atahuallpa, ruler of the Inca, 1532

DOCUMENT 3

"In this place were a number of savages who had come for traffic in furs, several of whom came to our vessels with their canoes, which are from eight to nine paces long, and about a pace or pace and a half broad in their middle, growing narrower toward the two ends. They are very apt to turn over, in case one does not understand managing them, and are made of birch bark, strengthened on the inside by little ribs of white cedar, very neatly arranged. They are so light that a man can easily carry one. Each can carry a weight equal to that of a pipe. When they want to go overland to a river where they have business, they carry them with them. From Chouacoet along the coast as far as the harbor of Tadoussac, they are all alike. After this agreement, I had some carpenters set to work to fit up a little barque [barge] of twelve or fourteen tons, for carrying all that was needed for our settlement . . . "

Samuel de Champlain, The Foundation of Quebec, 1608

DOCUMENT 4

Engraving of the 1609 battle between Champlain and the Iroquois

DOCUMENT 5

"Why will you take by force what you may obtain by love? Why will you destroy us who supply you with food? What can you get by war? . . . We are unarmed, and willing to give you what you ask, if you come in a friendly manner . . .

"I am not so simple as to not to know it is better to eat good meat, sleep comfortably, live quietly with my women and children and laugh and be merry with the English, and being their friend, trade for their copper and hatchets, than to run away from them . . .

"Take away your guns and swords, the cause of all our jealousy, or you may die in the same manner."

Powhatan, 1609, to English settlers in Jamestown

DOCUMENT 6

"This spring, also, those Indians that lived about their trading house there fell sick of the small pox, and died most miserably for a sorer disease cannot befall them; they fear it more than the plague; for usually they that have this disease have them in abundance . . .

William Bradford on Sickness among the Natives in History of Plimouth Plantation, 1633

DOCUMENT 7

"Worthy sr:

I received your loving letter, and am much provocked to express my affections towards you, but straitens of time forbids me; for my desire is to acquainte you with the Lords greate mercies towards us, in our prevailing against his & our enemies, that you may rejoice and praise his name with us . . .

Ther have been now slaine & taken, in all, aboute 700. The rest are dispersed, and the Indeans in all quarters so terrified as all their friends are afraid to receive them.

Yours assured,
Jo. Winthrop
The 28. of the 5. month, 1637."

ANSWERS AND EXPLANATIONS

MULTIPLE-CHOICE ANSWERS

1. C
The Algonquins built fairly permanent villages in the eastern region of the North American continent, though many tribes were seasonally nomadic. They depended on hunting and gathering as well as some agriculture for their livelihood. Their villages were community-centered. Algonquins may have had a well-developed system of trade, but that is not evident in the picture.

2. C
The Indian nations of the eastern half of North America tended to depend on farming, supplementing their harvest with hunting and gathering more food.

3. D
The introduction of the horse by the Spanish during the 16th century had a great impact. The relatively sedentary Plains Indians now had the opportunity to become nomadic, with the ability to follow their main food source, the buffalo, farther distances. At the same time, the ability to transport families and villages became very easy.

4. C
The mythology created by the Europeans that all Indians were nomadic and therefore did not own any land was the foundation for their policy of claiming the land Indians occupied and forcing them to move elsewhere at times.

5. A
Based on the information in the excerpt, the fact that the Great Plains Indians held organized hunts for buffalo and did, to an extent, depend on corn as a staple crop shows that they had a somewhat organized social structure. Of the four answer choices, (A) is the only answer that can be supported.

6. D
Based on studies of Cahokia, they had one of the most advanced societies in pre-Columbian North America. The excerpt denotes this with information on the large sedentary population and the well-developed cultural beliefs (burial mounds).

7. B
Cahokia, a sedentary Indian nation, had developed an extensive trade system and was much like its neighbors to the east, the Algonquin, who had permanent settlements and a rich culture, as evidenced by the burial mounds.

8. C
Each Indian nation adapted to its surroundings: If a tribe was located on a river system, it depended upon trade and tended to be an agrarian society; if it lived on the Great Plains, it tended to be nomadic; other groups who settled in other parts of the continent adapted to their surroundings as well.

SHORT-ANSWER QUESTIONS RESPONSES

1. (A) The major concern of the King of Spain was that the Indians they had encountered in the "New World" did not seem to live in a traditional community, at least one that was comprehended by the Spanish who occupied the region; therefore, the native population did not have an "ordered system."

   (B) The Spaniards had a hard time understanding how and why the Native American population did not have an organized community that would allow a system that was "conducive to their salvation and welfare." The Spaniards were convinced that their way of life was the only civilized way and that the Indians, who grossly deviated from the Spanish concepts of living, must be savages.

   (C) In what is now the Southwestern United States, the Spanish implemented the *encomienda* and mission systems. The native peoples were forced to work daily in the fields, essentially as slaves, for the holder of the *encomienda* or the mission's priests. In "exchange," the natives received religious instruction or Catholic indoctrination. The native population put up some resistance but would receive severe punishments for their "transgressions." The Spanish had difficulty understanding why the natives resisted salvation and education to be "civilized."

2. (A) The labor system portrayed in the picture is slave labor as it began to appear in the Spanish and English sugar cane colonies in the Caribbean region. Slaves were imported to the Caribbean as much of the native population fled from the Europeans or died after being exposed to European diseases to which it had no resistance.

   (B) Slavery began to impact the Atlantic World as it created a triangular trade—the organized trade between Europe, Africa, and the Americas that involved humans (slaves), sugar, and other raw materials. Human cargo from Africa would be transported to the Caribbean and sold, sometimes for cash, sometimes for molasses—a product of the sugar plantations where the slaves labored.

   (C) Slavery eventually spread to British North America in the next century as the population of indentured servants began to shrink because fewer people in England were selling themselves into that labor system. The growth of the plantation system in the southern and mid-Atlantic colonies began to flourish in the tobacco trade and more slave labor was needed. Therefore, slavery spread quickly from the Caribbean to British North America.

DBQ SAMPLE RESPONSE

As European nations began to claim different regions in the New World during the age of exploration, the relationships between the native population and the explorers grew distinct from each other as each of the three major European powers (the Spanish, the English, and the French) utilized their newfound territories in different ways. The motivations for the three European nations were similar in that each wanted to use its new territory to enhance the wealth and prestige of its home nation, but different in that each took a different path in creating distinctive patterns of colonial development.

The Spanish, the first European power to arrive in the New World, had two major goals: to enrich their kingdom and to spread Catholicism to the native population. With the blessings of the Pope, the Spanish were quick to claim the Western Hemisphere, but focused mainly on modern Central and South America because they were proven sources of precious metals, mainly gold. Along with the death of thousands of Aztecs and Incas due to exposure to disease, the Spanish were able to subjugate many natives, as the natives were not receptive to conversion to Catholicism. One reason may have been the language barrier and the lack of understanding of some of the concepts of the Spanish faith (Doc. 1). Another reason for the rejection of the faith was that although many of the native people were willing to accept the Spanish on an equal basis, they would not allow the Spanish to be superiors to the native Indians (Doc. 2). Because of the military weakness of the native population due to decimation by disease, and the superiority of Spanish weapons, the *conquistadores* were able to take control of the region with minimal resistance.

In their initial search for the fabled Northwest Passage, the French came across what is now the St. Lawrence River in eastern Canada and ultimately established the French empire in North America, mainly through lucrative trade with the native population. The French were different from the Spanish in their relationship with the native population. Although some armed battles did occur (Doc. 4), the French and the Native Americans established more of an economic relationship. While, like the Spanish, the French did try to spread Catholicism, the French and the natives were more cooperative in that the natives had fur pelts to trade and the French believed it was in their best interest to learn how to adapt to the New World. (Doc. 3) Overall, the more cooperative relationship led to alliances between the French and different American Indian nations. These alliances lasted for decades and benefited the French in wars that broke out with the English.

Unlike the economic and missionary goals of the Spanish and French, the English were more interested in establishing permanent communities in North America. Although England's first successful settlement (Jamestown) was economically based, by 1620 large numbers of English families began to settle in the New England region. Most were Puritans fleeing persecution in their homelands. Initial contact between the English and the Indians in the

Jamestown area was somewhat friendly, but within a few years it turned hostile mainly because of the rapid influx of English settlers and cultural misunderstandings (Doc. 5) until the famous marriage between John Rolfe (of tobacco fame) and Pocahontas created a temporary coexistence. In New England, the English carved out several permanent communities along the Atlantic coast, impacting the native populations that had lived there for generations. Not only did the English begin to take Native American land but they also, inadvertently, began to spread smallpox among the local population, killing a large percentage of the Indians (Doc. 6). In the mid-1630s, the Pequot War erupted between the English and New England natives. The English won, killing 700 Pequot and forcing the surviving Indians to disperse themselves amongst their allies or be sold into slavery. The result of the war ended Pequot influence in the region, giving the English control (Doc. 7).

Ultimately, the three European powers established colonies in the New World, each taking different paths. The Spanish, more domineering from the beginning, conquered the natives they encountered with disease and military might. The French, on the other hand, after some initial conflict, befriended many local Indian nations, creating lucrative trade relationships. The English, after initially settling in a peaceful manner, utilized warfare to maintain their permanence in North America. The common thread in the interaction between the Europeans and the American Indians was that the Europeans ultimately benefited more from their development of colonies in the New World.

Overall, this essay is very strong, well rounded, and balanced. The supporting evidence is good. The information from the documents and from outside of the documents is woven together to make a very clear argument that supports the thesis. However, more information from outside of the documents—especially in the paragraph on French settlement—could have been used to support the otherwise strong analysis.

The thesis for this essay would receive the 1 point credit (out of 1 possible); the inclusion of documents and outside information and their analysis would earn the 4 points possible. The contextualization is excellent, earning the 1 point possible, and the synthesis of the information would also earn the 1 possible point, giving this essay a 7 out of 7 possible points on the DBQ rubric.

CHAPTER 6: DIVERSE PATTERNS OF EUROPEAN COLONIZATION IN THE NEW WORLD

FRENCH COLONIZATION

Spain's New World empire altered the global economy's power balance: the land route to the East was supplanted by the Atlantic Ocean as the trading hub throughout the world.

A French fur-trading company sponsored Samuel de Champlain, who founded Quebec as a small, barricaded trading post in 1608. Almost 20 years later, France's New World territories were home to only 85 colonists, all of whom were male and based in Quebec. These Frenchmen depended on supply ships from the mother country for most of their sustenance and needed the altruism of the natives in order to survive and prosper.

Later in the 17th century, a Jesuit priest, Jacques Marquette, and French fur trader, Louis Joliet, found the Mississippi River. By 1681, French explorers René-Robert Cavelier and Sieur de La Salle reached the Gulf of Mexico, establishing France's claim to the entirety of the Mississippi River Valley region.

Despite this claim, the number of white colonists living in New France by 1700 was only 19,000. The French government sent fewer emigrants to the Americas, fearing that anything more significant would undermine its power in Europe or put its efforts to form a working relationship with Indians in jeopardy.

DUTCH COLONIZATION

Unlike other European nations, the Netherlands' goal in colonizing the New World was purely commercial, not missionary. In 1609, after being employed by the Dutch East India Company to find an eastern passage to Asia, Englishman **Henry Hudson** sailed into New York Harbor, prompting Dutch merchants to regularly send fur traders across the Atlantic and up the Hudson

River to exchange goods with the Indians. Five years after Hudson's voyage, the Dutch established a permanent base at Fort Nassau on the upper Hudson, which was home to only 50 Dutch West India Company employees.

In 1625, the Dutch established the town of New Amsterdam on Manhattan Island, which acted as the Netherlands' major New World seaport and government headquarters. New Amsterdam's tolerance of religious practice rendered the colony the most religiously and ethnically diverse colony in North America. However, despite this tolerance and the colony's location, it failed to attract enough settlers to compete with the populations of England's surrounding colonies.

THE ANGLO-DUTCH WAR

In 1664, the English took control of New Netherland, which the Dutch easily surrendered. In fewer than 20 years, New York's population grew from 9,000 to 20,000 under English rule.

ENGLISH COLONIZATION

Sixteenth-century England was a lesser European power due to its internal turmoil, which had many sources. In 1531, Henry VIII discontinued England's alignment with the Catholic Church after the Pope denied the king's request for an annulment of his marriage to Catherine of Aragon. In its place, Henry appointed himself as the head of the Church of England, or the Anglican Church, which was decidedly Protestant.

Between 1550 and 1600, England's population increased from 3 million to 4 million, which was not economically sustainable at the time, resulting in half the population living at or below the poverty line. It was these members of English society who were encouraged to emigrate to the New World, which was advertised as a utopia where the lower classes could achieve economic independence by obtaining property. It was this land ownership, which the English believed was the basis of liberty, that attracted many English emigrants. and caused half a million people to emigrate from England in the 17th century to not only North America but also Ireland and the West Indies.

Energy and funds that might have been directed toward early exploration of the New World went instead toward England's effort to subjugate Ireland, the Catholic population of which threatened the strength of Protestant England.

It was not until Henry VIII's successor, Elizabeth I, assumed the throne that England took note of what was happening in the Western Hemisphere. Parliament granted exclusive rights and privileges, known as **charters**, to Sir Humphrey Gilbert and Sir Walter Raleigh, permitting them to found colonies in North American at their own expense. Raleigh's colony, Roanoke, and Gilbert's colony on Newfoundland both failed.

Religion, profit, and prestige all played a role in England's early motives in colonizing the New World. Emphatically anti-Catholic, the English government asserted that it was obligated to free the New World from the Pope's authority, which had been established by Catholic nations such as Spain and France establishing settlements in the New World. More significantly, however, England, which at the end of the 16th century was still a relatively minor European power, believed it could gain standing on par with that of France and Spain. Those nations' respective explorations in present-day Canada and South America left the entirety of the land between the two open to England's exploration and colonization.

INDENTURED SERVITUDE

English emigrants who could afford passage to the New World arrived there as free and were quickly given land. However, nearly two-thirds of English colonists who emigrated during the 17th century offered up five to seven years of their freedom in exchange for passage to the Americas. These men and women could not marry without their master's permission, could be bought and sold, and were subject to corporal punishment. In addition, if a female servant became pregnant, her term of indenture was prolonged. These rules were upheld and imposed by courts. If an indentured servant survived, he or she received payment in the form of "freedom dues" and were thus considered free members of society.

PURITANISM

Puritanism, which emerged in England in the late 16th century, eventually described a religious code and a kind of societal organization that was perceived as ideal by its proponents. Puritans believed that the Church of England's religious ceremonies and teachings were too reminiscent of Catholicism. Puritans believed that religion was complex and that true believers ought to read the Bible for themselves and listen to the sermons of an educated clergy.

It seemed, in the 1620s and 1630s, that Charles I was reinstating ceremonies that resembled those of the recently replaced Catholicism. That shift coupled with the Church of England's dismissal of Puritan ministers and censorship of their writings encouraged the Puritans to emigrate to the New World where the sought freedom to worship and live in a society that adhered to what they believed to be truly Christian principles.

Puritans believed in domestic male authority as well as limiting married women's legal and economic liberties. A patriarch's control over his wife, children, and servants was deemed the foundation of social security. While women were cast lower in sociopolitical spheres, they were considered the spiritual equals of men and were allowed to be full church participants. A woman's responsibility as a wife and mother was the basis of her identity.

THE NAVIGATION ACTS

By the mid-1600s, it became clear to English authorities that they could profit from the New World colonies. **Mercantilism**, the theory that government control economic pursuits to advocate national power, emerged and elucidated the role of the colonies: to export raw materials to and import manufactured goods from England.

In 1651, British Parliament, then led by Oliver Cromwell, passed the **Navigation Acts**, which intended to supersede Dutch control of international trade. According to these laws, colonial commodities such as tobacco and sugar (the most profitable goods) had to be exported to England in English ships and sold in English ports before they could be re-exported to other nations' markets. This increased business not only brought income to English merchants but also profited the crown through the taxation placed on goods.

SPANISH COLONIZATION

In 1610, Spain settled the capital of New Mexico at Santa Fe, which became the first permanent European in settlement in the Southwestern United States.

THE PUEBLO REVOLT

In 1680, the small and relatively defenseless New Mexico population numbered fewer than 3,000 and consisted mostly of *mestizos*, descendants of Spanish and Native American unions. Throughout the 17th century, the relationship between the colonial rulers and the Pueblo Indian population of 60,000 deteriorated, as the exploitation of the Pueblo people had caused their numbers to dwindle to 17,000 in just 80 years.

The latter half of the 17th century saw an intensified Inquisition—the persecution of non-Catholics—in Spain and this was reflected in the Spanish New World colonies in which Franciscan friars attempted to eradicate Pueblo religious traditions by burning their idols, masks, and other sacred objects. These acts, attempts to convert Indians to Catholicism, resulted in the alienation of the indigenous people.

A prolonged drought starting and the Spanish authorities' failure to protect their villages and religious missionary settlements from Navajo and Apache Indian attacks contributed to the strife between the Pueblo Indians and the settlers. However, the colonists assumed the Pueblo could never unite against them, as the Pueblo Indians had long been internally divided.

In August 1680, a Pueblo man named Popé asserted himself as the head of an unexpectedly coordinated uprising, the intention of which was to drive the Spanish from the colony and restore the Pueblo's former independence. Two thousand Pueblo warriors attacked isolated farms and missions, killing 400 colonists. Among the 400 fatalities were 21 Franciscan missionaries. The natives then surrounded Santa Fe, leaving the Spanish no choice but to abandon the capital that they had established only 70 years before. The survivors, along with a few hundred converted Christian Indians, made their way south of New Mexico.

In a few weeks' time, nearly 100 years of Spanish colonization in the Southwest was dismantled in the most thorough Native American victory over Europeans and the only large-scale displacement of settlers in North American history.

AMERICAN SLAVERY

Not one of the European countries that had colonies in the Americas every intended on being reliant on African slavery for labor. Unlike indentured servants, African slaves could not claim the rights of Englishmen and had indefinite terms of labor. Also, African men were much more familiar with rigorous agricultural labor and were immune to European diseases unlike the Native American populations. These factors, coupled with pervasive anti-African stereotypes, rendered blacks perfect slaves in the eyes of the English.

THE MIDDLE PASSAGE

The **Middle Passage** was part of the Triangular trade among Europe, Africa, and the Americas, in which Africans were transported across the Atlantic to the New World. Because African men, women, and children were tightly crammed into ships in order to maximize profits, many succumbed to diseases such as measles and small pox. Twenty percent of enslaved Africans died before reaching the New World and fewer than 5 percent of these slaves went to the North American mainland, landing instead in Brazil or the West Indies to work on sugar plantations.

WEST INDIES SLAVERY

Bigotry alone did not prompt North American slavery. In the first half of the 17th century, the number of English emigrants to the West Indies outnumbered the number to North America. As a solution to the labor shortage caused by the decimation of the native populations by disease and unwillingness of white indentured servants to engage in the strenuous physical labor that sugar (the first crop to be mass-marketed to Europeans from the Americas) cultivation required, the colonists turned to importing African slaves.

CHESAPEAKE SLAVERY

The first Africans in North America, who arrived in Virginia in 1619, were treated as slaves with terms of labor that eventually ended, allowing them to acquire freedom. From the beginning of African residency in the New World, there were very strict laws governing their behavior and interactions with whites. In the 1620s, Virginia passed a law prohibiting blacks from serving in the militia. The government also executed harsher punishment for interracial, adulterous sexual relations more so than they did the same acts between two Europeans.

While there is evidence of blacks being enslaved as early as the 1640s, it was not until the 1660s when Virginia and Maryland laws explicitly referred to slavery. The introduction of slavery into the Chesapeake set the stage for the delineation of the area's elite class: the landowners and slaveowners, tobacco merchants, and lawyers who defended the actions of the former two groups.

CHAPTER 7: INTERCULTURAL CONTACT AND INTENSIFIED CONFLICT IN NORTH AMERICA

THE ENGLISH AND THE INDIANS

Unlike their colonizing counterparts, the English were not interested in intermarrying with Indians, converting them into subjects of the crown, or exploiting them for labor. Rather, the English wanted the land occupied by the natives. While Indians trade with the colonists and traveled through their settlements, the English sought to maintain a division.

Despite this division, many English recognized Indian ownership of the land based on occupation and obtained these areas by paying for them, often after forcing a treaty upon a tribe after conquering them in warfare, which was frequent. The recurrent English defeats of the natives imbued the colonists with a sense of superiority, which led to the most thorough displacement of the Indians among all of the European empires that colonized the Americas.

Natives who survived the European epidemics were deeply affected by the European invasion. Indians began to incorporate European products such as woven and metal goods, including guns, into their lives, dramatically altering the way they hunted, fished, and cooked. As the use of European goods in native culture increased, traditional skills declined.

THE INDIANS AT JAMESTOWN

The area surrounding Jamestown, prior to British arrival, was home to 15,000 to 25,000 natives who lived in many small agriculture-based communities. Despite the Virginia Company's instructions that colonists try to convert the Indians to Christianity, relations between the English and those they encountered were relatively pacific. The peace between the two groups was largely due to the fact that John Smith was aware of the settlers' dependence on trading. Despite his trying to prevent colonists from stealing Indian produce, he was captured by legendary Indian chief Powhatan and saved after an elaborate, possibly staged, execution ceremony by Powhatan's favorite daughter, Pocahontas, who brokered peace in 1614, which lasted for approximately eight years.

In 1622, Powhatan's younger brother Opechancanough planned and executed a surprise attack on Jamestown that killed 300 of the 1,200 Virginia colonists in the course of one day. The remaining settlers assembled, massacring the natives and destroying their communities, critically altering the balance of power in the region in favor of the English. Despite this retaliation and power shift, the Virginia natives continued to trade with the English for the remainder of the 17th century.

Another uprising in 1644 resulted in the deaths of 500 English settlers and prompted the colonists to establish a treaty with the surviving 2,000 or so natives in which they were forced to admit their subjection to the Jamestown government, relocate farther west, and refrain from entering European settlements without consent.

INDIANS IN NEW ENGLAND

New England's native population was approximately 100,000 when the Puritans arrived. While some settlers, like Roger Williams, believed Indians should be treated with justice, most colonists believed that Native Americans were savages, resembling Catholics with their false gods and rituals. Colonial leaders were also afraid that amoral Puritans would abandon civilized society to live with the "savages." While Puritans claimed that they wanted to convert Indians to Christianity, they did nothing to accomplish this; they primarily viewed natives as an obstacle to land.

THE PEQUOT WAR

The tribes on the coast of New England, whose populations had been significantly diminished by European disease, initially wanted to ally with the colonists to strengthen their standing against opposing tribes. In 1637, the Pequot tribe, which controlled the New England fur trade, killed an English fur trader. In retaliation, the Connecticut and Massachusetts soldiers surrounded the principal Pequot village at Mystic and set it on fire, killing any and all who attempted escape. More than 500 Indian men, women, and children were massacred and in a few months, the entirety of the Pequot tribe had been either killed or sold into Caribbean slavery. The Pequot War opened the Connecticut River Valley to English settlement and signaled to other tribes that the colonists' power could not be combatted.

KING PHILIP'S WAR

Also known as the First Indian War, **King Philip's War** was an ongoing battle between English colonists and the native inhabitants of the New England region. Fueled by the desire for land and entitlement, it began in the spring of 1675 when colonists at Plymouth captured, tried, and h three members of an Indian tribe for killing a converted native who had served as an informant for the English colonists. To retaliate, the Indian warriors began to attack colonial settlements. By the fall, they had attacked over half of the region's towns, bringing full destruction to 12. In the summer of 1676, the Indian resistance collapsed before the English and their Iroquois allies and Metacom, whom colonists referred to as "King Philip," was executed. The English victory expanded the access they had to the land previously inhabited by the natives.

RELIGIOUS CONFLICT IN NEW ENGLAND

In 1631, Protestant theologian **Roger Williams** emigrated to Massachusetts and shortly advocated for the separation of church and state as well as the retreat of colonial congregations from the Church of England. He believed that freedom of religion separate from government rule would strengthen faith among colonists. Because his theories went against Puritan values and teachings, Williams was banished from Massachusetts in 1636. He and his followers ventured south and established the colony of Rhode Island. Rhode Island had a more democratic government structure than Massachusetts. At the colony's onset, there was no established church, no religious voting requirements, and no stipulation that citizens attend church.

Anne Hutchinson and her husband followed their minister from England to Massachusetts in 1636. Hutchinson soon started hosting meetings during which she asserted that the Massachusetts ministers were erroneous in their delineation of the saved as those who attended church and exhibited moral behavior; she believed that salvation could not be earned through these means. She was soon condemned for violating church doctrine through her claims that God had spoken to her directly rather than through the proper channels (i.e., ministers and the Bible). She and her followers, banished, moved to Rhode Island and then Westchester, the area north of what is now New York City.

Prominent Puritan leader **Thomas Hooker**, after dissenting with the other Massachusetts authorities, moved to and established a settlement at Hartford, Connecticut in 1636. Three years later, the Hartford government was established in the **Fundamental Orders**, the first "constitution" in colonial America. While it modeled itself after the government of the Massachusetts Bay Colony, the document called for the power of government to be derived from the governed, who did not have to be church members to vote.

BACON'S REBELLION

Bacon's Rebellion of 1676 led to an increase in the demand for slaves by signaling the problems inherent in controlling former indentured servants.

Virginia's governor, **William Berkeley**, governed the colony based on the interests of the wealthy, elite tobacco planters. While tobacco had initially been lucrative for small farmers, tobacco farming began to spread inland and the governor gave the best tracts of land to the elite; former indentured servants who had filled their terms could only work as tenants or move to the frontier. Berkeley also advocated for good relations with the remaining Indians, disallowing the colonists from settling in areas reserved for the natives, to which colonists objected.

A young, newly arrived member of the House of Burgesses, **Nathaniel Bacon**, capitalized on the complaints of his fellow backwoodsmen by mobilizing them to form a citizens' militia. In 1676, Bacon's militia engaged in a series of raids against local native villages, massacring inhabitants. The mob was successful in defeating Berkeley's forces and then set fire to Jamestown. A short time later, Bacon died of dysentery, and the rebellion was finally crushed.

POLITICAL CHANGES IN ENGLAND

The year 1688 brought the "**Glorious Revolution**" to England and the overthrow of King James II. Parliament replaced James II with his daughter Mary II and her Dutch husband, William III of Orange. American colonists were excited, as the removal of James II signaled the end of his repressive measures that were aimed directly at Puritans and limited colonial self-governance. With **William and Mary** now at the helm, American colonists mistakenly believed that England would step away from the harsh policies of the Dominion of New England instituted by Parliament during James II's reign. Unfortunately for the colonists, Parliament continued restricting their ability to establish self-rule. Uprisings in several colonies erupted as it became clear that they would get no respite from repression. The English governors worked quickly to quell the unrest, but damage had already been done to the relationship between the colonists and the mother country.

LEISLER'S REBELLION

From 1689 to 1691, **Jacob Leisler**, a German merchant who had emigrated to New York, and his rebel militia took control of New York. **Leisler's Rebellion** separated the colonists based on ethnicity and economic status. The original New York settlers—the Dutch—too this opportunity to reclaim their power within the colony. The English colonists claimed that Leisler was a tyrant and eventually William of Orange dispatched a new governor, with military back up, to replace Leisler.

MORE CONFLICT IN NEW ENGLAND

The English crown replaced the Massachusetts charter in 1691, demanding that property ownership, not church membership, be the qualifications for voting in General Court elections. This led to Massachusetts's status as a royal colony, which demanded all inhabitants to follow the English Toleration Act of 1690, a document that called for the free worship of all Protestants, not just Puritans.

THE SALEM WITCH TRIALS

In 1692, a group of young girls in **Salem**, Massachusetts, began acting strangely after hearing tales of voodoo from their West Indian servant. The girls then began to accuse older, wealthy members of the community of witchcraft, leading to mass hysteria in Salem and surrounding areas. In the end, 20 people were executed, and the prestige of the traditional Puritan clergy was damaged beyond repair.

THE STONO REBELLION

During the course of the 18th century, many blacks, particularly recently enslaved young black men, chanced their lives in resistance to the slave societies to which they belonged. The first slave uprising in colonial America in New York City occurred in 1712: A group of slaves committed arson to colonial houses and murdered the first nine whites to oppose them. The white colonists responded by executing 18 conspirators, some of whom were physically tormented and then burned alive to send a threatening message to the slave population.

In 1739, a group of slaves in Stono, South Carolina, took control of a store that stocked various weapons. After arming themselves, they marched toward Florida, beating drums to signal followers and killing any whites they encountered, all while chanting, "Liberty." This rebellion, whose proponents eventually numbered over 100, incurred the deaths of more than two dozen whites and as many as 200 African slaves. The rebellion also caused the proprietors of South Carolina to make a stricter slave code and issue a temporary prohibitive tax on the import of slaves.

CHAPTER 8: THE DEVELOPMENT OF COLONIAL SOCIETIES IN NORTH AMERICA

THE CHESAPEAKE

Jamestown, which was founded in 1607 and had an original population of 104 colonists, was located next to a swamp that not only contained mosquitoes carrying malaria but also germs causing typhoid and dysentery bred from the waste settlers threw into local rivers. By the end of the colony's first year, the population had halved. New colonists, including two women, arrived in 1608, increasing the population, but after the winter of 1610, only 65 settlers were still living.

The colony would have failed completely had it not been for the rigorous military rule of **John Smith**, whose ironclad rule required colonists to partake in forced labor. Despite Smith's return to England, in 1609, after being injured in a chance gunpowder explosion, his inflicted regime was continued by his successors.

The until then failure prompted the Virginia Company to forgo its search for gold and in its stead aimed to find a commodity they could market in Europe and attract more colonists. To accomplish the latter, the Virginia Company established its use of the **headright system** in 1618, giving 50 acres of land to any settler who paid for his own—or someone else's—passage to the New World.

The Virginia Company also established the **House of Burgesses**, which upon its first meeting, in 1619, became the first elected assembly in the New World and served as a political model for subsequent English colonies. The limitations of the House of Burgesses were that only landowners had the right to vote and the Virginia Company and the governor it selected had the right to rescind any law or measure adopted.

There was no solid familial life in Virginia. This was partly because most of the women who emigrated came as indentured servants and had to complete their term of indenture before they could marry and start families. Both married and unmarried women had certain rights, however. If a married woman's husband died before she did, she was entitled to one-third of her deceased husband's property. Unmarried women had independent legal identities and were able to conduct business.

In 1624, the Virginia Company had not profited from the colony: Despite sending 6,000 settlers, the white population numbered only 1,200. The company conceded its charter, rendering Virginia the first royal colony whose governor was appointed by the crown.

THE TOBACCO BOOM

In 1611, **John Rolfe**, an influential leader of the colony, introduced the cultivation of tobacco, which soon became the English colonists' substitute for the gold they had not found, to Virginia farmers. By 1624, more than 200,000 pounds of tobacco were being cultivated in Virginia. In 1664, that amount increased to 15 million, which doubled in the 1680s.

The crown earned a profit from the taxes on the crop, the introduction of which motivated an aggressive entrepreneurial spirit as well as a need not only for land but also for laborers who, for the majority of the 17th century, were young men who came to the New World as indentured servants.

MARYLAND

Maryland was founded in 1632 as a **proprietary colony**: the crown allotted land and governmental command to one person. In Maryland's case, this person was Catholic Cecilius Calvert (also known as **Lord Baltimore**), a son of the recently deceased Charles I. Calvert wanted to feudally govern the colony, which he saw as a haven for his fellow Catholics who were being persecuted in England. The hope was that Protestants and Catholics could harmoniously coexist in Maryland. But while most of the officials Calvert designated were Catholic, the majority of the colony's population was Protestant. Calvert believed the average person had no say in governmental procedures or rulings even though the Maryland charter guaranteed that all colonists have the same rights and advantages as English citizens.

In 1689, after hearing news of the ousting of James II, a group of rebels decided that Lord Baltimore had grossly misled Maryland, which prompted William of Orange to revoke the charter and establish a government dominated by Protestants rather than Catholics. After this overthrow, Catholics maintained the right to practice their own religion but were not allowed to vote or hold office.

NEW ENGLAND PURITANS

The first Puritans to arrive in the New World were the **Pilgrims**, a group of **separatists**: A Puritan minority that had completely abandoned the Church of England to form its own independent churches that aimed to cleanse religion from within the infrastructure of worship. In 1620, fearing their surrounding culture in the Netherlands, to which they had emigrated twelve years prior, was corrupting their children, 150 Pilgrims sailed for Virginia aboard the Mayflower from England. However, they were blown off course and landed on what is now Cape Cod, where they founded the colony of **Plymouth**. Before arriving, the Pilgrims drafted an agreement to set up a *secular* body to administer the leadership of the colony, known as the **Mayflower Compact**. This document, the first written form of government in what is now the United States, set the stage for the concept of the separation of church and state and the rule of the majority.

The smallpox epidemic had decimated the Indian population in Plymouth, enabling the Pilgrims to found their colony at an abandoned Indian settlement, the fields of which had already been cleared by the former inhabitants. Having landed six weeks before winter without sustenance or livestock, only half of the Pilgrims survived and did so with the help of the local remaining natives. One Indian in particular, **Squanto**, who had previously been captured and transported to England where he learned English, acted as a translator for the Pilgrims and showed them how to plant corn and where to fish. Having survived to the autumn of 1621, the Pilgrims invited their Indian allies to harvest celebration, which is now considered the first Thanksgiving.

The Puritans, who were afraid of immoderate individualism and promoted social unity, organized themselves into self-governing towns, each with its own congregational church. The Massachusetts Bay Company owners emigrated to America, transforming their commercial charter into a kind of government, to rule the colony without interference or influence from non-Puritan outsiders. Only full church members could vote and to be a full church member, one had to attest to a conversion experience.

In 1641, the General Court issued a **Body of Liberties** that delineated the liberties and duties of Massachusetts settlers as outlined by the social order, which Puritans believed to be a result of God's will. The Body of Liberties allowed for free speech, assembly, and protection under the law, but also authorized the death penalty for the worship of false gods, blasphemy, and witchcraft.

THE GREAT MIGRATION

The Massachusetts Bay Company was founded in 1629 by a collective of London financiers who were advocates of the Puritan cause and wanted to profit from Indian trade in North America. Thus began the **Great Migration**, during which Puritan families ventured across the Atlantic during the 1630s, seeking religious freedom and a fresh start. By 1642, around 21,000 Puritans had emigrated to Massachusetts.

The Massachusetts Bay Colony saw a rapid growth in its population not only because of the more balanced gender distribution of colonists, but also because of the healthier climate. By 1700, New England's white population significantly outnumbered that of the Chesapeake and the West Indies combined.

THE HALF-WAY COVENANT

By 1650, fewer than 50 percent of the population had been admitted as full church members due to the ambiguous religious status of New England's third generation. While elected officials' children could be baptized, many never became full-fledged members of the church due to their inability to testify to a conversion experience.

In 1662, in response to this oversight, New England leaders established the **Half-Way Covenant**, which permitted Great Migration emigrants' grandchildren to be baptized and accept lower, or "half-way," church membership. This resulted in a shift from religious conversion to lineage as the basis for inclusion among the colony's leaders.

THE ENGLISH IN NEW YORK

After the English seized control of New York from the Dutch, many colonists asserted that they were being denied the given rights of Englishmen. In response to these complaints, an elected assembly was called and drafted a **Charter of Liberties and Privileges**, which mandated elections that male property owners and freemen could vote in every three years. The Charter also reinforced traditional English liberties like trial by jury, security of property, and Protestant religious toleration. The reinstatement of these rights was the result of the English colonists' desire to demonstrate their power over the older Dutch settlers.

THE CAROLINAS

In 1663, Charles II gave eight landholders the right to found an English colony to Florida's north to block off further Spanish expansion. Seven years later, the first settlers in the region established Carolina, which began as an branch of Barbados, which in the 17th century, was the richest plantation in the Caribbean. However, because of Barbados's small size, there was not enough land for the next generation prompting wealthy planters' sons to seek opportunities in Carolina.

Before even arriving, the proprietors issued the **Fundamental Constitutions of Carolina** in 1669 in which they aimed to create a feudal society replete with an inherited nobility, serfs, and slaves. Despite this hereditary social structure, colonial leaders established an elected assembly, religious toleration, and excessive headright system to attract emigrants to their colony.

PENNSYLVANIA

Pennsylvania was the last English colony to be founded in North America during the 17th century. Its founder, **William Penn**, wanted it to be a colony in which those being persecuted for their spiritual beliefs in Europe could enjoy freedom of religion and that Indians and settlers would be able to live side by side.

These beliefs stemmed from Penn's membership of the Society of Friends. Also known as **Quakers**, these people advocated that everyone was equal (including women, Africans, and Indians). In accordance, Pennsylvania had no established congregation, and it was not required that residents attend religious services. While personal faith was not monitored by the government, public conduct was: swearing, inebriation, and adultery were outlawed.

Penn owned all of the land in Pennsylvania and sold it to settlers at low costs rather than developing a headright system. The religious toleration, abundant climate, and low-cost land appealed to immigrants from all over western Europe. Pennsylvania's popularity and accessibility resulted in a decline in the number of indentured servants who emigrated to Virginia and Maryland. This decline in indentured servitude left a gap in labor that was shortly filled by African slaves.

GEORGIA

In the mid-18th century, the cultivation of rice spread into the land that now encompasses Georgia. Founded in 1733 by wealthy reformer James Oglethorpe, Georgia was envisioned as a haven for those who had been imprisoned in England and approved by London in hopes that the colony would protect South Carolina from the Spanish Floridians and their native allies. Georgia's proprietors initially banned slavery and alcohol from the colony, which led to many disputes among settlers. In 1751, the colony was surrendered to the crown, which repealed both bans.

CHARACTERISTICS OF COLONIAL SOCIETIES

The social structure of the English colonies closely modeled that of the social structure of towns in England. **Stratification** existed in the early years of the English colonies and became more apparent as the 17th century came to a close. The influx of more affluent immigrants and the continued development of the plantation economy in the South further increased the gap between rich and the poor. The Puritans in New England viewed wealth and success as a sign that one was a member of the **elect**, and in the South, social stratification had been carried over from the old feudal society of England. Led by men such as Virginia's governor, Sir William Berkeley, the royal sympathizers of the English Civil War, known as "Cavaliers," were recruited to build a society in the South that would honor the landed aristocracy.

The middle colonies did not have the same social rigidity as New England and the Chesapeake. Members of the middle classes enjoyed the diversity, acceptance, and tolerance of the middle colonies. The elite in New England and the middle colonies were made up mostly of successful merchants. However, the majority (some 90 percent of colonists) were involved in agriculture—many were subsistence and/or tenant farmers.

Family was very important to both the economic and social well-being of colonial societies. On average, colonial citizens married and bore children at a much younger age than citizens of the

European continent. More children meant more hands to tend the farm and, thus, more earnings for the family. The division of labor in most English colonies was clearly delineated by gender.

Men were mainly responsible for labor outside the home, while women were responsible for care of the homestead and child rearing. Women had very few rights or legal recourse in colonial society; however, many were "protected" by their husbands and society as a whole from abuse.

COLONIAL ECONOMIES

The economic theory of **mercantilism** was a reality for the 13 American colonies, particularly after the ascension of James II to the throne and the establishment of the Dominion of England in 1686. The colonies existed solely to provide raw materials and a market of consumers for the mother country. Nevertheless, the colonists did not let the Navigation Acts keep them from developing trade markets of their own that were not sanctioned by the English crown.

THE TRIANGULAR TRADE

The most prominent of these trade networks was the **Triangular Trade,** in which the New England colonies provided timber, fish, and manufactured goods to Caribbean islands in exchange for molasses, which would be used to make rum in New England. The rum would be taken to Africa in exchange for African slaves. Slaves would then eventually be taken to the colonies, thus completing the triangle. Therefore, rum-running became the trade of choice for New England merchants.

The middle colonies enjoyed a mixture of agriculture and light manufacturing, the largest market for goods being the West Indies. In the Southern colonies, tobacco was the main cash crop in the Chesapeake (Virginia and Maryland), while rice and indigo were the main cash crops in the Carolinas and Georgia. The Southern colonies traded extensively with England and the West Indies in exchange for manufactured goods and slaves.

RELIGION AND THE GREAT AWAKENING

By the middle of the 18th century, many colonists had lost touch with traditional Calvinist teachings that had been the cornerstone of the Puritan faith. Moreover, thousands of settlers on the frontier had little to no access to churches and religious services. In the late 1730s, a wave of preachers began delivering sermons that emphasized the power of an emotional connection to and a personal inspiration from God. Religious fervor spread across the colonies, with large revivals meeting under tents in the outskirts of towns. This religious spirit was called the "**Great Awakening**." "**New Light**" preacher **Jonathan Edwards** is credited with starting the Great

Awakening in 1734 by giving sermons that encouraged parishioners to absolve their sins and pay penance by praying for salvation. His most famous sermon was entitled "**Sinners in the Hands of an Angry God**," which he delivered in 1741. Churchgoers were told that God was angry with the sinners of the earth and only those who obeyed God's word would be free from damnation.

Emotional sermons evolved after Edwards with other "New Light" preachers, such as English-born **George Whitefield**. Whitefield and other "New Light" preachers crisscrossed the colonies speaking to large crowds about the "fire and brimstone" eternity all sinners would face if they did not confess their sins publicly. Whitefield also undermined the power and prestige of "Old Light" ministers by proclaiming that ordinary people could understand the gospel of the Lord without the leadership of a man of the cloth. Religious services changed drastically by the addition of emotional public admissions of sin and those sinners being "saved" right in front of the congregation.

The Great Awakening impacted the colonies in several ways. It was the first time that colonists across the 13 colonies could claim a common experience. Regardless of social class, country of origin, or occupation, the impact of the Great Awakening could be felt by all. Some historians believe this common religious experience was one of the foundations of the democratization of colonial society that occurred after the 1740s. Secondly, new sects and divisions within the Protestant faith arose as a result of the religious rebirth. Baptists and Methodists, who emphasized emotion in their sermons, attracted large numbers of followers, which led to increased competition in attracting congregants. Furthermore, many universities, such as Dartmouth, Rutgers, and Princeton, were founded to educate "New Light" ministers, who were in high demand. Indeed, the old intellectual approach to faith was largely overshadowed as a new emotional and personal connection with God came to define the American form of worship.

UNIT 2: REVIEW QUESTIONS

Multiple-Choice Questions

Directions: Choose the best answer choice for the following questions.

Questions 1–4 refer to the following image.

Peter Minuit (1589–1638), Director Of New Netherland Colony, Purchases Manhattan Island From The Native Americans In 1626, For Chests Of Goods, Unknown Artist, 1754

1. Based on the event illustrated in the picture, the Dutch were most similar to which other European colonizers?

   (A) The English as they settled in Jamestown

   (B) The Spanish in the Incan Empire

   (C) The French in Canada

   (D) The Spanish in the Caribbean

2. Which of the following best describes the influence and the origins of development of Dutch North American societies during the colonial period?

   (A) The Dutch were looking to establish permanent colonies in which to build a world empire.

   (B) The Dutch established colonies mainly for economic trade and the production of food for the mother country.

   (C) The overpopulation of the Netherlands motivated the Dutch government to seek more territory.

   (D) The Dutch wanted to challenge the Spanish for naval supremacy.

3. Socially, much like the French, the Dutch were successful at which of the following?

   (A) Intermarriage with Native Americans

   (B) Developing and promoting the slave trade

   (C) The establishment of permanent colonies by settling entire families in their colonies

   (D) Establishing colonies with tolerance for all religions

4. Which of the following European colonizers was least like the Dutch when it came to interrelationships with the native population and slaves?

   (A) The Spanish, because they did not believe in intermarriage with the native population

   (B) The French, as they maintained a peaceful, yet isolated, coexistence with the native population

   (C) The Portuguese, because of the rigid class system based upon race they established

   (D) The English, as they maintained a separation between themselves and the native and slave population

Questions 5–7 refer to the following quote.

". . . if enslaving our fellow creatures be a practice agreeable to Christianity, it is answered in a great measure in many treatises at home, to which I refer you . . .

. . . we are all apt to shift off the blame from ourselves and lay it upon others, how justly in our case you may judge. The Negroes are enslaved by the Negroes themselves before they are purchased by the masters of the ships who bring them here. It is, to be sure, at our choice whether we buy them or not, so this then is our crime, folly, or whatever you will please to call it."

—Peter Fontaine, "A Defense of Slavery in Virginia"

5. Based upon the excerpt, what was the justification for slavery in British North America?

   (A) Slavery was based upon principles of Christianity.

   (B) Those to be sold into slavery are held as slaves in Africa first; therefore, slavery is a business transaction.

   (C) Slavery was part of the "natural order" of the human races.

   (D) According to English law, "inferior people" were destined to serve as slaves.

6. Which of the following explains how slavery evolved in 17th-century British North America?

(A) Slaves were brought with the first settlers to Jamestown.

(B) Slavery was developed after the deaths of thousands of enslaved Native Americans because of exposure to European diseases.

(C) The Anglican Church encouraged the transport of slaves to the colonies in North America as a source of cheap labor.

(D) The influx of indentured servants had decreased, and cheap labor was needed for the developing plantation system.

7. Which of the following individuals would reject the argument of Peter Fontaine?

(A) A former indentured servant in Virginia

(B) A plantation owner in Carolina

(C) A Quaker in Pennsylvania

(D) An Anglican in Massachusetts

Questions 8–10 refer to the following quote.

". . . the Enlightenment slowly helped undermine the power of traditional authority—something the Great Awakening did as well. But unlike the Great Awakening, the Enlightenment encouraged men and women to look to themselves—not to God— for guidance as to how to live their lives and to shape society. Enlightenment thought, with its emphasis on human rationality, encouraged a new emphasis on education and a heightened interest in politics and government. Most Enlightenment figures did not challenge religion and insisted that rational inquiry would support, not undermine, Christianity."

—*American History* 14th edition, by Alan Brinkley, McGraw-Hill

8. Which of the following events from early British North American colonial history would reflect the sentiments of the previous quote?

(A) The approval of the Mayflower Compact

(B) The establishment of Jamestown

(C) The ideas expressed by Anne Hutchinson

(D) The motivation for the Salem Witch Trials

9. Advocates of the ideals of the Enlightenment, such as those expressed in the previous excerpt, would have most likely agreed with which of the following movements?

(A) Republicanism

(B) Mercantilism

(C) Antinomianism

(D) Deism

10. The ideals expressed in the previous excerpt would have a positive effect on the America colonies through which of the following events?

(A) The passage of the Navigation Acts

(B) The creation of the Dominion of New England

(C) The outcome of Bacon's Rebellion

(D) The Glorious Revolution

Short-Answer Questions

1. **Quote 1:**

   " . . . where Providence hath ordained to live as Servants, either in England or beyond Sea, endure the prefixed yoak of their limited time with patience, and then in a small computation of years, by an industrious endeavor, they may become Masters and Mistresses of Families themselves. And let this be spoke to the deserved praise of Mary-Land, That the four year I served there were not to me so slavish, as a two years Servitude of a Handicraft Apprenticeship was here in London . . . "

   —*A Character of the Province of Mary-Land,* George Alsop, 1666

   Quote 2:

   "Who therefore wishes to earn his bread in a Christian and honest way, and cannot earn it in his fatherland otherwise than by the work of his hands, let him do so in his own country and not in America; for he will not fare better in America. However hard he may be compelled to work in his fatherland, he will surely find it hard, if not harder, in the new country."

   —*Journey to Pennsylvania in the Year 1750 and Return to Germany in the Year 1754,* Gottlieb Mittelberger, 1754

   For this question, address all three parts:

   (A) Briefly explain the main argument of George Alsop in his passage supporting indentured servitude in America.

   (B) Briefly explain the motivation for Gottlieb Mittelberger's objection to indentured servitude in America.

   (C) Briefly analyze the reasons behind the development of indentured servitude as a labor system in the British North American colonies.

2. **Political Cartoon A:**

Benjamin Franklin, 1754

Political Cartoon B:

King George and the Colonial Rebels, 1773

For this question, address all three parts:

(A) Briefly explain the meaning of Political Cartoon A.

(B) Briefly explain the meaning of Political Cartoon B.

(C) Describe the change in the political attitude in the American colonies between the years 1754 and 1773. Provide one specific piece of historical evidence not used in Part A or B to support your answer.

Long Essay Question

Directions: You are advised to spend 5 minutes planning and 30 minutes writing your answer.

Some historians argue that the philosophy of self-government that drove the movement for independence was influenced by the ideals of the Great Awakening, Enlightenment beliefs, and the experience of local republican thought.

> "The Great Awakening subsided by 1750, . . . The Awakening, like its counterpart the Enlightenment, influenced the American Revolution and set in motion powerful currents that still flow in American life. It implanted in American culture the evangelical crusade and the emotional appeal of revivalism. The movement weakened the status of the old-fashioned clergy and state-supported churches, encouraged believers to exercise their own judgment, and thereby weakened habits of deference generally . . . the Awakening and the Enlightenment, between the urgings of the spirit and the logic of reason, led by different roads to similar ends. Both movements emphasized the power and right of individual decision making, and both aroused millennial hopes that America would become the promised land in which people might attain the perfection of piety or reason, if not both."

> —From *America: A Narrative History* by George Brown Tindall and David Emory Shi

Analyze events of the early 18th century and explain to what extent this statement was accurate.

ANSWERS AND EXPLANATIONS

MULTIPLE-CHOICE ANSWERS

1. C

The French also tried to establish a peaceful relationship with the native population in North America. Although they had some brief skirmishes with the natives, both the French and the Dutch established a peaceful coexistence with the Indians. The English did not have much interaction with the natives at first, followed by curiosity and some interaction, and within a few years a massacre at the hands of the Powhatan (Algonquin) Indians (in 1622). The Spanish took the Incan Empire and most of its Caribbean colonies by force.

2. B

The Netherlands's homeland was in a constant battle to reclaim territory from the sea and therefore sought more fertile land to produce food and gain wealth for the nation. Therefore, the Dutch claimed "New Netherland," now New York.

3. A

Both the French and the Dutch were able to successfully intermarry with Native American groups in North America. While all European colonizers were active in the slave trade, France and the Netherlands were the least involved. The French and the Dutch were less interested in establishing colonies in the English New England model, and while the Dutch did not tolerate all religious faiths, it was less important to them than to most other colonizing nations.

4. D

The English maintained a strict separation between themselves and the Native Americans and slaves. Their ideas were based on the rigid class system that existed in England and the idea that non-whites were inferior. On the other hand, the Dutch intermarried with natives and slaves, as did the Spanish, French, and Portuguese.

5. B

Slavery was viewed as a business transaction, since plantation owners did not originally enslave the population. British plantation owners could not compete with others from the colonies of Spain and France if they had to pay their labor.

6. D

As jobs became available in England, fewer individuals and families sought the opportunities available through indentured servitude in British North America. While prosperity was returning to England, the plantations needed more labor. Therefore, by the 1660s, different colonies began to pass legislation making persons of African descent slaves for life.

7. C

Quakers were the first group to publicly declare that slavery was immoral, as one human could not own another human. Former indentured servants usually inherited large tracts of land and, if they could afford them, would want to purchase slaves to work the land for them. Plantation owners in Carolina relied heavily on slave labor for their livelihood, and Massachusetts was the first colony in British North America to legalize slavery.

8. C

Anne Hutchinson held several conversations in her home after church services to discuss the ideas expressed in the sermon. This was not acceptable in Puritan society, as church leadership thought that Mrs. Hutchinson was questioning the sermon and its merits and that it was inappropriate for a woman to answer questions about biblical principles.

9. A

Republicanism developed in the colonies during the mid-18th century as a result of political ideas expressed during the Enlightenment. These ideas would eventually lead to ideas of independence.

10. D

The Glorious Revolution occurred when King William III and Mary I (of Orange) were brought to the throne in England, replacing the absolute rule of King James II. With them, William and Mary enacted the English "Bill of Rights," which became the foundation for English law and inspired Americans in their revolution almost one century later. The Navigation Acts and the Dominion of New England placed restrictions on American colonists. Although Bacon's Rebellion shared similar ideals as the Glorious Revolution, the Rebellion failed and any democratic measures passed by the Virginia House of Burgesses were rescinded.

SHORT-ANSWER QUESTIONS RESPONSES

1. (A) Benjamin Franklin produced one of the first political cartoons in American history to convince the colonies that in order to survive they must unite against common enemies. Franklin wanted the colonies to come together, under the control of the king of England, through Franklin's Albany Plan of Union.

   (B) The artist of this cartoon demonstrated that some Americans were beginning to believe that King George was controlling America through draconic parliamentary decisions without input from the colonists themselves—for example, the passage of the Stamp Act in 1765 without any input from the colonies.

   (C) The colonists began to change their attitude toward the British with the passage of restrictive laws and regulations such as the *writs of assistance*, which gave the English army the right to enter any American home and search for contraband. These searches were a violation of the English principle that a "man's home was his castle" and could not be entered unless there was a good purpose. As the years passed, there were more violations of the "rights of Englishmen" enforced on the colonists—to the point that the people began to resent the king.

2. (A) George Alsop explains that a person could be a servant in either England or in America. However, Alsop saw greater opportunity in America, for if a person went there as an indentured servant, he or she would earn freedom after a determined period of years and become master or mistress of their own plantation.

   (B) Gottlieb Mittelberger's argument is based on the idea that a worker would be better off in his homeland than he would be in America, as he would have to work harder in America and would not be familiar with the land.

   (C) As the plantation system in the British North American colonies developed and as work opportunities disappeared in England, impoverished English citizens were given the opportunity to come to America under the headright system. This system promised settlers that after their terms as indentured servants were completed, they would receive 50 acres of land (per family member) and have the opportunity to establish their own plantation. This system also provided the plantation owners with cheap labor, allowing the plantation owners to prosper.

LONG ESSAY SAMPLE RESPONSE

The idea of American independence from Great Britain began at least three decades before the outbreak of the war for independence in 1775. Americans had developed a semblance of self-rule with the disregard of the mercantilist policies of England through the policy of benign neglect, but added to that noticeable action was the underlying current of liberty and democratic rights of the Enlightenment and religious independence from the Great Awakening. Therefore, for several years Americans were arguably independent of Great Britain, although not in a legal sense but in spirit, making the official political separation from England in 1776 an easy one to accept.

The Enlightenment of the late 17th and early 18th centuries only added encouragement to the American economic independence that was unwittingly established in the early 18th century by Parliament. Benign or salutary neglect became the official policy of Britain, as the cost of oversight and protection of the British North American colonies became too expensive with the growing costs incurred by a series of worldwide wars with France. The colonies, it was believed, would adhere to British law and continue to be loyal to the Crown. Americans, however, began to establish business relationships that were not permitted under English mercantile law. Rhode Island soon gained the reputation of being a colony with an economy based on illegal trade with the French, Dutch, and Spanish. Although Americans were not adhering to English law, they were still politically and spiritually tied to the mother country.

While the ideas of the Enlightenment began to impress some Americans, it was the Great Awakening of the 1740s that demonstrated to Americans that the creation of institutions independent of the British Crown would thrive. The preaching of Jonathan Edwards and George Whitefield began a revival of American religious faith that inspired people to leave the established (Anglican) church within their colony and join more independent churches such as the Baptist and Methodist sects. Although still having to support the Anglican Church with tax revenue, the new churches were able to establish themselves with few repercussions. This demonstrates the value of religious toleration that was a cornerstone of Enlightenment philosophy.

Ideas of the Enlightenment began to trickle into America at the start of the 18th century, having some impact as Americans believed in their Rights as Englishmen, as espoused in the English Bill of Rights brought in by William and Mary in the Glorious Revolution. By the time of the American Revolution, many of the ideas of the philosophy were commonplace. Future founding fathers like George Washington, Thomas Jefferson, John Adams, and Benjamin Franklin were becoming more aware of political philosophy and began to adopt these ideals as they became more politically influential in their respective colonies. Most noteworthy would be Benjamin Franklin's Albany Plan of Union introduced in

1754, in which a representative-style government would be created to represent colonial interests, especially in matters of defense and economics.

Ultimately, by the time the British North American colonists made the decision to declare their independence from Great Britain, the ideas and the precedent had been long established. Arguably, the founding fathers had been influenced by two historically significant movements—the Enlightenment and the Great Awakening—as many of the founding documents of America, the Declaration of Independence, and some other works by Thomas Jefferson, such as the Virginia Statute of Religious Freedom, were deeply rooted in the ideas that had been introduced to Americans decades earlier. Also, the ideas of American liberty and the thought of independence from England was not a totally foreign concept as Americans had been practicing some form of independence for many years before July 4, 1776.

This analysis does an excellent job tying together three distinctive but interrelated reform movements from the antebellum era—all three movements were focused on the ideas of democracy and freedom. The amount of factual evidence is good, but could be stronger with the mention of a few more details like The Liberator and (later) Uncle Tom's Cabin—when discussing literature.

Overall, the essay demonstrates good synthesis by demonstrating the impact of both the Enlightenment and the Great Awakening on the development of American ideas on independence. Also, the essay clearly highlights the historical thinking skill of period and the skill of continuity and change over time that are the two main focuses of this task.

Based on the Long Essay Question rubric, this essay would receive a 6 out of 6 possible points.

CHAPTER 9: NEW CONFLICTS IN THE BRITISH COLONIES AND THE BIRTH OF THE UNITED STATES

THE FRENCH AND INDIAN WAR

England's efforts to assert its imperial domination eventually resulted in the **French and Indian War** in the colonies, which started in 1754 in the Ohio Valley. The French had been fortifying the Ohio Valley region to deter the British from settling further west. The British hoped to thwart French efforts by driving them from the North American continent. The colonial fight began in earnest in May 1754, when the governor of Virginia sent Lt. Colonel George Washington and his men to prevent the French from putting the finishing touches on Fort Duquesne (in modern-day Pittsburgh). Washington's forces proved weak in the face of a large combined French and Native American force and consequently retreated, finally surrendering on July 3, 1754. Recognizing that this was not going to be a quick and easy victory, British officials shortly called a meeting in Albany, New York to devise a defense plan. The Albany Congress, under the tutelage of **Benjamin Franklin**, constructed the **Albany Plan of Union**, which called for a confederation of colonies to provide defense from attack by European and native foes. However, the colonies rejected the plan because they felt it was too restrictive. Also, the British felt it allowed for too much colonial independence.

REMOVING THE FRENCH FROM NORTH AMERICA

British war efforts were ineffective in the early years of the war, until **William Pitt** took over as prime minister. He shifted British efforts from colonial skirmishes to the conquering of Canada, particularly Montreal, Quebec, and Louisbourg. The French surrendered Quebec in 1759, and Montreal in 1760. The result was the monumental **Peace of Paris** (1763), in which the British took control of French Canada and Spanish Florida, effectively removing France's presence from North America.

The French and Indian War was significant in many regards. The British emerged as the dominant colonial power in North America. No longer would the colonies have to worry about attacks launched by the French and Spanish or Native American tribes allied with either or both countries. However, the British had not been impressed with the colonial militias and felt that the colonists could not defend themselves adequately. The colonists, on the other hand, having tasted the fruits of victory, were proud of their ability to fend off French and Native American armies. They held the British military officers in contempt because of the poor treatment of colonial militiamen on the battlefield. More important to both the British and the colonists was the amount of debt left in the wake of war. British citizens were feeling the sting of war in the form of higher prices and skyrocketing taxes. The colonists, on the other hand, were not keen on the idea of paying for the war effort. The new government of Great Britain and young King George III had other plans for the colonies.

POST-WAR CONFLICTS WITH NATIVES

After the cession of Spanish and French territories to England after the Peace of Paris, the entire North American continent east of the Mississippi River belonged to England. The sudden removal of the French from North America shifted the power dynamics in the diplomacy between the English and Native Americans, who had primarily fought with the French in the Seven Years' War.

The long period of salutary neglect by the mother country came to an abrupt end by 1763. The British view that the colonists were not capable of protecting themselves was further solidified by the outbreak of **Pontiac's Rebellion** (1763). Native Americans in the Ohio Valley refused to hand over conquered lands to the British at the close of the war because of harsh treatment by the British. The Ottawa people, led by Chief Pontiac, led an attack on the new colonial settlements from the Great Lakes region of what is now Michigan all the way to Virginia. The damage to British forts and colonial settlements was significant, with many lives lost and homes destroyed. British regular forces were sent to protect the colonies, and the rebellion was finally subdued after 18 months of fighting.

To protect the British colonies from further Native American incursion, King George III signed the **Proclamation of 1763**. This proclamation set a line of demarcation that barred American colonists from settling west of the Appalachian Mountains. The British saw this as a quick and easy way to make peace with the Native American tribes of the region. British colonists, on the other hand, were incensed by the apparent permanent interference of the crown in their ability to take land they had won in battle. Most colonists simply ignored the Proclamation line and settled west in larger numbers than before the French and Indian War.

EFFECTS OF THE FRENCH AND INDIAN WAR

BRITISH MEASURES TO RAISE REVENUE

Strapped by large debt stemming from multiple wars, the British crown sought to make its colonies work to its advantage. Beginning with the Currency Act in 1764, which limited the use of colonial paper money, the British crown looked to the colonies to relieve some of the tax burden on its homeland citizens. Harsher tax collection began with the passage of the **Sugar Acts** of 1764, which raised the previous amount demanded on sweeteners (molasses and sugar) from the older Molasses Act of 1733. Britain wanted to collect the tax revenue it had been losing to the Triangular Trade by taxing molasses from the West Indies and abroad, but its primary purpose was to make money for the crown. In another blow to colonial autonomy, the **Quartering Act** of 1765 required colonial citizens to provide room and board for British soldiers stationed there. Nonetheless, these acts were tame in the eyes of the colonists—they were laxly enforced and rarely affected their everyday lives.

It was not until the passage of the **Stamp Act** in 1765 that colonists became truly aware of the impact of British taxation. The Stamp Tax was an attempt by Britain to collect revenues to build a new colonial army. The act required that all paper in the colonies have a stamp affixed, signifying that the tax had been paid. All colonial documents, from death and marriage certificates to newspapers, had to have the stamp. This was the first time the colonists had been subjected to a direct tax—a tax that was paid directly by the consumer of the paper good produced in the colony—as opposed to paying an indirect tax on an imported good. The act was justifiable in the eyes of the British prime minister, George Grenville, in that colonists were being asked to pay only their fair share of the burden of war. The colonists, however, did not see things this way.

COLONIAL REACTION TO BRITISH MEASURES

Colonials in all 13 colonies reacted to the Stamp Act with disdain. The young **Patrick Henry**, a lawyer from Virginia, expressed popular colonial sentiment when he stood in the Virginia House of Burgesses and accused the British government of usurping the rights guaranteed to colonists as Englishmen. He encouraged his fellow leaders to allow Virginians to be taxed only by Virginians, not by some distant royal authority.

Further north, **James Otis** of Massachusetts, the man most associated with the phrase "no taxation without representation," rallied representatives from 9 of the 13 colonies to meet in New York as the **Stamp Act Congress**. This body sent word to England that only colonial legislatures had the authority to tax the colonists. The colonists agreed that external taxes—levies imposed throughout the empire on traded goods—were within the rights of the crown to impose. However, they argued that internal taxes—taxes levied directly on the people of a region—were within the rights of only locally elected officials. Grenville responded by pointing out that since Parliament governed on behalf of the entire British Empire, the colonists did indeed have representation in Parliament—**virtual representation**.

COLONIAL BOYCOTT AND THE TOWNSHEND ACT

England's insistence that the colonists had "virtual representation" did not sit well, and violent reactions soon spread. **The Sons and Daughters of Liberty**, led by **Samuel Adams**, intimidated tax collectors by attacking their homes, burning them in effigy, and even tarring and feathering them. The Sons and Daughters even ransacked warehouses that held stamps and burned them to the ground. It became fashionable for colonists to protest the Stamp Act quietly by participating in *boycotts* of British goods by wearing homespun clothing and drinking Dutch tea. The boycotts negatively impacted British trade, and Parliament was ultimately forced to repeal the act in 1766. In its place, however, the British passed the **Declaratory Act**, which maintained the right of the crown to tax the colonies in the future.

The new chancellor of the exchequer (treasury), Charles Townshend, decided to punish the rebellious colonies by instituting a revenue plan of his own. The **Townshend Acts**, passed in 1767, brought harsher taxes on the purveyors of imported goods such as glass, paper, and tea. In addition, a special board of customs officials was appointed to enforce **writs of assistance**. These writs allowed customs officials to search colonial homes, businesses, and warehouses for smuggled goods without a warrant from a judge. While the colonists felt that any increase in taxes signaled an abuse by Parliament, they were slow to react to the Townshend duties because they were external, rather than internal, taxes. However, John Dickinson's *Letters from a Farmer in Pennsylvania* rekindled interest in the issue of taxation without representation and inspired Samuel Adams to pen the **Massachusetts Circular Letter** in 1768. The letter argued that there was no distinction between external and internal taxes and that the Townshend Act must be immediately repealed. The letter was copied and distributed throughout the colonies, sparking the rejuvenation of boycotts of British goods. Wishing to avoid the economic troubles caused by the Stamp Act, the new prime minister, Lord North, repealed the Townshend Acts in 1770.

BOSTON RESPONDS TO TAXATION

The colonies and Britain maintained relatively peaceful relations between 1770 and 1772, with one notable exception. The residents of Boston were particularly angered by the enforcement of the Quartering Act. Many British regulars had been stationed in the city to protect the port and collect customs duties for imported British goods. Eventually, a crowd of disgruntled Bostonians began to harass the troops guarding the customs house by throwing rocks and frozen oysters. The guards fired upon the crowd, killing five and wounding six protesters. The event became known in the colonies as the **Boston Massacre** through propaganda spread by the Sons of Liberty.

Samuel Adams and the Sons did not let the spirit of protest die during the period of calm. Aided by the **Committees of Correspondence,** Adams and other colonials continually circulated letters of protest against British policies. A favorite event of the propagandists was the *Gaspee* incident. The *Gaspee* was a British warship commissioned to capture vessels carrying smuggled goods before they reached the colonies. The *Gaspee* ran aground on the shores of Rhode Island, to the delight of some members of the Sons of Liberty. Dressed as Native Americans, the colonists boarded the ship, marched its crew to shore, and set fire to the boat. The event was celebrated and retold throughout coastal colonial towns as a victory for the tax-burdened consumer.

DAUGHTERS OF LIBERTY

Many women also played a part in the fight for independence. Some participated in riots or gave homespun, rather than imported, goods to the army while others even tipped the Continental army off to British military movements. Benjamin Franklin's daughter **Esther Reed** organized a **Ladies' Association**, the purpose of which was to raise funds to help Continental soldiers. Another woman, **Mercy Otis Warren**, advocated for independence through poems and plays. The Revolution saw the beginning of women's involvement in public activism.

The year 1773 brought renewed conflict to the British colonies with the passage of the **Tea Act**. Even though the new act actually lowered the price of tea, colonists were wary of any attempt by Britain to collect revenue and refused to purchase the tea. As a new shipment of tea sat in Boston Harbor awaiting unloading, a group of colonists, again dressed as Native Americans, boarded the ship, broke open the crates, and dumped the tea into the water. Colonists disputed whether this was to be applauded as a justified protest against oppression or it was simply childish destruction of property.

Prime Minister North was not pleased by the news of the **Boston Tea Party** and decided to punish the citizens of the city. He persuaded Parliament to pass the **Coercive Acts**, which would close Boston Harbor until the tea was paid for and revoke the charter of the colony of Massachusetts. This would put the colony under the control of the crown and expand the scope of the Quartering Act, allowing soldiers to be boarded in private homes. In addition, Parliament passed the **Quebec Act** (1774), which allowed the former French region to be self-sufficient and expand its borders, taking away potential lands from colonists in the Ohio River Valley. Enraged, the colonists named these acts the **Intolerable Acts**. They were angered more by the provision to allow Quebec citizens to practice Catholicism freely than by the other provisions.

THE AMERICAN REVOLUTION

THE COLONIES ORGANIZE—THE FIRST CONTINENTAL CONGRESS

The Intolerable Acts (also called the Coercive Acts) led colonial leaders to quickly organize in order to protect themselves from further British retaliation. Representatives from 12 of the 13 colonies traveled to Philadelphia in September of 1774 to discuss acceptable forms of protest and reaction. Leaders' reactions ranged from radical (Samuel Adams) to mild (John Jay). One thing was clear— the delegates needed to send a strong message asserting the rights of colonials to England by demanding the repeal of the Coercive Acts. Colonial leaders also urged colonies to expand military reserves and organize boycotts of British goods in the meantime.

The Continental Congress sent the ***Declaration of Rights and Grievances*** to the king to urge him to correct the wrongs incurred by the colonists while simultaneously acknowledging the authority of Parliament to regulate colonial trade and commerce. The Congress also created the Association, which called for the creation of "boycott committees" throughout the colonies to bring Britain to its knees, economically. Lastly, the delegates agreed to meet again in May of 1775 if their grievances had not been remedied by the crown. The king and Parliament did not respond to the demands of the **First Continental Congress**, as doing so would have legitimized the Congress's claim to wield political power. Before the congressional delegates could meet again, war would break out between American militiamen and British soldiers.

THE FIGHT BEGINS

Having experienced the brunt of British punishment, the citizens of Massachusetts were ready to fight. British general Thomas Gage, now the governor of Massachusetts, ordered his men to seize armaments and arrest rebels in the town of Concord. As the large force of British soldiers marched to carry out its orders, a forewarned group of American militiamen (minutemen) assembled in nearby Lexington to stop the British soldiers in their tracks. "The shot heard around the world" was fired at that fateful encounter on the Lexington Green. The American Revolution had begun. After losing eight men and finding themselves grossly overmatched, the American minutemen were forced to retreat, opening the way for the British to march to Concord. After the British inflicted minimal damage on Concord, the minutemen were able to force the British to retreat back to Boston and kill about 250 of them by day's end.

After fortifying the area around Boston, the minutemen found themselves embroiled in an intense battle for **Bunker Hill** on June 17, 1775. Even though the colonials lost the battle, they celebrated the massive casualties they were able to inflict on the most powerful military force in the world. Perhaps most importantly, the king officially declared the colonies in rebellion, a proclamation tantamount to a declaration of war. Shortly thereafter, the king hired Hessian mercenaries from Germany, known for their ruthlessness in battle, to invade the colonies. For Patriots, the conflict with Mother England had always been a family affair. When the Hessians entered the picture, the colonials increasingly saw the British motive for war as one of annihilation.

At the beginning of the war, the odds were in England's favor. With the most powerful navy in the world coupled with ample money and a plentiful supply of recruits, it seemed almost certain that the British would win a quick and decisive victory over the colonists. However, the colonists were able to take advantage of certain British weaknesses. The British troops were a long distance away from their own country. Thus, orders from above, munitions, and fresh soldiers took a long time to arrive. The Americans, on the other hand, had superb military leadership and a greater understanding of the terrain of the battlefield. The colonials, too, had their problems, however: There was fighting among colonies vying for positions of power, sinking morale of the

Continental troops due to lack of wages, and shrinking war supplies. These factors threatened to sink the colonial rebels once and for all.

THE FRENCH STEP IN

Lack of funding soon became a nonissue for the Americans, as the French were waiting patiently for an opportunity to exact revenge on their longtime British foes. France happily provided the colonials assistance after the **Battle of Saratoga** in 1777. This proved to be a turning point in the fight for independence and opened the doors for an American victory.

THE SECOND CONTINENTAL CONGRESS

Keeping their promise to reconvene, delegates from all 13 colonies met again in May 1775 to discuss their next steps. Even with skirmishes occurring nearby, the delegates widely varied in their opinions regarding the colonial position. Those from the New England colonies tended to be much more radical—many insisted on independence. Those from the middle colonies expressed a desire to reopen negotiations with Britain. Either way, it was clear that the Continental Congress needed to arrive at a consensus. Virginia's native son, George Washington, was appointed as the head of the Continental Army, a shrewd move on the part of Northern delegates, because the South would now rally behind the war effort. The Congress drew up the *Declaration of the Causes and Necessities of Taking Up Arms*, which urged King George III a second time to consider colonial grievances and provided for the raising of a professional colonial military force. As a last gesture of peace and a preventative measure against total war, the Congress voted to send the **Olive Branch Petition** to Britain in July 1775. This document reasserted colonial loyalty to the crown and asked King George III to intervene with Parliament on their behalf. The king, however, refused, once again, to recognize the legitimacy of the Congress.

In January 1776, **Thomas Paine**, a recent English immigrant to the colonies, published a pamphlet that would shift the radical notion of independence from England to the mainstream. Titled *Common Sense*, the pamphlet used John Locke's natural rights philosophy to argue that the citizens of the colonies were obligated to rebel against the oppression of Britain and that it would be contrary to common sense to allow the injustices to continue. Members of the Congress read the pamphlet with great interest, thereby integrating Paine's arguments into their deliberations in Philadelphia.

As a year of discussion and deliberation came to a close, the Second Continental Congress believed that independence was the only acceptable decision. On June 7, 1776, Richard Henry Lee called for a resolution declaring the colonies independent of Britain. A committee was chosen to draft a declaration document that would reiterate the June 7 resolution. **Thomas Jefferson** and four other delegates quickly set to work on writing the document that came to be known as the **Declaration of Independence**. It contained a preamble that heavily reflected the philosophy of John Locke regarding natural rights. Jefferson listed 27 grievances and charges of wrongdoing directed at the crown and Parliament. This declaration was the official break of the colonies from England, making the United States a country in its own right.

INDEPENDENCE, NOT DEPENDENCE

But the colonies could not mount a unified front against the British. Many historians believe that colonial citizens were divided roughly into thirds—one-third actively engaged in the fight for independence (**Patriots**), one-third siding with Great Britain (**Loyalists** or **Tories**), and the last third being uninterested or unaffected by the war altogether. Therefore, one of the major challenges for the new nation was limiting disagreement among its own citizens and educating those living in the west and removed from the turmoil. Loyalists were usually older, wealthy, educated citizens of the Middle or Southern colonies. They often sought to benefit from their loyalty to the crown by maintaining their social, economic, and political standing. After the war, some 60,000 to 80,000 Loyalists chose to flee into exile rather than remain in the United States. Patriots, on the other hand, were a small force of young New Englanders and Virginians who volunteered their time to the Continental Army. They would leave their homes, farms, and jobs for short tours of duty, return home for a short time, and return to the battlefield. Washington's forces were rarely paid for their services.

The war did not progress well for General Washington in the beginning. After losing New York City in 1776, Washington made a bit of headway by winning several small battles in New Jersey in 1777. Other American generals can be credited with winning the most important battle of the Revolution—the Battle of Saratoga (October 1777), fought by Generals Benedict Arnold and Horatio Gates. American forces were able to cut off the British charge on New England and secure the surrender of British General Burgoyne's army, thus convincing the French of America's military viability. The French had been waiting for evidence of an American success so they could justify entering the war on behalf of the revolutionaries. The entry of the French on the side of the Americans in 1778, and the Spanish and Dutch soon thereafter, turned the tide of the war in America's favor. The British were faced with the specter of another world war on the heels of the Seven Years' War and had to divert their resources elsewhere.

Having survived one of the coldest winters (1777–1778) on record at Valley Forge, Pennsylvania, Washington's troops were then able to take advantage of the depleted British forces and win battles on its march to Virginia. At Yorktown in 1781, the last major battle of the Revolution was waged. Washington's men, with the assistance of French forces, secured the surrender of British general Charles Cornwallis's regiment. Tired of the strain of the war on their economy, British citizens ousted their Tory government in favor of the Whigs, who wanted to end the war with the Americans.

At Paris in 1783, the warring sides came together to deliberate and reach a peace settlement. For their part, the Americans agreed to repay debts to British merchants and promised not to punish Loyalists who chose to remain in the United States.

THE U.S. OFFICIALLY BECOMES A COUNTRY

The resulting **Treaty of Paris** (1783) included a formal recognition of the United States as a country, a boundary that stretched west to the Mississippi River, and the retention of American fishing rights in Newfoundland.

INDIANS DURING AND AFTER THE REVOLUTION

During and after the American Revolution, many native tribes tried to build political alliances with each other and with Europeans who had a presence in America. The main goal of these attempted alliances was to keep and protect native land by controlling the migration of white settlers.

One of the most notable conflicts between Indians and Americans took place in and around the Ohio River Valley. The British openly sold firearms and alcohol to the Indians of the **Miami Confederacy**, or Western Confederacy, a group of eight Indian nations whose response to American encroachment on their lands was to terrorize them. The war chief of the Miami Confederacy, **Little Turtle**, informed Americans that the confederacy considered the Ohio River the northwestern boundary of the newfound United States. Open warfare broke out in 1790 and 1791. Little Turtle's troops devastated the American armies led by Josiah Harmar and Arthur St. Clair, killing 630 soldiers in the United States's worst defeat in the history of the frontier. In 1794, General "Mad Anthony" Wayne led 3,000 American soldiers in a sweeping defeat of Little Turtle's forces at the Battle of Fallen Timbers. The Indians turned to the British for help but were denied and soon surrendered.

The Battle of Fallen Timbers prompted the **Treaty of Greenville** of 1795, in which 12 Indian tribes ceded vast areas of the Old Northwest, including most of what is now Indiana and Ohio, to the federal government. In return, the tribes of the Miami Confederacy were given a payment of $20,000 and an **annuity** of $9,000. The "annuity" system in the United States began as a byproduct of this treaty and gave annual federal grants to Indian tribes in exchange for ceding ultimate control of Indian tribal affairs to the U.S. government.

CHAPTER 10: EXPERIMENTS WITH GOVERNMENT, RELIGIOUS, ECONOMIC, AND CULTURAL IDEAS

THE IMPACT OF THE ENLIGHTENMENT ON THE COLONIES

The ideas of political, philosophical, and social thinkers of Europe during the 17th and 18th centuries had a profound impact on the character and ideologies of many Americans. British philosopher **John Locke's** theory of natural rights challenged the absolute and divine rule of kings and queens by asserting that all men should be ruled by natural laws and that sovereignty was derived from the will of those governed. Locke went on to assert that the governed have a responsibility to rebel against a government that fails to protect the natural rights of life, liberty, and property. Men such as George Washington, Benjamin Franklin, Thomas Jefferson, and John Adams either experienced Enlightenment teachings firsthand while traveling in Europe, or had read the philosophies in their studies. With the addition of the writings of men such as the Baron de Montesquieu and Jean Jacques Rousseau, enlightened colonials began to emphasize the concept of reason over emotion. This shift in philosophy set the stage for a revolutionary spirit that abounded in late 18th-century America. Colonists now had justification for rebelling against a government they perceived as directly and deliberately violating their rights as Englishmen.

THE ARTICLES OF CONFEDERATION

Continental leaders did not idly sit around waiting for Britain to recognize their sovereignty during the Revolution. By 1777, all but three of the colonies had drafted and ratified their own "state" constitutions. These constitutions attempted to strike a delicate balance between law and order and the protection of natural rights. Most of the new constitutions provided suffrage for landholding male citizens and the protection of basic rights.

While colonies were busily forming governments of their own, the delegates of the Second Continental Congress set out to create a national government. With slight alterations made to a draft national constitution written by John Dickinson, the **Articles of Confederation** were accepted and sent to the states for ratification in 1777. After a dispute between the coastal states and inland states over the administration of westward lands, the Articles were finally ratified by all 13 states in 1781. The Articles of Confederation provided a template for government that the infant United States needed. They called for a central government with a unicameral legislative branch. To amend the Articles, a unanimous vote (13 representatives) was required, while a super-majority (two-thirds) was required to pass laws. The central government under the Articles could wage war, make treaties, and borrow money to pay debts. The Articles also established clear policies regarding the settlement and statehood of newly acquired lands to the west.

A NEW SET OF LAWS

The **Land Ordinance of 1785** required new townships to set aside a parcel of land for public education and stipulated that the sale of public lands would be used to pay off the national debt. The settlement of the Old Northwest would thus be orderly in contrast to relatively disorganized settlement in the South. The **Northwest Ordinance of 1787** established guidelines for attaining statehood: Territories with at least 60,000 people could apply for statehood. If accepted by Congress, the new state would have equal status with other states. Moreover, the Northwest Ordinance banned slavery north of the Ohio River, thereby guaranteeing future free states in the Midwest. While these examples show the successes of the Articles, the new central government was fraught with complications from the outset. To avoid tyranny and abuse of power by the new central government, the Articles did not allow for the taxing of citizens to raise revenue. Nor was the government given the authority to enforce its own laws. While the government could request taxes from the states, it could not enforce tax collection. This apparent weakness was deliberate; however, by limiting the strength of the central government, the states actually created more problems than they had bargained for. Because the central government could not tax its citizens for revenue, large war debts remained unpaid. This, coupled with the crippled American economy due to broken trade relationships and a depreciated currency, further drove the new nation into financial crisis. By not paying off its debts, the new government appeared weak and vulnerable to Europeans. Therefore, an invasion by Great Britain or Spain was a possibility.

SHAYS'S REBELLION AND ITS AFTERMATH

The greatest challenge to the strength of the Articles came not from abroad but from home. Angered by high taxes, debtors' prisons, and lack of valuable currency, **Daniel Shays** and a band of Massachusetts farmers rose up during the summer of 1786 and demanded tax and debt relief. **Shays's Rebellion** escalated in January 1787 when a mob undertook a seizure of the state **arsenal** in Springfield. At this stage, the Massachusetts militia marched in and quelled the rebellion. Although Shays's Rebellion seemed to be a minor local **insurrection**, Confederation leaders looked with concern at the implications of the event. The constitution of Massachusetts was one of the most thorough and well executed, thus Shays's Rebellion signaled a serious problem. With so much emphasis placed on the virtues of a republic, the delegates of Congress had failed to ensure that the states themselves would be able to protect faithfully the rights and liberties of their own citizens. It was clear to many congressional leaders that the Articles of Confederation needed to be overhauled.

To repair the problem of the regulation of commerce, a convention was called for Annapolis, Maryland, in 1786. It was sparsely attended (five delegates out of 13 states), and political heavyweights **James Madison** and **Alexander Hamilton** secured the calling of another convention, this time to be held in Philadelphia. Again, the focus of the meeting was to revise the existing Articles of Confederation. The tenor of this meeting soon shifted, and the meeting would become the **Constitutional Convention**.

THE CONSTITUTIONAL CONVENTION

The new nation experienced many challenges in the years immediately after the Peace of Paris was signed.

POSTWAR PROBLEMS

An economic depression occurred because of the lack and depreciated value of Continental currency. Farmers were hit particularly hard under the weight of high state taxes and high ratios of debt. The **sovereignty** of the United States was also challenged by several European nations and bands of pirates from North Africa. Even though Great Britain promised to respect the sovereignty of the United States, it refused to repeal the Navigation Laws, armed Native Americans along the western frontier, and failed to remove troops from posts along the Mississippi River. The Spanish closed the port of New Orleans to U.S. trade and also armed Native Americans in the southwest. France called for prompt repayment of the war debts owed and further deepened the economic crisis by limiting the ability of the United States to trade in the Caribbean. Taking advantage of the absence of British protection of U.S. shipping in the Mediterranean, North African **Barbary Pirates** attacked merchant ships, often seizing their goods and kidnapping crews. As a result of these problems, 12 of the 13 states agreed to send delegates to Philadelphia to improve the standing of the new nation both politically and economically by repairing the inadequate Articles.

A SECRET MEETING

The meeting had been scheduled to begin on May 14, 1787. However, troubles with travel and other engagements kept many delegates from arriving on time. While they were waiting for the others, the delegates from Virginia began working on a proposal that they would present to the full body once they convened. Finally, 55 delegates from all states but Rhode Island convened in secret on May 25, 1787. The meeting was composed of young, well-educated, wealthy men who were familiar with the conventions of republicanism and democracy. Most were practicing lawyers and had taken a direct hand in the writing of their own state constitutions. Some major names did not attend the convention owing to overseas business; some were not chosen because of their radical views; and one, Patrick Henry, refused to participate owing to his feelings about the danger of a strong central power. From his desk in Paris, Thomas Jefferson called the meeting a "convention of demigods." After great delays caused by the perils of travel, the group decided to continue meeting in private and to keep the work of the convention secret until it had been completed.

MADISON TAKES CHARGE

In an unanimous vote, George Washington was elected as chairperson, but his was by no means the strongest voice at the convention. **James Madison**, a delegate from Virginia, was well read in the areas of federalism, republicanism, and Lockean theory and quickly became the leading voice of the convention. Madison provided the cornerstones for the development of what is now the U.S. Constitution. First, he expressed the need for a **central government** whose power would exceed the power of the states. Second, he believed in the **separation of powers**—the executive, the legislative, and the judicial branches of government would be independent of one another but would be held accountable by each. Lastly, Madison outlined the dangers of "**factions**" and the power a strong national government would have to keep these groups in check. These views were somewhat radical. Many leaders, such as Thomas Jefferson and George Mason, did not believe that the national government should be supreme to the power of the states. "Early arrivals" from Virginia took control of the Convention, and soon it was clear that the Articles would be thrown out and a new document would be drafted to rebuild the national government.

A GREAT COMPROMISE IS REACHED

After the decision was made to scrap the Articles and start anew, divisive political, social, and economic issues came to light. First on the agenda was the issue of state representation in the legislative branch. Edmund Randolph and the delegates from larger states proposed an arrangement called the **Virginia Plan** that favored their states. This plan, presented on May 29, 1787, called for representation in both houses to be based solely on population or proportional representation. The small states, led by William Paterson, put forth their rebuttal to the large state proposal. The **New Jersey Plan** asked for equal representation, regardless of the number of citizens of a state, in a unicameral legislative body. At this point, June 9, 1787, the discussion was at a standstill, and the threat of the convention's collapsing was real. On June 11, Roger Sherman rose with this proposal: "That the proportion of suffrage in the first branch should be according to the respective numbers of free inhabitants and that in the second branch or Senate, each State should have one vote and no more." This was coined the **Great Compromise** (or Connecticut Compromise). Large states were satisfied because the lower chamber, or the **House of Representatives**, would be composed of members who reflected the population of individual states. Small states were satisfied because representation in the upper chamber, or **Senate,** was composed of membership that was equal regardless of state population. Large states stood to gain more from this compromise, as revenue bills would only go through the lower chamber, thus possibly easing the tax burden that large states would more likely have to pay.

AN EXECUTIVE DECISION AND THE THREE-FIFTHS COMPROMISE

Next, the delegates needed to discuss the issue of executive leadership. All of the men present were unwilling to hand the executive branch too much power; however, they understood all too well the dangers of a weak chief. After much debate, it was decided that the president would be elected by a representative body rather than by direct popular vote. The delegates were all worried about a "**mobocracy**" in which the uneducated would choose a president who was dangerous to the stability of the nation. Thus, by allowing the **Electoral College** to cast votes as representatives of their states, they controlled democracy, and mob rule was avoided. The president was given many more powers than the weak governors of the states. He would be commander in chief of the armed forces, act as chief diplomat, and have the ability to veto laws made by the legislative branch.

Just when the delegates thought the issue of representation was behind them, a conflict of geographic proportions arose. Southern delegates lived in large states, which had equally large populations of enslaved Africans who were not considered citizens. Southerners argued that although these people could not vote, they still had to be managed by the state and should thus be counted as part of the population. Northerners, some of whom disliked the practice of slavery but knew better than to ask for abolition, agreed to the **Three-Fifths Compromise** in exchange for the passage of the **Northwest Ordinance**. This compromise stipulated that each enslaved person in the South would be counted as three-fifths of a person. The South conceded to the end of the legal importation of slaves in 1808. Lastly, the Northern and Southern representatives decided on a compromise with regard to trade and taxes by agreeing that Congress could place taxes on imports but not exports.

THE DEBATE OVER RATIFICATION—FEDERALISTS VERSUS ANTI-FEDERALISTS

With the document complete, the delegates to the Constitutional Convention retired to their home states to campaign for *ratification*. Nine of the 13 states were required to ratify the national constitution. The discussion would rage on for almost a year. As word reached the state governments and citizens that the Articles of Confederation had been thrown out altogether, many feared a return to tyranny. States set out by selecting representatives to ratifying conventions. Several small states ratified quickly—Pennsylvania was the first large state to adopt the Constitution. Ratification debates occurred in statehouses, with those in favor of the Constitution and a strong central government called **Federalists** and those in opposition to the Constitution and in favor of strong states' rights called **Anti-Federalists**. Federalists were usually Northern merchants who had close ties with British trade networks. Anti-Federalists usually hailed from small Southern farms or western homesteads.

There were many battles to fight to garner the support of nine states necessary for ratification. Virginia was critical—it was the most populous state and had the largest concentration of Anti-Federalists, many of them concerned farmers. Soon enough, Virginia's native sons George Washington, James Madison, and John Marshall were able to persuade Anti-Federalists to ratify the document with the promise of an addition of a **Bill of Rights** to protect individual freedoms and state sovereignty. To encourage ratification in New York, James Madison, Alexander

Hamilton, and John Jay penned a series of 85 powerful essays collectively called *The Federalist Papers*. These papers were the *Common Sense* of the ratification period, urging ratifying conventions to set aside emotions when they considered the Constitution. Madison, Hamilton, and Jay refuted common doubts about whether a central government could effectively rule such vast territory. Soon after New York's vote to ratify, North Carolina and Rhode Island became the last states to ratify the Constitution.

If it had not been for the delay of delegates in arriving to the original convention in May 1787, Federalist Virginians might not have been able to take control of the meeting and, thus, convince the others to jettison the Articles instead of repairing them. In this respect, the new Constitution and resulting system of federalism was a victory for a very small minority. The addition of the Bill of Rights was the minority's concession. Congress acted quickly in 1789 to prepare the first 10 amendments promised to the Anti-Federalists. Penned mostly by James Madison, the 10 amendments served to protect states and individuals from possible abuses by the central government. They were ratified by the states in 1791.

STRUCTURING THE NEW REPUBLIC

Selected unanimously by the Electoral College, President George Washington took the oath of office on April 30, 1789, in the temporary national capital of New York City. John Adams was sworn in as the first vice president. Besides being the first president of the United States, Washington set many other important precedents that shaped the office of the presidency and the federal government as we know it today. The Constitution specifically assigns the president the task of designating departments of the executive branch to assist in government functions.

Washington appointed **Thomas Jefferson** as secretary of state, **Alexander Hamilton** as secretary of the treasury, Henry Knox as secretary of war, and Edmund Randolph as attorney general (appointed after the Judiciary Act of 1789). Washington called these four men his "cabinet" and met regularly with them to confer and gain advice. To this day, presidents regularly call advisory meetings of their cabinet members.

JUDICIARY ACT OF 1789

The smallest section of the Constitution is Article III—the Judiciary Branch. This article applies only to the federal court and is vague with regard to court structure. Therefore, Congress passed the **Judiciary Act of 1789**, establishing a Supreme Court consisting of one presiding chief justice and five associate justices. The act also provided for the establishment of 13 district courts and three circuit courts of appeal.

HAMILTON FIXES FINANCES

As economic problems had plagued the new nation ever since the Treaty of Paris, Secretary of the Treasury Alexander Hamilton set out to repair the nation's failing financial health. His ***Report on Public Credit*** (1790) explained how monetary and fiscal policy should favor the rich so that their good fortune would be spent within the economy and, thus, stimulate domestic growth. His ***Report on Manufactures*** (1791) promoted the industrialization of the United States and advocated strong protective tariffs to protect infant industries. His overall financial plan set out to place the United States on firm ground with regard to debt repayment, a stable currency, and a strong federal banking system. Made up of five components, the plan sought to boost national credit, create a "father/son" relationship between the federal government and the states, earn revenue by enacting heavy tariffs on imported goods and passing **excise taxes** on whiskey, and ensure stability by establishing a national bank. Each of these provisions was hotly contested, most strongly by Thomas Jefferson and the Anti-Federalists.

By "**funding at par**," Hamilton argued that the government should pay all debts at face value plus interest. Unfortunately for many government bond holders, the value of the bonds had dropped considerably because it was thought the new government would be unable to make good on its debts. Therefore, these original bond holders had sold to speculators, who were pleased to find that the government intended to pay face value on the bonds they now held. Hamilton was criticized for not alerting Americans about his plan before they sold their bonds.

The next issue was Hamilton's suggestion that the federal government assume all state debts. Northern states that had amassed large debts because of the war were thrilled, while smaller states in the South were not pleased with this plan. To appease both sides, Hamilton acquiesced to Thomas Jefferson's request to place the nation's permanent capital on the banks of the Potomac River, which straddled the states of Maryland and Virginia. The **Revenue Act of 1789** placed an 8 percent tariff on imports, a rate much lower than Hamilton had desired. He therefore imposed excise taxes on goods such as whiskey to make up the shortfall in revenue. These excise taxes became a problem for Hamilton and the new government when the Whiskey Rebellion broke out in 1794.

DISAGREEMENT OVER THE BANK OF THE UNITED STATES

The last and most contested part of Hamilton's plan was the establishment of a national bank—the **Bank of the United States (BUS)**. The federal government would hold the major financial interest in the bank, with private stockholders also contributing. The national treasury would keep its deposits in the bank, keeping the funds safe and available as loanable funds. Thomas Jefferson vehemently opposed the bank, stating that the Constitution did not provide for its creation. Jefferson was a **strict constructionist**, one who believed in the strict interpretation of the document. Hamilton, on the other hand, had a much broader, "loose" interpretation of the Constitution. He believed the Constitution supported the creation of a national bank because of the **"elastic" clause** (section 8, clause 18 of Article I of the Constitution). **Loose constructionists** like Alexander Hamilton believed this clause granted Congress "implied powers" to pass laws that were "necessary and proper" to run the country effectively. Hamilton argued that the creation of the Bank of the United States was justified under the elastic clause and by the need to keep and collect federal monies. His arguments won over George Washington, who signed the bank into law in 1791. This issue, however, caused the rift between Hamilton and Thomas Jefferson to widen.

RISE OF THE PARTY SYSTEM

The issues surrounding the ratification of the Constitution gave rise to a party system. Alexander Hamilton and the Federalists held fast to conservative *ideology*; the liberal states' rights and common man's viewpoint was held by the Anti-Federalists, soon to become the **Democratic-Republicans** championed by Thomas Jefferson.

Democratic-Republicans sought to limit the powers of the central government in favor of greater states' rights, while the Federalists believed in a strong national government whose powers were supreme over the states. These differences in opinion became clearer as conflict arose overseas.

DEVELOPMENT OF FOREIGN POLICY

Aside from developing political stability, President George Washington and his cabinet had to respond effectively to the demands of countries around the world. Soon after the new federal government was established, France experienced a revolution of its own. The war quickly extended beyond the borders of France and became a world war involving both Britain and the Caribbean. **The French Revolution** (1789–1793) challenged America's sovereignty, because Washington had to decide where U.S. loyalties would lie. Giving the French revolutionaries assistance as France had done for the Patriots during the American Revolution would strain the already delicate relationship with Britain. Initially, Americans were pleased about the overthrow of the king and queen of France, as it seemed an extension of the ideals of the American Revolution. It soon became clear, however, that this was a very different kind of revolution, a bloody and ruthless one. It did not take Americans long to become disgusted by the violence and radical nature of the French Jacobins.

Thomas Jefferson, a sympathizer with the French, urged that the United States should uphold the provisions of the Franco-American Alliance that had been forged in 1778 during the American Revolution. Alexander Hamilton, on the other hand, understood the necessity of maintaining trade relationships with Britain and, thus, called for U.S. neutrality. The president decided to side with Hamilton and declared the United States to be neutral in his landmark **Neutrality Proclamation of 1793**. Jefferson was furious. The French were not happy with the decision, either. Both the French and British began to seize American ships crossing the Atlantic, taking cargo and *impressing* sailors into military service. These seizures violated the Neutrality Proclamation, leading Washington to send Chief Justice of the Supreme Court John Jay in 1794 to negotiate with the British to seek the recognition of U.S. neutrality.

After almost a year of negotiations, **Jay's Treaty** did not settle the issue of British seizure or impressment of American sailors, but it did call for the removal of British forts in the west. The treaty further angered Democratic-Republicans and the French; the latter increased their harassment of American ships.

Jay's Treaty also worried Spain, which became concerned about a possible cozy relationship between Britain and the United States and sought to clear up any possible misunderstandings regarding the boundary between Spanish Florida and the new nation. President Washington sent Thomas Pinckney to negotiate a settlement of boundary, right of navigation along the Mississippi River, and right to deposit goods for transportation at the Port of New Orleans. The negotiations were successful and essentially removed Spain as a threat to further American settlement in the west. **Pinckney's Treaty** was unanimously ratified by Congress in 1796.

Upon leaving office in 1797, Washington delivered his **Farewell Address**, in which he warned the infant nation to remain neutral with regard to European affairs, to avoid entangling alliances, and to refrain from the formation of "factions," or political parties.

CHAPTER 11: MIGRATION WITHIN NORTH AMERICA AND A MULTIETHNIC, MULTIRACIAL NATIONAL IDENTITY

INTERNAL ISSUES FACING THE NEW GOVERNMENT

In addition to foreign policy issues, the fledgling nation had to deal with domestic challenges such as the constant threat of Native American attack, insurrection by angry citizens, and the settlement of newly acquired western lands. As American settlers pushed further and further westward, tensions with Native American tribes escalated. Having been given supplies and munitions by the British, the Shawnee, Miami, and other tribes rose up against the settlers and soldiers stationed in the region. In 1794, a U.S. force led by General Anthony Wayne defeated Native American fighters at the Battle of Fallen Timbers in the Old Northwest region of Ohio. The chiefs of the tribes agreed reluctantly to the Treaty of Greenville in 1795, whereby they surrendered tribal claims to land in what is now Ohio and Indiana. As these tribes moved west and away from their homelands, they were in almost continual battle with other tribes vying for land and power.

At nearly the same time, another uprising of backwoods farmers broke out in western Pennsylvania. These farmers were hit particularly hard by the excise tax imposed on the whiskey they distilled to supplement their incomes. Much as the Sons of Liberty had during the pre-Revolutionary era, some of these farmers violently protested the tax by tarring and feathering tax collectors or destroying public buildings. President Washington would not stand for such rebellion, and immediately sent a militia to quell the protest. A Shays-like fiasco was averted, and the new federal government proved that it had the power to maintain peace and stop the **Whiskey Rebellion**.

PUBLIC LAND ACT OF 1796

Modeled after the Northwest Ordinance of 1787, the Public Land Act of 1796 set clear procedures for the settlement, sale, and distribution of federal lands.

The original 13 states had surrendered a good amount of land in the West to be administered by the federal government. The fear of losing control of this land spurred Congress to act quickly.

ADAMS AS SECOND PRESIDENT

Foreign affairs and domestic troubles did not let up as the second president of the United States, **John Adams**, took office. As was provided for in the Constitution, Thomas Jefferson, runner-up in the race for president, became Adams's vice president.

THE XYZ AFFAIR AND AVOIDING WAR

Seeking to halt the incessant seizures of American vessels by the French, Adams sent a delegation to Paris in 1797 to negotiate an agreement. As the delegation arrived in France, they were approached by three French agents only named as X, Y, and Z. These agents demanded a large sum of money as a loan and an additional bribe from the American delegation just for the opportunity to speak with French officials. The delegation refused to comply, and word of the incident quickly spread across the Atlantic, where the American press dubbed it the **XYZ Affair**.

Federalists, including Alexander Hamilton, called for immediate military action. With war fever taking hold across the country, preparations for war began. An undeclared naval war, or "quasi-war," ensued. Most of the action took place in the West Indies between U.S. sailors and French vessels. From 1798 to 1800, this undeclared naval war strained trade in the Caribbean and was on the verge of escalating into a full-scale conflict. Adams, determined to keep the United States from engaging in total war with France, sent a team of envoys to meet with French foreign minister Talleyrand and Napoleon to negotiate a settlement. The meeting, dubbed the **Convention of 1800**, ended with the termination of the Franco-American Alliance, an agreement by the United States to pay for damages inflicted on French vessels, and the avoidance of an all-out war with France.

THE ALIEN AND SEDITION ACTS

Tension between the Federalists and the Democratic-Republicans intensified after the congressional elections of 1798. Emboldened by American anger over the XYZ Affair, Federalists swept control of Congress and began enacting laws aimed at silencing the opposition. The first of these laws were the **Alien Acts**, which increased the residency requirement for citizenship from 5 to 14 years and gave the president power to detain and/or deport enemy aliens in times of war. The second law aimed at silencing Democratic-Republicans was the **Sedition Act**. This law made it illegal to criticize the president or Congress, and imposed a heavy fine or a threat of imprisonment upon violators, such as editors of newspapers. Obviously, Jefferson and the Democratic-Republicans were angered by this violation of their protected right to free speech guaranteed by the First Amendment. Republicans fought back by encouraging states to pass their own statutes to *nullify* the Alien and Sedition Acts. By invoking the **compact theory**—that the federal government was formed because of a compact among states—Kentucky and Virginia passed resolutions overturning the Alien and Sedition Acts. However, no other states followed suit, and the issue of nullification disappeared for a short time.

"THE REVOLUTION OF 1800"—THE ELECTION OF THOMAS JEFFERSON

Through disagreements over going to war with France, the Alien and Sedition Acts, and increasing debts, the Federalists lost much of the momentum they had gained after the XYZ Affair, leading up to the election of 1800. The Federalists resorted to nasty mudslinging during the presidential election, accusing Thomas Jefferson of everything from being a thief to an atheist. These tactics backfired when the Federalists were swept from both the presidency and Congress. Although Thomas Jefferson defeated John Adams in the popular vote, he tied in the Electoral College with his vice presidential running mate, Aaron Burr. It was then up to the House of Representatives to decide who would take the presidency. Still in control of the House, the Federalists debated for four days over the issue. At the urging of Alexander Hamilton, who hated Aaron Burr, the House chose Thomas Jefferson as the third president of the United States.

This election was significant because there was a relatively peaceful (nonviolent) transfer of power from the Federalists to the Democratic-Republicans. This peaceful transfer of power was unprecedented in world history and proved that democracy could be strong in the face of adversity.

THE LOUISIANA PURCHASE

In his inaugural address, Thomas Jefferson looked to calm the fears encouraged by Washington's Farewell Address when he said, "We are all Republicans; we are all Federalists." Jefferson's Republican party, also known as the Democratic-Republican party, is an ancestor of the modern-day Democratic party. Although he was a staunch Republican, Jefferson understood that ideology could get in the way of the decisions that needed to be made for the betterment of the nation. In this, Jefferson's presidency was somewhat of a contradiction—in some cases, he adhered to the letter of the Constitution, while at other times, he adopted a somewhat "loose" interpretation. In either case, he argued that the decisions he made were for the good of the nation he so dearly loved. He kept many of the hallmarks of the Federalist Era intact (such as Hamilton's economic system) but had the citizenship requirement of the Alien Act reduced to five years and abolished the excise tax.

NEGOTIATIONS WITH NAPOLEON

A perfect example of Jefferson's loose constructionism is his purchase of the **Louisiana Territory** from Napoleon of France. In 1800, Napoleon obtained the territory from Spain under a cloak of secrecy. The United States had enjoyed the right of deposit at the Port of New Orleans since the signing of **Pinckney Treaty** in 1795 with Spain. In 1802, the Spanish (still in control of the port) revoked the right of deposit in New Orleans. Farmers on the western frontier pleaded for government intervention, since they depended on the ability to transport goods on the Mississippi and deposit them for trade in New Orleans. Jefferson, understanding the impact this would have on the economy and the possibility of getting mixed up in European affairs, dispatched ministers to Paris to negotiate with Napoleon.

Jefferson instructed his ministers to offer $10 million for New Orleans and a strip of land that extended to Florida. If the negotiations failed, the ministers were to travel directly to London to ask for a cross-Atlantic alliance between the United States and Britain. Much to the ministers' surprise, the French ministers were offering not just New Orleans and the strip of land that extended to Florida but the entire Louisiana Territory for the bargain price of $15 million. Napoleon had abandoned his dream of an American empire because of his failure to stop a slave uprising in Haiti and his desire to raise revenue to fund his conquest of Europe. The American ministers jumped at the opportunity, bringing the deal home for Jefferson's approval. The president was torn. If he accepted the deal, it would be in direct conflict with his strict constructionist views of the Constitution—the document does not specifically provide for the president to negotiate for and purchase land from a foreign power. If he did not accept the deal, the Union might be in peril—the doors would open for another country to purchase the land. Ironically, it was Federalists who voiced the loudest opposition to the **Louisiana Purchase** by arguing that Jefferson had no constitutional authority to negotiate the deal without the consent of the legislature. The president reluctantly sent the deal to the Republican-held Senate, which quickly approved the purchase.

LEWIS AND CLARK EXPLORE THE LAND

The Louisiana Purchase doubled the size of the United States for a mere three cents an acre. Both the French and the Spanish were removed as potential threats to U.S. sovereignty, the western frontier was opened to one of the most fertile valleys in the world, and Jefferson's dream of an agricultural empire was now closer to becoming a reality. Additionally, Jefferson hoped to find an all-water route connecting the Missouri River to the Pacific Ocean. To investigate this route, the president appointed a team, led by **Meriwether Lewis** and **William Clark**, to explore the vast territory beginning in 1804. The group traveled a route that began in St. Louis, Missouri, and took them to the Pacific Ocean on the coast of Oregon. They returned to St. Louis in 1806. By keeping meticulous field notes and drawings of the flora and fauna, as well as detailed accounts of encounters with native tribes, Lewis and Clark expanded America's knowledge of this vast new territory and warned of the hardships settlers would face moving west. However, Jefferson's most prized objective of finding an all-water route was not realized.

UNIT 3: REVIEW QUESTIONS

Multiple-Choice Questions

Directions: Choose the best answer choice for the following questions.

Questions 1–3 refer to the following quotation.

"SECTION 1. Be it enacted by the Senate and House of Representatives of the United States of America, in Congress assembled, That if any persons shall unlawfully combine or conspire together, with intent to oppose any measure or measures of the government of the United States, which are or shall be directed by proper authority, or to impede the operation of any law of the United States, or to intimidate or prevent any person holding a place or office in or under the government of the United States, from undertaking, performing or executing his trust or duty, and if any person or persons, with intent as aforesaid, shall counsel, advise or attempt to procure any insurrection, riot, unlawful assembly, or combination . . . "

—An Act in Addition to the Act, Entitled "An Act for the Punishment of Certain Crimes Against the United States"

1. This quotation refers to what piece of Federalist legislation?

   (A) Alien Acts

   (B) Sedition Acts

   (C) Quota Acts

   (D) Nationalization Acts

2. The main purpose of this legislation was to

   (A) prevent anti-American immigrants from coming to America

   (B) silence anti-Federalist critics of the current government policies

   (C) allow the president to deport any immigrants deemed a threat to the American republic

   (D) eliminate political corruption within federal offices

3. The Virginia and Kentucky Resolutions were a direct result of Federalist policies, and they

   (A) were designed to nullify Federalist laws that imposed on the individual rights of Americans

   (B) embodied the idea of seceding from the federal government because of tyrannical policies

   (C) advocated open relations with Britain to check the power of the Federalists

   (D) began negotiations to ally themselves with the French in response to a government that abused the power of the Constitution

Questions 4–6 refer to the following quote.

"And whereas it is just and reasonable, and essential to our Interest, and the Security of our Colonies, that the several Nations or Tribes of Indians with whom We are connected, and who live under our Protection, should not be molested or disturbed in the Possession of such Parts of Our Dominions and Territories as, not having been ceded to or purchased by Us, are reserved to them, or any of them, as their Hunting Grounds—We do therefore, with the Advice of our Privy Council, declare it to be our Royal Will and Pleasure, that no Governor or Commander in Chief in any of our Colonies of Quebec, East Florida, or West Florida, do presume, upon any Pretence whatever, to grant Warrants of Survey, or pass any Patents for Lands beyond the Bounds of their respective Governments, as described in their Commissions . . . "

—Proclamation of 1763

4. Following the Treaty of Paris in 1763, one of the biggest concerns of the British regarding North America was

   (A) creating a lasting peace with the French still residing in their new land acquisitions

   (B) settling the newly acquired lands to establish commerce with Indians

   (C) preventing westward expansion to mend relations with natives previously allied with the French

   (D) establishing governments that could control French Quebec and Spanish Florida

5. Following the French and Indian War, the American colonists were determined to

   (A) declare independence from Great Britain

   (B) settle lands in the Ohio River Valley

   (C) create commercial relationships with Indians in the interior of the continent

   (D) pay British merchants for the debt they incurred during the war

6. A direct result of colonial encroachment on native lands in the Great Lakes region led to

   (A) a renewed dispute between the *coureurs de bois* and American colonists

   (B) an uprising led by an Ottawa chief, Pontiac

   (C) hostilities between British regulars on the frontiers and American settlers wishing to venture west

   (D) taxes on colonials to prevent their expansion westward

Questions 7–10 refer to the following quote.

"Article 2

His Majesty will withdraw all His Troops and Garrisons from all Posts and Places within the Boundary Lines assigned by the Treaty of Peace to the United States. This Evacuation shall take place on or before the first Day of June One thousand seven hundred and ninety six, and all the proper Measures shall in the interval be taken by concert between the Government of the United States, and His Majesty's Governor General in America, for settling the previous arrangements which may be necessary respecting the delivery of the said Posts: The United States in the mean Time at Their discretion extending their settlements to any part within the said boundary line, except within the precincts or Jurisdiction of any of the said Posts.

Article 6

Whereas it is alleged by divers British Merchants and others His Majesty's Subjects, that Debts to a considerable amount which were bona fide contracted before the Peace, still remain owing to them by Citizens or Inhabitants of the United States, and that by the operation of various lawful Impediments since the Peace, not only the full recovery of the said Debts has been delayed, but also the Value and Security thereof, have been in several instances impaired and lessened, so that by the ordinary course of Judicial proceedings the British Creditors, cannot now obtain and actually have and receive full and adequate Compensation for the losses and damages which they have thereby sustained: It is agreed that in all such Cases where full Compensation for such losses and damages cannot, for whatever reason, be actually obtained had and received by the said Creditors in the ordinary course of Justice, The United States will make full and complete Compensation for the same to the said Creditors."

—Excerpt from Jay's Treaty, 1795

7. The significance of Article 2 was that it urged the British to

(A) remove troops and garrisons from American homes and buildings

(B) hand over American posts that had been occupied by the British during the Revolution

(C) remove British soldiers from forts in American territories according to the Treaty of Paris

(D) evacuate its citizens from the territory as American settlers began moving west

8. As a stipulation of the treaty, according to Article 6, America

(A) could not guarantee that British debts that existed before the war would be paid

(B) agreed to consume the debts of its citizens and pay the British for compliance with terms of the treaty

(C) believed that the British merchants were falsifying claims and refused to acknowledge them

(D) would only agree to the terms of the treaty if British merchants relinquished all debt claims held with the Americans

9. As a result of the treaty,

(A) the British immediately began evacuating their forts and posts in the Old Northwest

(B) citizen Edmund Genet, a French minister, began advocating war against the British

(C) many Americans were angry because they saw the treaty as a sign of weakness against their former enemy

(D) John Jay was hailed as a hero in America because of his efforts to prevent another war

10. In the years following the treaty,

(A) Britain upheld all of its agreements with the United States as set forth in Jay's Treaty

(B) relations began to deteriorate between the United States and Britain because Britain failed to follow through with its commitments of the treaty

(C) Spain became more hostile to American commercial interests because it saw the United States as a British ally

(D) Thomas Jefferson annulled the treaty because of his anti-British sentiments and decided to sign a similar treaty with the French

Short-Answer Question

1. "If men were angels, no government would be necessary. If governments were administered by saints, no checks upon it would be necessary. In framing a government which is to be administered by men over men, the great difficulty lies in this: you must first enable the government to control the governed; and in the next place oblige it to control itself."

—James Madison, Federalist #51, 1787

"To the citizens of the State of New York:

In my last number I endeavored to prove that the language of the article relative to the establishment of the executive of this new government was vague and inexplicit, that the great powers of the President, connected with his duration in office would lead to oppression and ruin.

. . . that the president cannot represent you because he is not of your own immediate choice, that if you adopt this government, you will incline to an arbitrary and odious aristocracy or monarchy, that the president possessed of the power given to him by this frame of government differs but very immaterially from the establishment in Great Britain."

—"Cato," Letter V, *The New York Journal*—November 22, 1787

For this question, address all three parts:

(A) Briefly explain the main point of Madison's argument.

(B) Briefly explain the main point of Cato's argument.

(C) Briefly discuss how the basis of ONE of the two arguments influenced the ratification debate of the United States Constitution.

Document-Based Question

Directions: Question 1 is based on the accompanying documents. The documents have been edited for the purpose of this exercise. You are advised to spend 15 minutes planning and 40 minutes writing your answer. Write your responses on the lined pages that follow the questions.

1. To what degree and for what reasons do you agree with this statement: "Political issues, compared to economic factors, caused the American Revolution." Construct your essay using the documents and knowledge from the period 1754–1776.

DOCUMENT 1

"The members of this Congress, sincerely devoted, with the warmest sentiments of affection and duty to His Majesty's Person and Government, inviolably attached to the present happy establishment of the Protestant succession . . . esteem it our indispensable duty to make the following declarations of our humble opinion, respecting the most essential rights and liberties Of the colonists, and of the grievances under which they labour, by reason of several late Acts of Parliament.

III. That it is inseparably essential to the freedom of a people, and the undoubted right of Englishmen, that no taxes be imposed on them, but with their own consent, given personally, or by their representatives.

IV. That the people of these colonies are not, and from their local circumstances cannot be, represented in the House of Commons in Great-Britain.

V. That the only representatives of the people of these colonies, are persons chosen therein by themselves, and that no taxes ever have been, or can be constitutionally imposed on them, but by their respective legislatures."

Resolutions of the Stamp Act Congress, October 19, 1765

DOCUMENT 2

"And We do further declare it to be Our Royal Will and Pleasure, for the present as aforesaid, to reserve under our Sovereignty, Protection, and Dominion, for the use of the said Indians, all the Lands and Territories not included within the Limits of Our said Three new Governments, or within the Limits of the Territory granted to the Hudson's Bay Company, as also all the Lands and Territories lying to the Westward of the Sources of the Rivers which fall into the Sea from the West and North West as aforesaid.

And We do hereby strictly forbid, on Pain of our Displeasure, all our loving Subjects from making any Purchases or Settlements whatever, or taking Possession of any of the Lands above reserved. without our especial leave and Licence for that Purpose first obtained."

King George, *Proclamation of 1763,* 7 October 1763, Web, Yale Avalon Project

DOCUMENT 3

"For quartering large bodies of armed troops among us;

For protecting them, by a mock trial, from punishment for any murders which they should commit on the inhabitants of these states;

For cutting off our trade with all parts of the world;

For imposing taxes on us without our consent;

For depriving us, in many cases, of the benefits of trial by jury;

For transporting us beyond seas, to be tried for pretended offenses;"

Source: Declaration of Independence, 1776

DOCUMENT 4

"Everything that is right or natural pleads for separation. The blood of the slain, the weeping voice of nature cries, 'TIS TIME TO PART. Even the distance at which the Almighty hath placed England and America, is a strong and natural proof, that the authority of the one, over the other, was never the design of Heaven. The time likewise at which the continent was discovered, adds weight to the argument, and the manner in which it was peopled increases the force of it. The reformation was preceded by the discovery of America, as if the Almighty graciously meant to open a sanctuary to the persecuted in future years, when home should afford neither friendship nor safety."

Thomas Paine, *Common Sense*, 1776: addressed to the inhabitants of America, on the following interesting subjects: I. Of the origin and design of government in general, with concise remarks on the English Constitution. II. Of monarchy and hereditary succession. III. Thoughts on the present state of American affairs. IV. Of the present ability of America, with some miscellaneous reflections.

DOCUMENT 5

Butterworth (1), Hezekia, ed., *Young Folks History of America*, Boston,
Estes and Lauriate, 1881

DOCUMENT 6

"The Revolution was effected before the war commenced. The Revolution was in the minds and hearts of the people."

John Adams to Hezekiah Niles, Feb. 3, 1818

DOCUMENT 7

"Men being . . . by nature all free, equal, and independent, no one can be . . . subjected to the political power of another without his own consent . . . To protect natural rights governments are established . . .

. . . Since men hope to preserve their property by establishing a government, they will not want that government to destroy their objectives. When legislators try to destroy or take away the property of the people, or try to reduce them to slavery, they put themselves in to a state of war with the people who can then refuse to obey the laws."

John Locke, Two Treatises on Government, 1690

ANSWERS AND EXPLANATIONS

MULTIPLE-CHOICE ANSWERS

1. B

The Sedition Acts were passed in 1798 in conjunction with the Alien Acts. They were both passed during the Quasi-War with France and were met with harsh criticism because they violated the Constitution.

2. B

The Sedition Acts were aimed at anti-Federalist critics of Adams's presidency and his approach to the French during the Quasi-War. Anyone who was accused of speaking out against the Federalist policies could be fined and/or jailed.

3. A

The Virginia and Kentucky Resolutions embodied the first ideas of nullifying a federal law that violated individual rights. Thomas Jefferson traveled to Kentucky while James Madison stayed in Virginia to implement their nullification ideas.

4. C

The French and Indian War pitted many Native Americans against the British, and many resided in the territories the British acquired in 1763. They believed that it was necessary to try to coexist with these tribes in the area to prevent expenditures on frontier soldiers and posts.

5. B

The Americans believed that they had fought for, and now were entitled to settle, the lands west of the Appalachian Mountains. Some had trickled in during previous years, but now that it was controlled by the British, they believed they had the right to settle these lands on their own accord.

6. B

Although the Proclamation Line of 1763 forbade settlement across the Appalachian Mountains, it was hard to enforce and American settlers began flooding into Indian lands. This caused a major uprising led by Pontiac, an Ottawa chief, and many lives were lost on both sides.

7. C

According to the terms of the Treaty of Paris in 1783, the British were supposed to evacuate their forts and posts in the Great Lakes region. They did not, which led Jay to once again call on them to follow the previous terms.

8. B

With the commercial relationship between English and American merchants intertwined before the Revolution, many English merchants were still owed money by Americans. The government agreed to consume these debts and pay them to the British in exchange for the British meeting the terms of the treaty.

9. C

John Jay was seen as a traitor once the public became aware of the treaty, and his body was burned in effigy in the streets. Most of the terms were never upheld on the British end.

10. B

The British never fully fulfilled their end of Jay's Treaty. Because they failed to evacuate forts or respect American interests and continued to arm hostile Indians in the Old Northwest, relations eventually deteriorated to the point of another war.

SHORT-ANSWER QUESTION RESPONSES

1. (A) Madison argues that government—a government with "checks and balances"—is necessary because our current society, and man himself, is not perfect. We must have checks and balances, separation of powers, and a division of power through federalism.

   (B) Cato—a pseudonym for a famous Anti-Federalist—explained that the president has too much power and is comparable in that way to King George. Many Anti-Federalists, such as Cato, were weary of the central government gaining too much power, which is why they were more comfortable strengthening the existing Articles of Confederation.

   (C) Madison's argument impacted the ratification debate because he and other Federalists, such as John Jay, demonstrated through *The Federalist Papers* that a strong central government is needed to foundationally build the United States, as opposed to simply strengthening the Articles of Confederation. Their arguments solidified the need for three separate branches of government, checks and balances, and a division of power between states and the federal government. Cato's argument impacted the ratification debate because it demonstrated the hesitation that people felt concerning the Constitution. Additionally, Anti-Federalists were also concerned that the "necessary and proper clause" gave too much power to the central government, the Supremacy Clause took away states' rights, and the lack of a bill of rights restricted individual freedoms. In fact, until Anti-Federalists were promised a bill of rights, they did not agree to ratify the Constitution.

DBQ SAMPLE RESPONSE

Although there were significant taxes stemming from the French and Indian War that caused an economic burden upon the colonists, these measures only perpetuated the colonists' desire to sever an already fleeting relationship with Great Britain. Thus, to a large degree, existing political motives such as the end of salutary neglect and enlightenment ideals of popular sovereignty greatly contributed to the colonists' beliefs that they should rebel from England and form a new, independent nation.

Before the French and Indian War, Great Britain practiced salutary neglect with the American colonists—combined with exclusive Navigation Acts, this policy allowed colonists to essentially form their own colonial governments and gave them generations of political freedom as long as they maintained Great Britain's mercantilist policies. However, this positive relationship abruptly ended with the French and Indian War (Doc. 2). Although England won the war, they incurred massive debt and needed the colonists' help to pay it off. Thus, the era of salutary neglect ended with the Proclamation of 1763, which banned colonists from settling west of the Appalachian Mountains and restricted colonists from trading with Native Americans. Although this did not cause the colonists to rebel, it was the first event to trigger a negative colonial response because the colonists felt rejected (Doc. 6). The colonists believed that since they aided Great Britain against the French, they should be rewarded by being allowed to settle west of the Mississippi; however, at the point where England passed the Proclamation, the colonists felt let down. Additionally, colonial Americans believed the war was triggered over competition for the very land that was now prohibited. This was an early indication of how "American" perspective had developed during the years of salutary neglect.

Another event that caused distress in the colonist/Great Britain relationship was the introduction (and repeal) of the Stamp Act (Doc. 1). Parliament passed the Stamp Act in 1765 as a way to raise revenue after the French and Indian War; it was essentially a duty/tax on all paper goods. However, Parliament did not expect colonial uproar in response to the Act. Some colonists were violent and rioted, while others even burned Massachusetts governor Thomas Hutchinson in effigy! The Stamp Act also led to the emergence of the Sons of Liberty, a secret political group that formed to protect colonists' political, social, and economic rights. Most notably, however, was the call for and subsequent meeting of the Stamp Act Congress of 1765. It is also worth noting that the Congress stipulated that Colonial Americans did not desire representation in Parliament, only representation in their own legislatures. Moreover, the Congress, which had 9 out of 13 colonies present at its meetings (which is quite an accomplishment given the nature of 19th-century travel) is indicative of the almost universal sentiment in the colonies that such a tax could not be legal. The earlier modification of the old Molasses Act did not produce the same reaction, as it was seen as just that—a modification of an existing policy.

Parliament eventually repealed the Stamp Act; however, the Congress was historically significant because it was the first united colonial response to any British measure.

In addition, compared to the Boston Tea Party, which lead to the negative Coercive/ Intolerable Acts, Parliament responded somewhat favorably to the Stamp Act, eventually repealing it (Doc. 5). Thus, the American response to the Stamp Act demonstrates how colonists politically banded together in opposition to a legislative policy.

In fact, even when the colonists declared their independence from Great Britain, our Founding Fathers specifically referenced political Enlightenment ideals such as popular sovereignty in the Declaration of Independence (Doc. 7). Locke, as well as other authors during that time such as Hobbes and Montesquieu, advocated for natural liberties, civil rights, and federalism—concepts that our own American government and Constitution would eventually utilize. It was important for the Founding Fathers to explain why we were "breaking up" with England: although suppressing trade and taxing the colonists was bothersome, the Founders asserted in the preamble that, "whenever any Form of Government becomes destructive of these ends, it is the Right of the People to alter or to abolish it" (Doc. 3).

Even though economic events such as the Stamp Act and Boston Tea Party negatively affected the relationship between the colonists and Great Britain, Americans had already developed a sense of political unity before the war started. The Enlightenment ideals stated in the Declaration of Independence echoed the colonists' pre-existing goals that Americans demand a right to assemble, form their own governments, and not have their speech censured. Thus, political motives contributed more to the colonists' rebelling against Great Britain than did economic issues.

The thesis directly addresses the issue of whether economic or political factors caused Americans to rebel—deciding in favor of political—and it would earn the full point.

There is plausible analysis of almost all of the documents, although depth varies (for example, Document 5 links the Boston Tea Party to the Coercive Acts; however, there could be more analysis of why Americans responded as they did). However, the rest of the student's analysis pertaining to the Stamp Act, the Proclamation of 1763, and the Declaration of Independence is strong as it incorporates cause/effect and outside information to support its claims; thus, the student would earn all 4 points in this section.

In terms of contextualization, the student clearly connects the documents and outside information to broader historical events—such as the Enlightenment, Sons of Liberty, and the American Revolution. The student would earn a full point in this category.

Lastly, the student would also earn a full point in the synthesis section of the rubric, as she appropriately extends and modifies the thesis statement throughout the essay.

Overall, this essay would receive a 7 out of 7 possible points on the DBQ rubric.

CHAPTER 12: DEFINING THE NATION'S DEMOCRATIC IDEALS

THE MARSHALL COURT

A few Federalists were still clinging to power during Jefferson's administration, mostly in the judicial system. In a last-minute piece of legislation before the Congress was to be turned over to the majority Republicans, the Federalists squeaked through the **Judiciary Act of 1801**, whereby 16 new judgeships were created. President John Adams worked through the nights of his last days in office, appointing so-called "**midnight judges**" who would serve on the bench during Jefferson's administration.

MARSHALL MAKES A DECISION

Incensed by the packing of Federalists into lifetime judicial appointments, Jefferson sought to block these men from taking the bench. He ordered his secretary of state James Madison not to deliver the commissions to the last-minute appointments, thereby blocking them from taking their judgeships. One of these "midnight judges," **William Marbury**, sued under the Judiciary Act of 1789, which granted the Supreme Court the authority to enforce judicial commissions.

Sitting as Chief Justice of the Supreme Court was Thomas Jefferson's cousin and staunch Federalist, **John Marshall**. Marshall knew that if the Supreme Court issued a **writ of mandamus** (an order to force Madison to deliver the commission), the Jefferson administration would simply ignore the order. On the other hand, if the Court did not issue a writ, then it would seem that the Court was weak compared to the other two branches. Eventually, Marshall declared that Madison should have delivered the commission to Marbury, but then he held that the section of the Judiciary Act of 1789 that gave the Supreme Court power to issue writs of mandamus exceeded the authority allotted the Court under Article III of the Constitution and was, therefore, null and void. With this decision, Marshall was able to reprimand the Republicans without compromising the stature of the Court. More importantly, Marshall had ruled a law passed by Congress to be unconstitutional, thereby establishing the precedent of **judicial review**. In this and subsequent decisions by the Marshall court, the power of the Supreme Court increased—it could check the authority of both the legislative and executive branches.

AN ATTEMPT TO FLUSH FEDERALISTS

President Jefferson was still determined to remove all remaining vestiges of the Federalists from the judicial branch. After the rebuke from Marshall and the Supreme Court in the *Marbury* decision, Jefferson turned his efforts to the **impeachment** of radical Federalist judges. The House successfully voted for the impeachment of Supreme Court Justice Samuel Chase owing to his highly **partisan** decisions. The Senate, however, refused to convict Chase because of the absence of any evidence of "high crimes and misdemeanors." Jefferson's attempt to flush Federalist judges out of the system was unsuccessful—most remained on the bench for life. The judges did tend to rule a bit more to the president's liking, however, as the threat of impeachment hung heavy over the judicial system. Nevertheless, this episode proved to be the last time that a Supreme Court justice would be impeached, maintaining the precious separation of powers between the legislative and judicial branches.

JEFFERSON'S CHALLENGES

Thomas Jefferson easily won re-election in 1804 and entered a much more difficult presidential term. His authority was challenged by his own former vice president, a threat from within his party, and foreign troubles.

A small, radical group of Republicans led by Jefferson's cousin John Randolph grew increasingly annoyed by the president's abandonment of his once staunch states' rights advocacy. The "Quids" accused Jefferson of entanglement in a faulty land deal in the western half of Georgia in 1804 (Yazoo River area, now Mississippi). Georgia had turned over her western lands to the federal government but not before granting much of it illegally to land companies. Desiring a quick end to the debacle, Jefferson and James Madison attempted to pay the land companies restitution for the illegally obtained land that the federal government was now taking. Randolph and his Quids leaped at the chance to portray Jefferson as corrupt by claiming that the president was paying a bribe. The Yazoo Land Controversy led to a schism within the Republican party, which would further challenge Jefferson during his second term.

BATTLES WITH AARON BURR

Before Jefferson ran for his second term, the Republicans decided not to select **Aaron Burr** as his vice presidential running mate. In 1804, the Constitution was amended by the **Twelfth Amendment**, which called for electors to the Electoral College to specify which ballot was being cast for the office of president and which was being cast for the office of vice president. The tie vote that occurred in 1800 between Jefferson and Burr would not happen again under the new amendment. Burr became very bitter over the snubbing by his own party and the injustice he believed he had endured back in 1800 at the hands of Alexander Hamilton. Seeking retribution, Burr joined forces with a small group of radical Federalists called the **Essex Junto**. This group was plotting for a New England state **secession** from the Union and had originally asked Hamilton if he would run for governor of New York to join in their exploits. Hamilton refused the offer, so the group then asked Burr if he would run. He gladly accepted and began his campaign.

Upon hearing the news of the campaign, Hamilton leaped at the chance to crush Burr's chances of election by leading the opposition faction. Fearing what an ex-Republican would do, Federalists in New York chose not to elect Aaron Burr as governor, and the plot faded away. After hearing of a snide remark made by Hamilton about his character, Burr challenged his enemy to a duel. Refusing such a challenge would have certainly affected Hamilton's stature as a leader and a man; therefore, the duel was set. Burr shot Hamilton, fatally wounding him, in 1804. Just when Americans thought Burr was gone, another secession plot arose in 1806 dubbed the **Burr Conspiracy**. His plan was to wrest Mexico from the Spaniards and join it with the Louisiana Territory to create a new country to the west. The plot was reported to President Jefferson, who called for Burr's immediate arrest and trial for treason. Chief Justice John Marshall sat on the bench of the jury trial, at which the prosecution could produce no credible witnesses. Burr was acquitted and freed.

THE ERA OF GOOD FEELINGS

With a renewed sense of independence and national pride, Americans elected **James Monroe** as their president in the election of 1816. However the "**Era of Good Feelings**" was not always as harmonious as the optimistic name ascribed to Monroe's two-term presidency by a U.S. newspaper. The period was rife with tension regarding tariffs, slavery, and political power within the Republican party.

Owing to the collapse of the Federalist Party, Monroe handily defeated his opponent in 1816 and easily won re-election in 1820. For an American electorate giddy with enthusiasm regarding the future of the country, he ushered in an age of intense patriotism and reverence for American heroes of the past. Portraits of presidents past and present were commissioned by the federal government and private citizens. Large pieces of canvas were adorned with the likenesses of Washington, Adams, and Jefferson by artists such as Gilbert Stuart and Charles Willson Peale. Children in public schools were taught patriotic alphabets, poems, and songs through the new readers of the day.

A NEW TARIFF AND ITS OPPOSITION

Coupled with this revival of patriotism was a desire to protect all things American, especially the burgeoning industrial economy. To deter cheap British goods from flooding the market and injuring American manufacturing, Monroe urged Congress to pass a stiff tariff to protect industry. The **Tariff of 1816** imposed a 20 percent duty on all imported goods and became the first truly "protective tariff" in American history. However, the passage of the tariff did not go over well in all areas of the United States.

A sectional crisis emerged, with three men leading the charge for their respective **constituents**. Former war hawk **John C. Calhoun** spoke for the South, saying that the tariff was an attempt to line the pockets of Northern merchants at the expense of farmers and plantation owners in his region. Speaking for the North was **Daniel Webster**, who complained that New England had not developed fully enough to withstand interruptions in her ability to trade freely with Britain. Lastly, Henry Clay of Kentucky argued on behalf of American mill and iron industries that the tariff, along with his **American System**, would help establish manufacturing and bring in much needed revenue for internal improvements to aid those in the South.

THE BEGINNING OF INFRASTRUCTURE

> Clay's American System included the recharter of the Bank of the United States; tariffs like the one passed in 1816; and the building up of American **infrastructure**, such as turnpikes, roads, and canals.

Congress had already created the Second Bank of the United States and established the first protective tariff, but President Monroe had strong misgivings about the plan for internal improvements. Monroe felt strongly that the Constitution did not expressly provide for the federal government to allocate monies to fund public works projects within the states. Therefore, he repeatedly vetoed bills regarding the building of roads or canals.

TROUBLE WITH THE BANK OF THE UNITED STATES

The Panic of 1819 threatened the Era of Good Feelings that Monroe had enjoyed his first presidential term. The Second Bank of the United States (BUS) caused this financial crisis—it **overspeculated** on land in the west and attempted to curb **inflation** by pulling back on credit for state banks. Typically, countries experience inflation during wartime and then a period of recession after a war. The United States was no exception to the rule. Hit hard by the drop in demand for American agricultural goods abroad and a widening trade deficit with Britain, the BUS was forced to demand payment from state banks in hard **specie** (coin). Unfortunately, frontier banks had very limited amounts of vaulted currency due to the high number of agricultural customers who had amassed large amounts of debt in the form of loans. Thus, these western or **"wildcat" banks** could not pay back the Bank of the United States in specie, and the amount of currency in circulation became dangerously low. The BUS demanded that western banks foreclose on farmers who could not pay back their debts, resulting in a significant rise of landless farmers. Western banks were deemed "evil" by frontier farmers and poor citizens, who were hit particularly hard by the depression. Nonetheless, James Monroe was re-elected for a second term in 1820.

THE RISE OF THE SECOND PARTY SYSTEM

As the United States emerged from the Panic of 1819 and experienced the massive economic and social changes of the 1820s, the old aristocratic tendencies transplanted from England were replaced by a new democratic spirit.

CHANGES IN THE ELECTORAL PROCESS

Americans across the nation favored equality for European American men. More and more men from the middle and lower classes began to become involved in the political process by voting, campaigning, and running for office. Sometimes called "the Rise of the Common Man," this era signaled a retreat from exclusive rule by the well-to-do and a shift to a more democratic society. By 1820, many states had adopted universal manhood **suffrage**, which eliminated the property-owning requirement that had once limited the voting population. These new political participants demanded leaders who better reflected their humble backgrounds—hardworking, modest, and Protestant.

Many other changes ushered in an age when the citizens of the nation had more say in the election of their leaders. The nominating caucus was replaced by nominating conventions, where large groups of people chose their party's slate of candidates. The state representatives to the Electoral College, who had once been chosen by state legislatures, were now chosen by the state's voters. New third parties, such as the **Anti-Masons** in 1832, arose to challenge the old two-party system. The popular election of electors led to the emergence of a new democracy, in which presidential candidates now had to run national campaigns and political parties had to grow to manage the task.

THE MUDSLINGING ELECTION OF 1824

The election of 1824 pitted four candidates from the Republican Party against each other for the presidency: John Quincy Adams, Henry Clay, William Crawford, and **Andrew Jackson**. The campaign was ugly, with Jackson slinging mud on the reputation of John Quincy Adams and Adams slinging mud right back. In the end, Andrew Jackson won the greatest number of popular votes, but with the votes split four ways, no one man had a majority of electoral votes. It was left up to the House of Representatives to choose the president. Henry Clay, a key opponent of Andrew Jackson's, used his influence to make John Quincy Adams president. When President Adams then appointed Clay as his secretary of state, the Jackson camp cried "Foul!" This "**corrupt bargain**" marred the selection of the new president. By 1828, Jackson wanted to run for president again. On one side of the political fence were the **Democrats** who supported Andrew Jackson, while those who supported Henry Clay on the other side were called **National Republicans**

(**Whigs** starting in 1836). The Whig ideology, which mirrored the platform of the old Federalist Party, was specifically crafted to oppose Andrew Jackson. Mudslinging ensued once again, with Jackson calling Adams's wife a bastard child and Adams accusing Jackson's wife of bigamy. Thus, the two-party system was reborn.

CHALLENGES TO FEDERAL AUTHORITY

Supreme Court Chief Justice John Marshall was still making his mark on American politics in the 1820s and 1830s. Still holding strong to his Federalist tendencies, Marshall continued to increase the power of the federal government over the states. The Court had to decide a case in 1819 that challenged the doctrine of federalism. The case of *McCulloch v. Maryland* involved the state of Maryland attempting to collect a tax from the Second Bank of the United States. In true Federalist fashion, Marshall used a "loose interpretation" of the Constitution to rule that the federal government had an implied power to establish the Bank and that the state had no right to tax a federal institution. He argued that "the power to tax was the power to destroy" and would signal the end of federalism. Most importantly, this ruling established that federal laws were the supreme law of the land and tantamount to state laws. The Marshall court also ruled in ***Gibbons v. Ogden*** (1824) that the state of New York could not issue a monopoly to a steamboat company because it was in direct conflict with the commerce clause of the Constitution, which gives the federal government control of interstate commerce. Prior to this decision, Marshall had also overturned laws and provisions states enacted to challenge the authority of the federal government.

THE DEATH OF THE BANK OF THE UNITED STATES

As a proponent of the common man, Andrew Jackson sought to separate government from the economy once and for all. His belief was that to ensure the success of every American, the government needed to stay out of economic affairs. This issue came to a head as the charter for the Bank of the United States (BUS) was set to expire in 1832. Jackson's key opponent, Henry Clay, favored the BUS and encouraged Congress to pass a rechartering bill prior to its demise. Jackson vetoed the bill and vowed to kill the BUS, which he considered a monopoly. The BUS's president, Nicholas Biddle, was successful in running the bank, but many accused him of favoring the wealthy. Upon winning re-election in 1832, Jackson came up with an elaborate scheme to kill the BUS once and for all. All federal funds were removed from the BUS and deposited in various state banks, which opponents dubbed "**pet banks**." When domestic prices for goods and land jumped dramatically and threatened to destroy the economy, Jackson issued the **Specie Circular**, which required the payment for purchase of all federal lands be made in hard coin, or specie, rather than banknotes. This caused the value of paper money to plummet and eventually led to the **Panic of 1837**. However, Jackson did succeed in killing the BUS. The United States did not have another federal bank until the creation of the National Banking System during the Civil War.

THE SOUTH'S CONTENTION OVER TARIFFS

Both John Quincy Adams and Andrew Jackson found themselves in a predicament due to separate tariffs passed during their presidencies. New England merchants had been pushing for the passage of a stiffer general tariff since 1824. Already the tariff had been upped from 20 percent to over 35 percent and would rise to a whopping 45 percent. New Englanders supported the passage of the **Tariff of 1828** to further protect them from foreign competitors. The outspoken **John C. Calhoun** of South Carolina secretly penned "**The Southern Carolina Exposition**," outlining the anger of the South in the face of the "Tariff of Abominations." The essay expressed the Southern contention that the tariff was unconstitutional and that it severely adversely altered trade with Europe that Southern farmers had become dependent on. Calhoun recommended that the Southern states declare the tariff to be null and void if the federal government refused to lower the duty requirement. This time around, Calhoun was alone in his protest.

WEBSTER AND HAYNE DEBATE

Senator **Daniel Webster** of Massachusetts and **Robert Y. Hayne** of South Carolina engaged one another in debate over the particulars of the tariff on the Senate floor in 1830. Hayne proposed that Calhoun's doctrine of nullification was the only way to preserve Southern interests and that an alliance between his region and the West was the only way to persevere in the face of the tariff.

Hayne claimed that the tariff was causing the economic troubles of South Carolina and that the union of states was a compact between the states and the federal government and could be broken. Webster, a powerful and respected orator, held the floor for two days as he decried the obvious abridgement of union. Webster argued that the Constitution was a compact between the people and the government, not to be broken by the states acting on their own behalf. Ending with these impassioned words, "Liberty and Union, now and forever, one and inseparable!" Webster successfully made nullification and secession equal to treason.

Despite Webster's passion, Calhoun would be joined by many other voices of protest as Jackson witnessed the passage of the **Tariff of 1832**. To appease the South, Jackson sought to lower the tariff from 45 percent to 35 percent. This change did little to placate Southerners, however. With Calhoun in the lead (having just resigned the vice presidency owing to severe differences with President Jackson), South Carolina nullified the Tariff of 1832 and threatened to secede from the Union if Jackson attempted to collect the duties by force. Jackson did make military preparations but stopped short of sending troops to South Carolina. Instead, he encouraged Congress to pass the **Force Bill**, which gave the president the power to use military force to collect tariffs if the need arose. Amid the possibility of civil war, Henry Clay proposed a compromise that would save the day. A new tariff was passed in 1833 that slowly reduced the tariff, and the "nullies" rescinded their ordinance for nullification. Andrew Jackson successfully protected the power of the federal government during the Nullification Crisis and averted a potentially dangerous clash of states' rights with federal power. In the end, the crisis signaled events to come, as the North and the South would continually go head-to-head over states' rights issues.

JACKSON EXERCISES VETO POWER

Andrew Jackson was a champion of states' rights, as long as the nation was not in peril. He believed that to protect the rights and guarantee the success of the common man, the president should exercise all due power. Therefore, Jackson vetoed more bills than the previous six presidents combined. States' rights were a hot topic, from the debate over nullification between Senator Robert Hayne of South Carolina and Senator Daniel Webster of New Hampshire that lasted for nine days, to Jackson's veto of the Maysville Road Bill. Jackson vetoed this bill because he was opposed to spending federal funds for infrastructure improvements that lay totally within one state (in this case, Clay's Kentucky). As Jackson increased the power of the presidency, he sometimes sought to expand democracy—but only when it served his interests.

JACKSON'S AMERICA—SUCCESSES AND LIMITATIONS

Jacksonians, though not necessarily Jackson himself, were successful in expanding democracy to the middle and lower classes of America. The "New Democracy" emerged in the 1820s, when many states reduced their voting requirements.

JACKSON'S GOVERNMENT OF THE PEOPLE

During Jackson's presidency, as in no time before, everyday Americans participated in the workings of the political system. Voter turnout increased, and new civil service opportunities arose for Jackson supporters. Andrew Jackson was a proponent of the **spoils system** in which he appointed those who supported his campaign to government positions. Many felt that this practice bred corruption and tainted the political process. Nonetheless, Jackson created jobs and appointed many friends to his unofficial cabinet, earning it the name "**kitchen cabinet**" from critics, who lamented that this group of advisers did not have to answer to Congress as they were not "official cabinet officers." Jackson also believed in rotating officials to discourage complacency and encourage fresh opinions. He felt that any man was as good as the next man, so there was no need for someone to hold an office indefinitely. This belief opened the door for many commoners to take an active role in governmental affairs. However, this "champion of the common man" did not feel that democracy should include all Americans—certainly not women, African Americans, and Native Americans. Universal manhood suffrage was intended for European American males only.

JACKSON VERSUS NATIVE AMERICANS

Jackson understood the positive impact continued western expansion could have on the country and wished to open up the frontier to European American settlers who longed to settle there. The problem was that large groups of Native Americans already lived on this land. Jackson believed that the solution was to move Native Americans to land set aside for them west of the Mississippi in what is now Oklahoma and Kansas. The **Indian Removal Act**, signed into law in 1830, provided for the immediate resettlement of Native Americans living in Mississippi, Alabama, Florida, Georgia, and present-day Illinois. By 1835, some 100,000 Cherokee, Chickasaw, Choctaw, Creek, and Seminole Native Americans had been forcibly removed from their homelands. The Cherokee Nation refused to leave without a fight and took its case against the state of Georgia to the Supreme Court. The Court ruled in *Cherokee Nation v. Georgia* (1831) that the tribe was not a sovereign foreign nation and, therefore, had no right to sue for jurisdiction over its homelands. In another Indian removal case, however, the Marshall Court ruled in favor of the Cherokee. In *Worcester v. Georgia* in 1832, John Marshall ruled that the state of Georgia could not infringe on the tribe's sovereignty, thus nullifying Georgia state laws within Cherokee territory. President Jackson was incensed and allegedly said, "John Marshall has made his decision; now let him enforce it." Jackson believed that as president, it was his duty to enforce the Constitution as he interpreted it, not how the Supreme Court interpreted it. Unfortunately for the Cherokee, the federal government did nothing to come to their aid.

THE TRAIL OF TEARS

By 1838, all the Cherokees had been forcibly removed from the state of Georgia. This trek is known as the **Trail of Tears**, as some 4,000 Cherokee died en route to Oklahoma.

A RELIGIOUS REVIVAL

The "Second Great Awakening" started well before revivalist preachers began touring the United States in the 1820s. Protestant traditionalists, such as the Calvinists, created a fervor in the 1790s in response to the liberal beliefs espoused by leaders such as Thomas Jefferson and other deists. These religious figures felt that liberal religious views were a direct threat to the moral fiber of America and sought to regain a foothold in the hearts and souls of followers. Unlike their Puritan ancestors, these Calvinists had a gentler approach to moral living and the afterlife, preaching free will and abandoning the idea of predestination.

Religious revivalism did not reach its full fever pitch until the 1820s, with the preaching of Presbyterian minister **Charles G. Finney**. Like Jonathan Edwards of the first Great Awakening, Finney appealed to his audience's emotions, rather than their reason. His "fire and brimstone" sermons became commonplace in upstate New York, where listeners were instilled with a fear of Satan and an eternity in Hell. Finney insisted that parishioners could save themselves through good works and a steadfast faith in God. This region of New York became known as the "burned-over district," as Finney preached of the dangers of eternal damnation across the countryside. Aside from Finney, other preachers set out across the nation, setting up tent revivals that resembled country picnics more than church services. Methodist and Baptist ministers, such as Peter Cartwright, traveled across the South and West, preaching at tent revivals and converting thousands. The Methodists and Baptists soon became the two largest denominations in the United States. As a result of this religious awakening, thousands of Americans were "saved." The new religious converts were mostly middle-class men and women, who then propelled a social reform movement that would last through the 1860s.

PASSIONATE REFORM

Many of the new religious converts believed in **perfectionism**, or the idea that humankind could reach a level of perfection that resembled the life of Jesus. People could obtain this level of perfection through faith, hard work, education, and temperance. In its earliest stages, this **antebellum** social reform movement operated on a local level, seeking only to affect individual morals. But reformers soon decided that to make their work effective, they would have to influence politics on a local, state, and national level.

TEMPERANCE AND AMERICA'S HEALTH

The evils of alcohol were one of the first areas of concern of antebellum reformers. Revival preachers joined forces in the mid-1820s to form the **American Temperance Society**, whose aim was to encourage drinkers to first limit their intake of alcohol and then eventually take a vow of abstinence. The consumption of alcohol was seen by these reformers as negatively impacting people's home and work lives. Soon state leaders would see that curbing alcohol use among their citizenry could lead to fewer on-the-job accidents and more overall productivity. Neal S. Dow led the way for the temperance movement to shift into the political arena with sponsorship of the **Maine Law** in 1851, which completely prohibited the manufacture and sale of alcoholic beverages in that state. Soon after, some 12 other states would pass similar laws, either severely limiting the sale of alcohol or prohibiting it altogether. The most active members of temperance societies tended to be middle-class women. When the temperance movement became overshadowed by the abolitionists in the 1850s, many of these women shifted their attention to ending slavery.

A RISE IN CONCERN FOR HEALTH

Aside from drinking, Americans' overall health became the next target of the reformers. From reforming insane asylums to the food Americans ate, a wave of smaller reform movements developed to assist Americans along their path to "perfection."

Dorothea Dix crusaded for the improvement of American institutions to care for the nation's mentally ill population. She worked relentlessly until patients were removed from prisons and other deplorable conditions and given proper treatment. Connected to the asylum reform movement was the crusade to change the penal system in the United States. As a result, some prisons instituted programs that taught prisoners job skills and increased access to religious services.

To cleanse the body and soul, men such as Sylvester Graham of graham-cracker fame and John Harvey Kellogg of the corn flake espoused the importance of diet. Dr. Kellogg established the Battle Creek Mental Institution to put his ideas about diet and health into practice.

THE ABOLITION MOVEMENT

The most politicized of all of the antebellum reform movements was the antislavery or abolition movement. Born from the teachings of the Second Great Awakening, abolitionists believed that slavery was sinful and, therefore, must be eliminated. In 1831, **William Lloyd Garrison** began publishing *The Liberator*, a newspaper dedicated to ending slavery in the United States. This outspoken and often radical leader of the abolitionist movement founded the **American Antislavery Society** in 1833 to combat the pro-slavery contingent. Garrison's radicalism soon alienated many moderates within the movement when he claimed that the Constitution was a pro-slavery document. Garrison's insistence on the participation of women in the movement led to a division among his supporters and the formation of the **Liberty Party**, which accepted the membership of women, and the **Foreign Antislavery Society**, which did not accept female participation.

Free African Americans had their own leadership within the abolition movement with **Harriet Tubman**, **Sojourner Truth**, and **Frederick Douglass**. Douglass published *The North Star*, an antislavery journal that chronicled the ugliness of slavery for readers, and argued that the Constitution could be used as a weapon against slavery. Thus, Douglass argued for fighting slavery through legal means in contrast to some other radical abolitionists, who advocated varying degrees of violence to achieve abolition. Tubman and Truth, along with many others, helped enslaved Africans escape bondage through an elaborate network called the **Underground Railroad**.

Some, however, chose to not participate in the snail's-pace progress of politics and took matters into their own hands, often with deadly results. Nat Turner, an enslaved African American from Virginia, organized a massive slave uprising in 1831. **Nat Turner's Rebellion** resulted in the deaths of over 50 European American men, women, and children and the retaliatory killings of hundreds of slaves. Unfortunately for the abolition movement, rebellions like these signaled to many Americans that enslaved African Americans would cause massive social problems that the country was unprepared to handle.

UTOPIAN SOCIETIES

The search for perfection spilled over into non-Protestant groups, who sought refuge from a society they disapproved of. Several groups, both religious and nonreligious, formed communal societies, which they hoped would be closer to a world in which everything and everyone was perfect.

THE BIRTH OF MORMONISM

According to Mormon tradition, the angel Moroni visited the young **Joseph Smith** in his western New York bedroom one autumn night in 1823. The angel told Smith of a sacred text that was inscribed on gold plates that had been buried by the fabled "Lost Tribe of Israel" nearby and revealed to him the exact location of the treasure. By 1830, Joseph Smith had allegedly translated the sacred text and formally organized the **Church of Jesus Christ of Latter-Day Saints** or, informally, the **Mormon Church**. The followers of Mormonism were ostracized and harassed later by their surrounding community and left New York to head west. Smith was murdered by a mob in Illinois, where a new leader, **Brigham Young**, collected his flock and moved further west into what is now the state of Utah. The Mormons remained outsiders owing to their religious practices and beliefs, notably the practice of polygamy (having multiple wives). Only after the Mormon Church agreed to forbid the controversial practice was Utah allowed to become a state.

THE TRANSCENDENTALISTS, SHAKERS, AND ONEIDAS

Meanwhile, Romanticism had swept over Europe, stirring emotion and an emphasis on the connection between man and nature. This romantic spirit was embraced in America through the writings of the **transcendentalists**. Close friends **Ralph Waldo Emerson** and **Henry David Thoreau** spoke throughout the country and wrote scathing essays about the state of man.

Spurning materialism and embracing self-reliance, they encouraged Americans to throw off the yoke of wealth and want and embrace the beauty and truth of the natural world. Thoreau's best-known book, *Walden*, chronicled a self-initiated experiment in which he removed himself from society by living in seclusion in the woods for two years.

INSPIRATION FOR FUTURE LEADERS

Perhaps more influential was Thoreau's essay **"On Civil Disobedience,"** in which he advocated passive resistance as a form of justifiable protest. This essay would inspire later social movement leaders Mahatma Gandhi and Dr. Martin Luther King Jr.

A group of transcendentalists settled in Massachusetts in 1841 to try to live the lifestyle espoused by Emerson and Thoreau. Brook Farm, a communal effort to practice transcendentalism, collapsed in 1849 because of massive debts.

Brook Farm was just one of many **utopian** communities that were established between 1830 and 1850. The **Shakers**, led by "Mother" Ann Lee, were known for their "shaking" as they felt the spirit of God pulse through them during church services.

They eventually died out owing to their forbidding of sexual relations. The **Oneida Commune**, founded by John Humphrey Noyes in 1848 to be a shining example of equality among all members, was controversial from the beginning. Oneida members shared everything, including spouses, which many on the outside believed to be immoral. The Oneida Commune died out after Noyes's death when a struggle over leadership and direction of the commune developed.

BIRTH OF AMERICAN CULTURE

Ralph Waldo Emerson encouraged the forging of a unique American identity as he traveled across the United States delivering lectures. A distinctive American culture, divorced from European influence, had already begun to bloom before Emerson's influence. American artists, writers, and architects had started to develop a unique American style that would express the pride of the growing nation.

Portraits of American presidents by Gilbert Stuart and Charles Wilson Peale, with their traditional lines and bold images, characterized American art in the early 1800s. These types of paintings faded in importance as the Romantic era influenced Americans and large-scale landscapes took center stage. These grand landscapes, by artists such as Thomas Cole and Frederic Church from the **Hudson River School** of painting, emphasized the beauty of the American landscape.

The nationalistic spirit that swept the nation after the War of 1812 continued to fuel American authors well into the 1850s. The **Knickerbockers** of New York, including Washington Irving, developed "American" fiction by using domestic settings and character types for their stories and tales. Tales such as *Rip Van Winkle, The Legend of Sleepy Hollow*, and *'Twas the Night Before Christmas* were all borrowed stories with an American twist. The tales of the frontier were glorified by James Fenimore Cooper, whose *The Last of the Mohicans* gained worldwide attention. Questions of religion and morality came front and center through the works of **Nathaniel Hawthorne** (*The Scarlet Letter*) and Herman Melville (*Moby-Dick.*)

American architects returned to the glory days of Rome and Greece by imitating ancient forms when designing landmarks, including Thomas Jefferson's home, Monticello, and rebuilding the nation's capital. Greek columns and Roman domes dotted the American landscape as builders expressed their pride in the Republic.

CHAPTER 13: TECHNOLOGICAL, AGRICULTURAL, AND COMMERCIAL DEVELOPMENTS

AN ECONOMIC AND SOCIAL REVOLUTION

A massive jump in America's population, along with advances in transportation, led to the creation of a national market economy in the United States between 1820 and 1860. The development of national roads, canals, steamboats, and railroads helped bring people, raw materials, and manufactured goods to the far corners of the country as never before. While this created a national market for goods manufactured in the United States, it also began to sectionalize the regions of the country with regard to ideology and economic specialization. The West became known for growing the grains needed to feed a hungry nation. The East emerged as the industrial powerhouse, with textile factories dotting the landscape. The plantation economy continued to grow in the South, owing to the invention of the **cotton gin** by Eli Whitney in 1793.

TRANSPORTATION ADVANCES LEAD TO NATIONAL CHANGES

Turnpikes, or toll roads, were the first transportation advance that served to link many towns in the eastern United States. The Lancaster Turnpike, built in the 1790s, spurred the building of many more toll roads across the United States—most importantly the Cumberland or National Road, which ultimately connected western Maryland with Illinois. Most turnpikes were built with private funds, as there was much opposition to the use of federal funds for internal improvements (recall the opposition to Clay's American System).

THE CREATION OF THE ERIE CANAL

The **Erie Canal**, completed in 1825 with funds provided by the state of New York, linked the Great Lakes with the Hudson River. Suddenly, the cost of shipping dropped dramatically and led to the growth of port cities along the length of the canal and its terminal points.

Robert Fulton promoted water transportation with his invention of the steamboat in 1807. Before the steamboat, river travel was done by flat- or keelboat, which relied on the current of the river or the strength of the men who would push the boat upstream. With the steamboat, goods and people could be transported two ways without relying on nature or brute strength.

Finally, the advent of the railroad brought an even cheaper method of transportation to the country and further connected the regions of the United States. The railroad was not bound by water and could traverse mountains and plains quickly and cheaply. The railroad came to be the fastest, most dependable, and most convenient means of traveling and shipping freight. By 1860, the country had constructed 30,000 miles of railroads.

While these exciting developments in transportation made life easier and cheaper for the average American, there were adverse social and political consequences. Divisions between rich and poor became much more distinct as manufacturers and plantation owners grew in prestige. Politically, regional divisions created difficulties that would soon become the early stages of sectionalism.

Naturally, the East and West were more closely connected because eastern manufacturers aggressively pursued a linkage between the regions through improved transportation. The South was largely cut off from the rest of the United States because the east-west railroad network rarely connected with the few Southern railroads that existed. This geographic division created tension between the North and the South politically and economically, which would continue to escalate through the 1850s.

IMMIGRANTS CHANGE THE NATIONAL SOCIAL STRUCTURE

Along with changes in the economic climate of the country came a shift in demographics that altered the social fabric of the United States. Since the nation had become independent, its population had doubled every 25 years because of the high birthrate of Americans. In the mid-1840s, a potato famine in Ireland and tough economic and political conditions in Germany led to an influx of immigrants to the United States. Between 1830 and 1860, Irish immigrants accounted for the single largest immigrant group; their impoverished ranks began to fill the country's cities. Boston and New York City were soon bursting with more Irish folks than lived in Ireland. The Irish were Roman Catholic and poor, and they competed for jobs with native-born

Americans—all traits that did not endear them to many Americans. Germans were not popular, either. Mostly displaced farmers, some 1.5 million Germans arrived at much the same time as the Irish. German immigrants often settled on the western frontier to farm and maintained some Old World customs. Members of the backlash movement against these immigrants became known as **nativists**. These Anglo-Americans believed that they were really the only true "Americans" and railed against the rights of those who had foreign blood. In 1849, an extreme wing of the nativist movement became a political party called the **American Party** or the **Know-Nothing Party**. The group opposed immigration and the election of Roman Catholics to political office. The members of the party met in secret and would not tell anyone what they stood for, saying, "I know nothing," when asked.

As more and more immigrants arrived and advances were made in technology, transportation, and business, the nation continued to change politically, socially, and economically. These changes would challenge Americans in all walks of life and would soon place enormous burdens on those leading the country.

THE INDUSTRIAL NORTH AND AGRICULTURAL NORTHWEST

The North included New England and the Middle Atlantic States. Improvements in transportation spurred massive economic growth and served to link these populous regions. Economic regionalization began to take hold across the country; the North was no exception. Textile factories led the way in industrial growth, followed distantly by other manufacturing, such as agricultural and consumer goods. As industry began to develop, the region's cities experienced massive expansion in their own right. Unfortunately, the nation's urban areas were not prepared for such sudden growth and suffered from overcrowding, disease, and rising crime rates.

Ohio, Indiana, Illinois, Michigan, Wisconsin, and Minnesota made up the Old Northwest region, which was closely tied to the industrial North by way of rail lines and canals. Economic regionalization in this area consisted of grain farming of corn and wheat. Shipping of grain products to the Northern cities of New York, Boston, and Philadelphia helped spur the growth of river and Great Lake port cities of St. Louis, Cleveland, and Chicago.

KING COTTON AND THE AGRARIAN SOUTH

The regional specialty of the South was planted long before the economic regionalization of the United States began. The plantation/cash crop economy that is now synonymous with antebellum Southern culture was emboldened with the invention of **Eli Whitney's** cotton gin in 1793.

This invention made the process of removing the seeds from raw cotton much easier and faster, making cotton the number one cash crop of the region. Southern plantation owners switched from growing tobacco to growing cotton to keep up with the demand from domestic and overseas markets. The growing demand for the fiber led to a rapid increase in the demand for slaves to work the fields. King Cotton caused the "**peculiar institution**" of slavery to grow; the number of enslaved Africans in the South increased from 1 million to almost 4 million in about 50 years. Southerners often justified and defended their dependence on slaves by citing the Bible as proof that God approved of the practice. As the population of enslaved Africans in the South increased, slave owners and other European American Southerners lived in fear of slave revolts. In some antebellum slave states, **Black Codes** were incorporated into the laws regulating enslaved Africans, which were known as **Slave Codes**. These laws were aimed at oppressing enslaved Africans, discouraging free blacks from living in the South, and preventing slave revolts.

Slave life was arduous and dehumanizing, but it was not the same from plantation to plantation. Some plantation owners treated their slaves humanely, while others beat their captives mercilessly. The goal of most plantation owners was to abase their slave population so as to drive any spirit of rebellion or humanity out of them. Families were split apart, marriages were either forbidden or forced, and women were under constant threat of sexual exploitation by their masters. Education was especially forbidden for fear of slave revolts. Many enslaved Africans found teachers in church or inside the plantation houses, where European American women and children often took it upon themselves to teach enslaved Africans to read and write. Even under these oppressive conditions, African Americans forged tight-knit communities that emphasized family, faith, and oral tradition. They also were known to resist their masters through passive resistance. Enslaved Africans would refuse to work or would work slowly to protest beatings or other injustices. By 1860, there were also 250,000 free African Americans in the South who had been emancipated or were the result of racial mixing. Many worked as field hands, craftspeople, or house servants.

The South's social structure had been transplanted from England in the 1620s and continued into the 19th century. At the top of the social pyramid were large planters (1,000 or more acres), who comprised less than 1 percent of the total number of European American families. Below them were the planters (100–1,000 acres), who made up approximately 3 percent of European American families. Next were small slaveholders (most were farmers, though some were merchants and owned fewer than 20 enslaved Africans); this group made up about 20 percent of European American families. Below them were non-slaveholding European Americans, who comprised 75 percent of antebellum Southern society. Next were free African Americans, who made up 3 percent of free families. At the bottom of this social pyramid were enslaved Africans, who numbered 4 million in 1860.

THE REALITY OF ANTEBELLUM SOUTHERN SLAVERY

Contrary to popular belief, most European American Southerners did not own slaves or owned only one. These people were called "white trash" by the other segments of Southern society but held fast to their belief in slavery, as they did not wish to be the lowest rung on the social ladder.

Along the Appalachian and Ozark Mountains lived scattered farmers and hill people, many of German descent. These "hillbillies," or mountain people, tended not to adopt traditional Southern cultural ways and felt more at ease with their Northern neighbors.

THE FRONTIER—WESTERN LANDS

Beyond the Mississippi River lay a vast territory that many Americans either longed to settle or wanted to avoid. Besides the writings of Lewis and Clark, little was known of this western region except its dangers. Native Americans who had been pushed west had settled in large numbers on the Great Plains and caused great concern for European American settlers moving into the frontier. Life was difficult for those who chose to venture into the vast territory. Many built log cabins or mud-thatched homes along rivers, streams, or lakes and lived off the land until farms could be established. The West was unique in that citizens tended to be more open to change than their counterparts in either the North or South. Granting women and African Americans more opportunities and having a more open governmental system were just some of the ways that the West differed from the East.

THE "CULT OF DOMESTICITY"

After the market revolution and transportation boom of the 1820s, the nature of "women's work" shifted. In many American homes, it was no longer necessary for the woman to work in both the fields and the home. The growth of industry moved men out of the fields and into factories, while women were left to tend the home and children. Children, too, became less important to the overall well-being of the family, as they were no longer required to work in the fields alongside their parents. Thus, the birthrate dropped into the 1860s among middle-class European American families. In this age of moral perfectibility, women's roles were clearly defined as homemakers and mothers—hence the "**cult of domesticity**."

Women also began to develop power within the antislavery movement and resent the second-class status even their fellow male abolitionists assigned them. A wave of female reformers left the abolitionist movement behind and started a women's rights movement to combat the "cult." Vehement abolitionists **Sarah and Angelina Grimke** voiced their opposition to male dominance within the movement in 1837, thus starting a dialogue about women's roles. Soon after, **Lucretia Mott**, **Elizabeth Cady Stanton**, and **Susan B. Anthony** organized a meeting of feminists at **Seneca Falls**, New York, to discuss the plight of women in the United States.

WOMEN AND FEMINISM

Encouraged and emboldened by their convention, the women at Seneca Falls drafted the **Declaration of Sentiments,** which was closely modeled after the Declaration of Independence, by declaring that "all men and women are created equal" and demanding true universal suffrage to include females as well as males.

Much like the earlier temperance movement, the women's crusade soon became eclipsed by the abolitionist movement and did not resurface until closer to the turn of the 20th century.

CHAPTER 14: SHAPING THE NATION'S FOREIGN POLICY

JEFFERSON AND TROUBLES ABROAD

Foreign troubles left over from his first term plagued Jefferson through his second term. The Barbary pirates in North Africa continued to seize U.S. merchant ships as they traveled in the Mediterranean. Presidents Washington and Adams reluctantly had paid leaders of North African nations a "protection fee" to reduce the number of times U.S. ships would be seized. Once Jefferson took office, the leader of Tripoli demanded a much higher sum for protection. Jefferson refused to pay the fee and instead sent a small fleet of naval ships to stop the pirates. The U.S. Navy fought the pirates in the Mediterranean Sea for four years in what came to be called the **Tripolitan War** (1801–1805). While chided for their efforts, the small American force was able to put a dent in the work of the pirates and gained the United States credibility overseas.

A much greater challenge to U.S. authority came with the continued escalation of the **Napoleonic Wars** that continued to rage in Europe. The British and French were busy punishing each other by issuing decrees that would blockade trade into one another's ports. Beginning with Napoleon's **Berlin Decree** in 1806, his attempt to cut Britain off from trading with the rest of the world meant that American ships traveling to Europe to deposit goods would get caught in the mess. The British quickly responded by issuing their **Orders in Council**, which retaliated against France by blockading all ports under French control—any American ship traveling to mainland Europe that did not stop first in Britain would be confiscated. In 1807, Napoleon fought back by issuing his **Milan Decree**, which authorized his navy to seize any foreign ship traveling to Europe that had first stopped in Britain. In other words, American shippers could continue trade at great risk but reap great profits.

Americans were growing increasingly concerned over the British practice of impressment and violations of U.S. neutrality. With thousands of American sailors forced into British military service on the high seas, the continued seizures of neutral ships, and a skirmish at sea with a British vessel, Jefferson was compelled to act. In 1807, the British ship *Leopard* fired upon the U.S. ship *Chesapeake* right off the coast of Virginia, killing three Americans, and the British impressed four sailors after they boarded the *Chesapeake* to search for deserters. Despite the war fever taking hold in the public sector, Jefferson sought to use the power of diplomacy and economic sanctions to keep the United States from fighting the British. He had no interest in going to war or getting involved in European affairs, but he hoped that the United States could hurt the British economically and, thus, force them to cease violating American neutrality.

THE EMBARGO ACT

Jefferson persuaded Congress to pass the **Embargo Act** in 1807, which prohibited U.S. merchant vessels from engaging in foreign trade. His hope was that Britain and France would be crippled economically by the loss of U.S. trade and would be forced to respect his country.

Unfortunately, Jefferson's plan was ruinous for the U.S. economy—most of the damage was inflicted on New England merchants and Southern farmers. A vast network of black market goods arose along the Canadian border to circumvent the embargo. This led to the passage of harsher enforcement laws that many, especially New Englanders, saw as punitive and oppressive. Congress repealed the Embargo Act in 1809, but soon replaced it with a similar bill.

MADISON PLAGUED BY EUROPEAN AFFAIRS

James Madison managed to defeat Federalist Charles Pinckney in the presidential election of 1808, and would carry on the legacy of Republicanism that Jefferson had left behind. Still, issues overseas would dominate U.S. politics during his presidency. **The Non-Intercourse Act of 1809** had been passed by Congress in the last days of Jefferson's presidency to replace the Embargo Act. This law, which expired one year from its enactment, allowed the United States to trade with foreign nations except Britain and France. Like its predecessor, the Embargo Act, it was difficult to enforce and mostly ineffective. Congress took up the issue again in 1810 and enacted **Macon's Bill Number 2**, which sought to lift trade restrictions against Britain or France but only after they agreed to honor U.S. neutrality. Napoleon happily repealed his Berlin and Milan Decrees in the hopes of stirring up tensions between the United States and Britain. Madison issued Britain an ultimatum—remove the orders in Council within three months, or U.S. trade restrictions would continue. Madison had been duped, however, by Napoleon, who never intended to honor his promise to remove the restrictions on shipping and trade. The British and French continued their practice of impressment and ship seizures, pushing the United States closer and closer to the brink of war.

"MR. MADISON'S WAR"—THE WAR OF 1812

A heightened sense of nationalism ushered in the first meeting of Congress in 1811. New, young Republican representatives and senators from the south and the west urged a war with Britain to secure a place in the global political structure for the United States. "War hawks," such as Henry Clay from Kentucky and John C. Calhoun from South Carolina, insisted that this war would finally clear Britain's influence from North America. Aside from dealing with the British at sea, the Americans were hoping to eliminate the threat of English-armed Native Americans, who continued to cause trouble for western frontier settlers.

The **Battle of Tippecanoe** in present-day Indiana caused many members of Congress from the frontier to feel justified in their call for war. Prior to the outbreak of the War of 1812, **General William Henry Harrison** sought to break up a large native confederacy that a pair of Shawnee brothers, **Tecumseh** and **The Prophet**, had organized in the face of an American advance westward. General Harrison and his men successfully fought back a surprise attack and subsequently burned a tribal settlement at Tippecanoe. Now with the Native American threat removed in the west, the war hawks looked to conquer Canada.

The British refusal to lift trade restrictions, and immense political pressure pushed President Madison to ask Congress for a declaration of war in June 1812. Ironically, the British at that very time had repealed the orders in Council. However, by the time word traveled across the Atlantic Ocean and reached Washington, D.C., the war had already begun. Few Americans and members of Congress were in favor of "Mr. Madison's War," with New Englanders voicing the greatest opposition. However, the war hawks were successful in amassing a large enough coalition to officially declare war.

"The Second War of Independence" was a small and disappointing war for the United States. The nation was not prepared to wage war—particularly not with the most powerful naval force in the world. The economy had been devastated by the Embargo Act, and America's standing military was small, poorly equipped, and undertrained. The "Mosquito Fleet," or U.S. Navy, was no match for the British Navy. U.S. ships were able to outmaneuver the British in the Great Lakes region, but the American invasion of Canada was a debacle.

With Napoleon under control in Europe by 1814, the British were able to focus their attention on North America. The Americans were able to repel a British attack on New York but could not save Washington, D.C., from being burned to the ground in August of 1814. The British amassed at Fort McHenry near the city of Baltimore, Maryland, but U.S. soldiers held the fort through a night of bombing, inspiring a prisoner on a nearby British ship to write a poem about it. Francis Scott Key put words to an old drinking song to express his love for his country, and called it "**The Star Spangled Banner**."

The formidable **General Andrew Jackson** led the American troops in their campaign in the south. He and his men were able to cut a swath through the British from Alabama to New Orleans and thwart the English attempt to control the Mississippi River at the **Battle of New Orleans**. Interestingly, the battle—while an impressive victory for the Americans—was completely unnecessary, as it was fought two weeks after the signing of the peace treaty that ended the war. Nonetheless, Jackson emerged as an American war hero.

The **Treaty of Ghent** that ended the War of 1812 was signed by American envoys and British diplomats in Belgium on December 24, 1814. The provisions of the treaty provided for the end of the fighting, the return of any conquered territories to their rightful owners, and the settlement of a boundary between Canada and the United States that had been set before the war. Essentially, the war ended in a draw—neither side gained any concessions, restitution, or apologies. Most Americans were pleased, however, because they had fully expected to lose territory. Despite their complaints, the war did allow manufacturing, especially in New England, to flourish. The country became a bit more independent from European markets. In effect, this was the beginning of America's industrial revolution.

IDEOLOGY DIVIDES THE UNITED STATES

A very serious ideological split divided the nation during the War of 1812—a split between the Federalists and the Republicans, which was essentially a split between New England and the rest of the nation. New England states were vehemently opposed to the war effort and the direction in which Republicans were taking the nation. A radical group of New England Federalists met at a convention in Hartford, Connecticut, during the winter of 1814–1815 to discuss ways to demand that the federal government pay them for the loss of trade due to the Embargo Act, Macon's Bill No. 2, and the War of 1812. The group also discussed possible amendments to the Constitution, which included a one-term limit for the office of president; a two-thirds vote for an embargo, declaration of war, and admission of new states; and an end to the Three-Fifths Compromise—all aimed at Republicans. A radical, small, vocal group even suggested secession from the Union. Hartford representatives were sent to Washington, D.C., to make the demands of the Convention clear to the federal government. However, before they could speak, news of the signing of the Treaty of Ghent and Jackson's victory at New Orleans drowned them out. With the war now over, the Federalists looked like a bunch of complainers and were labeled "unpatriotic." The **Hartford Convention** was basically the final nail in the coffin for the Federalist party, which was routed by Republican James Monroe in the election of 1816. These ideological divisions would continue to intensify and become sectional as the nation moved into the 1820s and began to expand further westward.

THE MISSOURI COMPROMISE

As the nation expanded westward and new states entered the Union, the debate over whether or not to allow slavery in these new states arose. New states in the Southern half of the frontier justified slavery by expressing the economic need for a large, stable workforce; those settling in the North had less need for slaves (although some Northern slavery did exist). The issue reared its ugly head in 1819 as Missouri applied for statehood.

A delicate balance existed in the Senate in 1819, with 11 free states and 11 slave states represented. This balance was extremely important to the Southern states, as they had previously lagged behind the North in population growth, thus losing sectional balance in the House in 1818. As long as this balance was maintained in the Senate, the South had the opportunity to block bills passed by the House that could hurt it. With Missouri now vying for statehood, each side had to weigh the possibility of this balance being tipped in the opposite direction. James Tallmadge of New York proposed an amendment to Missouri's bid for statehood. After the admission of Missouri as a state, the **Tallmadge Amendment** would not have allowed any more slaves to be brought into the state and would have provided for the **emancipation** of the children of Missouri slaves at the age of 25 years. Southerners were enraged by this abolition attempt by Northern representatives and crushed the amendment in the Senate. Thomas Jefferson was quoted as saying that the argument over the issue rang out as "a firebell in the night."

At this time, **Henry Clay** of Kentucky proposed three bills that would together make up the **Missouri Compromise** of 1820. The bills allowed for the admission of Missouri as a slave state,while also admitting Maine as a free state, to maintain the balance in the Senate. In addition, slavery would not be permitted in states admitted above the **36°30′ line** (with the exception of Missouri, which lay above the line). The compromise was accepted by both North and South and lasted for 34 years. Clay, "the Great Compromiser," had temporarily resolved the intense sectional issue of slavery. However the issue of slavery would now remain on the political center stage from this point until the Civil War.

THE MONROE DOCTRINE

The United States became a bit more aggressive with regard to foreign affairs as Monroe took the presidency. There were still lingering issues surrounding Canada, Florida, and the sovereignty of the United States. Back during Madison's presidency, the United States and Britain had signed a treaty to resolve issues involving Canada. The **Rush-Bagot Treaty**, signed in 1817, provided for the demilitarization of the Great Lakes and frontier borders and created the longest unfortified border in the world between the United States and British North America. In addition, the United States purchased Florida from Spain in 1819 through the **Adams-Onis Treaty** and gained Spanish assurances that Spain would abandon its claims in the Oregon Territory.

At the same time, many Latin American countries were experiencing revolutions of their own and were leaning toward more democratic forms of government. Americans were elated, but European powers were frightened by the possibility of losing influence in the Western hemisphere because of this change in political structure. Great Britain was interested in forming an alliance with the United States to maintain a foothold in the region. Some former American leaders urged President Monroe to enter such an alliance to keep the British in check. Secretary of State **John Quincy Adams** felt that the alliance was not as innocent as it looked. He believed that the alliance would serve to hinder U.S. expansion, and was simply a way for the British to protect their interests. Therefore, he penned President Monroe's annual address to Congress, which included a warning to the European powers to stay out of the Western hemisphere. The address, now known as the **Monroe Doctrine**, was delivered by the president in 1823. It quickly became the basis of U.S. foreign policy from that point forward. The Doctrine called for "nonintervention" in Latin America and an end to European colonization. It was more or less designed to check the power of Europe in the Western hemisphere and flex the muscles of the young nation. While the United States did not have the military means to enforce the doctrine in its early years, and a number of European countries were both amused and irritated by its contents, the United States increasingly enforced the policy throughout the late 19th and 20th centuries.

UNIT 4: REVIEW QUESTIONS

Multiple-Choice Questions

Directions: Choose the best answer choice for the following questions.

Questions 1–4 refer to the following quotation.

"SEC. 8. And be it further enacted. That in all that territory ceded by France to the United States, under the name of Louisiana, which lies north of thirty-six degrees and thirty minutes north latitude, not included within the limits of the state, contemplated by this act, slavery and involuntary servitude, otherwise than in the punishment of crimes, whereof the parties shall have been duly convicted, shall be, and is hereby, forever prohibited: Provided always, That any person escaping into the same, from whom labour or service is lawfully claimed, in any state or territory of the United States, such fugitive may be lawfully reclaimed and conveyed to the person claiming his or her labour or service as aforesaid."

—APPROVED, March 6, 1820

1. The Missouri Compromise became necessary because

   (A) Missouri wanted admittance to the Union as a slave state, which would have offset the balance between slave and free states

   (B) the French were not willing to give up this territory as a stipulation of the Louisiana Purchase

   (C) Texas still claimed areas in Missouri and vowed to fight for them if necessary

   (D) Maine was going to enter the Union as a free state, which would have offset the balance between slave and free states

2. The politician most notable for drafting the Missouri Compromise was

   (A) Andrew Jackson

   (B) James Monroe

   (C) Henry Clay

   (D) John Quincy Adams

3. The Missouri Compromise did all of the following except

   (A) outlaw the fugitive slave laws inside the state area ceded by France

   (B) forbid slavery north of the 36°30′ line inside the Louisiana Purchase

   (C) allow Missouri to enter as a slave state and Maine as a free state

   (D) relieve sectional tensions between free and slave state supporters

4. The Missouri Compromise would later be rendered unconstitutional as a result of

(A) the Kansas-Nebraska Act in 1854

(B) the Compromise of 1850

(C) John Brown's Raid on Harper's Ferry in 1859

(D) the *Dred Scott* decision

Questions 5–7 refer to the following illustration.

Source: National Park Service

5. President Jackson pushed through the Indian Removal Act of 1830

(A) to protect the natives from white settlers flooding into the area

(B) to punish the Indians for their alliances to the British and French in previous wars

(C) because these five tribes posed the biggest challenge to American claims in the southern states

(D) because these tribes inhabited some of most fertile farm land and locations and he believed white settlers had rights to the land

6. The Indian tribe that resisted the removal the most, which had a functioning, semi-sovereign government was the

(A) Creek

(B) Seminole

(C) Choctaw

(D) Cherokee

7. All of the following are false statements about the removal of Indians from their ancestral homelands except

(A) they were provided protection and supplies from the United States government that eased their transition

(B) they were removed from fertile land and placed in similar conditions in what became known as the Indian territory

(C) many Indians suffered as a result of the harsh winter and lack of food and supplies on their way west

(D) any Indian who agreed to assimilate into American culture was allowed to stay and coexist with white settlers

Questions 8–10 refer to the following excerpt.

1.1 *"Resolved,* That such laws as conflict, in any way, with the true and substantial happiness of woman, are contrary to the great precept of nature, and of no validity; for this is superior in obligation to any other.

Resolved, That all laws which prevent woman from occupying such a station in society as her conscience shall dictate, or which place her in a position inferior to that of man, are contrary to the great precept of nature, and therefore of no force or authority.

Resolved, That woman is man's equal—was intended to be so by the Creator, and the highest good of the race demands that she should be recognized as such.

Resolved, That the women of this country ought to be enlightened in regard to the laws under which they live, that they may no longer publish their degradation, by declaring themselves satisfied with their present position, nor their ignorance, by asserting that they have all the rights they want.

Resolved, That inasmuch as man, while claiming for himself intellectual superiority, does accord to woman moral superiority, it is pre-eminently his duty to encourage her to speak, and teach, as she has an opportunity, in all religious assemblies."

—Declaration of Rights and Sentiments, 1848

8. The main purpose of the Seneca Falls convention was to

   (A) declare the right to vote for women in the Northern states

   (B) advocate the education of women through establishing all-female colleges

   (C) assert the rights of women as equals to men morally, socially, and politically

   (D) demand that the word women be added to the Declaration of Independence along with the word men

9. Women gained more rights during the Second Great Awakening through all of the following except

   (A) being admitted to colleges and having all female colleges such as Mt. Holyoke and Troy Female Seminary

   (B) gaining notice as reformers in the areas of penal reform and abolitionism

   (C) being elected to political offices to allow them to advocate for more rights and privileges

   (D) being more involved in the religious fervor sweeping the nation at the time, which gave them more of a role in the church hierarchy

10. The main organizer of the Seneca Falls Convention and one of the most outspoken advocates of women's rights was

    (A) Lucretia Mott

    (B) Amelia Bloomer

    (C) Elizabeth C. Stanton

    (D) Alice Paul

Questions 11 and 12 refer to the following quote.

"Whereas the President of the United States, in his message of May 11, 1846, has declared that 'the Mexican Government not only refused to receive him, [the envoy of the United States,] or listen to his propositions, but, after a long-continued series of menaces, has at last invaded *our territory* and shed the blood of our fellow-citizens on our *own soil* . . .'

And again, in his message of December 8, 1846, that 'we had ample cause of war against Mexico long before the breaking out of hostilities; but even then we forbore to take redress into our own hands until Mexico herself became the aggressor, by invading *our soil* in hostile array, and shedding the blood of our citizens . . .'"

—Abraham Lincoln, Speech Before the United States House of Representatives, December 22, 1847

11. Abraham Lincoln, a senator at the time, spoke to Congress about his disagreement with President Polk on

    (A) the fact that blood had been spilled on American soil, leading to a conflict with Mexico

    (B) whether or not the rejection of the Slidell mission was true or fabricated to justify war

    (C) existing hostilities with Mexico and inevitability of war with that nation

    (D) invading Mexico to conquer its empire in the name of spreading slavery

12. Lincoln's speech to Congress ultimately challenged

   (A) America's justification for entering a war against Mexico

   (B) America's claim that the Rio Grande River was the official border between the United States and Mexico

   (C) the spread of slavery into areas already taken from Mexico by 1847

   (D) the authority of the president to declare war on a nonhostile nation

Short-Answer Questions

1. For this question, address all three parts:

    (A) Briefly explain ONE Supreme Court case during the Marshall court that asserted federal power over state laws.

    (B) Briefly explain another Supreme Court case during the Marshall court that asserted federal power over state laws.

    (C) Briefly explain an effect or challenge in enforcement of ONE of the aforementioned court cases in the period 1800–1848.

2.

    THE DOWNFALL OF MOTHER BANK.

    Using this 1833 image, address all three of the following parts:

    (A) Briefly explain the point of view about the National Bank from the perspective of the author.

    (B) Briefly explain ONE development from the period 1800–1848 that could be used to support the point of view expressed by the artist.

    (C) Briefly explain ONE development from the period 1800–1848 that could be used to challenge the point of view expressed by the artist.

Long Essay Question

Directions: You are advised to spend 5 minutes planning and 30 minutes writing your answer.

The period after the War of 1812 is commonly referred to as the "Era of Good Feelings." Support, modify, or refute this interpretation, providing specific evidence to justify your answer.

ANSWERS AND EXPLANATIONS

MULTIPLE-CHOICE ANSWERS

1. A

When Missouri wanted to enter the Union as a slave state, it threatened the sectional balance. Therefore, it was decided that Maine would be allowed to break away from Massachusetts and become its own state, and a free one at that.

2. C

Henry Clay, later known as the "Great Pacificator," authored and led the compromise. He was pro-states' rights, but in the end, he wanted to see the Union thrive. He was later responsible for resolving the tariff controversy and the issue over slavery in the Mexican Cession.

3. A

The Missouri Compromise settled sectional tensions, admitted Missouri as a slave state and Maine as a free state, and outlawed slavery north of the 36°30′ line. It also protected slave owners with a clause that any slaves would be sent back to Missouri in the event they escaped.

4. D

The Kansas-Nebraska Act annulled the Missouri Compromise, but the *Dred Scott* decision declared it unconstitutional. The Supreme Court ruled that Congress could not control the private property of citizens, and slaves were considered property, not people.

5. D

The Five Civilized Tribes coexisted with the whites more than other nations, but they had such large possessions, most of which rested on fertile farmland and waterways. Jackson's representation of the removal as a humane decision was a guise to move the Indians away from lands that the whites wanted.

6. D

The Cherokee nation had its own constitution, government, and system of laws in place. They appealed to the Supreme Court to retain their homelands. Marshall ruled that the Cherokee could keep their land, which allegedly prompted Jackson's famous words to John Marshall: "He has made his decision, now let him come down and enforce it."

7. A

The Indians were not given nearly the amount of resources and supplies promised to them in their trek west. Many starved or froze to death in the harsh winter. The Five Civilized Tribes were those who had actually assimilated the most, but they also suffered the worst casualties and hardships.

8. C

The Seneca Falls Convention was called for women to assert their rights. They believed they should have equal rights, and many were fighting against the "cult of domesticity," which declared that a woman's place was in the home.

9. C

Women were not elected to any political positions at this point in history. They did, however, gain more roles through reform, church association, and educational opportunities.

10. C

Elizabeth Cady Stanton was the main organizer of the Seneca Falls Convention, and she was extremely outspoken for women's rights. Susan B. Anthony took part, but much of her fame would come after the Civil War.

11. A

Lincoln did not believe that America was justified in its war with Mexico. His speech coined the term "spot resolution," where he continuously asked to know the spot on American soil where blood had been spilled.

12. A

Lincoln was not necessarily opposed to war, as is later evidenced, but it was more the causes put forth by Polk and Congress that he challenged.

SHORT-ANSWER QUESTIONS RESPONSES

1. (A) One Supreme Court case that increased federal power over state laws was *Marbury v. Madison*. This case established the precedent of judicial review, which dictated that the Supreme Court has the power to declare acts of Congress or the president unconstitutional. Because of this case, Marshall declared the Judiciary Act of 1789 illegal and did not allow Marbury to receive his commission, by which John Adams had appointed him justice of the peace in the District of Columbia.

   (B) Another Supreme Court case that asserted federal power over state laws was *McCulloch v. Maryland*. This case certified the constitutionality of the National Bank through the necessary and proper clause. Loose constructionists, such as Alexander Hamilton, were in favor of this decision, while strict constructionists, such as Thomas Jefferson, were against the decision.

   (C) One later effect of *McCulloch v. Maryland* was the extension and loss of the Second National Bank charter. Andrew Jackson, the seventh president of the United States, was adamantly opposed to the bank. President Jackson had all federal funds removed from the Second National Bank and redistributed into "Pet Banks," against the wishes of Nicholas Biddle, who was president of the Second National Bank.

2. (A) The artist is against the National Bank, as he is showing President Andrew Jackson holding a sign that says, "Order for the Removal of Public Money," as Major Jack Downing cheers him on. It is also apparent that the author is against the bank because Nicholas Biddle, the president of the Second National Bank, is portrayed as the devil (in devil horns, depicted smaller than Jackson, and seen running away).

   (B) "Pet banks," or moving federal money from the National Bank into state banks, is a historical development that supports the point of view of the artist. Andrew Jackson vetoed the re-charter of the bank and removed federal deposits into state banks, or "pet banks."

   (C) *McCulloch v. Maryland* could be used to challenge the point of view expressed by the artist because this Supreme Court case ensured the constitutionality of the National Bank through the necessary and proper, or "elastic," clause. Even though Andrew Jackson refused to extend the charter, the Bank was still considered constitutional.

LONG ESSAY SAMPLE RESPONSE

The term "Era of Good Feelings" is accurate to a certain extent in the period after the War of 1812: there were strong feelings of nationalism as Republicans during Monroe's Presidency began to develop American traditions independent of their European ancestors, and internal improvements dramatically improved our economy, which also increased nationalistic sentiments. However, the nation continued to divide itself into the increasingly anti-slavery industrial North and the pro-slavery agricultural South, which led to sectionalist controversies.

Although the Americans ended the War of 1812 with a "status quo ante" position with Great Britain, Andrew Jackson's win in the Battle of New Orleans, along with the Federalist Party's "death" after the Hartford Convention in 1814, contributed to James Monroe's easy win in the 1816 presidential election. This period became known as the "Era of Good Feelings" because after the war, most Americans subscribed to a one-party political system (Monroe easily won the 1820 election by a landslide) and became more patriotic. For example, during the War of 1812, John Philip Sousa wrote "In Defense of Fort McHenry," which later became our national anthem. This was important because now Americans had their own American anthem instead of singing British hymns.

Additionally, authors began to publish American history textbooks for students to read in school as opposed to learning from European textbooks. This also contributed to an emerging independent American ideology because students could now learn about the American Revolution and the American colonies. In terms of foreign policy, the Monroe Doctrine also led to an increased sense of nationalism because it demonstrated that under Secretary of State Adams's program, Americans refused to allow European nations to colonize the Western Hemisphere and implied that the United States was a major power in this hemisphere. Each of these examples added to strong nationalistic sentiments because they demonstrated America's growing patriotic spirit.

At the same time, however, increasing tensions between North and South contributed to sectionalist tendencies and fueled debates over issues such as slavery, the National Bank, and internal improvements. Henry Clay's American System advocated a protective tariff, internal improvements that connected the East to the West, and the establishment of the Second National Bank. Although Clay's intent was to improve the entire U.S. economy, the South felt otherwise because they did not benefit from many of the programs. For example, the Erie Canal, which connected the Hudson River to the Great Lakes, benefited the northern and western parts of the country, and national roads such as the Cumberland Road were created in the northern and western areas of the United States. The South did not receive any of these benefits and, from their perspective, got the "short end of the stick," as they had to comply with the Tariff of 1816. Although Southerners such as John C. Calhoun supported this tariff (he later rescinded his support with the

Tariff of Abominations of 1828), other Southerners believed the tariff was harmful to the Southern economy. Because the majority of their economy was dependent on cotton, Southern states had to pay an additional fee to the federal government in order to import goods from foreign nations. The North, however, with an expanding textile industry, would not suffer as much economically and thus supported the tariff because, since they were already producing goods, they could earn money by shipping through the newly created canals and national roads. Southern plantation owners, however, became gradually more upset as demonstrated by their opposition to both this tariff and the Tariff of Abomination in 1828. Thus, the dissent over the tariff and internal improvements only increased sectionalist tensions between the North and the South.

In addition to tensions over internal improvements, the North and South also debated over the issue of slavery. Up until the Missouri Compromise in 1820, there was a balance between slave and free states admitted into the Union. However, when Missouri applied for statehood, James Tallmadge offered an amendment that would have forbidden slavery in Missouri, which would have upset the delicate balance between slave and free states. The Tallmadge Amendment passed in the House but failed in the Senate (because there were more senators that were Southern). Southern senators were furious and believed that the amendment was unconstitutional because it placed unfair guidelines on whether they could apply for statehood. Thus, the Missouri Compromise, negotiated by Henry Clay, agreed for Maine to be admitted as a free state, Missouri to be admitted as a slave state, and all slavery banned north of the 36°30′ parallel. Although both sides compromised, the debate over slavery further increased tensions between the North and South, and the line would become a subject of great controversy in the years before the Civil War.

The Era of Good Feelings after the War of 1812 demonstrated an increased sense of patriotism, pride, and nationalism among Americans. However, the period also inadvertently caused greater tensions between the North and South. These tensions only intensified, as sectionalist differences later led the dissolution of Monroe's Republican stronghold in the election of 1824. Furthermore, the slavery issue never fully resolved itself, as the Kansas-Nebraska Act effectively repealed the Missouri Compromise, while the *Dred Scott* decision declared the Missouri Compromise unconstitutional and ultimately led to the split of the Union in 1861.

The thesis addresses all parts of the question, provides warrants to support its claims, and clearly explains how it will answer the question by outlining the essay into "nationalism" and "sectionalism" sections. It would earn a full point in this section.

In terms of support for argument, the paper supports the thesis by using specific evidence such as the Tallmadge Amendment, Missouri Compromise, Monroe Doctrine, and American System. Additionally, the essay clearly and consistently states how the evidence supports the thesis and establishes clear links between the thesis and the argument, so it is well focused. This essay, as per the College Board rubric, would earn the maximum 2 points in this section.

Regarding application, this essay would also earn the maximum 2 points in periodization because it fully analyzes the extent to which the Era of Good Feelings is similar and different to developments that preceded or followed (discussion of internal improvements has excellent analysis).

Finally, in terms of synthesis, the essay would earn another full point because it extends the thesis statement in the conclusion and connects it to other historical periods.

Based on the Long Essay Question rubric, this essay would receive a 6 out of 6 possible points.

CHAPTER 15: EXPANSIONIST FOREIGN POLICY IN THE WESTERN HEMISPHERE

MANIFEST DESTINY

SETTLERS MOVE WEST

Journalist John O'Sullivan coined the phrase "Manifest Destiny" in 1845. It would soon be the cry of European Americans who flocked the overland trails to settle the trans-Mississippi West. Manifest Destiny was the belief that it was God's will that the United States expand from sea to shining sea. The market revolution, advancements in transportation, and increasing nationalism drove Americans to seek opportunities to spread the virtues of the United States across the continent and beyond.

By 1840, thousands had moved into what is now Texas, with a trickle braving the overland trail to present-day Oregon. That trickle soon became a flood—by 1845, thousands more settlers had traversed the dangerous **Oregon Trail**. Caravans usually consisted of families in 10 to 20 covered wagons who traveled up to six months, covering a mere 12 to 15 miles a day depending on the weather. Many women did not wish to make the journey at all; those who did soon found their traditional roles as homemakers and mothers change shape. At the beginning of the journey, women took care of children, cooked meals, and cared for clothing. By midtrek, they were repairing wagon wheels, tending animals, and lifting the wagon covers. A sense of an established home was also lost on the journey; some women struggled to maintain some vestiges of "back home" by running prayer meetings and teaching "school."

EXPANSION AND NATIVE AMERICANS MEET

As European American settlers moved west, they encountered Native American tribes who had lived in the Great Plains region for centuries. Not only were Native Americans displaced by European Americans but also by the **Sioux**, who were moving west to hunt buffalo. While there were no large-scale clashes between Native Americans and European American settlers, stories abounded about the "ruthless savages" who lived on the plains.

The Sioux, on the other hand, did much to alter the way of life for many tribes that had lived in the Great Plains. The Sioux had moved steadily westward since the mid-18th century because of the spread of guns and horses, which they used to fight for territory and hunt their prized buffalo. Outbreaks of European diseases often cleared the way for the Sioux as they moved west by killing off tribes that would have otherwise stood in their way. By the beginning of the 19th century, the Sioux had control over much of the Great Plains. Yet because of relentless westward expansion, the Sioux and the other tribes of the Great Plains were unable to maintain their control of their lands.

TROUBLE WITH TERRITORIES

The era of westward expansion opened up politically with Martin Van Buren elected as president in 1836 and William Henry Harrison in 1840. A benefactor of Andrew Jackson's "spoils," Van Buren had a troubled presidency. Many believed he was simply a puppet of Jackson's. Van Buren also had to oversee a terrible economic depression that stemmed from his predecessor's policies. The Panic of 1837 was caused by many of the same problems that had caused the Panic of 1819. Overspeculation on western lands, faulty loans issued by "wildcat" western banks, the absence of a national bank, and Jackson's Specie Circular all placed enormous strains on the economy.

TIPPECANOE AND TYLER, TOO, AND NEW EXPANSION

Van Buren ran for re-election in 1840 against a vigorous campaign by the Whigs, who chose Battle of Tippecanoe hero William Henry Harrison as their candidate. As in recent previous elections, the mudslinging was fierce, with the Whigs blaming "Martin Van Ruin" for the economic crisis and Democrats accusing Harrison of being a drunk. The campaign was a lively one, with Whigs pushing large model log cabins and handing out hard cider in towns across America to boast of their candidate's supposed "poor" background. The "Tippecanoe and Tyler, too" ticket swept the elections, easily defeating Van Buren. However, Harrison fell gravely ill with pneumonia only four weeks into his term and died, leaving his vice president, John Tyler, to become president.

Maine, Oregon, and Texas soon became hotly sought-after pieces of real estate, as more and more Americans began settling these regions. Americans still harbored a deep-seated hatred for the British after the Revolutionary War and the War of 1812 and their continued presence along the U.S.-British North America border. This hatred came to a head when British lumber companies proposed building a road that would ease the transport of lumber and connect various regions of British North America. This road would cross sections of land whose boundaries were still being contested by the Americans and the British. In 1838, a group of British North American lumberjacks collided with the Maine militia as they claimed control over the Aroostook River Valley. The threatened Aroostook War was quickly averted, as Secretary of State Daniel Webster and British Foreign Minister Ashburton negotiated the terms that would settle the boundary dispute. The **Webster-Ashburton Treaty** (1842) divided the contested territory between the United States and Britain and settled the northern boundary of Minnesota.

The conflict between the United States and Britain would not end with the settlement over the Maine issue. The British had enjoyed a profitable fur-trading business in the Oregon territory and believed that gave them claim to the region. The United States contended that it had first found and settled the region and, therefore, could rightfully stake a claim on it. The most ardent proponents of expansion demanded that the United States take the entire territory up to the 54°40′ parallel, which lay even with the southern shore of Alaska. As Manifest Destiny "fever" swept the nation and the election of 1844 loomed, the Democrat **James K. Polk** sought to capitalize on the expansionist spirit with his campaign slogan "Fifty-four forty or fight!" which would make the U.S. border reach Russian Alaska. By the time he took office, Polk had backed down from his demand for all of the Oregon Territory by negotiating with Britain. The United States would obtain a boundary at the 49th parallel and reluctantly agreed to cede Vancouver Island and grant navigation rights on the Columbia River to the British. However, the Mexican War had erupted by this time, which overshadowed any concerns over the entrance of new free territories into the Union.

TEXAS JOINS THE UNION

Meanwhile, Texas was the biggest issue in the national spotlight. In 1821, Texas was officially a northern region of newly independent Mexico. Mexico had attracted many American farmers and ranchers into the region with cheap land and relative freedom from government intrusion. By the 1830s, whites and slaves outnumbered Mexicans in the region. Mexico decided to crack down on the Texans—it decided that slavery would be banned in the region and demanded that all residents become Catholic. The American settlers refused to abide by the new laws, and tensions grew. In 1834, Antonio Lopez de Santa Anna became military dictator of Mexico and attempted to force American settlers to abide by Mexican laws. The settlers, led by **Sam Houston**, staged a revolt in 1836 and declared Texas a republic independent of Mexico.

At present-day San Antonio, Santa Anna's forces attacked the Alamo, killing all the Americans stationed there, and marched to the San Jacinto River. There, a force led by Houston successfully routed the Mexican forces and captured Santa Anna. The Mexican dictator was forced to sign a decree granting independence to the Republic of Texas (the Lone Star Republic). Houston was chosen to lead the new country, and he quickly applied for annexation, or adoption as a state in the Union. His petitions were rejected early on by Jackson and Van Buren, who both feared tipping the balance in the Senate to favor slave states. Despite Tyler's support for annexation, Congress rejected his bid to bring Texas into the Union in 1844. The presidential election of 1844 brought expansionism and the fate of Texas to the forefront. Outgoing president Tyler saw the election of the expansionist candidate Polk as a **mandate** to drive the annexation of Texas through Congress. A joint resolution was passed in acceptance of Texas's bid for annexation. Mexico was unhappy about this development on its border.

THE MEXICAN WAR

President Polk had to react quickly to the impending crisis between Mexico and the United States. Mexico had ended the diplomatic relationship between the countries and demanded the return of Texas. Polk sent special envoy John Slidell to Mexico City to inform the Mexican government of U.S. intentions to honor the original Nueces River boundary of Texas and a desire to purchase California. In anticipation of the Mexicans not responding positively to Slidell's proposal, Polk amassed the U.S. Army, led by Zachary Taylor, along the disputed southern border of Texas at the Rio Grande River in January of 1846. In April, a Mexican force crossed the border and attacked Taylor's men, killing several American troops. Despite opposition from a small group of Whigs, led by Abraham Lincoln, a large majority of Congress voted to declare war on Mexico.

THE WILMOT PROVISO SPLITS NORTH AND SOUTH

The war caused immediate dissension among many Americans who opposed the fighting on principle. Many Whigs and Northerners accused Polk of falsely claiming that American blood had been shed on American soil when the Mexican force crossed the Rio Grande. In their eyes, the southern border lay some miles to the north at the Nueces, not at the Rio Grande. Secondly, the issue of expansion of slavery again reared its ugly head. Transcendentalists, such as Henry David Thoreau and Ralph Waldo Emerson, protested the war by refusing to pay taxes, with Emerson saying, "Mexico will poison us!" Sectional tension grew in Congress, as Representative David Wilmot proposed an amendment to a bill that would forbid slavery in any new lands acquired by the war with Mexico. The final bill passed in the House but failed in the Senate. More importantly, the **Wilmot Proviso** signaled the start of an even deeper crisis that would pit the North against the South over issues of slavery, states' rights, and representation.

THE MEXICAN CESSION

After quick, decisive military victories by the United States in California and Texas, the Mexican War was basically over by September of 1847. California had been declared independent as the **Bear Flag Republic** under the leadership of John C. Fremont, and Texas had been gained as the United States successfully overtook Mexico City. A peace was settled by the **Treaty of Guadalupe Hidalgo** in February 1848. The treaty granted California and most of the Southwest (current-day New Mexico, Arizona, Utah, and Nevada) to the United States. The American government agreed to pay war reparations in the sum of $15 million to the Mexican government. After bitter debate over the expansion of slavery, the treaty was ratified and the war officially over.

CHAPTER 16: THE ONSET OF THE CIVIL WAR

THE MORALITY OF SLAVERY

In 1853, President **Franklin Pierce** rounded out the Mexican cession by making the **Gadsden Purchase** from Mexico, which transferred to the United States the Mesilla Valley in the southernmost region of New Mexico and Arizona. As he did so, however, the controversy over the institution of slavery began to rage in Washington, D.C., and all over the nation. The discussion was political, social, economic, and, for many, moral.

After the Second Great Awakening, *abolitionists* spoke out about the evils of slavery in both the North and the South. After Nat Turner's Rebellion, however, some Southerners changed their tune by expressing concern over what the nation would do with the sudden release of "uncivilized" African American slaves. Pro-slavery advocates in the South began to strike back at their Northern opponents by defending the "peculiar institution." Some **apologists** used passages from the Bible to justify the institution of slavery, while others maintained that the "family-like" atmosphere slave owners provided for African Americans was preferable even to freedom. A large movement of apologists, led by **George Fitzhugh**, spoke of the happy lives of Southern slaves who were clothed, fed, and housed by benevolent slave owners. Fitzhugh argued in his book *Cannibals All* (1857) that African American slaves were much better off than the "Northern wage slave," who did not have basic living needs provided for him and his family.

THE FIRST ATTEMPTS AT COMPROMISE

The election of 1848 brought a third party into the political arena, encouraged by the Wilmot Proviso. The **Free-Soil Party** was made up of antislavery advocates from all political parties. Its campaign slogan was "Free soil, free speech, free labor, and free men." The party held some of the same beliefs the old Whigs (e.g., Clay's American System), but it opposed the expansion of slavery in total. The Free-Soilers nominated Martin Van Buren as their candidate to run against the Whig Zachary Taylor and the Democrat Lewis Cass. Cass had gained national attention with his proposal to use **popular sovereignty** to resolve the issue of slavery in the territories. He proposed that citizens of each territory should decide by vote whether or not slavery would be permitted. Taylor defeated Van Buren and Cass, as crucial Northern Democratic votes were split by the emergence of the Free-Soil Party and its candidate, former president Martin Van Buren.

With the discovery of gold in 1848 and the massive influx of **49ers** into the west to find their fortune, California quickly drafted a new constitution to gain statehood. The constitution forbade slavery, which would again alter the sectional balance in the Senate. Even though Taylor was an advocate of slavery, he understood the importance of adding California, and hopefully New Mexico, to the Union. His support of adding these free states sparked debate in Congress. Radical Southerners warned of possible secession, even going so far as meeting in Nashville to hatch their plans.

CLAY SEEKS COMPROMISE AGAIN

"The Great Compromiser" Henry Clay again came to the rescue with a plan to avert a national crisis. His plan would admit California as a free state, divide the Mexican cession into the New Mexico and Utah Territories with popular sovereignty serving as the basis for determining the status of slavery, ban the slave trade in Washington, D.C., enact a stricter **Fugitive Slave Law**, and give Texas monetary compensation for that state's willingness to drop its claims to part of New Mexico's territory.

Debate ensued quickly, as the "Great Triumvirate" of Clay, Calhoun, and Webster led the way with impassioned speeches on the floor of the Senate, with Calhoun in opposition and Clay and Webster in support of compromise. Calhoun argued that this was a states' rights issue, not a moral issue, and the federal government had no right to intervene. Webster argued that compromise might just save the Union and urged his fellow Northerners to be more conciliatory.

However, it seemed that a compromise might not be feasible. Northern radical William H. Seward argued that slavery should be banned on moral grounds, and President Taylor rejected any talk of compromise with the South. Compromise looked to be impossible until the sudden death of President Taylor due to cholera. Vice President Millard Fillmore took over the presidency and helped to usher in a compromise bill. The young Senator Stephen A. Douglas was able to break apart this compromise bill and garner enough votes to get each piece of it separately passed by the Senate. As each piece was passed, President Fillmore stood by to sign it into law.

The **Compromise of 1850**, in effect, "bought time" for the Union. The North actually fared a bit better—it gained the political upper hand with the admission of California as a free state, and time to grow economically. However the stricter Fugitive Slave Law and the concept of popular sovereignty became troublesome. Many Northerners were staunchly opposed to any enforcement of a law designed to re-enslave those **fugitives** who had made it to freedom. In addition, the new law denied legal rights to captured blacks and sentenced whites who had harbored fugitives to heavy fines or jail time. An **Underground Railroad** was established by abolitionists to assist slaves in escaping to freedom in either the Northern United States or British North America.

The harshness of this new law encouraged the daughter of a Northern abolitionist to write a novel chronicling the cruelty of slavery. **Harriet Beecher Stowe** wrote *Uncle Tom's Cabin* in 1852. The novel quickly gained fame in the North and scorn from the South. In essence, the Compromise of 1850 and *Uncle Tom's Cabin* galvanized more Northerners to believe that slavery was morally wrong, while Southerners grew in their conviction to protect it.

THE KANSAS-NEBRASKA ACT

The election of 1852 brought Democrat Franklin Pierce to the office of president and the Whig Party one step closer to the grave. The Whigs had decided to run a campaign that ignored the issue of slavery altogether. They discovered, however, that the sectional crisis could not be ignored. Another factor that would serve to challenge the tenuous sectional balance was a united government—the Democrats had control of both the executive and legislative branches.

A New Party Is Born

Illinois Senator Stephen A. Douglas came to the forefront of national politics once again with his proposal to divide the Nebraska Territory into two regions—Nebraska and Kansas. As with Cass's proposal back in 1848, the slavery issue would be decided by the citizens of the territory—popular sovereignty—with Nebraska presumably becoming a free state and Kansas a slave state. Douglas's motivation was not political as much as it was economic—he desired to give his state the eastern terminus for the transcontinental railroad, which needed Southern support to be secured. Thus, he introduced a bill that would garner Southerners' support in another way. Because both Kansas and Nebraska lay above the 36°30' line of demarcation established by the Missouri Compromise, passage of his bill would mean its repeal. With his great skills of oratory, Douglas was able to push his bill through both houses. It was signed into law by President Pierce in 1854.

The **Kansas-Nebraska Act** actually rekindled much of the controversy that had been quieted by the Compromise of 1850. By repealing the Missouri Compromise, Northern Democrats believed that the Union had "sold out" to the South with regard to the slavery issue. A new political party emerged due to the renewed sectional tension. Its ranks included Whigs, Democrats, Free-Soilers, and Know-Nothings, all from either the North or West. The new **Republican Party** was opposed to the expansion of slavery and the Kansas-Nebraska Act. Despite losing the presidential election of 1856 to the Democrat James Buchanan, the Republicans made a great showing by running the popular Californian John Fremont, who managed to win 11 of 16 free states in the Electoral College.

VIOLENCE IN KANSAS AND IN CONGRESS

Before the election, violence had erupted as Douglas's popular sovereignty concept was put to the test in Kansas. Little did anyone suspect that pro-slavery farmers from nearby Missouri would settle small areas along the border to vote in the election that would determine the slavery issue for Kansas. As Northerners learned of the Missourians or "**border ruffians**" setting up homesteads, they decided to fight back. Henry Ward Beecher and other abolitionists paved the way for antislavery settlers to travel and set up homes in Kansas. It was not long before fighting broke out between the pro- and antislavery factions. As a result, the region earned the name **Bleeding Kansas**.

The Missourians traveled across the border to Lecompton, Kansas, organized a pro-slavery government, and drafted a constitution that cleared the way for statehood. The constitution contained clauses protecting slaveholding and a bill of rights excluding free blacks. President Buchanan supported the **Lecompton Constitution**, which Douglas and others in the Senate loudly opposed. It was decided to remit the constitution back to Kansas for a re-vote. The antislavery faction refused to recognize the compromise re-vote by creating its own legislature in Topeka, Kansas. Unfortunately, as the politicos were busy arguing, violence escalated. In 1856, a band of armed border ruffians attacked the free-soil town of Lawrence, Kansas, killing two people and burning down buildings. In retaliation, fierce abolitionist John Brown and a band of followers savagely attacked a series of farms along Pottawatomie Creek, slashing five people to death.

TENSION IN CONGRESS LEADS TO VIOLENCE

All was not quiet on Capitol Hill either, as abolitionist Senator Charles Sumner spoke of the injustice in Kansas and in the process defamed the name of South Carolina senator Andrew Butler. South Carolina congressman Preston Brooks, who was Butler's nephew, was so enraged that he beat Sumner over the head with his gold-tipped cane some 30 times, nearly killing him. Even though many in the Senate were outraged by Brooks's actions, the Senate failed to censure or remove him from office.

DRED SCOTT DIVIDES THE NATION

The Supreme Court under Chief Justice Roger Taney added fuel to the already raging debate on March 6, 1857. In the case of ***Dred Scott v. Sanford***, the Court ruled the 36°30′ provision of the Missouri Compromise was unconstitutional and that all African Americans were not citizens, thus making them ineligible to sue in federal court. Dred Scott was a slave who had lived with his first master in Missouri and was then moved after his master's death to Wisconsin and Illinois for five years. Scott then returned to Missouri. Financed by Northern abolitionists, Dred Scott sued his master by claiming that the years he had lived in free territory made him a free man, even though he was currently living in a slave state. In his 22-page ruling, Taney argued that the Founding

Fathers had never had any intention of giving African Americans the protections of citizenship under the U.S. Constitution and, therefore, Scott had no right to sue in federal court. The opinion also maintained that Congress had no right to infringe on citizens' right to due process— in other words, an individual's property could not be denied him under the U.S. Constitution. Therefore, the Missouri Compromise of 1820, which forbade slavery north of the 36°30' line, was unconstitutional because it stripped slave owners of their "rightful" property once they moved northward. Both Democrat and Republican Northerners were horrified by the decision, while Southerners were thrilled. The decision served to widen the rift between the regions.

JOHN BROWN AND HARPER'S FERRY

John Brown of the Pottawatomie Creek massacre again entered national headlines, as he and his followers staged a raid on the federal arsenal at **Harper's Ferry**, Virginia. Brown, claiming he was following orders from God, hoped to arm slaves on the surrounding plantations to overthrow the institution of slavery and establish a free African American state. In October 1859, Brown and his gang seized the arsenal and managed to hold off the Virginia militia for two days. They were finally captured, tried for treason, and hanged. In the North, John Brown was hailed by some abolitionists as a martyr because of his conviction that his actions were guided by a higher moral purpose. In the South, Brown was labeled as a dangerous psychotic who was acting at the behest of Northern abolitionists. In response, Southerners formed citizens' militias designed to counteract possible slave uprisings and became more suspicious of the North's intentions.

THE RISE OF LINCOLN AND THE ELECTION OF 1860

Republican Abraham Lincoln was not a household name until the Illinois Senate election of 1858, which pitted the country lawyer against the powerful Democrat Stephen A. Douglas for the coveted seat. Lincoln was an eloquent orator and moderate who challenged his opponent to a series of public debates, which he hoped would garner both local and national attention from the press. The most celebrated debate occurred in the town of Freeport, Illinois, where Lincoln challenged Douglas to defend the concept of popular sovereignty under the *Dred Scott* decision. In what historians call his **Freeport Doctrine**, Douglas responded that communities would have to pass and enforce laws to protect the institution of slavery for it to exist. His doctrine caused an even deeper division within the Democratic party, as Southerners felt he had not done enough to support the *Dred Scott* decision. While his popular sovereignty stance won him the senatorial seat, Douglas injured his chances of winning the presidency in the election of 1860. The debates also brought the "unknown" Lincoln into the spotlight as a possible Republican hopeful for the next presidential election.

As the nominating conventions for the election of 1860 were underway, many Americans were of the opinion that the Union was on the verge of breaking apart. Most contentious was the Democratic convention, where Southerners walked out in protest over the nomination of Stephen A. Douglas, whom they considered a traitor. As they tried to reconvene and reconcile, it was clear that the party would not be able to nominate a single candidate for president. In the end, the Democratic party split in two—Northerners nominated Stephen A. Douglas, and Southerners chose moderate John C. Breckenridge. The Republicans decided against the nomination of the radical William H. Seward and chose instead the moderate orator Abraham Lincoln. As well as choosing Lincoln, the party adopted a broad platform that would appeal to a wide spectrum of voters. In addition to the barring the extension of slavery into the territories, the platform promised a protective tariff, rights for immigrants, a transcontinental railroad, federally financed infrastructure improvements for the west, and free homesteads for citizens out of publicly held land. Southern Democrats warned that they would leave the Union if Lincoln were elected president. Whigs and moderates were concerned that a Lincoln victory would mean the end of the Union. The **Constitutional Union Party** was formed and chose John Bell of Tennessee as its candidate, hoping to pull enough votes from the Republicans to keep the cotton states of the South from seceding.

Abraham Lincoln garnered about 40 percent of the popular vote; Breckenridge carried the South, and Douglas and Bell earned a scattering of votes. It was Lincoln's ability to carry states with large numbers of electoral votes that won him the election. Lincoln managed to win 180 electoral votes to Breckenridge's 72. Despite the fact that the South still maintained control of both the legislative and judicial branches, it still looked as if secession was inevitable.

THE SOUTH SECEDES

Just four days after the election results were tallied, the South Carolina legislature voted to secede from the Union. Within the next six weeks, six more Southern states decided to join South Carolina. A meeting of these states was called in February 1861 during which the **Confederate States of America** was formed, with Jefferson Davis named as its president.

In a final attempt at compromise, Kentucky senator John Crittenden proposed an amendment to the Constitution that would have protected the right of slave owners to hold their property below the 36°30′ line and instituted popular sovereignty in any new states. President-elect Lincoln rejected the compromise, as it was in opposition to the Republican Party platform, which had called for the nonextension of slavery.

Southerners felt leaving the Union was politically justified—the states had voluntarily entered into the Union to begin with and had every right to leave it. Based on the writings of John Locke and the American Founding Fathers, Southerners spoke of their responsibility and right to overthrow a government that no longer protected the rights of its citizens to life, liberty, and property. The South also drew upon the writings of Jefferson and Madison in the Kentucky and Virginia Resolutions, as well as the speeches delivered by South Carolina's John C. Calhoun with regard to nullification and the strength of Union. Southerners argued that these writings further supported their right to secede. The South was banking on the premise that the North would allow it to leave the Union quietly, because the regions were already economically independent of one another. The South did not take the resolve of Union into account.

CHAPTER 17: THE CIVIL WAR AND ITS AFTERMATH

TWO REGIONS AT WAR

Before the first shots were fired upon the Union stronghold of Fort Sumter off the coast of Charleston, South Carolina, in April 1861, the North and South had already become distinctly different regions within the same country. Now that each region was making preparations for war, each had to take advantage of its strengths and exploit the weaknesses of the enemy.

Advantages and Disadvantages of Each Region

Militarily, the Confederates only had to fight a defensive war on their own territory to a draw; thus, they required fewer troops overall. That, combined with high troop morale, well-trained generals, and very few landlocked regions, gave the South an advantage at the beginning of the war. The Union, on the other hand, was waging an offensive war in which the goal was to preserve the Union. This required many more men and munitions that needed to be moved long distances to the front lines.

However, the sheer size of the North's population gave it an early advantage that would be later bolstered by the emancipation of slaves, who would join the war effort on the side of the Union. In the 11 years between the Compromise of 1850 and the outbreak of war, the North's economy had grown in both the industrial and financial sectors. Northerners controlled the nation's banks, railroads, and factories. The Union had to levy the first-ever income tax to pay for the war. It also raised excise taxes, raised a previously low protective tariff, and issued **greenbacks** in place of gold as the wartime currency.

Largely **agrarian**, the South was at a distinct disadvantage with regard to basic resources needed to wage an effective war. As the war dragged on, Confederate soldiers lacked basic equipment such as shoes, blankets, and clothing. Because of the east-west network of railroad lines linking the North to the West, once Southern tracks were destroyed by Union forces, the Confederates had limited means to transport men, supplies, or goods for manufacture. The South had been banking on worldwide demand for cotton to keep it afloat during the war, and had even hoped for foreign assistance. This was not to be, however, as the French and British saw an alliance with the Confederates as a liability for a future relationship with the United States, and worldwide demand for cotton plunged in the mid-1860s. As a result, the Confederates had to issue a large number of bonds to pay for the war, raise duties on farm goods, and eventually overprint their paper currency, causing rampant inflation.

FINDING SOLDIERS TO FIGHT

The largest expression of dissent among Northerners and Southerners came when it was time to raise the forces that would actually fight the war. Desertion was common on both sides of the firing lines. The Union army originally consisted almost entirely of volunteers. As the pool of volunteers began to dwindle, the Union enacted the first federal **conscription** law to draft young men to military service in 1863. The draft caused dissension in many areas of the North, but none so violent as the **New York Draft Riots**, sparked by angry Irish Americans. In the end, some 500 people were killed, and whole city blocks were destroyed by fire. There were some African American soldiers fighting for the North early in the war; those numbers increased after the issuance of the Emancipation Proclamation.

The South relied on volunteers to fill its ranks, as well. With a smaller population to draw from, the Confederacy had to enact conscription a year earlier than the North. Class and regional divisions were much more evident in the South, as wealthy plantation owners were able to purchase the services of others to serve for them. Appalachian "hillbillies" refused to serve. Fear of arming slaves kept the Confederacy from using African Americans until the war was almost at an end.

DISSENSION IN BORDER STATES AND CONGRESS

Abraham Lincoln was deeply aware of the tenuous relationship between the North and the border states and the military necessity of keeping the border states in the Union. Delaware, Maryland, Missouri, and Kentucky each decided to remain in the Union, despite their slave-holding status. This is not to say that there were not citizens in these states who were opposed to the "War of Northern Aggression." Citizens militia groups sympathetic to the Confederate cause were active during the course of the war and had to be kept in check by Union forces. Dissent was also evident within the aisles of Congress. Speaking of the "unjust" nature of the war and their concern over the disruption of western trade routes, a group of Northern Democrats referred to as the **Copperheads** lashed out at President Lincoln's broad use of executive power and demanded an immediate end to the "unjust war." Despite heated debate, Lincoln continued to flex the muscles of the executive branch throughout the war.

MILITARY ENGAGEMENT AND FOREIGN INFLUENCE

The Union hoped to strike the state of Virginia quickly and deal the Confederacy a mortal blow. However, the Union military leadership miscalculated the tenacity and drive with which the Confederates would fight back. The first major battle of the Civil War would force the North to realize that this was going to be a long, bitter fight.

THE UNION HATCHES A PLAN

In July 1861, federal troops marched from Washington, D.C., to a position about 30 miles outside of the nation's capital. There at **Bull Run** (Manassas), Confederate troops stood at the ready for the oncoming attack. At the beginning, Union forces seemed to be gaining the upper hand. But more Confederate soldiers led by General "Stonewall" Jackson soon arrived, sending the Union troops scrambling back to D.C. The North was now awakened to the harsh reality that this was going to be a long and bloody war. Southerners, on the other hand, emboldened by their ability to send the "Blues" scrambling in retreat, grew complacent.

It was back to the drawing board for Union leadership, with General Winfield Scott at the helm. Scott drew up a four-phase plan to wear down the Confederacy gradually. The first phase was dubbed the **Anaconda Plan**, in which the Union Navy would blockade all Southern ports, cutting them off from supplies and trade. The second phase involved splitting the Confederacy in half by taking control of the Mississippi River. Third, the Union planned to cut through the heart of the South by marching through Georgia, then snaking up the southeast coast to the Carolinas. The last phase involved capturing the Confederate capital at Richmond and routing the last of the "Grays."

THE SECOND BATTLE OF BULL RUN AND ANTIETAM

President Lincoln's patience was wearing thin, as Eastern Union commander General McClellan refused to send untrained men into battle. Finally, he launched his troops into the peninsula region of Virginia in March 1862, only to be sent reeling by the Confederate general **Robert E. Lee**. As Union leadership in the east was being changed, General Lee took advantage of the lull by engaging Union troops again at Manassas in the **Second Battle of Bull Run**. This time, it was Union general John Pope who was sent scurrying back across the Potomac in retreat.

Now with two decisive victories under his belt and hopes that a third win would bring foreign aid, Lee led his men into enemy territory in Maryland. With McClellan back in command of the Union forces and advance knowledge of Confederate battle plans, Union forces were able to cut Lee off at **Antietam** Creek. The bloodiest day of the war ensued, as more than 22,000 men were killed or wounded. Lee's men, unable to break Union resolve, were forced to retreat to Virginia. However, General McClellan failed to pursue the retreating Confederates, enraging President Lincoln. Lincoln promptly relieved him from his command for the last time and replaced him with General Ambrose Burnside.

A TURNING POINT

> The September 1862 fight at Antietam was a turning point of the war—it kept the Confederates from gaining much-needed foreign assistance from Britain and France. In addition, President Lincoln now had the "victory" he had been waiting for. He promptly issued his preliminary Emancipation Proclamation on September 2, 1862.

IRONCLADS ENTER THE WAR

Union General Burnside was much more aggressive than McClellan had been; however, this was not necessarily an asset for the North. At the Battle of Fredericksburg in December of 1862, Lee defeated Burnside, who was subsequently replaced by General Joseph Hooker. Aside from land battles, 1862 also saw a revolution in naval warfare with the launching of the "**ironclads**." The South's *CSS Merrimac*, touted as a ship that could sink wooden naval ships with one blast, proceeded to pose a huge threat to the Union blockade. The Confederates had not, however, banked on the Union having its own version of the "ironclad," named the *USS Monitor*. In a five-hour skirmish in March 1862, the ironclads slowly shot each other to a draw. No longer would the United States depend on wooden ships for her navy.

CONTROL OF THE MISSISSIPPI AND GETTYSBURG

The war in the west was focused on the battle over control of the mighty Mississippi River. Union general **Ulysses S. Grant** was able to cut his way through Kentucky and Tennessee, fighting a bloody battle at Shiloh in April 1862. By the spring of 1863, Grant controlled the port city of New Orleans and almost all of the Mississippi River region. To complete the removal of the Confederates, Grant launched an attack on Vicksburg, Mississippi. Union forces lay siege for seven weeks to the fortified city in another turning point for the Union. It now controlled the length of the Mississippi River and the surrounding regions.

In 1863, the third year of war, Generals Lee and Jackson were still managing to keep their men fighting vigorously in the eastern United States. General Jackson's men successfully defeated Union General Hooker at Chancellorsville by flanking Northern forces. Unfortunately for the Confederates, General Jackson was killed by friendly fire in the battle. Despite the victory, the Confederates suffered great losses of some 13,000 men. In a last-ditch effort to invade the North, garner the attention of foreign supporters, and perhaps force the Union to negotiate for peace, General Lee launched an invasion of Pennsylvania while Union forces kept close tabs on the Confederates. The two huge armies converged at the small town of **Gettysburg** in southern Pennsylvania. The deadliest and most important battle of the war ensued from July 1 to 3, 1863, when some 53,000 men were either killed or wounded. Lee could not recover from the losses at Gettysburg and retreated to Virginia once again. The Confederates would not have another victory after Gettysburg.

SHERMAN CONTRIBUTES TO UNION VICTORIES

General Grant chose William Tecumseh Sherman to lead Union troops through the South. After winning the battle of Kennesaw Mountain in Georgia, Sherman's army captured Atlanta in September of 1864, but not before the Confederates had burned the city in retreat. Marching with some 100,000 men after winning the battle of Atlanta, Sherman cut a 60-mile swath through the heart of the South on his way to South Carolina. Sherman's **scorched-earth** policy ordered troops to burn and destroy fields, homes, and cities as they marched through Georgia. Sherman's goal was to inflict such misery on Southerners that they would be compelled to surrender. This strategy made the Civil War perhaps the first "modern war" in that civilians and their property became targets. Sherman was able to capture Savannah, Georgia, in December 1864 and finally Columbia, South Carolina, in February of 1865. By this time, Grant's forces in Virginia were on the verge of victory.

SOUTHERN SURRENDER AND ASSASSINATION

Lee's troop strength was wearing thin by the time his army abandoned the Confederate capital of Richmond, Virginia, in April 1865. Knowing that the end was near, Confederate leaders wished to negotiate with President Lincoln for peace terms. Lincoln refused anything short of an unconditional surrender of the South and a restoration of the Union; Jefferson Davis still clung to the dream of Southern independence. General Lee, surrounded by General Grant's forces west of Richmond, agreed to surrender. On April 9, 1865, the Confederate Army of Northern Virginia officially surrendered in the parlor of the house owned by Wilmer McLean in **Appomattox Court House, Virginia**. Tragically, President Lincoln would only relish the Union's victory for less than a week. He was assassinated by Southern sympathizer **John Wilkes Booth** on April 14, 1865, while attending a play in Ford's Theatre.

THE END OF SLAVERY AND FREE BLACKS

Ever the savvy politician, Abraham Lincoln had been extremely cautious with regard to the issue of slavery. As president, Lincoln was a master at gauging public opinion and reacting to it accordingly. Therefore, he understood that he needed to connect with residents of the Border States, prejudiced Northerners, and all types of American voters. He calculated the timing of his speeches and actions to coincide with the waves of public opinion and military victories.

In the first years of the war, the federal government passed Confiscation Acts designed to allow Union troops to seize enemy property that could be used in an act of war. Slaves fit under the loose definition of "property" and could, thus, be confiscated. The second of these acts freed slaves in any territory that was currently in rebellion against the Union. These were the first steps in the emancipation of slaves.

After the Battle of Antietam in September 1862, President Lincoln properly calculated that the nation was ready for a shift from an "offensive war" to save the Union to a "total war" to rectify a moral wrong. As promised after Antietam, the president issued the **Emancipation Proclamation** on January 1, 1863. The proclamation only applied to slaves living in Confederate states; slavery in the Border States was still legal. Despite its limitations, the proclamation did much to bolster the morale of Union troops and supporters at home. But it was not without its critics. Many in the North, particularly those in the border states, felt that Lincoln had gone too far. Moreover, many soldiers in the Union army felt betrayed by the proclamation, believing they had been duped into fighting a war for emancipation instead of merely for the Union's preservation. This discontent helped to fuel the New York Draft Riots. Nonetheless, the next great step toward emancipation had been taken.

The only remaining obstacle to freedom for slaves was the Constitution. Since its ratification, interpretations of the document either ignored the slavery issue or protected the institution and slave owners. President Lincoln would need an amendment to the Constitution to realize fully the Emancipation Proclamation and offer freedom to the slaves in the border states. The president worked tirelessly to garner enough votes in Congress to secure passage of what would become the **Thirteenth Amendment**. Sadly, President Lincoln was assassinated before he would see the amendment, which abolished slavery in the United States once and for all, ratified.

Even before ratification of the Thirteenth Amendment, thousands of **freedmen** had flocked to the North in search of refuge. Many joined the Union army, serving in segregated units, while others worked in supporting jobs along the battlefields. In fact, President Lincoln eventually credited the 180,000 African Americans who fought for the Union as having turned the tide of the war. The South simply could not compete with the overwhelming economic power of the North or the manpower of the Union army. However, not until after the war's end were full-scale efforts were made to assimilate former slaves into American society.

SOCIAL, POLITICAL, AND ECONOMIC CONSEQUENCES OF THE WAR

No part of America was left untouched, as a war of "brother against brother" had raged on for four long and bloody years. The North and the South lost a generation of able young men to death and injury, a loss that would take many years to recover from. About 2 percent of the American population, or 620,000 men, had lost their lives in the war. Over a million others had been wounded.

During and after the war, the plight of poverty became feminized, as many women suddenly became heads of the household because of the death or desertion of husbands. With men away fighting, women found themselves working the fields and in factories as well as at home. Women played a critical role on the battlefield as nurses and behind the lines as volunteers in veterans' hospitals. The Civil War opened doors for women and would give many the courage to fight for suffrage rights at the turn of the 20th century.

IMMEDIATE CONSEQUENCES

In 1865, the United States gained about 4 million new citizens instantly. With the ratification of the Thirteenth Amendment, these newly freed African Americans now had to find a place in the American social structure.

Southern whites came to the realization that their way of life would be forever altered and struggled to find peace among the chaos.

During the Civil War, President Lincoln exercised his power as the executive to limit Americans' civil rights and liberties to protect the Union. He suspended the **writ of habeas corpus**, which meant that the federal government could hold an individual in jail with no charges levied against him or her. For many "traitors," this meant long jail terms with no charges ever filed. Even though Lincoln suspended this guaranteed constitutional right, he planned for it to be restored as soon as the war was over.

The major long-term effect of the Civil War was a shift of political ideology away from one that protected states' rights to one that emphasized the preservation of Union and the supremacy of the federal government. The concept of "democracy" was expanded, as new African American citizens were guaranteed the rights and protections of the Constitution that whites had enjoyed since 1789. Much to the chagrin of many conservatives in Europe, the American experiment of democracy had survived a major challenge and looked more powerful than ever.

Economically, the war was devastating for the South—its infrastructure and industry stood in ruins. Jefferson's dream of an agrarian empire soon faded as the energy of the country shifted into industrializing the nation. During the recovery phase, many Northerners would move into the South to assist newly freed African Americans in their transition and to help organize the reconstruction of Southern governments.

Northerners experienced an industrial boom due to wartime demand for manufactured goods. Many amassed great fortunes by profiteering off of highly priced necessities, while average factory workers saw no improvement in their standard of living. The west benefited from wartime acts designed to stimulate settlement on the frontier. The **Homestead Act of 1862** granted 160 acres to any family that would agree to farm it for at least five years. The **Morrill Land Grant Act of 1862** gave federal lands to states for the purpose of building schools that would teach agriculture and technical trades. Perhaps most significantly, the **Pacific Railway Act of 1862** approved the building of a transcontinental railroad that would utterly transform the west by linking the Atlantic Ocean with the Pacific.

The Civil War resulted in devastating losses in population, wealth, and land, and the reunified United States would have a harrowing journey ahead, as the task of rebuilding the nation was at hand.

PRESIDENTIAL AND RADICAL RECONSTRUCTION

As the Civil War came to an end, the federal government had to figure out what to do with the former Confederate states that were buried under the weight of economic and physical destruction. Questions abounded about the treatment of Confederate leaders, the readmittance of former Confederate states into the Union, and the assimilation of 4 million freedmen and freedwomen into the social fabric of the nation. Standing in the way of any decision-making process were particular American views of government. As before the Civil War, Americans feared a large, powerful federal government. However, without the federal government leading the way to rebuild the nation, **Reconstruction** would be over before it started.

Many Americans believed that to reap the benefits of a democratic society, all one needed to do was work hard. Thus, when it came time to assist newly freed slaves begin their lives anew, white Americans were reluctant to provide too much assistance—they felt African Americans should work hard and earn their new place in the slave-free society. The enormous task of reconciling North and South fell upon the shoulders of President Andrew Johnson and Congress.

ASSIMILATING FORMER SOUTHERN STATES AND SLAVES

Before his assassination, President Lincoln had formulated some provisions for the rebuilding of the Union. His **Proclamation of Amnesty and Reconstruction** was issued in 1863 as a way to bring Southern states back under the wing of the federal government. The readmission process would begin with the re-establishment of state governments, which would gain legitimacy by having at least 10 percent of their voting populace swear an oath of loyalty to the United States and the Constitution. Secondly, the president was prepared to grant complete **pardons** to any former Confederate, as long as he also took the oath of allegiance and agreed to the elimination of slavery. Fellow Republicans were not thrilled with Lincoln's plan and decided to pass legislation of their own that would create a few more obstacles to full incorporation of former rebellious states. The **Wade-Davis Bill** was passed in 1864 by both houses. It required that 50 percent of Southern state voters take the oath of loyalty and allowed only those citizens who had not been active members or supporters of the Confederacy to approve of the new state constitutions. Exercising his executive power, President Lincoln pocket-vetoed the bill by refusing to sign it until after Congress had gone into recess.

To manage and assist the newly emancipated slaves of the nation, the federal government created the **Freedman's Bureau** in 1865. The bureau provided assistance in the form of food, shelter, and medical attention to African Americans. Eventually, the bureau would establish schools across the South and help to educate large numbers of former slaves. The Freedman's Bureau struggled as Congress refused to increase its funding, which expired in 1872.

THE UNEASY RULE OF ANDREW JOHNSON

After Lincoln's assassination, it looked as if President Johnson would continue his predecessor's basic Reconstruction plan, with some added conditions on former Confederates. Keeping

Lincoln's **10 Percent Plan**, Johnson added the disenfranchisement of some former Confederates, namely those who had been in leadership positions or who had assets of $250,000 or more. Johnson retained his right to grant full pardons to these former Confederates, which he exercised freely among the planter elite of the South. As a result, many former Confederate leaders and wealthy plantation owners were back in Congress as early as the end of 1865.

Johnson was no friend of Republican members of Congress, who felt that he was too friendly with the old Confederate guard and were angered by his continual refusal to support the rights of African Americans. With the congressional elections of 1866 just around the corner, Johnson decided to travel the country to bash his congressional foes and gain votes. Johnson took to the road in his "swing around the circle" tour, lodging attacks on his opponents who were running for congressional re-election. They did not sit by and allow Johnson to beat them to the punch, instead countering with accusations of alcoholism and anti-Unionism. In return, Republicans running for office resorted to emotionalism by "waving the bloody shirt," or invoking the pain of the Civil War for Northern voters in an attempt to turn them against Democrats. The election yielded a Republican victory, with moderates and radicals gaining more than a two-thirds majority in both houses.

The Republicans in Congress felt they had better ideas when it came to Reconstruction. Fearing a return of the Southern Democratic contingency, Republicans became more and more radical in their views as the election of 1866 forced them to work with Johnson, who was already in the White House.

THE BLACK CODES

While Congress was on hiatus, Southern legislatures adopted **Black Codes** to restrict the actions, movements, and freedoms of African Americans. Under these codes, African Americans could not own land, so they were tied instead to small plots leased from a landowner.

This began the system of **sharecropping**, in which African Americans were bound to the land under the crop-lien system. Sharecroppers would "lease" land and borrow supplies to till their plots, while giving a significant portion of their harvest to the landowner as payment for the "lien" or "loan." Never able to harvest quite enough to pay the landlord and feed their families, generations of African Americans remained tied to their plot of land until the civil rights movement of the 1950s and 1960s. Having refused to sign legislation that would revive the dying Freedman's Bureau and protect African Americans from the Black Codes, President Johnson assured himself a fight with Congress as he served out the remainder of his term.

THE FOURTEENTH AMENDMENT

Congressional or Radical Reconstruction occurred as many former Confederates took office. Republicans were furious that these former "rebels" were being allowed to rejoin Congress and were further angered by President Johnson's backtracking with regard to civil rights. After they modified the bill that would restore the Freedman's Bureau, Radical Republicans set out to protect the civil rights of African Americans. The **Civil Rights Bill of 1866** was designed to destroy the Black Codes by giving African Americans full citizenship. As expected, President Johnson vetoed the bill, and Congress overturned his veto. Many Republicans were concerned that a return of a Democratic majority in the future might mean the end of the bill they had worked so hard to pass. Therefore, they needed a more permanent solution to the civil rights problem. Proposed by Congress in 1866 and finally ratified in 1868, the **Fourteenth Amendment** protected the rights of all U.S. citizens, granted all African Americans full citizenship and civil rights, and required states to adhere to the due process and equal protection clauses of the Constitution. Furthermore, radical Republicans added some provisions aimed directly at the former Confederacy, which disallowed former Confederate officers from holding state or federal office and would decrease the proportional representation of any state that denied suffrage to any able citizen.

MORE TROUBLES FOR JOHNSON

Radical Republicans took aim directly at President Johnson when they outright rejected presidential Reconstruction and instead passed the Military Reconstruction Act of 1867 and then sought to remove him from office in 1868 by impeachment. The **Military Reconstruction Act** divided the South into five districts that would be governed by a Union general stationed there—in other words, martial law was in effect. The act further tightened the requirements for the readmission of former Confederate states by requiring petitioning states to ratify the Fourteenth Amendment and provide for universal manhood suffrage.

The impeachment crisis began when congressional Republicans passed the **Tenure of Office Act,** disallowing the executive to discharge a federal appointee without the express consent of the Senate. The act was an attempt by Republicans in Congress to protect their numbers from the angry hand of Johnson. The president chose to ignore the act and fired Secretary of War Edwin Stanton, who happened to be a Republican. The House of Representatives promptly submitted articles of impeachment to the floor by charging Johnson with 11 counts of "high crimes and misdemeanors." He was duly impeached by the House, but the Senate failed to convict Johnson by only one vote.

THE FIFTEENTH AMENDMENT

Needless to say, Johnson did not run for the presidency in 1868. The Republican nomination went to the Civil War hero Ulysses S. Grant, who eked out a win by gaining a large boost from the African American vote. During his tenure, radical Republicans such as Representative Thaddeus Stephens and Senator Charles Sumner continued pushing for the protection of civil rights in Southern states. The **Fifteenth Amendment** barred any state from abridging a citizen's right to vote on the basis of race, color, or previous servitude. The last of the Reconstruction-era civil rights acts was passed in 1875. This act made it a crime for any person to be denied full and equal use of public places, such as hotels, rail cars, restaurants, and theaters. Unfortunately this last act had a major shortcoming: It lacked any wording that would provide for enforcement of the law. The law was simply ignored by the majority of states, both Northern and Southern. It would take another 90 years before Congress penned an enforceable civil rights act.

DREAMS, SUCCESSES, AND REALITIES—SOUTHERN GOVERNMENTS

Despite being under federal martial law, Southern states hoped to return to statehood and quickly regain some semblance of stability. In the eyes of the Republicans on Capitol Hill, how quickly these state governments were recognized as legitimate depended on how soon the federal government's demands were met. African Americans soon realized the power of the vote, taking control of the lower house in South Carolina and seating several black representatives and senators in Congress. However, whites still maintained majority control of all other upper and lower houses and the governorships in all Southern states.

The Democrats remained the party of choice for Southerners, although the Republican Party did gain some strength through freedmen and Northerners who moved south. Southern Democrats named Southern Republicans **scalawags**, a derogatory term that meant they were pirates who sought to steal from state governments to line their own pockets. Northern Republicans who moved south to seek their fortunes were called **carpetbaggers**, a term that came from the stereotype of the Northerner who packed all of his worldly possessions in a suitcase made from carpet. Many white Southerners resented any incursion by Northerners, even if they were only in the South to aid in the rebuilding process.

Although tensions ran high during the military Reconstruction period, Southern governments did manage to piece together several successes. The South had never been a haven for solid public education. Reconstruction Southern legislatures created a system to provide state-funded public education. Southern infrastructure was given a boost as well, with the public rebuilding and improvement of roads, rail lines, and waterways. Hospitals and prisons were also modernized. Republican legislatures funded these improvements through better tax codes and collection services.

All was not harmonious, however, as Southerners continued to suspect wrongdoing among the Republicans. There were accusations of Republicans taking advantage of the weak Southern system by siphoning off monies. Many legislators were alleged to have arranged for government contractors to give them gifts of money in return for contracts. Others allegedly received bribes from companies and individuals who sought to bilk the system. Washington scandals, such as Crédit Mobilier, in the Grant administration did not help the Republicans shake off this perception.

Despite ratification of the Fourteenth and Fifteenth Amendments, racism still existed, and angry whites in the South sometimes resorted to violence to intimidate blacks. One of the most infamous examples was the **Ku Klux Klan**, an underground society of whites who ruthlessly and successfully used terrorist tactics to frighten both white and black Republicans in the South. Congress sought to abolish the Klan with the **Force Acts** of 1870 and 1871, which authorized the use of federal troops to quell violence and enforce the Fourteenth and Fifteenth Amendments. While these acts were moderately successful in limiting the Klan's activities, the group continued to exist, resurfacing in the 1920s in response to an influx of Southern and Eastern European immigrants.

There was also a growing movement to restore political control of the South to Southerners. This movement was fueled by a increasing resentment of any governing of Southern states by outsiders operating under the Reconstruction Acts. Those who wished to return control of the South to Southerners came to be known as the **Redeemers**.

FREEDMEN IN THE POSTWAR SOUTH

Reconstruction was a very confusing time for African Americans in the South—many were never told they had been emancipated. Slaves would be freed by Union armies marching through their region and then re-enslaved as soon as the soldiers left. Other plantation owners simply refused to recognize the Thirteenth Amendment and kept their "property." For their part, slaves themselves varied in their response to their newfound freedom. Some joyfully ran from the plantation looking for a new life. Others were reluctant to exercise their new freedom and initially remained with their masters. Yet others reacted with violence when freed by ransacking the main house or burning the fields. Eventually, all slaves in the South were freed, under federal martial law.

Once free, many went in search of a new life or to find family members and friends. Encouraged by a former slave named Ben Singleton, as many as 25,000 former slaves uprooted their families and moved toward Kansas between 1878 and 1880. These migrants called themselves **Exodusters**, because they believed that somewhere in the west lay their promised land. Word of their travels, as well as rumors about the federal government "setting aside" the entire state of Kansas for former slaves, spread through the vast church networks that connected black families across the South. The church became the central focus for most African Americans during the postwar period. It was here that one could receive comfort, food, and advice all under one roof.

"Forty acres and a mule" were supposed to make it into the hands of former slaves from confiscated Confederate land as per the Special Field Orders, no. 15, which were issued by General Sherman during his march through the South. However, the orders were in effect for only one year, and the promise went unfulfilled.

CREATION OF THE FREEDMEN'S BUREAU

Created in 1865 to assist in the assimilation of former slaves into American society, the Freedmen's Bureau acted as a pseudo-welfare agency in the early postwar years. Given the task of feeding, clothing, housing, and educating freed slaves and poor whites in the South, the Freedmen's Bureau struggled to stay alive throughout Reconstruction.

COMPROMISE OF 1877

The election of 1876 brought Republican **Rutherford B. Hayes** to the White House, but not without a fight. When the polls closed and the votes were counted, Democrat Samuel Tilden had won the popular vote. However, there was a problem with the electoral votes of three Southern states that Tilden needed to take the presidency. A federal commission was appointed to investigate and decide who should take the contested votes. The commission was made up of both Republicans and Democrats, and in-fighting between the parties on the commission led to the Democrats threatening a **filibuster** that would send the decision to the House of Representatives for a vote. As the Democrats held the majority, the Republicans changed their tactics, and the outcome of the election was ultimately decided by an unwritten negotiation. The **Compromise of 1877** provided that Rutherford B. Hayes would become president only if he agreed to remove the last remaining federal troops stationed in South Carolina, Florida, and Louisiana. The end of martial law in the South signaled the end of Reconstruction in the United States.

THE IMPACT OF RECONSTRUCTION

Historians today still cannot agree on the overall impact and effectiveness of the Reconstruction. It is clear, however, that white Southerners emerged from the Civil War and Reconstruction embittered and angry. They believed that their way of life had been forever altered and that they would not in their lifetimes see the South reclaim the glory of prewar days. Southerners were also angry about Northern interference in their politics and daily lives and the protections provided to African Americans by the federal government. As a result, many white Southerners turned radical in their resentment of freedmen and Northerners.

It is evident that President Lincoln, President Johnson, and Congress had no clear plan regarding how to change the postwar South. Republicans as a whole seemed to enter Reconstruction with rose-colored glasses of idealism and to leave exhausted by the reality of the process. By offering pardons and "quick" readmittance for former Confederate states, it was hoped that the South would readily rejoin the Union. Republicans in Congress, however, wished to protect the rights of African Americans while also advancing their own political agenda. Unfortunately for African Americans, it was the political agenda of Republicans that would ultimately stand in their path to realizing full rights and protections. In the end, African Americans were no longer held as involuntary servants, but they were widely relegated to inferior positions through economic, political, and social restrictions of their rights. Most found themselves trapped in a cycle of poverty due to the sharecropping system and without the rights and privileges guaranteed them in the Fourteenth and Fifteenth Amendments. In many respects, the prewar South was revived by the actions of Republicans who had sought to dismantle it once and for all. The social and political atmosphere of the postwar South would last well into the next century.

UNIT 5: REVIEW QUESTIONS

Multiple-Choice Questions

Directions: Choose the best answer choice for the following questions.

Questions 1–4 refer to the following figure.

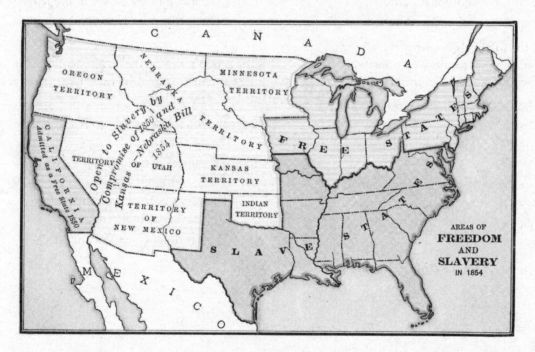

Freedom and Slavery in 1854, 1854
Charles Kendall Adams, *A History of the United States*, Boston, MA, Allyn and Bacon, 1909

1. The situation illustrated in the map was most clearly

   (A) a source of increased sectional conflict in the antebellum years

   (B) resolved by the decision in the *Dred Scott* case

   (C) a direct cause of U.S. entry into the Mexican American War

   (D) reflected in the strengthening of political party unity in the 1850s

2. The alignment of free and slaves states shown on the map directly led to

   (A) the passage of the Northwest Ordinance

   (B) the formation of the Republican Party

   (C) repudiation of manifest destiny

   (D) an increase in nativist sentiment

3. Opponents of the Kansas-Nebraska Act most likely supported

   (A) a continuation of the Missouri Compromise

   (B) a Free Soil position

   (C) expansion of suffrage to free blacks and women

   (D) annexation of additional territory

4. Which of the following events of the mid to late 20th century represents a continuation of the controversy illustrated in the map above?

   (A) Continued continental territorial expansion

   (B) Expansion of state segregation laws into the North

   (C) Resistance to development of the trans-Mississippi West

   (D) Challenges to states' rights

5. Which of the following groups would most likely support the perspective of the cartoon?

   (A) Supporters of the *Dred Scott* decision

   (B) Northern opponents of the war

   (C) Radical Republicans

   (D) Southern politicians

6. The situation portrayed in the cartoon most directly led to

   (A) Lincoln's decision to issue the Emancipation Proclamation

   (B) the emergence of sectional parties

   (C) the passage of the Fourteenth and Fifteenth Amendments

   (D) contraction in the power of the federal government

7. The action taken by the states mentioned in the cartoon most clearly shows the influence of which of the following?

   (A) The founding fathers' ability to resolve the slave question

   (B) Guarantees of European military and financial support for the Confederacy

   (C) The democratic philosophy of the Declaration of Independence

   (D) The creation of a national unified economy

Questions 5–7 refer to the following figure.

*Names written on illustrations include North Carolina, Tennessee, Mississippi, Kentucky, Missouri, Florida, Louisiana, Texas, Alabama, South Carolina, Virginia, and Baltimore.

Questions 8–11 refer to the following quote.

"... Disloyalty ... of any kind was a punishable offense ... If a newspaper promulgated disloyal sentiments, the paper was suppressed and the editor imprisoned. If a clergyman was disloyal in prayer or sermon, or if he failed to utter a prescribed prayer, he was liable to be treated in the same manner, and was sometimes so treated. A learned and eloquent Lutheran clergyman came to me for advice because he had been summoned before the provost marshal for saying that a nation which incurred a heavy debt in the prosecution of war laid violent hands on the harvests of the future; but his offense was condoned, because it appeared that he had referred to the "Thirty Years' War" and had made no direct reference to the debt of the United States, and perhaps for a better reason—that he had strong Republican friends among his congregation."

—*Baltimore and the Nineteenth of April, 1861: A Study of the War* by George William Brown, Chief Judge of the Supreme Bench of Baltimore and Mayor of the City in 1861

8. The situations described in the passage most clearly relate to

(A) support for Radical Reconstruction planning

(B) the success of Confederate strategy in mobilizing popular support

(C) Republican support for the Confederate cause

(D) Union concern over the allegiance of the border states

9. The controversy highlighted in the passage above most directly led to

(A) improvements in the Union's military leadership

(B) enlisting African Americans in the Union Army

(C) the establishment of martial law in some areas

(D) the opening of political opportunities for former slaves

10. Which of the following groups would most likely support the beliefs of the Lutheran clergyman expressed in the previous passage?

(A) Opponents of the Civil War

(B) Proponents of the Emancipation Proclamation

(C) Advocates of public education

(D) Detractors of sharecropping

11. The aforementioned events most clearly reflect which of the following continuities in United States history?

(A) Tensions between liberty and authority

(B) The changing relationship among the branches of the federal government

(C) The competition for territory and resources

(D) The expansion of religious freedom and toleration

Questions 12–15 refer to the following quote.

"With malice toward none, with charity for all, with firmness in the right as God gives us to see the right, let us strive on to finish the work we are in, to bind up the nation's wounds, to care for him who shall have borne the battle and for his widow and his orphan, to do all which may achieve and cherish a just and lasting peace among ourselves and with all nations."

—Abraham Lincoln's Second Inaugural Address, Saturday, March 4, 1865

12. The ideas expressed in the passage most directly led to the political controversies of the 1860s and 1870s over the

    (A) role of the federal government in settlement of the West

    (B) process of reconstructing the United States in the aftermath of war

    (C) authority of the states to promote economic development

    (D) extension of American democratic values abroad

13. Which of the following groups would most likely object to the perspective in the passage?

    (A) Radical Republicans

    (B) Moderate Republicans

    (C) Southern Democrats

    (D) Northern Democrats

14. Which of the following actions from the mid to late 19th century most closely parallels the ideas expressed in the passage?

    (A) Ratification of the Fourteenth and Fifteenth Amendments

    (B) Passage of state ratification laws

    (C) Expansion of the women's rights movement

    (D) Ratification of the Thirteenth Amendment

15. The previous beliefs most clearly reflect which of the following continuities in United States history?

    (A) Tensions between the executive and judicial branches

    (B) Changing relationship between state and local governments

    (C) Social change more difficult to achieve than political change

    (D) American military actions' impact on world politics

Short-Answer Questions

1. "When it became evident that the war [with Mexico] would result in the expansion of the United States to the southwest the question of the extension of slavery into the region to be acquired was raised; and, as Calhoun and other leaders had foreseen . . . a fierce struggle . . . was precipitated. Mississippi was prepared by the course of its development to align itself with the other states of the South in defense of the extension of slavery; but it did not assume a leading part in the beginning of the struggle . . . Mississippi awaited the initiative of the older slaveholding states to which the South was accustomed to look for leadership . . . "

   —Cleo Carson Hearon, *Mississippi and the Compromise of 1850*, 1913

   For this question, answer parts A, B, and C:

   (A) Based on the passage, explain the political relationship between the newer and older slaveholding states in the South.

   (B) Provide ONE piece of evidence from the period between 1820 and 1860, and explain how it supports a contention of the author.

   (C) Provide ONE OTHER piece of evidence from the period between 1820 and 1860 and explain how it supports a contention of the author.

2. "We affirm that these ends for which this Government [United States Government] was instituted have been defeated, and the Government itself has been made destructive of them by the action of the non-slaveholding States. Those States have assumed the right of deciding upon the propriety of our domestic institutions; and have denied the rights of property established in fifteen of the States and recognized by the Constitution; they have denounced as sinful the institution of slavery; they have permitted open establishment among them of societies, whose avowed object is to disturb the peace and to eloign the property of the citizens of other States. They have encouraged and assisted thousands of our slaves to leave their homes; and those who remain, have been incited by emissaries, books and pictures to servile insurrection."

   —Declaration of the Immediate Causes that Compel South Carolina to Leave the Union, 1860

Clashing political values and arguments escalated shortly before the Civil War. Use the passage and your knowledge of United States history to answer parts A, B, and C.

(A) Explain how South Carolina used either provisions from the Declaration of Independence or the United States Constitution to justify its secession.

(B) Explain how the non-slaveholding states used provisions from the Declaration of Independence to justify their reactions to the statement of South Carolina.

(C) Explain how the non-slaveholding states used provisions from the United States Constitution to justify their reactions to the statement of South Carolina.

Document-Based Question

Directions: Question 1 is based on the accompanying documents. The documents have been edited for the purpose of this exercise. You are advised to spend 15 minutes planning and 40 minutes writing your answer. Write your responses on the lined pages that follow the questions.

1. Analyze the impact of the Civil War on the economic, political, and social development of the United States during the period 1860–1877.

DOCUMENT 1

"... On the 25th of May, Mr. John Merryman, of Baltimore County, was arrested ... and confined in Fort McHenry. The next day ... his counsel ... presented a petition for the writ of *habeas corpus* to Chief Justice Taney, who issued the writ immediately ... [A couple of days later] a[n] aide-de-camp, came into court with a letter ... directed to the Chief Justice, stating that Mr. Merryman had been arrested on charges of high treason, and ... [which] ... authorized by the President of the United States in such cases to suspend the writ of *habeas corpus* for the public safety.

A startling issue was thus presented. The venerable Chief Justice had come from Washington to Baltimore for the purpose of issuing a writ of *habeas corpus,* and the President had thereupon authorized the commander of the fort to hold the prisoner and disregard the writ ... "

Baltimore and the Nineteenth of April 1861: A Study of the War by George William Brown, Chief Judge of the Supreme Bench of Baltimore and Mayor of the City in 1861 (1887)

DOCUMENT 2

"Office of the Union Pacific
Rail Road Company,
New York 23. Nov. 1863.

Sir:

If the Engineers are ready, it is proposed to break ground on the Pacific Rail Road, on the 1st or 2nd day of next month, at some point in Nebraska, through which, under the Act of Congress, the line will pass. This inauguration of the work will be followed up by early measures to complete, as soon as possible, the grading of one hundred miles of road authorized by the Board of Directors to report under contract.

In view of the vastness of the enterprise, and its probable influence upon the political and commercial prosperity of the country, it would be gratifying to receive a communication from you to be read on the occasion. I have the honor to be,

very respectfully,
Your obt. Servt.
 John A. Dix
Prest. U. P. R. R. Co. [Union Pacific Rail Road Company]"

John A. Dix to Abraham Lincoln, Monday, November 23, 1863

DOCUMENT 3

Labor Contract, 1866

"Transcript:

Bureau R.F. & A.L.

10th District, LEX. Subdistrict, KENTUCKY

CONTRACT

Know All Men by These Presents, That Abraham Bledsoe of the County of Mason, State of Kentucky, am held and firmly bound to THE UNITED STATES OF AMERICA, in the sum of FIVE HUNDRED DOLLARS, for the payment of which I bind my Heirs, Executors, and Administrators, firmly by these presents, in this contract: That I am to furnish the person whose name is subjoined (free laborer) quarters, fuel, substantial and healthy rations . . . and the amount set opposite his name, per month, one half to be paid at the expiration of every three months, for the services rendered for each three months preceding, the balance at the expiration of the year Henry Bledsoe agrees to work faithfully for the said Abraham Bledsoe obeying all his instructions in good faith, and in case he leaves his service before the expiration of this contract (provided not driven off or maltreated.) He is to forfeit all wages due at the time of his leaving.

Henry Bledsoe Age 17 Rate per month—$6.662/3 or $80 per annum

Said 'Bledsoe' further agrees to increase wages to one hundred dollars per year if he works well and briskly.

This contract is to commence January 1, 1866 and close with the year.

Given in triplicate, at Mayville, this 16th day of June, 1866."

Document 4

"AMENDMENT XIV

Section 1.

All persons born or naturalized in the United States . . . are citizens of the United States and of the State wherein they reside. No State shall make or enforce any law which shall abridge the privileges or immunities of citizens of the United States; nor . . . deprive any person of life, liberty, or property, without due process of law; nor deny to any person within . . . the equal protection of the laws.

Section 2.

Representatives shall be apportioned among the several States according to their respective numbers, counting the whole number of persons . . .

Section 4.

The validity of the public debt of the United States . . . shall not be questioned. But neither the United States nor any State shall assume or pay any debt or obligation incurred in aid of insurrection or rebellion against the United States, or any claim for the loss or emancipation of any slave . . . "

DOCUMENT 5

THE FIRST COLORED SENATOR AND REPRESENTATIVES.
In the 41ˢᵗ and 42ⁿᵈ Congress of the United States.

Published by Currier & Ives, 1872

DOCUMENT 6

"After the Civil War, our people had no money. We became a one-crop people. Cotton was ready money. Northern manufacturers and western farmers encouraged this, and we were without scientific knowledge. Speculators manipulated all the profit out of cotton by a system of exchanges, grades, and quotations. A system of credit was inaugurated by the State Lien Law. By this system the farmer paid tribute to the local Caesar, twenty-five to fifty times the price for plantation supplies."

Source: Mrs. Ella Gooding (aged 80) and her husband Robert (aged 82) lived in Winnsboro, South Carolina, when they were interviewed by the WPA Federal Writers Project in the 1938.

ANSWERS AND EXPLANATIONS

MULTIPLE-CHOICE ANSWERS

1. A

Concern over the free or slave status of the territory gained from Mexico increased sectional tensions in the late 1840s. After 1850, when California came in as a free state, upsetting the sectional balance in the U.S. Senate, the slave or free status of future states led to the outbreak of a civil war in Kansas.

2. B

Increasing tension over the possible expansion of slavery into the Kansas and Nebraska territories, due to the popular sovereignty provision in the Kansas-Nebraska Act, led to a major party realignment in the mid-1850s, including the creation of the Republican party.

3. B

Opponents of the Kansas-Nebraska Act included Republicans and others who wanted free soil or no extension of slavery into any additional territories, whether they were gained from Mexico or previously acquired in other territorial acquisitions.

4. D

The modern civil rights movement of the mid-1950s and 1960s continued the states' rights arguments unresolved during the Reconstruction era.

5. C

This 1861 political cartoon is strongly anti-Confederate, referring to those who supported secession as traitors. Moderate Republicans, such as Abraham Lincoln, did not want to destroy the secessionists. Radical Republicans were more punitive toward the South.

6. A

Lincoln's primary goal in fighting the Civil War, namely to keep the nation united, changed in 1863 with the Emancipation Proclamation. It broadened the goals of the war to include abolishing slavery,

although technically only in Confederate areas still in rebellion. The Emancipation Proclamation can be considered a turning point of the war.

7. C

Southern states, beginning with South Carolina, referred to the right of revolution, or the ability to alter or change a government when it no longer served the needs of the people, in justifying their secession. This idea of a social contract is a central concept to the democratic philosophy in the Declaration of Independence.

8. D

The loyalty or allegiance of the border states—slave states that remained in the Union such as Maryland—led to actions that challenged the constitutional rights of residents. The selection details life in Maryland during the early years of the Civil War and not Radical Republican planning for Reconstruction, which would develop in the coming years.

9. C

Concern over the loyalty of the border states led to the establishment of martial law in Maryland in 1861. This gave the military authority over the civilian population.

10. A

Opponents of the Civil War cited many reasons, including the huge financial cost to be paid by future generations, ambivalence at changing the goals of the war, hostility over the draft, concern over constitutional violations, and the concerns over the incredible loss of life.

11.   A

Challenges to freedom of speech, press, and expression became part of an effort to ensure that the border states remained in the Union during the Civil War. This tension between civil liberties and the authority of the nation often appears during wartime, e.g., the Alien and Sedition Acts of 1798 and the Sedition Act passed during World War I.

12.   B

In the aftermath of the Civil War, the United States went through several Reconstruction plans. President Lincoln, in his second inaugural address, introduced the philosophy for what would become his Ten Percent Plan.

13.   A

In contrast to Lincoln's call for ending Reconstruction as quickly as possible, Radicals within his own party wanted to treat the South as "conquered provinces." They created a much harsher policy in dealing with the South. Moderates initially sided with Lincoln. Democrats in both the North and South preferred Lincoln's position to that of his Radical critics.

14.   D

The Thirteenth Amendment's abolishment of slavery fulfilled the promise of the Emancipation Proclamation. Ratification of the Fourteenth and Fifteenth Amendments occurred after Lincoln's death.

15.   C

Despite Lincoln's call for moderation and tolerance, the aftermath of the war led to increased controversy. The political and constitutional changes of the Civil War/Reconstruction era failed to alter many of the social beliefs and attitudes of the 19th century.

SHORT-ANSWER QUESTIONS RESPONSES

1. (A) According to the author, Mississippi and possibly other, newer, slave states in the cotton-growing Deep South looked to political leadership from older slaveholding states such as Virginia or South Carolina. Southern states supported the expansion of slavery into the territory gained from Mexico as a way to ensure a sectional balance in the Senate.

   (B) The newer slave states of the Deep South tended to have a higher proportion of their total population enslaved and a higher percentage of their crops in cotton or sugar compared to the Old South. Even before South Carolina became the first state to secede from the Union after Lincoln's election, South Carolina had led the nullification crisis associated with the 1828 and 1832 tariffs.

   (C) Virginia was an influential slave state that maintained political leadership. As part of the Compromise of 1850, a Virginian drafted the Fugitive Slave Act, which required free states to return slaves to their owners in the South. Virginia was influential in supporting slavery and protecting the "rights" of slaveowners.

2. (A) South Carolina's 1860 secession statement draws upon the "right of revolution" argument in the Declaration of Independence. The concept of a social contract, an Enlightenment ideal, held that if the government no longer fulfilled the wishes of the people/populace, the government could be altered or abolished. South Carolina held that its compact with the United States government had been dissolved since the federal government was not keeping Northern states from encroaching on its property rights, namely slavery.

   (B) Abolitionists referred to the Declaration of Independence as a founding document that guaranteed all men are created equal. In addition, that all men have the freedom to pursue life, liberty, and happiness. The institution of slavery directly contradicted these principles. After the stricter Fugitive Slave Law passed as part of the Compromise of 1850, several Northern states passed personal liberty laws. These state laws tried to circumvent the stricter national law by using their reserved powers as contained in the Tenth Amendment to the United States Constitution to pass these personal liberty laws. Abolitionist speakers and societies, such as the Grimke sisters and Frederick Douglas, also exercised their constitutional rights of freedom of speech, press, and public assembly in their protests against the institution of slavery.

   (C) After the stricter Fugitive Slave Law passed as part of the Compromise of 1850, several Northern states passed personal liberty laws. These state laws tried to circumvent the stricter national law by using their reserved powers as contained in the TenthAmendment to the United States Constitution to pass these personal liberty laws. Abolitionist speakers and societies, such as the Grimke sisters and Frederick Douglas, also exercised their constitutional rights of freedom of speech, press, and public assembly in their protests againstthe institution of slavery.

DBQ Sample Response

In the early to mid-1860s, the United States, under the leadership of Abraham Lincoln, sought to keep the Union together during the devastation of the American Civil War. The demands and challenges of fighting a war that divided a nation, a war with changing goals, and a war that challenged the existing notions of freedom led to controversy and heated debate. Economically, the United States emerged into the beginnings of the second industrial revolution, leaving the devastated South to adjust to a post-slave plantation reality. Politically, the federal government gained power at the expense of the states and the former slaves sought to realize their new constitutional guarantees. Socially, those who resisted and resented the Freedmen sought to turn back gains made. The United States that emerged from the Civil War and the various stages of Reconstruction did so with distinction—a strengthened federal government, a national economy poised to burst into the second industrial revolution although with regional devastation, and a social system thrown into upheaval with the end of slavery.

When the South left the Union after Lincoln's election and the fall of Fort Sumter, the Union Congress passed a series of laws that would have a great economic impact in the latter half of the 19th century. Laws reminiscent of Henry Clay's American system included a stronger banking system and support for a transcontinental railroad. John Dix's letter to Lincoln (Doc. 2) recognizes the "vastness of the enterprise" in both the size of the project and its potential national impact. Although railroads had expanded dramatically in the 1850s, it wasn't until after the war that a number of transcontinental railroad lines were completed, beginning with the joining of the Union and Pacific railroads in Promontory Point, Utah, in 1869. After the war, creation of the Freedmen's Bureau sought to help Southerners, white and black, adjust to postwar life. Labor contracts, such as the one signed by Henry Bledsoe (Doc. 3), posed a dilemma for the Bureau. Cash and industrial jobs were scarce in the South. Labor contracts bound the Freedmen to the planter class and encouraged the development of a system of sharecropping. In many ways, the labor contracts of the Reconstruction era looked similar to the indentured servant contracts of the colonial era. The crop lien system that developed continued to tie the agricultural workers to the soil in a never-ending cycle of debt. Ella and Robert Gooding (Doc. 6) referred to this as "paying tribute." While industrialization increased in the North after the Civil War, the South's economy lagged behind due to devastation and government policy.

Politically, the federal government's power increased as a result of the Civil War, leading to controversy between the states and the national government and between the branches as well. President Lincoln suspended habeas corpus in the Merryman case (Doc. 1) as part of an effort to keep order and loyalty in the Union. Although Chief Justice Taney disagreed, Lincoln continued to expand presidential power to ensure the Union's victory. Tensions existed among the three branches over how habeas corpus could be constitutionally suspended. The strength of the presidency, as seen with Lincoln, would not be repeated for many years, until after the Reconstruction in 1877. The issue of which branch would control Reconstruction planning led, in part, to President Johnson's impeachment. In addition, ratification of the Thirteenth, Fourteenth, and Fifteenth Amendments to the Constitution (Doc. 4) abolished slavery, defined citizenship, restricted states, and gave black males the right to vote. The Fourteenth Amendment specifically stated that the states had to guarantee equal protection and due process. All of these amendments increased the power of the national government at the expense of that of the states, especially those of the former Confederacy. The Fourteenth and Fifteenth Amendments show the strength of the Radical Republicans in Congress during the latter phase of Reconstruction. These amendments would serve as a point of controversy for the next 90-plus years, leading historians to refer to Reconstruction as an "unfinished revolution."

Socially, the promise of equality proved fleeting for the Freedmen. While the Civil War/Reconstruction amendments seemed to offer the hope and promise of political equality, white Southern Democrats found ways to limit that potential. For a few years during Reconstruction, prominent black leaders (Doc. 5), free blacks, and former slaves, including Hiram Revels and Jefferson Long, were elected to Congress and the Southern state legislatures. The event was noteworthy enough for Currier and Ives to mass produce prints. Freedmen across the South looked to reunite and reconnect with family and friends. The promise, however, was fleeting. While some moved, most Freedmen stayed close to or on the plantations where they had been enslaved. Social equality could not be legislated and black codes emerged. African-American leaders in the years after Reconstruction would challenge the efforts to reintroduce legislated segregation. Nonetheless, emancipation was achieved and the bonds of slavery were broken after some 250 years.

The impact of Civil War actions and legislation resonated long after the war ended. As the nation moved into the Gilded Age and struggled with the problems and concerns of the industrial age, sharecropping increased across the South and the promise of the Reconstruction era amendments was temporarily suspended.

The response starts with a strong thesis that responds to the given question, takes a position, and states how each of the categories—economic, social, and political—will be addressed. In each of the sections, multiple pertinent documents are woven into the answer. Documents are used to support each other, as in the discussion of labor contracts and the crop lien system. Multiple pieces of outside information are included in each paragraph (e.g., Henry Clay's American system, Promontory Point, and UT). Use of documents goes beyond a restatement or summary of the information. The economic and political impacts are better developed than the social ones, but overall it is a well-organized and well-constructed response.

The thesis for this essay would receive the maximum credit of 1 point. The strong use of documents, including analysis, context, and outside information, would earn the maximum 4 points possible. Contextualization is excellent, earning this essay the maximum 1 point. Synthesis is also excellent, earning it the maximum 1 point. This essay would receive a 7 out of 7 possible points on the DBQ rubric.

CHAPTER 18: THE RISE OF BIG BUSINESS

RAILROAD TYCOONS AND ROBBER BARONS

During the Civil War, railroad building in the west took place at a rapid pace as railroad companies sought to earn profits by transporting goods and people between the rapidly growing towns and cities of the region, as well as between the east and west. To help the latter occur, the U.S. government subsidized the building of the transcontinental railroad and gave huge land grants to rail companies who sought to construct rail lines throughout the west.

VANDERBILT'S RAILROAD AND A TRANSCONTINENTAL SUCCESS

The railroad industry already had a foothold in the east, with men such as **Cornelius Vanderbilt** leading modernization of older tracks. Vanderbilt had amassed a fortune in the steamboat business before venturing into rail. He invested his fortune in the conversion of eastern lines to common-gauge steel rails and consolidated many smaller rail lines under one company—the New York Central Railroad. Before Vanderbilt's domination of the industry, there were dozens of small rail lines with varying widths of rail, mostly constructed of iron. Steel rails were safer because they did not rust and were stronger, allowing trains to carry heavier loads. By connecting and consolidating the smaller lines, Vanderbilt linked the major cities on the East Coast and in the Midwest.

The western half of the **transcontinental railroad** was constructed by the congressionally appointed Union Pacific Railroad and Central Pacific Railroad companies. The federal government gave the railroad companies generous land grants and federal loans for each mile of track that was laid as they progressed westward. The **Central Pacific Railroad**, led by Leland Stanford, set out to build the most difficult stretch of rail from Sacramento, California, through the Sierra Nevada mountains and eastward from there. The **Union Pacific** began building its portion of the transcontinental railroad in Council Bluffs, Iowa, moving westward. The rail lines of the Central Pacific and Union Pacific finally met on May 10, 1869, at **Promontory Point**, Utah, just north of the Great Salt Lake. Chinese laborers had been largely responsible for building the Central Pacific's line, while Irish American workers were largely responsible for constructing the Union Pacific's portion of the tracks. The completion of the transcontinental railroad ranks as perhaps the greatest American technological achievement of the 19th century. It linked the nation from sea to sea by both rail and telegraph. Furthermore, this vast railroad helped speed the development and eventual closure of the frontier.

RAILROAD CORRUPTION

Wishing to reap the rewards of land and money, some railroad owners underbuilt their lines or simply defrauded the federal government. Men such as Jay Gould earned the nickname "**robber barons**," as they artificially inflated the value of their company's stock, sold the stock to the public, and pocketed the profits. The company would then go bankrupt, leaving stockholders with nothing. Competition among rail lines was fierce, leading to dishonest businesses practices. Many companies offered rebates or kickbacks to certain high-volume customers, while charging exorbitant rates to smaller shippers, namely farmers. Another system the railroad tycoons invented was the **pool**, whereby competing rail companies would secretly agree to divide up business territories, artificially fix shipping rates, and split the profits among pool members.

The federal government largely kept out of the affairs of big business, with the exception of *Munn v. Illinois*, which the Supreme Court overturned with its decision in *Wabash v. Illinois* (1886). In this case, the Court broadly interpreted the Fourteenth Amendment (equal protection under the law) by deeming corporations to be "citizens" under the Constitution. This interpretation basically insulated corporations such as railroad companies from regulation by state governments.

INDUSTRIAL CONSOLIDATION AND MONOPOLIZATION

The hands-off approach of the federal government toward big business helped to fuel the growth of other large-scale manufacturing ventures after the Civil War. The United States experienced a "second industrial revolution," as the industrial sector of its economy shifted from light manufacturing to heavy industry with steel, oil, and heavy machinery now predominant.

ANDREW CARNEGIE AND THE BIRTH OF A STEEL INDUSTRY

The continued growth of the railroad industry after the Civil War served as a stimulus to the steel industry, since new rails and locomotives were constructed with steel, rather than iron. Thus, steel was the heart of the rise of heavy industry in the postwar period. Henry Bessemer revolutionized the production of steel when he discovered a way to produce it faster and make it stronger. What once took a week or more to produce now could be completed in as little as three hours. A young Scottish immigrant named **Andrew Carnegie** saw a future in the production of steel as he worked his way up in the railroad business in the 1860s. Carnegie emerged as one of the nation's wealthiest men by the late 1880s through his Carnegie Steel Company. By using the Bessemer process to produce steel to satisfy the demand of U.S. businesses, Carnegie soon was responsible for supplying over half of the world's steel. Steel production alone was not responsible for Carnegie's success, however. Carnegie used a business tactic called **vertical integration**, in which he controlled every aspect of the production process for steel from the mining of the ore to the distribution of the finished product. Carnegie was also a philanthropist, giving away much of his immense fortune to establish universities, endow libraries, and infuse culture to cities across the United States.

RISE OF J.P. MORGAN

Eventually, Carnegie retired from the steel business and sold his company to J. P. Morgan, who then created **U.S. Steel**, the country's first billion-dollar corporation. Still headquartered in Pittsburgh, Pennsylvania, U.S. Steel today remains one of the world's top producers of steel products.

ROCKEFELLER'S BUSINESS STRATEGIES

Meanwhile, the discovery of oil in the northwestern Pennsylvania hills in 1859 would revolutionize many other industries throughout the world. As a result, kerosene soon emerged as the fuel of choice for lighting, and the internal combustion engine would make work such as mining and farming faster. Another young businessman saw the potential in this "black gold" and soon joined Carnegie as one of the nation's wealthiest men. **John D. Rockefeller** turned a small petroleum company into a massive monopoly by using the business strategy of **horizontal integration**. Much more damaging to competition than Carnegie's vertical integration, Rockefeller's strategy was to control one aspect of the production process of oil, in this case the refining stage. His **Standard Oil Company** eventually controlled 95 percent of the refineries in the United States by employing the process of consolidation. Rockefeller offered an opportunity for stockholders in competing oil companies to enter a **trust,** in which they would sell him their shares of stock and control in exchange for trust certificates. The board of trustees would then control the business transactions of the now consolidated companies, driving other competitors out of business. Rockefeller was able to undercut his competition by cornering the market and driving prices dramatically downward. As a result, Americans were buying Standard Oil products whether they wanted to or not, as smaller companies were either aggressively taken over or driven out of business altogether. Taking a cue from Rockefeller's success and the government's "blind eye," other American industries developed trusts, creating a ruthless, Darwinian business environment.

The Panic of 1893 threw several financially overextended railroads into financial ruin, threatening the industry and the economy as a whole. J. P. Morgan and several other Wall Street financiers rushed to wrest control of the failing rail lines and merge them into single companies. The railway system then ran more smoothly, and shipping rates were consistent across the country. However, the governing boards of these companies were dominated by a few powerful men, principally J. P. Morgan. Morgan created **interlocking directorates**, or regional monopolies, which controlled almost two-thirds of the rail traffic in the United States.

GOVERNMENTAL POLICY TOWARD CAPITALISM

Hoping that states would control trusts on their own, the federal government was reluctant to intervene in the progress of big business. Adhering to the principle of *laissez-faire* articulated by the economist Adam Smith in his treatise *The Wealth of Nations*, American lawmakers believed that natural market forces, not governments, should regulate the marketplace. It soon became clear, however, that this was untenable. Natural competition was being ruthlessly choked out. Demands from small businesses, farmers, consumers, and even some big businesses pushed Congress to act.

Congress passed the **Sherman Antitrust Act** in 1890 in an attempt to break up the massive monopolies that were dominating the American economy. The act forbade the creation of trusts that were designed to restrain trade. However, the act failed to specify the difference between trusts that were beneficial to customers and those that were harmful. More importantly, the act failed to include any real method of enforcement. The Supreme Court further weakened the act in its ruling in *United States v. E. C. Knight* (1895), in which it interpreted the commerce clause of the Constitution to exclude manufacturing, thus rendering Congress incapable of regulating that sector of the economy. In essence, the Sherman Antitrust Act had no teeth, and businesspeople found ways to avoid its penalties.

THE THREE WESTERN FRONTIERS: MINING, CATTLE, AND FARMING

"The existence of an area of free land, its continuous recession, and the advance of American settlement westward explain American development." These words, taken from "The Significance of the Frontier in American History," a lecture delivered by historian Frederick Jackson Turner at the World's Columbian Exposition in Chicago in 1893, would become known as **Turner's "Frontier Thesis."** Turner argued that the American character was shaped by the existence of the frontier and the way Americans interacted with and developed the frontier. But as the Civil War ended and Manifest Destiny was complete, the frontier was closing. There was no longer any part of the continent that Americans had not touched. This was a dangerous time for Americans in Turner's eyes; he felt the frontier encouraged individualism and democracy. Without that "free land," would democracy and the American way close as well?

49ers and Immigrants in Search of Gold

With the discovery of gold in California and silver in Nevada, the spread of cattle ranching, and the flood of "homesteaders" rushing into the west, it was clear that this region would be uniquely American. After the discovery of gold at **Sutter's Mill** in northern California in 1848, thousands rushed to the region to pan the rivers and mine the hills to find their fortunes. The cities of San Francisco and Sacramento sprang up practically overnight due to the influx of "**49ers**."

California also experienced a flood of Chinese immigrants who came in search of the fabled "mountains of gold." Many Chinese immigrants had no intention of staying in the United States but were hoping to find enough gold to live like kings once back in China. In one year, more Chinese left the country than came in. Those who came found no "mountain of gold" but did find discrimination and poverty.

There were other later gold strikes across the west in Colorado, Arizona, and South Dakota, and the Comstock Lode in Nevada, discovered in 1859, had both gold and silver ores. The discovery and mining of gold and silver had an impact on the economy—the value of both metals fluctuated as more was discovered, which became a national issue in the last part of the 19th century. More importantly, the mining had an adverse effect on the environment of the west. Panning for gold soon led to hydraulic mining, which gored mountainsides and destroyed lakes, rivers, and streams.

Cattle Take Control

Miles and miles of open grassland were soon converted into vast cattle ranches in Texas, Kansas, and Nebraska. Additional rail lines were added in Kansas, Nebraska, Colorado, and Wyoming, which made the transport of beef more viable. Soon the Texas Longhorn was the most prized cattle in the United States. Trails were created for transporting the cattle on **long drives** from deep inside Texas to the rail junctions of Dodge City, Abilene, Denver, and Cheyenne. Cowboys and Mexican *vaqueros* drove and grazed thousands of heads of cattle along these trails, to the immense profit of the ranch owners. Before long, however, the lush grassland became the haven for new settlers—homesteaders and sheepherders—who built barbed-wire fences and small farms, impeding the long drives. In addition, overgrazing by cattle along the trails eventually made the long drive something of the past. Cattle ranchers turned to enclosing their herds, selectively breeding, and hiring only local ranch hands to tend their cattle.

Farmland Turns Unfarmable

The **Homestead Act of 1862** provided a settler with 160 acres of land if he promised to live on it and work it for at least five years. At one point, public lands were basically being given away to encourage Americans to settle and improve the frontier. About 500,000 families took advantage of the Homestead Act, while many more bought land from private purveyors. Unfortunately, the parcels of land on the Great Plains were often not farmable owing to lack of rain and hard-packed soil, forcing many homesteaders to leave the land behind and return home. Those who remained were often called "**sodbusters**," as they attempted to farm the land that they were given. Life was difficult on the Plains. Families often lived in houses built out of the sod they had dug up. Drought was always a problem. Plagues of insects were a constant nuisance. About two-thirds of the original homesteaders left the Great Plains, draining the region of half of its population by the turn of the 20th century.

THE FARMER'S PLIGHT

Falling farm prices and changing demand in the domestic and international markets crippled an already troubled sector of the U.S. economy. Farmers were dwindling in number owing to the mechanization of agriculture and the growth of industry across the country. The beginnings of **agribusiness**, large-scale cash crop farms, were growing, with small family farms falling by the wayside. Soil preparation, planting, and harvesting no longer required the same number of workers as before with the invention of better and faster machines to do the work. As a result, small farmers could not keep up with their large competitors in both buying expensive equipment and bringing goods quickly to market.

In the spirit of Turner's "Frontier Thesis," Midwestern farmers decided to fight their dilemma by organizing together. In 1867, Oliver H. Kelley organized the **National Grange of the Patrons of Husbandry** as a kind of fraternity of farmers and their families. Soon the social atmosphere of the Grange meetings was replaced by a more political climate. The Grange sought to break the hold of railroad owners and middlemen who kept raising the cost of farming by pocketing their profits. By the mid-1870s, there were Grange meetings across the country. Grangers organized farm cooperatives (member-owned businesses that sold farm products directly to the buyer), cutting out the middleman. The railroads and silo owners were under the watch of the Grangers because of the exorbitant prices they charged for the shipping and storage of grain. Due to the Grangers' political clout and expert lobbying, Granger laws, which regulated the rates farmers could be charged for shipping by rail or using grain elevators, were passed in many states.

The Supreme Court stepped into the controversy in the case *Munn v. Illinois* (1877) by ruling that a state had the right to regulate the practices of a business if that business served the public interest. Since railroad transportation was very much in the public's interest, according to the Court, state regulation of rates was appropriate. Despite these successes on the state level, farmers still had many of their laws overturned owing to federal laws protecting interstate commerce and railroad companies raising their long-haul rates to offset the losses on short hauls. Congress responded by passing the **Interstate Commerce Act** in 1887 and creating the **Interstate Commerce Commission (ICC)**, which would regulate and investigate railroad companies that participated in interstate rail trafficking. However, the ICC lacked enforcement powers and remained essentially a "paper tiger." Farmers did not gain much from the formation of the ICC, as they lost most of the cases brought before it. Nonetheless, farmers kept up the fight through the end of the 19th century as currency issues and railroad trusts made tough times even tougher.

IMPACT OF INDUSTRIALIZATION ON AMERICAN SOCIETY

The economic divide between the rich and poor grew steadily wider as the 19th century drew to a close.

OPINIONS ON WEALTH

Americans were quick to apply Charles Darwin's theory of evolution and the notion of "survival of the fittest" in an effort to explain people's disparate economic and social standings within American society. **Social Darwinists**, such as Yale's William Graham Sumner, argued that wealth belonged in the hands of those who were fittest to manage it. Many of Sumner's followers also believed that giving assistance to the poor went against the natural order. John D. Rockefeller stated that his "Puritan work ethic" was responsible for his success.

By the end of this period, 90 percent of America's wealth was controlled by only 10 percent of the population. Many lower-class Americans subscribed to the "rags-to-riches" myth propagated by the novelist **Horatio Alger**, whose titles such as *Ragged Dick* were intended to inspire the poor to become wealthy industrialists like Andrew Carnegie. In reality, even though opportunities for incredible success were available, the odds were slight that anyone would become another Andrew Carnegie.

TRICKLE-DOWN THEORY AND THE ACQUISITION OF WEALTH

Andrew Carnegie wrote the essay "The Gospel of Wealth" to explain that wealth was a result of God's will and that, in turn, the wealthy had an obligation to give money away to better society.

In addition, Carnegie subscribed to the **"trickle-down" theory** that wealth would benefit the lower classes via the spending and good nature of the rich and would, therefore, benefit society as a whole.

A GROWING MIDDLE AND WORKING CLASS

As American workers moved from farms to factories, the middle class expanded, and cities grew to accommodate them. Managerial positions developed—factories required people to make sure that human capital was working efficiently to increase profits. As the middle class grew, so did the professional service industry in the areas of medicine, law, and education.

The segment of the American society with the greatest population growth was the working class. Blue-collar workers, who often toiled 10 to 12 hours a day for barely enough money to scrape by, made up nearly two-thirds of the population of the United States by the end of the 19th century. In smaller numbers, women joined the workforce as clerical help but earned significantly less than their male counterparts. For the most part, factory work was reserved for men. Long hours, occasional 16-hour shifts, and unsafe conditions made factory jobs a horror for many Americans.

ORGANIZED LABOR FIGHTS BACK

This second industrial revolution was dramatically different from the one that had occurred after the Revolutionary War. No longer were skilled artisans in high demand; machines now took their place in the process of production. Craftsmanship declined, as Americans and those abroad demanded cheap goods. Increased demand for manufactured goods meant longer and harder hours for the American factory worker. Factory owners would sometimes paint windows shut to keep workers from "daydreaming." Conditions were dangerous in steel mills, where white-hot molten steel was poured day and night by men who had been on the job for 12 hours or more. Soon, American laborers had had enough and decided to organize for safer work conditions and better wages.

The first attempts at protest were often met with indignation and resistance by factory owners. Cheap replacement laborers, or **scabs**, were easy to come by when workers went out on strike. Factory owners would often hire private police forces, which would inflict violence on strikers as they attempted to protest. Locking out workers from their jobs could stop a strike before it started. Blacklisting could keep workers who were identified as "difficult" from being hired. Factory owners sometimes would force prospective employees to sign a **yellow-dog contract** or "ironclad oath" in which the worker agreed not to join a union as a condition of employment.

THE GREAT RAILROAD STRIKE

Unfortunately for organized labor, the federal government was reluctant to help, owing to its subscribing to *laissez-faire* theory and the sway of public opinion against organized labor. Factory owners were successful in taking advantage of the government's stance by obtaining court orders to ban strikes or gaining permission to fire all striking workers. One of the earliest attempts by labor to secure its rights also became one of the most violent. The **Great Railroad Strike** of 1877 occurred when rail companies cut wages by 10 percent in the wake of an economic **depression**. This was the second time in four years that the railroads had cut workers' wages. The strike began in West Virginia but quickly spread nationwide and paralyzed rail traffic across the United States. In addition, workers from other industries joined the strike, further injuring the economy. President Rutherford B. Hayes authorized the use of federal troops to break the strike. In the end, more than 100 workers were killed in clashes with federal troops, and the strikers gained nothing in return.

Unions Attempt to Protect Rights

Early labor unions often succumbed to their own idealistic vision of the future as they sought to include all workers under one organization. The first national union, the **National Labor Union**, was founded in 1866 to secure better working conditions, higher wages, shorter hours,and the inclusion of women and African Americans. After the violent Railroad Strike of 1877, the National Labor Union fell by the wayside.

EMERGENCE OF KNIGHTS OF LABOR

Meeting in secret so as to not lose their jobs, the **Knights of Labor** finally emerged in 1869 under the leadership of Terence V. Powderly. The union was inclusive—all workers, women and minorities included, were invited to join.

Much as had the National Labor Union before them, Powderly and his followers advocated both economic and social reforms, such as the development of labor cooperatives modeled after the Grangers, an eight-hour workday, government regulation of business, and **arbitration** to settle disputes between labor and management rather than violent strikes. Unfortunately for the Knights, a pivotal event would begin their demise. On May 4, 1886, a Knights of Labor protest in Haymarket Square in Chicago turned violent. Police were sent to break up the public meeting. Someone in the crowd threw a bomb, killing eight police officers and leading to chaos. It was alleged that an **anarchist** with ties to the Knights had thrown the bomb in an attempt to begin the overthrow of the government. Many Americans believed that the Knights were an anarchist movement that intended to take over their country violently. By the end of the 19th century, the once 700,000-member-strong Knights of Labor had declined to a membership of just 100,000.

Many of the former Knights had left to join Samuel Gompers and his **American Federation of Labor** (AFL) founded in 1886, an early federation of labor unions that became the country's largest. The Federation was a practical union (as opposed to a politically ideological union such as the Knights) that chose to concentrate on "bread-and-butter" economic issues—such as the eight-hour work day and higher wages—rather than involve itself in social change. Because the AFL was made up of skilled rather than unskilled laborers, Gompers was able to negotiate with employers more effectively, as his men were not as easily replaced by "scabs" if a strike was called. Gompers utilized the tactic of **collective bargaining** to make modest gains for workers,particularly through the establishment of **closed shops**, or businesses where all employees had to be a member of the union.

A STRIKEBREAKING GOVERNMENT

The end of the 19th century was difficult for organized labor, as the government time and time again sided with big business. One facet of that support was the practice of strikebreaking. Andrew Carnegie's manager of his Homestead Steel mill found himself in conflict with organized labor when he announced a 20 percent cut in worker wages in 1892. To stop a strike before it occurred, Henry Clay Frick locked out the members of the steelworkers union. As scabs attempted to enter the plant, the strikers became violent, scaring potential replacement workers away. To remedy the situation, Frick ordered hundreds of private Pinkerton police to surround the plant and rid the area of strikers. Violence erupted, with 16 workers killed and over 150 wounded. The governor of Pennsylvania ordered the state militia to assist the entrance of the replacement workers into the mill, and the strike received its death blow. This strike had been crushed by Carnegie and the state of Pennsylvania.

In response to the Great Railroad Strike of 1877, the **Pullman Palace Car Company**, which manufactured sleeping cars for the railroads, constructed a "model town" for its employees. When management announced a wage cut and fired the leader of their union, Pullman workers chose to stop working. With their homegrown union without a leader, the group sought assistance from the American Railway Union under the leadership of Eugene V. Debs. Rail workers across the nation joined the Pullman strikers by refusing to load, link, or carry any train that had a Pullman car attached. In effect, all rail traffic came to a screeching halt. To push the federal government to intervene, the rail owners began linking U.S. mail cars to Pullman cars. This way, they could claim that the strikers were impeding the flow of mail and, thus, violating the laws protecting interstate commerce. President Grover Cleveland encouraged the filing of an injunction to demand the workers stop striking and to get the mail running once again. Debs and his union leadership refused to abide by the court's ruling and were eventually arrested and jailed.

Organized labor was given yet another blow when the Supreme Court ruled in *In re Debs* (1895) that the use of court injunctions to break strikes was justified in the support of interstate commerce. In effect, the federal government had given employers permission to destroy labor unions.

CHAPTER 19: THE BIRTH OF AN INDUSTRIAL CULTURE

URBAN POLITICAL MACHINES

Politics in America's large cities was mired in corruption. Large, disciplined political groups called "machines" controlled party politics in cities such as New York, Chicago, and Baltimore.

THE TWEED RING OF TAMMANY HALL

The most famous of these machines, **Tammany Hall** in New York City, was led by **"Boss" Tweed**. Tweed and his fellow Irish gave aid to small business owners, immigrants, and the poor in exchange for votes. **Political machines** often provided coveted city jobs to those who promised to vote for their candidates. They also found housing for newly arrived immigrants and provided various forms of support to needy families, like distributing turkeys at Thanksgiving, handing out clothes, and providing job search assistance.

Not all members of this machine were honest in their intentions. George Washington Plunkitt, a lower boss in Tammany Hall, would pocket large sums of taxpayer money in what he called "honest graft." Plunkitt would gain advance notice of a city project from an insider sitting on the planning board. He would buy the land for the proposed project and then sell it to the city for as much as three times its original price. By 1870, the Tweed ring had bilked New York City taxpayers out of over $200 million. Urban citizens did not complain, however, as the political machines took care of them and threatened to harm those who spoke against them.

The end of the Tweed ring began in 1871 when a story ran in the *New York Times* alleging fraud, bribery, and graft by the political machine. **Thomas Nast**, a political cartoonist for *Harper's Weekly*, became Tweed's archenemy as he began drawing scathing commentaries regarding the machine's corruption and greed. Tweed's visage often graced the pages of the magazine, to the delight of readers and law enforcement. Having escaped serving jail time on a number of occasions, Tweed fled to Spain in 1876, where he was captured by Spanish police who recognized him from the Nast cartoons. Tweed finally was sent to jail in the United States, where he died of heart failure in 1878.

A SECOND WAVE OF REFORM

The often deplorable living conditions of immigrants and the greed of political machines spurred a new wave of reform, which would not fully take hold until the turn of the 20th century. These reformers were by and large middle-class Americans who were more concerned about a possible violent uprising of the poor and working class than they were about the well-being of the less fortunate.

THE SOCIAL GOSPEL AND THE HULL HOUSE

One of the most influential reform movements of this era was the **Social Gospel** movement. Leaders such as Walter Rauschenbusch believed that Christians had an obligation to improve the lives of those less fortunate, such as the citizens of the rough Hell's Kitchen area of New York City with whom he worked. In many ways, it was the work of Rauschenbusch that encouraged many middle-class Protestants to join reform efforts and bring on the Progressive movement.

Akin to the Social Gospel movement was the **settlement house** movement, which was begun by young, college-educated, middle-class women. In an age when women were expected to adhere to a strict ideal of femininity, young female activists sought to better society through volunteerism since they could not become involved in the political process. The most famous of all of the settlement houses was **Hull House** in Chicago (1889). The goal of its founder, **Jane Addams**, was to have immigrants live with college-educated people in order to ease their transition into American society. Settlement house guests were taught courses in English, hygiene, and cooking. Addams and others also pioneered some of the first instruction in child care. Many other settlement houses modeled themselves after Hull House as the 19th century came to a close. Moreover, settlement houses soon became a meeting place for young women activists.

THE TEMPERANCE MOVEMENT

The Victorian ideal of strict moral decorum and the concern over Catholic influences led to the revival of the **temperance** movement (which had been overshadowed by the abolitionist movement in the antebellum years). **Frances Willard** and the **Woman's Christian Temperance Union (WCTU)** gave the movement new life in 1874 by lobbying for laws to prohibit the sale of alcoholic beverages. They believed prohibition would cure society of a variety of ills, particularly poverty. **The Anti-Saloon League** followed in 1893, gaining more success as states across the country agreed to shutter bars. The most well-known WCTU member, Kentucky-born **Carrie A. Nation**, was inspired by the death of her alcoholic husband to travel across the United States, smashing bars with her trademark hatchet. Nation believed she was doing the work of God as she wreaked havoc across the Midwest. She was arrested over 30 times and became so well-known that she sold pewter hatchet pins to pay her jail fines. Nation also crusaded against the evils of smoking tobacco, fought for women's suffrage, and railed against the restrictive and sometimes dangerous women's fashions of the day.

The Changing Roles of Women

Nation was just one of the women who publicly fought for the rights of women. The industrial age brought women more independence—and more difficulties. Women married later in life (if at all) and bore fewer children. Divorce became more common. Despite newfound freedom, women still did not have a voice in politics. The women's movement had disappeared during Reconstruction—the issue of African American suffrage had taken precedence over women's suffrage. Understanding the need to revive the cause, some broke off from the WCTU and formed women's suffrage organizations from the 1870s to the 1890s. Activists **Elizabeth Cady Stanton** and **Susan B. Anthony** formed the **National American Woman Suffrage Association** in 1890, combining the once rival National Woman Suffrage Association and American Woman Suffrage Association to fight for a woman's right to vote. While gains for women were slow to come, a number of western states did allow women to vote by 1900.

CHAPTER 20: NEW CULTURAL AND INTELLECTUAL MOVEMENTS

REMOVAL OF THE PLAINS INDIANS

In 1865, some 400,000 Native Americans lived freely in the trans-Mississippi west. Some tribes had lived in the region for thousands of years, while others had been progressively forced westward from ancestral homelands by the push of white settlement. Plains Indians were largely nomadic, traveling by horse to hunt buffalo and wage war on neighboring tribes.

AN ATTEMPT AT A RESERVATION SYSTEM

Sioux Indians were able to control much of the upper west part of the country because of devastating European diseases that had removed potential resistance by other Native Americans. The Sioux were able to drive further resistance away through their aggressive warring tactics. The Pawnee pleaded with the federal government for assistance, as the Sioux were attempting to wipe them out. In response, the federal government created boundaries throughout the west that designated the land held by each tribe. These first attempts at a **reservation** system failed, as the white leaders in Washington, D.C., were ignorant of the nomadic nature and paternal tribal leadership system of most Native Americans on the Great Plains.

NATIVE AMERICANS AND WAR

More and more Native American tribes were becoming aggressive toward one another and against incoming white settlers. From the end of the Civil War to 1890, there was constant warfare. At Sand Creek, Colorado, in 1864, a U.S. militia slaughtered 400 unarmed Native Americans who had been promised protection. Colonel **George Custer** marched into the Black Hills of South Dakota, a section of the Sioux Indian reservation, and proclaimed the discovery of gold. As a result, the hills soon were flooded with gold seekers, which enraged the Sioux.

CUSTER'S DEFEAT

To quell a possible Sioux uprising, Custer marched his column of men deep into Sioux territory, only to discover some 2,500 Sioux warriors waiting for them at the Little Big Horn River. Custer and his men were cut down by the Native American warriors, who were soon hunted themselves by U.S. Army reinforcements.

Many other tribes (such as the Nez Perce led by Chief Joseph and the Apache led by Geronimo) were forced to fight for their land and lives throughout the end of the 19th century.

STRIPPING NATIVES OF THEIR RESOURCES AND IDENTITY

Warfare was not the only factor to affect the Native Americans living on the Great Plains. Plains tribes depended on the buffalo for meat, clothing, and fuel. As the railroad made its way across the West, mass killing of the buffalo ensued. Buffalo coats became fashionable, and the buffalo hunt became a favorite pastime. As a result, the American buffalo became an endangered species, with only a few surviving in the nation's zoos and preserves.

The 19th century did not end on a happy note for the Indian tribes of the Great Plains. Even though Helen Hunt Jackson's book *A Century of Dishonor* (1881) sparked debate over the government's treatment of Native American tribes, it seemed that no one could decide what to do now that the damage had been done. Many believed that the tribes needed to be assimilated into American society by being stripped of their culture and traditions. A new ritual was born in 1870 that promised a rebirth of Native American tradition and a repelling of white incursion. This **"Ghost Dance"** so frightened whites living near the Dakota Sioux that it was outlawed. The U.S. Army was called in 1890 to stop the Sioux from performing the dance, which led to the Battle of Wounded Knee. Two hundred Native American men, women, and children were slaughtered over the ritual.

In an attempt to "civilize" Native Americans, the federal government enacted the **Dawes Severalty Act of 1887**, which stripped tribes of their official federal recognition and land rights and would grant individual Indian families land and citizenship in 25 years if they "behaved." Former reservation land was sold, and the proceeds would fund "civilizing" ventures for Native Americans, such as Indian schools that taught Native Americans how to dress and behave like whites. This forced-assimilation policy remained the federal government's way to deal with Native Americans until 1934. The Dawes Severalty Act served to destroy tribal organization and strip Native Americans of the land they had been legally deeded by the U.S. government.

THE NEW SOUTH

Slow economic progress was a reality for the South after the Civil War. However, soon the South was back on its feet with the resurgence of tobacco as a cash crop. The South was also able to outperform the North in the textile industry because of an abundance of cheap labor and cotton. The emergence of a modern, viable railroad network further assisted the South in regaining and eventually surpassing its prewar financial strength.

SOUTHERN FARMERS STRUGGLE

But for the most part, Southern citizens still remained some of the most impoverished in the nation. The unprecedented postwar economic recovery came with strings attached; the North had financed a major portion of the South's war debt. Therefore, Northerners owned the lion's share of the industry that was being revived in the South. The majority of Southerners, both black and white, subsisted from day to day as sharecroppers and farmers. Owing to the South's steadfast belief in the plantation economy and lack of value placed on education and economic recovery, growth and innovation moved more slowly than in the North. Thus, the average Southern citizen did not reap any reward from the modest economic growth of the region, remaining below the poverty line.

As in the antebellum economy, cotton remained a major cash crop for the South—more and more farmers converted land to till cotton. They eventually glutted the worldwide marketplace with the fiber, driving the price to an all-time low in the 1890s. As a result, many small farmers lost their land because of their inability to pay back debts. Many tenant farmers were driven off land by landowners, who then needed to till it themselves. Most farmers, tenant or otherwise, remained tied to the land because of the use of crop-liens in which farmers paid for goods on credit to be paid back with the harvest of their next crop. A poor harvest drove farmers deeper into debt.

PLESSY v. FERGUSON AND JIM CROW LAWS

After the North removed federal troops and any other support for African Americans, white Southerners sought to enact policies that would create two distinct societies as before the war—one black and one white.

The Supreme Court aided the South's ability to discriminate through several decisions that more or less dismantled any Reconstruction protections of African-American civil rights. In the Civil Rights Cases of 1883, the Court decided that Congress had no jurisdiction to bar private citizens from practicing discrimination. In 1896, the landmark case of *Plessy v. Ferguson* was brought before the Court. In this case, a mixed-race man, Homer Plessy, who was seven-eighths white and one-eighth African American, refused to give up his seat on a "whites-only" railcar in the state of Louisiana and was arrested. He sued, claiming that his civil rights had been violated. Justice Henry Brown delivered the opinion of the Court, which ruled that because a car was provided for African American passengers, the state of Louisiana had not violated the Fourteenth Amendment.

The justices used the "separate but equal" doctrine to justify their decision. The South had now been given permission by the U.S. Supreme Court to discriminate on the basis of color in all public places. **Jim Crow laws**, which segregated public facilities from drinking fountains to hotel rooms, were immediately adopted by cities across the South.

FURTHER FORMS OF DISCRIMINATION

Discrimination did not end with Jim Crow. Southern states worked to disenfranchise African American voters through the use of **literacy tests, poll taxes**, and **grandfather clauses.**

Grandfather clauses would allow a man to vote only if his grandfather had voted in an election before 1865—that is, before Reconstruction. African Americans were not allowed to serve on juries and were subject to harsher penalties when convicted of crimes than their white counterparts. A new form of terrorism and intimidation called **lynching** developed in the post-war South. Lynching was the unauthorized execution of a person by a mob. Often the lynching would be publicized in advance so crowds of whites could gather to witness the event. In response, African Americans could do little but leave the South for other types of discrimination in the North. Self-educated former slave Booker T. Washington advocated the education of African Americans to make them more economically viable and indispensable to the economy. His Tuskegee Institute was founded to instruct African Americans in the industrial arts and the ability to "work within the system." With the turn of the 20th century, more radical African American thinkers would take umbrage at Washington's stance of "assimilation."

FLOOD OF IMMIGRANTS AND THE LURE OF THE CITY

Both push and pull factors brought millions of new immigrants to the United States in the years 1880 to 1924. Poverty, overcrowding, and religious persecution pushed immigrants from Southern and Eastern Europe. Stories of opportunity and freedom pulled them to cities such as New York, Chicago, and Boston. Clipper ships gave way to large ocean liners, which could carry both freight and passengers across the Atlantic relatively quickly. Cheap "steerage-class" tickets could be purchased for as little as $20. For some families, this was a life's savings; nonetheless, "new immigrant" families from Italy, Poland, and Russia gathered as much money as they could to take the one-way trip to America.

A BACKLASH AGAINST IMMIGRANTS

These "new" immigrants were markedly different from the "old" immigrants who had come to the United States in the 1820s and 1830s. Southern and Eastern European immigrants were often Catholic, Jewish, or Greek Orthodox Christians; the "old" immigrants were predominantly

English Protestants, although large numbers of Irish and Germans had begun to arrive in the mid-1840s. On the West Coast, Chinese immigrants continued to arrive in Los Angeles and San Francisco, prompting the passage of the **Chinese Exclusion Act** of 1882 to restrict Chinese immigration to the United States. Soon, Congress passed other acts aimed at restricting the tide of immigration flooding American cities. Many **nativists**, much like the old "Know-Nothings" during the first wave of immigration, feared domination by a population loyal to the Pope (Roman Catholics). Labor unions feared a loss of jobs to an eager immigrant work pool. In response, the American Protective Association was formed in 1887 to oppose the election of any Catholic to public office. The Reverend Josiah Strong echoed the sentiments of many Americans in his book *Our Country* (1885), in which he derided cities as a menace to American morality and social order. The tide could not be stemmed, however—by the turn of the 20th century, one out of every three New Yorkers was foreign born.

MAKING A NEW HOME IN AMERICA

Immigrants flocked to America's cities, where they could find affordable housing and abundant factory jobs. Ethnic neighborhoods popped up in New York, Chicago, and Philadelphia and other American cities. To handle the massive influx of bodies, landlords converted once single-family homes into apartments. The city of New York held a contest in 1879 for the best building design for urban dwellings. E. Ware won the contest with his "dumbbell **tenement**," which conformed to a law requiring windows for every dwelling. The design included an "airshaft" that was supposed to aid the distribution of fresh air through the apartments but in the end only helped the spread of infectious diseases, as more and more people were crammed into the buildings. New apartment buildings were built up rather than out, as land was at a premium and steel made taller buildings possible.

RISE OF THE EARLY SUBURBS

With the change in the inner-city populace, affluent and middle-class white Americans moved to burgeoning suburban neighborhoods, aided by the expansion of trolley car lines and subway services that could take them to their jobs in the city.

Ethnic groups often formed tight community bonds based on common language, customs, and foods. Even though immigrants often found themselves living in deplorable conditions, these urban neighborhoods began to feel more like home and provided a haven where many of the newest arrivals could get on their feet in America.

CULTURAL AWAKENINGS

As America's urban centers grew by leaps and bounds, cultural and intellectual endeavors were also given new life.

CHANGES IN EDUCATION

Publicly funded high schools and compulsory elementary attendance laws increased the literacy rate of Americans to almost 90 percent by the beginning of the 20th century. Higher education, already improved by the Morrill Land Grant Act of 1862, was further strengthened by the Hatch Act of 1887 and the philanthropy of men such as Carnegie, Rockefeller, Stanford, and Vanderbilt. American scholars began to apply the scientific method to social subjects, and "social science" emerged. Universities also professionalized the areas of medicine, law, and sociology by requiring research and practice to obtain a degree. "Normal" schools (teachers' colleges) were established across the country to train new educators to keep up with rising demand for qualified instructors.

ACHIEVEMENTS IN THE ARTS

Reacting to the Romanticism of the antebellum and Civil War eras, realist writers and artists sought to portray the conditions industrialized Americans were facing. One of the most famous and prolific of the realists was **Mark Twain** (Samuel Clemens), who captured the ruggedness of the frontier and South with humor and satire. It was Twain who coined the term **"the Gilded Age"** for this era. Bret Harte entranced Americans with his stories of the Gold Rush and Wild West.

As the era wore on, authors turned to stories of human nature and emotion in novels such as *Red Badge of Courage* by Stephen Crane and *Sister Carrie* by Theodore Dreiser. Many visual artists, such as Winslow Homer, remained tied to the romantic spirit of the Hudson River School and produced lush American landscapes and marine scenes, while others broke away from tradition and redefined American art. James Whistler and Mary Cassatt experimented with abstract color and composition in their works, which were heavily influenced by their time spent in Europe. Architects also reacted to the world around them as they designed buildings that would reach the sky but remain functional for everyday life.

BEAUTIFICATION OF CITIES

Many cities sought to beautify their surroundings by adding parks to the urban landscape.

Men such as **Frederick Law Olmsted** and Calvert Vaux focused on establishing open spaces in cities by designing vast parks that were densely planted and meticulously planned. Then Central Park in New York City set the standard for future urban beautification projects and with its use of winding trails, arched bridges, and open spaces that were nestled among the hustle and bustle of city life.

The music scene changed as new music traveled from communities in the South to Northern cities such as Chicago. Jazz developed from a blending of African American, European American, and European musical traditions.

Informing and entertaining the urban masses was now big business in cities such as New York and Chicago. Daily newspapers like **Joseph Pulitzer**'s *New York World* and **William Randolph Hearst**'s *New York Journal American* fought over circulation numbers in the city with their sensationalized stories and rock-bottom prices. Magazines also hit the newsstands in search of readership. *Ladies Home Journal*, *McCall's*, and *Vogue* all sought to reach women through advertisements and fashion tips.

City dwellers searching for a diversion looked forward to the big-tent shows that came rolling into town. The Barnum and Bailey Circus promised not only animals and tightrope walkers but a museum of "oddities," ranging from a bearded lady to the "fishboy," which patrons could walk through. William "Buffalo Bill" Cody traveled across the United States with Annie Oakley and his Wild West Show, thrilling audiences with sharpshooting, real "Indians," and bronco busting. Professional sports such as boxing and baseball were popular with young men, who would use their leisure time to bet on the results and hope for a win. Live vaudeville variety shows brought humor, drama, dance, and song to city dwellers. In the South, minstrel shows, in which whites would don black face paint and act as they imagined African Americans would, were popular among both whites and blacks.

UNIT 6: REVIEW QUESTIONS

Multiple-Choice Questions

Directions: Choose the best answer choice for the following questions.

Questions 1–4 refer to the following figure.

Mulberry St., New York, NY, 1900

1. The situation depicted in the photograph led most directly to

    (A) stricter federal immigration laws in the first decade of the 1900s

    (B) decreased importance of mechanized agriculture

    (C) widespread movement of southern and eastern Europeans to western farmland

    (D) the growth in power of urban political machines

2. Which of the following mid-19th century issues most clearly parallels the situation depicted in the photograph?

    (A) Increased nativism connected to Irish and German immigration

    (B) Political upheaval connected to the spread of slavery into the territories

    (C) Displacement of Native Americans connected to territorial expansion

    (D) Nullification connected to the growth of federal power

3. Which of the following events in the 1910s and 1920s represents a continuation of the event illustrated in the photograph?

    (A) Expansion of Jim Crow

    (B) Extension of Progressive reforms

    (C) Rejection of the Social Gospel

    (D) Increased interventionsim in the Caribbean and Pacific

4. Which of the following groups would be most likely to support the interests of the people in the photograph?

(A) Promoters of the New South

(B) Opponents of the settlement house movement

(C) Organizers for national unions

(D) Advocates of Social Darwinism

Questions 5–8 refer to the following quote.

". . . The first count in the declaration . . . {charges} that the Wabash, St. Louis & Pacific Railway Company had, in violation of a statute of the state of Illinois, been guilty of an unjust discrimination in its rates or charges of toll and compensation for the transportation of freight {from Illinois to New York State} . . . The court . . . holds as law that said act . . . cannot apply to transportation service rendered partly without the state . . . and cannot operate beyond the limits of the state of Illinois. The court further holds as matter of law that the transportation in question falls within the proper description of 'commerce among the states,' . . . "

WABASH, ST. L. & P. RY. CO. v. STATE OF ILLINOIS
118 U.S. 557 (7 S.Ct. 4, 30 L.Ed. 244)

WABASH, ST. L. & P. RY. CO. v. STATE OF ILLINOIS
Decided: October 25, 1886

5. Which change in American society most directly led to the situation described in the Supreme Court case?

(A) Dispersal of Native American tribes in the West to reservations

(B) Corruption in urban politics

(C) Support for expansion of the Social Gospel

(D) Increases in immigration and industrialization

6. Which action most directly resulted from the decision in the Supreme Court case?

(A) Accelerated migration to the Rocky Mountain states

(B) Development of the national park system

(C) Increased demand for federal legislation

(D) Increased immigration from Asia

7. The reasoning expressed in the Court's decision most directly reflects which of the following continuities in United States history?

(A) Debates over the role of government in regulating the economy

(B) Debates over the effect of expansion on indigenous peoples

(C) Debates over the environmental impact of demographic change

(D) Debates over industrialization's impact on national identity

8. Which of the following actions in the second half of the 20th century most closely parallels the reasoning of the Supreme Court's ruling in this case?

(A) Passage of a national highway speed limit to deal with the energy crisis of the 1970s

(B) Efforts of the Great Society programs of the 1960s to combat discrimination

(C) Republican attempts of the 1980s to limit the power of the federal government

(D) Policy debates over free trade in the last decades of the 20th century

Questions 9–11 refer to the following quote.

"Be it enacted by [Congress] That in all cases where any tribe or band of Indians has been . . . located upon any reservation created . . . [by Congress or the President] . . . [the President may] . . . allot the lands . . . :

• To each head of a family, one-quarter of a section;

• To each single person over eighteen years of age, one-eighth of a section . . . SEC. 6 . . . every Indian born within the territorial limits of the United States who . . . [resides] . . . separate and apart from any tribe of Indians . . . and has adopted the habits of civilized life, is . . . declared . . . a citizen of the United States . . . SEC. 10 . . . nothing in this act . . . [shall limit] . . . Congress to grant the right of way through any lands granted to an Indian, or a tribe . . . for the public use . . . upon making just compensation . . ."

—Dawes Act, 1887

9. Which of the following situations most directly resulted from the passage of this act?

(A) An increase in Native American tribal lands west of the Mississippi River

(B) A decrease in federal control over Native American affairs

(C) An increase in immigration from southern and eastern Europe after 1890

(D) A reduction in tribal autonomy

10. The process described in the Dawes Act most directly reflects which of the following continuities in United States history?

(A) Debates about expansion of voting rights

(B) Debates about the role of assimilation in national identity

(C) Debates about the growth of executive power

(D) Debates about economic globalization

11. The actions expressed in the excerpts of the Dawes Act most clearly show the influence of which of the following?

(A) Legislative supremacy as contained in the Articles of Confederation

(B) Orderly creation of new states as contained in the Northwest Ordinance

(C) Separation of powers as contained in the U.S. Constitution

(D) Civil liberties contained in the Bill of Rights

Questions 12 and 13 refer to the following quote.

"THE PLATFORM OF DEMANDS. [of the Farmers' Alliance]

. . .

First . . . . the abolition of National banks; . . . that the government shall establish sub-treasuries . . .

Second . . . . that Congress shall pass such laws . . . [to] prevent the dealing in futures on all agricultural and mechanical productions . . .

Third . . . . demand the free coinage of silver . . .

Fourth . . . . the passage of the laws prohibiting alien ownership of land . . .

Fifth . . . . 'equal rights to all and special privileges to none,' that our national legislation . . . not build up one industry at the expense of another, . . . remove existing heavy tariff; . . . a just and equitable system of graduated tax on incomes

Sixth . . . . State and National government control and supervision of the means of public communication and transportation . . . [or] government ownership of such

Seventh . . . . an amendment . . . providing for the [direct] election of United States Senators . . ."

—*Cleveland & Stevenson: Their Lives & Record,* edited by Thomas Campbell-Copeland, 1892

12. Which of the following groups would be most likely to support the demands in the previous passage?

(A) Supporters of the New South

(B) The People's (Populist) Party

(C) Proponents of "conspicuous consumption"

(D) Advocates of business consolidation

13. The reasoning expressed in the passage most directly reflects which of the following?

(A) Federalism contained in the U.S. Constitution

(B) Principles of republican self-government contained in the Declaration of Independence

(C) Disavowal of the Monroe Doctrine

(D) Support for the Missouri Compromise

Questions 14 and 15 refer to the following figure.

Cotton on the levee, New Orleans, 1898

14. Which of the following ideas is most clearly illustrated in the photograph?

(A) The limitations of the New South

(B) Opposition to the *Plessy v. Ferguson* decision

(C) Success of environmental efforts in the South

(D) Dominance of mechanized agriculture in the South

15. Which of the following debates from the middle of the 19th century most closely relates to the situation illustrated in the photograph?

    (A) Debates over the status of Native Americans and Hispanics as territorial expansion occurred

    (B) Debates over the expansion of American trade into China

    (C) Debates over nativist hostility to Catholic immigrants

    (D) Debates over the Mexican War and its aftermath

Short-Answer Questions

1. **Passage 1**

"This, then, is held to be the duty of the man of wealth: First, to set an example of modest, unostentatious living, shunning display or extravagance; . . . and, after doing so, to consider all surplus revenues which come to him simply as trust funds, which he is called upon to administer . . . to produce the most beneficial results for the community—the man of wealth thus becoming the mere trustee and agent for his poorer brethren, bringing to their service his superior wisdom, experience and ability to administer, doing for them better than they would or could do for themselves."

—From "Wealth," by Andrew Carnegie, *North American Review,* 1889

Passage 2

"In an age of free struggle and fierce competition for power, this old buccaneer, who was almost a septuagenarian at the break of the Civil war, was admired most of all for his unflagging aggressiveness. One incident . . .

Gentlemen:

You have undertaken to cheat me. I will not sue you, the law takes too long. I will ruin you.

Sincerely yours,
Cornelius Van Derbilt
And he did.

A characteristic expression of his, in another emergency, also became celebrated. "What do I care about the law?" he had exclaimed. "Hain't I got the power?""

—Matthew Josephson, *The Robber Barons,* 1934

Based on the two passages referring to the industrial capitalists of the mid to late 19th century, complete the following three tasks:

(A) Briefly explain the main point made by Passage 1.

(B) Briefly explain the main point made by Passage 2.

(C) Provide ONE piece of evidence that is from the mid to late 19th century that is not included in the passages, and explain how it supports the interpretation of either passage.

2.

NOTICE –
COMMUNIST
NIHILIST –
SOCIALIST
FENIAN
& HOODLUM
WELCOME
BUT NO
ADMITTANCE
TO
CHINAMEN

GOLDEN GATE OF LIBERTY

INDUSTRY

ORDER

THE ONLY ONE BARRED OUT.
ENLIGHTENED AMERICAN STATESMAN. —"We must draw the line *somewhere*, you know."

Use the image above and your knowledge of United States history to answer parts A, B, and C.

(A) Explain the point of view of the political cartoon.

(B) Explain how the point of view identified in part A helped to shape ONE specific United States government action between 1865 and 1898.

(C) Explain how the point of view identified in Part A helped to shape ONE OTHER specific United States government action between 1865 and 1898.

Long Essay Question

Directions: You are advised to spend 5 minutes planning and 30 minutes writing your answer.

Evaluate the effectiveness of the efforts of two of the following groups to deal with the challenges posed by the economic changes in the United States during the second half of the 19th century.

- Workers
- Farmers
- Native Americans
- Industrialists

ANSWERS AND EXPLANATIONS

MULTIPLE-CHOICE ANSWERS

1. D
The influx of immigrants to the cities of the Northeast increased the importance of urban political machines, such as Tammany Hall in New York City, which provided aid and assistance to immigrants in exchange for political support.

2. A
The increase in southern and eastern European immigrants in the late 19th/early 20th century, many of whom settled in the cities of the industrial Northeast, prompted renewed calls for immigration restrictions.

3. B
Urban problems associated with increased rapid industrialization, including sanitation, political corruption, and living conditions, became the focus of many Progressive-era urban reformers.

4. C
Unions, especially industrial ones, sought to represent the interests of labor, including the recently arrived immigrants, in a rapidly changing industrial world emerging in the United States during the late 19th/early 20th century.

5. D
Tremendous industrial growth and increases in immigration accelerated urbanization. This led to increased demand for foodstuff in the Northeast and the development of "industrial" farming with the expansion into the Great Plains. States, like Illinois, passed a number of regulatory laws.

6. C
The Supreme Court's ruling in the Wabash case effectively shut down state regulation of commerce within a state if it crossed state lines. The federal government's constitutional mandate to regulate interstate commerce formed the basis for the 1887 Interstate Commerce Act and 1890 Sherman Anti-Trust Act.

7. A
Questions and controversies over the role of government regulation, both state and federal, in an evolving market economy is a constant. Supporters of a free-market *laissez-faire* economy did not wish to see government regulation. Farmers and laborers looked to government to help control the power and excesses of big business.

8. A
The Supreme Court ruled in the Wabash case that only the federal government had the power to regulate interstate trade (across state lines). In an effort to deal with the Arab oil embargo, Congress passed a 55-mile-an-hour speed limit on all interstate highways as an effort to conserve gas. Lyndon Johnson's Great Society programs targeted racial and economic discrimination, not railroad rate discrimination.

9. D
While earlier government policy toward Native Americans sought to remove them from areas and place them on reservations, the Dawes Act sought to divide reservation land and create smaller farmsteads for individual American Indians. Excess tribal land could then be sold off to the increasing number of settlers looking to move onto the Great Plains. This resulted in less power or autonomy for tribal governments and greater control of federal agencies, such as the Bureau of Indian Affairs.

10. B
The Dawes Act attempted to alter the traditional tribal structure and governance of Native Americans. It sought to break up the reservations into a series of homesteads and assimilate American Indians into the American agricultural model. Conflicts over assimilation and distinctiveness relate to topics of immigration, race, class, and ethnic identity.

11. C

While the granting of citizenship would include the guarantees of the Bill of Rights, and Sec. 10 does reference part of the Fifth Amendment (just compensation), the overwhelming amount of information in this excerpt from the Dawes Act deals with separation of powers; specifically, the power of the Congress to place Native Americans on reservations and to allow the right of way across Indian land. In addition, the executive branch may allot the land parcels granted under the Dawes Act.

12. B

The Farmers' Alliance advocated on behalf of the American farmers in their struggle against the negative effects of industrial capitalism, including high freight rates and crushing debt. In the 1890s, the Populist or People's Party continued the political organization begun by the Farmers' Alliance and adopted in their political platforms of 1892 and 1896 many of the demands listed in the passage.

13. B

The demands of the Farmers' Alliance are a call for government action, including several which would increase the political power of the people. The call for direct election of U.S. senators is one example. This support for the consent of the governed is a key part of the democratic philosophy contained in the Declaration of Independence.

14. A

Despite the goals of some Southerners to create a New South based on a growing economy and increased industrialization, the Southern economy remained heavily agricultural. Sharecropping and the crop lien system tied many farmers to cotton farming using the technology of the antebellum years.

15. D

The expansion of cotton production during the middle decades of the 19th century impacted debates over the territorial expansion of the United States. The annexation of Texas, and the resulting Mexican War and its aftermath, fueled abolitionist fury at potential expansion of slavery and the growth of a slave power.

SHORT-ANSWER QUESTIONS RESPONSES

1. (A) Andrew Carnegie describes the duty of a man of wealth in his "Gospel of Wealth." It is to serve as a model for the working class and to serve as a steward of his wealth. That wealth should be used to benefit the community, but not used for direct charity.

    (B) Josephson, in *The Robber Barons*, characterizes Cornelius Vanderbilt negatively as a robber baron. The quotes used portray Vanderbilt as thinking he is above the law because of his wealth and industrial power.

    (C) Industrialist Andrew Carnegie's actions supported his words. As a young man, Carnegie credited his time learning in public libraries as one of the keys to his success. In his later years, Carnegie supported the work of Booker T. Washington's Tuskegee Institute and funded the building of libraries across the United States. This philanthropy was not without criticism, as some said he built the libraries but did not fund stocking them with books. Nonetheless, the money of many industrial capitalists funded schools, universities, foundations, and other institutions around the nation.

2. (A) Massive immigration answered the demands for cheap labor during the Age of Industrialization. While most immigrants to the United States came from Europe, Chinese immigration caused increased nativist reaction. This cartoonist portrays the Chinese wanting entry into the United States as hardworking, sober, and industrious. However, the doors to enter the United States allowed all other groups including ones with unsavory characteristics entry into the Land of Opportunity.

    (B) Nativist reaction called for greater restrictions on immigration. The first major congressional legislation to restrict an entire ethnic group came in 1882, with support from California nativists. The Chinese Exclusion Act barred entry to the United States from China, effectively cutting off Chinese immigration. Despite helping to build the transcontinental railroads, which facilitated western development, the Chinese had been viewed as a "yellow peril." More comprehensive immigration restrictions would not pass in Congress until the early 20th century.

    (C) The anti-Chinese immigration point of view depicted by the cartoon, also paved the way for the Scott Act in 1888. The Scott Act extended upon the Chinese Exclusion Act, but prohibiting Chinese laborers who returned to China from reentering the U.S. Over 20,000 Chinese laborers who returned to China before the bill was passed, were barred from reentering the U.S.

LONG ESSAY QUESTION SAMPLE RESPONSE

Mark Twain's *Gilded Age* of the late 19th century was marked by all the beauty and horror of the massive industrialization confronting the United States. The demand for goods and labor during that conflict spurred development and growth after the war, although some regions—the South—would not advance as quickly. The changeover to a massive industrial capitalism economy did not come without costs and disruptions. Even the industrial capitalists themselves had to adjust to the boom/bust cycles of the late 19th century. While the country was still primarily agricultural, farmers, especially those in the North Central Plains, had to adjust and battle corporations like the railroads in an attempt to achieve their vision of the American dream.

American industrial capitalists, such as Andrew Carnegie and John D. Rockefeller, had to adjust to the economic conditions of the late 19th century. Railroads introduced pooling as a way to control profit and competition, but that soon gave way to the trust. These massive attempts to monopolize industries were so successful that one cartoon at the turn of the century showed the Statue of Liberty covered in trust banners, while the *We, the People* ferry sank at her feet. Their attempts to generate profit using economies of scale and production efficiencies led them to worry about an eighth and quarter of a cent. In the world of the Chicago meatpackers, any part of the steer or hog that could be used for something to generate profit was used. "Everything but the squeal" was their motto.

The business cycle, with major panics and depressions in 1873 and 1893, impacted profits. Carnegie used the downturn as an opportunity to purchase failing companies and increase his investments. *George Pullman* cut wages, but not rents or the prices charged in his company town of Pullman, Illinois. This resulted in a labor action known as the Pullman Boycott. Usually challenges to an economic power by organized labor were met swiftly and decisively. Likewise, political attempts to regulate trusts led to vaguely worded laws and weak enforcement. It would take until the 20th century for the Interstate Commerce Act and the Sherman Anti-Trust Act to gain momentum against the power of the trusts.

American farmers in the heartland of the USA benefited from industrialism at first. Cyrus McCormick's reaper and John Deere's steel plow allowed the opening of the Great Plains to agricultural development. The North Central states challenged the South in the amount of acres cultivated by the end of the century. However, much of the grain crops were destined to feed the burgeoning immigrant populations in the eastern industrial cities. This meant that the farmers were at the mercy of the railroads and grain storage elevator operators. Farmers and their allies attempted political action. States such as Illinois passed several pro-farm laws known as the Granger laws. No surprise, court challenges came swiftly and frequently. The Munn case upheld the state action when it came to grain storage fees, but railroads that crossed state lines were another matter. The U.S. Supreme Court in the Wabash case overturned Illinois's law. While the Interstate Commerce Act passed in

Congress the following year, its enforcement was lax. Farmers also complained about too little money in circulation and demanded free coinage of silver. Their concerns were picked up by the Populists and Populist/Democratic presidential nominee, William Jennings Bryan, in 1896. But he was defeated by Republican William McKinley. The farmers would not enjoy true prosperity until a short-lived period during World War I, when they fed the United States and elsewhere, enjoying huge profits.

The challenges of late 19th-century industrialization concerned all those having to adjust. The basically *laissez-faire* period seemed to benefit industrialists the most, while those whose economic lives depended on them paid a higher price. Eventually, many of the farmers' proposals for change, including direct election of senators and a graduated income tax, would be taken up by Progressive era reformers.

The thesis is clear and goes well beyond a restatement of the question prompt. The score would be 1 out of 1 point for thesis. The quality of the argument and use of evidence is outstanding. Sophisticated arguments are made and strongly supported with abundant, specific detail. The score would be 2 out of 2 points for support of argument. Cause and effect suggested in this essay is abundant, interwoven, and strongly supported. The score would be 2 out of 2 for application of causation. Synthesis is outstanding as ties are made across geographic regions and there are strong correlations to other time periods. The score would be 1 out of 1 for synthesis. This essay would receive a 6 out of 6 possible points on the Long Essay Question rubric.

CHAPTER 21: EFFECTS OF LARGE-SCALE INDUSTRIALIZATION

THE "FORGETTABLE" ADMINISTRATIONS

Politics in the post-Reconstruction years was marked by lackluster performances by presidents many Americans have never heard of. Rutherford B. Hayes, James Garfield, and Chester A. Arthur all were elected to one term apiece from the years 1876 to 1884, but none did much to earn a place in the nation's collective memory. After the "big" government of the Reconstruction era, many in Washington, D.C., sought to limit the role of the federal government. This was not due so much to ideology but rather to concerns over job security. The **spoils system** got a makeover during the Gilded Age, as leaders in both parties played the game of party **patronage** much as the political machines did in large cities. For example, the Republican party during this time was comprised of three major factions. The **Stalwarts** supported the party patronage system and the **Halfbreeds** opposed it, while the **Mugwumps** remained neutral on the issue and sought modest reforms.

The presidency was not immune from the patronage that plagued the parties at the national level. After a less-than-stellar term by the Republican Hayes, the party chose to run the Halfbreed James Garfield for president with Stalwart Chester A. Arthur as his running mate. After winning the election, however, Garfield quickly set to work appointing party loyalists to coveted civil service positions. As Garfield prepared to leave for his vacation in 1881, an irate civil service job seeker shot him in the back. Garfield hung on for nearly three months, finally succumbing to infection from the wound.

Arthur began to separate himself from his Stalwart pals as he took the presidency. Unfortunately for him, the party chose another candidate for the next election, Senator James Blaine. Blaine did not succeed in winning the election of 1884, as his image had been tarnished by his connection to the Crédit Mobilier and other scandals. Instead, Democrat Grover Cleveland became the first of his party to take the executive office since before the Civil War.

ECONOMY AND CURRENCY ISSUES

Some accomplishments were made during in the "forgotten" administrations, such as passage of the **Pendleton Civil Service Act of 1881**, which reformed the corrupt patronage system. No longer could political cronyism secure government positions—all potential civil service employees had to take an exam to prove their worthiness. The economy became a hot-button issue during the Gilded Age. The money supply was tied to the gold standard, which limited the circulation of currency. As the country rebounded from economic panic after panic, it was clear to those who needed cash the most—farmers and other debtors—that the nation would have to adopt a bi-metal standard or use paper currency in place of limited hard coin. Some argued for the unlimited coinage of silver to loosen up the money supply. Others, such as those in the **Greenback Party**, looked to paper money not backed by hard specie as the answer to the country's economic woes. Currency issues, coupled with debate over the high protective tariff, carried over into the next election in 1888.

AGRARIAN DISCONTENT

Grover Cleveland did not win a second term in 1888, in part because of his support for a lower tariff that would benefit southern and western farmers. The Republicans were able to rally the votes of northern business owners to gain the upper hand in the Electoral College. The new president, Benjamin Harrison, presided over a unified government for two years, with Republicans also in control of the legislative branch. The unification was short-lived, however, as midterm elections gave Democrats back control of Congress.

THE BIRTH OF THE POPULISTS

Republicans also had competition from a rising third party. Taking a cue from the earlier Grange movement, farmers joined forces in several states across the country to form the **Farmers' Alliance**. The Alliance gained membership, successfully seated senators and governors in several Midwestern states, and eventually morphed into the **Populist** (People's) **Party**. Having drafted their political platform in Omaha, Nebraska, in 1892, the Populists advocated for the following: the unlimited coinage of silver; a graduated income tax; public ownership of railroads, telegraph, and telephone; government subsidies to assist in stabilizing agricultural prices; an eight-hour workday; the direct election of U.S. senators; and increased voter power with the use of the initiative, referendum, and recall.

Even though the Populists made an impressive third-party showing in the election of 1892 by garnering almost 1 million popular and 22 electoral votes, they failed to win. Vying for office were President Harrison and former president Cleveland. The Democrat Cleveland became the only president in history to win a second term after leaving the office for a term.

PANIC AND PROTEST

The Democratic victory celebration would be short, however, as the country soon was gripped with an economic depression, triggered by the **Panic of 1893**. Again, railroads and overspeculation by investors artificially inflated the price of stocks, which took a tumble and did not recover for almost four years. Investors began trading in their caches of silver bars for more valuable gold bars, depleting the already dangerously low supply of the latter metal. To mitigate the crisis, President Cleveland brokered a loan from the wealthy investment banker J. P. Morgan for a sum of $65 million and repealed the Sherman Silver Purchase Act. While these actions temporarily solved the gold shortage, they did much more to damage the president in the eyes of the American public, which already was wary of Washington's dealings with big business. The depression brought protesters to Washington under the leadership of Populist **Jacob Coxey**, whose "army" of jobless and homeless Americans proposed federally funded public works projects to employ those who needed work. The government did not listen but rather arrested the "army" for trespassing. Coxey's radical ideas, however, would soon become the cornerstone of policy for a future president who looked to emerge from an even greater depression.

GOLD VERSUS SILVER IN THE 1896 ELECTION

With the economic crisis, currency, and tariff issues still raging, candidates traveled across the country to tout their remedies for a renewed nation before the election of 1896. The Democrats were split over the gold and silver controversy, with "**Gold Bugs**" such as Cleveland on one side and pro-silver advocates without a leader on the other. The young William Jennings Bryan of Nebraska wowed the crowd at the Democratic National Convention with his famous **"Cross of Gold" speech**, which made him the spokesperson for the pro-silver advocates. In essence, the Democrats adopted the old Populist platform, and they nominated Bryan as their candidate for the 1896 election. Cleveland and his "Gold Bugs" were disgusted with the new party direction and left to make their own run for the presidency. The Republicans nominated William McKinley, a friend to labor and a proponent of the gold standard, as their candidate. With the Democratic ticket split and McKinley's use of the media, the Republicans easily took the presidency. Fortunately for McKinley, the country was finally on an economic upswing, and world events would soon turn American's attention away from domestic issues.

ORIGINS OF PROGRESSIVISM

The assassination of President McKinley during his second term brought his spirited, Progressive vice president **Theodore Roosevelt** into office. Reform movements had already established firm roots in local and state politics, but with the executive office now in the hands of the young Roosevelt, the spirit of change had a national champion. The **Progressive Era** began with the swearing in of Theodore Roosevelt in 1901 and lasted until the beginning of U.S. involvement in World War I in 1917.

Much like the reformers of earlier times, Progressives were largely white, middle-class Protestants who hoped to better society. They gained inspiration from earlier reformers such as Walter Rauschenbusch and the Social Gospel movement. The nation was changing at an alarmingly rapid rate, and thus reformers sought to preserve moral values while altering the social, economic, and political fabric of the country at the same time.

This reform movement did differ from past ones, however, as diverse groups such as women, African Americans, and organized labor gained voices as never before. But it was still the white, middle-class segment of the movement that had the greatest impact on legislation.

JOURNALISTS AND AUTHORS STIR CONTROVERSY

Just as newspaper giants Pulitzer and Hearst sought to attract and entertain their readers with sensational stories, a new breed of writer hoped to awaken the reformist spirit. Authors and journalists who wrote articles, essays, and books aimed at exposing scandal, corruption, and injustice were disparagingly called "**muckrakers**" by Theodore Roosevelt, who felt that they took sensationalism a bit too far. Nonetheless, these muckrakers were successful in gaining an audience and stirring up concerns among their readers. Magazines such as *McClure's* and *Collier's* were the first venues of the muckrakers. **Ida Tarbell's** series of articles titled *The History of the Standard Oil Company* (1904) caused a stir, as she detailed the ruthless business tactics of John D. Rockefeller. Starting his career in magazines, **Lincoln Steffens** moved into writing books with his *The Shame of Cities* (1904), which chronicled the corruption and greed of big-city political machines. To show the conditions of New York's tenements in the Lower East Side, Danish photojournalist **Jacob Riis** shocked the nation with his book *How the Other Half Lives*, published in 1890. Muckraking moved into fiction with the works of Theodore Dreiser (*Sister Carrie*) and Frank Norris (*The Octopus*) and became wildly popular through the early 1900s. However, as the era progressed, it became increasingly difficult for muckrakers to best their previous story. Soon the sensational became commonplace, as every newspaper, magazine, and novel had an "exposé." The muckrakers were successful in opening the eyes of many American readers and were moderately successful in gaining the attention of lawmakers and big business.

STATE, LOCAL, AND PRESIDENTIAL PROGRESSIVISM

Progressivism took hold in local and state politics long before it reached the national level. As early as 1888, voters in Massachusetts were using a "secret ballot" to vote in elections. Under the leadership of governor and later U.S. senator **Robert** "Fighting Bob" **La Follette**, Wisconsin became the model for increased voter power at the ballot box. Wisconsin was the first state in the Union to institute **direct primaries** in which state voters nominated their own slate of candidates, as opposed to selection of the party ticket by the state legislature. The **Wisconsin Experiment** led the way for other states to adopt reform laws with regard to taxes, representation, and commerce regulation.

Wisconsin and other states adopted the **initiative, referendum**, and **recall**, once touted by Populists, to increase the power of the voter in state and local politics. The initiative allows voters to propose a law and have it voted upon in an election, the referendum is the way in which voter-proposed public measures are voted upon, and recalls allow voters to remove an elected official from office through the ballot box. States also led the way in adopting the direct election of U.S. senators, with the federal government then making it the **Seventeenth Amendment** to the Constitution in 1913.

City governments looked to right the wrongs caused by political machines and overall voter complacency with massive reforms during the Progressive Era. Public utilities such as electric companies and street-car lines were forced to act in the public interest. Much like Wisconsin, the city of Galveston, Texas, became a model of reform when it became the first municipality in the nation to appoint a city planning commission.

ROOSEVELT AS A MODERN PRESIDENT

Theodore Roosevelt soon became known as the Progressive's president as he worked on issues ranging from labor disputes to land conservation. His **Square Deal** involved breaking up harmful trusts, increasing government regulation of business, giving labor a fair chance, and promoting conservation of the environment.

Theodore Roosevelt is often called the first "modern" president in that he actively set an agenda for Congress and expected it to listen to his legislative suggestions. Roosevelt's first test was a coal miners' dispute in eastern Pennsylvania. Past presidents had all sided with business owners at the expense of labor, but surprisingly, the young president decided to intervene by holding a private meeting in the White House between labor and management. When it was clear that neither side was willing to budge, Roosevelt threatened to take over the mines and run them with federal troops. Reluctantly, the mine owners agreed to lift the lockout, offer a 10 percent pay raise, and accept a nine-hour workday. Roosevelt's willingness to step in on the side of labor garnered him enough support to get him re-elected in his own right in the election of 1904.

Roosevelt's next major effort at reining in the unchecked power of business interests was an attempt to break up the **Northern Securities Company**, which Roosevelt considered a "harmful" trust. The railroad monopoly fought the president by taking its case all the way to the Supreme Court. The Court, however, upheld the president's positions. Roosevelt's victory gave him a reputation as a champion "trust buster." However, this was somewhat misleading, as President Taft had prosecuted twice as many trusts as Roosevelt did and in half the time. Nevertheless, this success gave the president reason to seek ways to regulate the railroad industry. Congress passed the **Elkins Act** in 1903, which gave the Interstate Commerce Commission (ICC) more power to prohibit rail companies from giving rebates and kickbacks to favored customers. The **Hepburn Act** in 1906 allowed the ICC to regulate maximum rates railroad lines could charge, ending the long-haul/short-haul price gouging that had been the bane of farmers. Along with targeting the rail industry, Roosevelt also sought to destroy other harmful trusts, such as Standard Oil.

LITERATURE LEADS TO REFORM

President Roosevelt did react to a piece of muckraking literature that had the nation up in arms. Author Upton Sinclair wrote *The Jungle* to expose the filthy conditions in which meatpacking plants were churning out their products. As a result of the public uproar, Roosevelt worked to establish major reforms that would regulate the food and drug industries.

Roosevelt had firsthand experience with the dangers of food-borne bacteria, as soldiers had suffered from food poisoning during the Spanish-American War that was caused by meat that was poorly preserved, chemically adulterated, and/or spoiled. The meat caused an unrecorded number of illnesses and deaths. To provide more consumer protections, Roosevelt worked to get the **Pure Food and Drug Act** and the **Meat Inspection Act** passed in 1906.

The fourth piece of Roosevelt's "Square Deal" was conservation of the environment. An ardent outdoorsman himself, Roosevelt sought to protect the nation's natural resources from industrialization and human habitation. Roosevelt could name among his friends the naturalist John Muir, and he visited the Yosemite Valley in California often during his presidency. Under Roosevelt's administration, millions of acres of land were protected after the creation of natural reserves and the National Conservation Commission.

TAFT'S PRESIDENCY

The next Progressive president came into the White House in 1909 after serving as Roosevelt's secretary of war. William Howard Taft continued his predecessor's policies of dismantling trusts and regulating business. The **Mann-Elkins Act** of 1910 placed the regulation of communications directly under the ICC. Taft also saw the ratification of the **Sixteenth Amendment** to the Constitution during his presidency, which authorized the federal government to collect an income tax.

Taft's policies were not enjoyed by some within his own party. Progressives were angry at Taft's support of a higher tariff bill, his firing of the popular conservationist Gifford Pinchot after he criticized another cabinet member, and his open support of conservative Republicans during the midterm elections. As a result, the Republican party was split, with liberal Progressives on one side and conservative "Old Guard" Republicans on the other. Taft further angered his predecessor, Roosevelt, by ordering the prosecution of an antitrust violation by U.S. Steel—a merger that Roosevelt himself had approved. Roosevelt took the case as a personal attack by Taft. The feud would encourage Roosevelt to seek presidential re-election for a splinter sect of the Republican party in 1912.

The election of 1912 saw Taft as the Republican candidate, Theodore Roosevelt as a Progressive Republican (or "Bull Moose") nominee, and Woodrow Wilson as the Democratic contender.

The Socialists hoped to make a dent in the election, with Eugene V. Debs again running for president. Taft was already faltering with low approval ratings, and Debs was not an option for most Americans owing to his radical views. Therefore, Roosevelt and Wilson competed for the Oval Office. Roosevelt introduced his vision of "New Nationalism," under which government would take a larger role in business regulations, women would be given the right to vote, and federal assistance programs would be offered to needy Americans. Wilson countered with "New Freedom," which promised a smaller, reformed government, less big business influence, and support for entrepreneurs and small businesses. Thanks to the split in the Republican Party, Wilson enjoyed an easy win but not enough to claim a mandate. Americans in large part supported the Progressive Party, a clear indication that the new president needed to take heed.

WILSON INTRODUCES NEW POLICIES

Wilson sought to break what he saw as the "triple wall of privilege": high tariffs, unfair banking practices, and trusts. In 1913, he persuaded Congress to pass the **Underwood Tariff Bill**, which significantly reduced tariff rates and protected consumers by keeping the price of manufactured goods low. To offset the loss of federal revenues from the lower tariff, Wilson used the power of the Sixteenth Amendment to have Congress enact a graduated income tax.

In light of the Panic of 1907, Wilson was deeply concerned about the financial health of the nation. He looked to Congress to address the problem of the money supply. Congress passed the monumental **Federal Reserve Act** in 1913, which created the **Federal Reserve System**. The new banking system consisted of 12 regional banks that were publicly controlled by the new Federal Reserve Board but privately owned by member banks. The system would serve as the "lender of last resort" for all private banks, hold or sell the nation's bonds, and issue Federal Reserve Notes— otherwise known as dollar bills—for consumers to purchase goods and services. This was the first time since Andrew Jackson killed the Second Bank of the United States that the country would have a national bank.

Another of Wilson's goals was to curb the power of monopolies. His first step was to gain passage of the **Clayton Antitrust Act** in 1914, which finally gave some teeth to the weak and ineffective Sherman Antitrust Act of 1890. The Clayton Act strengthened provisions for breaking up trusts and protected labor unions from prosecution under the Sherman Act. American Federation of Labor leader Samuel Gompers hailed the bill as the "Magna Carta of Labor." Wilson's second step in controlling monopolies was the creation of the **Federal Trade Commission** in 1914. This regulatory agency would monitor interstate business activities and force companies who broke laws to comply with government's "cease and desist" orders. Wilson's Progressive legislation after 1914 would be eclipsed by gradual U.S. involvement in the Great War.

AMERICAN BUSINESS AND CONSUMERISM

Big business continued to enjoy the government's *laissez-faire* policies as the country entered the 1920s. Presidents Harding, Coolidge, and Hoover all sang the praises of the wealthy businessmen of the nation and insulated them from litigation. A booming economy, after a brief recession in 1921, complemented this attitude. The country emerged from World War I as a creditor nation, and American industrial production rose dramatically in response to worldwide demand for manufactured goods. Despite losses that labor endured in 1920 and 1921, workers' wages actually were higher than they ever had been.

This did not mean the work of organized labor was finished. The labor movement suffered setbacks during the 1920s. Business owners fought for the end of the "closed shop" in which all employees had to become members of the union, sinking union membership to an all-time low. Although the standard of living for the average American was higher than in any other nation in the world, not all Americans enjoyed this prosperity. The poor, including many rural tenant farmers, struggled to make ends meet on incomes that were well below the poverty level. Farmers also suffered from a drop in the price of crops and heavy debt.

FORD AND CHANGING CONSUMERISM

Manufacturing fully shared in the prosperity of the new era. American productivity was greater than ever owing to advances in technology and the management systems of men like **Frederick W. Taylor** and **Henry Ford**. Many applied Taylor's principles of **scientific management** to make factory production faster and more efficient. Henry Ford applied Taylor's ideas to the assembly line in his automobile factories. By specializing the work that employees were hired to complete, Ford's factory could make cars at a speed previously unthinkable. Overall, American labor was producing 70 percent more than before the war.

This new prosperity, coupled with massive production of low-priced goods and the birth of modern advertising, led to the growth of a mass-consumption society. Ford's goal was to create an automobile that would be priced so an average American family could purchase one. His providing high wages in return for "thrifty habits" led to his being labeled a "traitor to his class" by other industrialists. By 1929, there were about 30 million automobiles in the nation, compared to barely 1 million before World War I. The car revolutionized American life economically and socially. Because of the increased demand for automobiles, related industries like steel, rubber, petroleum, and road construction experienced booms. Rail was no longer the method of choice for shipping goods on the short haul, as trains gave way to trucks. The way Americans viewed their country was altered; it was now easier to see other regions by driving rather than taking a train. One could stop and see the sights and then stay in a place far away from home. Suburbs grew, because it was now possible for middle-class families to move outside of the city limits and still commute to work in the city. Courting was also changed by the car, as young people could drive alone together to hidden spots in the privacy of their Model T.

New appliances that took advantage of the increasing availability of electric power became the must-have products of Americans looking to keep up with the rising standard of living. Refrigerators, vacuum cleaners, electric stoves, and clothes irons were soon in high demand, as American housewives looked to keep up with their neighbors. All of these must-have products needed to be purchased, and many consumers did not have enough cash to pay up front; therefore, the credit industry boomed.

REPUBLICANS TAKE THE HELM

Hoping to leave the stubborn, idealist presidency of Woodrow Wilson behind, Americans elected Republican Warren G. Harding president in 1920. Harding promised Americans a return to "normalcy," a word he invented to assure citizens that his administration would renew an interest in domestic prosperity and leave intervention in world affairs behind. The Progressive agenda was now a memory.

A SCANDALOUS PRESIDENCY

Harding's election began 12 years of conservative Republican rule. A poker-playing, handsome man from Ohio, Harding was a change from the more dour Wilson. Harding desired to surround himself with men who were familiar to him and capable to assist with running the country. His cabinet, dubbed the **Ohio Gang** or the **Poker Cabinet**, was made up of old friends from the president's home state who were knowledgeable in the areas in which they served. Some positions were filled by powerful men: Wall Street financier Andrew Mellon was secretary of the treasury, former Supreme Court justice Charles Evans Hughes was secretary of state, former head of the Food Administration Herbert Hoover was secretary of commerce, and former president William Taft was a justice on the Supreme Court. Some of his friends did more harm than good, however, as Harding's presidency soon became mired in scandal. It was discovered in 1923 that two of Harding's pals, Secretary of the Interior Albert Fall and Attorney General Harry Daugherty, had illegally leased government oil fields near Teapot Dome, Wyoming, in exchange for bribes of cash and cattle. Fall was charged with fraud and served one year in prison. He was the first cabinet official in history to be charged with a federal offense. As a result, Harding's administration would be labeled as dishonest, and it eventually gained the reputation among some historians as one of the worst presidencies in American history. While on a goodwill tour of the Pacific Northwest, President Harding fell ill and died of pneumonia in August 1923, leaving his vice president, Calvin Coolidge, to take over.

HARDING'S FOREIGN POLICY

In addition to dodging scandal, Harding ignored foreign policy issues and renewed the isolationist spirit. After refusing to join the League of Nations, the United States worked to avoid having the delicate postwar peace disturbed by other countries. A naval arms race had been developing since the end of World War I among the United States, Britain, and Japan. To keep the peace, Secretary of State Hughes organized the **Washington Naval Conference** in 1921 and 1922 to address disarmament issues. Several treaties were signed among the countries present—Belgium, China, France, Portugal, Japan, Italy, the Netherlands, and the United States—to limit the expansion of arms and build territorial respect among all present. The United States also sought to provide economic aid to Germany so it could pay war reparations to Britain and France, thus enabling those nations to repay the United States for their war debts. In 1924, Charles Dawes crafted a loan program that would enable Germany pay its war reparations, thus lessening the financial crisis in Europe. The **Dawes Plan** was successful until the program ended with the U.S. stock market crash in 1929.

COOLIDGE AND HOOVER TAKE OFFICE

After taking the oath of office as president of the United States in his parent's farmhouse in Vermont, Calvin Coolidge set out to promote the ideal of limited government. Less than a year after taking the oath, Coolidge won the presidency in his own right in the election of 1924. "Silent Cal" was a man of few words who worked very little as president. Where Woodrow Wilson would often put in 12- to 15-hour days, Coolidge would rarely work more than four hours a day. Aside from the growth of big business aided by Coolidge's inaction, he is mainly known as a president who refused to pay World War I veterans their promised bonuses and twice vetoed the **McNary-Haugen Bill**, which would have assisted farmers who badly needed price supports. His announcement that he would not seek re-election did not surprise the Republican Party, which had Herbert Hoover waiting in the wings to run for office in 1928.

Running against Democrat Alfred Smith, a New York Catholic "wet" (meaning he opposed prohibition), Hoover won relatively easily on a conservative platform that promised a continuation of prosperity and progress. Unfortunately for the new president, economic disaster befell just eight months from his inauguration. Hoover believed in the strength of the American businessperson. He abided by the idea of "**rugged individualism,**" which held that anyone could become a success if he or she worked hard enough.

At the end of Coolidge's term, world peace was fostered with the signing of the **Kellogg-Briand Pact** in 1928, which made offensive wars illegal throughout the world. Unfortunately, the pact did not have any teeth—it did not prohibit defensive warfare or provide for punishment of countries that disobeyed the pact. Hoover did react in a mild way after Japanese aggression toward Manchuria in 1931. The **Hoover-Stimson Doctrine** of 1932 declared that the United States would not recognize territorial gains made by nations that violated the Kellogg-Briand Pact. Hoover also initiated the **Good Neighbor Policy** with Latin America, withdrawing American forces from Nicaragua to establish more normalized relations.

CAUSES OF THE GREAT DEPRESSION

The United States had experienced economic crises every 20 years or so, usually labeled "panics," from the years 1819 to 1907. Most of these panics were short-lived and corresponded with the natural business cycle. By 1929, the New York Stock Exchange had reached an all-time high, with many stocks selling for more than their actual worth. This **bull market** was a façade, however, as Americans ignored the signs that a serious economic crisis was on the horizon. Millions of Americans sought to "get rich quick" by gambling their life savings in the stock market. Until late September 1929, this seemed a worthwhile risk. In October, however, the financial "bubble" burst, and the stock market collapsed.

"**Black Tuesday**," October 29, 1929, witnessed a selling frenzy on Wall Street—days before, stock prices had plunged to desperate levels. Investors were willing to sell their shares for pennies on the dollar or were simply holding on to the worthless certificates. The signals of impending doom were clear well before the crash. Americans had spent themselves far into debt by purchasing stocks with loans (**buying on margin**). Investors also artificially drove stock prices sky-high by overspeculation, gambling that the value of the stocks would continue to rise. An overproduction of manufactured goods, both consumer and industrial, flooded the American marketplace. When it became apparent to manufacturers that consumer spending was slowing down, especially in the realm of durable goods, they laid workers off or cut wages to maintain their profit levels. Farmers too suffered, as the demand for agricultural goods never rose back to World War I levels. To keep up with technological innovations in agriculture, farmers had to purchase new equipment like tractors on credit, which drove them further into debt. This new equipment added another dimension to their problems, as improved methods led to overproduction.

The American banking system suffered as a result of its own risky practices. Overspeculating on property and issuing risky personal loans led to numerous defaults and foreclosures. Bank customers' deposits were not protected from poor banking practices; as the stock market failed, many of these people lost the money they had deposited.

Republican policies of the 1920s did not help the situation, as *laissez-faire* policies reigned supreme. Globally, economic depression was just around the bend—heavy debt burdens, war reparations, and the suspension of loan programs to assist the rebuilding of Europe drove countries such as Germany and Britain deeper into recession.

HOOVER'S REACTION

Initially, President Hoover believed that Europe was the force behind the economic crisis. In response, Hoover made a grave mistake in hopes of protecting American business from further injury by signing the **Hawley-Smoot Tariff** into law. The tariff on imported goods increased from 30 percent to almost 50 percent and spurred the retaliation of foreign governments, who passed protective tariffs of their own. Hoover also called for a worldwide debt moratorium to ease the struggle of nations paying back loans and reparations from World War I. Hoover's foreign policy was not his downfall; his refusal to address domestic issues was.

A staunch believer in "rugged individualism" and volunteerism, Hoover was reluctant to give direct aid to Americans who were suffering. When it seemed that something had to be done, Congress created the **Reconstruction Finance Corporation** (RFC) in 1932. Too little, too late, the corporation was given authority to issue loans to assist railroads, banks, and municipalities to prevent them from collapsing. Hoover held fast to his belief in "trickle-down" economics, in which the wealthy are given more to spend so eventually they stimulate the economy and the benefits reach the poor. The RFC benefited only the wealthy instead of those truly in need. Hoover continually refused to provide any kind of government assistance to those who were being crushed under the weight of the economic crisis. He believed that private charity groups should be responsible for assisting the needy.

This charity-based solution was not enough for a group of World War I veterans, who marched on Washington in 1932 to demand the early release of bonuses Congress had promised to pay in 1945. The **Bonus Army** arrived in the nation's capital and set up a makeshift encampment around the Capitol. Many Americans who had become homeless had set up similar makeshift camps, which they named "Hoovervilles" as a jab at the current administration. Eventually, the original campers were joined by thousands more veterans and their families, who protested and marched around the Capitol and the White House. The Bonus Bill, however, was not passed by Congress, and a clash between veterans and local police resulted in the deaths of two protestors. President Hoover called in the U.S. Army to stop the ensuing riot, and soldiers used tear gas and tanks on the unarmed protesters. The U.S. Army also burned the encampment, driving the veterans from Washington, D.C. Across the nation, Americans looked on in horror. Many saw Hoover as a heartless coward.

FRANKLIN DELANO ROOSEVELT AND THE NEW DEAL

The election of 1932 took place during the worst year of the depression. The Democratic Party looked for a household name to run for president and chose the governor of New York, **Franklin Delano Roosevelt** (FDR). Roosevelt promised Americans a "new deal" and criticized the ineffective policies of the Hoover administration for massive government spending that had led to a large budget deficit. FDR also promised the repeal of the Eighteenth Amendment. Americans responded and overwhelmingly elected him to office. The president-elect had made a name for himself through a career in politics that had begun in state politics during World War I and then took him on the path of his distant cousin, Theodore Roosevelt. FDR almost left politics permanently when he was stricken by polio in 1921, which paralyzed him from the waist down. If not for the tenacity of his wife, Eleanor Roosevelt, who nursed her husband to health and campaigned for him when he was ill, he might never have become president.

The "new deal" FDR promised as he campaigned was a mystery to Americans—and the president himself—as he entered the Oval Office. Roosevelt knew that he had three goals, which he labeled the "**three Rs**": relief, recovery, and reform. But aside from this, the president had no specific plan of action to release the country from the grip of depression. During his presidential campaign, FDR appointed a group of economists, professors, and politicians he would dub the **Brain Trust** to advise him on matters of economic and political policy. Within the first three months of taking office, FDR managed to get Congress to pass an unprecedented amount of new legislation, which would alter the role of the federal government from that point on. This "**First Hundred Days**" saw the passage of bills aimed at repairing the banking system and restoring American's faith in the economy, starting government works projects to employ those out of work, offering subsidies to farmers, and devising a plan to aid in the recovery of the economy's industrial sector.

The period of 1933 to 1935, called the first **New Deal**, began with a banking holiday. FDR ordered all financial institutions to close for two days; only those banks that were deemed solvent could reopen their doors on the third day. The other banks' assets were taken over by the federal government. To inform Americans of the **Emergency Banking Relief Act** passed on March 9, 1933, that reopened solvent banks, the president gave the first of his "**fireside chats**." FDR delivered these weekly radio addresses to inform and soothe an American public that was reeling from the pain of unemployment and poverty. To shore up the nation's currency, the president took the United States off of the gold standard and recovered all of the gold held by private banks and individuals in exchange for Treasury notes (dollar bills). The **Glass-Steagall Act** prohibited commercial banks from performing the functions of investment banks and paved the way for the Federal Deposit Insurance Corporation (FDIC), which would protect Americans' banking deposits up to $5,000 per deposit. Now Americans could bank with confidence, knowing that their investments could not be used in high-risk financial ventures and that the government was standing by in case of a banking collapse.

Several acts designed to assist in the relief effort were also passed in this period. Beginning what was called an "alphabet soup" of government agencies, the first hundred days saw the birth of such programs as the **Public Works Administration** (PWA), designed to employ thousands of Americans to rebuild the country's infrastructure; the **Civilian Conservation Corps** (CCC), which employed young college- and high school–aged young men to reforest America; and the **Tennessee Valley Authority** (TVA), which worked to electrify the impoverished Tennessee Valley with hydroelectric power. The **National Recovery Administration** (NRA) started industrial relief. The "blue eagle" of the NRA was displayed in the windows of businesses that adhered to the regulations of the agency, which included fair labor practices, price ceilings and floors, and temporary "monopolies" of companies joining forces to increase production. Before long, however, the blue eagle would be shot down—the Supreme Court, under the leadership of Charles Evans Hughes, ruled it unconstitutional in the case of *Schechter v. United States*. This would be the first in a long series of battles between the president and the Supreme Court over his New Deal policies. The next program, the **Agricultural Adjustment Administration** (AAA), was also deemed unconstitutional by the Supreme Court in 1935, but not before it aided many of America's farmers. The AAA paid farmers subsidies to destroy or plow under fields so as to create artificial scarcity, thereby increasing the price of foodstuffs and the profits of farmers.

A SECOND NEW DEAL

The **Second New Deal**, which ran from roughly 1935 to 1938, focused more on relief and reform. Another round of congressional acts continued to increase the federal government's role in the lives of Americans. To encourage more public works projects and the employment of "nontraditional" workers, such as artists, writers, and young people, the **Works Progress Administration** (WPA) employed Americans to build bridges, refurbish parks, write plays, and paint murals. The **Social Security Act** (SSA), passed in 1935, guaranteed income for retirees, the disabled, and the unemployed. Unfortunately, the law was biased—it did not apply to millions of agricultural and service workers, such as domestics, nannies, and janitors, who were largely African American. Nonetheless, the SSA provided a guaranteed pension to shield many of America's most vulnerable from abject poverty.

Watching the American economy from overseas was the British economist John Maynard Keynes. Keynes questioned *laissez-faire* policies and argued that demand determined the health of an economy. Even though Roosevelt was willing to experiment with government policies, he was both unwilling and uninterested in tinkering with fiscal and monetary policy. Keynesian theory proposed that instead of attempting to balance the budget and imposing new taxes on an already "taxed" system, the government should spend that which it did not have—in other words, resort to deficit spending. By the government increasing spending, it would "prime the pump" by spurring an increase in demand that would eventually increase the need for employees. Roosevelt had to do something; the "**Roosevelt Recession**" occurred in 1937 and 1938 because the president had decided to do less government spending. FDR then initiated an increase in spending on public works projects and other programs, which increased investment. It should be noted, however, that even during the best times of recovery during the Great Depression, the unemployment rate never dipped below 16 percent. It took **mobilization** for World War II to finally get the country out of the Great Depression.

ORGANIZED LABOR GAINS

The **National Industrial Recovery Act** (NIRA) passed during the "first" New Deal was the most proactive legislation to date in protecting the rights of workers and organized labor. The provisions of the act were administered by the National Industrial Recovery Administration, which was composed of a board of trustees responsible for setting policy for industry in the United States.

The board set maximum work hours, minimum wages, and price floors. It was also responsible for setting production quotas and inventories to prevent overproduction or price gouging. Most importantly for organized labor, **Section 7a** of NIRA formally guaranteed organized labor the right to collectively bargain and organize. No longer was the old "yellow-dog contract" or "iron-clad oath" an issue; unions could actively recruit members in American factories and workplaces. Finally, organized labor had gained recognition of its rights.

To further the gains of labor, the **National Labor Relations Act** of 1935—also called the Wagner Act after it's sponsor, who penned the bill—strengthened the language of Section 7a of NIRA. Even though all labor unions fought for the protections of workers, not all agreed on whom should be protected. The **American Federation of Labor** (AFL) comprised mainly skilled workers who did not agree that unions should protect all workers. Members of the AFL who wished to extend union membership to all workers broke away and joined other labor groups to form the **Congress of Industrial Organizations** (CIO) under the leadership of John L. Lewis of the United Mine Workers. The CIO focused on organizing unskilled laborers in America's heavy industrial sector such as steel, automobiles, and mines. By 1938, the CIO was completely independent of the AFL. During the Second New Deal, the **Fair Labor Standards Act** established a federal minimum wage and maximum hours for interstate businesses and ensured an end to child labor.

This is not to say that organized labor was entirely happy throughout the New Deal. Some industries resisted unionization. To drive a point home to General Motors in Flint, Michigan, the **United Auto Workers** (UAW) organized a "sit-down strike" of assembly line employees in the plant in 1936 and 1937. When the government refused to intervene between labor and management, the companies reluctantly went to the bargaining table and officially recognized the UAW as an official party with which to negotiate worker contracts. The UAW did not fare as well at the Ford plant, however, as workers were driven away violently before they could strike. The steel industry was also slow in its recognition of unions, with most plants finally accepting their workers' unions by the arrival of World War II.

NEW DEAL SUPPORTERS AND CRITICS

The New Deal was largely supported by Democrats, who stood by their charismatic president from the day he took office. Organized labor became an ally of both FDR and the Democratic Party, as the administration continued to support workers and workers' rights throughout the New Deal. African Americans also became ardent supporters of the Democrats and FDR as the New Deal continued. President Roosevelt, at the urging of his wife Eleanor, appointed more African Americans to executive department positions than had any president before him. His **"Black Cabinet"** advised him on issues ranging from the repeal of Jim Crow laws in the South to anti-lynching legislation. Unfortunately for African Americans, FDR needed to maintain the support of Southern Democrats and did not sign any legislation designed to end either of these practices.

Changing Party Politics and Anti-FDR Sentiments

The Republicans and Democrats both experienced changes in the makeups of their parties as the role of government changed. Southern Democrats struggled with FDR's liberal values with regard to race and gender relations, while many considered fleeing to the "party of Lincoln." The Republicans were experiencing an influx of conservative Northerners and Southerners who had been lifelong Democrats but disagreed with FDR's handling of the Great Depression. Supporters argued that the New Deal had been successful in keeping millions of Americans from the clutches of poverty.

FDR had critics both inside and outside his party. It seemed that in some respects FDR could do nothing right. Extremists on both ends of the political spectrum charged that the president was either not doing enough or doing too much. Socialists argued that the administration needed to do more with regard to the "forgotten man," or the poor. Conservatives were frightened by the increasing role of the government in every aspect of Americans' lives. Claiming that the New Deal was "socialism," anti-Roosevelt Democrats formed the **American Liberty League** to promote the concerns of big business and advocate for small government. They were so convinced that the New Deal and FDR were bad for America that they sought to unseat FDR as he ran for president in 1936.

Some of FDR's critics used the airwaves to reach Americans, much as the president did with his Fireside Chats. Playing to the fears of the average citizen, Catholic priest Father Charles E. Coughlin attacked the New Deal as a benefit to only the well-to-do and big business. He was extremely popular; almost 40 million Americans tuned in to his radio show every week. Father Coughlin eventually digressed into **anti-Semitic** and **fascist** tirades before Catholic leaders pulled him from the air. Before the passage of the Social Security Act, **Dr. Francis Townsend** advocated a federal pension that would provide $200 a month for every retired American over the age of 60. His plan gathered millions of supporters, who agreed that if retirees were given this pension and required to spend it all within a month, it would stimulate the economy. Roosevelt decided that he would opt for a much less radical plan, which became the Social Security Act. After its passage, Townsend criticized the president for not pushing for more.

From within Congress, Roosevelt found a critic in the senator from Louisiana, **Huey P. "Kingfish" Long**. Long had long advocated a "Robin Hood" plan to take from the rich and give to the poor called "Share Our Wealth." His plan would impose heavy taxes on inheritance and estates to fund a minimum salary of $2,000 a year for every American. Long argued that the New Deal was not enough to aid the country's most needy citizens. Felled by an assassin's bullet in 1935, Long might have challenged Roosevelt for the Democratic nomination in 1936.

The Supreme Court offered another challenge for Roosevelt as he continued to drive more and more legislation through Congress and further increase the power of the executive and legislative branches. Fed up with Court decisions that had effectively killed two important pieces of New Deal legislation (the NRA and the AAA), Roosevelt decided that he was going to reorganize the Supreme Court with the hope that his legislation might find a more sympathetic audience. His **Judicial Reorganization Bill** (1937) would allow the president to appoint one justice for every seated justice over 70 years old. At the time, the bill would have given FDR the ability to seat six justices on the court, bringing the number to 15. Conservatives and Republicans immediately opposed it and dubbed the bill a "court-packing scheme." Neither side would back down, but the bill finally died when some of FDR's biggest supporters refused to back it. It may have been the threat of the reorganization or a softening of the Court, but by the time the "court-packing" bill was killed, the Court was backing down from its previous hard-line stance. Roosevelt eventually was able to make eight appointments to the Supreme Court during his presidency, leaving a liberal legacy on the bench. After the "Roosevelt Recession" in 1937, the economy had only modestly rebounded, and many problems such as high unemployment and poverty remained. Americans voiced their concerns during the midterm elections of 1938, when some Republicans and moderate Democrats replaced supporters of the New Deal. This, coupled with worldwide attention turning to Hitler's actions, signaled an end to the New Deal.

CHAPTER 22: THE NEW MASS CULTURE

WOMEN'S ROLES: FAMILY, WORK, EDUCATION, AND SUFFRAGE

Many Progressive politicians were not so liberal as to believe that women should have a voice in politics. Still, women's roles in the United States continued to shift as industrialization took hold in more parts of the country. No longer was it necessary for most American families to have many members to care for the family farm. Very few urban families had more than two children; thus, the role of the woman as mother and homemaker decreased.

More and more women entered the workforce as factory jobs opened up. Women were mainly involved in the textile industry, working in spinning mills or large garment factories. Other women found work as telephone or telegraph operators, secretaries, or typists. Some women entered the world of academia, as women's universities opened across the nation. Mount Holyoke, Wellesley, and Barnard all offered women the opportunity to attain a liberal arts education.

Not all women could afford to attend college; they had to enter the workforce to help support their families. Some even broke through the male-dominated world of labor unions to promote better working conditions for females. The International Ladies' Garment Workers Union (ILGWU) organized women who worked in sweatshops in cities like New York and Chicago. On March 25, 1911, the unspeakable happened in a New York City sweatshop. The **Triangle Shirtwaist Factory** was housed in the top floors of the Asch building, where women and girls, some as young as 15 years old, were crammed in. Windows, doors, and fire exits were completely blocked by people, machines, and trash cans. That night, just before closing, a fire broke out on the ninth floor. With no way to escape, many of the young women died in the building, while others jumped from windows to the pavement below. After the flames were finally tamed, the fire had taken 146 of 500 employees' lives. The ILGWU organized protest rallies to inform others around the country of the tragedy. As a result, the state of New York made massive reforms in the conditions of its garment factories. This victory was bittersweet, however, as the owners of the factory were later acquitted of any wrongdoing, even though they had known the exits and fire escapes were all locked.

Active among the railroad workers and coal miners, female activist **Mother Jones** traveled the country protesting and lobbying for the rights of all workers. Even as she lost her ability to write and walk without assistance, Mother Jones continued to fight for labor rights up until her death at the age of 93 in 1930.

College-educated women were emboldened by the successes of their male Progressive counterparts and looked to improve their standing in the United States. The **National American Woman Suffrage Association** (NAWSA) gained a new president in 1900 with the election of **Carrie Chapman Catt**. Catt was an outspoken advocate of women's suffrage. She believed that women could only guarantee protections for themselves and their children through voting. The NAWSA would soon have some inner conflict, as more radical members of the group wanted to push for more immediate action. Led by **Alice Paul**, this splinter group left the NAWSA to form the **National Women's Party**. The women in this group often picketed important sites, such as the White House and the Capitol, to demand the right to vote. Arrests occurred, and the women were known for going on hunger strikes while in jail. President Woodrow Wilson was disgusted with these militant protesters, who would chain themselves to the White House gates, yell insults at the president, and carry signs intending to embarrass the chief executive. He did, however, listen to Carrie Chapman Catt, who skillfully used the American mobilization for entrance into World War I to advance her cause. She claimed that armed with the vote, American women would support their president and country as it entered the worldwide crisis. Her message, delivered on the eve of the congressional vote on women's suffrage, hit home. President Wilson gave his public support for the amendment.

Because of the efforts of women such as Catt, the **Nineteenth Amendment**, which granted women the right to vote, was ratified in 1920. Catt formed the **League of Women Voters** to assist these new voters, while Paul continued working with the National Woman's Party and shifted her focus to the Equal Rights Amendment (ERA), which repeatedly failed passage and finally succumbed in the early 1980s.

AFRICAN AMERICANS AT THE TURN OF THE CENTURY

As mentioned before, the Progressives were largely white, middle-class citizens who were interested in reforming American society. African Americans were largely ignored by Progressive agendas at the local, state, and national levels. Progressive President Woodrow Wilson even issued an executive order to segregate federal buildings and named the racist silent film *Birth of a Nation*—which glamorized the history of the Ku Klux Klan—as one of his personal favorites. Since the end of Reconstruction, the protection of African American civil rights had decreased as the federal government failed to take stands against segregation, disenfranchisement, and lynching. It was up to African Americans themselves to fight for their own rights.

Having risen to prominence during the late 1890s, **Booker T. Washington** continued to argue that African Americans needed the skills necessary to work within the white world. In essence, he argued that blacks needed to make themselves successful economically before they could become equal to whites. This view came to be known as "**accommodation**." On the other side of the fence was Harvard-educated **W.E.B. Du Bois**, who disagreed vehemently with Washington. Du Bois believed that African Americans should demand nothing less than social and political equality with whites; only then would blacks gain economic success. In 1905, Du Bois held a meeting in Niagara Falls to discuss possible forms of protest and to formulate a plan of action. This group, called the **Niagara Movement**, joined forces with other concerned African Americans and whites to form the **National Association for the Advancement of Colored People (NAACP)** on February 12, 1908. Founding members W.E.B. Du Bois, Ida Wells-Barnett, Henry Moscowitz, Mary White Ovington, Oswald Garrison Villiard, and William English Walling answered what they deemed the "call" to end all racial discrimination, segregation, and disenfranchisement. The NAACP became one of the largest and most active civil rights groups in the country. It was so influential that it pushed President Wilson to make a public statement condemning lynching in 1918.

The activism of the NAACP and Booker T. Washington was spurred by the increase in discriminatory practices throughout the country. In the period between 1910 and 1930, a "**Great Migration**" of millions of African Americans moved from the southern to northern cities in search of jobs and a better life. Just as the cities had lured European immigrants during the 1880s, the promise of factory work and less discrimination brought blacks to urban centers. Unfortunately, northern African Americans experienced horrible living conditions, low-paying jobs, and racial discrimination. African Americans would find the fight against discrimination just as difficult in the north as it was in the south.

BIRTH OF MODERN CULTURE

America's new mobility—aided by the automobile and later by air travel—and the rise of radio and film as forms of mass communication helped spawn a new American sensibility, which would excite some and frighten others.

THE ROARING TWENTIES

Often called the **Jazz Age** or the **Roaring Twenties,** the era from 1920 to 1929 experienced a cultural explosion similar to that of the antebellum period. Jazz music began to change as it moved from the Deep South into Northern cities like Chicago and Philadelphia. It became the music of choice for the young and "hep" urbanites.

American families had more leisure time and looked to entertainment to fill their evenings and weekends. Commercial radio began in 1920 with the first broadcast of limited range by KDKA in Pittsburgh and expanded with the establishment of the National Broadcast System (NBC) in 1924, which reached some 5 million homes across the country. A radio listener in California was often listening to the same program as someone in New York City. A common cultural identity was established, as Americans listened to comedy, drama, and sports from all corners of the nation. Movies became wildly popular; Americans flocked to the theaters to see these "moving pictures." Early films were silent, with text at the bottom of the screen for the actor's dialogue and a live orchestra playing the film's score. The release of *The Jazz Singer* in 1927 began the age of the "talkies," so now audiences could listen to actors converse onscreen. Hollywood, California, became the glamorous entertainment capital of the country, home to such stars as Rudolph Valentino and Lillian Gish. Radio and movies altered the standard for the "true American hero" as movie stars, radio personalities, and professional athletes took the place of presidents and world leaders. Professional sports also gained a large following. Big boxing matches between Jack Dempsey and Gene Tunney mesmerized fans, and the legendary Babe Ruth hit home runs out of Yankee Stadium.

Some Americans were not as pleased by the more materialistic, mass-consumption society of the 1920s. A group of authors and artists, increasingly concerned about the influence of money and conservatism on society, began to express themselves. The "**Lost Generation**" was made up of authors and poets such as F. Scott Fitzgerald, Gertrude Stein, Ezra Pound, and Ernest Hemingway. Artists such as Georgia O'Keeffe and Thomas Hart Benton reacted to the impact of technology and business by painting realist or early surrealist works that portrayed American themes without the glitter of consumerism.

Harlem, a neighborhood of New York City, became the center of African-American culture in the 1920s. Here African-American artists, poets, and musicians gave birth to a movement now called the **Harlem Renaissance**. Deeply critical of white society in some respects, writers such as Countee Cullen, Langston Hughes, and Zora Neale Hurston wrote poems, essays, and novels expressing the joy and pain of being an African American. Artists such as Sterling Brown and Augusta Savage brought African American and African culture to life and into the homes of many white New York socialites. Jazz musicians like Louis Armstrong and Duke Ellington became wildly successful as they traveled the country playing concerts for all Americans. The Harlem Renaissance helped to change the perception of African Americans in particular and fostered a greater social consciousness of the abilities and worth of all Americans in general. When the stock market crashed in 1929, white patronage for artists slowed; however, many musicians continued to prosper.

A CONSERVATIVE REACTION

The 1920s stereotype of flappers and speakeasies does not reveal the underlying cultural struggle between the conservative right and the modernist left. Many Americans were frightened by the changes occurring around them and sought to protect their communities from perceived moral degradation. Fundamentalists, prohibitionists, and nativists all hoped to stop these changes from impacting American lives.

A FIGHT OVER EVOLUTION

Fundamentalist Christians had new fuel for their fight when the American Civil Liberties Union (ACLU) found a Tennessee science teacher willing to become its test case regarding a state statute that barred teaching the theory of evolution. **John Scopes**, a biology teacher in Dayton, Tennessee, was arrested and brought to trial in 1925. The ACLU appointed the famous lawyer Clarence Darrow to represent Scopes, while the state of Tennessee chose the outspoken Christian fundamentalist and former presidential candidate **William Jennings Bryan** as its counsel. The trial was a spectacle, as newspaper and radio press swarmed the town of Dayton. Darrow got Bryan to fumble and contradict himself as Bryan tried to use the Bible to justify the statute while testifying as a religious expert. In the end, however, Scopes was found guilty. The conviction was later overturned.

PROHIBITION AND ORGANIZED CRIME

Prohibitionists continued to protect their coveted constitutional amendment, although it was ineffective and largely unenforced. The **Volstead Act** of 1920, the enforcement arm of the Eighteenth Amendment, had many Americans finding ways to skirt the law. Many in America's cities visited secret clubs called **speakeasies** where visitors needed to know the password and whisper it, or "speak easy," to gain entrance. Even President Harding defied the law by serving alcohol in the White House to guests and dignitaries. The underground or "bootleg" network of illegal alcohol began first with small-time distillers, who would brew "bathtub gin" for sale to local clients. Soon organized crime took hold of the bootlegging industry and grew in size, influence, and violence. The infamous Chicago crime boss Al Capone ran a network of illegal activities that began with alcohol and soon included drugs, prostitution, and illegal gambling. Violent turf wars between rival gangs made Chicago one of the most dangerous cities in the United States. Soon many called for the repeal of the Eighteenth Amendment, as it looked as if the "noble experiment" engendered more disgust than respect for the law.

IMMIGRATION RESENTMENT AND RACISM CONTINUE

Meanwhile, European immigrants and African American migrants continued to move into American cities well into the 1920s, and they were met by a resurgence of the nativist feelings that the Know-Nothing Party had embraced in the 1850s. In response, Congress passed several laws aimed at curbing the tide of immigrants coming from European countries. The **Quota Act**, or **Immigration Act**, of 1921 set a 3 percent limit on individuals from each nation of origin based on the 1910 census. The second was the **National Origins Act** of 1924, which set the limit at 2 percent based on the 1890 census; this act was directed at Southern and Eastern European and Asian immigrants.

The once-powerful racist organization the Ku Klux Klan experienced a rebirth during the 1920s with an ire directed not just at African Americans but at Jews, Catholics, and communists.

The new KKK used the terror tactics it had employed in the Reconstruction era, such as cross burnings, whippings, and lynchings. Klan members included government officials and police in many Southern and Midwestern cities. In 1925, a former Grand Dragon of the Klan was convicted of murder, and the public nature and membership of the Klan dipped significantly.

The case of Nicola Sacco and Bartolomeo Vanzetti best illustrates the injustice of nativism. The robbery and murder of a paymaster in South Braintree, Massachusetts, resulted in the arrest of two Italian anarchists, Sacco and Vanzetti. The evidence in the case was contradictory and confused. However, the two were convicted and sentenced to death by electric chair. Many Americans—such as Albert Einstein and the Italian American community—came to their defense, but to no avail. After multiple appeals, Sacco and Vanzetti were executed in 1927.

THE CONTINUING STRUGGLE FOR EQUALITY

Immigrants were not alone in their struggle for an equal place in American society. African Americans and women continued to fight for basic civil rights and equality. Some had radical solutions to the problems of inequality, while others chose to work within the system to better their lives.

Amidst the Harlem Renaissance, a young Jamaican immigrant named Marcus Garvey had formed the **United Negro Improvement Association** and encouraged African Americans to form a separate community from white society. He eventually advocated a "Back to Africa" movement. Unfortunately for the movement, Garvey was arrested and convicted for tax fraud. Garvey was deported back to Jamaica in 1929, and the "Back to Africa" movement collapsed. Other African Americans, such as W.E.B. Du Bois and the NAACP, continued to fight for social justice and equality as the number of lynchings increased in the South.

The "cult of domesticity" continued to be a reality for American women, particularly those of the middle class. New inventions, such as the vacuum cleaner and dishwasher, left many American women wondering what to do with their spare time. But this leisure time was not experienced by all women, as lower-class women had to work outside of the home to make ends meet. Young women began to break away from the Victorian style, to the disgust of many of their elders. The "**flappers**," so named because they were not unlike baby birds flapping their wings and leaving the nest, cut their hair into short "bobs," wore short skirts, rolled down their stockings to reveal their knees, drank alcohol, and danced the Charleston. Their numbers were few, but their behavior was very public and raised concerns among America's conservatives. Also of great concern to America's conservatives was the increase in divorce during the 1920s. Now that women were voting, legislators had to listen to their concerns. One concern was maintaining the ability to divorce. As a result of more liberal laws regarding divorce, divorces happened in much greater numbers than before. Women also benefited from new laws making attendance in school compulsory until age 16. This opened doors for many women to gain a college education. Margaret Sanger caused controversy when she advocated the use of birth control, founding the American Birth Control League in 1921. Sanger encouraged young women to discuss openly issues ranging from menstruation to the prevention of pregnancy and worked to help put a stop to poverty, abuse, and premature death of young women.

AMERICAN SOCIETY THROUGH THE DEPRESSION

The Great Depression had a profound impact on those who experienced it. Many of these Americans were insecure about their personal finances well into the 1940s and 1950s, despite new prosperity. Americans from all walks of life had to "make do" with what was available to them. Depression cookbooks would include recipes for dishes such as "dandelion soup" made with water, a potato, and dandelion greens that could be picked from the lawn. Desperate unemployed businessmen would turn to selling apples on the street for a nickel to avoid having to accept charity. Even with the ingenuity of Americans, soup kitchens and bread lines became an everyday sight across the country as citizens looked for a meal. Many proud Americans were not happy about having to take a handout and did so reluctantly.

THE ROLE OF WOMEN AND THE DUST BOWL

Certain groups of Americans faced special challenges during the Depression. Women were often left with the burden of caring for children alone, as many were left behind by their husbands; many men deserted their families out of shame because they could not find work to support a wife and child. Women entered the workforce when possible to supplement meager incomes brought in by husbands and other family members. Scraping together enough money to keep the family fed, clothed, and housed was a daily struggle for women during the Depression.

That plight was even more difficult for the wives of farmers in the Great Plains region. A severe drought hit the Great Plains, killing all of the crops. The topsoil turned to a fine, powdery dust that blew away with the severe, hot winds that wreaked havoc on the farmers who remained. The area was called the **Dust Bowl**, as Plains farmers saw their land literally blow away. With no opportunity to save their land from foreclosure, many of these families packed their belongings onto trucks and sought a new life in the west. California picking companies blanketed the Dust Bowl region with flyers promising jobs, money, housing, and fields of beautiful produce. As a result, many of these farmers and their families flocked to California and earned the name

"**Okies**," as many came from the panhandle regions of Oklahoma or Texas. If they survived the journey, many of these migrants realized upon arrival that they were not in the "Promised Land." Bouncing from migrant camp to migrant camp, Okies experienced discrimination, abuse, and humiliation. Nonetheless, many remained in California, finally settling in its Central Valley region to begin a new life.

MINORITIES IN THE DEPRESSION

American minority groups fared much worse than whites during the depression. African Americans struggled to survive, as there was little work available to them. Moreover, because of discrimination all across the nation, many African Americans were not given assistance from their states or cities. Despite FDR's need for the support of Southern Democrats, African Americans did find a friend in him and Eleanor Roosevelt. Several New Deal programs openly accepted African Americans, and after a threatened march on Washington to be organized by Rail Porters Union president A. Philip Randolph, the **Fair Employment Practices Committee** (FEPC) was established to prohibit employment discrimination in the defense industry. Native Americans regained self-governance with the **Indian Reorganization Act** of 1934, which repealed the Dawes Act of 1887 and returned lands to the tribes and gave support to Native Americans to re-establish and preserve tribal culture. Mexican Americans continued to face discrimination in areas where they had lived for years. The federal government was of no assistance, and many Mexican Americans chose to go to Mexico.

CHAPTER 23: RENEWED DEBATES OVER THE NATION'S VALUES

NEW IMPERIALISM VIA POLITICS AND ECONOMICS

With the closing of the western frontier, many Americans felt that Manifest Destiny had still not been fulfilled. That, coupled with the rise of American economic power, led many to believe that the time was ripe to expand beyond the contiguous United States.

SEWARD'S FOLLY

The United States first set its sights on Alaska, a region then held by Russia on the northwestern edge of North America. Secretary of State William H. Seward brokered a deal to purchase the land from Russia for a sum of $7.2 million in 1867. At the time, Seward was seen by many as a laughingstock, and Alaska was nicknamed "**Seward's Folly**" or "**Seward's Icebox**." Not until the 20th century, when oil drillers found that Alaska was rich with fossil fuel, would Americans realize the sweet deal they had gotten.

OVERSEAS EXPANSION

Charles Darwin had not realized the extent to which people throughout the world would take his theory of evolution and distort it to fit their specific agendas. Industrialists had used it to justify their wealth with "social Darwinism," and imperialists would use it to justify their expansionism in the late 19th and early 20th centuries. **Imperialism** was not a new idea. European nations had been establishing new colonies as early as the mid-1800s in places such as Africa and Asia. It was this early expansion that led President Monroe to unveil his Monroe Doctrine in 1823. This "new" imperialism was spurred by the concept of **jingoism** (extreme **nationalism** that encourages a very aggressive foreign policy stance), the desire to find new markets in which to sell American goods, and social Darwinism.

One proponent of overseas expansion was U.S. Naval Captain Alfred Thayer Mahan. His influential book *The Influence of Sea Power upon History* (1890) focused on the idea that the

United States needed to pour money and resources into the building a powerful, world-class navy to become a major world power broker. To do this, Mahan contended that the United States would need to occupy sites around the world to establish refueling stations and naval bases. The most logical areas for such bases were Hawaii and Cuba. Mahan also advocated the building of a canal across the Isthmus of Panama to provide a quick route from the Pacific to the Atlantic. Thus, the focus for early expansion was on Pacific islands and Central America. American minister to Hawaii John Stevens perfectly illustrated the U.S. view of the islands when he said, "The Hawaiian pear is now fully ripe, and this is the golden hour for the United States to pluck it." He uttered these words as an unauthorized battalion of U.S. troops landed on the islands to assist a planter revolt, led by the American pineapple exporter Sanford B. Dole. The revolt began when a new, nationalist queen named Liliuokalani took the throne and began to expel whites from the islands. Dole and a small band of planters revolted against the queen and demanded assistance from the United States. But by the time word had reached President Cleveland, the damage had been done. A treaty to authorize the **annexation** of the islands was passed by Congress. Cleveland was outraged and refused to sign the treaty, instead demanding the reseating of the queen on the throne and the immediate removal of American troops. He was unsuccessful, however, as Dole and his followers declared Hawaii an independent republic in 1894. Hopes of annexation faded until 1898, when Dole was appointed to serve as provincial governor of the islands.

THE SPANISH-AMERICAN WAR

The debate regarding overseas expansion moved to the Caribbean, as trouble reared its head on the Spanish-held island of Cuba. Americans had moved to Cuba after the Civil War to establish large sugar plantations on the lush, tropical island. Cuban natives had been growing more and more irritated by the presence of foreigners, American and Spanish, who amassed huge fortunes while natives toiled on the plantations and subsisted from day to day. The Spanish sensed the seeds of revolt and set to nip a revolution in the bud by "**reconcentrating**" the Cuban natives into central locations under direct Spanish control. Many Cubans died as a result of this effort to rid the country of revolutionaries.

Americans heard of the atrocities, real and sensationalized, from the American popular press. Papers such as Hearst's *Journal* and Pulitzer's *World* radically altered the truth of stories coming out of Cuba in the effort to sell papers. This kind of writing was dubbed "**yellow journalism**," after a popular color comic strip called "Yellow Kid" that ran exclusively in Hearst's paper. As a result, many Americans and Cuban immigrants in the United States grew increasingly concerned over the events in Cuba. American jingoism also contributed to concerns over the island. Presidents Cleveland and McKinley did not favor intervention, however. It would take a supposed attack on the United States to make war an option for McKinley.

Popular opinion on Cuba began to shift toward war when, in 1898, a letter was leaked to Hearst's *Journal*. In this letter, Spanish minister to the United States Dupuy de Lome insinuated that President McKinley was corrupt. Americans immediately took this as a direct insult from the

Spanish. The next event made war inevitable in the eyes of most Americans. On February 15, 1898, the *USS Maine* exploded in Havana Harbor under mysterious circumstances. The ship had arrived in the Cuban harbor to provide protection and act as an escape vessel for the Americans currently living on the island. The ship exploded while anchored in the harbor, killing 260 sailors and injuring many more. The Spanish immediately responded by denying any role in the tragedy. The Americans sent down a team to investigate the wreckage and declared that a submarine mine had sunk the ship. Hearst and Pulitzer took to the story and blamed the Spanish for the tragedy, further fanning the flames of war. Americans now cried "Remember the *Maine*!" to push President McKinley to declare war on Spain. The president was reluctant to issue the war decree without some caveats. The **Teller Amendment** was added to the war declaration to assure Cuba and the world that the United States intended to grant Cuba her independence once the war ended.

The **Spanish-American War** officially began on April 11, 1898. Fighting did not begin in Cuba but rather in the Spanish colony of the Philippines. U.S. Naval Commodore George Dewey was sent with his fleet to Manila Bay and opened fire on May 1. This naval battle was short-lived—the U.S. Navy was able to rout the Spanish fleet in a matter of hours. But as the battle made landfall, it was not quite as easy. Many Filipinos fought to oust both the Spanish and American forces. The United States was able to convince the Filipino revolutionary Emilio Aguinaldo to assist in the fight against the Spanish in exchange for independence after the war's end. As a result, the American and Filipino fighters were able to take Manila by August.

The fight in Cuba would be much more difficult—not because of better Spanish fighters but because of tropical diseases and the inexperience of the American forces. Most American causalities, some 5,000, were attributed to diseases, with just 10 percent due to actual combat. The most celebrated American battle was for the high ground of San Juan Hill. Theodore Roosevelt and his volunteer force of college students, cowboys, and adventurers called the "**Rough Riders**" were able to take the Hill with the heavy assistance of the Fourteenth Regiment Colored Calvary.

UNITED STATES INVADES PUERTO RICO

After the United States claimed victory in Cuba on July 1, it invaded the Spanish colony of Puerto Rico. Unwilling to fight any longer, the Spanish signed a cease-fire with the United States in August 1898.

The resulting peace treaty, signed in Paris, gave the United States the Pacific island of Guam and the Caribbean island of Puerto Rico. The most difficult decision was what to do with the Philippines. President McKinley was between a rock and a hard place. On one hand, he could give the Philippines their independence as promised, or he could take the islands and face the court of world opinion. He decided that the United States would take the Philippines and deal with the independence issue at a later date.

PROBLEMS WITH THE NEW EXPANSION

The debate over imperialism intensified with the end of the Spanish-American War. Anti-imperialists such as **William Jennings Bryan** even formed an organization to oppose U.S. expansion publicly. Citizens living in newly conquered territories brought cases regarding their constitutional rights to the U.S. Supreme Court. In 1901, the Court ruled in the **Insular Cases** that the Constitution and its protections did not follow the flag. In other words, a citizen in a conquered territory did not necessarily have the protection of the Constitution. It was up to Congress to decide the rights of the peoples in the newly conquered territories. As Cuba set to draft its constitution, the United States ignored the Teller Amendment and its promise to give Cuba independence. Thus, the United States issued the **Platt Amendment** in 1903, which Cubans would now have to incorporate into their new constitution. The provisions of the Platt Amendment were that Cuba had to have all treaties approved by the United States, the United States had the right to interfere in Cuban affairs both politically and militarily, and the United States would be given access to naval bases on the island. In essence, the Cubans had not gained their independence at all.

The United States then turned its attention to other parts of the world. The Filipinos, under the leadership of the once–American ally Aguinaldo, revolted against the American presence. Horrible guerrilla warfare broke out between the Filipino revolutionaries and Americans on the islands in 1899. Aguinaldo and his fighters were finally subdued by the Americans in 1901, when the leader was captured. The Philippines did not gain its independence until 1946.

China was another area of interest for Americans, especially investors. Japan and European nations had already carved China up into **spheres of influence** in which they basically controlled the economic dealings of specific regions. Hoping to get a piece of the action, Secretary of State John Hay announced the "**Open Door Policy.**" Under the Open Door Policy, China and would be open and free to trade with any nation. The policy was wildly popular in the United States but, unsurprisingly, was denounced and resisted in China. In 1900, a young group of Chinese nationalists revolted against the Open Door Policy and foreign intervention. The **Boxer Rebellion** sought to remove all foreigners from China by force. The Boxers killed some 200 whites, and a multinational force, including U.S. forces, was sent to Peking and ended the rebellion. It was clear that the Chinese were not interested in foreign intervention in their political and economic affairs.

THE PANAMA CANAL

The canal that Mahan had suggested became a reality, as Americans and Europeans built one across the Isthmus of Panama. Construction was begun by Ferdinand de Lesseps, who had constructed the Suez Canal. Unfortunately, the construction effort was plagued with setbacks—workers fell to disease and engineering troubles ensued due to the tropical climate and geography, respectively. The United States was more than willing to take over the building of the canal, but several issues stood in the way. First, the United States needed to secure the right to build the canal from Colombia, since the canal would go right through the country. The Colombian government did not recognize the **Hay-Pauncefote Treaty**, in which the British granted full construction rights to the Americans. The nation of Panama would have to be created, and quickly.

In secrecy and with the aid of the French, President Theodore Roosevelt raised a revolutionary force to fight for Panamanian independence from Colombia. The "revolution" ended as quickly as it began; Roosevelt immediately recognized the new nation. It came as no surprise that the Panamanian government quickly signed an agreement to allow the United States to build the canal in 1903. The building was completed in 1914. Critics of Roosevelt's policy regarding Panama branded his actions "**gunboat diplomacy**." Latin American countries were becoming increasingly alarmed at the way the "Colossus of the North" was flexing its muscles throughout the region.

THE ROOSEVELT COROLLARY CHANGES RELATIONS ABROAD

President Roosevelt had his own imperialist aims aside from the Panama Canal. The president was growing increasingly concerned over problems he was having with attempts by Britain and Germany to collect debts from Venezuela. In an attempt to protect Venezuela from European intervention, President Roosevelt amended the Monroe Doctrine with the **Roosevelt Corollary**, which stated that the United States would come to the aid of any Latin American nation experiencing financial trouble. In essence, the United States gained total control of Latin America through the Corollary.

Under this new imperialism, the United States used force to "protect" the Dominican Republic and Cuba from political chaos. Roosevelt also intervened in the Russo-Japanese War of 1904. Russia and Japan were feuding over land and ports in Korea and Manchuria. Roosevelt did not want either nation to win control over the region and approached Japan to assist in the settlement of the war. The **Treaty of Portsmouth** was signed in 1905 to end the war. A year later, Theodore Roosevelt won the Nobel Peace Prize for his role in negotiating the treaty.

NEGOTIATIONS WITH JAPAN

U.S.–Japanese relations were not harmonious at the end of the war, however. An influx of Japanese immigrants flooded the city of San Francisco to escape financial crisis in their homeland and to start life anew. White San Franciscans were concerned about of the presence of the Japanese in their city, and they began passing restrictive laws aimed directly at the incoming immigrants, such as banning Japanese children from attending public school. The Japanese were enraged at the discrimination, and Theodore Roosevelt decided to step in. The president was able to craft a "**Gentleman's Agreement**" between the San Francisco School Board and the Japanese government. The school board would allow Japanese students to enter public school if the Japanese government would help stem the tide of immigrants coming to California. From this point on, U.S.–Japanese relations were amiable but strained.

TAFT AND WILSON ON IMPERIALISM

President Taft used a different approach to foreign relations. Taft's **Dollar Diplomacy** encouraged American businesses to send their dollars to foreign countries, such as those in Latin America, to weaken European bonds and strengthen ties with the United States. However, when these American investments were endangered, Taft on several occasions sent U.S. forces to invade Latin American countries and protect American interests. These actions further alienated the United States from Latin America.

President Wilson, in contrast, believed imperialism was immoral. Yet he also believed in the superiority of American democracy and thought it was his duty to spread that ideal to protect nations under threat of totalitarianism. This policy became known as **Moral Diplomacy**. As a result, Wilson sent troops to invade Nicaragua and the Dominican Republic and purchased the Virgin Islands. Wilson also intervened in the Mexican Revolution to capture the revolutionary Pancho Villa after he had killed Americans in the towns of Santa Ysabel, Mexico, and Columbus, New Mexico. The United States was finally forced to withdraw from the civil war in Mexico in 1917. However, another, dramatically larger war was in progress that would soon trouble President Wilson.

THE GREAT WAR AND INITIAL NEUTRALITY

Initially, President Wilson sought to keep the United States out of the affairs of Europe. However, political alliances all over Europe, militarism, and extreme nationalism made war inevitable after the assassination of the **Archduke Franz Ferdinand** of Austria-Hungary by a Serbian nationalist in 1914. For the United States, there was no desire to enter the war. Many Americans did not feel that U.S. national security or interests were in danger.

Yet Americans were affected by the war in the early years. The outbreak of war in Europe had devastating effects on the American economy. A deep recession was spurred by the drain of hard specie, as European nations looked for debt repayment in the form of gold and silver. There was also a loss of profitable overseas markets for U.S. products. However, by 1915, Britain and France looked to the United States to supply them with munitions for war, giving the economy a much-needed boost. Also, overseas demand for U.S. foodstuffs became a boon to the American farmer.

DEBUT OF THE GERMAN U-BOAT

U.S. neutrality was severely tested after both Britain and France imposed naval blockades against the Germans. The Germans had a new weapon that they would use to terrorize shipping traffic across the Atlantic. The German **U-boat** (submarine) would strike ships as they crossed the Atlantic, whether civilian or military.

The Germans claimed that these ships might be carrying munitions for Britain or France and must be stopped. By September of 1915, German U-boats had sunk 90 ships in the Atlantic and surrounding waters. One such ship was the British luxury liner *Lusitania*. Almost 1,200 people died (about 130 of those American) as the ship was sunk off the coast of Ireland. Wilson, still not wishing to enter the war, issued a stern warning to the Germans to cease submarine warfare on unarmed ships. After the sinking of another liner that cost the lives of two Americans, the Germans finally agreed to stop this type of attack.

The promise was short-lived. In March 1916, the Germans attacked the French passenger liner *Sussex*, killing four Americans. Wilson issued the **Sussex Ultimatum**, in which he warned the Germans to stop submarine warfare or the United States would break off all diplomatic relations with Germany. This move clearly signaled America's willingness to go to war. Germany again agreed to stop submarine warfare but only if the United States convinced Britain to lift its blockade.

In January 1917, an announcement came from Germany—it would again start unrestricted submarine warfare and would sink any ship entering the war zone, including American ships. Wilson immediately broke off relations with Germany. On March 2, 1917, Wilson received word that a British agent had intercepted and decoded a letter from the German Foreign Secretary Zimmerman to the German ambassador to Mexico. The letter contained a promise from the German government to the Mexican president that if his country assisted Germany in a possible war against the United States, Mexico would be given back the territory lost in the Mexican-Ameican War after Germany's victory. Wilson had the ammunition he needed—the security of the United States had been directly threatened. After the news of the telegram and the German sinking of four unarmed American merchant vessels, the United States was now poised to enter the "**Great War**."

IMPACT OF THE WAR AT HOME

The United States was woefully unprepared to enter the war in Europe. Woodrow Wilson's idealism, stubbornness, and belief in American exceptionalism led the country through the crisis. Wilson truly believed that the Great War was the "war to end all wars." He also believed that the American way of life, including democracy, was better than any other system in the world and that it was his duty to "make the world safe for democracy." In advancing his postwar vision, Wilson delivered his **Fourteen Points** speech to Congress on January 8, 1918. Wilson's points provided for the abolishment of secret treaties, freedom of the seas, economic freedom, reduction of arms, the end of colonialization, freedom of **self-determination** for all peoples, and the formation of an international organization for collective security. This last point was the most important to Wilson, but it would also be a thorn in his side as the war ended.

The United States mobilized for war reluctantly. The country was aided by the formation of the **Committee on Public Information**, headed by George Creel. This department was given the task of gaining the support of Americans for the war through a massive propaganda machine.

Posters, speeches, and "liberty leagues" throughout the country encouraged Americans to buy war bonds and support the war effort. Herbert Hoover headed up the Food Administration, which encouraged Americans to have "meatless" Mondays, to grow "victory gardens," and to limit the amount of food they ate. Americans also renamed "German" foods, such as frankfurters (liberty sausages) and sauerkraut (liberty cabbage). Americans ceased playing German music, and the German language was no longer taught in schools. American factories soon found themselves under the **War Industries Board**, headed by Bernard Baruch, which sought to control production, wages, and the prices of manufactured goods.

Raising an army was another difficult task for the government, as allies were begging for fresh men to fight the Germans. In response, Wilson urged the passage of the **Selective Service Act** (1917), which authorized the conscription of American males into military service. Within months of its passage, the army had enough men to relieve the Allied forces overseas.

Americans experienced a curbing of their civil liberties during wartime. Mostly aimed at German Americans and antiwar protesters, the **Espionage Act** of 1917 and **Sedition Act** of 1918 curbed the right to free speech. **Socialists** such as Eugene V. Debs were targeted, arrested, and jailed. In the pivotal ruling of *Schenck v. United States*, the Supreme Court, with Justice Oliver Wendell Holmes writing the majority opinion, upheld the Espionage Act by stating that Congress could limit the right of free speech if it represented a "clear and present danger" that would bring about "evils" that the government was seeking to stop. Unfortunately, the war years were an ugly time for civil liberties—many Americans served time well into the 1920s and 1930s for wartime "crimes."

NEGOTIATING PEACE AT VERSAILLES

As the fighting ended and it was time to negotiate peace, President Wilson hoped to promote his Fourteen Points in the treaty talks at **Versailles**, located just outside of Paris. The president had lost some pull at home, however, as the 1918 midterm elections brought a narrow Republican majority to Congress. Wilson infuriated the legislative branch when he traveled without any Republicans to Versailles to negotiate the peace terms with the European powers. This would later haunt him when he worked to get the treaty ratified by Congress.

The peace conference began on January 18, 1919, with the "**Big Four**"—Woodrow Wilson, Georges Clemenceau of France, Vittorio Orlando of Italy, and David Lloyd George of Great Britain—meeting at Versailles Palace. Germany and Russia were conspicuously absent from the meeting. Being a rather stubborn idealist, Wilson was determined to see his Fourteen Points come to fruition, especially his fourteenth point (the call for the creation of a League of Nations). The other European leaders were interested in exacting **reparations** from Germany, which they believed was responsible for the war. This made Wilson's job difficult—he had to compromise to see his ideas become a reality. One of the first areas of compromise was the idea of **mandates**, in which conquered territories would not become the property of the conquering nation but would rather be under the trusteeship of the League.

Eventually, Wilson would have to compromise on most of his Fourteen Points and give in to the desires of the European powers to assign full blame for the war and its consequences on Germany. Woodrow Wilson did get his **League of Nations**, and **Article X** of the League's charter called for members to stand at the ready if another member nation's sovereignty was being threatened.

It was Article X, along with other mistakes Wilson made in the eyes of the Republicans, that would derail ratification of the Versailles Treaty in the United States. One of the most outspoken opponents of the president and of the treaty was Republican senator Henry Cabot Lodge. Those who were opposed to ratification of the treaty fell into two camps: **reservationists** and the **irreconcilables**. Lodge and his reservationists would only agree to ratify the treaty if "reservations," such as the ability to leave the League and international acceptance of the Monroe Doctrine, were added to the League's Covenant. The irreconcilables, led by Senators Hiram Johnson and William Borah, refused to ratify the treaty under any circumstances. Wilson had to act quickly to save the treaty and the League of Nations.

President Wilson got on a train and traveled the United States to speak directly to the American public about the treaty and its importance. While in Colorado, the president collapsed from exhaustion. A few days later, he suffered a stroke, which left him partially paralyzed and unable to meet with his cabinet for seven months.

The Senate voted on the treaty twice in 1919, both times failing to ratify it. Eventually, the fight over the treaty turned on whether or not it would be accepted with or without reservations. Democrats were split: some voted with the reservationists; loyal Wilson supporters voted to reject the treaty rather than accept it with reservations. The election of 1920, in Wilson's eyes, would be a "solemn referendum" on the treaty, as he hoped Americans would give his Democratic Party a majority in Congress and continued control of the White House. It was the Republicans, however, who dominated the election. The United States did not officially end its war with Germany until 1921 and never ratified the Treaty of Versailles. As a result, the United States did not join the League of Nations, weakening the organization.

POST-WORLD WAR I AMERICAN SOCIETY AND ECONOMY

Returning from war was a difficult transition for American soldiers. The federal government did not have any plans for helping war veterans re-establish themselves in civilian life. The realities of trench warfare and the horrors of war left many veterans scarred both physically and mentally. Many American veterans returned from Europe with missing limbs, facial disfigurements, and "shell shock" (now called post-traumatic stress disorder). While most war veterans found work quickly when they returned to the States, they displaced thousands of women and African Americans who had held these jobs during the war years.

TROUBLES ABROAD

Tensions rose as society shifted from wartime to peacetime. Aside from the end of the war, other developments in Europe frightened Americans and caused social unrest as the country entered the 1920s. The 1917 **Bolshevik Revolution** in Russia frightened middle- and upper-class Americans, as the Bolsheviks overthrew the Provisional Government of Russia and pledged to destroy capitalism. Socialists and anarchists in the United States had been persecuted throughout the war, and their problems intensified as fears over communism rose. Attorney General A. Mitchell Palmer fanned the flames of unrest after a series of bombings, including one that occurred in his neighborhood that was attributed to anarchist groups. Palmer immediately ordered the rounding up of suspected anarchists, socialists, aliens (usually Russian), and agitators and started what is known as the **Red Scare**. During the Palmer Raids, some 6,000 people were arrested in a two-month period, and 500 were deported on "Soviet Arks," which sent the passengers back to Europe.

LABOR AND RACE ISSUES

Fears of a socialist or communist takeover spilled over into labor conflicts, which peaked in 1919. Organized labor felt the need to protect workers as the nation fell into a recession. Many companies had to lay off employees and drastically cut wages. As labor strikes grew increasingly violent, many Americans began to believe the labor unions were being infiltrated and funded by communist groups. As a result, the federal government began to take a hard-line stance with regard to strikes, especially in cases where the public safety was at risk.

One of the most notable strikes occurred in Boston, when police officers refused to work because they wanted the right to collectively bargain and a wage increase. Governor of Massachusetts Calvin Coolidge felt that the police had no right to strike because doing so would place the public safety at risk. As a result, Coolidge sent in the National Guard to break the strike, making him an instant hero in the eyes of some Americans.

Racial issues also came to the surface as the nation moved into the new decade. Having been fired in favor of war veterans returning from Europe, African Americans in many cities began to express their frustrations. Riots broke out in Chicago, Baltimore, and Omaha in which African Americans destroyed property to express their anger and resentment toward discrimination and poverty.

WORLD PROBLEMS AND AMERICAN NEUTRALITY

Most Americans were not keen on getting involved in another world war, since the country had fought in the Great War just two decades earlier. Americans were intensely concerned with the Great Depression, even as Germany's Adolf Hitler continually violated the provisions of the Treaty of Versailles. President Herbert Hoover ushered in the 1930s using diplomacy instead of military force to stave off potential threats around the world. With his diplomatic intervention crisis in Manchuria (see the Hoover-Stimson Doctrine) and the initiation of the Good Neighbor Policy with Latin America, it was clear that Americans were interested in maintaining their distance from world affairs through a policy of isolationism. It was Franklin Delano Roosevelt who gave a name to the relationship with Latin America, promising to be "good neighbors" by staying out of their affairs. At the **Montevideo Conference** in 1933, the president personally pledged that the United States would not engage in armed intervention in the region.

Economically, FDR looked to rid the world of the high protective tariffs that had crippled many nations' economies throughout the Depression. To open up new markets, FDR formally recognized the Soviet Union as a sovereign nation in 1933. But even FDR, occupied with getting the United States out of the Great Depression, could not ignore the crisis that was worsening across both the Atlantic and Pacific Oceans.

TROUBLE BREWS ABROAD

Totalitarian regimes had gained power in Europe and Japan during the 1920s and early 1930s because of the impact of the worldwide economic depression. The grim reality of being blamed wholly for the Great War caused many Germans to feel betrayed by their new government. They were for strong leadership. Faced with runaway inflation caused by the printing of German marks to pay the massive war reparations debt, Germans saw Adolf Hitler as the way to return their nation to power. Italians, too, felt that their government had "sold them out" to other world powers during the Versailles treaty negotiations, as they lost valuable territories and prestige. They found hope in the words of "**il Duce**"—the leader of their Fascist movement, **Benito Mussolini**. Faced with a trade imbalance that would cripple their island nation, the Japanese looked for a return to power. The United States watched from afar, not wishing to become involved again in a foreign war. Several neutrality acts were passed from 1935 to 1937 in response to the increasing turmoil and threat of war in Europe and Asia. The United States sat and watched as her allies in Europe and Asia enacted diplomatic policies aimed at keeping these dictators at bay, even as Hitler and Mussolini used the Spanish Civil War as a testing ground for their military tactics.

FDR BEGINS TO PREPARE

For his part, President Roosevelt did not make the same mistake as his predecessor, Woodrow Wilson. FDR started increasing military spending in 1938 to begin preparation for war. Part of his "pump priming," this increase in government spending ultimately took the country on the road to full economic recovery. Even as early as 1940, FDR was realistic about the potential of U.S. involvement in a war; he pressured Congress to pass the **Selective Service Act,** which provided for all American males between the ages of 21 to 35 to register for compulsory military service. This was the first time a peacetime military draft had been initiated, signaling that the president's stance was shifting from isolationism to interventionism.

THE ROAD TO WAR

Mussolini and Hitler understood the fragility of the League of Nations and hoped to take advantage of its weaknesses in their bid to take over Europe and the world. Mussolini first sent troops to invade the African country of Ethiopia in 1935; the League condemned his actions but did nothing to intervene. Hitler invaded the demilitarized region between France and Germany, the Rhineland, in 1936, thus violating the Versailles Treaty. The year 1937 brought the Japanese invasion of China and a potential U.S.-Japanese war as the Japanese "accidentally" sank an American ship on the Yangtze River.

European leaders were at a loss as to how to handle Hitler's increasingly aggressive actions. He claimed an area of Czechoslovakia called the **Sudetenland** in 1938. In a bid to keep the peace, the British prime minister Neville Chamberlain and French president Edouard Daladier met with Hitler to negotiate a settlement over the disputed territory. Surprisingly, Czechoslovakia was not invited. At the conference, held in Munich in 1938, the policy of "**appeasement**" was born. Hitler would be allowed to take the Sudetenland in exchange for his promise to not invade any other territories. Hitler agreed, and Chamberlain and Daladier were pleased that they had dodged another bullet.

THE WAR BEGINS

The peace was short-lived, however, as Hitler invaded the rest of Czechoslovakia six months later and set his sights on Poland. The general secretary of the Soviet Union, **Joseph Stalin**, had good reason to want to keep Poland as a neutral "buffer zone" between Germany and Russia. His country had been invaded through Poland many times throughout its history; he hoped a free Poland would keep his people safe. The world was surprised when it was announced that Stalin and Hitler had signed a secret nonaggression pact in 1939, which freed Germany to invade the western half of Poland with no resistance; the Soviets would take the eastern half. The British and French pledged their support of Poland by stating they would declare war on Germany if the invasion took place. Then, on September 1, 1939, Hitler's forces rolled into Poland and started World War II.

As former American allies Britain and France were now engaged in a war with Germany and Italy, the United States took measures to maintain its neutrality while supplying munitions to them. The **Neutrality Act of 1939** again proclaimed U.S. neutrality but only in name—not in deed. The act provided for the sale of U.S. weapons to European allies on a "**cash-and-carry**" basis only. In other words, countries such as Britain and France would have to pay cash and provide their own transport for whatever war munitions they bought. This would eliminate the need for war loans to allies that could cause problems in a fragile postwar economy and would keep U.S. merchant ships out of the war zone. September 1940 would bring increased U.S. involvement in the war. The new British prime minister, **Winston Churchill**, pleaded for more assistance in the face of continual bombings of his country by the German air force (the *Luftwaffe*) and the threat of U-boats in the Atlantic and English Channel. The two sides brokered the **Destroyers-for-Bases Agreement**, whereby the United States would provide Britain several older U.S. naval ships in return for the right to establish U.S. military installments on British-held Caribbean islands.

RE-ELECTION FOR FDR AND PLANS WITH CHURCHILL

With the election of 1940 looming, President Roosevelt broke the precedent set by George Washington by running for a third term. Running against Republican Wendell Willkie, Roosevelt was able to convince Americans that electing him again was choosing a voice of experience in the face of war. He won the election with 54 percent of the popular vote.

Growing more and more concerned over the fate of U.S. allies, President Roosevelt believed that his re-election was a mandate from the American people to end isolationism and become more involved in the war. He still emphasized diplomacy over military force, but it was clear to many that the president was not unwilling to enter the war if necessary. In his State of the Union Address to Congress in 1940, the president offered his vision of U.S. involvement. FDR argued that offering Great Britain loans to buy U.S.-made munitions would further stimulate the economy and aid in the protection of the "**Four Freedoms**": Freedom of Speech, Freedom of Religion, Freedom from Want, and Freedom from Fear. His proposal was to end the "cash-and-carry" program and institute the **Lend-Lease program** (March 1941), which would provide Britain with U.S. war materials. FDR arranged a secret meeting with Prime Minister Churchill to discuss postwar aims in response to the secret nonaggression pact signed by Hitler and Stalin. The two men drew up the **Atlantic Charter**, which declared that the self-determination of peoples and free trade would be the cornerstones of a world free of fascism.

ATTACK ON PEARL HARBOR

As Hitler continued to conquer Europe, with Paris falling in June 1940, the United States struggled to maintain amiable relations with Japan. Japanese forces remained in China and were poised to take French Indochina, which prompted FDR to cut Japan off from U.S. raw materials. As an island nation with few natural resources, the Japanese relied heavily on imports of American oil. Hoping to secure the removal of Japanese troops from China and Indochina in return for lifting the oil embargo, FDR sent Secretary of State Cordell Hull to negotiate with the Japanese government. Amidst the negotiations, the new Japanese leader, General Hideki Tojo, changed course unexpectedly and backed out. Little did Hull know that the general was planning a secret attack on the Pacific fleet that he hoped would cripple the United States.

On December 7, 1941, the entire U.S. Pacific fleet was attacked at **Pearl Harbor**, Hawaii, in the early morning hours. The surprise attack killed 2,400 American sailors and wounded 1,200. Eight battleships were either sunk or severely damaged, including the *USS Arizona*, which lost 1,100 sailors. Ten other ships were severely damaged and almost 200 planes destroyed in the attack. Immediately, FDR asked Congress to declare war on Japan, and it responded with but one dissenting vote. Three days later, Germany and Italy responded by declaring war on the United States.

A TWO-FRONT WAR

By the time the United States entered the war in Europe, the focus of the Allies had shifted from the western front to the east, as Hitler broke his promise to Stalin and invaded Russia through Poland in late 1941. The Soviet leader joined the Allies, making the "Big Three" of Roosevelt, Churchill, and Stalin. The three agreed to focus on stopping Hitler before turning to Japan.

FOCUS ON GERMANY

In the European "theater," the Allies concentrated on ridding the seas of German U-boats and the skies of the German *Luftwaffe*. The new British invention of radar turned the tide of war against the Germans, as the Royal Air Force was able to down German planes and the U.S. Navy was able to locate and sink U-boats. In Africa, the Allies struggled to rout the Germans from the North African theater as they cut their way northward under the leadership of the German tank commander, General Erwin "the Desert Fox" Rommel. Operation Torch, led by U.S. general Dwight D. Eisenhower and British general Bernard Montgomery, successfully flanked Rommel in Tunisia in May 1943. Next, the Allies looked across the Mediterranean Sea to the island of Sicily, which they invaded in September 1943. Facing fierce resistance from both Italian and German troops, the United States finally took the island in May 1945.

Understanding the need to liberate Nazi-occupied France, the Allies began planning an invasion of the beaches of Normandy. Operation Overlord, now known as the **D-Day** invasion, was an amphibious landing that required the utmost secrecy and favorable weather conditions. The perfect opening arose on June 6, 1944. General Eisenhower led a multinational force to storm the beaches in northern France. Despite enormous loss of life, the invasion proved to be a success, as the Allies liberated Paris by the end of August. The final Allied push into neighboring Belgium was met with an attack by the Germans in December 1944 at the **Battle of the Bulge**. Even after suffering heavy losses in the battle, the Allies were able to recover and continue their push toward Germany. The British and U.S. air forces were successful in crippling Germany by bombing her urban centers. With German defeat imminent, Hitler took his own life in April 1945, and Nazi forces surrendered unconditionally on May 7. As Allied troops marched further into Nazi-held territory, they came upon unspeakable horrors. Massive concentration camps were discovered throughout Germany, Poland, Austria, and Czechoslovakia, where much of Hitler's **genocidal "Final Solution"** had been carried out.

FOCUS ON JAPAN

After **V-E Day** (Victory in Europe Day), the Allies could focus on defeating the Japanese. By the end of 1942, the Japanese had extended their sphere of influence far beyond China and Indochina, occupying the Korean peninsula, the Philippines, Indonesia, and many Pacific islands. The Pacific theater was different from the one in Europe—here the Allies had to rely heavily on naval power and the destruction of the Japanese air force to win.

Early in the Pacific theater, two naval battles served as turning points for the Allies. In the Battles of Coral Sea and Midway (May 1942 and June 1942, respectively), the Allies were able to stop a Japanese aircraft carrier from reaching Australia. They also broke the Japanese code, enabling them to intercept and destroy four more aircraft carriers. U.S. admiral Chester Nimitz soon adopted the strategy of "island hopping," in which the U.S. Navy would focus only on strategic Japanese-held Pacific islands and surround them to engage the enemy. Eventually, this tactic would lead the Allies to the southernmost Japanese islands.

The Japanese were not about to back down, however, and several other bloody battles raged between 1943 and 1945. By 1945, the United States had come close enough to the Japanese mainland to launch air raids on major cities, such as Tokyo. As the Japanese grew more desperate, sending suicide bombers called **kamikazes** into U.S. aircraft carriers, new president Harry Truman believed that the only way to end the war would be to invade Japan. (President Roosevelt had died in April 1945, and the presidency had passed to Vice President Truman.) Not wishing to launch an invasion that would more than likely cost many thousands of American lives, Truman decided instead to use a new secret weapon on Japan. On August 6, 1945, "Little Boy," an atomic bomb, was dropped from the *Enola Gay* over the industrial city of Hiroshima, killing 80,000 people instantly. With the Japanese still unwilling to agree to an unconditional surrender, a second bomb, "Fat Man," was dropped on August 9 on the city of Nagasaki. Another 60,000 Japanese were killed immediately. Japan surrendered on September 2, 1945.

DIPLOMACY AND CONFERENCES

Throughout World War II, the Big Three met to discuss wartime concerns and postwar desires. Meetings in Casablanca, Tehran, Yalta, and Potsdam all yielded agreements and concessions among Britain, the United States, and the USSR that would shape the course of the war and impact the coming Cold War.

The first of these war meetings, which took place in Casablanca in 1943, only included Roosevelt and Churchill—Stalin declined the invitation. Here they decided to invade Sicily and settle for nothing less than "unconditional surrender" from the Axis powers. November 1943 brought Roosevelt, Churchill, and Stalin together in the Iranian city of Tehran. The seeds of the D-Day invasion were sown here. It was also here that the first disagreements between the Soviet leader and the Western powers came to light. Stalin claimed the right to use Eastern Europe to create a buffer zone between his country and Western Europe. Churchill, on the other hand, demanded a free Europe and the preservation of a unified Germany at the war's end. Roosevelt mediated an understanding between the two by promising peace through the proposed United Nations.

The Big Three met once again at Yalta in February 1945 to finalize the plans for postwar Europe. Here, Stalin agreed to enter the war against Japan within three months of Germany's surrender and signed an agreement to create a free Eastern Europe with free elections. Additionally, the **Yalta Conference** yielded a skeleton framework for the United Nations and the division of Germany into four occupied military zones.

The Big Three suffered two losses after Yalta. The first was the death of President Roosevelt on April 12, 1945. The president struggled with failing health while at Yalta. Worn down and exhausted, he died suddenly while resting at his vacation home in Georgia. A saddened nation soon learned that Vice President Harry S. Truman had taken the oath of office and, in doing so, had taken on enormous responsibilities. The second occurred when the British elected a new prime minister, Clement Attlee.

WARTIME MOBILIZATION

The Selective Service System, having already instituted the draft in 1940, expanded to include all 18- to 64-year-old males when the United States declared war on Japan. In addition, some 260,000 women enlisted as members of the **Women's Army Corps** (WACs), **Women Appointed for Voluntary Emergency Service** (WAVES), and **Women's Auxiliary Ferrying Squadron** (WAFs). These women supported the war effort by flying supply missions, decoding enemy communications, and repairing machines. By the war's end, almost 16 million American men and women had served in some capacity in the war effort.

The **Office of War Mobilization** took over from the earlier War Production Board to transition the country from a peacetime to a wartime economy. Soon outproducing the Axis powers, U.S. manufacturers devoted most of their their productive capacity to making war supplies. Unemployment, the scourge of the nation 10 years earlier, had all but vanished, as Americans went to work to fuel the war machine. The **Office of Price Administration** (OPA) and **Office of Economic Stabilization** set forth to keep the wartime economy under control by setting price floors and ceilings, regulating the tax code, and instituting rationing. Rationing stamps were issued to every American family for goods such as sugar, coffee, and gasoline. Rationing made these goods available to troops overseas and freed up manufacturers to focus on supplying war munitions rather than consumer goods. Because of the lack of consumer goods for sale, American families sank the money they made during the war into savings, which would impact the postwar economy by funding expansion and bolstering consumer spending.

Americans were asked to sacrifice and save voluntarily in addition to enforced rationing. Women saved bacon fat for the manufacturing of artillery shells, and children donated their bicycle tires for recycling. As at no time before, it seemed the entire country was willing to sacrifice to win a war.

WW II AND THE ECONOMY

World War II saw the national debt rise by some $200 billion, as the government increased spending to finance the war. To fund this deficit spending, the federal government borrowed money from Americans in the form of war bonds, which would be repaid after the war was over.

THE WAR'S IMPACT ON AMERICAN SOCIETY

The war impacted Americans from all walks of life. Citizens could not escape war propaganda as they walked to work, listened to the radio, ate their meals, and went to the movies. The **Office of War Information** (OWI) produced radio shows and news reels to keep Americans apprised of events overseas. Many sat riveted as USO shows from overseas featuring Bob Hope and Francis Langford were broadcast across the nation. Movies of the day often glorified American war involvement, reaching audiences of millions. Posters and cartoons were created to encourage compliance with rationing, the saving of grease, and the purchasing of war bonds. The OWI aimed to keep American morale high and to increase support for the war.

WOMEN AND MINORITIES DURING WARTIME

Women were specifically targeted by OWI propaganda. As many as 5 million women joined the workforce during the war in response to propaganda that glorified women's war work. "**Rosie the Riveter**" was glorified in songs, posters, and movies as an American heroine and everyday woman, able to work all day and still manage to run the household. Despite the urging of women such as Eleanor Roosevelt to make women's pay equal to that of their male counterparts, companies typically paid female workers just two-thirds of what male workers earned.

America's minority groups also experienced changes in their lives due to the war. African Americans again flocked to industrial centers in the North to seek jobs in factories as they had during World War I. Just as before, racial tensions ensued. The summer of 1943 saw disturbances in cities such as Detroit and Baltimore. The NAACP experienced a surge in membership during the war. Mexican Americans, many of whom had moved to Mexico during the Great Depression, were encouraged to return to the United States as migrant farm laborers in the *bracero* program. Under this program, both former U.S. residents and Mexican nationals crossed into the United States to work during harvest season, and many remained north of the border to live permanently. Tensions between sailors stationed in Los Angeles and Long Beach awaiting deployment to the Pacific theater and young Mexican-American men reached a boiling point in the summer of 1943. The **Zoot Suit Riots** occurred when the sailors roamed the streets of Los Angeles and Long Beach attacking young "zooters"—Mexican-American teens who wore long coats, flashy colors, and long hairstyles. A special commission appointed by Governor Earl Warren found that the riots were not caused by the sailors and the police.

Native Americans served the country by enlisting in the armed services and working in thousands of factories across the United States. Most famous were the **Navajo Code Talkers**, who translated U.S. documents into their Native American language so that enemy forces could not decipher their content.

WARTIME TREATMENT OF THE JAPANESE

The individuals most adversely affected by the war domestically were the Japanese Americans living along the West Coast. Some 100,000 Japanese-American citizens were ordered to leave their homes for internment camps located across the west. President Roosevelt issued **Executive Order 9066** in reaction to the paranoia of the War Department that American citizens of Japanese ancestry might turn against their adopted country to aid Japan in an invasion of the West Coast. Of the 100,000 Japanese Americans interned, only 30 percent were foreign born. These citizens were given less than 48 hours to vacate their homes and businesses. Carrying only what they could in a few suitcases, the internees arrived in these camps and lived there until the war's end. Once these families returned to their homes after the war, they found their property, land, and homes taken over by other families. Japanese Americans lost millions of dollars in potential income, property, and land. The Supreme Court upheld the decision to intern these citizens in the case *Korematsu v. United States* (1944), stating that in times of war, the curbing of civil rights was justified and that the Court could not second-guess military decisions. The federal government finally agreed in 1988 to apologize formally for internment and pay surviving families $20,000 in restitution.

POST-WORLD WAR II RECOVERY

World War II certainly made its mark on the United States. The war cost the country 400,000 men and over 800,000 causalities, more than all other U.S. wars combined, excluding the Civil War. Monetarily, the war cost some $360 billion and led to the largest budget deficit in U.S. history. Approximately 55 million people died worldwide, and 38 million were either wounded or missing. To promote peace in the postwar world, the **United Nations**, chartered in October 1945, set to work to peacefully mediate disputes among nations.

Hoping to avoid the mistakes of World War I regarding returning veterans, Congress acted quickly to create a plan to aid those returning from war beginning life again as civilians. In 1944, Congress passed the **GI Bill** (Servicemen's Readjustment Act), which provided funding for a college education, as well as low-interest home and small business loans. For 15 million soldiers returning from war, the GI Bill provided the opportunity for veterans to secure a career and purchase a home. Returning GIs married and had babies, leading to a "baby boom" that lasted from 1945 to 1963.

The war opened doors of opportunity to many groups, forever changing the United States. Women and African Americans felt a sense of hope, as they enjoyed steady employment and increased social standing. President Truman hoped not only to continue the New Deal programs of Roosevelt but to improve upon them by striving for full employment and increased rights for African Americans. Congress passed the **Employment Act of 1946** in an attempt to keep the United States at full employment at all times. Like most postwar economies, the United States experienced inflation as rationing and price regulations were lifted. Workers struggled to earn wages that kept up with inflation, even though the standard of living for the average American was higher than ever before. With regard to civil rights, President Truman alienated Southern Democrats by ending racial segregation in the federal government and armed forces.

However, Americans elected enough Republicans to give the GOP a majority in Congress during the midterm elections of 1946. Under their leadership, the Constitution was amended to avoid the repeat of a four-term presidency (FDR) by limiting a president to two terms. In addition, Congress passed the **Taft-Hartley Act** in 1947 in an attempt to garner the support of big business. The bill, which was vetoed by Truman but enacted by a congressional override, outlawed "closed-shop" workplaces, limited boycotts, and allowed the president to obtain an 80-day injunction against any strike deemed a danger to national health or safety. Under Taft-Hartley, organized labor lost much of the ground it had gained during the New Deal.

The population of the country shifted to **Sun Belt** states, such as Florida, California, Texas, and Arizona, with families moving from the former **Rust Belt** of Michigan, Ohio, and Illinois. Suddenly, once prosperous Northern and Midwestern states were burdened with the loss of tax revenues and sagging economies as families fled in search of warmer climates. Wartime technologies gave way to consumer conveniences, such as plastics and faster public air travel. But it was the political realm that would impact Americans most, as fears of fascism soon gave way to fear of nuclear war.

UNIT 7: REVIEW QUESTIONS

Multiple-Choice Questions

Directions: Choose the best answer choice for the following questions.

Questions 1–4 refer to the following quote.

"The general sanitary investigation of 1912 included 45 cities of the State, and covered 1,338 industrial establishments, . . . 125,961 wage-earners . . . employed . . . in the different industries of the State . . .

Laws Passed as a Result of the Commission's Second Year's Work [1913]

1. Reorganization of Labor Department . . .

5. Fire escapes and exits; limitation of number of occupants; . . .

7. Prohibition of employment of children under fourteen, in cannery sheds or tenement houses; . . .

8. Physical examination of children employed in factories . . .

11. Night work of women in factories.

12. Seats for women in factories . . .

The enactment of these laws marked a new era in labor legislation . . . It placed the State of New York in the lead in legislation for the protection of wage earners . . . "

—Fourth Report of the Factory Investigating Commission, 1915, pages 5–7

1. Which of the following terms most clearly relates to the goals of the work described in the passage?

(A) Social Gospel

(B) Americanization

(C) Social Darwinism

(D) Gilded Age

2. Which of the following movements from the 1930s most clearly parallels the ideas of the passage?

(A) Isolationism

(B) Socialism

(C) *Laissez-faire*

(D) New Deal

3. The actions in the previous passage were most likely the result of an alliance between which of the following?

(A) African-American activists and Southern Democrats

(B) Urban political machines and Progressive reformers

(C) Industrial capitalists and labor unions

(D) Republicans and industrial capitalists

4. The actions in the previous passage most clearly reflect which of the following continuities in United States history?

   (A) Debates over the proper degree of government activism

   (B) Debates over the gender inequality

   (C) Debates over the challenges of urbanization

   (D) Debates over the increased consumerism

Questions 5–7 refer to the following figure.

Americans All! Victory Liberty Loan/Howard Chandler Christy; Forbes, Boston, 1919

5. Which change in American society in the early 20th century most directly led to the situation described in the poster?

   (A) Increased support for American imperialism

   (B) Demographic shift in immigration patterns

   (C) Decreased support for immigration quotas

   (D) Increased xenophobia

6. Which event of the post–World War I era most directly challenged the sentiment in the poster?

   (A) The Great Migration out of the South

   (B) Unrestricted immigration from the Western Hemisphere

   (C) The first Red Scare

   (D) The "closing" of the American frontier

7. The ideas expressed in the poster most clearly show the influence of which of the following?

   (A) Violations of civil liberties

   (B) Wartime patriotism

   (C) Support for women's suffrage

   (D) Nativism

Questions 8–11 refer to the following quote.

"The President of the United States of America and the Prime Minister . . . met together . . . [and] make known . . . their hopes for a better future . . .

First, their countries seek no aggrandizement, territorial or other;

Second, . . . no territorial changes that do not accord with the freely expressed wishes of the peoples . . . ;

Third, . . . the right of all peoples to choose [their] form of government . . . ;

Fourth, . . . access, on equal terms, to the trade and to the raw materials of the world . . . ;

Fifth, . . . the fullest [economic] collaboration between all nations . . . ;

Sixth, after the final destruction of the Nazi tyranny, . . . freedom from fear and want;

Seventh, . . . traverse the high seas and oceans without hindrance;

Eighth, . . . the establishment of a . . . permanent system of general security, [and] disarmament . . . "

—The Atlantic Charter, 1941

8. Which of the following events of the early 20th century most clearly represents a continuation of the ideas illustrated in the passage?

(A) Creation of the League of Nations

(B) Development of a unilateral foreign policy

(C) Violations of civil liberties during wartime

(D) Support for isolationism

9. The ideas expressed in the passage most directly reflect which of the following continuities in United States history?

(A) Migration and population patterns affecting American life

(B) Changes in transportation and technology affecting American society

(C) Difficulty of maintaining a balance between liberty and order

(D) Finding acceptable ways to pursue international and domestic goals

10. Which of the following actions of the late 20th century most clearly reflects the perspective of the passage?

(A) Decolonization movements in Africa, Asia, and the Middle East

(B) American support of non-communist regimes in Latin America

(C) Post–World War II partitioning of Korea and Vietnam

(D) Development of nuclear arsenals in the United States and USSR

11. The actions referred to in the previous passage most directly contributed to which of the following?

(A) The Cold War

(B) The creation of the League of Nations

(C) The internment of Japanese Americans

(D) The Allied victory over the Axis powers

Questions 12–15 refer to the following figure.

12. Which change in American society most directly led to the situation described in the poster?

(A) Rise of political corruption

(B) Result of unrestricted immigration

(C) Impact of severe business cycle fluctuation

(D) Massive internal migrations

13. Which situation most directly resulted from the actions portrayed in the poster?

(A) The Great Depression

(B) Increased support for *laissez-faire* economic policies

(C) Electoral dominance of the Republican Party

(D) Rise of a limited welfare state

14. The ideas illustrated in the poster most clearly show the influence of which of the following?

(A) National power as defined by the Articles of Confederation

(B) Beliefs of American cultural superiority connected with manifest destiny

(C) Constitutional amendments of the Reconstruction era

(D) Social justice reforms of the Progressive era

15. The policy illustrated in the poster above most directly led to political controversies in the last decades of the 20th and early 21st century over

(A) the impact of demographic change on the environment

(B) the difficulty of reforming popular "big government" programs

(C) the challenges raised by the end of the Cold War

(D) the growth of religious fundamentalism

Short-Answer Questions

1. **Passage 1:**

"The more economical methods of production did not begin all at once . . . (p. 78)

A Ford car contains about five thousand parts—that is counting screws, nuts, and all . . . (p. 79)

The first step forward in assembly came when we began to taking the work to the men instead of the men to the work. . . .(p. 80)

. . . The idea came in a general way from the overhead trolley that the Chicago packers use in dressing beef . . . the result is this: by aid of scientific study one man is now able to do somewhat more than four did only a comparatively few years ago . . . (p. 81)

The idea is that a man must not be hurried in his work—he must have every second necessary but not a single unnecessary second . . . (p. 82)

—*My Life and Work* by Henry Ford, 1922, pp. 78–82

Passage 2:

"January 23, 1914
 My Dear Mr. Ford-

. . . I am the wife of one of the final assemblers in your institution and neither one of us want to be agitators and thus do not want to say anything to make anyone else more aggravated but Mr. Ford <u>you</u> do not know the conditions in your factory . . . or you would not allow it.

. . . The chain system you have is a <u>slave driver!</u> . . . My husband has come home and thrown himself down and can't eat his supper—so done out! . . . Couldn't there be a man ready to step in and relieve a man when nature calls . . . That $5 a day is a blessing—a far bigger one than you know but <u>ok</u> they earn it . . . <u>Please investigate</u> . . . "

—Letter to Henry Ford from wife of assembly line worker, 1914

Based on the two sources dealing with American business practices at the turn of the 20th century, complete the following three tasks:

(A) Briefly explain the main point made by Passage 1.

(B) Briefly explain the main point made by Passage 2.

(C) Provide ONE piece of evidence dealing with American business practices at the turn of the 20th century, and explain how it supports the interpretation in either passage.

2.

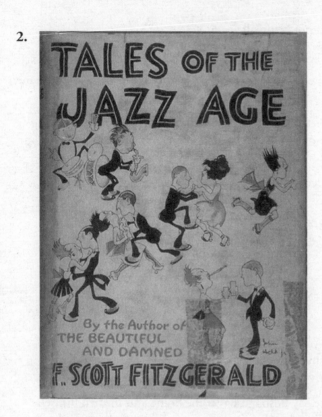

Use the image here and your knowledge of United States history to answer parts A, B, and C.

(A) Explain the point of view reflected in the image.

(B) Provide ONE piece of evidence from the era of the Jazz Age and explain how it supports the interpretation in the image.

(C) Provide ONE piece of evidence from the era of the Jazz Age and explain how it refutes the interpretation in the image.

Document-Based Question

Directions: Question 1 is based on the accompanying documents. The documents have been edited for the purpose of this exercise. You are advised to spend 15 minutes planning and 40 minutes writing your answer. Write your responses on the lined pages that follow the questions.

1. Evaluate the impact the December 7, 1941, attack on Pearl Harbor had on the American home front. Confine your response to the period between 1939 and 1946.

DOCUMENT 1

Mr. Wilkie:

Were you now the President of these United States, possessing the comprehensive and intelligent views gained by many years of service in all phases of national and international experiences and being fully cognizant of serious emergencies now facing our nation, would you as an American looking out for the welfare of all Americans be satisfied to turn over the management of this great nation to a layman, inexperienced in government affairs except as a front man and mouthpiece for utility companies.

Answer this Mr. Wilkie — without evasion - yes or NO.

Mail this card to a friend who is as yet undecided.

1940 Election FDR Campaign Card

DOCUMENT 2

Women shipfitters worked on board the *USS NEREUS* . . . U.S. Navy Yard, Mare Island, CA, *c.* 1943

DOCUMENT 3

Year	Total labor force (*1,000)	of which Male (*1,000)	of which Female (*1,000)	Female share of total (%)
1940	56,100	41,940	14,160	25.2
1941	57,720	43,070	14,650	25.4
1942	60,330	44,200	16,120	26.7
1943	64,780	45,950	18,830	29.1
1944	66,320	46,930	19,390	29.2
1945	66,210	46,910	19,304	29.2
1946	60,520	43,690	16,840	27.8

DOCUMENT 4

" . . . we propose that ten thousand Negroes MARCH ON WASHINGTON FOR JOBS IN NATIONAL DEFENSE AND EQUAL INTEGRATION IN THE FIGHTING FORCES OF THE UNITED STATES . . .

It will shake up official Washington.

It will give encouragement to our white friends to fight all the harder by our side, with us, for our righteous cause.

It will gain respect for the Negro people.

It will create a new sense of self-respect among Negroes.

But what of national unity?

We believe in national unity which recognizes equal opportunity of black and white citizens to jobs in national defense and the armed forces, and in all other institutions and endeavors in America. We condemn all dictatorships, Fascist, Nazi and Communist. We are loyal, patriotic Americans all . . . "

The Call to Negro America to March on Washington, A. Philip Randolph, 1941

DOCUMENT 5

U.S. Active Military Personnel (1939–1945) Year	Army	Navy	Marines	Total
1939	189,839	125,202	19,432	334,473
1940	269,023	160,997	28,345	458,365
1941	1,462,315	284,427	54,359	1,801,101
1942	3,075,608	640,570	142,613	3,858,791
1943	6,994,472	1,741,750	308,523	9,044,745
1944	7,994,750	2,981,365	475,604	11,451,719
1945	8,267,958	3,380,817	474,680	12,123,445

DOCUMENT 6

Office of War Information poster

DOCUMENT 7

"Executive Order

Authorizing the Secretary of War to Prescribe Military Areas

Whereas the successful prosecution of the war requires every possible protection against espionage and against sabotage to national-defense . . .

Now, therefore, by virtue of the authority vested in me as President of the United States, and Commander in Chief of the Army and Navy, I hereby authorize and direct the Secretary of War, and the Military Commanders . . . to prescribe military areas in such places and of such extent . . . from which any or all persons may be excluded, and with respect to which, the right of any person to enter, remain in, or leave shall be subject to whatever restrictions the Secretary of War or the appropriate Military Commander may impose in his discretion . . . .

Franklin D. Roosevelt
The White House,
February 19, 1942"

ANSWERS AND EXPLANATIONS

MULTIPLE-CHOICE ANSWERS

1. A

In the aftermath of the Triangle Shirtwaist fire in New York City in 1911, New York State created a series of investigating commissions to look into working conditions across the industries in the state. The philosophy behind the Social Gospel, a call by mostly Protestant clergy at the turn of the century, focused on social justice and lessening the problems of industrialization, including poverty and political corruption. The Social Gospel's results were mixed, but it influenced many urban progressive reformers to call for local and state government action.

2. D

Progressive era reforms influenced the thinking and proposals of President Franklin Roosevelt in dealing with the problems of the Great Depression of the 1930s. As a former governor of New York, Roosevelt was profoundly influenced by Progressivism.

3. B

Politicians who owed their allegiance to moneyed interests often blocked urban reform. By the Progressive era, urban political machines, especially Tammany Hall in New York City, realized that much of their political support came from immigrant communities demanding government action. These voters, combined with the actions of urban middle class reformers, swayed political machines to more robustly support reform in order to retain political power.

4. A

As American capitalism has developed, calls for government action to address the problems and limitations periodically increase. This has led to debates over the role of government in the economy and the proper amount of government intervention necessary to limit the worst abuses of capitalism. While issues related to gender, work equality, and urbanization are debated, how much government regulation is appropriate and acceptable in American society is key.

5. B

This World War I era poster calls upon all Americans, whatever their ethnic background as illustrated in the listing of names, to participate in a bond drive to fund the war effort. After 1890, more immigrants came from southern and eastern Europe than from northern and western Europe. The emphasis in the poster is on assimilation, rather than xenophobia or fear of foreigners.

6. C

Shortly after World War I and the Bolshevik Revolution, concern over the spread of communism and anarchism led to the first Red Scare in the United States. It was marked by increased xenophobia and a limitation on civil liberties.

7. B

With posters such as this one, the American government appealed to the wartime patriotism of its entire population, including its large immigrant population. Liberty bond drives raised money for the war effort from across a wide demographic of the American population.

8. A

Prior to American entry into World War II, President Roosevelt met with British prime minister Winston Churchill off the coast of Newfoundland and agreed to a general statement of war principles. This Atlantic Charter articulated many of the goals of President Wilson's Fourteen Points prior to U.S. entry in World War I, including an organization to promote "general security," namely the League of Nations.

9. D

While the Atlantic Charter established an idealized set of world goals, the decision to act on those goals involves complex questions of federal policy, public opinion and resolve, and the economic resources necessary to achieve public policy goals at home and abroad.

10. A

The dismantling of pre–World War II colonial empires accelerated after the war in Africa, Asia, and the Middle East. While self-determination of peoples formed a core principle of Wilson's Fourteen Points and the Atlantic Charter, these movements generated controversy and conflict. Cold War competition led to American support of regimes in Latin America with differing support of democracy.

11. D

During World War II, President Roosevelt and Prime Minister Churchill formed a strong alliance, later joined by Joseph Stalin, which defeated the Axis powers of Italy, Germany, and Japan. Their diplomatic meetings during the course of the war, although at times strained, determined Allied strategy and the initial plans for the postwar world, including the formation of the United Nations.

12. C

The boom-bust cycle of the late 19th century continued into the twentieth with the massive Great Depression. The reform legislation of the New Deal, including the Social Security Act, attempted to make the population more economically secure through federal government action. These reforms are part of the legacy of President Franklin Roosevelt's New Deal.

13. D

The reform legislation that created various agencies during the New Deal, including the Social Security Act, the National Labor Relations Act, and the Federal Deposit Insurance Corporation, made the national government more responsible for the economic safety and well-being of its citizens. Not without controversy, this increased role for government forms the basis of the limited welfare state.

14. D

During the early 20th century, Progressive era reformers at the local, state, and national level sought to increase the role of government to protect American consumers, workers, and citizens. They sought to control the worst abuses of industrial and finance capitalism.

15. B

By the late 20th century, many economic and demographic challenges confronted the United States. Slow economic growth, in part, led to an increasing budget deficit in the early 21st century. Calls for decreasing "big government" became problematic when popular programs such as social security, Medicare, and Medicaid became the targets of reform.

Short-Answer Questions Responses

1. (A) Henry Ford, in his autobiography, explains the process by which the assembly line came to dominate the production of Ford automobiles. Inspired by Chicago's meatpackers, he used division of labor to efficiently take 5,000 parts and assemble a car.

   (B) From a worker's perspective, work at a Ford plant was brutal and dehumanizing. A worker's spouse identifies key problems—lack of bathroom breaks and an exhausting schedule caused by assembly-line chain—that need investigating by Henry Ford. The spouse and her husband believe Henry Ford is unaware of conditions.

   (C) Inspiration for Henry Ford's assembly-line process innovations came from a number of different sources. Chicago meatpackers like Armour and Swift and their "disassembly" line served as one source. Taylorism, a system of scientific management developed by Frederick Winslow Taylor, sought the most efficient way to break down the production process using time-motion studies. High wages were a part of Fordism, but they came at a cost.

2. (A) The cover image from F. Scott Fitzgerald's book portrays the 1920s, the era of the Jazz Age, as a time of close dancing, drinking, and affluence.

   (B) The flappers of the 1920s portrayed one view of the new, modern woman. Bobbed hair, flesh-colored stockings, short skirts, and a boyish figure embodied in celebrities such as Clara Bow challenged the rural, girl-next-door view of American middle-class womanhood. The rise of the city and prohibition and the end of World War I accelerated change in America.

   (C) Conservative reaction to the intense changes confronting America in the 1920s also marked the Jazz Age. Prohibition became the law of the land when the Volstead Act was passed to enforce the Eighteenth Amendment to the Constitution. Although speakeasies and bootlegging sought to circumvent prohibition, it was the law of the land until the Twenty-First Amendment repealed it as the Great Depression took hold.

DBQ SAMPLE RESPONSE

For Americans, the Japanese attack on Pearl Harbor, Hawaii, on Sunday, December 7, "a day which will live in infamy" officially brought World War II home to America. Congress answered FDR's call the following day with a declaration of war, but the United States home front had already begun to transition toward war in the year or so prior. Increased aid to the Allied powers and the institution of a peacetime draft predated America's entry into the war and affected life at home. The Japanese attack would lead to violations of civil liberties, new economic opportunities for women and minorities, and disruptions to the peacetime consumer economy.

After Nazi Germany invaded Poland in 1939, America reevaluated its isolationist policies of the 1930s. Cash-carry was replaced by lend-lease, and American manufacturing geared up to produce arms and equipment to fight fascism on several continents. American production capacity increased astronomically. The total labor force increased to meet demand (Doc. 3). War work was coordinated by the War Production Board, a federal agency similar in intent to those established during World War I. Consumer production facilities transitioned over to producing war products; for example, the Ford Motor Company plants produced jeeps. While the need for more labor helped move the United States beyond the Great Depression years, the first peacetime draft of 1940 began to target able-bodied young men for military service (Doc. 5). Who would fill the labor shortage?

Rosie the Riveter, a fictional character, sought to turn America's patriotic females into war production laborers. Many women did heed the call (Docs 2 and 3). But workplace relations weren't always "rosie." Women met with discrimination and prejudice, more often in older, more established industries. Married women with small children had issues with child care if they sought wartime employment. Some women even joined the various branches of the armed forces. The official view, as seen in the U.S. Navy official photograph (Doc. 2), was that there were few problems. The work crew pictured is integrated, but not all workplaces were, as African Americans sought to have equal access to wartime employment.

Labor organizer and activist A. Philip Randolph proposed a march on Washington in 1941 as a show of patriotism and, in part, a call for equal access to jobs (Doc. 4). While this march did not occur, it did give a political push to President Roosevelt's decision to issue an executive order banning discrimination in defense industries. But life on the home front was still segregated—Jim Crow was alive and well in the South, and America's military would not be desegregated until after World War II was over. But the changes and challenges here would strengthen after the war. A war against tyranny and democratic values illustrated some of the paradoxes in the American experience. While Americans, regardless of race or geographic area, had to contend with rationing and food shortages (Doc. 6), some were targeted for discrimination.

The attacks on Pearl Harbor led to a public hysteria and belief that a Japanese attack or invasion of the West Coast was a real possibility. Decades of Japanese immigration and settlement had led to a significant Japanese presence in California and other West Coast states. Nativist reaction, fears of sabotage, and racial prejudice supported FDR's executive order (Doc. 7), which allowed for the creation of internment camps. Abandoning personal possessions and property, persons of Japanese ancestry, including Japanese Americans in the areas in question, were rounded up and sent inland to internment camps in desolate areas. Ironically, one could leave the camps if one enlisted in the military. Many did, but were not sent to the Pacific theater. Rather, they distinguished themselves in combat in the European theater of operations. Challenges to this treatment reached the Supreme Court in cases like *Korematsu v. USA*, but it was wartime. The Supreme Court upheld the action of the federal government. An official apology would not come for decades.

Although President Roosevelt did not live to see the war end, his leadership, policies, and vision at home and abroad helped achieve Allied success. This feeling got him elected in 1940, breaking the two-term limit established by George Washington (Doc. 1). Actions on the home front during World War II illustrated strengths and limitations of the American experience. When the war ended, so did some of the employment gains made by women, but the seeds were sown for changes to come in the following decades.

This response starts with a strong thesis that answers the question, takes a position, and identifies multiple categories. All of the documents are used in this essay. Document usage goes beyond a simple summary; context is often provided. Note the sentence suggesting the U.S. Navy photo was more propaganda than reality. Outside information is appropriate, strong, and abundant. It is woven throughout each paragraph. Contextualization is also very strong. Note that the response goes backward and forward in time when appropriate, demonstrating a good sense of chronology. Synthesis is also demonstrated throughout the essay.

The thesis for this essay would receive the maximum credit of 1 point. The strong use of documents, including analysis, context, and outside information would earn the maximum 4 points possible. Contextualization is excellent, earning this essay the maximum 1 point. Synthesis is also excellent, earning it the maximum 1 point. This essay would receive a 7 out of 7 possible points on the DBQ rubric.

CHAPTER 24: THE U.S. IN THE POSTWAR WORLD

ORIGINS OF THE COLD WAR

It was clear to Roosevelt and Churchill, and later Truman and Atlee, that Joseph Stalin was focused on carving out spheres of influence in Eastern Europe. The "shotgun marriage" between the Soviets and the United States during World War II would soon crumble as it became clear that Stalin could not be trusted. The Soviets' refusal to sign a plan eliminating atomic weapons and to join the World Bank also caused Western powers to grow increasingly alarmed about Stalin's intentions. Despite his agreement to allow free elections in Eastern Europe at the Yalta Conference, when time came for these elections, Stalin refused to allow them in Poland and other Eastern European countries. From 1946 to 1948, many communist leaders were installed by Moscow, with the Soviets taking these countries under their wing as "satellite" nations. This was a clear violation of the agreements reached at the war conferences, where the world powers had set forth to protect the self-determination of peoples.

As the United States, Great Britain, and France looked to unify Germany once again as a sovereign nation, the Soviets turned East Germany into a communist state. By tightening control over its sector, the USSR hoped to constrain Germany and avoid another world war. It also sought to force the other three world powers to give up their sectors of the capital city of Berlin, since it lay within the Soviet-controlled region of East Germany. In March 1946, Winston Churchill delivered a speech in Fulton, Missouri, where he said, "An iron curtain has descended across Europe." The "iron curtain" he spoke of was communism.

THE POLICY OF CONTAINMENT

Heavily influenced by his top advisers, Secretary of State George Marshall, Undersecretary of State Dean Acheson, and Soviet expert George Kennan, President Truman was interested in "containing" the spread of world communism. Kennan had recently penned an article in which he outlined his predictions of Soviet world domination if the United States and United Nations did not act to stop it. The containment policy was first implemented in reaction to communist threats in Greece and Turkey.

THE TRUMAN DOCTRINE

In March 1947, President Truman asked Congress for funding to assist these countries in repelling a possible communist takeover. Now known as the **Truman Doctrine**, the president's speech explained that the United States had a duty to give financial assistance to free nations under communist threat. The Truman Doctrine passed its first test, as both Greece and Turkey successfully thwarted communism.

THE MARSHALL PLAN

In rebuilding war-torn Europe, the Truman administration wanted to act quickly to avoid the troubles that had besieged the region after World War I. Postwar conditions were on the side of extremist political parties, which stood poised to take advantage of the hungry, tired, and poor. These parties included hard-line communists, who were building momentum in France and Italy. To curb the success of the communists, the Truman administration needed to supply funding to rebuild the economies of Western Europe.

In June 1947, Truman's secretary of state, George Marshall, masterminded a plan to give Western Europe massive amounts of financial assistance to rebuild. Congress readily approved the **Marshall Plan**, which would supply $3 billion in aid over a four-year period. The Marshall Plan was a stunning success. By the end of the 1950s, Western Europe was entirely self-sufficient, and communism had been contained.

THE BERLIN WALL AND THE WARSAW PACT

It looked as if the Cold War was about to get hot in June of 1948. Stalin had grown tired of U.S. intrusion into his country's affairs. Stalin angrily cut off the city of Berlin from Western contact. In an effort to eliminate American influence in an area mostly under Soviet control, all land routes into and out of the city were blockaded by Soviet troops. Not wishing to provoke Stalin, Truman decided to fly supplies to the city's citizens by air. The **Berlin Airlift** delivered supplies to the city, day after day, for 11 months. The world held its breath while the possibility of a world war loomed, but Stalin finally reopened the city.

President Truman broke a tradition dating from Washington's presidency—he joined an alliance with European countries when the **North Atlantic Treaty Organization (NATO)** was formed in 1949. Stalin responded by forming the **Warsaw Pact** in 1955, which provided the same military protection, but at a cost—once a country was a member, it could never leave the alliance. These alliances created an atmosphere in which each side attempted to one up the other by growing their armed forces and developing superior large-scale weapons. After the Soviets exploded their first atomic bomb in 1949, the atomic race was on. By 1952, the United States had developed and tested its first hydrogen bomb, which was at least 1,000 times stronger than the bombs dropped on Hiroshima and Nagasaki.

THE NATIONAL SECURITY ACT AND NSC-68

Domestically, President Truman urged the passage of the **National Security Act** in 1947, which created the **Department of Defense** (formally the Department of War), the **National Security Council**, and the **Central Intelligence Agency** (CIA). To keep the country always at the ready, a permanent peacetime draft was enacted in 1948. As a boost to Truman's belief in the need for increased defense spending, a classified report labeled NSC-68, written by the National Security Council, was released just after China fell to communism and the Korean crisis was about to begin. The report detailed the Soviet Union's plans for worldwide domination and encouraged an immediate buildup of the nation's military. Where the Truman Doctrine had provided for financial support in preventing the spread of communism, NSC-68 now provided the rationale for the use of U.S. troops to achieve containment.

COLD WAR POLICY IN ASIA

Containment in Asia was not as easy as containment had been in Europe. To keep Japan away from communism, the United States occupied the islands until 1951. The new constitution, written with the assistance of General Douglas MacArthur, retained a ceremonial emperor and a limited military. Americans assisted Japan in rebuilding economically and politically after the war's end. Other regions in Asia would not take to democracy so readily.

CHINA FALLS TO COMMUNISM

A corrupt regime had taken control of China with the support of the United States during World War II. The **Nationalists (Kuomintang)**, under the leadership of Chiang Kai-shek (Jiang Jieshi), received financial aid from the United States to keep the country from falling prey to the Japanese. Once that support was removed after the war, the Nationalists and the Communists, the latter under the leadership of **Mao Tse-Tung** (Mao Zedong), re-engaged in a civil war that had started before World War II. Many Chinese citizens began to turn to Mao and the Communists as they became more and more disgusted by the corruption, inflation, and inequality they experienced under Chiang. President Truman sent George Marshall to mediate between the two parties but to no avail. More money was sent to the Nationalists, but much of it was misspent. China finally fell to the Communists in 1949; Chiang and the Nationalists fled to the nearby island of Formosa, now called Taiwan. Americans were taken aback by this spread of communism and blamed the Truman administration for its lack of strength. Another blow to containment came in 1950, when Joseph Stalin and Mao Tse-Tung signed a pact that linked their two large nations in one communist bloc.

WAR IN KOREA

Soon the former Japanese colony of Korea seemed ripe for the picking to the Soviets. When the Japanese withdrew from the northern region of the peninsula, they left it in the hands of the communist Soviet Union, while the United States controlled the southern half. Supplied with Chinese and Soviet weapons, the North Korean army invaded the South over the 38th parallel in

June 1950. President Truman reacted immediately by urging the United Nations Security Council to intervene on behalf of the South Koreans. Luckily, the Soviet Union—a permanent member of the council—had boycotted the UN, opening the door for a quick decision. The Security Council and U.S. Congress authorized a "police action" of military force to liberate South Korea. Congress did not declare war.

The fighting in Korea was a fiasco, as the North Koreans cut their way easily to the heart of the South. General MacArthur was later able to push the North Koreans back across the 38th parallel with a surprise landing of UN forces at Inchon, near the border of the two Koreas. MacArthur pushed the enemy back almost to the Chinese border. However, MacArthur was taken by surprise as Chinese forces crossed the border and forced the UN troops to retreat back across the 38th parallel. At this point, MacArthur was convinced that if he had more resources, he could win the war and possibly take China as well. Truman had already called for a "limited war" and sternly told MacArthur that he was not to make any statements that were critical of American policy in Asia. In a letter that was later leaked to the press, the general said that "there is no substitute for victory" and alleged that the president was weak.

MacArthur then ignored Truman's wishes and demanded an unconditional surrender of the North Koreans. Upon hearing this news, Truman immediately removed General MacArthur from his command and had him return to the United States in April 1951. He returned to a hero's welcome, as most Americans had never experienced a U.S. military loss and could not understand the objectives of containment. Nonetheless, Truman's action signified that civilian rule in the United States was supreme; it was the military's responsibility to follow the president's orders, not make them. In the end, the Korean conflict ended in a stalemate, with the original division at the 38th parallel remaining—Communists in the North and Nationalists in the South. Now that the United States had "lost" two Asian nations to communism, Republicans were beginning to claim that the Democrats did not have what it took to rid the world of communism.

EISENHOWER AND KENNEDY

World War II hero General **Dwight D. "Ike" Eisenhower** took the reins of the presidency in 1952 with the anti-communist-crusading Richard M. Nixon as his vice president. Eisenhower chose John Foster Dulles as his secretary of state. Dulles advocated a departure from Truman's Cold War policies. American foreign policy would now actively support nations that sought liberation from communism through his policy of **brinksmanship**—the United States would push the aggressor nation to the brink of nuclear war, forcing it to back down and make concessions in the face of American superiority. The aspect of this new approach to foreign policy affected the composition of American armed forces. Dulles believed that the United States needed to place more emphasis on nuclear and air power and less on conventional troops and weapons. This led to his advocacy of **massive retaliation**, whereby the United States would unleash its arsenal of nuclear weapons on any nation that attacked it. This new approach, however, did not address the problem of small countries under communist threat.

The Geneva Convention and Troubles in Vietnam

As colonial governments collapsed in Asia, the Pacific, and Africa, the United States struggled to keep up with the need to avoid communist takeover of these vulnerable countries. Along with brinksmanship and massive retaliation, Dulles also championed the use of covert action to fight the Cold War. In 1953, the CIA staged a coup that led to the return of the liberal, corrupt, and ruthless shah of Iran. Similarly, the CIA aided in the overthrow of a left-leaning government in Guatemala in 1954.

The French were losing control of their colonies in Indochina, with the final ouster at the Vietnamese city of Dien Bien Phu in 1954. Without American assistance, the French were forced to give up the colony entirely. As a result of the **Geneva Convention** (1954), the region was divided into three nations: Vietnam, Cambodia, and Laos. The convention also decided to divide Vietnam at the 17th parallel, with the Communists led by Ho Chi Minh in the north and Nationalists led by Ngo Dinh Diem in the south. It was further decided that elections to reunite Vietnam would occur in two years. Fearing a communist win in the elections, Ngo Dinh Diem never allowed them to take place and became increasingly dictatorial. Eisenhower, fearing what he called the "domino theory" (where one Asian nation would fall to communism and the rest would follow), urged Dulles to action. He created the **South East Asian Treaty Organization (SEATO)**, which resembled NATO, to give mutual military assistance to member nations and hold up Diem's crumbling regime.

Eisenhower and the Middle East

Aside from Iran, other Middle Eastern countries concerned Eisenhower. When the Egyptian leader Nasser asked the United States for assistance in building the **Aswan Dam**, he was assured the deal would be easy. The United States refused, however, as Egypt seemed to threaten the security of the new Jewish state of Israel. Nasser took this rebuke very seriously and seized the foreign-held Suez Canal. The free flow of oil from the Middle East to Europe and the United States was now cut off. Unbeknownst to Eisenhower, Britain, France, and Israel launched a surprise attack on Egypt and regained control of the Suez Canal. An angry Eisenhower called upon the UN Security Council to denounce the surprise action and call for the immediate removal of the multinational forces. The UN complied, and Britain and France fell from their role as world leaders.

THE EISENHOWER DOCTRINE

Eisenhower seized this opportunity to become more of a presence in the Middle East by proclaiming the **Eisenhower Doctrine,** which was much like the Truman Doctrine. Eisenhower's document was pointed at the Middle East.

THE SOVIET UNION AND HUNGARY

The tensions between the United States and the Soviet Union would continue to plague Eisenhower just as they had Truman before him. After Stalin's death in 1953, many looked for relief from Cold War tensions, and signs existed that this was a possibility. Agreements to "open skies" and the end to some postwar Soviet occupations gave some members of the Warsaw Pact a glimmer of hope. One such member was Hungary, which in 1956 successfully overthrew a Soviet puppet government. The new government demanded Hungary's removal from the Warsaw Pact. The new Soviet premier, Nikita Khrushchev, ordered Soviet troops to crush the resistance. There was no American response. Eisenhower feared that sending in U.S. troops would begin World War III. The USSR brutally crushed the Hungarian resistance, killing many.

SPY PLANES OVER THE SOVIET UNION

Berlin was again in the news when in 1958 Khrushchev demanded the removal of Westerners from the city within six months. Eisenhower called an urgent meeting with the Soviet premier, and they agreed to hold off on any decision until they could meet again in Paris in 1960. Unfortunately, this meeting would never occur, as a U.S. U-2 spy plane was shot down over the Soviet Union two weeks prior. It was then revealed that the United States had been flying regular spy missions over the USSR since 1955. Khrushchev called off the scheduled Paris talks.

CASTRO COMMUNIZES CUBA

Communism found a new home just 90 miles off the coast of the United States on the Caribbean island of Cuba. There the brutal dictator Batista had been overthrown by the revolutionary **Fidel Castro** in 1959. Cuban exiles living in the United States rejoiced, as it looked as if their nation was now free from oppression. The "honeymoon" with Castro soon faded, as he nationalized businesses owned by Americans and introduced massive land reforms. After Eisenhower cut diplomatic relations with Castro, the Cuban leader looked to the Soviets for help. Castro then set about building a communist state on the island. Before he left office, Eisenhower approved of a covert plan to invade Cuba and overthrow Fidel Castro. However, Eisenhower would not see the plan through.

BAY OF PIGS AND THE BERLIN WALL

John F. Kennedy was the next president who had to deal with Cold War politics. The young president would agree to allow an invasion to take place in April 1961 at the **Bay of Pigs** (Bahia de Puerco). Using faulty intelligence, the CIA-trained forces landed and were immediately defeated by armed Cubans. The invasion was a failure and an embarrassment for the new president. Kennedy had little time to rest, as he was scheduled to meet with Khrushchev soon in Vienna. The Soviet leader used this opportunity to threaten President Kennedy with regard to Berlin. Kennedy did not back down, refusing to remove U.S. troops from the city. The Soviets responded by building a wall around West Berlin to stem the flow of East Berliners escaping to the West. The president did not stop the building of the wall, but he did travel to West Berlin in 1963 to proclaim U.S. support for its citizens.

THE CUBAN MISSILE CRISIS

The nation was gripped with fear as Fidel Castro and Khrushchev joined forces to threaten U.S. national security. U.S. spy planes discovered the building of nuclear missile sites on the island of Cuba in October 1962. These medium-range and long-range nuclear missiles decreased the existing warning time of a nuclear attack on the United States from 30 minutes to 30 seconds. The missiles in Cuba also left no place in North America safe from nuclear attack. Kennedy ordered the immediate removal of the missiles, but Castro and Khrushchev refused. JFK was left with a grave decision and enlisted a group of advisers to assist him. Headed by his brother, Attorney General Robert Kennedy, the group decided that a naval blockade would be the least dangerous option. After several days of Soviet ships being turned back in the Atlantic Ocean and tense negotiations, Khrushchev decided to remove the missiles from Cuba, as long as the United States promised never to invade Cuba again and removed its own nuclear missiles from Turkey. As close as the two nations had been to nuclear war, the **Cuban Missile Crisis** was effective in opening up channels of communication between Washington, D.C., and Moscow. A direct "**red phone**" or hotline was installed so that the world leaders could have immediate contact in the case of emergency.

Upon assuming the presidency, Kennedy did not believe that Dulles's "new-look" military would be effective in a world where colonial governments continued to fall in small Asian and African nations. His "flexible-response" military looked to use conventional tactics and elite special forces units to root out communists in nations such as Vietnam and Congo.

THE SECOND RED SCARE

To dislodge potential "disloyals" from the inner workings of the federal government, Congress, against the wishes of President Truman, took several actions aimed at communists and other subversives. The **Smith Act** of 1940 was designed to arrest people who were advocates of overthrowing the government, even if they had no intention of ever doing so. The **House Un-American Activities Committee** (HUAC), established in 1939 to look for former Nazis who had made it to the United States, was reactivated in the postwar years to find communists.

AMERICAN ESPIONAGE AND SENATOR MCCARTHY

Paranoia about a potential communist takeover swept the nation in the 1950s, much as it had after World War I. Fueling this fear were actual cases of espionage in which American spies were handing U.S. secrets to the Soviets. HUAC made headlines in 1948 when American communist Whittaker Chambers testified in the case of a State Department employee who had supposedly leaked secrets to the communists. A young lawyer named Richard M. Nixon linked Chambers to a man who had assisted President Franklin Roosevelt during the Yalta Conference, **Alger Hiss**. Hiss denied any connections to the Communist Party or any spy networks. Nonetheless, he was convicted and sent to prison for perjury; Hiss had falsely testified under oath that he had never been a member of a communist party.

The FBI successfully uncovered a spy network that led to the arrest of a husband and wife duo, Julius and Ethel Rosenberg. The couple was accused of delivering atomic bomb secrets to the Soviets. The trial was a press spectacle, and a conviction was finally handed down in 1951. Convicted of treason and espionage, the Rosenbergs were sentenced to death and executed by electric chair.

Republican senator **Joseph McCarthy** ceaselessly raised suspicions that communists besides Alger Hiss were still working in the State Department. Using the media to his advantage, McCarthy widely cast his anti-communist net as he accused many within the Truman administration and other well-known Americans of anti-American activities. While his accusations were mostly false, Republicans did little to stop him, as he helped their chances in the upcoming presidential election. McCarthy painted himself into a corner however, when in 1954, he turned his ruthless tactics on the military. The Senate committee hearings investigating communists in the army showed McCarthy in a poor light as he questioned those on the stand. Soon, fellow members of Congress decided that **McCarthyism** had gone far enough and voted to censure the senator.

LIVING IN FEAR—AMERICANS AND THE COLD WAR

Americans were hoping for some peace after World War II, but they traded fear of Hitler and Tojo for fear of nuclear war. It seemed that every time they turned around, U.S. citizens were faced with images of nations falling to communist rule, American spies, and nuclear threat. After the launch of the Russian space satellite *Sputnik* in 1957, Americans were convinced that they had better get moving if they were to keep up with the Soviets. Congress responded by allocating millions of dollars to schools and universities across the nation to prepare students in mathematics, science, and foreign languages. Eisenhower also urged the creation of the **National Aeronautics and Space Administration (NASA)** in 1958 to get the United States back in the running with the Soviets.

Bomb shelters were big business in the United States, with Americans spending upwards of $5,000 to protect their families. These buildings, constructed underground, had provisions for a family of four to survive after a nuclear attack. Children in schools practiced "duck and cover" drills in which they would fall out of their seats, hide under desks, and remain until the "all clear" signal sounded. Americans purchased canned goods, bottled water, and Geiger counters for their homes and bomb shelters. Once novelty items, "spy gear" became popular as Americans hoped to be able to outsmart neighbors who might be Russian double agents. The **National Highway Act** of 1956, which created the nation's interstate system, looked as if it was intended solely to improve the county's infrastructure, but the 42,000 miles of road were also meant to provide for the quick evacuation of large urban centers, the emergency landing of planes, and the transport of nuclear missiles.

The Cold War had a profound effect on the entertainment industry, as well. Comic characters such as Captain America and movies like *The Invasion of the Body Snatchers* fueled the American thirst for "commie hunting." Eisenhower himself reacted negatively to Cold War developments as he warned the nation of their ill effects in his farewell address. Eisenhower warned of the "military-industrial complex," whereby the nation would be driven by the needs of the arms race and war machine.

KENNEDY TO JOHNSON—CHANGING IDEOLOGIES

Despite leaving the presidency more popular than ever, Eisenhower was unable to transfer that enthusiasm to the Republican candidate **Richard M. Nixon** in the 1960 election. A former vice president, Nixon believed his campaign would be an easy one, as the Democrats chose Massachusetts senator **John F. Kennedy** as their candidate. Kennedy's charisma and good looks carried him through the primaries to the Democratic convention, where he chose Texas senator Lyndon Baines Johnson as his running mate. The campaign was an uphill battle for Kennedy— he was a Roman Catholic and would be the youngest elected president in history. The choice of Lyndon Johnson as a running mate was a shrewd one because it secured the support of Southerners. Kennedy's youth actually played in his favor, as Americans were drawn to his style and vitality. His religion would be his most difficult hurdle to clear. Many questioned whether or not a Catholic president could effectively rule the nation without the influence of the Pope. Kennedy laid all fears to rest when he reassured an audience of Protestant ministers that he would in no way allow his religious beliefs to interfere with his role as chief executive.

"Ask not what your country can do for you; ask what you can do for your country." With these words from his inaugural address, John F. Kennedy began a shift in the White House that would deeply impact American society. His domestic policy was named the "**New Frontier**," with promises of equality, full employment, and financial aid to the needy. The young president would run into many roadblocks as he attempted to get his legislative agenda through Congress. Republicans and conservative Democrats, a coalition that had earlier stalled the New Deal in 1938 and thwarted Truman's attempts to expand it in the late 1940s, repeatedly blocked the president's attempts. Kennedy did have some success in creating the Peace Corps, raising the minimum wage, and advancing urban renewal. Aside from these instances, the majority of Kennedy's domestic legislative initiatives were not passed until after his assassination.

NIXON AND KENNEDY DEBATE ON TV

For the first time in U.S. history, the four presidential debates were televised nationally. These debates sealed the election for JFK. Kennedy's poise and vitality proved effective weapons against the seemingly nervous Nixon. Americans who watched the debates believed that Kennedy had won, while those who listened on the radio gave their nod to Nixon. It was clear that Kennedy would benefit from media coverage, and he used it to his advantage as the election neared. In a narrowly contested race, Kennedy edged Nixon by the slimmest margin ever in an American presidential election. Despite unsubstantiated cries of election fraud and ballot tampering from the Republicans, JFK was declared the next president.

KENNEDY'S ASSASSINATION

While on a trip to Texas to gain support for his policy agenda programs, John F. Kennedy was assassinated. On November 22, 1963, Lee Harvey Oswald shot the president from the window of a building in downtown Dallas as the president's motorcade drove by. Americans sat riveted to their televisions as they waited for news of their beloved president. It was with great sadness that news anchors announced the president's death and the swearing in of Lyndon Baines Johnson (LBJ) aboard Air Force One. As his first act as president, LBJ ordered the appointment of a special investigatory commission to investigate the assassination of JFK. The **Warren Commission**, headed by Chief Justice Warren, concluded that Oswald had acted alone in killing the president. Many conspiracy theories abounded after the commission delivered its report, and to this day many question the conclusions of the Warren Commission.

LBJ AND THE GREAT SOCIETY

President Johnson had a difficult task in taking over for an immensely popular president. After winning the presidency in his own right in 1964, LBJ was determined to continue along the liberal path of his predecessor and expand upon some of the New Frontier ideas he thought too modest. Johnson named his program **The Great Society**, and he was determined to expand civil rights and eliminate poverty. Johnson was heavily influenced by a book by Michael Harrington titled *The Other America*. In it, Harrington explained that 20 percent of Americans and more than 40 percent of all African Americans lived in poverty. In response, the president created the **Office of Equal Opportunity** (OEO), which oversaw the creation of the Job Corps, a program that provided career training to inner-city and rural citizens. The OEO was also in charge of the Head Start program, which provided free or low-cost preschool to low-income children to ready them for elementary school. In many ways, LBJ continued and strengthened the New Deal programs started by FDR. The Great Society also saw the creation of Medicare and Medicaid, which provide low-cost medical care for the elderly and poor, respectively. The **Department of Housing and Urban Development** was created in 1965 to provide low-cost housing and federal funding to rid cities of urban blight. The **Immigration Act of 1965** repealed the discriminatory practices of the Quota Acts of the 1920s. This monumental law helped change the face of American society by allowing millions of people from all over the world to immigrate to the United States over the course of the next four decades. President Johnson oversaw the creation of the National Endowment for the Humanities, which provided federal funding for artistic and cultural endeavors. The Johnson administration created the Department of Transportation, increased funding for universities and colleges, and enacted laws to protect consumers and the environment. Aside from FDR, no other president had passed this amount of legislation.

THE COLD WAR GETS HOT

President Kennedy shared Eisenhower's belief that Asian countries would fall like dominoes if left alone and unprotected from communism. Therefore, when it became clear that the French were pulling completely out of Vietnam, Kennedy increased financial and military assistance to the government of South Vietnam.

THE GULF OF TONKIN RESOLUTION

However, the Ngo Dinh Diem regime, which Eisenhower had worked to prop up with SEATO, was becoming more and more of a liability. Buddhist monks in the South Vietnamese capital set themselves on fire to protest Ngo's policies discriminating against fellow Buddhists, who made up more than 75 percent of the country's population. Just before JFK's death, Diem was assassinated in the first of several coups d'etat that led to an unstable Vietnamese government in the early 1960s. Later, Lyndon Johnson refused to allow Vietnam and Southeast Asia to fall to communists. Yet Vietnam was falling apart just as he took the oath of office. Johnson's secretary of defense, Robert McNamara, urged the president to take more forceful action to prevent the fall of South Vietnam to communism. In August 1964, LBJ claimed that a North Vietnamese gunboat had carried out an unprovoked attack on two U.S. destroyers in the Gulf of Tonkin off the coast of North Vietnam. The president immediately used the incident to ask Congress for an increase in his authority to wage war in Vietnam without an actual war declaration. The **Gulf of Tonkin Resolution** greatly increased the power of the executive branch to engage in this war. It was later discovered that the U.S. destroyers had actually been assisting the South Vietnamese in attacking their northern neighbor and, thus, the attacks were not "unprovoked." Johnson used the Gulf of Tonkin Resolution to widen the war further after he won re-election in 1964.

JOHNSON HEIGHTENS AMERICAN INVOLVEMENT

As Vietnam sank further and further into chaos, Johnson chose to escalate American involvement in the war. He thought it was not a viable option to back out of Vietnam, as the country would have certainly fallen into communist hands. But escalation meant diverting resources from his beloved Great Society programs—funding was needed to fuel the war machine. He hoped the war would be a quick one, and the first-strike Operation Rolling Thunder in 1965 called for bombing raids over North Vietnam. A quick victory was not in the cards, however, as **Ho Chi Minh's Vietminh** and the **South Vietnamese Vietcong** continued to bounce back with more supplies and more men in the face of the American assault.

The United States relied on air and ground forces to fight in the heavily forested jungles of Vietnam. U.S. tactics focused on destroying the **Ho Chi Minh Trail**, which linked the South Vietnamese Vietcong fighters with the North Vietnamese supply lines. The United States dropped more bombs on North Vietnam than were used in all of World War II. The ground war would prove to be much more difficult and dangerous for Americans. The heavy rain forest canopy and moist tropical climate made fighting a conventional war impossible. General William Westmoreland developed a controversial "search and destroy" method of rooting South Vietnamese Vietcong sympathizers out of villages by burning homes to the ground. Finding the enemy proved to be most difficult, as Vietcong soldiers dressed in the same peasant clothing as ordinary villagers. In an attempt to clear the countryside, the United States uprooted villagers and moved them to cities. Controversy at home escalated as the "hawks" (those who supported the war) and "doves" (those opposed to the war) battled it out in Congress and across America. As the election of 1968 loomed, events in Vietnam would change course.

THE WAR CHANGES COURSE

The Vietnamese Lunar New Year, known as Tet, marked the beginning of a massive Vietcong offensive that moved the war away from rural areas to the cities of South Vietnam. In January 1968, Vietcong forces surprised American troops by attacking military bases and regional capitals. Even as General Westmoreland said that the war's end was near, it was clear to those watching on television that the communists had no intention of surrendering. The psychological impact of the **Tet Offensive** would change the course of the war both in Vietnam and at home. American public opinion now shifted against the war, and increasingly people demanded that the United States pull out of the war-torn country. In effect, Tet was the beginning of the end of U.S. military involvement in Vietnam. Having lost almost half of his support in presidential approval ratings, LBJ decided that he would not run for re-election in 1968.

THE ELECTION OF 1968

John F. Kennedy's younger brother, Robert, decided to continue the Kennedy presidential legacy and entered the race for president in 1968. RFK had shown an uncanny ability to garner the votes of working-class and liberal Democrats. Therefore, it came as no surprise when he won the California Democratic primary in June 1968. The events after his victory speech were a shock, however, when a young Palestinian activist by the name of **Sirhan Sirhan** shot and killed RFK as he walked through the kitchen of the Ambassador Hotel in Los Angeles. The Democrats eventually nominated Vice President Hubert Humphrey as their candidate.

THE CONVENTION RIOT OF 1968

The Democratic National Convention was held in Chicago that year. Mayor Richard Daley made sure his city was prepared for possible trouble. Antiwar protesters had mobilized to the convention to express their distaste for a candidate (Humphrey) whom they believed would continue to support Johnson's war in Vietnam. A massive number of demonstrators lined the streets of downtown Chicago, with an equal number of police present to keep the peace. In an event that would be broadcast on national television, Chicago police harassed and beat protesters, resulting in a riot that caused the nation to question both Daley and Humphrey.

The Republicans decided to give Richard M. Nixon another shot at the presidency, with vice presidential candidate and Southerner Spiro Agnew at his side. A third party rose to prominence; the **American Independent Party** chose Alabama governor George Wallace as its candidate. This party organized itself around the issue of states' rights to pursue a segregationist agenda. Nixon won the election by a slim margin over Humphrey, while Democrats maintained their majority in Congress. Without a clear mandate from American voters, Nixon would struggle at the start of his presidency.

CHAPTER 25: LIBERALISM AND THE POLITICAL AND CULTURAL RESPONSE

THE EARLY CIVIL RIGHTS MOVEMENT

Segregation and discrimination against African Americans was nothing new in American society, and neither were the voices of protest. The social climate was changing, however. President Truman desegregated the armed forces in 1948. Before that, in 1947, the Brooklyn Dodgers had broken the color line in professional baseball by drafting the Negro League star Jackie Robinson. As African Americans moved to northern cities during the Great Migration, they began to exercise the rights granted them by the Fourteenth and Fifteenth Amendments, with no barriers. There was an a contradiction within America—the country had just fought a war to liberate people to make their own decisions, but it could not offer that same freedom to many of its own citizens. African Americans had experienced welcoming societies in Europe when they fought in two world wars and wanted that same treatment from their home country.

BROWN V. BOARD OF EDUCATION AND THE LITTLE ROCK NINE

The civil rights movement gained an important ally when President Eisenhower appointed former California governor Earl Warren as Chief Justice of the Supreme Court. Unbeknownst to Eisenhower, the **Warren Court** would be one of the most liberal in history. As early as the mid-1940s, the NAACP had begun to challenge segregation in Southern colleges and universities, making modest gains in breaking down the wall of segregation. However, not until the organization found a test case involving an elementary school student in Topeka, Kansas, did any widespread progress take place. Linda Brown, a first grader, had to leave her home an hour and a half early to travel across town to attend an all–African American school, when there was a white neighborhood school less than a mile from her house. The NAACP encouraged the Brown family to file suit against the Topeka school board on the grounds that Linda's right to equal protection had been violated by its segregation policy. The case made it to the Supreme Court in 1954. The NAACP's Thurgood Marshall (later, the first African American to serve on the Supreme Court) represented the Brown family. He argued that the Fourteenth Amendment guaranteed all citizens equal protection under the law, which translated into equal opportunity. The Warren Court agreed with Marshall, and the ruling in *Brown v. Board of Education* (1954) overturned the 1896 decision in *Plessy v. Ferguson*. The Court decision read that "separate facilities were inherently unequal" and had no place in public education. The Court ordered the desegregation of all public school facilities with "all deliberate speed."

The decision was not well received by many Southerners and other Americans. Many states claimed they would simply close their public schools if they had to integrate. White families refused to send their children to integrated schools, and some state legislatures even passed laws to resist the ruling. In 1957, the situation came to a head in Little Rock, Arkansas, as the governor of the state, Orval Faubus, ordered the Arkansas National Guard to bar the entrance of nine African American students into the all-white Central High School. The "**Little Rock Nine**" gained admission to the campus by a federal court ruling, but violent protests immediately broke out in the city. President Eisenhower looked on with despair. The president eventually ordered federal troops into the city to restore order and escort the students safely to their classes. Within a year of the forced integration, all Little Rock public schools had been shuttered; white families sent their children to segregated private schools or public schools outside of the city. It was not until another Warren Court ruling that the Little Rock School Board finally relented and integrated its public schools.

ROSA PARKS AND A BUS BOYCOTT

A petite woman would soon make big headlines when she was arrested in Montgomery, Alabama, for refusing to give up her bus seat to a white patron. The African-American population, almost 65 percent of the total, drank from separate water fountains, rode at the back of buses, and ate in separate areas of restaurants. **Rosa Parks**, a recent volunteer for the local chapter of the NAACP, had seen many African American men and women arrested and mistreated for refusing to comply with the Jim Crow laws that ruled the bus system. Parks decided enough was enough when, on December 11, 1955, she refused to give up her seat to a white man on a city bus. Arrested and fined, Parks started the ball rolling. A young minister from Georgia, **Dr. Martin Luther King Jr.**, along with other African American leaders, organized a bus boycott to last until the buses were desegregated. This would be an enormous blow to the city's revenues, as African Americans made up about 95 percent of bus riders. The boycott lasted around 400 days, with the black community organizing car pools and walk buddies for the hundreds of people needing to get to school, work, and home. The Warren Court ruled that segregation on public buses was unconstitutional, and soon the boycott was over. The negotiations between Dr. King and city managers and downtown business owners helped to keep the crisis from exploding into violence.

Dr. King and Protests Across the Country

Dr. Martin Luther King Jr. and the Southern Christian Leadership Conference (SCLC) built on the lessons of the Montgomery boycott and began to challenge more Jim Crow laws in Alabama and other Southern states. King believed in the teachings of Thoreau and Gandhi and practiced the tenets of civil disobedience and nonviolent resistance. He believed that engaging in violence would only feed the negative stereotypes of African Americans. Other boycotts took place as followers across the country took King's message to heart. Greensboro, North Carolina, became the stage for a new kind of protest in 1960, when local college and high school students entered a Woolworth's drug store and sat at the whites-only lunch counter, refusing to leave until they were served. Beginning with four students, the sit-in grew to a nationwide effort with a thousand students, who rotated on and off lunch counter seats until the store owners gave in six months later. Several other sit-ins occurred across the nation in motel lobbies, on beaches, at public pools, and in libraries. Students soon became the leaders of the movement, as the **Student Nonviolent Coordinating Committee** (SNCC).

President Eisenhower was a reluctant participant in the civil rights movement, preferring to maintain the support of Southerners and the status quo. He did sign two modest civil rights bills as president, however. The Civil Rights Bill of 1957 sought to ensure that African Americans would be able to exercise their right to vote by supporting a new division within the federal Justice Department to monitor civil rights abuses. Furthermore, a bipartisan report was to be written by representatives of both major political parties on the issue of race relations. By the time the bill was enacted as law, it had been watered down so as to not have much impact. The Civil Rights Act of 1960 gave the federal government authority to monitor local and state elections. After an intense fight in Congress, the final bill was just as weak as its predecessor in securing voting rights for African Americans.

THE "AFFLUENT SOCIETY"

As Eisenhower looked to balance the federal budget and maintain the prosperity that flourished in the 1950s, the gap between the rich and poor widened. The country as a whole experienced economic growth with little inflation and stable employment rates. The average American family saw its income more than triple during the decade and enjoyed the world's highest standard of living. Modern conveniences became easier for Americans to purchase. "Keeping up with the Joneses," or keeping pace with the prosperity of one's neighbors, became the American mantra. As a result, America experienced a second major consumer revolution as cars, televisions, and household appliances were purchased in large quantities. The mass-consumption culture of the 1920s would be eclipsed by spending of the 1950s. Since consumer goods were in short supply during the war, Americans had significant savings and were ready to spend. The National Highway Act and the GI Bill fueled the growth of American suburbs and the construction industry, as young families moved out of cities and into suburbs. The American dream was now reality for an increasing number of Americans.

That American dream remained elusive for a large number of citizens, however. Despite civil rights gains made in the South, African Americans throughout the nation did not share equally in the nation's postwar economic expansion and abundance.

CONFORMITY IN MIDDLE-CLASS SOCIETY

The stereotypical picture of the 1950s usually consists of teenagers sipping ice cream malts and dancing at the sock hop, and men in gray flannel suits coming home to a pipe, newspaper, and beautiful wife after work. Just as Americans looked to keep up with the mass consumption of goods that surrounded them, they also strove to blend in to the middle-class conformist mold. Television was a major contributor to the American myth, as viewers often consumed as many as five hours a day of the "boob tube." Situation comedies such as *Father Knows Best* and *I Love Lucy*, along with advertisements for branded products, painted portraits of the "perfect" American family, wife, and household. Corporate America had an impact on society, as middle-class, white-collar workers donned similar clothes and left each day to make enough money to live the "American dream."

BEATNIKS AND NONCONFORMISTS

Not all Americans bought into the middle-class, suburban myth. Many in the academic field called the conformity of the era into question in essays, books, and research papers. While most Hollywood films celebrated the consumerist/conformist lifestyle of the 1950s, some filmmakers challenged it with movies such as *The Man in the Gray Flannel Suit*, based on the novel by Sloan Wilson. Artists such as Jackson Pollock shocked the world with paintings that did not follow form or function. Novelists of the era often mocked or satirized the American dream, challenging readers to think for themselves. J. D. Salinger's *The Catcher in the Rye* told the adventures of the anti-hero and nonconformist Holden Caulfield.

Another group of nonconformists rocked America with their poetry and alternative culture. The **beatniks**, led by alternative writers such as writer Jack Kerouac and poet Allen Ginsberg, encouraged individuality in an age of conformity.

Sometimes using mind-altering drugs and often rebelling against the social standards of the day, beatniks studied art, poetry, and philosophy and openly criticized the society in which they lived. Poetry readings often included "free verse," and participants were invited to the open microphone and encouraged to speak their minds. The Beatniks provided the mold from which the "hippie" movement of the 1960s would emerge.

Women too rebelled, as conformity to traditional roles created a climate that stifled free thought and individuality. In her book ***The Feminine Mystique*** (1963), Betty Friedan encouraged women to leave homemaking behind and pursue fulfillment outside of the home. She called into question the notion that women were meant to remain at home to care for family and instead spoke of opportunities for women to become successful in the business world.

WOMEN AND THE CULT OF DOMESTICITY

Women of the 1950s were expected to take care of the "baby boom" generation as outlined by the baby care book by nationally renowned Dr. Benjamin Spock. Homemaking was venerated as a noble "profession," and women working outside the home were looked down upon by their more traditional counterparts. The "cult of domesticity" was alive and well in the 1950s, but not all women were content with their situation. Alcoholism became an increasing problem, as bored housewives looked to liven up the hours they spent alone when their husbands and children were away for the day. Depression was also a burgeoning problem for American women, but it was often considered a "weakness" and left untreated.

THE CIVIL RIGHTS MOVEMENT EXPANDS

In his early days as president, Kennedy was reluctant, like many before him, to take a public stand with regard to African-American civil rights. Because he needed the support of Southern Democrats to get legislation passed, he did not want to alienate them. As a result, JFK satby for the first two years of his presidency while the civil rights movement continued to gain momentum. The president, however, reacted in 1961 when a voter registration campaign in the South was initiated by the Congress of Racial Equality (CORE). Kennedy took a public stand and voiced support for CORE's efforts. Three years later, Johnson had a domestic crisis on his hands when another group of activists, again led by CORE organizers, boarded integrated buses in the North bound for the Deep South to show their support for the desegregation of public transit and bus stations, as ruled by the Supreme Court. As the buses reached Alabama, waiting mobs firebombed and severely beat the Freedom Riders as state troopers and local police stood by and watched. Attorney General Robert Kennedy at first asked the **Freedom Riders** to stop, but more and more boarded buses and traveled to the South. The attorney general then sent federal marshals to protect the bus riders, signaling a victory for the civil rights movement.

MARTIN LUTHER KING'S PEACEFUL PROTESTS

In 1962, JFK sent federal marshals to protect University of Mississippi student James Meredith as he attended classes on the once all-white campus. Meanwhile, Dr. Martin Luther King Jr. began a peaceful assault on the town of Birmingham, Alabama. The city had closed all of its public facilities to avoid integration. King and his followers staged a march on Good Friday 1963 and were arrested and jailed. While spending two weeks in his cell, Dr. King penned his "Letter from Birmingham Jail," which he wrote to explain to other black ministers why he and his followers could not "wait" for the whites to come around. The nation and world later watched in horror as Birmingham police commissioner Eugene "Bull" Connor had his officers use dogs, fire hoses, and cattle prods to disperse the nonviolent protesters, many of whom were children. Pressure was mounting on the president to take a more vigorous stand. Federal troops were dispatched to the state of Alabama, as Governor George Wallace attempted to stop African-American students from attending the University of Alabama in 1963. This was the last straw for JFK. After theBirmingham marches and the debacle with George Wallace, the president actively began to seek legislation to protect African-American civil rights. On August 28, 1963, Dr. King organized the single most successful march in U.S. history to show support for civil rights legislation on the Mall in Washington, D.C. His "I Have a Dream" speech touched citizens and lawmakers, and a civil rights bill was passed by Congress just after JFK was assassinated.

THE CIVIL RIGHTS ACT AND THE VOTING RIGHTS ACT

Continuing to pass and expanding the scope of civil rights legislation was a major goal for Lyndon Johnson. LBJ saw the ratification of the Twenty-Fourth Amendment, which abolished another barrier to voting rights by outlawing the poll tax. Having years of congressional experience under his belt aided the president as he worked to get Kennedy's civil rights bill pushed through the Senate. The monumental **Civil Rights Act of 1964** outlawed unequal application of voter registration requirements, prohibited segregation of public schools and other public accommodations, and expanded the powers of the Civil Rights Commission established by the Civil Rights Act of 1957. The greatest legislative success of the civil rights movement signaled the end of *de jure* (by law) segregation in America. Unfortunately, the Civil Rights Act did not effectively address many problems associated with African American voting rights. To show lawmakers just how serious this problem was, Dr. King organized a march from Selma to Montgomery, Alabama, in 1965. The march came to a violent end outside of Selma, as state police beat and harassed marchers. King tried again but was stopped just outside Selma. This time, President Johnson sent an urgent message to King asking him to stop marching until he could finalize work on a voting rights bill. As promised, the **Voting Rights Act of 1965** was passed, making literacy tests illegal and prohibiting states from denying the right to vote to any U.S. citizen on the basis of race.

MALCOLM X AND THE BLACK PANTHERS

Even though African Americans had made great strides in securing their civil rights, many within the African American community were not convinced that integration was either attainable or desirable. Radical African American groups rose up, as some grew tired of the goals and tactics of Dr. King. The **Nation of Islam** (Black Muslims) followed the teachings of Elijah Muhammad as delivered by his disciple **Malcolm X**. Malcolm X openly criticized Dr. King and his followers for having sold themselves out to whites. While not advocating the use of violence, Malcolm X did encourage his followers to respond to violence perpetrated against them with self-defense. Malcolm X took his requisite Hajj (pilgrimage) to Mecca and returned a changed man in 1964. Preaching integration and understanding, Malcolm X left the Nation of Islam and was assassinated by members of the Nation as he gave a speech in February 1965. Meanwhile, the once nonviolent SNCC changed course under the leadership of **Stokely Carmichael** in 1966, when it rejected integration and began advocating "Black Power." Carmichael left SNCC for the Oakland, California–based Black Panthers, who openly carried weapons and clashed with police on a regular basis. The Black Panthers were successful in organizing the community of Oakland to serve as a self-sufficient network for citizens, providing free day care and food for low-income African Americans. The Panthers finally succumbed to government harassment as well as the arrests and deaths of major leaders by the 1970s.

MARTIN LUTHER KING IS ASSASSINATED

The frustration of African Americans in urban areas resulted in race riots, which broke out during the summers of 1964 through 1968 in cities such as Los Angeles, Chicago, and Atlanta. The Johnson-appointed **Kerner Commission** concluded in 1968 that frustrations over extreme poverty and a lack of opportunity had sparked the riots. Unfortunately for the civil rights movement and its supporters, Dr. Martin Luther King Jr. was assassinated as he stood on a Memphis motel balcony in April 1968. Because it was rumored that King's assassin was white, many felt that the efforts toward equal rights for blacks and whites had permanently stalled. Dr. King had lost some support when he publicly opposed increased American involvement in the war in Vietnam, but in reaction to his death, riots broke out across the country as African Americans expressed their frustration and anger with society.

THE COUNTERCULTURE AND ANTI-VIETNAM WAR MOVEMENTS

As the 1950s became the 1960s, America's "baby boomers" were now teenagers hoping to break away from the conformity that their parents subscribed to. Many American teens grew their hair longer or wore clothing that their parents did not approve of. Only a small percentage of the teen and young adult population was truly involved in the counterculture and antiwar protests. Nonetheless, these students were outspoken and willing to protest publicly the wrongs they saw in American social, economic, and political policy.

College students met in Port Huron, Michigan, in 1962 to form the Students for a Democratic Society (SDS), led by Tom Hayden. The meeting yielded the **Port Huron Statement**, in which the students demanded the expansion of democracy. This signaled the birth of the "New Left." Soon afterward, the Free Speech Movement (FSM) would begin in 1964 on the campus of the University of California–Berkeley. Berkeley students staged sit-ins in administration buildings to protest university policies and teach-ins to hear speeches and lectures regarding issues from civil rights to the Vietnam War. Students across the nation took cues from SDS and the FSM to form protest and social change movements of their own.

Nothing typified the new youth culture like the 1969 music festival on a farm in New York State called **Woodstock**. Hippies gathered at the concert for a three-day party that involved peace, love, and music. Artists such as Jimi Hendrix and Janis Joplin wowed the crowd, and young people found a connection with the work of folk singers such as Arlo Guthrie and Joan Baez, whose protest songs galvanized the counterculture. The "flower children" of Woodstock would soon change course to protest the Vietnam War with their shouts of "Make love, not war!"

The counterculture led to a sexual revolution in which Americans' views regarding sexual relationships and gender roles softened. With the advent of the birth control pill and the beginnings of the feminist movement in the mid-1960s, many Americans believed that the old sexual mores of their parents were repressive. The feminist movement also gained momentum as a result of the liberal nature of the counterculture. After the founding of the **National Organization for Women** (NOW) in 1966 by Betty Friedan, women began to become morevocal in demanding a more equal role in American society. With the Civil Rights Act of 1964 already making discrimination on the basis of gender illegal, women looked to strengthen their rights by amending the Constitution. In 1972, Congress passed the **Equal Rights Amendment**, which would bar states and the federal government from discriminating on the basis of sex. Unfortunately for the women's movement, the amendment fell short of the required number of ratifying states and died in the 1980s.

CHAPTER 26: POSTWAR ECONOMIC, DEMOGRAPHIC, AND TECHNOLOGICAL CHANGES

REVOLUTIONS IN SCIENCE, TECHNOLOGY, AND MEDICINE

The electronics industry experienced the most growth in the 1950s. As 95 percent of American homes were electric powered, the industry worked to keep up with the demand for new and innovative products. Record players, refrigerators, and the new "transistor radio" revolutionized the lives of Americans. Super computers opened doors for engineers and designers in space, aeronautics, and automobiles. What once took weeks to calculate, the computer could churn out in a matter of hours. Air travel was no longer affordable only for the ultra wealthy, as commercial airlines began to fly Americans across the nation and around the world.

Americans experienced an increase in their life expectancy as new medical discoveries and inventions emerged in the 1950s. Another discovery in the 1940s improved the chances of someone surviving infection by bacteria. Penicillin, an antibiotic, became widely available to doctors in the United States. It soon became very rare that an American would die from a simple bacterial infection.

DR. SALK AND THE POLIO VACCINE

Polio was a constant threat to people all over the world. The debilitating disease could cripple children and adults and confine them to a life of pain. In 1955, **Jonas Salk** discovered the serum that would immunize humans against polio. Using a live strain of the virus, Salk was successful in developing a vaccine that would almost eradicate the disease within the United States by the 1960s.

NIXON FACES THE WORLD

Richard M. Nixon promised the United States change and a return of "law and order." First and foremost on the new president's agenda was the Vietnam War.

SLOWLY LEAVING VIETNAM

Over 500,000 American men and women were serving overseas in a very unpopular war; Nixon wished to get out, but on his terms. He wanted a way to pull back slowly but still end the conflict with an "honorable peace." Even as he promised during the 1968 presidential campaign that he had a "secret" plan to end the war, Nixon really had no idea how he was going to accomplish this task. Soon after his inauguration, Nixon announced a plan to turn the war over to those who should be fighting it—the Vietnamese. This process of **Vietnamization** involved the U.S. military instructing the South Vietnamese how to fight the war on their own. The number of U.S. troops in the country slowly decreased. Within the span of three years, the number of U.S. troops in Vietnam decreased from over 500,000 in 1969 to just under 30,000 in 1972.

PROTESTS, SECRETS, AND STAGGERING LOSSES

Nevertheless, many Americans were not pleased with the president's plans. He seemed to be talking out of both sides of his mouth—he wished to reduce the number of troops in Vietnam, but then he escalated the war by secretly bombing Cambodia in 1970 to shut down the Ho Chi Minh Trail, which facilitated a massive flow of men and goods from North Vietnam into the South. Protests across the nation broke out as news of the secret bombing missions reached the airwaves. The nation did not know that the bombings had already occurred. As a result of two of these protests, four students at Kent State University in Ohio (who happened to be innocent passers-by during the protest) and two students at Jackson State in Mississippi were shot and killed by National Guard troops sent to keep the peace. The nation was shocked again when news of a 1968 massacre of Vietnamese women and children by U.S. troops in the village of My Lai was revealed in 1969. Eventually, the lieutenant in charge of this slaughter was court-martialed, convicted, and sentenced. However, his sentence was soon reduced from life in prison to 10 years. News of this aroused even more protesters, who now dubbed U.S. troops in Vietnam "baby killers." Then, secret documents regarding the Vietnam War under the Johnson administration were leaked to *The New York Times* by a former Defense Department analyst, Daniel Ellsberg. The documents showed that Congress had been lied to about the war in Vietnam during the presidency of LBJ. All the while, Nixon had Secretary of State **Henry Kissinger** meet secretly with the North Vietnamese to negotiate a settlement. It was clear to Nixon that the South Vietnamese would not be able to hold the communists off for very long on their own, and he wanted to get out quickly.

As the talks ground to a screeching halt, Nixon ordered some of the heaviest bombings yet to get North Vietnam back to the negotiating table. In 1973, the sides returned to the table in

Paris to hammer out an agreement. As a result, the North Vietnamese regained control of areas in the South, while the United States agreed to pull out troops in exchange for prisoners of war (POWs). March 29, 1973, saw the last of the U.S. troops pull out of South Vietnam. The South Vietnamese capital of Saigon fell to the communist forces in April of 1975, with the United States evacuating the last of its diplomatic corps and South Vietnamese sympathizers. In the end, the war caused the deaths of 58,000 Americans with 300,000 wounded and almost 2,600 missing in action. The Vietnamese lost over 2 million people, both military and civilian. The United States had spent a staggering $176 billion on the war through the Kennedy, Johnson, and Nixon administrations. After learning of the secret bombings of Cambodia, Congress passed the **War Powers Act**, which severely limits the president's ability to wage war without the consent of the legislative branch.

DÉTENTE WITH CHINA AND RUSSIA

President Nixon and Secretary of State Kissinger did make headway in another part of Asia, with results that would alter the very fabric of world affairs. Together they crafted a **détente**, or the relaxing of tensions among the United States, the Soviet Union, and China. In February 1972, Nixon became the first U.S. president to visit communist China in an attempt to discuss foreign policy with Mao Tse-Tung. Kissinger and Nixon had also been mediating between the two communist superpowers behind the scenes, as the nations had split over differing opinions about how communism should work in practice. In a rare reversal, president Nixon agreed to support China's bid to be admitted to the United Nations and officially recognized the Chinese Revolution. Moscow watched this all with fascination and concern. Nixon also visited Moscow in 1972 to encourage the USSR to sign a nuclear arms limitation treaty. In the **Strategic Arms Limitation Treaty (SALT I)**, signed by the United States and the USSR in May 1972, each nation agreed to reduce the number of nuclear missiles in its arsenal in exchange for the United States supplying the Soviets with much-needed grain over the next three years. While not ending the arms race or Cold War, détente did do much to relieve the world of tension created by the struggle among the three world superpowers.

THE YOM KIPPUR WAR AND GAS SHORTAGES

In October 1973, war broke out on the Jewish holy day of Yom Kippur between Israel and a coalition of Arab states led by Syria and Egypt. President Nixon reacted by sending military aid to Israel. The war was over quickly, as the aid from the United States greatly bolstered Israeli forces. Trouble was far from over for the United States, however. The **Organization of Petroleum Exporting Countries** (OPEC) initiated an embargo of oil exports to the United States as punishment for its involvement in the **Yom Kippur War**. Immediately, the U.S. supply of gasoline and petroleum products plummeted. Americans waited in lines that stretched as much as a mile long at gas stations to purchase the coveted liquid. The impact of the gas shortage was most devastating to the economy—the nation fell into a deep recession as companies decreased investment, laid off workers, and reduced inventories. Inflation was growing at an alarming rate, and there was little the government could do.

DOMESTIC CRISES

Nixon's presidency is now known as an "imperial presidency," after a thesis posited by historian Arthur Schlesinger. At various times, President Nixon abused his power as executive by claiming a right to protect documents from Congress and refusing to spend funds appropriated by Congress by "impounding" them. President Nixon's presidency also saw the emergence of a new economic phenomenon called "**stagflation**," in which high inflation was coupled with high unemployment.

The stagnant economy was difficult to repair, and Nixon first attempted to curb inflation by cutting government spending. He did not know this would prove to be disastrous. Fortunately, the president enacted a new monetary policy near the end of 1971, taking the country once again off the gold standard to bring its currency's value down relative to foreign currencies. This stimulated foreign investment and spending in the United States and helped to spur an economic recovery.

NIXON AND WATERGATE

To garner more support from conservatives across the nation, Nixon appealed to the so-called "silent majority"—conservative Democrats who were most likely to be either Southern, working-class, or elderly citizens who had become disenchanted by the liberalism of their party. He appealed to these voters by attempting to block forced busing of students to integrate public schools and becoming more vocal in his disdain for antiwar protesters.

The Nixon presidency would be damaged beyond repair, however, after the election of 1972. A break-in at the Democratic Party National Headquarters at the **Watergate** Hotel in Washington, D.C., in June would be his political demise. Through the investigations of *Washington Post* journalists Bob Woodward and Carl Bernstein, it was discovered that the burglars were connected to the Nixon administration. Eventually the duo of Woodward and Bernstein uncovered evidence that the Watergate break-in was just the tip of an iceberg of illegal activities linked to the Oval Office. As the chips began to fall, the president insulated himself with an ever-shrinking circle of supporters. A voice-activated tape system was discovered in the Oval Office and led to Congress's insistence that the tapes be released for investigation. President Nixon refused by claiming he was protected by **executive privilege** and fought with Congress for over a year. Just as things could not get worse, Vice President Spiro Agnew was convicted of tax evasion committed during his tenure as governor of Maryland and was forced to resign. Nixon chose Representative Gerald R. Ford as his new vice president.

Facing certain impeachment and conviction by Congress on the charges of obstruction of justice, abuse of power, and contempt, President Nixon resigned from office on August 9, 1974. The

Oval Office tapes, finally released owing to a Supreme Court ruling in *Nixon v. United States* in July 1974, had contained the "smoking gun" that directly linked the president to the Watergate scandal. Vice President Gerald R. Ford took the oath of office.

President Ford caused a great controversy early in his administration, and certainly hurt his prospects for securing a second term, when he formally pardoned Nixon of all charges. Ford's biggest challenge was to try to address stagflation. Nothing he attempted worked for very long. President Ford witnessed the failure of U.S. foreign policy in Southeast Asia, as Saigon and Cambodia both fell to the communists in 1975.

HIGHS AND LOWS OF CARTER'S PRESIDENCY

The Democrats seized on Ford's ineffectiveness and chose a "Washington outsider" to run for the office of president in 1976. Former Georgia governor and peanut farmer Jimmy Carter was a conservative Democrat from the South who appealed to Americans. Carter squeaked out a narrow victory by garnering 51 percent of the popular vote, managing to take 97 percent of the ballots cast by African Americans. The Democrats also were able to secure majorities in both houses of Congress. Carter was thought to be one of the most intelligent presidents ever to serve but was plagued from the start by his inability to play politics.

Carter's greatest success occurred when he crafted a peace agreement between Egypt and Israel in 1978. The president invited Egyptian president **Anwar Sadat** and Israeli prime minister **Menachem Begin** to meet at the presidential retreat at Camp David in Maryland. Sadat and Begin discussed peace options while Carter acted as mediator. A peace agreement was signed in September 1978. The **Camp David Accords** served as the first step toward peace in the Middle East since the turmoil that had followed the founding of the state of Israel in 1948. Carter enjoyed another foreign policy success when he negotiated a treaty with Panama in 1977 that relinquished American control over the Panama Canal.

Unfortunately, another peace would soon be shattered as Islamic fundamentalists overthrew the shah and seated the **Ayatollah Khomeini** as ruler of Iran in 1979. The United States now had no ally in the oil-rich region, and the ayatollah suddenly cut off the flow of petroleum to OPEC, causing yet another gasoline shortage. As if this was not enough, later that year, Iranian college and high school students, angry over U.S. protection of the shah, seized the American embassy in the Iranian capital, Tehran, and took hostages, many of whom were women. After a few days, the women and African Americans were released, but 52 white men were held captive for 444 days. President Carter froze Iranian assets in the United States and ordered a rescue mission that became an embarrassing failure.

Carter also had to deal with increasing tensions between his country and the Soviet Union. SALT I was set to expire in 1977, so Carter and the Soviets were set to sign a renewal treaty. **SALT II** was negotiated and sat ready for ratification when another world crisis got in the way. The USSR invaded the nation of Afghanistan in December 1979 in a move to play a greater role in the

Middle East. Americans were now certain that the Soviets intended to take control of the precious oil transportation region of the Persian Gulf. The United States immediately ceased supplying the USSR with grain shipments and withdrew SALT II from the table.

In protest, President Carter also boycotted the 1980 Olympic Games, which were held in Moscow. President Carter would be plagued by this decision and the Iran hostage crisis, which cost him the election in 1980. Domestically, Carter had difficulties eclipsing the troubles he was facing in foreign policy. He did uphold his promise to grant amnesty to the 10,000 young men who had fled the country during the Vietnam War draft. He created the Department of Education to address the problems of the nation's public schools and the Department of Energy to try to deal with the nation's energy crisis. The nation's energy woes were coupled with staggering inflation and high unemployment (stagflation), but even with the most conservative monetary policy, the nation did not emerge from the depths of the economic crisis until the mid-1980s.

UNIT 8: REVIEW QUESTIONS

Multiple-Choice Questions

Directions: Choose the best answer choice for the following questions.

Questions 1–4 refer to the following quote.

"IV.

A vital element in keeping the peace is our military establishment. Our arms must be mighty, ready for instant action . . .

Our military organization today bears little relation to that known by any of my predecessors . . .

Until the latest of our world conflicts, the United States had no armaments industry. American makers of plowshares could, with time and as required, make swords as well. But now we can no longer risk emergency improvisation of national defense . . .

This conjunction of an immense military establishment and a large arms industry . . . we must not fail to comprehend its grave implications . . .

In the councils of government, we must guard against the acquisition of unwarranted influence, . . . by the military-industrial complex. The potential for the disastrous rise of misplaced power exists . . . "

—President Dwight D. Eisenhower speech, 1961

1. Which United States governmental stance most directly led to the situation described in the passage?

   (A) Increased internationalism after World War II

   (B) Development of the limited welfare state after the Great Depression

   (C) Expansion of opportunities for minorities after the *Brown* decision

   (D) Increased isolationism after the Korean Conflict

2. Which action from the second half of the 20th century most clearly supported the position stated in the passage above?

   (A) Elimination of United States factory jobs in the 1980s

   (B) Lyndon Johnson's Great Society programs

   (C) Development of a homogenous mass culture

   (D) Vietnam era protests

3. The reasoning expressed in the previous passage most directly reflects which of the following continuities in United States history?

(A) Debates about the role of the federal government in the economy

(B) Debates about the changing relationships among the federal branches

(C) Debates about the balance between liberty and security

(D) Debates about the impact of American foreign policy on the world community

4. Which of the following from the first half of the 20th century most closely resembles the argument raised in the previous passage?

(A) Reasons for the first Red Scare

(B) Reasons for economic collapse during the Great Depression

(C) Reasons for American intervention in Latin America

(D) Reasons for United States entry into World War I

Questions 5–9 refer to the following figure.

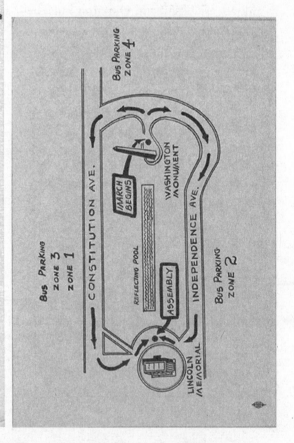

The official program handed out during the March on Washington for Jobs and Freedom on Aug. 28, 1963.

5. The actions identified in the document were most likely the result of an alliance between which of the following?

    (A) African-American activists and Southern Democrats

    (B) New Dealers and labor union members

    (C) Supporters of the *Brown* Supreme Court decision and religious leaders

    (D) Korean War veterans and northern liberals

6. Which of the following from the second half of the 19th century most clearly parallels the events identified in the document shown?

    (A) New South

    (B) Gilded Age

    (C) Radical Reconstruction

    (D) Populism

7. The list of speakers in the document shown most clearly illustrates which of the following continuities in United States history?

    (A) Debates over the relationship between the state and federal government

    (B) Debates over the expansion of gender roles

    (C) Debates over the impact of economic globalization

    (D) Debates over conflicting views of group identity

8. Which of the following actions resulted most directly from the event listed in the document?

    (A) Increased federal government regulation

    (B) Expansion of American military presence in Vietnam

    (C) Clashes between environmentalists and business interests

    (D) Migration to the Sun Belt

9. The ideas expressed in the document most clearly show the influence of which of the following?

    (A) Electoral guarantees contained in the Fifteenth Amendment

    (B) Civil liberties contained in the Bill of Rights

    (C) Belief in separation of power as contained in the U.S. Constitution

    (D) Divisiveness of political parties contained in Washington's Farewell Address

Questions 10 and 11 refer to the following figure.

United States stamps, 1975

10. Which of the following events from the second half of the 20th century most clearly parallels the situation in the images above?

    (A) President Reagan's negotiations with Soviet leader Mikhail Gorbachev

    (B) Containment policy of the Korean War

    (C) Collective security agreement which created NATO

    (D) Energy crisis resulting from the Arab oil embargo

11. The idea expressed in the previous images most directly reflects which of the following continuities in United States history?

    (A) Debates over economic values and role of the federal government in economy

    (B) Debates over separation of powers as contained in the U.S. Constitution

    (C) Debates over the impact of immigration policy

    (D) Debates over public support of the arts

Questions 12–15 refer to the following figure.

Levittown, NY, 1951

12. Which change in American society most directly led to the situation depicted in the image?

(A) Expansion of the electorate to include women

(B) Decreasing social and economic mobility

(C) Growth of a car culture

(D) Increasingly restrictive immigration laws

13. Which of the following groups most likely benefited from the situation seen in the image?

(A) Smart-growth planners

(B) World War II veterans

(C) Mass transit users

(D) Civil rights activists

14. The situation depicted in the photograph most directly led to the

    (A) increasingly heterogeneous mass culture of the 1960s

    (B) dominance of the Democratic Party in the 1950s

    (C) passage of new immigration laws in the 1960s

    (D) rapid expansion in higher education in the 1960s

15. Which of the following innovations from the early 20th century is most clearly seen in the photograph?

    (A) Efficiencies in production techniques

    (B) Expanded cultural opportunities for America's diverse population

    (C) Increased opportunity for women in the workforce

    (D) Development of mass media

Short-Answer Questions

1. **Passage 1:**

"To promote the maintenance of international peace and security in Southeast Asia.

Whereas naval units of the communist regime in Vietnam . . . have deliberately and repeatedly attacked United States naval vessels lawfully present in international waters, and . . . created a serious threat to international peace; and . . .

Whereas the United States is assisting the peoples of Southeast Asia to protect their freedom and has no territorial, military or political ambitions in that area, but desires only that these peoples should be left in peace to work out their own destinies in their own way . . .

Resolved . . . That the Congress approves and supports the determination of the President, as Commander in Chief, to take all necessary measures to repel any armed attack against the forces of the United States and to prevent further aggression . . .

Sec. 3. This resolution shall expire when the President shall determine . . . or . . . it may be terminated earlier by concurrent resolution of the Congress."

—Text of Joint Resolution of Congress, August 7, 1964

Passage 2:

"To the House of Representatives:

I hereby return without my approval House Joint Resolution 542—the War Powers Resolution. While I am in accord with the desire of the Congress to assert its proper role in the conduct of our foreign affairs, the restrictions which this resolution would impose upon the authority of the President are both unconstitutional and dangerous to the best interests of our Nation . . .

House Joint Resolution 542 would attempt to take away, by a mere legislative act, authorities which the President has properly exercised under the Constitution for almost 200 years . . .

We may well have been unable to respond . . . [as] we did during the Berlin crisis of 1961, the Cuban missile crisis of 1962 . . . —to mention just a few examples . . . "

—Message to the House of Representatives from President Nixon, October 24, 1973

Based on the two sources dealing with American foreign policy in the second half of the 20th century, complete the following three tasks:

(A) Briefly explain the main point made by Passage 1.

(B) Briefly explain the main point made by Passage 2.

(C) Provide ONE piece of evidence dealing with American foreign policy in the second half of the 20th century, and explain how it furthers the understanding of either passage.

2.

October, 1973

Use the image shown and your knowledge of United States history to answer parts A, B, and C.

(A) Explain the situation reflected in the image regarding ONE of the following:

- Technology
- Domestic politics
- Foreign policy

(B) Explain how the situation you identified in part A helped to shape ONE specific United States government action during the 1970s.

(C) Explain how the situation you identified in Part A helped to shape ONE OTHER specific United States government action during the 1970s.

Long Essay Question

Directions: You are advised to spend 5 minutes planning and 30 minutes writing your answer.

Evaluate the effectiveness of the Lyndon B. Johnson administration's response to the economic, social, and political problems confronting the United States between 1963 and 1968.

ANSWERS AND EXPLANATIONS

MULTIPLE-CHOICE ANSWERS

1. A

The participation of the United States in the United Nations, NATO, and other security organizations led to increased military presence and an acceleration of the arms race after World War II. These changes, in part, led President Eisenhower to speak about the growing power and connection between the interests of the military and arms contractors. He stated that they may have undue influence on the direction of American policy decisions.

2. D

The Vietnam era protests challenged the prevailing power and attitudes in Washington regarding the use of American military power in Southeast Asia. While development of a mass media culture made Vietnam "the living room war" because of its coverage on television, the challenge to existing policy was vocalized by the Vietnam era activists and protestors.

3. C

Well before President Eisenhower delivered his farewell address, wartime and periods of national security stress brought concerns that the solutions limited personal liberty. After World War II, concerns over the Cold War with the Soviet Union gave way to concerns over global terrorism from a number of rogue states and terrorist groups. To deal with these concerns, new military technologies, surveillance techniques, and other methods of securing the nation and its citizens have been developed. However, these policies have been challenged because of their effects on individual privacy, liberty, and national identity.

4. D

Post–World War I congressional investigations into what led the United States into World War I led to accusations that American munitions makers helped push the country into the war. This sentiment contributed to America's noninterventionist sentiment in the 1930s.

5. C

The *Brown* decision in 1954 ruled school segregation unconstitutional. This decision helped usher in the modern civil rights movement. In the 1950s and 1960s, many leaders of the civil rights movement came from African-American church leadership in the South. Southern Democrats, the white majority of the "Solid South," resisted the changes supported by the *Brown* decision.

6. C

The Radical Republican program for Reconstruction called for greater economic and political equality for the Freedmen. Often referred to as an "unfinished" revolution, many of the issues and goals of the Radical Republicans, including equal treatment in public accommodations, did not become public policy until the modern civil rights movement of the 1950s and 1960s.

7. D

There are multiple civil rights groups listed in this 1963 program. By the mid-1960s, movement leadership expanded and different philosophies and tactics developed, creating tensions within the civil rights movement. Dr. King's call for direct action and passive resistance were challenged as violence and resistance increased.

8. A

Passage of the Civil Rights Act of 1964 and the Voting Rights Act of 1965 during the Johnson years came in the aftermath of the events that preceded the March on Washington. The movement would turn more militant and clashes more frequent as the 1960s unfolded and civil rights activity spread nationwide.

9. B

The First Amendment guarantees freedom of speech, assembly, and the right to petition the government for redress of grievances. The 1963 March on Washington sought to do all of the above. Goals of the march called for specific action by the federal government to end segregation and achieve the promise of the Fourteenth Amendment to the Constitution.

10. A
While the Cold War dominated American foreign policy from the post–World War II era until the fall of the Soviet Union in the early 1990s, there were periods of mutual coexistence or détente. Joint efforts between the United States and the Soviet Union, such as the Apollo-Soyuz mission, illustrate this, as did the negotiations between President Reagan and Soviet leader Gorbachev that resulted in the 1997 Intermediate-Range Nuclear Forces (INF) Treaty.

11. A
Because the space race became part of the Cold War tensions between the United States and the Soviet Union, U.S. government expenditures for space missions and exploration became associated with the cost of the Cold War. As the United States faced a series of economic crises at the end of the twentieth and beginning of the 21st century, federal expenditures for NASA and its programs came into question.

12. C
Development of the interstate highway system, road construction, and increased car ownership encouraged suburban development. Low-cost single-family homes, the hallmark of suburbanization in the post–World War II years, brought home ownership to millions of Americans. What some historians have called an Age of Affluence, the 1950s and early 1960s saw a rising middle class and new opportunities for economic and social mobility.

13. B
Benefits of the 1945 Servicemen's Readjustment Act, or GI Bill, included low-cost mortgages that allowed World War II veterans to consider home ownership. Critics argued that suburbanization contributed to the cultural conformity of the 1950s, including whites-only deed restrictions.

14. D
In the post–World War II years, a number of changes impacted American society. The move to the suburbs, GI Bill benefits, a rising middle class, and the baby boom contributed to increased demand for higher education. A college education was increasingly seen as an achievable goal to enhance economic and social mobility.

15. A
The construction techniques of Levittown borrowed many ideas from the Ford assembly line methodology. Developing a limited number of house options and using mass production techniques allowed affordable, single family, suburban subdivisions to characterize the 1950s. Detractors criticized the suburbanization of America for its conformity and lack of diversity.

SHORT-ANSWER QUESTIONS RESPONSES

1. (A) The joint resolution of Congress, otherwise known as the Gulf of Tonkin Resolution, gave the President "all necessary power" to fight communist aggression in Southeast Asia. This came as a result of North Vietnamese attacks on American ships in the Gulf of Tonkin in July of 1964. As a result of this resolution, a declaration of war by Congress was unnecessary.

   (B) President Nixon vetoed the War Powers Resolution of Congress, which sought to limit the president's ability to send the military into action without their approval. He claimed the restrictions placed on the president's power as commander-in-chief were unconstitutional.

   (C) By 1973, the Vietnam War was a source of political and social discord. Despite the escalation of United States involvement in the aftermath of the Gulf of Tonkin Resolution, by the late 1960s no clear victor had emerged. Popular protests, especially among the young, over the tactics used in the war, the draft, and the Americans' role in the world accelerated. Congress sought to regain lost control by passing the War Powers Act, which established time limits for presidential action without approval of Congress. Congress overrode the veto. The war in Vietnam was coming to a close, but the repercussions of that war would linger.

2. (A) Technology—the gas crisis of the 1970s put a damper on America's love affair with the car. The car culture that developed after World War II and was aided by the development of the interstate highway system suffered from the shortages of gas. The various crises in the Middle East led to an Arab oil embargo, which in turn led to a rethinking of American energy policy. Big gas-guzzling cars became a liability.

   (B) The development of the trans-Alaskan pipeline resulted from the energy crisis of the 1970s. But it was not the only national policy change or alteration to occur in the 1970s. New emissions standards for cars, a national 55-mile-an-hour speed limit, and year-round daylight saving time were all efforts to conserve energy resources. Not all lasted and concerns about energy conservation and energy shortages continue to this day.

   (C) The oil crisis of 1973 spurred interest in and the development of alternative energy. Solar power and wind power were utilized, as well as a greater dependence on coal and nuclear energy. In addition, there was a larger interest in mass transit, to offset the amount of oil being consumed on a daily basis by commuters.

LONG ESSAY SAMPLE RESPONSE

The 1960s, an era of incredible and profound change in the United States and the world, presented a number of problems and issues that no single president or administration could solve successfully. Lyndon Johnson, a Texas New Deal–era Democrat chosen to balance the Kennedy ticket in 1960, became President of the United States on a plane after JFK's assassination. Johnson took power as the nation continued to enjoy postwar prosperity, but not every segment of the population benefited. America's love affair with suburbia was leading to trouble in the cities as white flight and racial tensions increased. And politically, Johnson's attempt to create a Great Society was eventually overshadowed by the political and economic costs of the war in Vietnam. Despite starting in tragedy, LBJ's presidency started in a period of comparative prosperity with the beginnings of major social and political upheaval that would define the 1960s. His administration's policies would fundamentally alter the role of government in the United States, but not be able to peacefully and successfully deal with all the crises confronting the nation from 1963 to 1968.

In the early and mid 1960s, the United States still enjoyed the postwar boom and economic expansion of a peacetime economy. As the middle class grew, consumerism and affluence rose. However, not all Americans enjoyed this prosperity. Pockets of poverty bothered the Texas politician who had been part of FDR's New Deal. Johnson used the momentum of Kennedy's assassination and his own overwhelming electoral victory in 1964 to push Congress toward passing his War on Poverty programs, part of his plan for a Great Society. These included what would become very popular entitlement programs, such as Medicare (medical assistance for the elderly), Medicaid (medical assistance for the poor), and an expansion of Social Security benefits. While these did not eradicate poverty in America, they did mark a significant expansion of the federal government in the daily economic life of a significant number of Americans. Funding problems for these programs would increase as defense spending associated with the Cold War, especially the war in Vietnam, increased.

American society faced two distinct and somewhat interconnected challenges in the 1960s that undermined the Johnson administration's goals. The activities connected to the civil rights movement gained momentum and increasing militancy in the 1960s. Racial unrest moved out of the South and into America's Northern cities, the so-called "long, hot summers" of 1964–1967. Johnson's support of civil rights, including pushing for the passage of the Civil Rights Act of 1964 and even the Voting Rights Act of 1965, marked a new era in presidential support. But new and more militant voices, including the Black Muslims and the Black Panthers, challenged the leadership and tactics of groups like the NAACP and the Southern Christian Leadership Conference. Growing resistance to the escalation of the war in Vietnam led to youth resistance and a growing counterculture. Add to that a Supreme Court that seemed to decide cases in favor of criminals (Miranda) and individual rights (no school prayer), and white working class Americans began to feel that law and order were leaving America. These challenges undermined the effectiveness of Johnson's vision of a Great Society.

The strong political support Johnson enjoyed in the early years of his presidency, even considering hard-fought battles to achieve passage of civil rights legislation, unraveled by 1968. This largely dealt with the growing unpopularity of the war in Vietnam. When Congress passed the Gulf of Tonkin Resolution in 1963, the president had vast power to fight communist aggression in Southeast Asia. The resulting escalation of the war, including the draft, proved very unpopular and generated no clear military victories. By the time of the Tet Offensive in 1968, student unrest and protest were high and public support was rapidly declining. The cost of the war hurt Johnson's domestic program. Chants of "Hey, hey, LBJ, how many kids did you kill today?" and other setbacks eventually led Johnson to pull out of the 1968 presidential race. The assassinations of Martin Luther King and Bobby Kennedy in 1968 along with other violence led many to question the results of the progressive change earlier in the decade, resulting in a Republican victory in 1968.

Lyndon Johnson and his administration hoped to continue the promise and fulfill America's postwar "American dream." While the ideas of New Deal government activism served as a model, the Great Society and the War on Poverty did not deliver as expected. Problems and controversies of the second half of the 1960s would lead to a rising conservative tide in the United States in the decades to come.

The strong thesis suggests a complex understanding of the time period in the essay prompt. The score would be 1 out of 1 point for thesis. Quality of argumentation and use of evidence is strong as well. Rich detail supports all three categories in the prompt and ties back to the thesis. The score would be 2 of 2 points for argumentation. Application of the targeted skill of causation in analyzing the effectiveness is also strong. The score would be 2 of 2 points for causation. Connecting the Great Society to both the New Deal of the 1930s and the rising conservatism of the post–1968 years demonstrates strong synthesis. The score would be 1 of 1 point for synthesis. This well-developed essay would receive a 6 out of 7 possible points in the Long Essay Question rubric.

CHAPTER 27: NEW CONSERVATISM

CONSERVATIVE REVOLUTION

President Carter faced stiff competition from the right when Republicans chose former California governor Ronald Reagan as their candidate for the election of 1980. The Democrats were reeling from the notion that Carter was ineffectual both domestically and abroad amidst a severe economic downturn. Conservatism was gaining popularity across the nation as taxpayers sought to control where their money was spent. Christian fundamentalists became more influential, and Americans looked to "traditional family values" for strength. Americans cast their ballots for the former movie star and elected Ronald Reagan as their 40th (and oldest) president.

REAGAN BRINGS NEW POLICIES

The "**Reagan Revolution**" was a blow to the New Deal coalition and ushered in a new era of conservative policy making in Washington. Reagan promised lower taxes, smaller government, and a stronger military. Helped by the sudden release of the Iranian hostages on the day of his inauguration, Reagan set forth to enact his agenda.

First the new president looked to strengthen the economy by rejecting widely accepted Keynesian demand-side theory and adopting a supply-side model. Much as had Andrew Carnegie of the 1920s, Reagan believed in the "trickle-down" theory, which maintains that offering tax cuts and investment incentives to the wealthy will lead to the creation of jobs and that the wealth created this way will trickle down to the middle and lower classes. Congress agreed and passed a federal bill in 1981 that would cut taxes by 25 percent over a three-year period. As a result, many federally funded social programs were either cut or eliminated altogether, while defense spending increased at an unprecedented peacetime rate.

During his first term, President Reagan enacted deregulation of the telephone and the trucking industries. Other government regulations, such as clean air standards for automobiles and large factories were lifted. Owing to government deregulation of the savings and loan industry, many in the 1980s began making risky investments to increase profits. By the mid-1980s, many of these institutions were collapsing, and taxpayers would have to foot the bill for the failure of the government to regulate this industry. A potentially costly strike for the American economy and safety concerns loomed over the president in August 1981 as the nation's air traffic controllers decided to walk off the job illegally. In a controversial stand, Reagan fired every one of the controllers and replaced them with military personnel until civilians could be trained to take their places permanently. As a result, the air traffic controllers' union was destroyed.

It had been a promise of Reagan to reconfigure the Supreme Court to promote more conservative rulings, and he fulfilled his promise. Reagan successfully seated the first woman on the Court, Sandra Day O'Connor, and placed conservatives Antonin Scalia and Anthony Kennedy on the bench as well. The new court pleased conservatives by scaling back laws protecting women and African Americans.

REAGAN'S SECOND TERM

Running against the first woman vice presidential candidate on the Democratic ticket, Reagan and Vice President George H.W. Bush successfully won re-election in 1984. Reagan's second term would be marked by continued conservative policies, as Congress worked to lower taxes even further and to limit illegal immigration. But the **Iran-Contra scandal** left a stain on Reagan's presidency. It was discovered that money had been secretly diverted from the sale of American weapons to the Nicaraguan Contras, to whom Congress had specifically forbidden aid. It was also discovered that as part of the deal, the United States had secretly sold military equipment to Iran in exchange for the release of the American hostages. This money was then illegally diverted to the Contras. The president denied any knowledge of the scandal, but he took full responsibility for the actions of his subordinates who were found during subsequent congressional investigations to have been involved.

Reagan also witnessed stock markets around the world crash on Black Monday, October 19, 1987. Congress responded by reducing taxes further, fearing a return of recession.

THE *CHALLENGER* DISASTER

Reagan had to soothe Americans when, on January 28, 1986, the NASA space shuttle *Challenger* exploded shortly after takeoff, killing all seven astronauts aboard, including the first teacher to serve as an astronaut, Christa McAuliffe.

CHAPTER 28: THE END OF THE COLD WAR

THE COLD WAR ENDS

After the Soviet invasion of Afghanistan in 1979 and the subsequent U.S. boycott of the 1980 Olympic Games, it was clear that détente was a thing of the past. President Reagan promised Americans a stronger military and had some tough words for what he called the "evil empire" of the Soviet Union. The president delivered on his promise of increased defense spending by pushing for funding of the Strategic Defense System (SDI), more popularly known as "**Star Wars**." The system was designed to station satellites in orbit that could defend the United States against nuclear attack with lasers. While critics and many in the scientific community spoke of the impossibility of SDI, Reagan used the idea of the system as a scare tactic against the Soviets. The United States shifted its focus to promoting an arms race. This buildup of U.S. military capacity put intense pressure on the Soviet economy, as it struggled to keep up.

GORBACHEV'S *GLASNOST* AND *PERESTROIKA*

In 1985, a new leader came to power in the USSR who intended to change his country. Mikhail Gorbachev introduced two important reforms—*glasnost* and *perestroika*. The first reform, *glasnost*, or "openness," was designed to rid the country of the old Stalin totalitarian state byeasing laws designed to limit the freedoms of Russians. Secondly, *perestroika*, or "restructuring," was aimed at opening up the once-closed Soviet economy to free-market mechanisms. Gorbachev made a difficult decision to cease the arms buildup in his country to ease the shift toward his new vision. In December 1987, President Reagan and Premier Gorbachev signed an agreement to rid the world of intermediate-range missiles. From this point on, the two leaders worked to ease tensions.

GEORGE H.W. BUSH, THE BERLIN WALL, AND THE COLLAPSE OF THE SOVIET UNION

The United States was in a very interesting position on the eve of the election of 1988. With the Cold War now almost at an end, what would happen to the hyper-military society Ronald Reagan had set up? The Republicans ran Vice President **George H.W. Bush** as their candidate against the Democrat Michael Dukakis. Bush was able to take the presidency easily, with his promise to be tough on crime and his statement of "Read my lips: no new taxes." However, the Republicans were not successful in uniting government, as the House and Senate went to the Democrats.

Communism around the world was under fire from the moment George Bush took the oath of office. In the spring of 1989, China experienced a student uprising that demanded democratic reforms. Beijing crushed this uprising with force. An unknown number were killed and many more imprisoned for their role in the protests. On the other side of the globe, the Eastern Bloc countries were experiencing challenges of their own. Needing to cut back on military spending, Gorbachev warned communist governments in countries such as Poland, Hungary, and Czechoslovakia that the Soviet Union would no longer be providing them assistance. With the rise of the **"Solidarity" movement** in Poland and the collapse of the Romanian government in 1989, the "iron curtain" was falling in Europe. President Reagan's famous words "Mr. Gorbachev, tear down this wall," became a reality, as the **Berlin Wall** was torn down by a crowd in October 1989 after the fall of the East German government. Despite his attempts at reform, Gorbachev watched as his own country struggled under the weight of protest. The Soviet republics of Estonia, Latvia, and Lithuania declared their independence in the spring of 1990. Gorbachev was forced from power, as the Soviet Union collapsed on Christmas Day, 1991. Boris Yeltsin became president of Russia, which joined with the 14 other former Soviet republics to create the temporary **Commonwealth of Independent States**. Presidents Bush and Yeltsin immediately began to dismantle the nuclear arms that had been built up over the past four decades. They signed **START I** in 1991, which drastically reduced the number of nuclear warheads possessed in both countries. **START II** was signed by both men in 1993 to reduce further the number of warheads, with an added promise of U.S. aid to the Russian economy. Both Bush and Yeltsin continued to witness former Soviet republics fall into turmoil.

LIVING IN A MULTICULTURAL SOCIETY

As the world became globalized through mass communication and the Internet and as immigration increased from 1965 to 2000, America became more diverse. For example, in the city of Los Angeles in 1990, a full third of residents were foreign born. California now has residents from all over the world, with many having come from Southeast Asia and Mexico. Most Californians embraced this demographic shift; unfortunately, this increased diversity has also led to the re-emergence of nativism. Many neo-nativists focus their energies on limiting undocumented workers' access to public services such as education and medical care. There has even been a push to make English the state's official language.

AFFIRMATIVE ACTION DEBATES

California continued to be at the forefront of multicultural clashes as laws were passed that undid the progress made during Johnson's Great Society. **Affirmative action,** the policy of increasing minorities' access to jobs and education, first took a blow in 1978 when the Supreme Court ruled in *Bakke v. UC Board of Regents* that the University of California (UC) system's admissions process resulted in "**reverse discrimination**" such that qualified white applicants were being denied admission in favor of less-qualified minority applicants. Later, in 1996, **Proposition 209** was passed, barring affirmative action laws in the state of California. As a result, minority enrollment in the UC system plummeted, with classrooms not reflecting the ethnic diversity of the state as a whole. Several other states, such as Michigan, followed suit, enacting laws abolishing affirmative action.

CLINTON'S POLITICAL DEVELOPMENTS

Winning the election for president in 1992, **President William (Bill) Clinton** worked to reform healthcare and the welfare system amid the remaining vestiges of Reagan conservatism on Capitol Hill. Clinton faced the challenge of not having a united government—after the midterm election of 1994, Congress was in the hands of Republicans under the leadership of House Speaker Newt Gingrich. The president and speaker were headed for a showdown, as Clinton threatened to veto the Republican budget and force the closure of all government offices until a new budget could be drawn up. The Republicans were ultimately forced to back down, and Clinton was able to pass a federal budget that would better enable him to pursue his domestic policy objectives. However, because of opposition from Republicans and conservative Democrats, Clinton was unable to enact any healthcare reform. He did manage to secure passage of the **Personal Responsibility and Work Opportunity Reconciliation Act of 1996**, which reformed America's welfare system. During the midterm elections of 1994, which witnessed Republicans taking control of the legislative branch, that party unveiled its **Contract with America**, which promised to balance the federal budget by cutting taxes and limiting spending on social programs while still supporting massive expenditures for the American military. Much of Clinton's second term was consumed with defending himself against an array of charges of personal and political misconduct leveled by political opponents. The American economy grew rapidly during the Clinton years, and when he left office, the United States enjoyed a massive budget surplus.

CHAPTER 29: THE 21st CENTURY

DEMOGRAPHIC SHIFTS

Many domestic and foreign developments altered the demographic makeup of the United States after 1965. First and foremost, the Johnson-era passage of the **Immigration Act of 1965** opened the doors to foreigners seeking a new life or an escape from oppression. Cubans fleeing the oppressive dictatorship of Fidel Castro, Vietnamese fleeing communist rule, Filipinos seeking economic opportunity, and Mexicans looking for a better life all came to the United States between 1965 and 2000. While these were the largest groups seeking citizenship, many others joined their ranks from countries such as India, Pakistan, Korea, China, and the Dominican Republic. States such as Texas, California, Arizona, and Florida experienced massive population growth. As immigration continued to increase, local and state governments sometimes struggled to keep pace with providing education, medical care, and and other essential services to these new Americans. Moreover, this rapid increase in immigration led to a neonativist backlash targeted at "illegal" or undocumented workers. Aiming to put a damper on illegal immigration, Congress passed the **Immigration and Control Act** in 1986. This measure has proven to be largely ineffective, and the issue of immigration continues to polarize the American electorate and political leaders.

Americans were also on the move during this period, as they picked up from the former "steel belt" states and moved to the Sun Belt. Steel-producing states, such as Michigan, Pennsylvania, and Ohio, became known as the **Rust Belt**, as large steel mills closed because of decreasing domestic demand and increasing competition in the global market. Americans flocked to California, Texas, Arizona, Florida, and New Mexico to take advantage of their climates, as well as new job opportunities. Americans were on the move during leisure time too, thanks to the Interstate Highway Act, which provided easy-to-navigate freeways that connected every point across the United States from Newport, Rhode Island, to Newport Beach, California.

PRESENT-DAY GRAYING OF AMERICA

The United States is today experiencing an aging population, as the baby boomers of the post–World War II era begin to reach the later stages of life. The "graying" of America began in the mid-1990s and will continue through the 2050s. Taxing the Social Security system set forth by FDR during the New Deal and the nation's health care system, the number of Americans over 65 will skyrocket as the baby boomers age and improved health care increases the average life span. By the year 2030, about 25 percent of all Americans will be over 85 years old. The possible effects of such a demographic shift are still being debated, but certainly the nation will experience challenges as a result.

SCI-FI BECOMES A REALITY

What was once the stuff of science fiction movies became reality between the years 1965 and 2000. Advances in biotechnology, mass communications, and computers have made the world a much smaller place, bringing excitement and danger along with progress.

ADVANCES IN HEALTH

The average life span of an American well exceeds the life expectancy of just 50 years ago. Through advances in medicine, such as organ transplant, artificial life support, and advanced drug therapy, human life can be extended greatly. Previously deadly bacteria can now be treated with a single regimen of antibiotics. Polio, which was once the scourge of Americans, has been all but eradicated from the North American continent. Other diseases have taken its place, though, with much deadlier effect and with no cure in sight. In an effort to find cures for diseases such as AIDS, cancer, and diabetes, researchers in the United States successfully completed mapping the entire human genome in 2003. The medical research community has been experimenting with human stem cells in an effort to regenerate damaged cells to cure a variety of illnesses. The use of embryos in stem cell research has proven to be highly controversial in the United States.

THE AIDS CRISIS

The outbreak of Acquired Immune Deficiency Syndrome, or **AIDS,** in the 1980s began in Africa and soon spread worldwide. By 2009, the number of known cases of HIV (the virus that causes AIDS) in the United States had reached 1.7 million.

ADVANCES IN COMMUNICATION

The idea of portable communication in the 1960s usually appeared in spy stories such as those featuring James Bond or Maxwell Smart, who used tiny telephones that could be hidden in a watch or shoe. The first consumer portable telephones were introduced in the 1980s at prices that only the very wealthy could afford. The phones looked like two-way radios and needed the frequent charging of a huge battery pack. Currently, cellular phones seem to be everywhere. These telephones are small and lightweight. More advanced smartphones are essentially computers that can fit in a pocket. The advent of pay television revolutionized the airwaves in the late 1970s and early 1980s as consumers scrambled to get cable television. Not held to the same programming standards as broadcast television, cable networks pushed the boundaries with more explicit programming. Cable news stations soon eclipsed the standard network stations, changing television news coverage into a 24-hour-a-day affair. Satellite communications opened up the world to television audiences, as news from around the globe could be transmitted in seconds.

No technological development has impacted society more than the information boom caused by the creation of the Internet. Although the **World Wide Web** gained prominence when it moved from the academic and political worlds into the public arena, the system (ARPANET) had been in place since the mid-1960s. Then used mostly by universities and government officials, this small network of computers would be the foundation for what is now a global system. A young computer science student named Bill Gates, who dropped out of Harvard University, revolutionized the computer industry by developing an operating system for personal computers. Mainframes, long the industry standard, could take up entire floors of office buildings. Gates's MS-DOS software now made it possible for people to purchase computers for their homes. IBM adopted MS-DOS for its personal computer line in 1980 and began the personal computing revolution. More companies entered the business, making personal computers more affordable and increasing their speed through the development of microprocessors. By the mid-1990s, personal laptop computers had the ability to outperform their mainframe predecessors by a hundredfold. In 1990, the once-cumbersome network of computers began using domain names and hypertext links that made navigation quick and easy. By the late 1990s, most Americans had used the **Internet** at some point. With the spread of Internet use have come many challenges as well. It is difficult to manage misinformation, information theft, and other criminal activities. Users are left to protect their own personal information and protect themselves from other dangers that lurk online.

GLOBALIZATION IN THE UNITED STATES

As at no time before, the United States in the 21st century is linked to a broader global economy. Economic crises in distant lands can impact the United States before most Americans have had their morning coffee. The late 1990s and the late 2000s decade witnessed a global economic crisis that highlighted the potential risks associated with economic globalization. In the 1990s, Asian financial markets collapsed. Japan, the Philippines, and Korea experienced severe economic downturns caused by the overvaluing of real estate and risky investments. Thailand soon responded by closing banks across the nation, causing a ripple effect of bank patrons rushing to withdraw their deposits across Asia. Quickly, once-vast fortunes became worthless as currency and stock values crashed in many countries. Countries that relied on exports to Asia suffered as their supply of goods rose and Asian demand fell. Oil-producing nations found themselves strapped with large reserves of crude and no buyers. The Russian and Venezuelan economies were especially hard hit. The **International Monetary Fund** (IMF) supplied billions in loans to faltering nations. Some economies rebounded quickly, but future global economic crises remained a possibility.

President Clinton worked in his first term to promote economic globalization. His **North American Free Trade Agreement (NAFTA)** created a free-trade pact with Canada and Mexico that allowed the free flow of goods, services, and jobs in North America. NAFTA was hotly contested by organized labor and other progressive groups, who saw the agreement as moving American jobs across the border to Mexico while compromising America's sovereignty. NAFTA was signed in 1993, and its value and effects continue to be the subject of debate.

THE FEAR OF TERRORISM

Throughout the 20th century, Americans had watched from afar as other nations dealt with terrorism. Occasionally, American lives were lost at the hands of a hijacker or suicide bomber, but for the most part, the United States would remain isolated from the effects of terrorism. That all changed in 1995, when the Murrah Federal Building in Oklahoma City, Oklahoma, was destroyed by a large bomb that killed 168 people. It was discovered that the terror in Oklahoma was homegrown. Right-wing extremist **Timothy McVeigh** and two accomplices were convicted. Americans were stunned by the nature of the attack and grieved over the loss of so many innocent lives.

In the meantime, fundamentalist Islamist groups opposed to American foreign policy and presence in the Middle East were forming in countries such as Saudi Arabia, Iran, Syria, and Afghanistan. While some were established solely for protest purposes, others created networks of terrorist cells. One such group had already attacked Americans both on and off U.S. soil. **Al-Qaeda**, led by **Osama Bin Laden**, a Saudi national, had established a military training camp in Afghanistan to prepare members to attack Western targets. Bin Laden had successfully created a multinational force of terrorists by the early 1990s. Al-Qaeda began by attacking the World Trade Center in New York in 1993, killing six people but inflicting minimal damage. From that point on, Americans grew increasingly concerned as more and more attacks were carried out against them around the world. Soon, al-Qaeda and Bin Laden would become infamous among Americans.

SEPTEMBER 11 AND A NEW AMERICA

September 11, 2001, began as a normal workday in New York City, as employees of the businesses in the World Trade Center rushed off the subways and streets into their offices. At 8:46 AM Eastern Time, American Airlines Flight 11 crashed into the north tower of the World Trade Center. The flight had originated in Boston's Logan Airport and was supposed to be en route to Los Angeles with a belly full of fuel, 81 passengers, and a full flight crew. Many thought this was a freak accident, until approximately 15 minutes later, when United Flight 175 crashed into the south tower of the World Trade Center. It was then clear that the United States was under attack. Two other commercial planes remained unaccounted for until American Flight 77 crashed into the Pentagon and United Flight 93 crashed into a wooded area of Pennsylvania. All flights were immediately grounded and the airspace over the entire country closed to any traffic. Pledging immediate action, **President George W. Bush** promised that the perpetrators would be caught and justice would be served. The towers soon collapsed, killing occupants and rescue workers who had rushed in to save anyone they could. In the end, nearly 3,000 lives were lost in the **9/11** attacks, and the city of New York faced enormous financial damages. The impact on American business was staggering—commercial airlines begged for assistance to avoid bankruptcy, and travel destinations around the country remained empty. Lost too was the sense of security of the American public, who had previously considered themselves safer here than anywhere else in the world.

WAR ON IRAQ

President Bush invaded another Muslim country in March 2003 in an effort to remove a potentially threatening dictator and his alleged cache of **weapons of mass destruction**. Iraq had been a thorn in the side of the Bush family since his father's action to liberate Kuwait in 1991. With **Saddam Hussein** still in power and refusing to cooperate fully with United Nations weapons inspections, Bush, along with British prime minister Tony Blair, convinced Congress and most of the United States that Iraq posed a serious threat to the United States and the world if left in power. The invasion of Iraq was not officially sanctioned by the United Nations and was condemned by many U.S. allies around the world. Saddam Hussein was quickly removed from power, but weapons of mass destruction were never located, and the United States did not remove its forces entirely until nearly 10 years later.

ENVIRONMENTAL ISSUES

The world's population continues to grow at a rapid rate. It is unknown whether or not the planet will be able to sustain future population growth. Issues such as biodiversity, genetically engineered foods, overpopulation, global warming, resource conservation, and natural disasters will continue to concern human beings in the foreseeable future.

Domestically, the United States has experienced its fair share of environmental problems since 1965. President Carter was one of the first presidents to address the issues surrounding the environment and energy sources when he created the Department of Energy and superfund sites were identified. Superfund sites are chemical waste dump sites that the federal government takes over and cleans for future use. Carter also encouraged the use of solar power in place of nonrenewable energy sources and started the **Drive 55** plan to reduce the amount of gasoline consumed by Americans.

Nuclear power seemed to be viable alternative fuel until 1979, when the nuclear plant at **Three Mile Island** in Pennsylvania sent a cloud of radioactive gas into the air. It was soon discovered that in a rush to get the plant online, many shortcuts had been taken that ultimately threatened the safety of Americans living near the plant. After this incident, nuclear power was no longer a palatable option for most Americans.

Many of the measures taken to protect the environment would be reversed by Presidents Reagan and George H.W. Bush in an effort to stimulate the nation's economy by lifting restrictions on waste dumping and pollution emissions. Now, many Americans live in areas where the air poses health risks. The nation faces serious choices regarding resource conservation, energy sources, and environmental protection in the coming years.

UNIT 9: REVIEW QUESTIONS

Multiple-Choice Questions

Directions: Choose the best answer choice for the following questions.

Questions 1–3 refer to the following table.

Place of Birth for the Foreign-Born Population in the United States

Top ten countries	2010	2000	1990
Mexico	11,711,103	9,177,487	4,298,014
China	2,166,526	1,518,652	921,070
India	1,780,322	1,022,552	450,406
Philippines	1,777,588	1,369,070	912,674
Vietnam	1,240,542	988,174	543,262
El Salvador	1,214,049	817,336	465,433
Cuba	1,104,679	872,716	736,971
South Korea	1,100,422	864,125	568,397
Dominican Republic	879,187	687,677	347,858
Guatemala	830,824	480,665	225,739
All of Latin America	21,224,087	16,086,974	8,407,837
All Immigrants	39,955,854	31,107,889	19,767,316

1990 and 2000 Decennial Census and 2010 American Community Survey

1. The trends expressed in the chart most directly reflect which of the following continuities in United States history?

   (A) Debates about the extension of American ideals abroad

   (B) Debates about the relationships among the three branches of the United States government

   (C) Debates about gender equality

   (D) Debates about national identity and democratic ideas

2. Which action most directly resulted from the demographic information illustrated?

(A) Shifting of political power to Southern and Western states

(B) Greater consensus on the direction of American foreign policy

(C) Growth in the power of organized labor in the Northeast

(D) Decline in the number of clashes between conservatives and liberals

3. Which of the following events from earlier in United States history most clearly parallels the situation illustrated in the chart?

(A) Growth of a cotton economy in the antebellum period

(B) Rise of an industrial culture in the Gilded Age

(C) Great Migration of the post–World War I period

(D) Suburbanization of the post–World War II period

Questions 4–7 refer to the following quote.

" . . . the new Republican majority will immediately pass the following major reforms, aimed at restoring the faith and trust of the American people in their government:

- **FIRST,** require all laws that apply to the rest of the country also apply equally to the Congress;

- **SECOND,** select a major, independent auditing firm to conduct a comprehensive audit of Congress for waste, fraud or abuse;

- **THIRD,** cut the number of House committees, and cut committee staff by one-third;

- **FOURTH,** limit the terms of all committee chairs; . . .

- **SIXTH,** require committee meetings to be open to the public;

- **SEVENTH,** require a three-fifths majority vote to pass a tax increase;

- **EIGHTH,** guarantee an honest accounting of our Federal Budget by implementing zero base-line budgeting."

—Republican Contract with America, 1994

4. Which of the following groups would be most likely to support the perspective of the previous passage?

(A) Union leaders from the Sunbelt states

(B) Supporters of 1980s Reagan federalism

(C) Proponents of 1960s federal programs

(D) Internet social network members

5. The reasoning expressed in the previous passage most directly reflects which of the following continuities in United States history?

(A) Debates about the cost of involvement in foreign wars

(B) Debates about the changing relationship between state and local governments

(C) Debates about separation of powers

(D) Debates about the values that guide the political system

6. The concerns expressed in the Contract with America most closely resemble the goals associated with which of the following periods in United States history?

(A) The period of Manifest Destiny

(B) The Civil War years

(C) The progressive era

(D) Lyndon Johnson's Great Society

7. The beliefs expressed in the document above most directly led to political controversies from the 1990s to the present over

(A) immigration policy

(B) size and scope of social safety net programs

(C) globalization and loss of American jobs

(D) dependence upon fossil fuels

Questions 8–10 refer to the following figure.

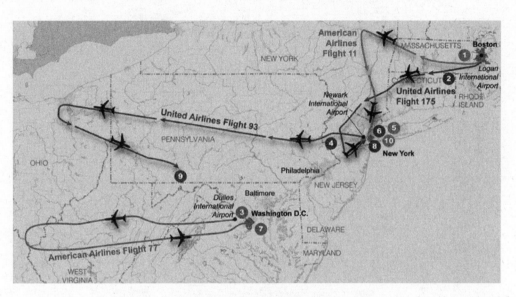

Flight Paths, September 11, 2001

8. Which of the following events from the 20th century most closely parallels the situation depicted in the image shown?

(A) Advocacy of American interventionism in Latin America in the early 20th century

(B) Woodrow Wilson's call for the defense of democracy in 1917

(C) Support for voluntary armed services post in 1975

(D) Opposition to the war in Vietnam in the 1960s and 1970s

9. The situation illustrated in the image most directly reflects which of the following continuities in United States history?

(A) Debates about the impact of airline deregulation in the 1980s

(B) Debates about economic globalization

(C) Debates about domestic security and civil rights

(D) Debates about federalism and states' rights

10. The situation illustrated in the image shown
    most directly led to

    (A) sustained economic growth

    (B) a growth in executive power

    (C) strengthening of World War II–era
        international coalitions

    (D) increasing Cold War tensions

Short-Answer Questions

1. **Source 1:**

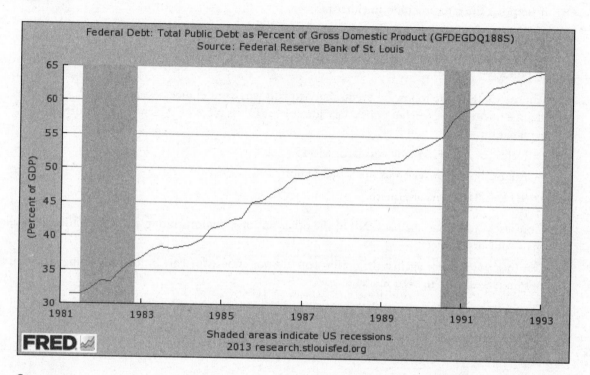

Source 2:

"When I visited this Chamber last year as a newcomer to Washington, critical of past policies which I believed had failed, I proposed a new spirit of partnership between this Congress and this administration and between Washington and our State and local governments. In forging this new partnership for America, we could achieve the oldest hopes of our Republic—prosperity . . . peace . . . and the blessings of individual liberty . . .

The last decade has seen a series of recessions. . . . unemployment increased and inflation soon turned up . . . We coined the word "stagflation" to describe this . . .

Together, after 50 years of taking power away from the hands of the people in their States and local communities, we have started returning power and resources to them.

Together, we have cut the growth of new Federal regulations nearly in half . . .

Together, we've begun to mobilize the private sector . . .

Together, we've begun to restore that margin of military safety that ensures peace. Our country's uniform is being worn once again with pride.

Together, we have made a New Beginning, but we have only begun."

—President Ronald Reagan, State of the Union Address, January 26, 1982

Based on the two sources dealing with the American economy in the 1980s, complete the following three tasks:

(A) Briefly explain the main point made by Source 1.

(B) Briefly explain the main point made by Source 2.

(C) Provide ONE piece of evidence dealing with the American economy in the 1980s, and explain how it supports the interpretation in either passage.

2. United States historians have used various events to mark a significant shift or change in American foreign policy.

(A) Choose ONE of the following events, and explain why your choice best represents a significant change in American foreign policy. Provide at least ONE piece of evidence to support your explanation.

- Defeat of Nazi Germany and Japan, 1945
- Fall of the Berlin Wall and the Soviet Union, 1989–1991
- 9/11/2001 and its aftermath

(B) Contrast your choice against ONE of the other options, demonstrating why that option is weaker than your first choice.

(C) Contrast your choice against the option you did not choose for Part B, demonstrating why that option is weaker than your first choice.

Document-Based Question

Directions: Question 1 is based on the accompanying documents. The documents have been edited for the purpose of this exercise. You are advised to spend 15 minutes planning and 45 minutes writing your answer. Write your responses on the lined pages that follow the questions.

1. Use the following documents and your knowledge of United States history to answer the previous question.

   Evaluate the effectiveness of American foreign policy in achieving and maintaining the safety and security of the United States in the period after 1972.

DOCUMENT 1

The United States of America and the Union of Soviet Socialist Republics . . .

Conscious that nuclear war would have devastating consequences for all mankind,

Proceeding from the Basic Principles of Relations . . . of May 29, 1972,

Attaching particular significance to the limitation of strategic arms and determined to continue their efforts begun with the Treaty on the Limitation of Anti-Ballistic Missile Systems and the Interim Agreement on Certain Measures with Respect to the Limitation of Strategic Offensive Arms, of May 26, 1972,

Convinced that the additional measures limiting strategic offensive arms . . . will contribute to the improvement of relations between the Parties, help to reduce the risk of outbreak of nuclear war and strengthen international peace and security, . . .

Reaffirming their desire to take measures for the further limitation and for the further reduction of strategic arms, having in mind the goal of achieving general and complete disarmament,

Declaring their intention to undertake in the near future negotiations further to limit and further to reduce strategic offensive arms,

Have agreed as follows . . . "

Treaty between the USA and the USSR signed in Vienna, June 18, 1979

DOCUMENT 2

"The 1980s have been born in turmoil, strife, and change. This is a time of challenge to our interests and our values and it's a time that tests our wisdom and our skills. . . .

Three basic developments have helped to shape our challenges: the steady growth and increased projection of Soviet military power beyond its own borders; the overwhelming dependence of the Western democracies on oil supplies from the Middle East; and the press of social and religious and economic and political change in the many nations of the developing world, exemplified by the revolution in Iran . . . "

President Jimmy Carter, State of the Union Address, January 23, 1980

Source: http://www.jimmycarterlibrary.gov/documents/speeches/su80jec.phtml

DOCUMENT 3

"The truth is that a freeze now would be a very dangerous fraud, for that is merely the illusion of peace. The reality is that we must find peace through strength.

Yes, let us pray for the salvation of all of those who live in that totalitarian darkness—pray they will discover the joy of knowing God. But until they do . . . they are the focus of evil in the modern world . . .

. . . But if history teaches anything, it teaches that simple-minded appeasement or wishful thinking about our adversaries is folly. It means the betrayal of our past, the squandering of our freedom.

So, I urge you to speak out against those who would place the United States in a position of military and moral inferiority . . . beware the temptation . . . to ignore the facts of history and the aggressive impulses of an evil empire, to simply call the arms race a giant misunderstanding and thereby remove yourself from the struggle between right and wrong and good and evil . . ."

President Ronald Reagan, speech to National Association of Evangelicals meeting in Orlando, Florida, March 8, 1983

DOCUMENT 4

"We last met in an hour of shock and suffering . . .

Our nation will continue . . . First, we will shut down . . ., disrupt . . . , and bring terrorists to justice. And, second, we must prevent . . . chemical, biological or nuclear weapons from threatening the United States and the world.

My hope is that all nations will heed our call, and eliminate the terrorist parasites who threaten their countries and our own. Many nations are acting forcefully . . .

But some governments will be timid in the face of terror. And make no mistake about it: If they do not act, America will.

States like [Iraq and North Korea], and their terrorist allies, constitute an axis of evil, . . . the price of indifference would be catastrophic.

We will work closely with our coalition to deny terrorists and their state sponsors the materials, technology, and expertise to make and deliver weapons of mass destruction. We will develop and deploy effective missile defenses to protect America and our allies from sudden attack. And all nations should know: America will do what is necessary to ensure our nation's security."

President George W. Bush, State of the Union Address, January 29, 2002

DOCUMENT 5

"Responding to . . . [an] observation that a transatlantic rift has deepened since the 1970s, Kissinger said, "There's an enormous difference between the environment of the present situation and the environment then.

"The period we're talking about was dominated by our consciousness of the Soviet Union as a superpower. Every crisis had to be conducted against a background of the possibility of escalating into nuclear war. Every ally realized there was a limit beyond which breaking with the United States was too risky," Kissinger said.

"The challenge of the '70s was how to construct a creative foreign policy in the midst of an undisputed permanent tension. The challenge of the present period is how to build a creative foreign policy in which there is no agreement on what the danger is, and therefore, the definition of positive objectives is much more difficult," [Kissinger] said."

Henry Kissinger, June 2003, remarks made at roundtable "Reevaluating the Nixon/Ford/Kissinger Era: Transatlantic Relations and U.S. Foreign Policy in the 1970s and Beyond"

DOCUMENT 6

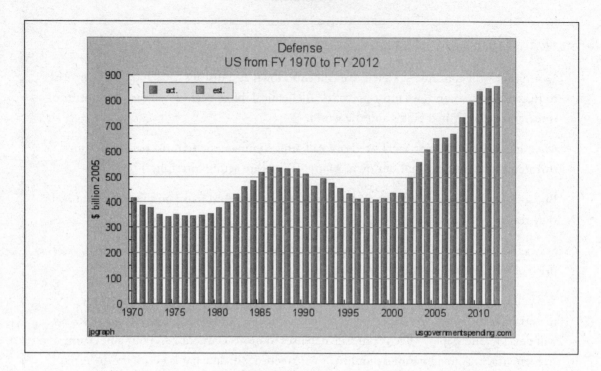

DOCUMENT 7

President Barack Obama and Vice President Joe Biden, along with members of the national security team, receive an update on the mission against Osama bin Laden, May 1, 2011

ANSWERS AND EXPLANATIONS

MULTIPLE-CHOICE ANSWERS

1. D

After over two centuries of European-dominated immigration to the United States, more people arrived from Asia and the Americas by the turn of the 21st century. This influx of new immigrants has led to controversies and debates, including those about immigration policy and national identity.

2. A

Many of the recent immigrants to the United States have settled in Southern and Western states. California, Texas, and Florida are among the most populous states in the United States and therefore have among the largest delegations in the United States House of Representatives.

3. B

Gilded Age industrialization led to a huge demand for labor. Immigrants from southern and eastern Europe poured into the United States at the turn of the 20th century. They challenged existing immigration patterns, since late 19th/early 20th century "new immigrants" no longer came from the once-dominant areas of northern and western Europe.

4. B

The Contract with America, released by Republicans during the midterm election period in 1994, attempted to regain Republican conservative control of the federal government. The Republicans wished to continue the limitations of the power of the federal government, especially in domestic affairs, begun during the Reagan administration in the 1980s.

5. D

While the Contract with America outlined the role that Congress, especially the House of Representatives, would take, at its core it challenged the concept of big government. It envisioned a government that would continue to roll back its size and scope, well beyond levels created by the Great Society programs of the 1960s. These proposals presented an alternative to "big government" values of the earlier decades.

6. C

Both the progressive era and the Republican Contract with America spotlight the need for government reform. Proponents of both believed that the control of government had gotten away from the wishes of the citizenry and called for greater political power to be given back to the people. While many progressive policies actually led to an increased regulatory role for the government, calls for government's being more responsive to the wishes of the electorate are similar.

7. C

Republican policy, especially since the 1980s, has sought to limit the size and scope of the power of the federal government. A series of budget crises and economic downturns has led to concerns that the United States government's economic policies are limiting future economic growth and stability. Popular programs like Medicare, Medicaid, and Social Security have proven difficult to reform.

8. B

The attacks on 9/11 led to a War on Terror for the United States. The belief that the United States stood as a country of liberty and freedom and would take action against those who actively challenged that belief echoed Wilson's call to "make the world safe for democracy" before the United States entered World War I.

9. C

The attacks on 9/11 led to increased security across the United States, including the changes in procedure in the nation's airports and many public buildings. Passage of the Patriot Act by Congress, which included increased surveillance, has increased the debate between domestic security and civil rights.

10. D

In the aftermath of 9/11 actions, the Bush administration launched a War on Terror. American armed forces were sent to Afghanistan and Iraq with limited international support. President Bush issued an executive order authorizing military tribunals for noncitizens accused of terrorism. While executive authority to combat terrorism increased, critics argued against constitutional violations.

SHORT-ANSWER QUESTIONS RESPONSES

1. (A) The federal deficit as a percentage of GDP more than doubled in the period from 1980 to 1993, rising from just over 30 percent in 1981 to almost 65 percent in 1993. The rate of increase was relatively consistent, even through periods of recession.

   (B) President Reagan, early in his first term in office, outlined a program to reduce the size of the federal government to help the nation recover from the economic problems of the 1970s. His hope was that this would help restore confidence and spur economic recovery.

   (C) President Reagan, a conservative, developed a number of proposals, another New Federalism, to reduce the size of the federal government. These proposals included significant tax cuts and a reduction in the size of the federal government. However, increases in defense spending in the years before the fall of the Soviet Union and the difficulty in reforming popular programs like Social Security and Medicare/Medicaid led to an increasing federal debt.

2. (A) Defeat of the Axis powers in 1945 heralded a new era in American foreign policy. Since George Washington's years in office, the United States had followed a policy of neutrality and general noninvolvement when it came to European affairs. Even after involvement in World War I, the United States rejected any major international role in the interwar years. That all changed in 1945 when the United States emerged as the leading Allied victor. The creation of the United Nations and, a few years later, the North Atlantic Treaty Organization put the United States in the forefront of a more internationalist foreign policy. This internationalism led to American interventionism in many areas across the world in the decades after WWII.

   (B) The attacks on 9/11 led to a change in American foreign policy as well. The United States became less insulated from events in the world. Terrorism struck at home and the USA launched its War on Terror, leading to intervention in Iraq and Afghanistan, a war that involved actions in nation-states and against groups such as Al-Qaeda and the Taliban. While exceedingly significant, this interventionism and, indeed, some of the underlying concerns such as American policy in the Middle East date back to the changes occurring in the years after the defeat of the Axis powers in 1945. Consequently, the changes occurring post-1945 are more significant.

   (C) The fall of the Berlin Wall and the Soviet Union led to a change in American foreign policy as well. The United States became the world's undisputed super power after the fall of the Soviet Union. The United States began to cooperate with Russia and other satellites to help them democratize and to secure nuclear weapons. This was done through the Nunn-Lugar Act. Although this was a significant shift in United States foreign policy, as they went from being in a Cold War with Eastern Europe to cooperating together, it is not as significant as the defeat of the Axis powers in 1945. The defeat of the Axis powers is the event that propelled the United States into the position of a world superpower.

DBQ SAMPLE RESPONSE

Escalating protests over American involvement in the Vietnam War marked the beginning of the 1970s, and the American Cold War foreign policy was about to undergo significant change. President Nixon's détente with the Soviet Union seemed dead by the Reagan years of the 1980s, but by the end of the 1980s, the Soviet Union was dead. During the Cold War, American safety and security focused primarily on the relations between the United States and the Soviet Union, with alternating periods of freeze and thaw. After a short "peace dividend" in the 1990s, the end of the Cold War brought serious challenges to American security from other sources. While the threat of nuclear holocaust dominated Cold War security, and concerns led to real diplomatic gains in the 1970s and 1980s, the start of the 21st century showed that national security threats are always evolving.

As the war in Vietnam ended, President Nixon and his chief foreign policy adviser looked to lessen America's commitment to being the world's foremost fighter against communism with policies such as Vietnamization. Although the controversial Vietnam conflict ended after years of American commitment and bloodshed, the end of the war did allow for more peaceful overtures between the United States and the major communist powers. Nixon pursued a policy of détente, which led to meetings and visits with the leaders of the USSR and China. These policies resulted in a lessening of tensions between these nations and the signing of SALT I, a major nuclear disarmament treaty. Problems in the Middle East between Israel and its Arab neighbors would lead to more significant issues in the next decades and into the 21st century.

American support of Israel would lead to the Arab oil embargo in the 1970s, which caused tremendous disruption of the economy, lessening national security. Inflation skyrocketed amid a stagnant economy and the term "stagflation" was born. Jimmy Carter's handling of this economic crisis overshadowed his attempts to continue the rollback of nuclear weapons that Nixon started (Doc. 1). SALT II was never ratified by the United States Senate because the Soviet Union invaded Afghanistan. Another problem in the Middle East involved the Iranian Revolution, which led to the capture of American embassy personnel for over a year (Doc. 2). Viewed as another Carter failure, continued destabilization in the Middle East would eventually overshadow the USSR as the dominant threat to the United States.

Ronald Reagan's presidency seemed to reenergize Cold War rhetoric with his speeches focusing on an "evil empire" and proposing his Star Wars or SDI defense idea. However, in some strange way it seemed to help end the threat of the USSR. Changeover in the Soviet Union put Mikhail Gorbachev in power, a leader who recognized that the USSR did not possess the capital to outspend American defense numbers. Glasnost and perestroika gave way to START negotiations and eventually the Intermediate-Range Nuclear Forces Treaty. Post-WWII tensions seemed to be permanently on the decline. When the Berlin Wall did eventually come down, and the Soviet Union and the Warsaw Pact ended, the United States and its allies seemed to sigh with relief. Many hailed an economic "peace dividend" that would result from decreased defense spending. That didn't last long (Doc. 6). While the United States enjoyed a prosperous 1990s, problems anchored in the Middle East conflicts would spread well beyond those geographic borders and attack Americans right at home.

The attacks on 9/11 robbed Americans of the belief that they were safe at home. When the World Trade towers came down, so did American innocence. Evil was still a key word as President Bush talked of "an axis of evil" (Doc. 4). But the challenge was in defining the target of American military action. As Henry Kissinger, foreign policy adviser to Nixon and Ford, stated, "There is no agreement on what the danger is," leading to much more difficult policy decisions (Doc. 5). Osama bin Laden, mastermind of the 9/11 attacks, hid out in Afghanistan and Pakistan. But in addition, the United States also attacked Saddam Hussein's regime in Iraq, confusing some Americans as to where the 9/11 attacks originated. The American War on Terror continues after over a decade. And despite bin Laden's death on President Obama's orders and an increase in defense spending, al-Qaeda and the threat to the American security still exist (Doc. 6 and Doc. 7).

The threats to American safety and security have changed since 1972. The world is a much more fragmented place, where major threats to national security are not from traditional nation-states with highly sophisticated weapons. Rather, non-state terrorist groups and a few rogue leaders, like Kim Jong-il in North Korea, have emerged as serious threats to American safety and security. While diplomatic and military efforts have proven successful in avoiding another attack like that of 9/11, the world is still a dangerous place.

The opening paragraph provides historical context for the question and a setting for the thesis, which goes beyond a restatement of the question. The score would be 1 out of 1 point for the thesis. The use of evidence, argumentation, and causation is strong. Analysis of the documents focuses primarily on historical context and, occasionally, on purpose.

The student should develop the ability to note point of view and intended audience to make a more richly developed essay, but the work done with all of the documents used fulfills the rubric's guidelines. The score would be 3 out of 3 points for analysis of documents. Many outside examples were introduced to further support the thesis. The score would be 1 out of 1 point for analysis of outside examples. There is strong contextualization made throughout essay to set events in broader context and show change over time. The score would be 1 out of 1 point for contextualization. Synthesis is demonstrated throughout essay. The score would be 1 out of 1 point for synthesis. This essay would receive a 7 out of 7 possible points on the DBQ rubric.

Part Four

PRACTICE TESTS

HOW TO TAKE THE PRACTICE TESTS

The next section of this book consists of four full-length practice tests. Taking a practice AP exam gives you an idea of what it's like to answer these test questions under conditions that approximate those of the real test. You'll find out which areas you're strong in and where additional review may be required. Any mistakes you make now are ones you won't make on the actual exam, as long as you take the time to learn where you went wrong.

The four full-length practice tests in this book each include 55 multiple-choice questions, four short-answer questions, one document-based question, and your choice of two long essay questions. You will have 55 minutes for the multiple-choice questions, 50 minutes for the short-answer questions, 55 minutes for the document-based question (which includes a required 15-minute reading period), and 35 minutes for the long essay question. Before taking a practice test, find a quiet place where you can work uninterrupted. Time yourself according to the time limit given at the beginning of each section. It's okay to take a short break between sections, but for the most accurate results, you should approximate real test conditions as much as possible. Use the 15-minute reading period to plan your answers for the document-based question, but don't begin writing your response until the 15 minutes are up.

As you take the practice tests, remember to pace yourself. Train yourself to be aware of the time you are spending on each problem. Try to be aware of the general types of questions you encounter, as well as being alert to certain strategies or approaches that help you to handle the various question types more effectively.

After taking a practice exam, be sure to read the detailed answer explanations that follow. These will help you identify areas that could use additional review. Even when you answered a question correctly, you can learn additional information by looking at the answer explanation.

Finally, it's important to approach the test with the right attitude. You're going to get a great score because you've reviewed the material and learned the strategies in this book.

Good luck!

Practice Test 1 Answer Grid

1. Ⓐ Ⓑ Ⓒ Ⓓ

2. Ⓐ Ⓑ Ⓒ Ⓓ

3. Ⓐ Ⓑ Ⓒ Ⓓ

4. Ⓐ Ⓑ Ⓒ Ⓓ

5. Ⓐ Ⓑ Ⓒ Ⓓ

6. Ⓐ Ⓑ Ⓒ Ⓓ

7. Ⓐ Ⓑ Ⓒ Ⓓ

8. Ⓐ Ⓑ Ⓒ Ⓓ

9. Ⓐ Ⓑ Ⓒ Ⓓ

10. Ⓐ Ⓑ Ⓒ Ⓓ

11. Ⓐ Ⓑ Ⓒ Ⓓ

12. Ⓐ Ⓑ Ⓒ Ⓓ

13. Ⓐ Ⓑ Ⓒ Ⓓ

14. Ⓐ Ⓑ Ⓒ Ⓓ

15. Ⓐ Ⓑ Ⓒ Ⓓ

16. Ⓐ Ⓑ Ⓒ Ⓓ

17. Ⓐ Ⓑ Ⓒ Ⓓ

18. Ⓐ Ⓑ Ⓒ Ⓓ

19. Ⓐ Ⓑ Ⓒ Ⓓ

20. Ⓐ Ⓑ Ⓒ Ⓓ

21. Ⓐ Ⓑ Ⓒ Ⓓ

22. Ⓐ Ⓑ Ⓒ Ⓓ

23. Ⓐ Ⓑ Ⓒ Ⓓ

24. Ⓐ Ⓑ Ⓒ Ⓓ

25. Ⓐ Ⓑ Ⓒ Ⓓ

26. Ⓐ Ⓑ Ⓒ Ⓓ

27. Ⓐ Ⓑ Ⓒ Ⓓ

28. Ⓐ Ⓑ Ⓒ Ⓓ

29. Ⓐ Ⓑ Ⓒ Ⓓ

30. Ⓐ Ⓑ Ⓒ Ⓓ

31. Ⓐ Ⓑ Ⓒ Ⓓ

32. Ⓐ Ⓑ Ⓒ Ⓓ

33. Ⓐ Ⓑ Ⓒ Ⓓ

34. Ⓐ Ⓑ Ⓒ Ⓓ

35. Ⓐ Ⓑ Ⓒ Ⓓ

36. Ⓐ Ⓑ Ⓒ Ⓓ

37. Ⓐ Ⓑ Ⓒ Ⓓ

38. Ⓐ Ⓑ Ⓒ Ⓓ

39. Ⓐ Ⓑ Ⓒ Ⓓ

40. Ⓐ Ⓑ Ⓒ Ⓓ

41. Ⓐ Ⓑ Ⓒ Ⓓ

42. Ⓐ Ⓑ Ⓒ Ⓓ

43. Ⓐ Ⓑ Ⓒ Ⓓ

44. Ⓐ Ⓑ Ⓒ Ⓓ

45. Ⓐ Ⓑ Ⓒ Ⓓ

46. Ⓐ Ⓑ Ⓒ Ⓓ

47. Ⓐ Ⓑ Ⓒ Ⓓ

48. Ⓐ Ⓑ Ⓒ Ⓓ

49. Ⓐ Ⓑ Ⓒ Ⓓ

50. Ⓐ Ⓑ Ⓒ Ⓓ

51. Ⓐ Ⓑ Ⓒ Ⓓ

52. Ⓐ Ⓑ Ⓒ Ⓓ

53. Ⓐ Ⓑ Ⓒ Ⓓ

54. Ⓐ Ⓑ Ⓒ Ⓓ

55. Ⓐ Ⓑ Ⓒ Ⓓ

PRACTICE TEST 1

Section I

Part A: Multiple-Choice Questions

Time: 55 Minutes
55 Questions

Directions: Choose the best answer choice for the following questions.

Questions 1–3 refer to the following passage.

"Maize swept into Africa as introduced disease was leveling Indian societies. Faced with a labor shortage, the Europeans turned their eyes to Africa. The continent's quarrelsome societies helped them siphon off millions of people."

—From *1491* by Charles C. Mann, Vintage Books: New York, 2006, p. 224

1. The main impact of European exploration on American Indians at the onset of the establishment of the Columbian Exchange was

   (A) the native population was forced off their land as slave labor was imported from Africa

   (B) the introduction of diseases like smallpox led to a decimation of the American Indian population

   (C) Spanish and Portuguese explorers cut American-Indian nations off from trade routes, leading to mass starvation

   (D) the introduction of the horse by the Spanish-led American Indians to hunt more and depend upon maize and other crops less

2. The most significant impact of the introduction of sugarcane in the West Indies was

   (A) the need for slave labor from Africa to maintain constant production of sugar

   (B) the desire of the Spanish to settle the Western Hemisphere with permanent settlements made up of families

   (C) the development of a continuous war between Spain and Portugal over Caribbean islands

   (D) the destruction of the ecosystem of many Caribbean islands resulting in the death of thousands of natives

GO ON TO THE NEXT PAGE

3. As described, the Columbian Exchange was significant in that it had the greatest impact on which group of people?

(A) Africans; they received a greater variety of foodstuffs from Europe, in turn increasing their population significantly.

(B) Europeans; their wealth increased.

(C) Native Americans; they were enslaved by the *encomienda* system by the thousands.

(D) Europeans; new, easier-to-grow foodstuffs such as corn and potatoes were brought from the New World and allowed impoverished population groups to survive and increase their numbers.

Questions 4–6 refer to the following passage.

"We, whose names are underwritten, the loyal subjects of our dread Sovereigne Lord, King James, by the grace of God, of Great Britaine, France and Ireland king, defender of the faith, etc. having undertaken, for the glory of God, and advancement of the Christian faith, and honour of our king and country, a voyage to plant the first colony in the Northerne parts of Virginia, doe by these presents solemnly and mutually in the presence of God and one of another, covenant and combine ourselves together into a civill body politick, for our better ordering and preservation, and furtherance of the ends aforesaid; and by virtue hereof to enact, constitute, and frame such just and equall laws, ordinances, acts, constitutions and offices, from time to time, as shall be thought most meete and convenient for the generall good of the Colonie unto which we promise all due submission and obedience."

—Excerpted from the Mayflower Compact, November 11, 1620

4. The main idea of this document influenced which of the following ideals of the British North American colonies?

(A) The idea of separation of church and state

(B) The concept that the colonies need to be governed by a constitution

(C) The concept of rule by majority, as in town meetings

(D) The foundation for social equality

5. Which of the following groups would most likely support the main concepts of the Mayflower Compact?

(A) Delegates to the Stamp Act Congress

(B) Supporters of the Articles of Confederation

(C) Persons living in the New Harmony, Indiana communal society

(D) Delegates to the Constitutional Convention in 1787

6. The excerpt from the Mayflower Compact clearly reflects which of the following?

(A) The English were establishing North American colonies based on the Spanish *encomienda* system.

(B) The English were attempting to establish permanent communities.

(C) The English were prepared to challenge French claims in North America.

(D) Instructions that the English settlers in North America were to establish communities identical to those in England.

GO ON TO THE NEXT PAGE

Questions 7–9 refer to the following image.

The Burning of Jamestown by Howard Pyle © 1905, depicting the burning of Jamestown, Virginia, during Bacon's Rebellion

7. The major cause of Bacon's Rebellion was the competing perceptions of power in 17th-century Virginia. Which of the following best describes the differing perceptions?

   (A) The difference in the amount of land available to settlers in the Tidewater region and in western Virginia; settlers in the Tidewater region had more land.

   (B) The competing desires for economic equality and power between the different regions of Virginia

   (C) The difference in political power between the eastern plantation owners and the newer settlers in the west, with the advantage going to the plantation owners in the east

   (D) The fact that settlers in the western portion of the colony were mainly former indentured servants who had no political rights

8. The philosophical ideology that led to Bacon's Rebellion would have motivated which of the following groups later in America?

   (A) South Carolina politicians who supported nullification of the federal tariff in the 1830s

   (B) Western Pennsylvania farmers who opposed the Whiskey Tax in the 1790s

   (C) Americans in Texas who opposed the conditions Mexico imposed on them for moving into Texas in the 1830s

   (D) Abolitionists who were becoming more radically antislavery in the 1850s

9. The event expressed in the picture most clearly demonstrates the influence of which of the following?

   (A) Royal authority that tended to discount lower-class groups during the 17th century

   (B) Belief of the people that there should be separation between church and state

   (C) Desire for more economic equality between the plantation and yeoman farmer classes

   (D) The strong desire for social equality during the colonial era

GO ON TO THE NEXT PAGE

Questions 10–13 refer to the following passage.

War Song, 1776

Hark, hark the sound of war is heard,
And we must all attend;
Take up our arms and go with speed,
Our country to defend.

Our parent state has turned our foe,
Which fills our land with pain;
Her gallant ships, manned out for war,
Come thundering o'er the main.

There's Carleton, Howe, and Clinton too.
And many thousands more,
May cross the sea, but all in vain,
Our rights we'll ne'er give o'er.

Our pleasant homes they do invade,
Our property devour;
And all because we won't submit
To their despotic power.

10. What is the main point of the lyrics in the excerpt?

    (A) The lyrics warn that Americans should be aware of an impending English invasion of their homes.

    (B) The words are meant to inspire American colonists to take up arms and fight against the despotic mother country.

    (C) There was a fear of a French attack and Americans needed to be ready to fight.

    (D) There was a continued fear of an impending attack by Native Americans and Americans must take up arms to protect their homes.

11. Based on the previous lyrics, what were Americans fighting for?

    (A) Americans were fighting for their rights as Englishmen.

    (B) Americans were fighting for economic liberty and to be able to practice free trade.

    (C) Americans were fighting for the right to replace their despotic royal governors

    (D) Americans were attempting to replace British Enlightenment philosophy with their own ideas on government.

12. Despite the strength of the patriotic "call to arms" attitude in the lyrics, which of the following events would discourage the American spirit in 1776?

    (A) The fact that Native Americans were attacking British colonists from the west while the British navy was attacking from the east

    (B) The fear of a massive slave rebellion

    (C) The lack of economic means to support a war effort against England

    (D) The presence of Loyalists throughout the colonies

13. Based on the lyrics, which of the following is the most plausible reason for the reaction described in the song?

    (A) The passage of restrictive regulations on the British North American colonies by Parliament

    (B) The continued violation of American freedom of the seas and free trade

    (C) The fear of invasion of American ports by the English Navy in order to stop American trade with the Spanish and French Caribbean colonies

    (D) The continuous attack by Native Americans on frontier settlements west of the Appalachian Mountains

GO ON TO THE NEXT PAGE ⟩

Questions 14–16 refer to the following passage.

" . . . we are enabled this Day to add one more Step to universal Civilization by removing as much as possible the Sorrows of those, who have lived in undeserved Bondage . . .

And whereas, the Condition of those Persons who have heretofore been denominated Negroe (sic), has been attended with Circumstances which not only deprived them of the common Blessings that they were by Nature entitled to . . . In Justice therefore to Persons so unhappily circumstanced and who, having no Prospect before them whereon they may rest their Sorrows Commemoration of our own happy Deliverance, from that State of unconditional Submission, to which we were doomed by the Tyranny of Britain."

—Excerpted from the Pennsylvania Emancipation Act, 1780

14. The ideas expressed in the excerpt are most similar to which of the following?

(A) The idea that slavery is immoral and must be ended

(B) The public education reform movement, because education was considered the great social equalizer and therefore should be offered to slaves

(C) The abolitionist movement as part of the Second Great Awakening, which valued religious awakening and service to society

(D) The prison reform movement, the idea that prisons should be made more humane and focus on rehabilitation

15. Which of the following groups would have been most likely to agree with the previous excerpt?

(A) The Locofoco wing of the Democratic Party in the 1830s

(B) The Liberty Party of the 1840s

(C) The Free Soil Party of the 1840s and 1850s

(D) Members of the American Party in the 1850s

16. Which of the following best explains the motivations behind this declaration?

(A) The king had forced slavery upon the Americas and was no longer in power over the newly independent states.

(B) Slavery had been declared illegal in several Northern states, and Pennsylvania was pressured to free their slaves.

(C) Just as Americans had fought for their freedom from Britain, so too did Pennsylvanians believe it right to free those held in bondage within their state along with other Northern colonies.

(D) The tyranny of Great Britain had forced slavery onto the people of Pennsylvania; Pennsylvania was now independent and ended the institution.

GO ON TO THE NEXT PAGE >

Questions 17–20 refer to the following passage.

"The authority given to the Supreme Court by the act establishing the judicial system of the United States to issue writs of mandamus to public officers appears not to be warranted by the Constitution.

It is emphatically the duty of the Judicial Department to say what the law is. Those who apply the rule to particular cases must, of necessity, expound and interpret the rule. If two laws conflict with each other, the Court must decide on the operation of each.

If courts are to regard the Constitution, and the Constitution is superior to any ordinary act of the legislature, the Constitution, and not such ordinary act, must govern the case to which they both apply."

—*Marbury v. Madison* decision written by John Marshall, 1803

17. According to this excerpt, which of the following has supremacy in American law?

   (A) The Supreme Court
   (B) The Judicial branch
   (C) Writs of Mandamus
   (D) The Constitution

18. The previous excerpt would have been most strongly supported by which group?

   (A) New England Federalists in the 1810s
   (B) South Carolina plantation owners in the 1830s
   (C) Kentucky legislature in the 1790s
   (D) Southern slave owners in the 1850s

19. In reaction to changing events in American history, interpretation of the Constitution by the Supreme Court can allow subsequent decisions to change initial court rulings. Which of the following pair of Supreme Court decisions illustrates this change of interpretation?

   (A) *Fletcher v. Peck* and *Gibbons v. Ogden*
   (B) *Scott v. Sandford* and *Schenk v. United States*
   (C) *Plessy v. Ferguson* and *Brown v. Board of Education*
   (D) *Cherokee Nation v. Georgia* and *Worcester v. Georgia*

20. Which of the following presidential actions of the first half of the 19th century challenges the main principles behind the previous quote?

   (A) James Madison's Declaration of War in 1812
   (B) James Madison's veto of internal improvements in 1817
   (C) James Monroe's issuing of the Monroe Doctrine
   (D) Andrew Jackson's veto of the bill that called for the re-charter of the Second Bank of the United States

GO ON TO THE NEXT PAGE

Questions 21–23 refer to the following image.

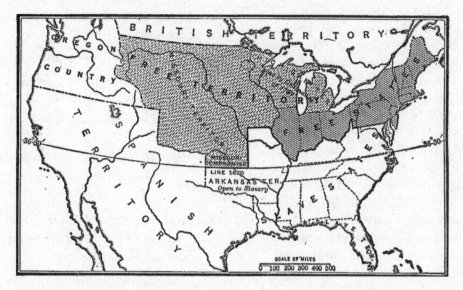

Robert Hall, Harriet Smither, and Clarence Ousley, *A History of the United States*
(Dallas, Texas, The Southern Publishing Company, 1920), courtesy of Maps ETC

21. Based on the information in the map, which of the following best describes the circumstances of events in the early 19th century?

   (A) Slave territory was beginning to encroach on free territory.

   (B) The United States had intentions of taking the Spanish Territory in the West.

   (C) The United States was attempting to maintain a balance between free and slave states.

   (D) Free states were looking to add Oregon Country to their territory to have access to the Pacific Ocean.

22. Based on the map, which of the following groups would have most likely objected to the outcome of the events that were established in the compromise of 1820?

   (A) Slave owners in the newly emerging cotton-growing states

   (B) New England factory workers

   (C) Quakers in the Northeast

   (D) Poor whites in the South

23. The event portrayed in the map was the center of controversy later in the first half of the 19th century when

   (A) the events depicted in the map caused the war with Mexico in 1846

   (B) legislation passed in the 1850s overturned the laws established in 1820, allowing a state to rid its territory of slavery

   (C) the Supreme Court determined the outcome of the compromise that created the above map to be unconstitutional

   (D) the Free Soil Party began to win elections in the western territories where it had been determined that popular sovereignty would determine the outcome of a territory's slave status

GO ON TO THE NEXT PAGE

Questions 24–26 refer to the following passage.

"And be it further enacted, That when a person held to service or labor in any State or Territory of the United States, has heretofore or shall hereafter escape into another State or Territory of the United States, the person or persons to whom such service or labor may be due, or his, her, or their agent or attorney, duly authorized, by power of attorney, in writing, acknowledged and certified under the seal of some legal officer or court of the State or Territory in which the same may be executed, may pursue and reclaim such fugitive person, either by procuring a warrant from some one of the courts, judges, or commissioners aforesaid, of the proper circuit, district, or county, for the apprehension of such fugitive from service or labor, or by seizing and arresting such fugitive, where the same can be done without process, and by taking, or causing such person to be taken, forthwith before such court, judge, or commissioner, whose duty it shall be to hear and determine the case of such claimant in a summary manner . . . "

—Sixth provision of the Fugitive Slave Act of 1850

24. One of the immediate effects of the passage of the Fugitive Slave Act of 1850 was

(A) the passage of "personal liberty laws" in northern states

(B) the pronouncement by Senator John C. Calhoun that slavery was a "necessary good"

(C) the beginning of "Bleeding Kansas"

(D) the start of the Underground Railroad

25. Which of the following was written after the passage of the Fugitive Slave Act of 1850 and raised awareness of the treatment of slaves in the South?

(A) *The Liberator* by William Lloyd Garrison

(B) *An Appeal to the Colored Citizens of the World* by David Walker

(C) *Uncle Tom's Cabin* by Harriet Beecher Stowe

(D) *The Adventures of Huckleberry Finn* by Mark Twain

26. Reaction in the North to the Fugitive Slave Act was similar to American reaction to which of the following?

(A) Pronouncement of the Monroe Doctrine

(B) The outcome of Bacon's Rebellion

(C) The passage of the Stamp Act

(D) The Glorious Revolution

GO ON TO THE NEXT PAGE

Questions 27–29 refer to the following passage.

"Resolved, That we, the delegated representatives of the Republican electors of the United States in Convention assembled, in discharge of the duty we owe to our constituents and our country, unite in the following declarations:

[Plank] 8. That the normal condition of all the territory of the United States is that of freedom: That, as our Republican fathers, when they had abolished slavery in all our national territory, ordained that "no persons should be deprived of life, liberty or property without due process of law," it becomes our duty, by legislation, whenever such legislation is necessary, to maintain this provision of the Constitution against all attempts to violate it; and we deny the authority of Congress, of a territorial legislature, or of any individuals, to give legal existence to slavery in any territory of the United States."

—Republican Party Platform, 1860

27. Which of the following best explains the Republican stance on slavery?

(A) They supported the concept of popular sovereignty.

(B) They wanted to ban slavery in the United States.

(C) They adopted the Free Soil position of not allowing slavery to spread from where it existed.

(D) They called for the passage of the Emancipation Proclamation.

28. Concepts such as those expressed in the previous excerpt led to which of the following developments in American identity?

(A) A stronger link between the agricultural Midwest and South because of their dependence upon slave labor

(B) Further division of the nation based on sectional political issues

(C) A stronger bond between Southern cotton growers and New England factory workers

(D) An economic relationship between the South and West

29. The ideas expressed in the previous excerpt are most similar to those in which of the following movements?

(A) The labor movement of the late 19th century

(B) The new nativist movement of the turn of the 20th century

(C) The women's suffrage movement

(D) The American Temperance Union

GO ON TO THE NEXT PAGE

Questions 30–32 refer to the following image.

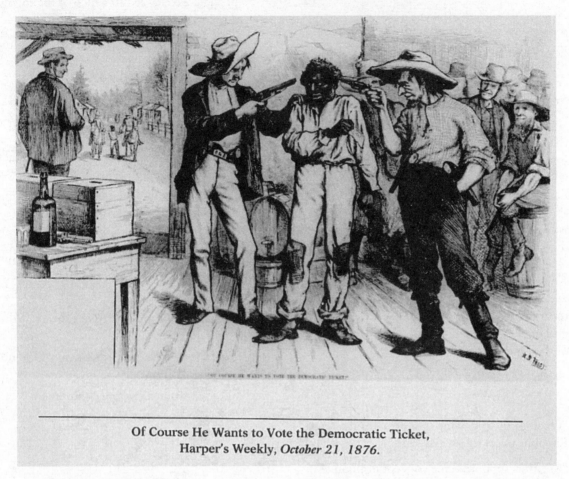

Of Course He Wants to Vote the Democratic Ticket,
Harper's Weekly, *October 21, 1876*.

A.B. Frost, "Of Course He Wants to Vote the Democratic Ticket," cartoon, *Harper's Weekly*, October 21, 1876

30. Which of the following statements best describes the event in the political cartoon?

(A) Radical Republicans resorted to threats and intimidation against the Freedmen to coerce them into voting.

(B) Despite the right to vote granted to Freedmen in the Fifteenth Amendment, white supremacists intimidated them to vote for their candidates.

(C) The South passed legislation eventually eliminating the Freedmen's right to vote.

(D) Southern Democrats, known as Redeemers, did their best to exclude the Republicans from Southern politics.

31. Which of the following codified the rights granted to Freedmen during Reconstruction?

(A) Civil Rights legislation written during the New Deal

(B) Legislation passed after the Montgomery Bus boycott during the Eisenhower administration

(C) Anti-lynching legislation written during the Progressive Era

(D) Legislation passed under the Great Society of the Johnson administration

GO ON TO THE NEXT PAGE

32. Which of the following 20th-century actions most closely parallels the civil rights issue portrayed in the illustration?

    (A) *Brown v. Board of Education* decision

    (B) Civil Rights Acts of 1964 and 1965

    (C) Racial integration of the U.S. military

    (D) *Korematsu v. United States* decision

Questions 33–35 refer to the following passage.

"The old South rested everything on slavery and agriculture, unconscious that these could neither give nor maintain healthy growth. The new South presents a perfect democracy, the oligarchs leading in the popular movement—a social system compact and closely knitted, less splendid on the surface, but stronger at the core—a hundred farms for every plantation, fifty homes for every palace—and a diversified industry that meets the complex need of this complex age."

—Henry Grady, *The New South*, 1886, 1889

33. Based on the excerpt of Henry Grady's *New South*, which of the following statements best describes the change in the description of the American identity?

    (A) After the Civil War, the South accepted the new status of the African American as an equal citizen.

    (B) The South had done away with the hierarchical plantation system and replaced it with a more egalitarian society.

    (C) The new South was the first region to grant political equality to women.

    (D) The South had become as industrialized as the North.

34. Which of the following pieces of evidence would counteract the ideal of the new South as described by Henry Grady?

    (A) The development of the iron and steel industry in Birmingham, Alabama

    (B) Industrial development in New Orleans and other Gulf Coast cities

    (C) The restructuring of the South's agricultural system

    (D) The existence of sharecropping and the crop-lien system

35. Which of the following would more accurately fit Grady's description of the new South?

    (A) The antebellum South

    (B) The South of the Great Depression

    (C) The South during the World War II era

    (D) The reconstruction South

GO ON TO THE NEXT PAGE

Questions 36–38 refer to the following passage.

"Herbert has finished his course at the academy, and is about to enter the manufactory as an office clerk. Mr. Cameron means to promote him as he merits, and I should not be at all surprised if our young friend eventually became junior partner. He and his mother have bought the house into which they moved, and have done not a little to convert it into a tasteful home. The invention has proved all that Mr. Cameron hoped for it. It has been widely introduced, and Herbert realizes as much from his own half as Mr. Cameron agreed to pay for that which he purchased. So his father's invention has proved to be Herbert Carter's most valuable legacy."

—From *Herbert Carter's Legacy* by Horatio Alger, 1875

36. Which of the following best summarizes the main idea of the excerpt?

(A) Reform was needed in American industry.

(B) Industrialization was of value to all Americans.

(C) The American Dream was attainable by only a few.

(D) Through hard work, anyone could become a success.

37. Which of the following groups would most strongly disagree with the previous excerpt?

(A) Social Darwinists

(B) Labor union members

(C) Factory owners

(D) City dwellers

38. Which of the following historical ideals explains the core of the passage and others like it?

(A) The Puritan work ethic

(B) The ideals of Republican Motherhood

(C) The philosophy behind Jeffersonian democracy

(D) Jacksonian democracy

GO ON TO THE NEXT PAGE

Questions 39–42 refer to the following image.

Joseph Keppler, "The Bosses of the Senate," political cartoon, *Puck*, January 23, 1889

39. The main point of this political cartoon most directly reflects which of the following ideas?

(A) The Social Gospel, a Protestant intellectual movement to help the plight of the poor at the turn of the 20th century

(B) Progressivism, from 1900 to 1924

(C) Populism, a pro-agricultural political movement, from 1890 to 1896

(D) Social Darwinism, a belief that only the fittest would survive in business, from the 1870s and 1880s

40. The ideas expressed by the artist in the political cartoon illustrate which of the following issues of the Industrial Revolution?

(A) Labor unions had too much influence in the government.

(B) The U.S. Senate was able to pass legislation to promote fair business practices.

(C) The belief that monopolies controlled the U.S. Senate.

(D) The economy was producing an equitable society.

GO ON TO THE NEXT PAGE

41. Which of the following ideas developed and became prominent in 20th-century American politics based on the issues expressed in the cartoon?

    (A) New Deal ideas for redistribution of wealth

    (B) Progressive ideas to break up monopolies

    (C) Populist ideas calling for the direct election of Congress

    (D) Great Society voting rights legislation

42. Which of the following 20th-century events most closely parallels the events in the cartoon?

    (A) New Deal legislation to control big business authority in Congress

    (B) The *laissez-faire* attitude of 1920s politics

    (C) Post–World War I to World War II business development

    (D) The government's reaction to the lack of environmental regulation in the 1970s

Questions 43–45 refer to the following image.

Darling, "There Are Moments When Married Life Seems Quite Endurable Even to a Man Who Thinks He's Henpecked," cartoon, *New York Tribune*, 1919

43. Which of the following statements on labor is most closely related to the views expressed in this cartoon?

    (A) "Reds," along with labor, were attempting to take control of the United States.

    (B) U.S. labor was an instrument to protect democracy from "Red" influence.

    (C) It was feared that U.S. labor was in danger of being influenced by "Reds."

    (D) U.S. labor and capitalism were strong enough to defeat the "Reds" and their threat to America.

44. Which of the following 19th-century events created American fear of anarchists and socialists?

    (A) The apparent lawlessness of Ku Klux Klan dominance in parts of the unreconstructed South

    (B) The resulting court case from the Haymarket Square Riot in Chicago

    (C) The events leading to the Homestead Steel Strike in Pittsburgh, Pennsylvania

    (D) Jacob Coxey's "March on Washington" as a protest to the Panic of 1893

45. Which of the following international events is considered to have had the most influence in creating a fear of "Reds" in the United States during the first quarter of the 20th century?

    (A) Worldwide Great Depression

    (B) The inconclusive ending to World War I

    (C) The emergence of dictatorships in Europe

    (D) The Russian Revolution

GO ON TO THE NEXT PAGE

Questions 46–48 refer to the following image.

Courtesy of the Lyndon B. Johnson Library

46. Which of the following statements is most accurate, based on this photograph taken in the 1970s?

(A) For the first time, a large number of American youth protested a political matter.

(B) American youth had always voiced their opinion about major social and political issues.

(C) The youth of America were influenced by other groups that had opposed American involvement in the Vietnam War.

(D) Youth protest against the Vietnam War was widespread but did not influence political policy regarding the war.

47. Which event expressed the sentiments of the photograph and had the most substantial impact on American politics in the late 1960s?

(A) The riots across America after the assassination of Martin Luther King, Jr.

(B) The antiwar backlash after the assassination of Robert F. Kennedy

(C) The violent radical youth-group-led protests at the 1968 Democratic Party Convention in Chicago

(D) The Woodstock Music Festival that had a theme of peace

48. Which of the following forms of pop culture evolved most during the 1960s and 1970s as a result of the events surrounding the photograph?

(A) Fictional literature aimed at young adults focused more on social justice.

(B) The visual arts became more oriented toward social causes.

(C) Television programming became more focused on youth culture.

(D) Popular music became more focused on antiwar and social themes.

GO ON TO THE NEXT PAGE

Questions 49 and 50 refer to the following passage.

"The conditions which brought us to this point are well known. Two decades of low productivity and stagnant wages; persistent unemployment . . . years of huge government deficits . . . exploding health care costs . . . educational and job training opportunities inadequate to the demands of a high wage, high growth economy. For too long we drifted . . . paralyzed by special interest groups, partisan bickering and the sheer complexity of our problems.

I know we can do better . . . . If we have the vision, the will and the heart to make the changes we must, we will enter the 21st century . . . having secured the American dream for ourselves and future generations."

—President Bill Clinton, State of the Union Address, February 17, 1993

49. According to the excerpt, which of the following events most impacted the United States during the 1990s?

(A) Labor issues were causing massive unemployment.

(B) America was facing an economic recession.

(C) Record numbers of high-wage jobs were being exported.

(D) America was entering a new era of bipartisan cooperation.

50. Which 21st-century issue was not a major concern at the time this speech was given?

(A) The advent of the Internet and social media

(B) With dramatic advancements in technology, the loss of jobs for many Americans

(C) A war on terrorism

(D) The collapse of the Soviet empire and concerns about the Cold War

Questions 51–55 refer to the following cartoon.

51. Based on the image and its title, which of the following best describes the sentiments of the cartoon above?

(A) hateful

(B) sarcastic

(C) critical

(D) serious

52. Which of the following groups would have most strongly appreciated the cartoon above?

(A) Shipbuilders who hired women

(B) Armed forces generals

(C) Women who had joined the workforce

(D) Child psychologists

GO ON TO THE NEXT PAGE

53. The ideas expressed in the cartoon above most clearly show which of the following?

(A) The belief that women had limitations

(B) The training needed to "retool" for wartime

(C) The growing need for childcare in American society

(D) The shifting roles of women in American society

54. The ideas expressed in the cartoon above most clearly show the influence of which the following prior events?

(A) The ratification of the Nineteenth Amendment

(B) The women's rights movement of the 19th century

(C) The expansion of factories in the 19th century

(D) The growth of trade unions in the 19th century

55. Though some "Rosie the Riveters" left their jobs to return to homemaking following World War II, the number of U.S. women who worked outside the home rose steadily during the 1950s and 1960s. Based on this fact, which of the following conclusions can be drawn?

(A) The "Rosie the Riveters" could not sustain their roles as breadwinners without the presence of childcare.

(B) The role of "Rosie the Riveters" in the war effort helped lead to the expansion of jobs for women.

(C) Women realized that obtaining a college degree was necessary in order to improve their status in the workplace.

(D) Women helped the U.S. defeat the enemy.

IF YOU FINISH BEFORE TIME IS CALLED, YOU MAY CHECK YOUR WORK ON THIS SECTION ONLY. DO NOT TURN TO ANY OTHER SECTION IN THE TEST.

STOP

Part B: Short-Answer Questions

Time: 50 Minutes
4 Questions

1. The exchange of goods in the Atlantic World altered the environment of North America and affected interactions among various groups.

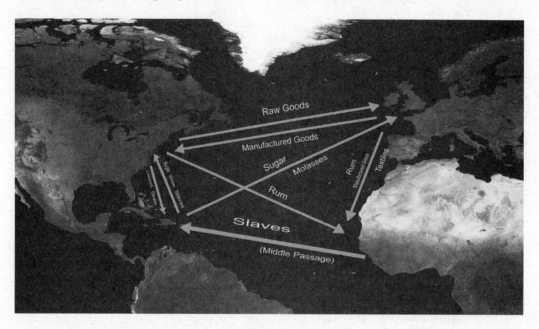

Use the image and your knowledge of United States history to answer parts A, B, and C.

(A) Select one group from the Atlantic World and briefly explain how that group was impacted by this exchange of goods.

(B) Select a second group from the Atlantic World and briefly explain how that group was impacted by this exchange of goods.

(C) Briefly discuss how the two groups used in parts A and B were changed because of the interaction that occurred during this exchange.

GO ON TO THE NEXT PAGE

2. "Here was a population, low-class and mostly foreign, hanging always on the verge of starvation, and dependent for its opportunities of life upon the whim of men every bit as brutal and unscrupulous as the old-time slave drivers; under such circumstances immorality was exactly as inevitable, and as prevalent, as it was under the system of chattel slavery. Things that were quite unspeakable went on there in the packing houses all the time, and were taken for granted by everybody; only they did not show, as in the old slavery times, because there was no difference in color between master and slave."

—From *The Jungle* by Upton Sinclair, 1906

Use the quote to address all three parts of the following question:

(A) Briefly explain the main point of the passage.

(B) Briefly explain how the passage reflects the Progressive Era.

(C) Identify and briefly explain one political impact the situation described and others similar to it had on American society.

3. **Quote 1:**

"But what of the negro? Have we solved the problem he presents or progressed in honor and equity toward solution? . . . No section shows a more prosperous laboring population than the negroes of the South, none in fuller sympathy with the employing and land-owning class. He shares our school fund, has the fullest protection of our laws and the friendship of our people . . . . Our future, our very existence depends upon our working out this problem in full and exact justice. We understand that when Lincoln signed the emancipation proclamation, your victory was assured, for he then committed you to the cause of human liberty, against which the arms of man cannot prevail—while those of our statesmen who trusted to make slavery the corner-stone of the Confederacy doomed us to defeat as far as they could . . . ."

—Henry Grady in his address to "Sell the New South" before The New England Club of New York City, 1886

Quote 2:

"In every expression of every line where the Negro is mentioned the old spirit of Negro hatred is manifest. The beautifully phrased compliments so charmingly paid the North are but a disguise to conceal the hand which one strove to stab it. That hand still holds the knife, kept bright and keen by disappointed hopes of twenty years and more . . .

In Georgia . . . the Negro's real wealth is $20 million. Its population of Negroes is 752,132. Twenty millions of dollars divided among that number will give each person $27.58 . . . In those 15 (other) states (of the South) the Negro has . . . amassed a fortune of $1.00 per year (since the end of the Civil War)."

—Joshua A. Brockett in "Response to Mr. Grady," 1890

Use these quotes to answer all three parts of the following question:

(A) Briefly explain the main idea made by Henry Grady in Quote 1.

(B) Briefly explain the main idea made by Joshua A. Brockett in Quote 2.

(C) Provide one piece of factual evidence from the post-Reconstruction time period that could support the argument of one of the two quotes.

GO ON TO THE NEXT PAGE ⇨

4. **Quote 1:**

"The world must be made safe for democracy. Its peace must be planted upon the tested foundations of political liberty. We have no selfish ends to serve. We desire no conquest, no dominion. We seek no indemnities for ourselves, no material compensation for the sacrifices we shall freely make. We are but one of the champions of the rights of mankind. We shall be satisfied when those rights have been made as secure as the faith and the freedom of nations can make them."

—Woodrow Wilson, Declaration of War speech, April 2, 1917

Quote 2:

"Let us say to the democracies: 'We Americans are vitally concerned in your defense of freedom. We are putting forth our energies, our resources, and our organizing powers to give you the strength to regain and maintain a free world. We shall send you in ever-increasing numbers, ships, planes, tanks, guns. That is our purpose and our pledge.'

In fulfillment of this purpose we will not be intimidated by the threats of dictators that they will regard as a breach of international law or as an act of war our aid to the democracies which dare to resist their aggression. Such aid—Such aid is not an act of war, even if a dictator should unilaterally proclaim it so to be."

—Franklin Delano Roosevelt, The Four Freedoms, January 6, 1941

Use these quotes to answer all three parts of the following question:

(A) Briefly explain the motivation for Woodrow Wilson's statement in Quote 1.

(B) Briefly explain the motivation for Franklin Delano Roosevelt's statement in Quote 2.

(C) Select a third 20th-century conflict in which the United States took part, and briefly explain the motivations for American involvement. Compare that motivation to one of the two conflicts alluded to in the previous quotes.

Section II

Part A: Document-Based Question

Time: 55 Minutes
1 Question

Directions: Question 1 is based on the accompanying documents. The documents have been edited for the purpose of this exercise. You are advised to spend 15 minutes planning and 40 minutes writing your answer. Write your responses on the lined pages that follow the questions.

1. Analyze the origins of the two-party system and how the philosophy of the Federalists and Democratic-Republicans developed and changed; focus your answer on the time period between 1791 and 1833.

DOCUMENT 1

"It is conceded that implied powers are to be considered as delegated equally with express ones. Then it follows, that as a power of erecting a corporation may as well be implied as any other thing, it may as well be employed as an instrument or mean of carrying into execution any of the specified powers, as any other instrument or mean whatever. The only question must be in this, as in every other case, whether the mean to be employed or in this instance, the corporation to be erected, has a natural relation to any of the acknowledged objects or lawful ends of the government. Thus a corporation may not be erected by Congress for superintending the police of the city of Philadelphia, because they are not authorized to regulate the police of that city. But one may be erected in relation to the collection of taxes, or to the trade with foreign countries, or to the trade between the States, or with the Indian tribes; because it is the province of the federal government to regulate those objects, and because it is incident to a general sovereign or legislative power to regulate a thing, to employ all the means which relate to its regulation to the best and greatest advantage."

Alexander Hamilton on the Constitutionality of the U.S. Bank, 1791

DOCUMENT 2

"I consider the foundation of the Constitution as laid on this ground: That "all powers not delegated to the United States, by the Constitution, nor prohibited by it to the States, are reserved to the States or to the people." To take a single step beyond the boundaries thus specially drawn around the powers of Congress, is to take possession of a boundless field of power, no longer susceptible of any definition.

The incorporation of a bank, and the powers assumed by this bill, have not, in my opinion, been delegated to the United States, by the Constitution."

Thomas Jefferson's Opinion on the Constitutionality of the U.S. Bank, 1791

GO ON TO THE NEXT PAGE

DOCUMENT 3

"But every difference of opinion is not a difference of principle. We have called by different names brethren of the same principle. We are all Republicans, we are all Federalists. If there be any among us who would wish to dissolve this Union or to change its republican form, let them stand undisturbed as monuments of the safety with which error of opinion may be tolerated where reason is left free to combat it."

Thomas Jefferson, First Inaugural Address, March 4, 1801

DOCUMENT 4

Louisiana Purchase, 1803

Source: National Atlas of the United States

GO ON TO THE NEXT PAGE

DOCUMENT 5

"Resolved, That the following amendments of the constitution of the United States be recommended to the states represented as aforesaid, to be proposed by them for adoption by the state legislatures, and in such cases as may be deemed expedient by a convention chosen by the people of each state . . .

Second. No new state shall be admitted into the Union by Congress, in virtue of the power granted by the constitution, without the concurrence of two thirds of both houses . . .

Fourth. Congress shall not have power, without the concurrence of two thirds of both houses, to interdict the commercial intercourse between the United States and any foreign nation or the dependencies thereof.

Fifth. Congress shall not make or declare war, or authorize acts of hostility against any foreign nation, without the concurrence of two thirds of both houses, except such acts of hostility be in defence of the territories of the United States when actually invaded . . . "

Excerpted from the Report and Resolutions of the Hartford Convention, January 5, 1815

DOCUMENT 6

"The bill 'to modify and continue' the act entitled 'An act to incorporate the subscribers to the Bank of the United States' was presented to me on the 4th July instant. Having considered it with that solemn regard to the principles of the Constitution . . . and come to the conclusion that it ought not to become a law . . .

A bank of the United States is in many respects convenient for the Government and useful to the people. Entertaining this opinion, and deeply impressed with the belief that some of the powers and privileges possessed by the existing bank are unauthorized by the Constitution, subversive of the rights of the States, and dangerous to the liberties of the people, I felt it my duty at an early period of my Administration to call the attention of Congress to the practicability of organizing an institution combining all its advantages and obviating these objections. I sincerely regret that in the act before me I can perceive none of those modifications of the bank charter which are necessary, in my opinion, to make it compatible with justice, with sound policy, or with the Constitution of our country."

Andrew Jackson, Veto Message of the U.S. Bank, July 10, 1832

GO ON TO THE NEXT PAGE

DOCUMENT 7

"King Andrew," 1832 political cartoon
Source: http://apush-xl.com/Parties.html

IF YOU FINISH BEFORE TIME IS CALLED, YOU MAY CHECK YOUR WORK ON THIS SECTION ONLY. DO NOT TURN TO ANY OTHER SECTION IN THE TEST.

STOP

Part B: Long Essay Question

Time: 35 Minutes
1 Question

Directions: Choose ONE question from this part. You are advised to spend five minutes planning and 30 minutes writing your answer.

1. Analyze the impact the Market Revolution had on internal migration during the first half of the 19th century and the effect this migration had on the United States as a whole.

2. Analyze the cause and effect of the Great Migration of African Americans from 1890 through 1930 and its social and economic impact on the development of 20th-century America.

IF YOU FINISH BEFORE TIME IS CALLED, YOU MAY CHECK YOUR WORK ON THIS SECTION ONLY. DO NOT TURN TO ANY OTHER SECTION IN THE TEST.

STOP

PRACTICE TEST 1 ANSWER KEY

1.	B	15.	B	29.	C	43.	C
2.	A	16.	C	30.	B	44.	B
3.	D	17.	D	31.	D	45.	D
4.	C	18.	D	32.	B	46.	A
5.	D	19.	C	33.	B	47.	C
6.	B	20.	D	34.	D	48.	D
7.	C	21.	C	35.	C	49.	B
8.	B	22.	C	36.	D	50.	C
9.	A	23.	C	37.	B	51.	B
10.	B	24.	A	38.	A	52.	C
11.	A	25.	C	39.	D	53.	D
12.	D	26.	C	40.	C	54.	B
13.	A	27.	C	41.	B	55.	B
14.	A	28.	B	42.	B		

ANSWERS AND EXPLANATIONS

SECTION I

PART A: MULTIPLE-CHOICE ANSWERS

1. B

Although it is not possible to know exactly how many American Indians died due to pandemic diseases like smallpox, it is estimated that anywhere between 50 and 90 percent of the number of persons living in the Western Hemisphere perished at the time of European "discovery."

2. A

To maintain constant productivity, the Spanish, and later the English, needed to have thousands of slaves work the sugar plantations for up to 14 hours per day. The difficult and tedious labor led to a high mortality rate, which in turn required a continuous flow of slave labor into the Caribbean from Africa.

3. D

Corn and (more significantly) potatoes were imported to Europe as easy-to-grow crops. Countries with large numbers of poor, such as Ireland, the German states, Sweden, and France, grew in population as more people were healthier and lived longer. They therefore produced more children who survived into adulthood; the population in some areas increased by 500 percent.

4. C

The major concept in the Mayflower Compact is the idea that decisions will be made by majority rule like that developed in early New England town meetings (" . . . combine ourselves together into a civill body politick, for our better ordering and preservation, and furtherance of the end aforesaid . . . ").

5. D

The delegates to the Constitutional Convention in the summer of 1787 agreed to abide by majority rule in establishing a new and stronger government of the United States. The rule by majority is a main reason for the establishment of so many compromises in developing the Constitution.

6. B

The English were attempting to make inroads in North America as Spain and France were establishing outposts in their growing economic empires. The English hoped that sending families and forming a set of rules would help in this establishment.

7. C

Between 1650 and 1675, the population of the western portion of Virginia surpassed that of the Tidewater region. Bacon's Rebellion began as Nathaniel Bacon desired to gain political rights, among other demands, for the underrepresented (in the House of Burgesses) western population so that funding for internal improvements and protection from attacks by American Indians could be improved.

8. B

Western Pennsylvania farmers in the 1790s believed they were being unfairly taxed with the new excise tax under Alexander Hamilton's financial plan. They felt that their interests were not proportionately represented in Congress because most congressmen were wealthy and well educated and did not take their local population's interest to heart.

9. A

The royal governor of Virginia, William Berkeley, and the House of Burgesses tended to ignore the requests of the Virginians on the western frontier for protection from raids by the Native Americans and a desire for better transportation routes to the Tidewater region. Also, there was no recognition of political rights of the frontiersmen: By 1670 the population of western Virginia was greater than that of the Tidewater region, yet the Tidewater region had a larger representation in the House of Burgesses.

10. B

The words were written to give Americans cause for alarm that the British were going to prevent Americans from fighting for their rights and all Americans needed to "take up [their] arms and go with speed [their] country to defend."

11. A

Americans began fighting in 1775 for their "rights as Englishmen." In 1776, the Americans began to focus on fighting for independence. Free trade and economic liberty would come with independence but that was not the goal of the Revolution. The removal of despotic royal governors had already begun with the advent of the Committees of Safety, and American political leaders were greatly influenced by the Enlightenment and wished to see those ideas implemented in America.

12. D

Loyalists made up approximately one-third of the colonial population; many took up arms and fought alongside the British against American patriots. Native Americans did help the English, but some assisted the Americans in their fight against Britain; the English did not attack from only the east. There was some fear of slave rebellion, but this fear was not too great. Although America was short on hard currency, the colonial government (Second Continental Congress) did authorize the printing of Continental Dollars, and later in the war Americans were able to get loans from France and Spain.

13. A

The English had passed several restrictive acts targeting the Americans since 1765 (Stamp Act) continuing into the 1770s (Townshend Act, Coercive Acts), and Americans believed their "rights as Englishmen" had been violated and were continuously ignored.

14. A

The Pennsylvania Emancipation Act called for the gradual emancipation of slaves in Pennsylvania toward the end of the American Revolution. Some Americans were beginning to understand the hypocrisy of Americans holding slaves as well as fighting to free themselves from the bondage of Britain.

15. B

The Liberty Party advocated the abolition of slavery. The movement was a political alternative to the radical abolitionist movement that emerged in the 1830s. The Liberty Party believed in outlawing slavery through the legal process. The Locofoco wing of the Democratic Party was associated mainly with the state of New York and was labor-friendly and anti-bank; the Free Soilers were mainly people who wanted to keep slavery and free blacks out of the new territories so that there would not be a lot of competition for jobs from people who would accept lower salaries; the American Party was focused on nativist ideas, and its philosophy transcended regional boundaries.

16. C

After the American Revolution, the Northern states began to outlaw slavery. They believed it hypocritical to have slaves as they themselves had just freed themselves from the bondage of service to Britain.

17. D

According to *Marbury v. Madison*, the U.S. Constitution is "superior to any ordinary act of the legislature." Ultimately, this court case made the U.S. Constitution the supreme law of the land.

18. D

Southern slave owners would have accepted the Supreme Court being able to interpret the U.S. Constitution (as supreme law) as a result of the *Dred Scott* decision of 1857.

19. C

While *Plessy v. Ferguson* established the precedent of "separate but equal" in 1896, the court case *Brown v. Board of Education* overturned that decision by stating "separate" was inherently unequal and ordered the integration of public schools.

20. D

Andrew Jackson vetoed the bill that rechartered the Second Bank of the United States, although in 1819 the Supreme Court established the constitutionality of the bank in the Supreme Court case *McCulloch v. Maryland*. It was Jackson's personal opinion that the bank was unconstitutional.

21. C

In 1819, Missouri applied to join the Union as a slave state. This would have offset the balance between free and slave states, giving the advantage to the slave states. In 1820, Kentucky senator Henry Clay created a compromise that admitted Missouri as a slave state and Maine (part of Massachusetts) as a free state.

22. C

Quakers were the first group in America to openly oppose slavery, especially the spread of slavery. Adding a new slave state was not acceptable to those in the early abolitionist movement.

23. C

The Supreme Court *Dred Scott* decision declared that slaves were property protected by the "due process clause" of the Fifth Amendment, and the decision also declared the Missouri Compromise unconstitutional.

24. A

Several Northern states passed personal liberty laws, which in general did not require state authorities to cooperate in the recapture of runaway slaves. Southern states believed it was their right to recapture "runaway property" and return it to the rightful owner. In 1859, the Supreme Court case *Abelman v. Booth* guaranteed this right.

25. C

In 1852, a series of chapter-length stories was put together and published as *Uncle Tom's Cabin*, which told of the horrendous treatment of slaves in the South in the antebellum years. This novel caused the abolitionist movement to grow rapidly.

26. C

The Stamp Act, passed by British Parliament in 1765, led to a vocal and occasionally violent reaction in the American colonies. Colonists objected to this law raising taxes on Americans that was passed without their consent.

27. C

The Free Soil Party, formed in the late 1840s, did not want to allow slavery to expand to the new territories being created from the Mexican Cession and acquisition of Oregon. Although the Republicans seemed to be accepting the idea of slavery in the South, the party attracted a lot of abolitionists, as there was an understanding that the days of slavery would be limited.

28. B

The Republican Party platform, on the whole, drove the North and South farther apart, creating a stronger regional sense of identity in their residents. The Midwest was not dependent upon slave labor, and although New England factory workers depended on a consistent cotton crop for their jobs, they realized that slave labor was becoming more of a moral issue and began to oppose it more. Though the South and West had a minor economic relationship, the West was more aligned with the North.

29. C

Women's suffragists wanted the right to vote, which was starting to be granted in the western states and territories. Their fight was based on rights granted in the Constitution, just as the equal protection clause would state in the Fourteenth Amendment.

30. B

With the passage of the Fifteenth Amendment, adult male Freedmen were granted the right to vote. As Reconstruction was ending across the South, different white supremacist groups began to intimidate the Freedmen into either voting for Democrats or not voting at all.

31. D

Two major pieces of legislation passed in 1964 and 1965 guaranteed the equal protection clause of the Fourteenth Amendment and the voting rights of the Fifteenth Amendment, giving the federal government the authority to enforce these laws.

32. B

The Civil Rights Acts of 1964 and 1965 codified the integration of society and protected the rights of African Americans to register to vote and actually participate in the electoral process.

33. B

Henry Grady wanted to portray the South as a more egalitarian region than it had been before the Civil War. Although agriculture was still prevalent, most of the economy was based on sharecropping and impoverished Freedman labor.

34. D

The idea of sharecropping and the crop-lien system does not fit in well with the optimistic description of the new South. The "fifty homes" tended to be more like the old shacks that slaves would live in under the plantation system. Sharecroppers were not financially well off compared to other agricultural workers in the post–Civil War years.

35. C

Henry Grady's description of the South would more appropriately fit the description of the South beginning in the 1950s with the development of the Sun Belt and the growth of industrialization and suburbanization in the region.

36. D

The premise behind Horatio Alger's stories was that anyone who worked hard and lived an honest life could become a success and live the American Dream.

37. B

Members of labor unions tended to work long hours for low wages, some for many years, and did not advance or become wealthy.

38. A

The Puritan work ethic of working hard and becoming successful is the main theme of Alger's stories. All of his main characters, as exemplified by Herbert in the passage, were honest and hardworking.

39. D

Social Darwinism was the belief that the strongest and the best in society would be the most successful. During the Industrial Revolution, it was commonly believed that business tycoons who controlled the trusts (and in this political cartoon controlled the U.S. Senate) were the strongest of society.

40. C

The artist promoted the idea that the U.S. Senate was a corrupt body because it was controlled by the monopolists (trusts). There is no evidence that labor unions had any influence in the U.S. Senate; in fact, the opposite was true, and the U.S. Senate passed legislation that helped business owners and big industry grow at the expense of the safety of the workers. American society was far from equitable in the late 19th century.

41. B

The corruption that existed in the U.S. Senate, especially in the late 19th century (due to the influence of trusts), led to the 20th-century Progressive movement demand to break up trusts. This would create fair business practices that would allow small businessmen to survive the power of the giant trusts.

42. B

Although trusts had been broken up by the 1920s, it was believed that the *laissez-faire* attitude of the three main branches of government allowed the development of the economic crisis known as the Great Depression in the 1930s, just as the trusts forced small businessmen out of business and workers to accept low wages and unsafe working conditions in the late 19th century.

43. C

A fear existed in the United States that labor unions were strongly influenced by "Reds," or communists; the recent Russian Revolution and other protests that occurred before the revolution itself were led by labor unions. The point of view of the artist is that while labor may not be happy with capitalism (based upon the "henpecked" comment), it would be more successful with a capitalist economy rather than one based on "Red" ideology.

44. B

The Haymarket Square Riot in Chicago, Illinois (May 4, 1886), led to a celebrated court case. Eight anarchists were arrested (many of whom were not present at the incident) for conspiracy and murder of Chicago policemen who died when an unknown assailant tossed a bomb into a crowd.

45. D

The Russian Revolution created a panic or "Red Scare" in the United States as in the post–World War I years. Many European nations, fearing a communist or socialist takeover, were forcing known anarchists and socialists to leave; many of those individual ended up coming to the United States. Coupled with labor strikes in the United States and mysterious letter bombs being received by prominent Americans, many American citizens feared the nation was heading down the path to revolution.

46. A

For the first time in American history, a large number of American youth took a cause and made it popular. Beginning on college campuses and then spreading to mainstream America, protests against the Vietnam War became more prominent as the war continued.

47. C

Several anti–Vietnam War protests turned into anti–Lyndon Johnson protests. This was especially true at the 1968 Democratic Party National Convention held in Chicago. Although Lyndon B. Johnson withdrew from the presidential race in March 1968, the Vietnam War and the Johnson administration were still the targets of the protesters. A nationwide television audience witnessed the protest as it became very violent.

48. D

As the 1960s and 1970s progressed, music targeted at the youth culture became more prominent in mainstream culture. At the same time, this music began to reflect the antiwar movement (usually through rock and roll and folk music).

49. B

In 1993, the United States was in the middle of an economic recession that had created high unemployment and higher than average inflation.

50. C

A war on terrorism began in the late fall of 2001. The concept of a war against a movement, as opposed to another nation, was not considered in the early 1990s.

51. B

Answer choice B is the best answer. The image depicts two "Rosie the Riverters" with tools in hand, involved in the difficult work of building a ship. At the same time, children surround one of the workers. The image, along with its title, convey a sarcastic sentiment; the women do not have any spare time.

52. C

Answer choice C is the best answer. Women who had joined the workforce during World War II to build ships, planes, weapons, and other necessities of war would have probably appreciated the humorous depiction of a woman doing hard physical work while still tending her children.

53. D

Answer choice D is the best answer. The cartoon clearly reflects the shifting roles of women as new situations and opportunities presented themselves in American society.

54. B

Answer choice B is the best answer. The women's rights movement of the 19th century, led by such figures at Susan B. Anthony, focused attention not only on the lack of voting rights for women but on the need to address the roles of women in society and how they played out in both the home and workplace.

55. B

Answer choice B is the best answer. Based on the information provided, one can conclude that the role of the "Rosie the Riverters," along with other factors, helped lead to the expansion of jobs for women in the decades that followed.

PART B: SHORT-QUESTION RESPONSES

1. (A) Africans were greatly impacted by the exchange of goods in the Atlantic World since they were considered, by the Europeans, to be part of the "goods" to be sold or exchanged. Eventually millions of people were taken from Africa, brought to the New World, and sold as slaves to plantation owners. The Africans' life span was greatly cut short due to harsh working conditions and treatment. However, this practice of kidnapping people and selling them into involuntary servitude became profitable for the Europeans for over three centuries.

    (B) Native Americans were greatly impacted by the exchange in the Atlantic World as they were exposed to disease that wiped out untold millions. Also, as the European settlers moved farther into the wilderness in the Americas, Native Americans found themselves losing their traditional homeland.

    (C) The interaction between Native Americans and Europeans had a continent-wide impact. Perhaps millions of Native Americans were wiped out due to disease and enslavement, while only a portion of Africans were impacted by the slave trade. Only the Africans who were transported to the Western Hemisphere were impacted; most other populations of Africa were not changed at all.

2. (A) Upton Sinclair is explaining that immigrant factory workers during the industrial revolution worked much as slaves did in the South during the antebellum era. The only difference was that race was not a factor in this relationship. The factory owner was the master and the laborer was the slave.

    (B) The ideals behind the Progressive Era included higher salaries and safer working conditions for the factory workers. Upton Sinclair was using his novel, *The Jungle*, to expose the plight of the workers so that society might rise up and demand better for them.

    (C) The passage from *The Jungle* expresses the need for change in society during the Progressive Era. A group of writers known as "muckrakers" exposed the wrongdoings of society and government, hoping to cause change. Laws were passed on the state and national level that gave more democratic power to the people, thus diluting the power of politicians and industrialists. President Theodore Roosevelt promoted his "square deal" for the American people. One major impact of *The Jungle* was the passage of two consumer safety laws: the Pure Food and Drug Act and the Meat Inspection Act—both pieces of legislation were intended to protect citizens who consumed these products.

3. (A) In regard to the Freedmen, Henry Grady stated that the new South has made great progress in bringing African Americans into society opportunity for jobs and a good education. Therefore, the "liberty" created by President Lincoln was very evident in the new South.

(B) Joshua Brockett paints a very different picture of the life of the Freedman by stating that throughout the South the average Freedman has amassed a "fortune" of about $1 per year since the end of the Civil War and civil rights do not seem to be evident.

(C) Possible responses:

The passage of literacy laws and poll taxes in order to be allowed to vote was a violation of the civil rights of African American men, since they were given the right to vote by the Fifteenth Amendment. As a result, as the 19th and early 20th centuries progressed, there was less voter participation from the African American community.

OR

In the Supreme Court civil rights cases of 1883, the court ruled that Congress lacked the constitutional authority to enforce various aspects of the Fourteenth Amendment regarding discrimination by individuals or organizations. This basically legalized discrimination against African Americans across the South when it came to public accommodations, opening up the legalization of Jim Crow Laws.

An alternative view might be:

The passage of the Fourteenth and Fifteenth Amendments to the Constitution granted citizenship to all persons born in the United States except Native Americans, regardless of their former position of servitude. The Fifteenth Amendment granted all adult male citizens the right to vote.

4. (A) President Woodrow Wilson justified his request for the United States to enter "the Great War," or World War I, to "make the world safe for democracy." Although Wilson had tried to keep America neutral, events of recent months forced Wilson's hand.

(B) President Franklin Delano Roosevelt laid out his vision of how the United States could help the democratic allies in their struggle against dictatorships that wanted to crush freedom. Most specifically, FDR was speaking to Great Britain and explaining how the United States could help them without actually declaring war.

(C) [Vietnam]: President Lyndon Baines Johnson asked for unlimited war powers with the passage of the Gulf of Tonkin Resolution as North Vietnamese gunboats allegedly attacked an American naval ship in international waters. LBJ justified his actions by stating that America must stop the spread of communism in Southeast Asia.

[Korea]: President Harry S. Truman requested that the United Nations send troops into the Korean peninsula to stop North Korean aggression against South Korea. Truman was able to convince the United Nations Security Council that North Korea had violated the freedom of the people of South Korea with an unprovoked attack. The majority of UN troops were from the United States.

SECTION II

PART A: DBQ SAMPLE RESPONSE

Although the founding fathers advised against the establishment of "political factions" as the Constitution was going through the ratification process, a split between men in President George Washington's cabinet initiated the move toward the idea of political party. By the end of the first decade, the existence of the United States under its current constitution, a two-party system, had begun. Although these two political entities were steadfast in their initial ideals, both parties had to modify some of their original positions on various issues as they faced the reality of governance.

George Washington assembled some of the best political thinkers of the time in his group of advisers, known as the presidential cabinet. Two of these members, Alexander Hamilton, Secretary of the Treasury, and Thomas Jefferson, Secretary of State, soon found themselves at odds with each other on many facets of the Washington administration. The first schism occurred when Hamilton requested a Bank of the United States be formed to bring order to the American economy and trade, using the "elastic clause" of the Constitution to justify his request (Doc. 1). Thomas Jefferson argued against the Bank as it was not permitted by the Constitution, therefore illegal and a violation of states' rights (Doc. 2). From this debate emerged two interpretations of the Constitution, Hamilton's *loose construction*, where if the Constitution does not deny something, then it is permissible, and Jefferson's *strict construction*, where if the Constitution does not explicitly call for an entity, it cannot exist. These philosophies became the foundation of the first two political parties, as did the philosophy about whether the federal or state government should have more authority. Hamilton was joined by Vice President John Adams leading the Federalists, who avowed a strong central government. Jefferson was joined by protégé James Madison leading the Democrat-Republicans, who believed power rested with the states.

However, as the nation progressed and developed, it became clear that the unwavering views of the two political parties needed to moderate if the country was to grow. Jefferson made the first step toward reconciliation and moderation of his political philosophy with the Federalists by offering an olive branch of sorts in his First Inaugural Address (Doc. 3). Jefferson stated, "We are all Republicans, we are all Federalists," meaning Americans are all in this nation together and together they make the nation great. Jefferson and his party had to further moderate their ideals when the opportunity to purchase the Louisiana Territory from France arose in 1803 (Doc. 4). There was no provision in the Constitution for a president to buy more territory. However, the opportunity may have not remained available for long, and Jefferson changed his own "strict construction" views and doubled the size of the United States.

The United States, against its will, became involved in European affairs as the Napoleonic War was fought, interfering with American shipping and trade. Ultimately, the United States went to war with Great Britain to protect its right to "freedom of the seas." Federalists, who by now were out of power in the executive branch and a minority in the legislative branch, began to protest America's involvement. They formulated a set of demands in Hartford, Connecticut, which would have given more power to the minority party, something they were against in the 1790s (Doc. 5). Thus, by the conclusion of the War of 1812, both parties had moderated their core beliefs to the point that their ideology had almost switched roles. The Democrat-Republicans were more of a party that supported "loose construction" and the Federalists the opposite.

After the election of 1816, the Federalist Party basically ceased to exist, giving the Democrat-Republicans an opportunity to shape the United States in its own image. As the Democrat-Republicans changed, so did the nation as different classes of people were granted suffrage rights, first in the new western states and then in the established states on the Atlantic Coast. These new voters influenced the Democrat-Republican party to eventually give them more attention as the old "aristocracy" of leadership was fading away. In the election of 1828, the Democrat-Republican party split into two factions, the Democrats and the National Republicans. From the Democrats emerged the first "common man" president in Andrew Jackson. Jackson claimed to be ruling from the will of "the People," and from this philosophy he took it upon himself to protect the country from the political and economic abuses of the past. To do this, Jackson vetoed several bills that he believed would harm the nation or violate his principles in the name of the "common man," but he may have vetoed some bills for vindictive reasons. The Maysville Road veto was made because it was an extension of the National Road but "exclusively within the state of Kentucky," so it was a state issue. In reality, Jackson was trying to hurt the political reputation of one of his political rivals, Henry Clay of Kentucky. Jackson also vetoed the National Bank recharter in 1832 (Doc. 6), mainly because of his personal distrust of banks. President Jackson's political enemies labeled him "King Andrew" or "King Veto" because of the unprecedented power he seemed to be wielding (Doc. 7).

The two-party system evolved significantly from 1791 to 1832. The Federalist Party went from an organization that held broad beliefs and a loose interpretation of the Constitution to one that adopted a stricter interpretation and then disappeared. However, the Federalists were reborn in 1828 as the National Republicans, taking on a broader belief that the central government should be more dominant than the state governments. The Democrat-Republicans began as a minority party that believed the Constitution was a clear and strict document to be followed to the letter, until they were in power and their ideology loosened, as did their interpretation of the Constitution. By the time of the re-emergence of the two-party system, the old philosophy of state governments having more authority over its people, in most cases, became prevalent in the Democratic Party.

Overall, this essay is balanced and very thorough, considering there is a 45-minute suggested time limit for writing the DBQ essay. This essay utilizes all seven documents very clearly; the analysis of each document is woven very neatly into the narrative along with excellent use of outside factual support.

This essay has a strong thesis, very clear and relevant, and the context of the question is also very clear. This thesis would earn the 1 point possible for the thesis. The use of factual information is exceptional, and the information is explained very well and is nicely linked to the analytical information. This essay would receive all 4 possible points for the analysis of historical evidence and support. The context of the analysis is very clear, and the reader can tell exactly when the events are taking place in American history. (One point out of 1 is awarded for the context.) The evidence and analysis are all synthesized into a clear and well-developed narration. (One point out of 1 is awarded for synthesis.) The total score for this essay would be a 7 out of 7 possible.

PART B: LONG ESSAY SAMPLE RESPONSES

SAMPLE 1

It was apparent during the War of 1812 versus the British that the Jeffersonian agrarian republic was evolving into a more industrialized nation with factory production of large quantities of war material. Americans realized that to develop as an industrialized country, it had to grow physically as well as develop a strong infrastructure. Overall, a Market Revolution emerged and changed the United States in several capacities, all of which influenced the migration patterns of the American people and developed America as a modern nation by developing a self-sufficient economy.

Initially migration occurred on a regional basis, impacting only local economies yet at the same time laying the groundwork for economic development in the nation. During the 1820s, the Lowell Mills in New England employed young women who left the farms of the region looking for honest work and a good salary. Women worked 10 to 12 hours a day, six days a week, producing cloth, much of it from cotton that was grown on Southern plantations. Cotton was fast becoming the staple crop of the South, due in large part to the invention of the cotton gin by Eli Whitney in 1791. Because the fertility of the land of the plantations was quickly expended by constant cotton growing, many plantation owners migrated westward. There they could develop larger crops on larger plantations, in turn earning a larger profit.

As the economy developed, the Market Revolution became more predominant and migration became more inter-regional. Early 19th-century migration patterns were influenced by the building of a more extensive transportation network through the development of a road and canal system. The National Road linked points east of the Appalachian Mountains to the interior, eventually linking the east coast to St. Louis, Missouri. The Erie Canal literally opened an American network that connected the growing port of New York City with the interior of the nation at the western terminus in Chicago via the Great Lakes system. Americans took advantage of this new "highway" and moved westward along with tons of raw materials and foodstuffs. The water highway quickly made America one of the largest economies in the world.

The factory system in New England gave way to larger factories in growing cities like New York and others on the Great Lakes, all bolstered by protective tariffs and a Second National Bank. As a result, Americans migrated westward, settling west of the Appalachian Mountains in large numbers in developing cities like Pittsburgh, Cincinnati, and Detroit. Therefore, American markets moved deeper into the North American continent, pulled by economic opportunity and transported by new technological developments like the steamboat and the beginnings of a railroad system. With the migration of Americans from east to west, the American economy began to develop as a more self-sufficient entity.

This essay begins with a good setup of the context of the time period and a strong thesis statement that is addressed throughout the essay. The chronological development is very clear, demonstrating a progression in the Market Revolution and illustrating the impact it had on migration in America.

There is ample factual support for the thesis, making the narrative very clear and easy to understand. The information clearly addresses all aspects of the question.

The conclusion is strong and clear. This essay would receive a 6 on the 6-point scale of the Long Essay Question rubric.

SAMPLE 2

One of the most significant internal migrations of modern America was the Great Migration of African Americans from the rural South to the industrialized North. This mass movement changed the dynamics of both North and South and the economic situation of the people who moved, as well as creating a new unifying culture. As with all migrations, either domestic or international, there were "push" and "pull" factors that motivated thousands of people to leave their more traditional homes for a new and unknown location. The most significant of these factors was the potential to take on higher-paying jobs with less discrimination.

In the post-Reconstruction South, African Americans faced much discrimination and continued threats to their safety. Two major employment opportunities for Freedmen in the years following the Civil War were those of sharecropper and tenant farmer. Either way, the Freedmen were always in debt to the landowner or the institution that loaned them the money to produce crops. The Freedmen could never get ahead financially. In parts of the South, if African Americans tried to better themselves or be more aggressive in business, they often faced threats from local vigilante groups. Even though white supremacist organizations were outlawed in the early 1870s, the threat of lynching or property destruction remained a constant. To avoid these problems, many African Americans sought refuge in the industrialized North at the turn of the 20th century.

Around 1890, immigration from Europe began to change from primarily northern and western Europeans to those from the southern and eastern parts of the continent. Being much poorer and less educated, the new immigrants did not have the means to travel much farther than the port where they landed, mainly New York City. This situation often left factories in the Midwest, around Chicago, Detroit, Milwaukee, and Cleveland, for example, in need of more workers. Industrialists began advertising for workers in need of steady salaries in newspapers that had a predominant African American audience. This resulted in a growing number of African Americans leaving behind the trappings and debt of sharecropping for the potential of living in a less threatening environment with a consistent income. This gave rise to a dramatic growth of African-American communities in the upper Midwest region.

As more African Americans arrived in the North, many found that the jobs were not as plentiful as they had been led to believe. Although many African Americans had been attracted by newspapers advertisements, recruiting agents, and by letters from relatives who had preceded them northward, many discovered that jobs were difficult to find and living conditions more crowded than they had ever experienced. At the outbreak of World War I, more jobs were available, but when the war ended in 1919 many African Americans were forced out of their positions to be replaced by whites returning from the war. Tension built in several cities, and this often led to violence between the two races. The most notorious race riot occurred in Chicago in the summer of 1919.

Although there were some opportunities for African Americans, more migrated to the North than there were available jobs. Through the 1920s, job opportunities were not as strong as they were for whites, and at the end of the decade, African Americans were usually the first to lose their jobs. Overall, the Great Migration provided some opportunity for some African Americans; however, most still lived in poverty. A major social impact of the migration of African Americans was the creation of a more positive racial identity within the African-American community. The Harlem Renaissance and its many associated artists began to spread the idea "I am a Negro and beautiful" of Langston Hughes. Also, African-American music and dance began to cross over into the mainstream as jazz and the jitterbug became popular with young white Americans.

The Great Migration, while not such a success economically for African Americans as had been hoped, effected the redistribution of the African American population across the North. With the development of an African American identity, a community was established that would be poised to change the status quo of the United States in the way of economic and civil rights in the coming decades.

Overall, the essay addresses the entire scope of the question with a strong narrative. Although more facts might be desirable, there are enough facts in this analysis to support the points.

The essay is also developed chronologically. Based on the learning objectives and the key concepts, it seems that most essays might be best if they were written in a chronological framework, rather than plugging in a fact whenever it seems to work. This would demonstrate that the student has a stronger command of U.S. history and how events and ideas evolved over time.

This essay would receive a 6 on the 6-point scale for the redesign.

Practice Test 2 Answer Grid

1. Ⓐ Ⓑ Ⓒ Ⓓ
2. Ⓐ Ⓑ Ⓒ Ⓓ
3. Ⓐ Ⓑ Ⓒ Ⓓ
4. Ⓐ Ⓑ Ⓒ Ⓓ
5. Ⓐ Ⓑ Ⓒ Ⓓ
6. Ⓐ Ⓑ Ⓒ Ⓓ
7. Ⓐ Ⓑ Ⓒ Ⓓ
8. Ⓐ Ⓑ Ⓒ Ⓓ
9. Ⓐ Ⓑ Ⓒ Ⓓ
10. Ⓐ Ⓑ Ⓒ Ⓓ
11. Ⓐ Ⓑ Ⓒ Ⓓ
12. Ⓐ Ⓑ Ⓒ Ⓓ
13. Ⓐ Ⓑ Ⓒ Ⓓ
14. Ⓐ Ⓑ Ⓒ Ⓓ

15. Ⓐ Ⓑ Ⓒ Ⓓ
16. Ⓐ Ⓑ Ⓒ Ⓓ
17. Ⓐ Ⓑ Ⓒ Ⓓ
18. Ⓐ Ⓑ Ⓒ Ⓓ
19. Ⓐ Ⓑ Ⓒ Ⓓ
20. Ⓐ Ⓑ Ⓒ Ⓓ
21. Ⓐ Ⓑ Ⓒ Ⓓ
22. Ⓐ Ⓑ Ⓒ Ⓓ
23. Ⓐ Ⓑ Ⓒ Ⓓ
24. Ⓐ Ⓑ Ⓒ Ⓓ
25. Ⓐ Ⓑ Ⓒ Ⓓ
26. Ⓐ Ⓑ Ⓒ Ⓓ
27. Ⓐ Ⓑ Ⓒ Ⓓ
28. Ⓐ Ⓑ Ⓒ Ⓓ

29. Ⓐ Ⓑ Ⓒ Ⓓ
30. Ⓐ Ⓑ Ⓒ Ⓓ
31. Ⓐ Ⓑ Ⓒ Ⓓ
32. Ⓐ Ⓑ Ⓒ Ⓓ
33. Ⓐ Ⓑ Ⓒ Ⓓ
34. Ⓐ Ⓑ Ⓒ Ⓓ
35. Ⓐ Ⓑ Ⓒ Ⓓ
36. Ⓐ Ⓑ Ⓒ Ⓓ
37. Ⓐ Ⓑ Ⓒ Ⓓ
38. Ⓐ Ⓑ Ⓒ Ⓓ
39. Ⓐ Ⓑ Ⓒ Ⓓ
40. Ⓐ Ⓑ Ⓒ Ⓓ
41. Ⓐ Ⓑ Ⓒ Ⓓ
42. Ⓐ Ⓑ Ⓒ Ⓓ

43. Ⓐ Ⓑ Ⓒ Ⓓ
44. Ⓐ Ⓑ Ⓒ Ⓓ
45. Ⓐ Ⓑ Ⓒ Ⓓ
46. Ⓐ Ⓑ Ⓒ Ⓓ
47. Ⓐ Ⓑ Ⓒ Ⓓ
48. Ⓐ Ⓑ Ⓒ Ⓓ
49. Ⓐ Ⓑ Ⓒ Ⓓ
50. Ⓐ Ⓑ Ⓒ Ⓓ
51. Ⓐ Ⓑ Ⓒ Ⓓ
52. Ⓐ Ⓑ Ⓒ Ⓓ
53. Ⓐ Ⓑ Ⓒ Ⓓ
54. Ⓐ Ⓑ Ⓒ Ⓓ
55. Ⓐ Ⓑ Ⓒ Ⓓ

PRACTICE TEST 2

Section I

Part A: Multiple-Choice Questions

Time: 55 Minutes
55 Questions

Directions: Choose the best answer choice for the following questions.

Questions 1–3 refer to the following quotation.

"The common ways mainly employed by the Spaniards who call themselves Christian and who have gone there to extirpate those pitiful nations and wipe them off the earth is by unjustly waging cruel and bloody wars. Then, when they have slain all those who fought for their lives or to escape the tortures they would have to endure, that is to say, when they have slain all the native rulers and young men (since the Spaniards usually spare only the women and children, who are subjected to the hardest and bitterest servitude ever suffered by man or beast), they enslave any survivors. With these infernal methods of tyranny they debase and weaken countless numbers of those pitiful Indian nations."

—Bartolome de Las Casas, *A Brief Description of the Devastation of the Indies* (1542)

1. Which of the following Spanish practices is de Las Casas referring to?

    (A) Asiento system
    (B) Headright system
    (C) *Encomienda* system
    (D) Hacienda system

2. Bartolome de Las Casas is most known for

    (A) speaking out against the atrocities by the Spanish against the native peoples of the Americas
    (B) advocating the conversion of indigenous people to Christianity by allowing Spanish conquistadors to own them and teach them scripture
    (C) suppressing native people in order to gain new land for Spanish Christians wishing to start religious societies in the New World
    (D) starting missions in the New World as sanctuaries for native peoples fleeing persecution by Spanish conquistadors

3. Through his view of the Spanish treatment of native peoples, de Las Casas most likely influenced which of the following?

    (A) Columbian Exchange
    (B) Triangular Trade
    (C) The Black Legend
    (D) Middle Passage

GO ON TO THE NEXT PAGE

Questions 4–6 refer to the following illustration.

4. The "Middle Passage" of Triangular Trade was most known for transporting

   (A) cotton and sugar

   (B) slaves

   (C) manufactured goods

   (D) tobacco, cotton, sugar, and molasses

5. What conclusion can be drawn from the illustration?

   (A) Slaves were sold from Africa to Europe in exchange for manufactured goods.

   (B) Europe depended on manufactured goods to trade for tobacco, cotton, sugar, and molasses.

   (C) European merchants were most likely the transporters of slaves from Africa to the Americas.

   (D) Merchants often exchanged raw materials for African slaves.

6. Triangular trade was part of what colonial economic practice?

   (A) Imperialism

   (B) Mercantilism

   (C) Utopianism

   (D) Unitarianism

GO ON TO THE NEXT PAGE

Questions 7 and 8 refer to the following quotation.

"When Europeans first touched the shores of the Americas, Old World crops such as wheat, barley, rice, and turnips had not traveled west across the Atlantic, and New World crops such as maize, white potatoes, sweet potatoes, and manioc had not traveled east to Europe. In the Americas, there were no horses, cattle, sheep, or goats, all animals of Old World origin. Except for the llama, alpaca, dog, a few fowl, and guinea pig, the New World had no equivalents to the domesticated animals associated with the Old World, nor did it have the pathogens associated with the Old World's dense populations of humans and such associated creatures as chickens, cattle, black rats, and *Aedes egypti* mosquitoes. Among these germs were those that carried smallpox, measles, chickenpox, influenza, malaria, and yellow fever."

—Alfred Crosby, "The Columbian Exchange"

7. Perhaps the most devastating aspect of the Columbian Exchange was

(A) the extinction of animals in the New World by invasive species

(B) the European diseases that decimated indigenous populations in the Americas

(C) the slave trade that became part of the Columbian Exchange between Africa and the New World

(D) the wave of explorers that ensued and began to populate the Americas and push the native peoples out of their homelands

8. Which of the following had a profound effect on the growth of agriculture in the New World?

(A) The introduction of maize, white potatoes, and sweet potatoes to the Americas

(B) The waves of settlers and explorers that began to populate the New World

(C) The horses, cattle, sheep, and goats that came from the Old to New World

(D) The rise of African slavery that originated as part of the Middle Passage

Questions 9 and 10 refer to the following picture.

9. Perhaps the most influential and successful group to convert natives in the New World were the

(A) English Protestants

(B) Catholic Jesuits

(C) Spanish conquistadors

(D) All attempts to convert natives to Christianity failed in the New World.

10. Attempts to convert natives were often coercive and led to violence, which in turn led to what uprising in 1680?

(A) Pontiac's Rebellion

(B) Battle of Acoma

(C) Pueblo Revolt

(D) Bacon's Rebellion

GO ON TO THE NEXT PAGE ⟶

Questions 11–13 refer to the following quote:

"Now the onely way to avoyde this shipwracke and to provide for our posterity is to . . . knitt together in this worke as one man, wee must entertaine each other in brotherly Affeccion, . . . soe shall wee keepe the unitie of the spirit in the bond of peace, the Lord will be our God and delight to dwell among us, as his owne people and will commaund a blessing upon us in all our ways . . . that men shall say of succeeding plantacions: the lord make it like that of New England: for wee must Consider that wee shall be as a Citty upon a Hill, the eies of all people are uppon us; soe that if wee shall deale falsely with our god in this worke wee have undertaken and soe cause him to withdrawe his present help from us, wee shall be made a story and a byword through the world, . . . wee shall shame the faces of many of gods worthy servants, and cause theire prayers to be turned into Cursses upon us till wee be consumed out of the good land whether wee are going."

—John Winthrop, "City upon a Hill" sermon, 1630

11. To what group of people is John Winthrop speaking?

    (A) Pilgrims

    (B) Puritans

    (C) Separatists

    (D) Parliament

12. What city is Winthrop referring to as the "City upon a Hill"?

    (A) Boston

    (B) New York

    (C) Jamestown

    (D) Plymouth

13. Which of the following supports Winthrop's vision for his "Citty upon a Hill"?

    (A) He sought to establish a religious society that was accepting of all peoples and different religious beliefs.

    (B) He wanted to create a city based on purified Anglicanism and devoted to a Protestant work ethic.

    (C) He wanted to establish a religious missionary to convert native peoples to Protestantism to gain favor within the Anglican Church.

    (D) He wanted his community to be a successful economic venture to pay off the joint-stock company that financed his establishment of a new city.

Questions 14 and 15 refer to the following quote.

"If they dare to come out in the open field and defend the gold standard as a good thing, we shall fight them to the uttermost, having behind us the producing masses of the nation and the world. Having behind us the commercial interests and the laboring interests and all the toiling masses, we shall answer their demands for a gold standard by saying to them, you shall not press down upon the brow of labor this crown of thorns. You shall not crucify mankind upon a cross of gold."

—William Jennings Bryan, "Cross of Gold Speech," 1896

GO ON TO THE NEXT PAGE ⇨

14. Which of the following was most likely the result of Bryan's speech?

    (A) It boosted production in the United States to bring them out of the depression of 1893.

    (B) It revived the gold standard in the United States, which had been abandoned since 1873.

    (C) He united the Populist Party with the Democratic Party to run against the Republicans.

    (D) Bryan's speech played no role, as he lost the nomination for president to William McKinley.

15. Which of the following least represents the argument over bimetallism as expressed in Jennings's speech?

    (A) Laborers and farmers tended to support an inflationary money policy through the silver standard.

    (B) Industrialists favored the silver standard because it allowed them to grow their businesses by putting more money in their pockets.

    (C) The use of the gold standard was supported by Republicans and industrialists because it allowed them to control financial policies.

    (D) The use of the silver standard was widely accepted in the southern and western portions of the United States because of its agricultural industry.

Questions 16–18 refer to the following quote.

"Many courageous fellows were unwilling to come out, and fought most desperately through the palisadoes, so as they were scorched and burnt with the very flame, and were deprived of their arms, in regard the fire burnt their very bowstrings, and so perished valiantly. Mercy they did deserve for their valor, could we have had opportunity to have bestowed it. Many were burnt in the fort, both men, women, and children. Others forced out, and came in troops to the Indians, twenty and thirty at a time, which our soldiers received and entertained with the point of the sword. Down fell men, women, and children: those that scaped us, fell into the hands of the Indians, that were in the rear of us; it is reported by themselves, that there were about four hundred souls in this fort, and not above five of them escaped out of our hands. Great and doleful was the bloody sight to the view of young soldiers that never had been in war, to see so many souls lie gasping on the ground so thick in some places, that you could hardly pass along."

—Excerpt from Vol. I. *The Transplanting of Culture: 1607–1650* by Captain John Underhill

16. This account is a detail of what Anglo-Indian conflict?

    (A) King Philip's War

    (B) The Powhatan Wars

    (C) The Pequot War

    (D) Pontiac's Rebellion

17. The main reason the conflict described occurred was most likely because of what reason?

    (A) The Indians had been raiding settlements along the Chesapeake Bay.

    (B) The English were avenging a killed trader and looking for an excuse to remove Indians from valuable land.

    (C) The Indians burned an English fort, which caused Captain Underhill to avenge the fallen colonists.

    (D) The Indians were pro-French and allied themselves to fight with the French against encroaching English settlers.

GO ON TO THE NEXT PAGE

18. Which of the following best characterizes the overall approach of English settlers to New England Indians in the 17th century?

   (A) They often befriended the Indians and wished to assimilate them into their culture.

   (B) The colonists learned to coexist with the natives and created a strong economic relationship.

   (C) The settlers wanted the land the Indians possessed and pursued a policy of conquest against many tribes.

   (D) The English enlisted many of the natives in their armies to fight against the French and Spanish.

Questions 19–21 refer to the following quote.

Such is the Crime which you are to judge. The criminal also must be dragged into the day, what you may see and measure the power by which all this wrong is sustained. From no common source could it proceed. In its perpetration was needed a spirit of vaulting ambition which would hesitate at nothing; a hardihood of purpose insensible to the judgment of mankind; a madness for Slavery, in spite of Constitution, laws, and all the great examples of our history; also consciousness of power such as comes from the habit of power; a combination of energies found only in a hundred arms directed by a hundred eyes; a control of Public Opinion through venal pens and a prostituted press; an ability to subsidize crowds in every vocation of life—the politician with his local importance, the lawyer with his subtle tongue, and even the authority of the judge on the bench—with a familiar use of men in places high and low, so that none, from the President to the lowest border postmaster, should decline to be its tool: all these things, and more, were needed, and they were found in the Slave Power of our Republic.

—"The Crime Against Kansas: The Apologies for the Crime; The True Remedy Delivered to the United States Senate," 19–20 May 1856 by Hon. Charles Sumner

19. What prompted this speech by Charles Sumner to Congress in 1856?

   (A) John Brown's Osawatomie massacre of pro-slavery supporters in Kansas

   (B) The admission of Kansas as a free state

   (C) The Kansas-Nebraska Act, authored by Stephen Douglas

   (D) The ratification of the Lecompton Constitution which secured slavery in Kansas

20. Sumner's incendiary words and condemnations were directed to

   (A) the president

   (B) the people of Kansas

   (C) Southern slave expansionists

   (D) framers of the Constitution

21. Because of his speech in Congress, Sumner was

   (A) dismissed from his Congressional seat

   (B) caned by Preston Brooks in the Congressional chamber

   (C) successful in repealing the Kansas-Nebraska Act

   (D) appointed secretary of state by President Buchanan

GO ON TO THE NEXT PAGE

Questions 22–24 refer to the following illustration.

22. This illustration of a religious revival most likely occurred during which decades in American history?

    (A) 1820 to 1830s

    (B) 1850s to 1860s

    (C) 1900s to 1930s

    (D) 1880s to 1890s

23. This revival occurred during an era of reform known as

    (A) the First Great Awakening

    (B) the Progressive Era

    (C) the Second Great Awakening

    (D) the Industrial Revolution

24. The "camp meeting," in the illustration, was most beneficial to what denominations?

    (A) Catholics, because it helped boost their membership in a dominantly Protest society

    (B) Mormons, because it converted more people to grow their fledgling religion

    (C) Baptists and Methodists, because it stressed the importance of personal conversions rather than predestination

    (D) Southern Protestants, because they were amenable to allowing change into their churches

Questions 25–27 refer to the following illustration.

25. This pro-temperance poster was designed to

    (A) illustrate the success of men involved in the business of distilling

    (B) show the effects of alcohol consumption on a family

    (C) gain support for women's suffrage

    (D) show how prohibition hurt American families

26. The temperance movement of the late 19th century was given most of its support from which region of the country?

    (A) The South

    (B) The Northwest

    (C) The West

    (D) The Midwest

27. Which of the following was not associated with the temperance movement of the late 19th century?

    (A) The Anti-Saloon League

    (B) The National Prohibition Party

    (C) Women's Christian Temperance Union

    (D) Order of the Star-Spangled Banner

GO ON TO THE NEXT PAGE ⟩

Questions 28–30 refer to the following cartoon.

Credit: Berryman, Clifford Kennedy, artist. "The President's Dream of A Successful Hunt," 1907. Prints and Photographs Division, Library of Congress

28. Theodore Roosevelt was a president who

(A) was personally and directly involved with government policies

(B) practiced *laissez-faire* when it came to big business

(C) believed in bringing down all trusts in America

(D) allowed the private business sector to rule over the government

29. When it came to his policies with trusts, Roosevelt

(A) believed that all trusts were evil and needed to be brought down

(B) only accepted trusts that could benefit him politically

(C) believed in regulating good trusts and bringing down those he determined to be too powerful

(D) realized that they were too powerful and gave in to the interests of big business

30. During his presidency, President Roosevelt was responsible for all of the following in regards to private business except the

(A) Elkins Act

(B) Hepburn Act

(C) Meat Inspection Act

(D) Federal Reserve Act

Questions 31–33 refer to the following quote.

"Our greatest primary task is to put people to work. This is no unsolvable problem if we face it wisely and courageously. It can be accomplished in part by direct recruiting by the Government itself, treating the task as we would treat the emergency of a war, but at the same time, through this employment, accomplishing greatly needed projects to stimulate and reorganize the use of our natural resources."

—Excerpt from Franklin Roosevelt's first Inaugural Speech, 1932

31. When Franklin Roosevelt became president in 1932, his most daunting task was

(A) relieving unemployment

(B) uncovering political corruption

(C) controlling big business

(D) regulating trusts

32. Which of the following was not a major goal of the New Deal?

(A) Creating employment through rebuilding America's infrastructure

(B) Regulating and controlling banking policies through government intervention

(C) Expanding America's overseas empire to import more raw materials

(D) Reducing overproduction in the agricultural and industrial sector

GO ON TO THE NEXT PAGE

33. The Supreme Court ruled the Agricultural Adjustment Act unconstitutional on the grounds that

(A) Congress could not control interstate commerce, especially local businesses

(B) Congress could not use taxes to regulate any sector of the economy

(C) the president did not have the authority to authorize tax breaks for farmers

(D) the federal government could not pay to relocate farmers from the Dust Bowl

Questions 34–36 refer to the following quote.

"I stand up here in a more solemn court, to assist in a far greater cause; not to impeach the character of one man, but of a whole people; not to recover the sum of a hundred thousand dollars, but to obtain the liberation of two millions of wretched, degraded beings, who are pining in hopeless bondage—over whose sufferings scarcely an eye weeps, or a heart melts, or a tongue pleads either to God or man. I regret that a better advocate had not been found, to enchain your attention and to warm your blood. Whatever fallacy, however, may appear in the argument, there is no flaw in the indictment; what the speaker lacks, the cause will supply."

—William Lloyd Garrison, address to the American Colonization Society, 1829.

34. Garrison was an outspoken opponent of

(A) immigration restriction

(B) westward expansion

(C) slavery

(D) executive power

35. The goal of the American Colonization Society was to

(A) relocate free blacks to Africa

(B) free slaves in the South through the Underground Railroad

(C) provide education for free blacks after the Civil War

(D) use politics to promote emancipation of slaves

36. The abolitionist movement

(A) became a popular movement in the South that led to many slaves being emancipated by their owners

(B) was generally unpopular throughout the United States prior to the Civil War

(C) gained much support in Congress, which in turn issued gag orders on any pro-slavery laws

(D) accepted the institution of slavery in the South but opposed its expansion west

GO ON TO THE NEXT PAGE

Questions 37–39 refer to the following document.

"The question of the relation which the States and General Government bear to each other is not one of recent origin. From the commencement of our system, it has divided public sentiment. Even in the Convention, while the Constitution was struggling into existence, there were two parties as to what this relation should be, whose different sentiments constituted no small impediment in forming that instrument. After the General Government went into operation, experience soon proved that the question had not terminated with the labors of the Convention. The great struggle that preceded the political revolution of 1801, which brought Mr. Jefferson into power, turned essentially on it; and the doctrines and arguments on both sides were embodied and ably sustained— on the one, in the Virginia and Kentucky Resolutions, and the Report to the Virginia Legislature—and on the other, in the replies of the Legislature of Massachusetts and some of the other States."

—John C. Calhoun, Fort Hill Address, July 26, 1831

37. John C. Calhoun's reference to the Virginia and Kentucky Resolutions embodies his belief of

(A) national supremacy

(B) executive power

(C) states' rights

(D) judicial review

38. Calhoun's sentiments in his Fort Hill Address led to what major crisis in American history?

(A) The Indian Removal Act in which the president declared that he had power over the Supreme Court's rulings

(B) The Nullification Crisis in which South Carolina refuted the Tariff of 1832 and threatened secession

(C) The annexation of Texas by John Tyler, which led to the Mexican War

(D) Nat Turner's slave rebellion in Virginia, which caused the deaths of over 50 whites

39. Calhoun's comment about the "great struggle" was in reference to the

(A) debate over the Supreme Court's ability to review any laws passed by Congress

(B) battle between supporters of states' rights versus those who supported federal power

(C) argument over whether or not slaves would be counted for Congressional representation

(D) War of 1812 between the United States and Great Britain for control of North America

GO ON TO THE NEXT PAGE ⟶

Questions 40–42 refer to the following quote.

"Commotions of this sort, like snow-balls, gather strength as they roll, if there is no opposition in the way to divide and crumble them. Do write me fully, I beseech you, on these matters; not only with respect to facts, but as to opinions of their tendency and issue. I am mortified beyond expression that in the moment of our acknowledged independence we should by our conduct verify the predictions of our transatlantic foe, and render ourselves ridiculous and contemptible in the eyes of all Europe."

—Letter from George Washington to David Humphreys, October 22, 1786

40. The major weakness of the Articles of Confederation, and the one that sparked the "commotion" that Washington addresses, was that Congress could not

   (A) create treaties

   (B) levy taxes

   (C) control the sale of lands

   (D) draft militia soldiers into service

41. Shays's Rebellion occurred in Massachusetts as a result of

   (A) foreclosures on the lands of farmers in Massachusetts

   (B) unfair taxes placed on farmers by Congress

   (C) mandatory enlistment into the militia of Massachusetts

   (D) Indian raids on the frontier

42. Washington's fear, along with many other politicians' fears, of a rebellion sweeping through the nation uncontrollably eventually led to

   (A) a renewed debate over a stronger central government

   (B) amendment of the Articles of Confederation

   (C) emergence of pro-British sentiments through America

   (D) alliances with foreign nations to improve America's military forces

GO ON TO THE NEXT PAGE

Questions 43 and 44 refer to the following illustration.

43. After war broke out in Europe, President Wilson's biggest challenge was

   (A) keeping the United States neutral

   (B) providing arms and ammunitions to the allied powers

   (C) mobilizing troops to invaded Europe

   (D) convincing the American public to support war against the Central Powers

44. Which of the following best describes the reason that American ultimately entered the First World War?

   (A) Americans discovered German saboteurs planning to invade the United States.

   (B) The Germans attempted to convince Canada to invade the United States.

   (C) Germany began to practice unrestricted submarine warfare on the open seas.

   (D) The United States mobilized for warfare to bring itself out of an economic depression.

GO ON TO THE NEXT PAGE

Questions 45–48 refer to the following illustration.

Udo J. Keppler, 1872–1956, artist, courtesy of the Everett Collection

45. Perhaps one of the most powerful trusts of the Gilded Age, as illustrated, was controlled by

(A) William Vanderbilt

(B) John Rockefeller

(C) Andrew Carnegie

(D) William Marcy Tweed

46. The Gilded Age was an economic period known for

(A) strong presidents who controlled the private industry and often regulated it

(B) Congressional laws that disenfranchised trusts in order to give power back to the federal government

(C) an era when big business controlled almost every aspect of government and the American economy

(D) major advancements in workers' rights and their ability to be paid equal wages

47. The Interstate Commerce Act, one of the first anti-trust legislations, had the effect of

(A) allowing railroad owners to ship goods across state lines without inspection

(B) giving the federal government the power to regulate rates of interstate commerce

(C) regulating trusts' abilities to control commerce and rates across state lines

(D) lowering tariffs for certain goods that America needed from foreign countries

GO ON TO THE NEXT PAGE

48. The trusts of the Gilded Age gained their power through all of the following methods except

(A) fairness and equality in the eyes of the government and the courts

(B) eliminating competition through buying them out or bankrupting them

(C) horizontal or vertical integration of competition

(D) infiltration of government to receive favorable treatment for their businesses

Questions 49 and 50 refer to the following illustration.

Credit: Library of Congress, Prints & Photographs Division

49. After the Great War, one of America's greatest internal concerns was

(A) losing its overseas possessions in the Treaty of Versailles

(B) bringing its troops home who were still stationed in Europe

(C) a fear of communism and socialism infiltrating American life and politics

(D) integrating returning soldiers back into the workforce

50. All of the following were causes of the Red Scare except

(A) American soldiers returning from Europe with socialist ideals

(B) the emergence of workers' unions that opposed America's involvement in the Great War

(C) a fear of American socialism after Russia fell to the Bolsheviks

(D) a series of violent strikes which were blamed on anarchists

GO ON TO THE NEXT PAGE

Questions 51–55 refer to the following cartoon.

THE AGE OF BRASS.
or the triumphs of Woman's rights

51. Which of the following best describes the sentiments of the cartoon above?

(A) very respectful

(B) bitterly sarcastic

(C) mildly critical

(D) seriously concerned

52. Which of the following ideas in the cartoon is expressed by the woman to the right, standing with her husband and baby?

(A) concern about reversal of gender roles in the U.S.

(B) concern about the reduced size of families in the U.S.

(C) concern about husbands and wives voting the same way

(D) concern about exposing children to rough elements of society

53. Which of the following groups would be most likely to support the perspective of the cartoon?

(A) early suffragists, such as Elizabeth Cady Stanton and Lucretia Mott

(B) attendees at the World's Anti-Slavery Convention in 1840

(C) leaders in the temperance reform movement

(D) a majority of elected politicians in the U.S.

54. The ideas expressed in the cartoon above directly reflect which of the following continuities in United States history?

(A) Debates about federal vs. states' rights

(B) Debates about access to education

(C) Debates about access to voting rights

(D) Debates about our democratic form of government

GO ON TO THE NEXT PAGE

55. Which of the following issues over the last 20 years most closely parallels the controversy depicted in the cartoon above?

(A) Campaign financing

(B) Immigration reform

(C) Military action following 9/11

(D) Women in the military

Part B: Short-Answer Questions

Time: 50 Minutes
4 Questions

1.

Credit: Clifford Kennedy Berryman, 1869-1949, probably published in the Washington Star.

Use the image and your knowledge of United States history to answer parts A, B, and C.

(A) Describe President Roosevelt's role in this illustration and how it relates to the other figures.

(B) Use ONE element from the image to defend your answer in part A.

(C) Explain how the point of view expressed in part A helped to reform ONE major sector of the economy during the Great Depression.

GO ON TO THE NEXT PAGE

2. United States historians have proposed various events that illustrated a shift in American foreign policy from internal interests to external.

(A) Choose ONE of the events listed below, and explain why your choice best represents the shift in American foreign policy. Provide at least ONE piece of evidence to support your explanation.
   - Spanish-American War (1898)
   - Building the Panama Canal (1901)
   - World War I (1914–1918)

(B) Contrast your choice against ONE of the other options, demonstrating why the other option is not as good as your choice.

(C) Contrast your choice against the option you did NOT choose in Part B, demonstrating why it is not as good as your choice from Part A.

3. **Quote 1:**

"THESE are the times that try men's souls. The summer soldier and the sunshine patriot will, in this crisis, shrink from the service of their country; but he that stands it now, deserves the love and thanks of man and woman. Tyranny, like hell, is not easily conquered; yet we have this consolation with us, that the harder the conflict, the more glorious the triumph. What we obtain too cheap, we esteem too lightly: it is dearness only that gives every thing its value. Heaven knows how to put a proper price upon its goods; and it would be strange indeed if so celestial an article as FREEDOM should not be highly rated."

— *The Crisis* No. I, written December 19, 1776; published December 23, 1776

Quote 2:

"THESE are times that tried men's souls, and they are over—and the greatest and completest revolution the world ever knew, gloriously and happily accomplished. But to pass from the extremes of danger to safety—from the tumult of war to the tranquility of peace, though sweet in contemplation, requires a gradual composure of the senses to receive it. Even calmness has the power of stunning, when it opens too instantly upon us. The long and raging hurricane that should cease in a moment, would leave us in a state rather of wonder than enjoyment; and some moments of recollection must pass, before we could be capable of tasting the felicity of repose. There are but few instances, in which the mind is fitted for sudden transitions: it takes in its pleasures by reflection and comparison and those must have time to act, before the relish for new scenes is complete."

— *The American Crisis: Philadelphia*, April 19, 1783

Based on the quotes above by Thomas Paine, complete the following three tasks related to the question.

(A) Briefly explain the historical context in Passage 1.

(B) Briefly explain the historical context in Passage 2.

(C) Provide ONE piece of evidence from the era of the American Revolution that is not included in the passages, and explain how it supports the interpretation in either passage.

GO ON TO THE NEXT PAGE

4. Historians often contend that World War I had major effects on certain groups in America.

   (A) Choose ONE of the following groups listed, and explain why you believe World War I had an effect on it. It can be a positive or negative effect. Provide at least ONE piece of evidence to support your explanation.

      • Women

      • Immigrants

      • Labor Unions

   (B) Contrast your choice against ONE of the other options, demonstrating why one group was affected differently from the other.

   (C) Contrast your choice in Part A against the option you did not choose in Part B, demonstrating why one group was affected differently from the other.

IF YOU FINISH BEFORE TIME IS CALLED, YOU MAY CHECK YOUR WORK ON THIS SECTION ONLY. DO NOT TURN TO ANY OTHER SECTION IN THE TEST.

STOP

Section II

Part A: Document-Based Question

Time: 55 Minutes
1 Question

Directions: Question 1 is based on the accompanying documents. The documents have been edited for the purpose of this exercise. You are advised to spend 15 minutes planning and 40 minutes writing your answer. Write your responses on the lined pages that follow the questions.

1. Analyze the shift in America from a feeling of reconciliation with the crown to the decision to declare independence from Britain in the period 1765–1776.

DOCUMENT 1

"The members of this Congress, sincerely devoted, with the warmest sentiments of affection and duty to His Majesty's Person and Government, inviolably attached to the present happy establishment of the Protestant succession, and with minds deeply impressed by a sense of the present and impending misfortunes of the British colonies on this continent; having considered as maturely as time will permit the circumstances of the said colonies, esteem it our indispensable duty to make the following declarations of our humble opinion, respecting the most essential rights and liberties of the colonists, and of the grievances under which they labour, by reason of several late Acts of Parliament."

Resolutions of the Stamp Act Congress, 1765

GO ON TO THE NEXT PAGE

DOCUMENT 2

Woodcut of Boston Massacre, Paul Revere, 1770

DOCUMENT 3

Dickinson Letters

"Let these truths be indelibly impressed on our minds—that we cannot be happy without being free—that we cannot be free, without being secure in our property—that *we* cannot be secure in our property, if, without our consent, others may, as by right, take it away— that taxes imposed on us by parliament, do thus take it away—that duties laid for the sole purpose of raising money, are taxes—that attempts to lay such duties should be Instant*ly* and firmly opposed—that this opposition can never be effectual, unless it is the united effort of these provinces—that therefore benevolence of temper towards each other, and unanimity of councils, are essential to the welfare of the whole—and lastly, that for this reason, every man amongst us, who in any manner would encourage either dissension, diffidence, *or* indifference, between these colonies, is an enemy to himself, and to his country . . ."

John Dickinson, Letters from a Farmer in Pennsylvania, Letter 12

GO ON TO THE NEXT PAGE

DOCUMENT 4

Declaration of Rights and Grievances

"To these grievous acts and measures, Americans cannot submit, but in hopes that their fellow subjects in Great-Britain will, on a revision of them, restore us to that state in which both countries found happiness and prosperity, we have for the present only resolved to pursue the following peaceable measures:

1. To enter into a non-importation, non-consumption, and non-exportation agreement or association.

2. To prepare an address to the people of Great-Britain, and a memorial to the inhabitants of British America, &

3. To prepare a loyal address to his Majesty; agreeable to Resolutions already entered into."

Drafted by First Continental Congress on October 14, 1774, and submitted to the King

DOCUMENT 5

"Knowing, to what violent resentments and incurable animosities, civil discords are apt to exasperate and inflame the contending parties, we think ourselves required by indispensable obligations to Almighty God, to your Majesty, to our fellow subjects, and to ourselves, immediately to use all the means in our power not incompatible with our safety, for stopping the further effusion of blood, and for averting the impending calamities that threaten the British Empire."

Excerpt from the Olive Branch Petition, submitted on July 8, 1775

DOCUMENT 6

"Until an independence is declared the continent will feel itself like a man who continues putting off some unpleasant business from day to day, yet knows it must be done, hates to set about it, wishes it over, and is continually haunted with the thoughts of its necessity."

Thomas Paine, *Common Sense*, 1776

GO ON TO THE NEXT PAGE ⇨

DOCUMENT 7

A group of radical, or Patriot, Whigs pulls down a statue of King George III in New York City's Bowling Green in 1776 (William Walcutt, 1854).

IF YOU FINISH BEFORE TIME IS CALLED, YOU MAY CHECK YOUR WORK ON THIS SECTION ONLY. DO NOT TURN TO ANY OTHER SECTION IN THE TEST.

STOP

Part B: Long Essay Question

Time: 35 Minutes
1 Question

Directions: Choose ONE question from this part. You are advised to spend five minutes planning and 30 minutes writing your answer.

1. Some historians argue that Manifest Destiny rekindled sectional tensions and led to the American Civil War that began in 1861. Support, modify, or refute this contention using specific evidence.

2. Some historians that Shays's Rebellion tested the Articles of Confederation, which led to the Constitutional Convention and the call for a stronger central government. Support, modify, or refute this contention using specific evidence.

PRACTICE TEST 2 ANSWER KEY

1.	C	15.	B	29.	C	43.	A
2.	A	16.	C	30.	D	44.	C
3.	C	17.	B	31.	A	45.	B
4.	B	18.	C	32.	C	46.	C
5.	C	19.	C	33.	B	47.	C
6.	B	20.	C	34.	C	48.	A
7.	B	21.	B	35.	A	49.	C
8.	C	22.	A	36.	B	50.	A
9.	B	23.	A	37.	C	51.	B
10.	C	24.	C	38.	B	52.	A
11.	B	25.	B	39.	B	53.	D
12.	A	26.	C	40.	B	54.	C
13.	B	27.	D	41.	A	55.	D
14.	C	28.	A	42.	A		

ANSWERS AND EXPLANATIONS

SECTION I

PART A: MULTIPLE-CHOICE ANSWERS

1. C

The *encomienda* was a system that allowed Spanish colonists to take control of native peoples to convert them. Most of the time, these people were used as slaves and many perished from European diseases.

2. A

De Las Casas was an outspoken opponent of the Spanish treatment of native peoples in the New World. He spoke out mostly against the *encomienda* system.

3. C

The Black Legend started in the 16th century, and was an anti-Spanish historical view that illustrated the Spanish as barbaric. It was created to try and decrease the influence of power of the Spanish empire throughout the world.

4. B

The Middle Passage was infamous for being the route that transported slaves across the Atlantic. Africans were packed in the ships and often chained up for weeks. The mortality rate was extremely high.

5. C

European merchants traveled along the coast of Africa trading goods, which then led them to begin trading for African slaves. Once their holds were full, they traveled across the Atlantic and sold them in the Americas. This slave labor was used in the growing economies of the New World.

6. B

Mercantilism was an economic philosophy practiced by many European countries during colonization. It was the idea that colonies should ship raw materials to their mother country to be used in the manufacture of goods.

7. B

Diseases of the Europeans decimated indigenous populations in the Americas. While technology and other products did lead to new economic opportunities in the New World, diseases led to the deaths of countless native peoples.

8. C

With the introduction of livestock into the New World, farming and agriculture began to thrive in the Americas. The horse also revolutionized warfare, especially among the Plains peoples of the Southwest.

9. B

Catholic Jesuits set out on a mission to convert many native peoples of the Americas. While Spanish conversions often led to cruel treatment of natives, the French Catholics were often the most accepting of native cultures.

10. C

The Pueblo peoples of the American Southwest, mostly New Mexico, were sick of being enslaved and mistreated. Therefore, a major revolt, led by Pope in 1680, led to many Catholic missions being destroyed as the natives revolted against Spanish rule.

11. B

John Winthrop led the first non-separatist Puritans from England in 1630 when he founded the Massachusetts Bay Colony. He sought to create a religious society free from the influences of Europe, as he wanted to purify the Anglican Church in the colonies.

12. A

Boston became the main city in the Massachusetts Bay Colony. Its natural harbors led it to be a hub of trade and maritime activity that benefited the colony.

13. B

Winthrop believed that a religious community based on hard work and piousness could thrive in the colonies. He wanted to practice a purified Anglican religion and build an economy based on community and hard work.

14. C

The Populist movement began to gain momentum in the late 19th century as farmers and laborers were exploited more by industrialists. Bryan's speech against big business and bimetallism helped unite the Democrats with the Populist movement to run against William McKinley in 1896.

15. B

Industrialists favored the gold standard because it allowed them to control the financial policies of the economy. Farmers and lower classes tended to favor the silver standard and inflationary monetary policies because it allowed more money in circulation.

16. C

The Pequot War was an early Anglo-Indian conflict that occurred in Connecticut. It led to the deaths of nearly 400 Pequots, most notably in the Mystic River Massacre in 1637.

17. B

Although the English used the death of a trader as their cause for war, it is generally noted that the Pequot possessed valuable tracts of land along the Mystic River.

18. C

While the English colonists often befriended many native peoples initially, they eventually began to wage war against them. As the overwhelming numbers of English colonists began to flock to the colonies, it only became a matter of time before the Indians were defeated or used as allies in colonial wars.

19. C

The Kansas-Nebraska Act was a scheme created by Illinois senator Stephen Douglas. It was proposed to allow these two territories to vote on slavery based on popular sovereignty, which caused a major uproar in Congress and the United States population.

20. C

Charles Sumner of Pennsylvania directed his words against the slave expansionists, fire-eaters, of the South. He believed in the "slavocracy" of the South in which they sought political power by spreading slavery throughout the entire country.

21. B

Charles Sumner suffered a near-fatal beating at the hands of Preston Brooks for Sumner's remarks against Brooks's uncle, Andrew Butler of South Carolina. Sumner had to travel to England for treatment, but kept his seat and returned to it during Reconstruction, where he became a staunch Radical Republican.

22. A

The Second Great Awakening was a time of religious revivalism and reform throughout the United States. The "camp meetings" occurred throughout the Northeast mostly and were led by such evangelists as Charles Grandison Finney.

23. A

This era of revivalism and reform was known as the Second Great Awakening in which social and religious reform became major aspects of the era. Temperance, penal, and anti-slavery reform became major goals of reformers during this time.

24. C

Baptist and Methodist denominations depended heavily on the personal aspect of the religion, and the idea of personal conversions led to an influx in their membership. Their numbers grew exponentially during this era because of the field revivals of the time.

25. B

During the temperance movement of the late 19th century, many reformers sought to show the effects that alcoholism had on families. This specific poster illustrated the progression of a man "from the first drink to the grave" and the neglect of his wife and child in the process.

26. C

The West was a major target for temperance advocates because of the saloons of the boom-towns. While temperance did appear in other sections of the country, the focus of these reformers became the West through avenues such as the Anti-Saloon League and Carrie Nation.

27. D

The Order of the Star-Spangled Banner was a nativist group that appeared during the mid 19th century as a result of the influx of immigration. They were not generally associated with any type of temperance movement.

28. A

Theodore Roosevelt believed in being a direct activist when it came to the presidency. He was very active and involved in policy making and ensuring that policies were carried out by Congress and other sectors of the government.

29. C

Roosevelt was not a trust buster, he was a trust regulator. He believed that keeping the trusts under control through government policies could serve the American economy better. His approach to most trusts was regulation and using them to serve the economy and government policies together.

30. D

The Elkins, Hepburn, and Meat Inspection Acts were all designed to control and regulate the trusts and protect the consumers during Roosevelt's presidency. The Federal Reserve Act was banking reform that occurred under Woodrow Wilson in 1913.

31. A

Unemployment was the biggest issue facing Roosevelt as president. In 1932, the unemployment rate was approximately 23 percent. Other reforms would come later through other New Deal legislation.

32. C

If anything, Roosevelt retreated from foreign endeavors to focus more on America's internal issues rather than focus on overseas possessions and politics. He did make concessions to lower tariffs to boost international trade, but he also refused to send delegates to the London Conference that was designed to stabilize currency.

33. B

The Agricultural Adjustment Act (AAA) was created to regulate production of crops and livestock, but it came under heavy scrutiny, as it used taxes to coerce farmers and ranchers into minimizing production. It was revised after the Supreme Court declared the first AAA Constitutional, where incentives were used rather than taxes.

34. C

William Lloyd Garrison was an outspoken opponent of slavery, and his newspaper, *The Liberator*, was designed to protest against slavery and promote abolition. He was threatened many times, even as a Bostonian, for his radical views and approach to abolition.

35. A

The American Colonization Society was created to send freed blacks back to Africa on their own accord. The state of Liberia was created with Monrovia as its capital, and the success of the program was minimal due to a lack of funding.

36. B

The abolitionist movement was not a popular movement in the years prior to the Civil War. It was a minority movement and often discouraged in Congress through gag rules and media censorship throughout the country. Some abolitionists, such as

Garrison and the Tappan brothers, almost lost their lives because of their views, and Reverend Elijah Lovejoy was killed by an angry mob for speaking out against slavery.

37. C

The Virginia and Kentucky Resolutions were prompted by Thomas Jefferson and James Madison in response to the Alien and Sedition Acts of 1798. They promoted the idea that a state could nullify a federal law if the law violated their constitutional rights.

38. B

Calhoun's speech led South Carolina to declare the Tariff of 1832 null and void, which led to a secession crisis and a feud between South Carolina and the federal government, most notably, Andrew Jackson. South Carolina embraced the states' rights idea and refuted the tariff for its supposed anti-Southern stipulations. It was only after Henry Clay negotiated a compromise tariff in 1833 that the crisis ended.

39. B

Calhoun, and many of the Southern states, believed that the battle between states' rights and a strong central government was an ongoing battle. This was not the first, nor the last, argument between the two factions over who had the last say, and would not be settled until the Civil War's conclusion in 1865.

40. B

After living in tyranny under Parliament and the king, American politicians were fearful of creating a government that granted too much power to a central authority and lawmaking body. They also did not want to give the government the ability to tax, because of the unfair taxes levied on the colonies by Parliament. This led to states proposing taxes to pay debts, most of which were extremely unfair and aimed at poorer Americans.

41. A

Shays's Rebellion erupted because of farm foreclosures and extreme debt caused by heavy taxes levied by the Massachusetts legislature. Farmers, many of whom were Continental veterans, amassed a force to rebel against unfair taxes but ended before any major violence took place.

42. A

Shays's Rebellion led many politicians to realize the need for a government that could regulate and control aspects that the Articles could not. Because of the fear of losing the freedom they had fought for in the Revolution, many American lawmakers began to promote a stronger government.

43. A

When war erupted in 1914 in Europe, America had to remain neutral as the war spread. The American people and politicians did not want to get involved in a war overseas, but as America became more involved economically with the Allied powers, it led America on a path to war.

44. C

Because America began to trade heavily with England and France, Germany began to practice unrestricted submarine warfare. Although Wilson gave Germany ultimatums, they refused those and sank the Lusitania, attacked American ships, and sent the infamous Zimmerman Telegram. In the end, Wilson felt he had no choice but to get involved in the war.

45. B

J. D. Rockefeller controlled Standard Oil, a company based in Ohio. At its height, the company controlled 95 percent of America's oil production and distribution in the United States. Rockefeller, also known as "Reckafellow," used horizontal integration to control businesses and take control of the industry.

46. C

The Gilded Age was known for weak presidents and powerful "robber barons." These wealthy trusts and industrialists often controlled politics from local, state, and federal offices and were able to find loopholes in legislation to build financial empires. The government gradually began to regulate these trusts, gaining momentum in the Progressive Era in the early 20th century.

47. C

The Interstate Commerce Act, the first major piece of anti-trust regulation in 1886, was weak in the beginning but a step in the right direction. It was designed to regulate railroad and interstate shipping rates to create fairness and eliminate price-gouging and favoritism.

48. A

The trusts were anything but fair and equal in gaining their power. They often destroyed other companies by buying them out or just simply lowering prices to eliminate competition. They used political corruption, integration and consolidation, and bribery.

49. C

Although America had plenty to worry about overseas, the threat of socialism and communism in America emerged during and after the war, especially after the Bolsheviks took control of Russia. People such as Eugene Debs and the IWW also ignited fears that led to widespread xenophobia.

50. A

The soldiers returning from Europe had not been introduced to socialist ideals, and most of the threats came internally. With the Bolshevik revolution, violent strikes were started by anarchists (or at least blamed on them) and workers' unions that opposed the war. The threat was more imminent to American politics.

51. B

Answer B is the best answer. The artist depicts in an unflattering and bitterly sarcastic way two candidates, "Susan Sharp-tongue the Celebrated Man-Tamer" and "Miss Hangman for Sheriff." Other details in the cartoon reinforce the tone of bitter sarcasm.

52. A

Answer A is the best answer. On the right, an angry-looking woman threatens her husband with her fist as he holds the baby and looks scared. This expresses the concern held by some people in the 19th century that women's rights would lead to unwanted role reversal of genders in society.

53. D

Answer D is the best answer. Elected politicians would most likely support the perspective of the cartoon, since their own political futures might be affected by the ability of women to gain the right to vote.

54. C

Answer C is the best answer. This political cartoon most directly reflects the continuing debate over voting rights.

55. D

Answer D is the best answer. Though immigration reform has certain parallels with this controversy in the sense that it represents another change in society that some people fear, the role of women in the military has the most direct parallels to the controversy depicted in the cartoon because it involves women.

PART B: SHORT-QUESTION RESPONSES

1. (A) President Roosevelt believed that his New Deal programs were going to remedy America's problems during the Great Depression. Uncle Sam represented the United States as being sick while FDR represented a doctor, who admits that his medicine may need to be adjusted if America does not get better. Congress represents the caretaker who will be administering the medicine prescribed by FDR.

    (B) In the image, Uncle Sam represents a sickly America who has already been prescribed and taken many "remedies," as seen by the numerous labeled bottles to his right. This symbolizes how fast many of the New Deal programs were pushed through Congress in the First 100 Days. FDR is admitting that these may need to be changed in the event that they do not work.

    (C) One of the areas FDR sought to reform, as seen in the image, was the banking sector, and we can see the FDIC (Federal Deposit Insurance Corporation) as one of the remedies. This was designed to provide insurance to private investments and citizens putting their money back into the banks. When the stock market crashed, many Americans lost their entire savings when the banks crashed. The FDIC is still in place today throughout America's banking system.

2. (A) The Spanish-American War represented a major shift in foreign policy because America became an imperial power when it gained Cuba, the Philippines, and Guam in the Treaty of Paris of 1898. America now had territorial possessions in both hemispheres and began turning its focus to overseas possessions.

    (B) During the Spanish-American War, America was ready for a fight, and yellow journalism played a major role in America's declaration of war. However, America was not interested in joining a European conflict that broke out in 1914. America found reasons to declare war against the Spanish, especially the mistreatment of Cubans by the Spaniards. Yet it took the threat of American lives through unrestricted submarine warfare to goad America into a foreign war.

    (C) The Spanish-American War preceded the building of the Panama Canal and gave the U.S. territorial possessions in both hemispheres. The building of the Panama Canal enabled the U.S. navy to travel much more quickly from the Pacific to the Atlantic oceans, to support the imperialistic shift in foreign policy that came with the Spanish-American War.

3. (A) Given the date the first Crisis was written, America was very unsure of its future in the war. It was very early in the conflict, and it seemed as though nothing could go America's way. Congress could not fulfill the demands of the Continental Army, and many were starving and suffering miserably and not getting paid. Paine also realized that something more had to be defended, which is why he uses FREEDOM as a motivation against British tyranny.

(B) *This Crisis* is written at the conclusion of the war, after the trying times of the Revolution. Paine expresses his excitement of victory and gratitude of the colonists. However, he is cautious about celebrating too soon given the fact that America is a new country and has many challenges ahead, hence his statement about wonder rather than enjoyment.

(C) Paine anticipated that the Patriots were going to suffer major hardships during the war, such as the experience of the Army at Valley Forge during the winter of 1777–1778. He also realized that Congress could not fulfill the needs of the Army during the war, and it would take a mutual belief in freedom from tyranny to unite the colonists and overcome hardships.

4. (A) World War I had a profound effect on the rights and roles of women. Women filled jobs in the factories, war departments, and other important sectors of the economy while the men were off fighting the war; they were essential to the war effort at home. Because of their dedication and contributions, they eventually gained the right to vote with the Nineteenth Amendment. Woodrow Wilson realized that they earned the respect necessary to be granted the right to vote.

(B) Although World War I had a positive effect on the role of women, the war in Europe had a negative effect on immigrants arriving in America. Even during the war, German Americans were often mistreated and their civil liberties denied because of their ethnic ties to Germany. When Russia fell to the Bolsheviks, anti-immigration surged as nativist sentiments once again emerged in America. The Alien Acts were aimed at immigrants, who could be seen as an internal threat. As the 1920s emerged, more restrictions against immigrants would be ushered in by Congress.

(C) World War I had positive effects on unions while it was going on, but government support for unions ended once the war was over. During World War I, union membership skyrocketed and made up a larger percentage of the workforce, as the government needed materials and supplies for the war. However, after World War I, the AFL launched a series of failed strikes that put unions back at their pre-war status.

SECTION II

PART A: DBQ SAMPLE RESPONSES

In 1763, the French were defeated on the North American continent after their surrender at the Treaty of Paris, which left the British in complete control. However, with such a massive acquisition of land, and the debt that the British incurred in a long, bloody war with the French, it was necessary for the British to control their new North American empire and refill their empty coffers. This led Parliament to levy heavy taxes, which strained an already fragile relationship between the colonies and the mother country. With the end of salutary neglect, the British began to reassert their control over the economic policies of the American colonies. It was the emergence of an American identity and the resolve of Parliament to reign over the colonies that ultimately led the colonies to declare themselves independent of Britain.

With all of the debt that the British incurred during the war, their first attempt to raise revenue came with the Sugar Act in 1764, but it was ultimately unsuccessful. This led to the passage of the Stamp Act, which levied taxes on paper goods such as legal documents, licenses, and newspapers. The cry from the colonists became "no taxation without representation." Parliament countered that they "virtually represented" all of their British subjects throughout the empire. This was not what the colonists wished for, and they began to tar and feather tax agents. Eventually, colonists organized the Stamp Act Congress to protest Parliamentary taxes and claim their rights as Englishmen (Doc. 1). At this point, the colonists did not want independence, and they appealed to the king directly. They still believed that the king and Parliament acted separately. John Dickinson, a lawyer and not a farmer, wrote his letters expressing the future fear of British policies interfering with colonial commercial interests, and he even refers to those who would speak against a peaceful union of Britain and the colonies as enemies (Doc. 3). Even as the colonies spoke out against British economic policies, they still remained loyal to the Crown.

As the Stamp Act was repealed and Parliament vowed to tax the colonies in all cases whatsoever through the Declaratory Act, the next round of taxes was the Townshend Acts, which placed taxes on goods such as glass, lead, and other small imported goods. Many of the colonists refused to pay the taxes outright because of principle, and also for the reason that these taxes were earmarked to pay, and in turn control, colonial governors. When Bostonians refused to pay the taxes, British regulars were dispatched to collect these taxes, which in turn led to the Boston Massacre in 1770 in which five colonists were killed (Doc. 2). Even with the bloodshed of Americans on their own soil, the ties between the mother country and Britain were only stretched but not broken. However, the passage of the Tea Act in 1773 consequently led to the Boston Tea Party, which led to tons of tea being dumped in the Boston Harbor as a protest against British control. In response, Britain passed the Coercive Acts against the colonies, which led to widespread protest and an emerging colonial unity against British policies.

In 1774, the First Continental Congress met to discuss their common grievances against Britain. They drafted the *Declaration of Rights and Grievances*, which was an appeal to the king. As noted, they asked for a peaceable solution and listed their demands to King George (Doc. 4). The leaders at this meeting agreed to meet in another year if their grievances were not met, and they felt their plea for the rights of Englishmen was fair. The thought of reconciliation with Britain may have been on the minds of American leaders, but before American leaders could reconvene, the citizens were fed up. After British troops landed in Boston to search for John Hancock and Samuel Adams, both of whom were opponents of the crown and had spread their ideas through the Committees of Correspondence, a fight broke out between the Massachusetts militia and British regulars at Lexington and Concord in 1775. It seemed as though all attempts to settle their differences failed as blood was shed there.

But the Continental Congress pled one last time with the Olive Branch Petition that appealed directly to the king for a resolution without any further bloodshed (Doc 5). However, King George had already declared the colonies in open rebellion. All attempts at reconciliation had failed, and it now seemed that the only option was to fight and declare independence from the Crown. In his famous pamphlet, *Common Sense*, Thomas Paine instilled the idea of independence as he spoke of a country free from tyrants and one that could subsist on its own (Doc. 6). Additionally, Paine convinced much of the American public that the king was as much at fault as Parliament for leading the colonists down the road to revolution. Dickinson made one last effort to convince Congress that it was not the answer, because separating from the Crown would render the colonies weak. However, the thought of independence was already spreading through the colonies, and on July 4, 1776, the colonies declared themselves the United States of America. In the declaration, Thomas Jefferson spoke of numerous attempts at reconciliation but how the British refused to listen and accommodate the needs of the colonies, which in turn led America to separate itself from the mother country. The news of independence made its way through the colonies as more support surfaced against British tyranny. Even a statue that was once raised in honor of King George III in New York was toppled by patriots, melted down, and used to make musket balls to fight the British (Doc. 7).

The end of the French and Indian War marked the beginning of the path to revolution. As the British levied taxes to repay their war debts, the colonies bore the burden of the war. In the beginning, the colonists pled for the rights of Englishmen and tried to reconcile their differences with the Crown. However, the British were unwilling to back down from their policies and further imposed their will on the colonies. Throughout the period of salutary neglect, the colonial economy thrived under the banner of the British flag, but any attempt to stymie this growth was met with resistance. The American colonies expended all efforts to prevent bloodshed, but the emergence of an American identity ultimately shifted from reconciliation to revolution as the colonists sought to determine their own future as a republic rather than a monarchy.

This essay provides a strong thesis that revolves around the British economic policies and the emergence of an American identity as the main cause of the shift from reconciliation to independence. The introduction provides valid background information that illustrates the writer's argument.

This essay is loaded with valid evidence and information that builds a strong argument to support the thesis. The chronology, paired with analysis and development of the thesis, makes this essay easy to read.

This essay would receive a 7 out of 7 possible points on the DBQ rubric.

PART B: LONG ESSAY SAMPLE RESPONSES

SAMPLE 1

Manifest Destiny reached its height in the 1840s as more Americans began flooding into the western United States to claim land and opportunity. With this expansion, an already existing sectional conflict amplified and ultimately led to a point of war between the North and the South. Sectional tensions over western land had already occurred when Missouri applied for statehood as a slave state in 1819, which ended in a compromise that allowed Missouri to become a slave state and Maine to gain statehood as a free state. Another component of the Missouri Compromise was the outlawing of future slavery inside the Louisiana Purchase above the 36°30′ line. However, compromise only forestalled the inevitable as more settlers, both Northern and Southern, began to flood into the frontier lands of the West. Americans have always looked to the West for more land and opportunities, which was a trend that began even during colonial times.

In 1837, Texas fought for independence from Mexico and eventually won its freedom. It remained an independent republic for eight years, partly because the United States was fearful that the acquisition of such a large piece of land would offset the sectional balance in favor of the slave states. It was not until 1845 that President John Tyler, during his lame-duck period, decided to grant Texas statehood. This caused major tensions in the United States as Texas was such a large tract of land, and now it was a slave state. However, the acquisition of Texas caused a war with Mexico that broke out in 1846 and lasted two years. With the Treaty of Guadalupe-Hidalgo, the United States doubled in size and its borders now extended from the Atlantic to the Pacific and from the Rio Grande to Canada. Manifest Destiny had been fulfilled, but the Mexican Cession reignited the sectional tensions to the near point of armed conflict, and would only be resolved by another compromise.

After gold was discovered in 1849 in California, enough settlers reached California to allow it to apply for statehood. California applied for statehood as a free state, which angered many Southerners, who were fearful of a shift in power in the federal government. Once again, Henry Clay tried to alleviate tensions. He authored the Omnibus Bill, better known as the Compromise of 1850. The stipulations of the compromise were that California be admitted as a slave state, Texas be paid for the land it wanted in the New Mexico territory, the slave owners be granted a stricter Fugitive Slave Law, and all western territories would decide on slavery through popular sovereignty. It seemed as though compromise had once again prevented an armed conflict over sectional tensions, but 1854 posed new problems for this uneasy peace.

In 1854, Stephen Douglas proposed the Kansas-Nebraska Act, which would allow these two territories the opportunity to vote on slavery through popular sovereignty. Southern slave owners had never thought of Kansas as a potential slave state because it was north of the 36°30′ line established by the Missouri Compromise. An armed conflict ensued, which became known as Bleeding Kansas, in which pro-slavery and anti-slavery supporters vied for power, leading to much destruction and bloodshed in the process. Eventually, the status of Kansas as a state was tabled, and the sacred Missouri Compromise was nullified. Yet, in 1857, a former slave named Dred Scott sued for his freedom based on the fact that he had resided in free territories with his owner, who had recently died. His case made it to the Supreme Court, and in the conclusion of *Dred Scott v. Sanford*, the Supreme Court declared the Missouri Compromise unconstitutional based on the fact that Congress cannot control the private property of citizens. In the eyes of the law, slaves were considered property, not citizens. This bombshell sparked an uproar in Northern states and was applauded throughout the South because it seemed now that slavery could exist anywhere in the United States, regardless of what Congress or anyone else said.

With compromises over sectional tensions, there eventually was nothing else to compromise as tensions grew out of control. Northern Free Soilers and abolitionists began to gain power in the government as the Republican Party gained strength in the North. They were dead set on preventing the spread of slavery into "free" territories while the Southern expansionists devised ways to spread the peculiar institution, going so far as to look at expanding it into Latin America. With the election of Abraham Lincoln in 1860, a Free Soiler and a Republican, the South had the only excuse it needed to secede, and South Carolina was the first to go. Even the Crittenden Compromise failed to alleviate the tensions; decades of discontent, mistrust, and disagreements over slave and free states finally led the Southern states to secede and declare war on the United States of America. In 1861, a deadly conflict broke out between the Confederate States of America and the United States of America, and a major cause of this was the sectional tensions that grew more pronounced with westward expansion.

This essay begins with some important background information that sets the tone for the rest of the essay. This allows the writer to tie in prior tensions that escalated at a much faster pace through Manifest Destiny. The chronology of the essay is accurate and further supplements the argument that sectional tensions were intensified as Manifest Destiny was fulfilled.

There is clear and specific evidence that supports the thesis, which makes the essay easy to follow and comprehend. The evidence is used to support the thesis rather than to list random facts.

The conclusion is strong and ties the thesis in to the Civil War. This essay would receive a 6 on a 6-point scale of the Long Essay Question rubric.

SAMPLE 2

In 1786, angry farmers in western Massachusetts banded together to fight back against the high taxes and foreclosures initiated by Massachusetts politicians. These taxes were placed on farmers to pay back the debts that the colony incurred during the Revolution, but they were deemed unfair and unjust by many in the state. The Articles of Confederation, the states' first written constitution, was ratified in 1781, and it was designed to be weak. The Continental Congress wanted a decentralized government because of the fact they did not want to trade one oppressive government for another. With the weaknesses of the Articles, it would take a rebellion to save the republic, and Shays's Rebellion ultimately led to a stronger government.

The major weakness of the Articles of Confederation was its inability to levy taxes through the national government. With no source of revenue, it could not raise and pay an army. This stemmed from the uproar against unfair taxes that was a major cause of the American Revolution. This in turn left it up to the states to levy taxes on their own, and many states suffered destruction during the war, and Massachusetts took the brunt of the fighting and British occupation. Therefore, with no central government to regulate or levy taxes, the legislature of Massachusetts began to levy taxes on its citizens, which were so high that many could not afford to pay them. Because of the weaknesses of the Articles, states were left to rebuild their own economy and infrastructure, which in this case, led to a second revolution against unfair taxes.

Farmers in Massachusetts, many of them Revolutionary War veterans, suffered the brunt of state taxes. With the colonial economy in shambles after the war, many sectors of the economy were recovering, and farmers were no exception. Only three years after the war concluded, farmers in western Massachusetts banded together to dispute the unfair taxes, and their original plea was to forestall farm foreclosures and debt arrests. However, the legislature would not budge, and the farmers turned to violence. Although the rebellion was put down before it led to widespread bloodshed and anarchy, it definitely struck fear into the hearts of the Founding Fathers, who feared that what they had fought for during the Revolution would be for naught if something was not done.

With massive debt and the fear of anarchy looming over the heads of Congress, they granted the wishes of Alexander Hamilton to hold the Annapolis Convention in 1786. This meeting was called to inspect the Articles and propose changes to the federal government to save the fledgling republic. The representation was minimal as only five states sent delegates. Consequently, these delegates then used the failure of the convention to convince Congress to call for another convention to amend the Constitution. In 1787, delegates from 12 states (Rhode Island did not send delegates) sent representatives to meet in Philadelphia, Pennsylvania, with strict orders from Congress to revise the Articles.

However, the delegates in Philadelphia decided to scrap the Articles and create a new constitution to protect and secure the future of the republic.

Although America won its independence from the British in 1783, an insurrection in Massachusetts threatened the validation and establishment of the independent nation. With unfair taxes levied on citizens in Massachusetts, the farmers decided to take matters into their own hands and fight back as they had done three years before. Because the Articles could not levy taxes, they could not raise an army to protect its citizens. Both of the limitations stemmed from fears of oppressive governments. In the end, Shays's Rebellion was the main catalyst for the call to create a stronger central government that eventually led to the drafting of a new Constitution that addressed the flaws of the Articles.

This essay begins with a strong thesis that is supported throughout the essay. Although there is no clear-cut evidence that Shays's Rebellion led to the drafting of the Constitution, the writer makes a valid argument that it played a major role.

There is sufficient evidence to support the thesis, which makes the essay clear and easy to understand. The writer provides a narrative approach along with ample inclusion of the role of Shays's Rebellion.

The conclusion is strong and clear. This essay would receive a 5 on a 6-point scale of the Long Essay Question rubric.

Practice Test 3 Answer Grid

1. Ⓐ Ⓑ Ⓒ Ⓓ
2. Ⓐ Ⓑ Ⓒ Ⓓ
3. Ⓐ Ⓑ Ⓒ Ⓓ
4. Ⓐ Ⓑ Ⓒ Ⓓ
5. Ⓐ Ⓑ Ⓒ Ⓓ
6. Ⓐ Ⓑ Ⓒ Ⓓ
7. Ⓐ Ⓑ Ⓒ Ⓓ
8. Ⓐ Ⓑ Ⓒ Ⓓ
9. Ⓐ Ⓑ Ⓒ Ⓓ
10. Ⓐ Ⓑ Ⓒ Ⓓ
11. Ⓐ Ⓑ Ⓒ Ⓓ
12. Ⓐ Ⓑ Ⓒ Ⓓ
13. Ⓐ Ⓑ Ⓒ Ⓓ
14. Ⓐ Ⓑ Ⓒ Ⓓ

15. Ⓐ Ⓑ Ⓒ Ⓓ
16. Ⓐ Ⓑ Ⓒ Ⓓ
17. Ⓐ Ⓑ Ⓒ Ⓓ
18. Ⓐ Ⓑ Ⓒ Ⓓ
19. Ⓐ Ⓑ Ⓒ Ⓓ
20. Ⓐ Ⓑ Ⓒ Ⓓ
21. Ⓐ Ⓑ Ⓒ Ⓓ
22. Ⓐ Ⓑ Ⓒ Ⓓ
23. Ⓐ Ⓑ Ⓒ Ⓓ
24. Ⓐ Ⓑ Ⓒ Ⓓ
25. Ⓐ Ⓑ Ⓒ Ⓓ
26. Ⓐ Ⓑ Ⓒ Ⓓ
27. Ⓐ Ⓑ Ⓒ Ⓓ
28. Ⓐ Ⓑ Ⓒ Ⓓ

29. Ⓐ Ⓑ Ⓒ Ⓓ
30. Ⓐ Ⓑ Ⓒ Ⓓ
31. Ⓐ Ⓑ Ⓒ Ⓓ
32. Ⓐ Ⓑ Ⓒ Ⓓ
33. Ⓐ Ⓑ Ⓒ Ⓓ
34. Ⓐ Ⓑ Ⓒ Ⓓ
35. Ⓐ Ⓑ Ⓒ Ⓓ
36. Ⓐ Ⓑ Ⓒ Ⓓ
37. Ⓐ Ⓑ Ⓒ Ⓓ
38. Ⓐ Ⓑ Ⓒ Ⓓ
39. Ⓐ Ⓑ Ⓒ Ⓓ
40. Ⓐ Ⓑ Ⓒ Ⓓ
41. Ⓐ Ⓑ Ⓒ Ⓓ
42. Ⓐ Ⓑ Ⓒ Ⓓ

43. Ⓐ Ⓑ Ⓒ Ⓓ
44. Ⓐ Ⓑ Ⓒ Ⓓ
45. Ⓐ Ⓑ Ⓒ Ⓓ
46. Ⓐ Ⓑ Ⓒ Ⓓ
47. Ⓐ Ⓑ Ⓒ Ⓓ
48. Ⓐ Ⓑ Ⓒ Ⓓ
49. Ⓐ Ⓑ Ⓒ Ⓓ
50. Ⓐ Ⓑ Ⓒ Ⓓ
51. Ⓐ Ⓑ Ⓒ Ⓓ
52. Ⓐ Ⓑ Ⓒ Ⓓ
53. Ⓐ Ⓑ Ⓒ Ⓓ
54. Ⓐ Ⓑ Ⓒ Ⓓ
55. Ⓐ Ⓑ Ⓒ Ⓓ

PRACTICE TEST 3

Section I

Part A: Multiple-Choice Questions

Time: 55 Minutes
55 Questions

Directions: Choose the best answer choice for the following questions.

Questions 1–3 refer to the following quotation.

"During the sixteenth century, the European colonizers had expected to live as economic parasites on the labor of many Indians, but the epidemics upset their best-laid plans. Left with large tracts of fertile but depopulated lands, the colonists cast about for a new source of cheap and exploitable labor that was less susceptible to disease. Beginning in 1518 to Hispaniola, the colonizers imported growing numbers of slaves from West Africa. Prior to 1820, at least two-thirds of the twelve million emigrants from the Old to the New World were enslaved Africans . . . . Most of the slaves were put to work on tropical or subtropical plantations raising crops—primarily sugar, rice, indigo, tobacco, cotton, and coffee—for the European market."

—Alan Taylor, *American Colonies: The Settling of North America*, 2001

1. Beginning in the 16th century, Spanish colonizers imported increasing numbers of slaves from West Africa for all of the following reasons except

   (A) the native peoples did not make good slaves because most of them died of disease

   (B) they had no other readily available source of labor to work on their plantations

   (C) the number of immigrants from Spain to their colonies remained small

   (D) in the half-century after 1518, European demand for tobacco increased dramatically

2. During the 16th century, the number of people from England and continental Europe who immigrated to Spain's New World colonies and settled there

   (A) grew exponentially with each passing decade

   (B) remained small

   (C) fluctuated wildly due to the frequent wars among the great powers

   (D) never dropped below 10,000 per year

GO ON TO THE NEXT PAGE

3. Prior to 1607,

   (A) Spain remained the dominant colonial power in the New World

   (B) the Portuguese claimed large tracts in the New World, but were unable to retain any of them because they lacked enough soldiers and settlers to hold them

   (C) the English established far more colonies in the New World than other European powers

   (D) the French had already replaced the Spanish as the dominant colonial power in North America

Questions 4–7 refer to the following excerpts from the lyrics of a popular song.

"Well come on Wall Street don't be slow,

Why man this is war go go go,

There's plenty good money to be made,

By supplying the army with the tools of the trade,

Just hope and pray that if they drop the bomb

They drop it on the Vietcong.

And its 1, 2, 3 what are we fighting for?

Don't ask me I don't give a damn,

The next stop is Vietnam . . .

Well come on generals let's move fast,

Your big chance is come at last,

Gotta go out and get those reds,

The only good commie is one that's dead,

And you know that peace can only be won,

When you blow them all to kingdom come"

—Country Joe and the Fish, "I Feel Like I'm Fixin' to Die Rag," 1965

4. Although the song "I Feel Like I'm Fixin' to Die Rag" was written and first performed in 1965, it did not achieve great popularity until several years later, most notably in August 1969, when it was performed twice at the Woodstock Music and Art Fair. An important reason that this song had become much more popular by 1969 was as a result of the

   (A) decline in popularity of folk music

   (B) escalation of the Vietnam War

   (C) increase in popularity of country music

   (D) end of the civil rights movement

5. The sentiments expressed in this song were shared by which of the following groups of Americans in the late 1960s?

   (A) Radical feminists

   (B) Advocates of black power

   (C) Political supporters of President Lyndon Johnson

   (D) Students for a Democratic Society

6. Those Americans in the late 1960s who were strongly offended by the sentiments contained in this song and who expressed their opposition to it most vocally were

   (A) construction workers

   (B) hippies

   (C) yuppies

   (D) CEOs of large corporations

GO ON TO THE NEXT PAGE

7. Young people in the United States in the late 1960s who enjoyed listening to music but did not enjoy listening to songs like "I Feel Like I'm Fixin' to Die Rag" usually preferred to listen to

(A) jazz, such as that performed by Miles Davis

(B) country music, such as "Okie from Muskogee" performed by Merle Haggard

(C) folk music, such as that performed by Pete Seeger

(D) classical music, such as that performed by the Chicago Symphony Orchestra

Questions 8–10 refer to the following cartoon.

1893 political cartoon by Joseph Keppler

8. Which of the following groups would be most likely to oppose the perspective of the cartoon?

(A) Supporters of the immigration laws passed in the 1920s

(B) Members of the Ku Klux Klan

(C) Nativists in support of government actions during the Red Scare

(D) All of the above

9. The 1891 Immigration Act

(A) granted responsibility for immigration to the states

(B) repealed the Chinese Exclusion Act of 1882

(C) created a federal office to supervise the admission or rejection of immigrants at U.S. ports of entry

(D) specifically limited immigration from Latin America

10. The influx of which immigrant groups gave rise to the sentiments in the cartoon?

(A) Immigrants from Northern and Western Europe

(B) Immigrants from Central and South America

(C) Immigrants from East Asia and Central Asia

(D) Immigrants from Southern and Eastern Europe

Questions 11–13 refer to the following quote.

"Act XII. Children got by an Englishman upon a Negro woman shall be bond or free according to the condition of the mother, and if any Christian shall commit fornication with a Negro man or woman, he shall pay double the fines of a former act."

—Virginia statute of 1662

GO ON TO THE NEXT PAGE

11. The provisions of the quoted statute, approved in 1662, indicate that by that time slavery in Virginia

(A) had been abolished

(B) did not exist as yet

(C) was legal and at least some of its defining features had been written into law

(D) existed, but there was no discrimination against African Americans

12. Given the fact it has been estimated that there were fewer than 1,000 African American slaves in all of the North American colonies in 1660, it seems clear that the Virginia statute of 1662

(A) was passed in reaction to the rapid growth of the slave population in the early 1660s

(B) was written to address the status of mixed-race children

(C) banned marriage between the races

(D) made Virginia the first colony to legalize slavery

13. Combined with the Virginia statute of 1662, which of the following had the most negative impact on African American women?

(A) Banning the importation of slaves after 1808

(B) The *Dred Scott v. Sanford* decision

(C) The 1850 Fugitive Slave Act

(D) The 1820 Missouri Compromise

Questions 14–16 refer to the following quotation.

"In 1739 arrived among us from Ireland the Reverend Mr. Whitefield, who had made himself remarkable there as an itinerant preacher. He was at first permitted to preach in some of our churches; but the clergy, taking a dislike to him, soon refused him their pulpits, and he was obliged to preach in the fields. The multitudes of all sects and denominations that attended his sermons were enormous, and it was a matter of speculation to me, who was one of the number, to observe the extraordinary influence of his oratory on his hearers . . . . It was wonderful to see the change soon made in the manners of our inhabitants. From being thoughtless or indifferent about religion, it seemed as if all the world were growing religious . . . ."

—From *The Autobiography of Benjamin Franklin*, begun in 1771 and completed in 1788

14. As Benjamin Franklin has testified, George Whitefield's sermons during his first two religious revival tours of England's North American colonies in 1739 and 1740

(A) were so full of hateful rhetoric that he alienated most of the clergymen who heard him

(B) won so many converts that historians regard his tours as the beginning of the First Great Awakening

(C) nearly caused a rebellion in Puritan New England, where the clergy regarded him as a heretic

(D) helped transfer the intellectual currents of the European Enlightenment to the colonies

15. When Benjamin Franklin notes that "the clergy, taking a dislike to him, soon refused him their pulpits," he is alluding to

(A) the eventual split of many congregations into New Lights and Old Lights

(B) Whitefield's offending of the clergy by refusing to share the money he collected with them

(C) congregations protesting that they would prefer to listen to their own minister's sermons

(D) Whitefield's unwillingness to reimburse the churches for the use of their facilities

GO ON TO THE NEXT PAGE

16. Benjamin Franklin's admiration for the power of Whitefield's oratory and the positive impact that it had on ordinary colonists is especially noteworthy because Franklin

    (A) was so busy with his inventions that he had never before listened to a sermon

    (B) found Whitefield's Loyalist political views objectionable

    (C) greatly admired the colonial clergymen who refused to share their pulpits with Whitefield

    (D) was not a religious individual and did not pay much attention to most preachers

Questions 17–19 refer to the following image.

"The Bloody Massacre," 1770 engraving by Paul Revere

17. The event depicted in this engraving of 1770 entitled "The Bloody Massacre"

    (A) quickly led to the outbreak of war between the British and the American colonists

    (B) had relatively little immediate impact because it coincided with the repeal of four of the five Townshend duties

    (C) was strongly condemned by John Adams, winning him the admiration of the Patriots

    (D) never actually occurred; it was a product of Paul Revere's imagination

18. When John Adams described the victims of the massacre as "a motley rabble of saucy boys, negroes and mulattoes, Irish teagues and outlandish jack tarrs," he was

    (A) implying that one motive behind the disturbance that led to the massacre might have been resentment of British soldiers by those who were competing with them for jobs

    (B) affirming the right of the common people to organize a demonstration against oppressive British policies

    (C) making a plea to his fellow colonists to respect the rights of immigrants and members of racial and ethnic minority groups

    (D) criticizing the British soldiers for firing on a group of poor innocent victims

GO ON TO THE NEXT PAGE

19. In the immediate aftermath of the Boston Massacre, many of the citizens of the city of Boston

    (A) decided to enlist in the British army in order to obtain weapons to defend themselves

    (B) organized the Boston Tea Party

    (C) became more receptive to the pleas of radicals such as Samuel Adams, who saw the need for vigilance in view of signs of increasing British oppression

    (D) looked to George Washington to organize and lead a new colonial military force

Questions 20–23 refer to the following quotation.

"Most of the basic changes which set modern America off from its premodern past were clearly apparent to astute observers of the 1820s and 1830s. Between the first decades of the nineteenth century and the years of Andrew Jackson's presidency, American changed from a traditional society that was slow to accept innovations, to a modern capitalistic state in which people believed that society could be transformed. The mid-1840s, therefore, were well within the modern era."

—Douglas T. Miller, *The Birth of Modern America 1820–1850*

20. Events that had occurred by the mid–1840s that might serve as evidence to support Professor Miller's interpretation include all of the following EXCEPT

    (A) telegraphic messages that carried the news that Henry Clay and James K. Polk had been nominated for the presidency

    (B) the opening of the Boston and Albany Railroad

    (C) transatlantic Cunard steamships arriving regularly in Boston Harbor

    (D) Thomas Edison installing electric lights at the New York Stock Exchange

21. One of the "basic changes" that set modern America off from its premodern past that was clearly apparent by the 1830s was the

    (A) proliferation of large, mechanized textile factories such as those constructed in Lowell, Massachusetts

    (B) building of transcontinental railroads in the North as well as the South

    (C) expansion of the steel industry from Pittsburgh to places such as Birmingham, Alabama

    (D) mass production of the automobile at several locations near Detroit, Michigan

22. To make the argument that the opening of the Erie Canal was one of the important events of the 1820s that helped transform American society, historians such as Professor Miller might point to

    (A) the proliferation of steamships on America's rivers

    (B) the rise of New York City to become America's largest city and busiest port

    (C) large-scale imports of horses to pull the barges along the canal

    (D) the decline of the railroad as the major carrier of goods between East Coast and Midwest cities

GO ON TO THE NEXT PAGE

23. The idea that American politics as well as American society had entered the modern era by the mid-1840s seems plausible when one recognizes that by that time

    (A) all adult white males had the right to vote

    (B) two well-organized political parties had been formed, able to compete with each other in elections in every section of the country

    (C) the Constitution had been amended to provide for the direct election of U.S. senators

    (D) contributions from a small number of large donors was already determining the outcome of most national elections

Questions 24–26 refer to the following quote.

"We want Homesteads; we were promised Homesteads by the government. If It does not carry out the promises Its agents made to us, If the government Having concluded to befriend Its late enemies and to neglect to observe the principles of common faith between Its self and us Its allies In the war you said was over, now takes away from them all right to the soil they stand upon save such as they can get by again working for your late and their all time enemies. If the government does so we are left In a more unpleasant condition than our former. We are at the mercy of those who are combined to prevent us from getting land enough to lay our Fathers bones upon . . . "

—Excerpt from a letter from the Freedmen of Edisto Island, South Carolina to General O.O. Howard, head of the Freedmen's Bureau, in October 1865

24. The Freedmen who petitioned General Howard in October 1865

    (A) had learned that Congress had appropriated money to give away "forty acres and a mule"

    (B) recognized that they needed to obtain land of their own to be truly free

    (C) were trying to avoid having to work in order to earn a living

    (D) were more concerned with gaining the right to vote than with obtaining land

25. The "promises its agents made to us" refers to

    (A) President Lincoln's Emancipation Proclamation

    (B) President Andrew Johnson's plan for Reconstruction

    (C) the Wade-Davis bill, passed by Congress in 1864 but vetoed by President Lincoln

    (D) offers of assistance that the Freedmen had received from agents of the Freedmen's Bureau during the months after the surrender at Appomattox

26. An important reason that the idea that the federal government would make "homesteads" available to the Freedmen seem plausible in 1865 is that

    (A) President Lincoln had promised to do so in the Emancipation Proclamation

    (B) President Johnson promised to do so when he announced his plan for Reconstruction

    (C) Congress had passed and President Lincoln had signed the Homestead Act in 1862

    (D) Congress had authorized the Freedmen's Bureau to give away "forty acres and a mule"

GO ON TO THE NEXT PAGE

Questions 27–29 refer to the following quotation.

"The vision of America as melted into one people prevailed through most of the two centuries of the history of the United States. But the twentieth century has brought forth a new and opposing vision . . . In a nation marked by an even stranger mixture of blood than Crevecoeur had known, his celebrated question is asked once more, with a new passion—and a new answer. Today many Americans disavow the historic goal of 'a new race of man.' . . . A cult of ethnicity has arisen both among non-Anglo whites and among nonwhite minorities to denounce the idea of a melting pot, to challenge the concept of 'one people,' and to protect, promote, and perpetuate separate ethnic and racial communities."

—From Arthur M. Schlesinger, Jr., *The Disuniting of America*, 1991

27. This passage from *The Disuniting of America* represents one of Professor Schlesinger's most important contributions to the so-called "Culture Wars" of the early 1990s, a contribution that emphasizes which issue of the time period?

    (A) Progress made as a nation toward the goal of full equality

    (B) Shortcomings of the capitalist economic system in the United States

    (C) Importance of preserving American identity as an inclusive, unified nation

    (D) Superiority of American conservative ideology

28. The idea that the United States has been a "melting pot," an idea that Professor Schlesinger goes on to clearly disavow, has been increasingly challenged and rejected by other historians as well because

    (A) most racial and ethnic groups have preserved their own identities into the 21st century

    (B) other metaphors, such as that of a "mosaic," appear to be more accurate

    (C) many European Americans continue to discriminate against nonwhite minorities

    (D) All of the above

29. Those contemporaries and historians who agree with Professor Schlesinger that "a cult of ethnicity has arisen both among non-Anglo whites and among nonwhite minorities" might correctly point to which of the following as corroborating evidence?

    (A) Black Power movement of the 1960s

    (B) Feminist movement of the 1960s

    (C) Founding of the Student Non-Violent Coordinating Committee (SNCC)

    (D) Immigration and Nationality Act of 1965 (Hart-Cellar Act)

Questions 30–33 refer to the following quotation.

"Let . . . the bellowing voice of Bessie Smith singing the Blues penetrate the closed ears of the colored near intellectuals until they listen and perhaps understand. Let . . . Rudolph Fisher writing about the streets of Harlem . . . cause the smug Negro middle class . . . to catch a glimmer of their own beauty. We younger Negro artists who create now intend to express our individual dark-skinned selves without fear or shame. If white people are pleased we are glad. If they are not, it doesn't matter. We know we are beautiful. And ugly

GO ON TO THE NEXT PAGE ⇒

too . . . If colored people are pleased we are glad. If they are not, their displeasure doesn't matter either. We build our temples for tomorrow, strong as we know how, and we stand on top of the mountain, free within ourselves."

—Langston Hughes, "The Negro Artist and the Racial Mountain," *The Nation*, 1926

30. What most likely prompted Langston Hughes to write the words in the excerpt?

(A) The racial violence in Chicago and other northern cities in 1919 and the early 1920s

(B) His disagreements with other African American writers and intellectuals concerning the most appropriate way to depict and represent his fellow African Americans

(C) To combat the lurid crime stories published in prominent white newspapers such as *The New York Times* depicting most African Americans as criminals

(D) President Calvin Coolidge's refusal to endorse the civil rights bill that was then being debated in Congress

31. Which of the following were most offended and most critical of the views expressed by Langston Hughes in this essay?

(A) African American intellectuals who sought respectability in the eyes of whites

(B) White Americans who regarded African Americans as members of an inferior race

(C) White Americans, who preferred traditional forms of expression in the arts and literature to innovative approaches

(D) Americans, white and black, who celebrated all of the writers and artists of the Harlem Renaissance

32. Langston Hughes chose the example of "Bessie Smith singing the Blues" primarily because he wished to call attention to

(A) the new technology of phonograph records to record and play songs

(B) leaders of the new feminist movement and their accomplishments

(C) one of the distinctive forms of African American culture represented by such songs

(D) his own talents as a singer and songwriter

33. The sentiments expressed by Langston Hughes in the previous passage were later amplified and popularized in

(A) the 1960s by advocates of Black Power and "Black Is Beautiful"

(B) the 1950s by advocates of U.S. superiority in the Cold War

(C) the 1940s by jazz musicians such as Count Basie and Charlie Parker

(D) the 1930s by Franklin Roosevelt and supporters of a New Deal for African Americans

GO ON TO THE NEXT PAGE

Questions 34–38 refer to the following two tables, which provide statistical data relating to industrialization and urbanization.

Table 1. Percentage Urban

Year	Percentage Urban
1790	5.1
1800	6.1
1810	7.3
1820	7.2
1830	8.8
1840	10.8
1850	15.3
1860	19.8

W. Elliot Brownlee, *Dynamics of Ascent, A History of the American Economy*, second edition (New York: Alfred Knopf, 1979), pp. 127 and 133

Table 2. Shares of Agriculture and Manufacturing in Total Labor Force Participation

Year	Agriculture	Manufacturing
1800	82.6%	Not Available
1810	83.7%	3.2%
1820	79.0%	Not Available
1830	70.7%	Not Available
1840	63.4%	8.8%
1850	54.8%	14.5%
1860	53.2%	13.7%

Paul David, "The Growth of Real Product in the United States Before 1840: New Evidence, Controlled Conjectures," *Journal of Economic History*, Vol. 27, No. 2 (June 1967), p. 196

34. It can be inferred from Tables 1 and 2 that the War of 1812

(A) accelerated the rate of urbanization in the United States

(B) did not lead to any increase in manufacturing in the United States

(C) was followed by an increase in the westward movement

(D) retarded industrialization for more than two decades

35. The increase in textile manufacturing, especially the construction of large factories such as the ones in Lowell, Massachusetts, is most directly reflected in the

(A) large increase in urban percentage between 1840 and 1850

(B) significant increase in the percentage of the labor force engaged in manufacturing by 1840

(C) substantial increase in the percentage of the labor force engaged in manufacturing between 1840 and 1850

(D) large percentage of the labor force engaged in manufacturing by 1860

GO ON TO THE NEXT PAGE

36. The increasing use of steamboats on major rivers in the United States and the boom in canal building that followed the completion of the Erie Canal are best reflected by the

   (A) sustained growth in the urban percentage between 1820 and 1860

   (B) increase in manufacturing between 1840 and 1850

   (C) increase in the urban percentage between 1850 and 1860

   (D) increase in the agricultural labor force between 1800 and 1810

37. The great increase in railroad building in the United States is mostly directly reflected in the

   (A) great increase in the manufacturing workforce between 1840 and 1850

   (B) sharp increase in the urban percentage between 1820 and 1830

   (C) sharp decline of the agricultural labor force between 1830 and 1840

   (D) substantial increase in the urban percentage between 1840 and 1860

38. Which region of the United States benefited most from the industrialization and increase in urbanization reflected in these two tables?

   (A) Old Northwest

   (B) New England

   (C) Southwest

   (D) Southeast

Questions 39–42 refer to the following excerpt from what is popularly known as Washington's Farewell Address.

"One of the expedients of party to acquire influence within particular districts is to misrepresent the opinions and aims of other districts . . . The inhabitants of our Western country have lately had a useful lesson on this head; they have seen, in the negotiation by the Executive, and in the unanimous ratification by the Senate, of the treaty with Spain, . . . decisive proof how unfounded were the suspicions propagated among them of a policy in the General Government and in the Atlantic States unfriendly to their interests in regard to the Mississippi; . . . the . . . two treaties, that with Great Britain, and that with Spain, . . . secure to them everything they could desire, in respect to our foreign relations, towards confirming their prosperity."

—Address of General Washington to the People of the United States, September 19, 1796

39. The excerpt from President George Washington's Farewell Address makes reference to both Jay's Treaty (Treaty of London of 1794) and Pinckney's Treaty (Treaty of San Lorenzo of 1795), in part for the purpose of

   (A) increasing the president's popularity with the American people

   (B) encouraging the development of a stronger national identity

   (C) discrediting criticisms of the president made by Thomas Paine

   (D) discouraging radical New Englanders from seceding from the Union

40. President Washington's references to "the expedients of party" and to "the inhabitants of our Western country" indicate that he feared that

   (A) the Federalist Party might lose seats in Congress in the next election

   (B) people living in the West might form a new political party

   (C) attacks by Native Americans might devastate frontier settlements

   (D) Westerners' regional identity might be exploited for partisan political purposes

GO ON TO THE NEXT PAGE

41. President Washington was aware that, during the previous decade, John Jay, a trusted collaborator and the negotiator of the Treaty of London of 1794, had given "the inhabitants of our Western country cause to suspect that he was "unfriendly to their interests in regard to the Mississippi" when he negotiated the Jay-Gardoqui Treaty in 1786. Therefore, in the previous passage from his Farewell Address, the president was careful to allude to the fact that Pinckney's Treaty

   (A) guaranteed United States navigation rights on the Mississippi

   (B) contained several provisions unfriendly to England

   (C) stopped the Atlantic States from discriminating against Westerners

   (D) protected the United States from the threat of a French invasion

42. The partisan conflict President Washington was alluding to in his Farewell Address was between American supporters of which two competing European powers?

   (A) Britain and France

   (B) Spain and France

   (C) Russia and Japan

   (D) Britain and Russia

Questions 43–45 refer to the following quotation.

" . . . [A]lthough disastrous for American natives, the post-1492 exchange of New and Old World microbes and plants provided a double boon to Europeans. First, they obtained an expanded food supply that permitted their reproduction at an unprecedented rate. Second, they acquired access to fertile and extensive new lands largely emptied of native peoples by the exported diseases. In effect, the post-Columbian exchange depleted people on the American side of the Atlantic while swelling those on the European and African shores. Eventually, the surplus population flowed westward to refill the demographic vacuum created on the American side of the Atlantic world."

—Alan Taylor, *American Colonies. The Settling of North America*, 2001

43. It is important to remember that the "fertile and extensive new lands" that the Spanish, French, Dutch, and English colonized in the 15th, 16th, and 17th centuries had been "largely emptied of native peoples by the exported diseases" because

   (A) most important historical events are caused by climatic and biological changes

   (B) the defeat of the native peoples of the Americas was due largely to their lack of knowledge

   (C) the native peoples failed to prosper despite the fertility of their extensive lands

   (D) European conquest of the native peoples was due primarily to the impact of disease

44. The "expanded food supply" made possible by exporting plants such as maize, cassava (manioc), potatoes, and sweet potatoes from the Americas, which made possible a significant increase in population in both Europe and Africa, paved the way for the largest population flow westward in the 16th, 17th, and 18th centuries. What caused this largest population movement?

   (A) The African slave trade

   (B) Immigration from the British Isles and Western Europe to North America

   (C) Immigration from Spain and Portugal to Central and South America

   (D) Irish immigration to the English colonies of North America

GO ON TO THE NEXT PAGE

45. Another important aspect of the post-Columbian exchange that had a significant impact on the native peoples and their relationship with the European colonizers was the importation into the New World of

   (A) venereal diseases, especially syphilis

   (B) plants such as tomatoes and cabbage

   (C) animals such as horses and sheep that helped the native peoples resist the Europeans

   (D) beavers and other fur-producing animals, which initiated the lucrative fur trade

Questions 46–48 refer to the following political cartoon.

Credit: Coffin, George Yost, "The Kneipp cure up to date, or the Populistic panacea for all political aches and ailments," September 7, 1896. Cartoon Drawings, Prints and Photographs Division, Library of Congress.

46. The political cartoon represents which issue that was controversial during the Gilded Age?

   (A) Currency

   (B) Voting rights

   (C) Tariff

   (D) Women's suffrage

47. Divisions over this issue, and others, would help lead to the formation of which political party?

   (A) American Liberty Party

   (B) Dixiecrat Party

   (C) Whig Party

   (D) People's (Populist) Party

48. People who agreed with the argument for "free silver" would most likely also recommend what other actions?

   (A) The end to "separate but equal" established by *Plessy v. Ferguson*

   (B) A return to a *laissez-faire* economic approach by the federal government

   (C) Laws to limit the power of labor unions

   (D) Laws to increase the power of the federal government's role in the economic system

GO ON TO THE NEXT PAGE ⟩

Questions 49 and 50 refer to the following images.

49. The economic activity of maize cultivation, depicted on the left, most directly relates to which native population?

(A) Societies in the Northeast

(B) Societies in the Northwest

(C) Societies in the Great Plains

(D) Societies in the Southwest

50. The development of a mixed agriculture and hunter-gatherer economy that resulted in more of a permanent village society most directly relates to which native population?

(A) Societies in the Northeast and Southwest

(B) Societies in the Southwest and Great Plains

(C) Societies in the Great Plains and Atlantic Seaboard

(D) Societies in the Northeast and Atlantic Seaboard

GO ON TO THE NEXT PAGE

Questions 51–55 refer to the following image.

51. Based on the sentiments expressed in the image, one can conclude which of the following about the Salem witchcraft trials?

(A) They were religious events.

(B) They were controlled by both men and women.

(C) They were filled with emotion and hysteria.

(D) They were led by an impartial judge.

52. The controversy highlighted in the image above most likely led to

(A) the establishment of U.S. courts of law.

(B) the questioning of the existence of witchcraft.

(C) the belief that witchcraft could not be controlled.

(D) the improved education of young girls.

53. The ideas expressed in the image above most directly reflect which of the following continuities in United States history?

(A) Debates about freedom of religion

(B) Debates about social class

(C) Debates about the rights of individuals

(D) Debates about the pursuit of happiness

54. Which of the following movements was in direct contradiction to the practices of Salem witchcraft trials?

(A) The Reformation

(B) The Enlightenment

(C) The Great Awakening

(D) The Inquisition

55. Which of the following events in U.S. history most closely parallels the controversy depicted in the image above?

(A) The Montgomery Bus Boycott in 1950s

(B) The battle of Little Big Horn in 1876

(C) The House Committee on Un-American Activities in 1940s and 1950s

(D) The assassination of Abraham Lincoln in 1865

IF YOU FINISH BEFORE TIME IS CALLED, YOU MAY CHECK YOUR WORK ON THIS SECTION ONLY. DO NOT TURN TO ANY OTHER SECTION IN THE TEST.

STOP

Part B: Short-Answer Questions

Time: 50 Minutes
4 Questions

1. **Excerpt 1:**

The dense undergrowth of the Indians' recent history [laid] violent hazards in the way of the "plan of civilization," and the most vital and stubborn of the strands took the form of prophetic nativism. Between 1795 and 1815, individual prophets and groups of Indian claiming supernatural inspiration posed direct challenges to those leaders who advocated political and even cultural accommodation to the power of the United States. Insurgent nativists drew upon their histories of intertribal cooperation. They looked to their shared beliefs in the ritual demands of power. Turning to the spirits as well as to their intertribal comrades, they attempted to rally support against those tribal leaders who cede land to the Americans. Prophetic parties . . . broke with their accommodating countrymen to prepare an intertribal, Indian union against the expansion of the United States . . .

—Gregory Evans Dowd, *A Spirited Resistance: The North American Indian Struggle for Unity, 1745–1815*. Johns Hopkins University Press (1993)

Excerpt 2:

Some Cherokees believed that "civilization" was their best protection against forced removal. Consequently, they spoke English, sent their children to school, and converted to Christianity. They established a Cherokee republic with written laws, a court system, and a national police force. They also tried to conform to Anglo-American notions about appropriate behavior for men and women . . .

The Cherokees who are most visible in the historical record succeeded in this transformation. They reacted to the crisis of the late eighteenth and early nineteenth centuries by trying to re-create Cherokee culture and society in ways that accommodated "civilization."

—Theda Perdue, *Cherokee Women: Gender and Culture Change, 1700–1835*. University of Nebraska Press (1998)

Using the excerpts, answer parts A, B, and C.

(A) Briefly explain ONE major difference between Dowd's and Perdue's interpretations of how Indians responded to westward movement.

(B) Briefly explain how ONE development from the early 1800s not directly mentioned in the excerpts supports Dowd's argument.

(C) Briefly explain how ONE development from the early 1800s not directly mentioned in the excerpts supports Perdue's argument.

GO ON TO THE NEXT PAGE

2. Answer parts A, B, and C.

(A), (B) Identify TWO aspects of expansionism in the late 19th century and early 20th century.

(C) Briefly explain ONE way this led to domestic debates about U.S. expansionism.

3. Debates about the use of natural resources and the protection of the natural environment were particularly frequent during the period 1901–1910 and again during the period 1962–1972.

Answer parts A, B, and C.

(A) Briefly explain ONE of the major controversies about the use of natural resources or the protection of the natural environment that occurred between 1901 and 1910.

(B) Briefly explain ONE of the major controversies about the use of natural resources or the protection of the natural environment that occurred between 1962 and 1972.

(C) Briefly explain ONE important reason for the continuity or change between the controversy that occurred during the period 1901–1910 and the one that occurred during the period 1962–1972.

4. Question 4 is based on the following photograph, taken at the Geneva summit meeting in November 1985.

Credit: Courtesy Ronald Reagan Library

Using the photograph, answer parts A, B, and C.

(A) Briefly explain the point of view expressed in the photograph toward ONE of the following:
- Relations between the United States and the Soviet Union during Reagan's presidency
- President Reagan's foreign policy
- The value of summit meetings as a method of resolving important differences

(B) Briefly explain ONE development from the period 1981–1985 that led to the point of view expressed in the photograph.

(C) Briefly explain ONE way in which developments in the years 1985–1989 challenged or supported the point of view expressed in the photograph.

IF YOU FINISH BEFORE TIME IS CALLED, YOU MAY CHECK YOUR WORK ON THIS SECTION ONLY. DO NOT TURN TO ANY OTHER SECTION IN THE TEST.

Section II

Part A: Document-Based Question

Time: 55 Minutes
1 Question

Directions: Question 1 is based on the accompanying documents. The documents have been edited for the purpose of this exercise. You are advised to spend 15 minutes planning and 40 minutes writing your answer. Write your responses on the lined pages that follow the questions.

1. "While conservatives upset with a series of Supreme Court decisions aimed at expanding democracy and individual freedoms were the first to issue the call for mobilization, by 1964 the new conservative movement had shifted its focus and grew over the next decade largely in response to other issues. Support, modify or refute the preceding assertion on the basis of the documents and your knowledge of the period 1954–1973."

DOCUMENT 1

The whole slogan of "civil rights," as used to make trouble in the South today, is an exact parallel to the slogan of "agrarian reform" which they used in China. And the Communists, who are pulling innocent and idealistic Americans into promoting this agitation for them, have no . . . real interest in the welfare of the Negroes . . .

But for the dirtiest deal in American political history, participated in if not actually engineered by Richard Nixon in order to make himself Vice-President (and to put Warren on the Supreme Court as part of that deal), Taft would have been nominated at Chicago in 1952. It is almost certain that Taft would then have been elected President by a far greater plurality than was Eisenhower, . . . and that we wouldn't even be in this mess that we are supposed to look to Nixon to lead us out of.

—Presentation given by Robert Welch at the founding meeting of The John Birch Society in Indianapolis, December 9, 1958.

GO ON TO THE NEXT PAGE

DOCUMENT 2

DOCUMENT 3

. . . It is supremely urgent that the effort be made, gloriously encouraging that we are mobilized to make it: . . . To those who remark the danger of demoralization by talk about impending defeat, it is necessary to remark the danger of demoralization after November 3. I fear that the morale of an army on the march is the morale that is most easily destroyed in the event of unanticipated defeat. I . . . [fear] a national demoralization of the conservative movement the day after the campaign ends . . .

Now is precisely the moment to labor incessantly to educate our fellow citizens. The point is to win recruits whose attention we might never have attracted but for Barry Goldwater; to win them not only for November 3, but for future Novembers: to infuse the conservative spirit in enough people to entitle us to look about, on November 4, not at the ashes of defeat but at the well-planted seeds of hope, which will flower on a great November day in the future, if there is a future.

— William F. Buckley, Jr., "The Impending Defeat of Barry Goldwater," An Address to the Young Americans for Freedom's National Convention, September 11, 1964

GO ON TO THE NEXT PAGE

DOCUMENT 4

DOCUMENT 5

— Jeff MacNelly, Richmond News Leader, 1972

GO ON TO THE NEXT PAGE

DOCUMENT 6

The questions presented in the present cases . . . involve the right of privacy, one aspect of which we considered in *Griswold v. Connecticut*, 381 U.S. 479, 484, when we held that various guarantees in the Bill of Rights create zones of privacy . . .

The Griswold case involved a law forbidding the use of contraceptives. We held that law as applied to married people unconstitutional . . .

The District Court in Doe held that Griswold and related cases

'establish a Constitutional right to privacy broad enough to encompass the right of a woman to terminate an unwanted pregnancy in its early stages, by obtaining an abortion . . . '

—Concurring Opinion of Justice William O. Douglas in the cases of *Roe v. Wade* and *Doe v. Bolton*

The Court simply fashions and announces a new constitutional right for pregnant mothers and, with scarcely any reason or authority for its action, invests that right with sufficient substance to override most existing state abortion statutes . . . I find no constitutional warrant for imposing such an order of priorities on the people and legislatures of the States . . . This issue, for the most part, should be left with the people and to the political processes the people have devised to govern their affairs.

—Dissenting Opinion of Justice Byron White in the cases of *Roe v. Wade* and *Doe v. Bolton*

DOCUMENT 7

There are those in our Party who favor complete support for the Supreme Court decision which permits abortion on demand. There are others who share sincere convictions that the Supreme Court's decision must be changed by a constitutional amendment prohibiting all abortions. Others have yet to take a position, or they have assumed a stance somewhere in between polar positions.

We protest the Supreme Court's intrusion into the family structure through its denial of the parents' obligation and right to guide their minor children. The Republican Party favors a continuance of the public dialogue on abortion and supports the efforts of those who seek enactment of a constitutional amendment to restore protection of the right to life for unborn children.

— Excerpt from the Republican Party Platform of 1976

IF YOU FINISH BEFORE TIME IS CALLED, YOU MAY CHECK YOUR WORK ON THIS SECTION ONLY. DO NOT TURN TO ANY OTHER SECTION IN THE TEST.  STOP

Part B: Long Essay Question

Time: 35 Minutes
1 Question

Directions: Choose ONE question from this part. You are advised to spend five minutes planning and 30 minutes writing your answer.

1. "While the reform movements of the period 1815–1860 and the so-called Market Revolution that many historians believe was taking place during that time were both centered in New England, reformers paid little attention to the effects of the Market Revolution and leading merchants and industrialists showed little enthusiasm for reform." Support, modify, or refute the preceding interpretation using at least two reform movements and one merchant or industrialist from the period 1815–1860 as evidence.

2. "The reform movements of the late nineteenth and early twentieth century focused primarily on the effects of the accelerating Industrial Revolution, especially its impact on the natural environment." Support, modify, or refute the preceding interpretation using at least two reform movements and one environmental issue from the period 1880–1920 as evidence.

IF YOU FINISH BEFORE TIME IS CALLED, YOU MAY CHECK YOUR WORK ON THIS SECTION ONLY. DO NOT TURN TO ANY OTHER SECTION IN THE TEST.

STOP

PRACTICE TEST 3 ANSWER KEY

1.	D	15.	A	29.	A	43.	D
2.	B	16.	D	30.	B	44.	A
3.	A	17.	B	31.	D	45.	C
4.	C	18.	A	32.	C	46.	A
5.	D	19.	C	33.	A	47.	D
6.	A	20.	D	34.	C	48.	D
7.	B	21.	A	35.	C	49.	D
8.	D	22.	B	36.	A	50.	D
9.	C	23.	B	37.	D	51.	C
10.	D	24.	B	38.	B	52.	B
11.	C	25.	D	39.	B	53.	C
12.	B	26.	C	40.	D	54.	B
13.	A	27.	C	41.	A	55.	C
14.	B	28.	D	42.	A		

ANSWERS AND EXPLANATIONS

SECTION I

PART A: MULTIPLE-CHOICE ANSWERS

1. D

The dramatic increase in tobacco production in response to European demand did not occur until after 1607, and for several decades thereafter it was indentured servants, not slaves, who were the principal labor force in the tobacco fields.

2. B

The number of Europeans who immigrated to Spain's New World colonies was small, not only during the 16th century, but also for several centuries thereafter. One of the reasons that Spain had difficulty defending its colonies, especially those in North America, against the English and later the Americans, was that it had so few colonists to occupy the land or serve as soldiers.

3. A

Spain remained the dominant colonial power in the New World throughout the 16th century. It was not until after 1607 that the English began to challenge Spain for dominance; the French did not make a significant effort to expand their colonies in the New World until much later as well.

4. C

The antiwar movement did not gain strength and attract widespread popular attention until it became evident that President Johnson's escalation of the war in 1966 and 1967 was not bringing about a military victory. Controversy and dissent grew dramatically after the Tet Offensive in early 1968.

5. D

In comparing the differing attitudes of outspoken groups of Americans in the late 1960s, it is clear that those most disillusioned by the war in Vietnam were not feminists or advocates of black power, but rather Students for a Democratic Society, a group that started the first student antiwar protests.

6. A

In comparing the differing attitudes of groups of Americans in the late 1960s who were critical of antiwar protesters, construction workers or "hard hats" were the group that was most offended and most outspoken.

7. B

In comparing the differing musical preferences of different groups of Americans in the late 1960s, it is apparent that those who strongly supported the war in Vietnam were those who were wedded to traditional values, and such individuals usually listened to country music.

8. D

The 1890s cartoonist Joseph Keppler criticized those descendants of previous immigrant groups who were then opposing the entrance into the United States of new immigrants. Supporters of the immigration laws passed in the 1920s, members of the revived Ku Klux Klan, and nativists who favored the deportation of recent immigrants during the Red Scare of 1919–1920 would all have disagreed with the cartoonist's perspective.

9. C

The Office of the Superintendent of Immigration was created to oversee basic immigration procedures. The service collected passenger lists from incoming ships and, after questioning, admitted or rejected the immigrants. The Chinese Exclusion Act was actually renewed the following year, and immigration from Southern and Eastern Europe, not Latin America, was the main concern in the 1890s.

10. D

The number of immigrants from Southern and Eastern Europe greatly increased during the mid-1880s. The influx of so many non-Protestant

Christians and Jews was a source of concern for many Protestant Americans.

11.   C

Slaves were imported into the English colonies in North America as early as 1619, and slavery was not abolished anywhere in the future United States until the era of the American Revolution. The excerpt from the statute clearly indicates that slavery was legal in Virginia by 1662 and being written into law. It also shows the growing discrimination against African Americans, because existing English law granted a child the hereditary status of the father.

12.   B

The statute of 1662 establishes hereditary slavery, based on the status of the mother, to address the issue of children born to white male colonists and African American women. During the period prior to Bacon's Rebellion in 1676, indentured servants continued to dominate the labor force in Virginia, marriage between races was not encouraged but not illegal yet, and Massachusetts was the first colony to legalize slavery.

13.   A

Once the importation of slaves was banned, the value of childbearing African American women increased, because a slave owner also owned the female slave's children. This negatively impacted female slaves more than male slaves, because female slaves were often forced to bear children against their will. The other laws impacted men and women equally.

14.   B

George Whitefield played an important role in initiating the First Great Awakening, which began in the middle of the 18th century. Benjamin Franklin makes no reference to hateful rhetoric or Puritan New England. Colonists attracted to the ideas of the European Enlightenment were usually rationalists rather than profoundly religious people.

15.   A

One of the most important effects of the First Great Awakening was to divide many congregations along the lines of New Lights, supporters of emotional preaching like Whitefield's, and Old Lights, those who preferred less emotional appeals by ministers expounding on passages from the Bible. There is no mention by Franklin of collecting money, of congregants rather than ministers objecting to Whitefield's style of preaching, or of any request for reimbursement.

16.   D

Benjamin Franklin was an admirer of Enlightenment thinkers, most of whom said little about personal religious beliefs. Nothing in the excerpt from his autobiography suggests that Franklin was religious or that he listened to very many preachers. The question of Loyalist political views had not yet arisen in 1739–1740, and Franklin gives no indication in this excerpt as to whether he admired or was critical of clergymen who refused to share their pulpits with Whitefield.

17.   B

The Boston Massacre occurred in March 1770, but actual fighting between British troops and colonial militia did not occur until April 1775. In the immediate aftermath of the massacre, another event had an even more decisive short-term impact: the repeal of four of the five Townshend duties, an action that helped reduce tensions for the next two to three years. John Adams defended the accused British soldiers in a court of law.

18.   A

John Adams's characterization of the victims is an implied comparison with the supposedly more upstanding British soldiers. The context was the animosity that the presence of British troops in Boston had caused, particularly the resentment on the part of many laborers. They resented the competition that British soldiers caused in the search for menial jobs.

19.   C

The Boston Tea Party was a response to the Tea Act of May 1773, not the Boston Massacre of March 1770. George Washington's appointment to lead a new colonial military force did not occur until June 1775. And few citizens of Boston decided to enlist in any military force in 1770, much less the British army.

20. D

The telegraph, the opening of an early railroad line, and the beginning of transatlantic steamship voyages all occurred prior to 1850, while Thomas Edison did not make his mark as an inventor until the late 1870s and early 1880s.

21. A

The first large mechanized textile factory was constructed in Lowell, Massachusetts, in the early 1820s and, by the 1830s, a number of others had been constructed nearby. Construction on the first transcontinental railroad did not begin until the early 1860s. The expansion of the steel industry resulted from the introduction of the Bessemer process in the 1850s; mass production of the automobile began much later.

22. B

The Erie Canal competed with, rather than stimulated, both the proliferation of steamships on America's rivers, which began earlier, and large-scale railroad building, which occurred later. New York City was connected to the Great Lakes and surrounding region by the Erie Canal and the Hudson River. The city grew and prospered as a result of the improvement to the speed and lowering of the cost of transportation.

23. B

Modern American politics had clearly come into being by the time of the election of 1840, in which two well-organized parties, the Democrats and the Whigs, competed with each other in every section of the country.

24. B

In the context of emancipation after the Civil War, many Freedmen, like those living on Edisto Island, recognized that without land of their own, they would have to return to work for their former masters. Sympathetic whites focused on helping the Freedmen gain equal rights, but the Freedmen themselves realized that economic independence was, in the short run, even more important.

25. D

The agents of the Freedmen's Bureau were not all that helpful to the Freedmen, but compared to President Lincoln, President Johnson, and even the Republican majority in Congress, they were offering to help with everyday concerns rather than ignoring those concerns (Lincoln and Johnson) or focusing on obtaining equal rights (Radical Republicans).

26. C

In the context of the aftermath of the Civil War, neither President Lincoln, nor President Johnson, nor the Republican majority in Congress made a significant effort to help the Freedmen obtain land. The Freedmen were aware that the government was making land available to white settlers and wanted the government to make it available to them as well.

27. C

Professor Schlesinger, although sympathetic to the movements for equal rights, is arguing that some outspoken representatives of certain minority groups, especially those African Americans advocating Afrocentrism, had gone too far and were dividing the nation into separate communities rather than uniting the American people.

28. D

In the context of the 1990s and more recent decades, most historians have abandoned the idea of the United States as a "melting pot" and have chosen to emphasize other aspects of the relationship between group identity and national identity. Some historians emphasize the preservation of group identities, others the metaphor of the "mosaic," and still others continued discrimination against people of color.

29. A

The term "cult of ethnicity" applies very well to advocates of black separation and black power during the 1960s, but not to feminists, advocates of equal voting rights, or those working for immigration reform.

30. B

Langston Hughes was moved by his disagreements with more culturally conservative African American writers and intellectuals, such as W. E. B. DuBois, to assert his pride in the activities and culture of ordinary African Americans.

31. D
Langston Hughes was criticized in the 1920s by culturally conservative African Americans seeking respectability, whereas most whites were indifferent.

32. C
The Blues emerged during the 1920s as a distinctively African American musical form, and the recordings and performances of Bessie Smith brought that musical form to the attention of the American public.

33. A
In his 1926 essay and in much of his poetry, Langston Hughes expressed pride in African Americans as a race and in African American culture. His assertion that "we know we are beautiful" was echoed by a large number of African Americans in the 1960s.

34. C
Manufacturing increased during and after the War of 1812 and accelerated thereafter, but urbanization did not accelerate until the 1820s. The fact that the percentage of the labor force engaged in agriculture declined only slightly after the War of 1812 helps confirm the observation of contemporaries that the westward movement increased in the immediate aftermath of the war.

35. C
The growth of manufacturing initially took place in rural, not urban, areas and did not accelerate significantly until the 1840s. The fact that the agricultural sector of the economy continued to expand significantly as late as the 1850s ensured that, relatively speaking, the growth of manufacturing slowed during the final decade before the Civil War.

36. A
The increased use of steamboats on major rivers stimulated the growth of river cities such as Cincinnati and St. Louis, and the opening of the Erie Canal fed the growth of cities on the Great Lakes, such as Buffalo, Cleveland, and Chicago from the 1820s onward, not just in the 1850s.

37. D
This question tests the skills of periodization and causation. The great increase in railroad building did not reach its peak until the 1850s, when it contributed greatly to urban growth by connecting towns and cities along its major routes.

38. B
The only section of the United States that contained significant numbers of factories prior to 1860 was New England, and by 1860, industrialization had begun to contribute to urban growth.

39. B
President Washington tried to encourage the development of a stronger national identity by appealing to settlers living in the West and trying to convince them that the national government was working to promote their best interests as well as that of all other U.S. citizens.

40. D
President Washington warned his countrymen not to be swayed by appeals to one's regional identity because those appeals were not genuine, but rather were being used to manipulate voters for partisan political purposes.

41. A
President Washington's reference to securing for Westerners "everything they could desire, in respect to our foreign relations, towards confirming their prosperity" is designed to remind them of their newly guaranteed navigation rights on the Mississippi.

42. A
Britain and France had been at war since 1793. Thomas Jefferson and James Madison had begun to organize a Republican opposition that criticized the Washington administration for pursuing a policy favorable to Britain and detrimental to France, the country that had helped the United States win independence from Britain.

43. D
At the time and for many years thereafter, Europeans attributed their ability to defeat the

native peoples of the Americas to the superiority of their weapons and civilization. However, more recent research conducted during the past half-century has demonstrated that the high death rate among the native peoples when exposed to diseases such as smallpox, to which they had no immunity, was the most important factor.

44. A
The largest population movement between the Old World and the New after the "discovery" of the New World but prior to the upsurge of European immigration in the 19th century was the African slave trade. Irish immigration, for example, surged dramatically only in the 1840s.

45. C
This question tests the skill of recognizing causation. While venereal disease and plants such as tomatoes and cabbage were exported from the New World to the Old, the European colonizers brought with them domesticated animals such as horses and sheep. The native peoples were able to make use of these animals to resist further European encroachments.

46. A
In the debate over whether the gold standard or a bimetallic currency best served the interest of the country, William Jennings Bryan advocated the expansion of a bimetallic currency through the free coinage of silver.

47. D
The debate over the coinage of silver was one of the most important issues around which the Populist, or People's Party, coalesced in 1892. This became its primary focus in the election of 1896.

48. D
The platform of the People's Party in the election of 1892 and again in the election of 1896 included such measures as a graduated income tax and stricter government regulation of railroads, banks, and big businesses.

49. D
Native peoples such as the Pueblos, whose culture revolved around the cultivation of maize, lived in

the Southwest, which today includes the states of Arizona, New Mexico, and Colorado.

50. D
It was the English who encountered native peoples engaged in agriculture as well as hunting and gathering when they first settled in the Northeast and along the Atlantic Seaboard.

51. C
Answer C is the best answer. Based on the facial expressions of the people in the image, once can conclude that the Salem witchcraft trials were filled with much emotion and hysteria.

52. B
Answer B is the best answer. The Salem witchcraft trials are now viewed as classic instances of mass hysteria, in which people's attitudes fueled other's fears. Ultimately, the trials caused many to begin questioning the existence of witchcraft.

53. C
Answer C is the best answer. The Salem witchcraft trials most directly reflect the ongoing debate about the rights of individuals—particularly the right to a fair trial.

54. B
Answer B is the best answer. Beginning in the Renaissance, European philosophers began to emphasize the importance of science and reason, looking beyond religious beliefs to better understand their lives. This led to the seventeenth-century movement known as the Enlightenment, which would have been in direct contradiction to the practices of trying and executing people for witchcraft.

55. C
Answer C is the best answer. In the 1950s, excessive concern about the influence of Communism in the United States led to the interrogation and accusation of many individuals who were thought to be Communist sympathizers. Many were sent to prison; others were blacklisted and thus unable to work. This event in American history parallels the mass hysteria responsible for the Salem witchcraft trials.

PART B: SHORT-QUESTION RESPONSES

1. (A) Dowd is writing about how certain groups of Native Americans that were "most vital" worked to bring tribes together in order to hold back the United States and settlers that were expanding westward, challenging other Native American leaders who were working for "accommodation." Perdue is focusing on how some Native Americans, particularly the Cherokees, felt the "best protection" was to accommodate to the ways of the United States and take on customs and ways that were considered "civilized."

    (B) An example to support Dowd's argument would be Tecumseh and his brother, the Prophet. They worked to unite various tribes in the Great Lakes region by stressing the rejection of the whites' ways. They were able to mobilize a number of tribes to unite in the Indiana Territory who were willing to fight against the government in the Battle of Tippecanoe.

    (C) Even after taking on the "civilized" ways of the whites, the Cherokee were still going to be forced off their land in Georgia. However, instead of uniting with other tribes being forced off their land and going to war, the Cherokee tried protesting through the American court system, and their case went all the way to the Supreme Court in *Cherokee Nation v. Georgia* and *Worcester v. Georgia*.

2.   (A), (B) Expansionists during this time period would justify their policies toward Imperialism with ideas of racialized Social Darwinism and American exceptionalism. This was supported by Josiah Strong and his popular book, *Our Country*, which espoused the idea that the United States and the Anglo-Saxon race was unique and justified in spreading their democracy and civilization. Also, others would push for the United States to expand to secure markets and raw materials. This would see the United States looking to annex new territories (Hawaii, Cuba, and Philippines, for example) and being the protectorate of others (Dominican Republic).

        (C) As a result, this would lead to debates at times between imperialists and anti-imperialists. After the Spanish-American War, controversy would arise about whether the United States should annex the Philippines. Anti-imperialists questioned whether the takeover of this territory would violate basic principles developed in the Declaration of Independence and whether the United States should try to rule a large population that was of a different race and culture.

3. (A) The Ballinger-Pinchot affair, which occurred in 1909–1910, pitted the head of the forest service, Gifford Pinchot, against the new secretary of the interior, Richard Ballinger, regarding the protection of an important natural resource, our forests. Pinchot objected to Ballinger's opening up previously protected forest land to logging, and when he said so publicly, President Taft sided with Ballinger and fired Pinchot.

(B) One of the most famous controversies regarding the protection of our natural environment was touched off in 1962 by the publication of Rachel Carson's book, *Silent Spring*. Carson documented the harmful effects of the pesticide DDT on humans and animals. Chemical companies that produced and sold DDT tried to silence Carson, but she succeeded in igniting a popular movement that led within a few years to the banning of the use of DDT.

(C) Although both the Ballinger-Pinchot affair and Rachel Carson's efforts to ban the use of DDT sought to protect natural resources and the environment, Carson took a very different approach to these issues than Pinchot had. Whereas Pinchot focused primarily on conserving our forests by replanting trees to replace those that were being cut down, Carson was an environmentalist who focused on protecting plants, animals, and humans from harm and possible extinction. Pinchot wanted to limit the amount of logging that took place, while Carson wanted to prohibit the use of DDT and other dangerous pesticides entirely.

4. (A) The photograph portrays relations between the United States and the Soviet Union during Ronald Reagan's presidency as two countries engaged in serious, carefully planned negotiations. It shows that both President Reagan and General Secretary of the Communist Party Mikhail Gorbachev came to the Geneva summit meeting in November 1985 with a full staff of advisers, prepared to discuss a wide range of issues.

(B) Although President Reagan had previously called the Soviet Union an "evil empire" and had dramatically increased U.S. military spending, his attitude changed when Mr. Gorbachev became the new leader of the Soviet Union. President Reagan recognized that Mr. Gorbachev was not a "cold warrior" like his predecessors, that he was someone who was willing to negotiate a mutual relaxation of tensions and a mutual reduction of nuclear weapons.

(C) When President Reagan became convinced that Mr. Gorbachev was sincere in wanting a mutual reduction of nuclear weapons, he and his advisers, including Secretary of State George Schulz (pictured lower right), negotiated and signed the INF treaty with the Soviet Union. The Intermediate-Range Nuclear Forces Treaty, signed in 1987, dramatically reduced the number of intermediate-range nuclear missiles that each side had aimed at the other.

SECTION II

PART A: DBQ SAMPLE RESPONSES

SAMPLE 1

During the time period from 1954 to 1976, the Supreme Court would make a number of decisions that made conservatives angry. The conservatives would want to mobilize against the Supreme Court and then over other issues. From 1954 to 1976, conservatives would be upset with the Supreme Court over their expanding democracy and individual freedoms and also over many other issues.

In the 1950s, the Supreme Court would rule that schools should not be separate for races anymore, and that white and black students should be able to go to school together. This would make a lot of people angry, especially in the South. In document 4, it shows a billboard saying "Save our Republic! Impeach Earl Warren." This is meant to be propaganda because it is on a billboard. Also, in the 1970s, even the police would help people in trying to stop the buses from bringing black students to white schools. This is biased because it comes from a newspaper in Virginia.

Besides getting angry about the Supreme Court, conservatives were also angry about other issues. William Buckley, Jr., would say, "To those who remark that danger of demoralization by talk about impending defeat, it is necessary to remark the danger of demoralization after November 3. I fear that the morale of an army on the march is the morale that is most easily destroyed in the event of unanticipated defeat. I . . . [fear] a national demoralization of the conservative movement the day after the campaign ends . . ." (Doc. 3). Phyllis Schlafly was also angry and said, "The result of Nixon's surrender was that . . . Nixon pulled his punches and failed to campaign on the fundamental issues. He beat a steady retreat from the conservative and anti-Communist principles which alone could bring victory for Republicans . . ." (Doc. 2). The conservatives would be upset with other issues besides the Supreme Court and schools.

During this time period, there would be a lot of anger and protests about what was going on in the country. It wasn't just the hippies protesting the war, but also conservatives would be upset and protesting. They were upset with the Supreme Court and their decisions on schools, and also other issues would make them upset.

Weak Response: The thesis is just restating the question and doesn't address the required skill adequately. The author is not analyzing the documents, but rather describing what is in them or just providing long quotes. The use of the documents also fails to meet the requirement of using all or all but one of the documents. Attempts at providing purpose and point of view are inadequate and not fully explained or analyzed in relation to the document. There is no outside information (besides mentioning that schools in the 1950s were being desegregated). The essay also does not provide contextualization regarding how these events were relevant to issues throughout the country. The last requirement is synthesis, and the essay doesn't meet one of the following criteria: extending or modifying the thesis, accounting for contradictory evidence, or connecting the topic to other periods/areas/contexts. This essay would not earn any points on the scoring rubric.

SAMPLE 2

In response to *Brown v. Board of Education* in 1954 (and the ensuing civil rights activism into the early 1960s), conservative activists started to mobilize in defense of states' rights and a limited role of government. These activists succeeded in getting the Republican Party to nominate Barry Goldwater as their presidential candidate in the upcoming election; however, in 1964, Republican presidential candidate Barry Goldwater would lose in a landslide by winning only states in the Deep South (besides his own home state). Some felt this represented the death of the conservative movement. However, with further efforts to expand the desegregation of schools, the rights of criminals, the rights of women, and the legalization of abortion (*Roe v. Wade*, 1973), the new conservative movement would energize various groups to unify in the fight over the proper role of the government and in the defense of traditional values.

In 1954, the Supreme Court, led by Chief Justice Earl Warren, would overrule the "separate but equal" policy established by the *Plessy v. Ferguson* case in relation to public schools in the case *Brown v. Board of Education*. They would call for schools to desegregate with "all deliberate speed." This case would unify many in the South and lead to organized "massive resistance" against the call for integrating schools. This call for resistance would not be limited to the South or limited to the integration of schools. Politicians and newly formed organizations alike would expand this debate throughout the country and call for warnings against the Supreme Court and the federal government for expanding their power beyond the limits of the Constitution. Politicians like Republican Barry Goldwater would argue that the decisions by the Supreme Court were an abuse of the power delegated by the Constitution and in violation of states' rights. It was not only Republican politicians who would try to organize around the Supreme Court, but citizens like Robert Welch and William Buckley would also be influential by starting private organizations that would rally support from outside the traditional Republicans and outside just the South. Robert Welch founded the John Birch Society to help in the cause in fighting for states' rights and anticommunism. The Birch Society saw the Supreme Court and its decisions as infringing on states' rights and would even call for the impeachment of Chief Justice Warren (Doc. 4). The sign purposely uses propaganda tools like the word "Republic" and the American flag in hopes of defending their argument in a patriotic appeal. They would even combine the two causes and compare those who fight for civil rights in the South the same as communists in China, and that they had no real interest in the helping the African Americans but only to spread their cause through "agitation" (Doc. 1). However, it is not surprising that Welch would criticize civil rights activists as communists, because he was looking to gain support from Southern Democrats, as well as others throughout the country. So by linking civil rights to communism it could build support for the states' rights and anticommunism argument without sounding racist.

Brown v. Board of Education and President Eisenhower's use of federal troops to enforce the integration of Central High School in Little Rock in the late 1950s were important in energizing conservatives. The Supreme Court's role in the late 1960s and early 1970s around rights of the accused criminals and busing to integrate schools was instrumental in energizing a new conservative movement and expanding it beyond the South. In reaction to the Supreme Court, new conservatives would be energized and successful in pushing their candidate, Barry Goldwater, for the Republican Party nomination in 1964, centered around fighting for states' rights (and anticommunism). Even though they lost, new conservatives like William Buckley would represent this energy in calling for others to realize that the fight had just begun (Doc. 3). Buckley might be trying to use this speech to be an inspiration and call for the new young wing of the Republican Party to keep fighting, not just against the liberal Democrats but also against the traditional moderates within the Republican Party. The Supreme Court would supply Buckley and other conservatives with more ammunition with rulings like *Miranda v. Arizona*. Right-wing activists accused the Supreme Court of contributing to the social breakdown in society and asserted that this increased liberalization toward criminals was only contributing to greater crime in the country. The Supreme Court would also rule by the early 1970s that school districts were allowed to bus in students to support the integration of schools. Anger over this would lead to galvanizing people against the Supreme Court and supporting the conservative movement over this single issue (Doc. 5). It is not surprising that this viewpoint came from a newspaper in the South (Virginia), as this state had been a leader in the "massive resistance" fight against school integration. Yet anger over this would also be seen in the North in cities like Detroit and Boston. With further Supreme Court rulings revolving around the issue of busing that now brought desegregation out of the South, the new conservative movement would expand its support.

Conservative activists, especially in the growing influential areas of the South and West, would also help create this new movement around the fight for traditional beliefs toward morality and family. Two central issues it would benefit from were the fight against the growing women's movement and push for the Equal Rights Amendment (ERA) and the Supreme Court 1973 decision of *Roe v. Wade*. The dissenting viewpoint in *Roe v. Wade*, written by Justice Byron White, would echo the continuing argument made by those on the right who claimed, "The Court simply fashions and announces a new constitutional right . . . I find no constitutional warrant for imposing such an order of priorities on the people and legislatures of the States" (Doc. 6). Because this is a ruling by the Supreme Court and looked at by the nation as the highest law, Justice White is going to want to provide clear arguments for his opposition and support with strong language how he thinks the other side has gone too far. This decision did not calm the dissenters, though, and the New Right gained more supporters. Supporters who weren't necessarily Republican but were "social conservatives" angered by this Supreme Court felt this was the most important issue for them. Understanding the importance of the social conservative backlash that was gaining momentum and fueling the New Right during the 1970s, the Republican Party made sure to include this issue in their party platform for the presidential election of 1976 (Doc. 7). Still reeling from the Watergate scandal and its damage to the Republican Party, the New Right and Republicans knew they had to appeal to an audience on other issues, such as abortion. Besides abortion, the revived ERA movement, led by the National Organization of Women (NOW), caused a backlash that brought traditional women to the New Right. Phyllis Schlafly formed the organization STOP ERA, bringing together groups from around the country, especially in the South and West (Doc. 2). With the rise of the Sunbelt after WWII, this area had a growing political power and led the way with many of these new "single issue" groups forming the New Right. Schlafly was able to build a coalition from various religious groups and traditionalists who feared the growing feminist movement. Going state-to-state warning against such things as women having to fight in a war and legalized abortion, she would be able to stop the ERA movement. But this also was a victory for the conservative movement and to the building of the Christian Right coalition that would become so important for the new conservative movement.

While the Supreme Court was able to expand democracy and increase individual freedoms for many people in the United States during this time period, it would also unite groups of people who opposed these decisions. The New Right would bring together grassroots organizations that rallied against what they felt was the expansion of the federal government and decaying of the moral fabric of society. The uniting of these various groups would help create a new conservative movement that 16 years after their loss in 1964 would come back with a victory in 1980 led by Ronald Reagan.

Strong Response: The thesis statement establishes a clear argument that addresses all parts of the question and establishes how the author is "modifying" the statement. In addition, the author addresses the emphasized historical skill. The thesis establishes the causes for the new conservative movement and also deals with how it would change and develop over the time period.

The author does a nice job of incorporation all documents. She doesn't just say what is in the documents, but analyzes their contents and uses them to support her thesis. She also analyzes all of the documents for such elements as intended audience, purpose, historical content, and author's point of view. For example, she analyzes purpose for Document 1 and why the author might be trying to link "communism" to the civil rights movement. She also offers plenty of outside historical examples ("massive resistance," Little Rock, Miranda, etc.) that help support the documents and the thesis statement.

She also earns the last points for contextualization and synthesis. The author was able to connect other events, such as the rise of the Sunbelt, to the argument and issues discussed in the essay.

She also shows how the rise of the Sunbelt was not just a regional event, but how it also dealt with historical phenomena going on around the country. Overall, she did synthesize the evidence, documents, and context of the question into a coherent essay, while modifying the statement to show how the new conservative movement was about the Supreme Court decisions, as well as other "single issues" that came up during this time period. The author showed the causes and that it was a continuous and growing movement throughout the years 1954–1976. The total score for this essay would be a 7 out of 7 possible points.

PART B: LONG ESSAY SAMPLE RESPONSES

SAMPLE 1

Both the so-called "Market Revolution" and the most influential reform movements of the period 1815–1860 took place throughout the United States, not just in New England, and at least some leading merchants and industrialists were enthusiastic supporters of reform. It is true that New England was home to a substantial number of reformers, especially several important leaders of the abolitionist movement, such as William Lloyd Garrison and Wendell Phillips. It is also true that the two most influential reform movements, the temperance and abolitionist movements, were not primarily concerned with the effects of the Market Revolution. Yet the spread of the Market Revolution did significantly increase the number of employers who supported the temperance movement, if for no other reason than to try to ensure that their employees came to work sober and ready to do their jobs.

Although there were numerous reform movements founded during the period 1815–1860, from the New York Female Moral Reform Society to the Lowell Female Labor Reform Association to the Woman's suffrage movement, the two largest and most influential reform movements were the temperance movement, initiated by the American Temperance Society, and the abolitionist movement, first organized effectively in the American Anti-Slavery Society. Both the American Temperance Society and the New England Anti-Slavery Society, the precursor of the American Anti-Slavery Society, began in New England. The American Anti-Slavery Society was founded in Philadelphia. These organizations quickly spread throughout the country, opening hundreds of local chapters. Among the most important, most dedicated leaders of the abolitionist movement were the New York brothers Arthur and Lewis Tappan, wealthy merchants who gave strong financial support to the anti-slavery movement.

While some reformers such as the Tappan brothers and Robert Owen, the founder of a utopian community at New Lanark, Indiana, were successful merchants and industrialists, a much larger number of prominent reformers, including most of the leaders of the temperance and abolitionist movements, were motivated primarily by their religious beliefs. This was certainly true of Reverend Lyman Beecher, one of the founders of the American Temperance Society and a leading abolitionist; Charles Grandison Finney, an evangelist and leading anti-slavery advocate; and Finney's disciple, Theodore Dwight Weld, a leading abolitionist and husband of prominent female anti-slavery speaker, Angelina Grimke. And, of these four famous reformers, only Beecher was a New Englander.

Thus, although New England was home to a substantial number of reformers during the antebellum period, it was only one of a number of centers of reform. Like the so-called Market Revolution, reform movements flourished throughout the nation during these years, and while some merchants and industrialists were leading reformers, the largest number of prominent reformers appear to have been motivated by religious beliefs rather than a desire to combat any of the evils attributed by contemporaries to the Market Revolution.

This thesis statement establishes a clear argument that addresses all parts of the question and makes a clear argument, earning the point for thesis. The essay does a good job arguing that reform was taking place throughout the United States and that some industrialists supported it and some reform was affected by the Market Revolution. The argument also addresses the targeted skill of causation by dealing with the causes and effects of the events mentioned in the question, earning two points.

The essay uses specific evidence to support the argument, which earns the 2 possible points. For example, it points out that the Anti-Slavery Society and Temperance Society were not just limited to New England and that some of the important leaders were merchants. You also identify reformers such as Charles Finney and use these examples to support arguments that some reformers were affected more by their beliefs than by the Market Revolution. These examples also address the targeted skill by showing the cause and effect of these events on merchants and reformers in relation to the reform movements.

The essay also earns the point for applying the skill of synthesis. It modifies the thesis statement and connects the topic to other areas besides New England. This essay would score a 6 out of 6 possible points.

SAMPLE 2

While a number of the most important reform movements of the late 19th and early 20th centuries grew out of efforts to combat the negative effects of industrialization, the main focus of their efforts was not the impact of the Industrial Revolution on the natural environment. Although some reformers, such as Theodore Roosevelt and Gifford Pinchot, were deeply worried about the consequences of economic development on the natural environment, the most influential, most effective reformers were primarily concerned with the impact of the rise of big business on small businesses, industrial workers, and consumers, and with corruption in government that reformers believed resulted from the economic power of large corporations.

Farmers were upset at what they regarded as arbitrary and excessive railroad rates and abuses such as rebates to big business like Standard Oil. These farmers were among the first and most outspoken advocates of reform in the late 19th century. Pressure from the Farmers' Alliances convinced Congress to pass and President Cleveland to sign the Interstate Commerce Act of 1887, a piece of legislation designed to regulate railroad rates and prohibit corrupt practices such as rebates. By 1890, these Farmers' Alliances had entered politics in a number of Southern and Midwestern states and succeeded in pressuring Congress to pass the Sherman Antitrust Act, outlawing all "combinations in restraint of trade." By 1892, a national People's Party had been organized, nominating a third-party presidential candidate and electing several members of Congress. The Populist movement, a reform movement attempting to combat the negative effects of industrialization and the rise of big business, was now in full swing.

Beginning at the state level and with strong support in many urban areas, a new progressive movement reached the national level during the first years of the 20th century. Supported by President Theodore Roosevelt, progressive reformers, like the Populists, sought to strengthen railroad regulation and both enforce and further strengthen the antitrust laws. In 1902, President Roosevelt not only forced mine owners to submit to arbitration to settle a nationwide coal strike, he also asked his attorney general to file an antitrust suit against the Northern Securities Company, a large railroad holding company. After the Supreme Court upheld a lower court decision to break up the Northern Securities Company in 1904, Roosevelt went on to strengthen the Interstate Commerce Commission's ability to regulate railroad rates by pushing the Hepburn Act through Congress in 1906. A few years later, another progressive reformer, Woodrow Wilson, succeeded to the presidency, and he managed to further strengthen the antitrust laws by pushing the Clayton Antitrust Act through Congress in 1914.

While railroad regulation and antitrust actions attracted the most attention of reformers during the period 1880–1920, some efforts were made by reformers to mitigate the effects of industrialization and commercial expansion on the natural environment. President Roosevelt used his executive authority to put thousands of acres of public lands aside for national parks, saving them from commercial exploitation. In 1908, he convened a conservation conference at the White House in an effort to further mitigate the damage that mining and manufacturing were doing to the natural environment, especially in the West. President Roosevelt also pushed for the establishment of the forest service and appointed a conservation-minded ally, Gifford Pinchot, to head that agency. Finally, even after retiring from office, Roosevelt supported Pinchot in his efforts to prevent President Taft's secretary of the interior, Richard Ballinger, from opening additional public lands to commercial exploitation.

Thus, both the populist and progressive movements sought to combat the negative effects of industrialization and economic expansion by focusing primarily on railroad regulation and the strengthening and enforcement of antitrust legislation. Nevertheless, some progressive reformers like Theodore Roosevelt and Gifford Pinchot did pay significant attention to preventing further damage to the natural environment and helped to found the modern conservation movement.

This thesis statement establishes a clear argument that addresses all parts of the question and makes a clear argument, earning one point. It does a nice job of demonstrating that at least two reform movements were not just aimed at the effects of the Industrial Revolution, but also at the impact on small business, workers, and consumers, as well as corruption in government. Through its clear thesis, the essay is also able to address the targeted skill of causation by dealing with the causes and effects of the events mentioned in the question, for which it earns both of the possible points.

In its body paragraphs, the essay also does a very good job of identifying and using specific evidence to support its argument. It cites the Farmers' Alliances and their role in pushing for the Interstate Commerce Act and Sherman Antitrust Act. In addition, the essay uses a lot of pertinent information from the presidency of Theodore Roosevelt to support the thesis statement and also addresses how there were some reforms that dealt with the natural environment, i.e., national parks and the forest service. These examples also address the targeted skill by showing the cause and effect of these events in relation to the reform movements, earning two more points.

You also are able to meet the last point by applying the skill of synthesis. You modified the statement in developing your argument and employed the use of other categories. This essay scores a 6 out of a possible 6 points.

Practice Test 4 Answer Grid

1. Ⓐ Ⓑ Ⓒ Ⓓ
2. Ⓐ Ⓑ Ⓒ Ⓓ
3. Ⓐ Ⓑ Ⓒ Ⓓ
4. Ⓐ Ⓑ Ⓒ Ⓓ
5. Ⓐ Ⓑ Ⓒ Ⓓ
6. Ⓐ Ⓑ Ⓒ Ⓓ
7. Ⓐ Ⓑ Ⓒ Ⓓ
8. Ⓐ Ⓑ Ⓒ Ⓓ
9. Ⓐ Ⓑ Ⓒ Ⓓ
10. Ⓐ Ⓑ Ⓒ Ⓓ
11. Ⓐ Ⓑ Ⓒ Ⓓ
12. Ⓐ Ⓑ Ⓒ Ⓓ
13. Ⓐ Ⓑ Ⓒ Ⓓ
14. Ⓐ Ⓑ Ⓒ Ⓓ

15. Ⓐ Ⓑ Ⓒ Ⓓ
16. Ⓐ Ⓑ Ⓒ Ⓓ
17. Ⓐ Ⓑ Ⓒ Ⓓ
18. Ⓐ Ⓑ Ⓒ Ⓓ
19. Ⓐ Ⓑ Ⓒ Ⓓ
20. Ⓐ Ⓑ Ⓒ Ⓓ
21. Ⓐ Ⓑ Ⓒ Ⓓ
22. Ⓐ Ⓑ Ⓒ Ⓓ
23. Ⓐ Ⓑ Ⓒ Ⓓ
24. Ⓐ Ⓑ Ⓒ Ⓓ
25. Ⓐ Ⓑ Ⓒ Ⓓ
26. Ⓐ Ⓑ Ⓒ Ⓓ
27. Ⓐ Ⓑ Ⓒ Ⓓ
28. Ⓐ Ⓑ Ⓒ Ⓓ

29. Ⓐ Ⓑ Ⓒ Ⓓ
30. Ⓐ Ⓑ Ⓒ Ⓓ
31. Ⓐ Ⓑ Ⓒ Ⓓ
32. Ⓐ Ⓑ Ⓒ Ⓓ
33. Ⓐ Ⓑ Ⓒ Ⓓ
34. Ⓐ Ⓑ Ⓒ Ⓓ
35. Ⓐ Ⓑ Ⓒ Ⓓ
36. Ⓐ Ⓑ Ⓒ Ⓓ
37. Ⓐ Ⓑ Ⓒ Ⓓ
38. Ⓐ Ⓑ Ⓒ Ⓓ
39. Ⓐ Ⓑ Ⓒ Ⓓ
40. Ⓐ Ⓑ Ⓒ Ⓓ
41. Ⓐ Ⓑ Ⓒ Ⓓ
42. Ⓐ Ⓑ Ⓒ Ⓓ

43. Ⓐ Ⓑ Ⓒ Ⓓ
44. Ⓐ Ⓑ Ⓒ Ⓓ
45. Ⓐ Ⓑ Ⓒ Ⓓ
46. Ⓐ Ⓑ Ⓒ Ⓓ
47. Ⓐ Ⓑ Ⓒ Ⓓ
48. Ⓐ Ⓑ Ⓒ Ⓓ
49. Ⓐ Ⓑ Ⓒ Ⓓ
50. Ⓐ Ⓑ Ⓒ Ⓓ
51. Ⓐ Ⓑ Ⓒ Ⓓ
52. Ⓐ Ⓑ Ⓒ Ⓓ
53. Ⓐ Ⓑ Ⓒ Ⓓ
54. Ⓐ Ⓑ Ⓒ Ⓓ
55. Ⓐ Ⓑ Ⓒ Ⓓ

PRACTICE TEST 4

Section I

Part A: Multiple-Choice Questions

Time: 55 Minutes
55 Questions

Directions: Choose the best answer choice for the following questions.

Questions 1 and 2 refer to following quote.

" . . . (a) major consequence of the Pueblo Revolt was the opportunity it afforded Indian rebels to acquire hundreds of coveted Spanish horses. The Pueblos in turn established a thriving horse trade with Navajos, Apaches, and other tribes . . . (horses) soon spread across the Great Plains, the vast rolling grasslands extending from the Missouri River valley in the east to the base of the Rocky Mountains in the west."

—George Brown Tindall and David Emory Shi in *America: A Narrative History,* 8e

1. Which of the following was a major impact of the introduction of the horse to the Plains Indians?

   (A) The horse allowed Plains Indians the ability to become sedentary.

   (B) The horse stopped the intense competition between the various Indian nations over food and land.

   (C) The horse consumed the primary food source of the bison, causing the bison population to dwindle.

   (D) The horse allowed the Plains Indians to become more efficient in hunting and caused them to become more nomadic.

GO ON TO THE NEXT PAGE

2. Which of the following describes the Spanish reaction to the Pueblo Revolt?

(A) The Spanish enslaved the natives.

(B) The Spanish decided that it would be advantageous to work with the Pueblo as allies rather than enemies and sided with the Pueblo to conquer their neighboring enemies.

(C) The Spanish killed several Pueblo and mutilated or enslaved the survivors.

(D) For the first time in their new empire, the Spanish implemented the *encomienda* system to Christianize the Pueblo.

Questions 3–5 refer to the following quote.

" . . . though under the greatest Enjoyment of Civil Liberties, if abridged of the Freedom of their Consciences, as to their Religious Profession and Worship: And Almighty God being the only Lord of Conscience, Father of Lights and Spirits; and the Author as well as Object of all divine Knowledge, Faith and Worship, who only doth enlighten the Minds, and persuade and convince the Understandings of People, I do hereby grant and declare, That no Person or Persons, inhabiting in this Province or Territories, who shall confess and acknowledge One almighty God, the Creator, Upholder and Ruler of the World; and profess him or themselves obliged to live quietly under the Civil Government, shall be in any Case molested or prejudiced, in his or their Person or Estate, . . . "

—William Penn, *Pennsylvania Charter of Privileges,* October 28, 1701

3. In what way was the main idea in the excerpt a departure from the other colonies in British North America?

(A) With few exceptions, other British North American colonies had one established faith.

(B) Pennsylvania was the first colony to tolerate all religious beliefs.

(C) Settlers in Pennsylvania were required to attend church services.

(D) Puritan ideas were banned from the colony.

4. Which of the following events from the colonial era is most like the ideas expressed in the excerpt from the *Charter of Privileges*?

(A) The ideas of John Locke and their influence on the Enlightenment

(B) The theological beliefs of Roger Williams in his founding of Rhode Island

(C) The Carolina Charter

(D) The Maryland Act of Toleration

5. The previous excerpt is most similar to the sentiments expressed in which of the following?

(A) The Declaration of Independence

(B) The South Carolina Exposition and Protest

(C) The Bill of Rights

(D) The Alien and Sedition Acts

GO ON TO THE NEXT PAGE ⇨

Questions 6–8 refer to the following quote.

"With the (cotton gin), a single operator could clean as much cotton in a few hours as a group of workers had once needed a whole day to do . . . Soon cotton growing spread into the upland South and beyond, within a decade the total crop increased eightfold . . . The cotton gin not only changed the economy of the South, it also helped transform the North. The large supply of domestically produced fiber was a strong incentive to entrepreneurs in New England and elsewhere to develop an American textile industry."

—Alan Brinkley from *American History: Connecting With the Past,* 14e

6. Based on the above analysis by Dr. Alan Brinkley, which of the following best explains the political development based on the economy of the North and South in the late 18th and early 19th centuries?

   (A) The North and South were cooperative in their development of a profitable textile industry and therefore politically cooperative.

   (B) Both the North and South depended upon legislation that supported the institution of slavery.

   (C) A wedge developed between the North and South because of the North's rapid industrialization and the South's dependence on agriculture.

   (D) The South began to develop industrially, and by the early 19th century realized they could be both politically and economically independent of the North.

7. The invention of the cotton gin had as much impact on the development of slave labor in the first half of the 19th century as which of the following did toward the end of the 19th and early 20th centuries?

   (A) The development of the assembly line

   (B) Development of the Bessemer process in the steel industry

   (C) The application of steam power to factories

   (D) The invention of the sewing machine

8. Which of the following was a direct impact of the invention of the cotton gin?

   (A) The invention of the steel plow to allow for more rapid planting of cotton crops

   (B) The spread of the plantation system into Northern states

   (C) The development of the Lowell factory system in New England

   (D) The introduction of the factory system in the South

GO ON TO THE NEXT PAGE

Questions 9–12 refer to the following map.

1784 Map prepared by John Hartley from Thomas Jefferson's *Land Ordinance of 1784*
Courtesy of the William L. Clements Library, University of Michigan, Ann Arbor

9. Based on the ideas in *Land Ordinance of 1784*, the information in the above map indicates Thomas Jefferson intended which of the following?

(A) That the Western Territories be evenly divided into free and slave states

(B) That the United States, under the Articles of Confederation, should create states equal with the original 13

(C) That the Western Territories should be sold off in fourteen lots to pay off the national debt

(D) That the United States must purchase New Orleans as an outlet to the sea for the new Western Territories

10. In reference to the Western Territories, which of the following events impacted American migration westward in the pre-Revolutionary years?

(A) The Proclamation of 1763

(B) The English defeat of the French and Indians in the Seven Years' War

(C) The proclamation of the writs of assistance

(D) The passage of the Declaratory Act

11. As the United States began to occupy the region west of the Appalachian Mountains, which of the following developed as the most significant issue to impact the country in the late 18th century?

(A) The question of whether the new states should be slave or free

(B) The development of industrialization

(C) The settlers' desire for free navigation of the Mississippi River

(D) The issue of whether the new states should be on an equal level with the 13 original states

12. As the United States expanded westward, which of the following was the most significant departure from government policy toward American Indians?

(A) Signing of the Treaty of Greenville of 1795

(B) The Trail of Tears

(C) The Indian Appropriations Act of 1851

(D) The Dawes Severalty Act of 1887

GO ON TO THE NEXT PAGE

Questions 13–16 refer to the following quote.

" . . . to the amicable relations existing between the United States and those powers, to declare, that we should consider any attempt on their part to extend their system to any portion of this hemisphere, as dangerous to our peace and safety. With the existing colonies or dependencies of any European power we have not interfered, and shall not interfere. But with the governments who have declared their independence, and maintained it, and whose independence we have . . . acknowledged, we could not view any interposition for the purpose of oppressing them . . . by any European power in any other light than as the manifestation of an unfriendly disposition towards the United States. . . . in the judgment of the competent authorities of this government, shall make a corresponding change, on the part of the United States, indispensable to their security."

—Excerpt from the Monroe Doctrine from President James Monroe's annual message to Congress, 1823

13. Based on the excerpt, which of the following statements best describes the change in American foreign policy in 1823?

(A) The United States would become more active in European affairs.

(B) The United States would consider any attempt of European interference in the Western Hemisphere as unfriendly toward the United States.

(C) The United States intended to end European colonialism in the Western Hemisphere.

(D) The United States declared its intention to gain a world empire.

14. The ideals expressed in the Monroe Doctrine augment the ideals expressed in which of the following previously established American policies?

(A) The concept of "free trade" inaugurated in Jay's Treaty

(B) The idea of "right of deposit" established in Pinckney's Treaty

(C) The statement of "no entangling alliances" expressed in President George Washington's Farewell Address

(D) The acquisition of new territory, as established in the Greenville Treaty in 1795

15. The United States maintained the foreign policy of the Monroe Doctrine until which of the following?

(A) The war against Mexico in order to gain new western territory

(B) Efforts made by the Union to keep Great Britain and France out of the Civil War

(C) America's acquisition of an overseas empire as a result of a war with Spain

(D) American participation in World War I

16. The establishment of the Monroe Doctrine was a reaction to which of the following events?

(A) The outcome of the War of 1812

(B) The intention of the European powers to reclaim Spanish colonies in the Western Hemisphere

(C) The unsettled results of the Napoleonic Wars in Europe

(D) European economic encroachment in the Western Hemisphere

GO ON TO THE NEXT PAGE

Questions 17–19 refer to the following quote.

"I thank you, dear sir, for the copy you have been so kind as to send me of the letter to your constituents on the Missouri question . . . But this momentous question, like a firebell in the night, awakened and filled me with terror. I considered it at once as the knell of the Union. It is hushed, indeed, for the moment. But this is a reprieve only, not a final sentence. A geographical line, coinciding with a marked principle, moral and political, once conceived and held up to the angry passions of men, will never be obliterated; and every new irritation will mark it deeper and deeper."

—Letter from Thomas Jefferson to John Holmes, April 22, 1820

17. Which of the following divisive issues is Thomas Jefferson warning the reader about in the above excerpt?

(A) The protective tariff

(B) States' rights questions that were before Congress

(C) The economic panic that began in 1819

(D) The issue of slavery

18. Which of the following events best illustrated Thomas Jefferson's fear that the issue discussed in the excerpt had come to realization?

(A) The issuing of the South Carolina Exposition and Protest

(B) The passage of the Indian Removal Act in 1830

(C) Bleeding Kansas

(D) The destruction of the U.S. Bank

19. Which of the following was a reason Congress believed it necessary to enact a measure in response to the "Missouri Question" in 1820?

(A) The federal government wanted to maintain the balance of free and slave states

(B) The fear that expansion could worsen the effects of the Panic of 1819

(C) The continuing debate over the concept of the protective tariff

(D) The controversy of expanding west of the Mississippi River would cause the Mexican government to react aggressively

Questions 20–24 refer to the following quote.

" . . . we are the nation of progress, of individual freedom, of universal enfranchisement. Equality of rights is the cynosure* of our union of States, the grand exemplar of the correlative equality of individuals; . . . We must onward to the fulfilment of our mission—to the entire development of the principle of our organization—freedom of conscience, freedom of person, freedom of trade and business pursuits, universality of freedom and equality. This is our high destiny, and in nature's eternal, inevitable decree of cause and effect we must accomplish it. All this will be our future history, to establish on earth the moral dignity and salvation of man—the immutable truth and beneficence of God. For this blessed mission to the nations of the world, which are shut out from the life-giving light of truth, has America been chosen; and her high example shall smite unto death the tyranny of kings, hierarchs, and oligarchs, . . . Who, then, can doubt that our country is destined to be the great nation of futurity?"

—John L. O'Sullivan on *Manifest Destiny,* excerpted from "The Great Nation of Futurity," 1839

GO ON TO THE NEXT PAGE

20. Based on the excerpt from John L. O'Sullivan's opinion on Manifest Destiny, what was the purpose of American expansion?

   (A) To expand the ideals of equality and freedom

   (B) To demonstrate to the world American political superiority

   (C) The only hope for the salvation of mankind

   (D) America must avoid tyrannical rulers

21. Who of the following would most likely agree with the excerpt written by John L. O'Sullivan?

   (A) A male Irish immigrant living in Boston

   (B) A white male squatter from Tennessee

   (C) A female factory worker in New England

   (D) A plantation owner from Georgia

22. The motivations behind which of the following actions from the late 19th century are similar to the ideals of O'Sullivan's excerpt?

   (A) The American annexation of Hawaii

   (B) The takeover of the Philippine Islands after the Spanish-American War

   (C) The acquisition of American Samoa in 1898

   (D) The liberation of Cuba from Spanish rule

23. Which of the following events allowed for an almost immediate realization of the goals of Manifest Destiny in the 1840s?

   (A) The full realization of the ideals of Jacksonian democracy

   (B) The election of war hero Zachary Taylor as president of the United States

   (C) The conclusion of the Indian Removal policy enacted in the 1830s

   (D) The American victory in the Mexican War

24. Which of the following environmental factors led to the further development of the growing division between the North and South in the antebellum period?

   (A) The discovery of gold in California

   (B) The extensive river systems in the Southwest allowed for more internal migration

   (C) The fact that a good portion of the new territory in the Mexican Cession was south of the 36°30′ parallel

   (D) The western mountains were not conducive to the spread of slavery; therefore, the North would not challenge the existence of slavery in the new territory

GO ON TO THE NEXT PAGE

Questions 25–27 refer to the following quote.

"Resolved, that it is both the part of patriotism and of duty to recognize no political principle other than THE CONSTITUTION OF THE COUNTRY, THE UNION OF THE STATES, AND THE ENFORCEMENT OF THE LAWS, and that, as representatives of the Constitutional Union men of the country . . . we hereby pledge ourselves to maintain, protect, and defend, separately and unitedly, these great principles of public liberty and national safety, against all enemies, at home and abroad; . . . the rights of the People and of the States re-established, and the Government again placed in that condition of justice, fraternity and equality, which, under the example and Constitution of our fathers, has solemnly bound every citizen of the United States to maintain a more perfect union . . ."

—From the Platform of the Constitutional Union Party of 1860

25. This excerpt addresses which of the following continuing antebellum issues?

(A) The continued public debate over slavery

(B) The failure of compromise

(C) The continued debate over the tariff

(D) Disputes created after the *Dred Scott* decision

26. According to the excerpt, which of the following was the main reason for the formation of the Constitutional Union Party for the election of 1860?

(A) To end slavery

(B) To promote the equality of all citizens

(C) To preserve the "more perfect Union"

(D) To protect the nation from all enemies

27. The ideas expressed in the Constitution Union Party platform most directly reflect which of the following continuities in history?

(A) Justification for immigration restriction in the 1920s

(B) The passage of the Progressive Amendments to the Constitution

(C) The ideals of the New Deal

(D) Justification for America's entry into World War I

GO ON TO THE NEXT PAGE

Questions 28 and 29 refer to the following image.

Ruins on Carey Street, Richmond, Virginia, April 1865

28. The impact of battles on the South, such as the siege of Richmond as shown in the above photograph, impacted the outcome of the American Civil War in which of the following ways?

(A) Not only was the Confederate Army defeated, but the infrastructure of the South was also destroyed, leading to an unconditional surrender.

(B) Despite the destruction of major cities, the surrender of the Confederacy surprised much of the Southern population.

(C) Even with the destruction of the South, the Confederate's advantage in the amount of resources caused the war to last longer than anticipated.

(D) The Civil War had little impact on the South's infrastructure.

29. Which of the following led to a Union victory over the South?

(A) The capture of Richmond, the Confederate capital

(B) The ability to maintain an effective sea blockade on the South

(C) The mobilization of free African American soldiers throughout the duration of the war

(D) The superiority of Union military leadership

Questions 30–32 refer to the following quote.

"The laboring man in this bounteous and hospitable country has no ground for complaint. His vote is potential and he is elevated thereby to the position of man. Elsewhere he is a creature of circumstance, which is that of abject depression. Under the government of this nation, the effort is to elevate the standard of the human race and not to degrade it. In all other nations it is the reverse. What, therefore, has the laborer to complain of in America? By inciting strikes and encouraging discontent, he stands in the way of the elevation of his race and of mankind."

—Henry Clews from "The Organizing of Labor Into Unions Is Dangerous," *North American Review,* 1886

30. Henry Clews's opinion was most likely a reaction to which of the following?

(A) Rapid industrialization after the Civil War

(B) Increasing immigration to the United States from Europe

(C) The lack of work opportunities for Americans in factories

(D) The results of violent events like the Great Railroad Strike of 1877 and the Haymarket Affair

GO ON TO THE NEXT PAGE

31. Who of the following would most likely support the sentiments of the previous excerpt?

    (A) Samuel Gompers

    (B) Grover Cleveland

    (C) Terence V. Powderly

    (D) Mother Jones

32. Which of the following 20th-century events share similar sentiments with the above excerpt?

    (A) The creation of the War Labor Board during World War I

    (B) The passage of the Taft-Hartley Act after World War II

    (C) Passage of the Wagner Labor Relations Act of 1935

    (D) Fair Deal proposals regarding labor

Questions 33–35 refer to the following quote.

"In our day the market rate determined the price of labor of all sorts, as well as of goods. The employer paid as little as he could, and the worker got as much. It was not a pretty system ethically, I admit; but it did, at least, furnish us a rough-and-ready formula for settling a question which must be settled then thousand times a day if the world was ever going to get forward. There seemed to be no other practical way of doing it. "Yes," replied Dr. Leete, "it was the only practical way under a system which made the interests of every individual antagonistic to those of every other; but it would have been a pity if humanity could never have devised a better plan, for yours was simply the application to the mutual relations of men of the devil's maxim, 'Your necessity is my opportunity.'"

—Edward Bellamy from *Looking Backward, 2000–1887*

33. Which of the following best describes the social conditions in the United States when Bellamy wrote the excerpt?

    (A) The political attitude was that of economic equality for all.

    (B) Major industries were supportive of the growth of large unions.

    (C) A great maldistribution of wealth existed in American society.

    (D) Most workers found it difficult to find work.

34. Which of the following were Bellamy and similar commentators criticizing?

    (A) Rapid industrialization

    (B) Unlimited immigration

    (C) Mechanization of the workplace

    (D) Capitalism

35. Which of the following groups from the antebellum era most closely resembles the ideas expressed by Edward Bellamy's excerpt?

    (A) Utopian communities

    (B) Abolitionists

    (C) Advocates for Indian Removal

    (D) Transcendentalists

GO ON TO THE NEXT PAGE

Questions 36–38 refer to the following image.

Clifford Kennedy Berryman, *The Washington Star*,
March 9, 1937

36. What was the motivation for Franklin D. Roosevelt's idea that is portrayed in the above political cartoon?

   (A) Congress was beginning to question some of the more radical ideas of the New Deal that were introduced in FDR's second term.

   (B) FDR wanted to be able to appoint new Supreme Court justices, as the Court had declared some of his key New Deal legislation unconstitutional.

   (C) The Democratic Party began to react in a negative manner to the radical ideas of the New Deal.

   (D) FDR's second term was not as successful as the first, and he wanted more federal justices to help declare his ideas as constitutional.

37. Which of the following groups would have most likely supported the main idea of the political cartoon?

   (A) Liberal Republicans

   (B) Southern farmers

   (C) Union Democrats

   (D) Southern Democrats

38. Which of the following presidents reacted to a Supreme Court decision in a manner similar to the one depicted in the political cartoon?

   (A) Thomas Jefferson's reaction to *Marbury* v. *Madison*

   (B) Andrew Jackson's reaction to *Worcester* v. *Georgia*

   (C) Chester Arthur's reaction to the civil rights cases of 1883

   (D) Grover Cleveland's reaction to *Plessy* v. *Ferguson*

Questions 39–41 refer to the following quote.

"Despite the public hostility, the frequent strikes, the business failures, and the long depression, the magicians of money were still managing to make it. Without always consciously setting out to do so, they were creating the foundations of monopoly capitalism. Economic indicators were good. Throughout the Gilded Age, a high savings rate (18–20 percent) meant much investment capital was available. A positive balance of trade, with exports exceeding imports, emerged in 1876–80—the first time this had ever happened for five years in a row."

—From *Rebirth of a Nation: The Making of Modern America, 1877–1920* by Jackson Lears, 2009 (pg. 88)

39. Which of the following events would support the main argument made by historian Jackson Lears?

   (A) The Haymarket Riot greatly slowed down American economic growth.

   (B) The development of the steel industry by Andrew Carnegie made America one of the largest exporters of steel in the world.

   (C) The union movement of the late 19th and early 20th centuries boosted the American economy.

   (D) The Populist movement encouraged rapid industrial growth.

GO ON TO THE NEXT PAGE ⟶

40. Which of the following encouraged the development of "monopoly capitalism"?

(A) The development of the assembly line

(B) The Bessemer process

(C) The development of the Taylor scientific management system

(D) Vertical and horizontal integration

41. Which of the following best describes the government's response to "monopoly capitalism"?

(A) The Supreme Court used the Fourteenth Amendment to support the growth of big business

(B) Congress passed the Sherman Antitrust Act

(C) The passage of the Clayton Antitrust Act

(D) Ratification of the Hepburn Act

Questions 42 and 43 refer to the following quote.

"The cars of the migrant people crawled out of the side roads onto the great cross-country highway, and they took the migrant way to the West. In the daylight they scuttled like bugs to the westward; and as the dark caught them, they clustered like bugs near to shelter and to water. And because they were lonely and perplexed, because they had all come from a place of sadness and worry and defeat, and because they were all going to a new mysterious place, they huddled together; they talked together; they shared their lives, their food, and they things they hoped for in the new country."

— *The Grapes of Wrath* by John Steinbeck, chapter 17

42. The phenomenon described in the excerpt from *The Grapes of Wrath* by John Steinbeck is best described by which of the following?

(A) The mass exodus of African Americans from the South during the Great Migration at the time of World War I

(B) The immigration of *braceros* from Mexico to the American Southwest during World War II

(C) The exodus of Okies from the Dust Bowl to California

(D) A metaphor for the trip made across the Atlantic Ocean by the eastern and southern Europeans who immigrated to the United States during the early 20th century

43. Which of the following best describes the motivation for the move made by the migrant people described in the Steinbeck excerpt?

(A) They were looking for work as they escaped the impact of the Great Depression on their hometown.

(B) They sought opportunity for new and better jobs due to the opportunities created by the war industry.

(C) The migrants were heading west to take advantage of promised jobs through the New Deal.

(D) Jobs in new industries in Western cities attracted thousands of migrants from the American Midwest.

GO ON TO THE NEXT PAGE

Questions 44–46 refer to the following quote.

"The truth is that the newest immigrants came for many of the same reasons as the old. They typically left countries where populations were growing rapidly and where agricultural and industrial revolutions were shaking people loose from old habit of life—conditions almost identical to those in nineteenth-century Europe. And they came to America, as previous immigrants had done, in search of jobs and economic opportunity. Some came with skills and even professional degrees, from India or Taiwan or the former Soviet Union, and they found their way into middle-class jobs. But most came with fewer skills and less education, seeking work as janitors, nannies, farm laborers, lawn cutters, or restaurant workers."

— *The American Pageant,* 14e by David M. Kennedy and Lizabeth Cohen Wadsworth, Cengage Learning © 2010

44. Which of the following best describes Kennedy's and Cohen's interpretation of modern immigration?

   (A) The modern immigrants were very similar to those of the "old" and "new" immigrants of the late 19th and early 20th century.

   (B) The modern immigrants were much like the Irish immigrants of the 19th century who were distrusted and disliked because they took traditional American jobs at lower salaries, causing Americans to form a political party opposing them.

   (C) Although many modern immigrants arrived as skilled laborers, they usually found work that pays less and requires little skill.

   (D) Most modern immigrants found no work or opportunity when they arrived in the United States.

45. Which of the following historical periods of immigration is most similar to the passage in the previous excerpt?

   (A) The "old immigration" of Northern and Western Europeans 1865–1890

   (B) The influx of French immigrants during the French Revolution and Napoleonic Wars

   (C) The arrival of Chinese immigrants during the gold rush era

   (D) The immigration of Irish fleeing the potato famine in the 1830s and 1840s

46. Reactions in the 21st century to the events described in the excerpt are similar to which of the following?

   (A) Similar to the Adams administration passage of the Alien and Sedition Acts

   (B) The formation of the Know-Nothings in the 1850s

   (C) The call for immigration restriction in the 1920s

   (D) Widespread belief in the ideals expressed by Emma Lazarus in her poem engraved on the base of the Statue of Liberty, "Give me your tired, your poor . . . "

GO ON TO THE NEXT PAGE

Questions 47–50 refer to the following quote.

"The black man forfeits his opportunity to speak forcefully and clearly for his race, and he justifies this in terms of expediency. Thus, when one talks of a 'Negro Establishment' in most places in this country, one is talking of an Establishment resting on a white power base; of hand-picked blacks whom that base projects as showpieces out front. These 'black leaders' are, then, only as powerful as their white kingmakers will permit them to be. This is no less true of the North than the South . . . "

—Stokely Carmichael and Charles V. Hamilton *Black Power: The Politics of Liberation in America,* 1967

47. Which of the following organizations would agree with the sentiments of the previous statement?

    (A) National Association for the Advancement of Colored People

    (B) Congress on Racial Equality

    (C) Black Panthers

    (D) Southern Christian Leadership Conference

48. Which of the following leaders from the 1960s would agree most with the sentiments of the above statement?

    (A) John R. Lewis of the Student Non-Violent Coordinating Committee

    (B) Martin Luther King, Jr.

    (C) Ralph Abernathy, Baptist minister and founding member of the SCLC

    (D) Eldridge Cleaver, author of *Soul on Ice*

49. Which of the following most directly caused the belief in the existence of the "Negro Establishment" and its failure to address the needs of African Americans?

    (A) The passage of civil rights legislation in the 1960s and the continued existence of inequality in society

    (B) The continued existence of Jim Crow laws throughout the nation in the late 1960s

    (C) The failure of school integration to bring about equal opportunity for African Americans

    (D) The disproportionate conscription of African American men to fight in the Vietnam conflict

50. The position on equality and civil rights expressed by Carmichael and Hamilton is most similar to the

    (A) work of the suffragists in the 19th century

    (B) concerns of progressives over the living conditions in tenements in the early 20th century

    (C) demands of the members of the American Federation of Labor during the late 19th century

    (D) the ideas espoused by Malcolm X in his support for the Black Muslim movement

GO ON TO THE NEXT PAGE

Questions 51–55 refer to the following photograph.

51. Based on the sentiments expressed in the photograph, one can conclude which of the following?

   (A) Sacco and Vanzetti were not given a fair trial.

   (B) The Sacco and Vanzetti trial drew worldwide attention.

   (C) Many people in other countries did not support the death penalty.

   (D) Freedom of speech is a basic right in England.

52. Which of the following groups at the time would have most likely supported the sentiments shown in the photograph above?

   (A) U.S. businessmen

   (B) U.S. lawmakers

   (C) U.S. immigrants

   (D) U.S. soldiers

53. Which of the following Bill of Rights would most directly support the sentiments expressed in the photograph above?

   (A) The right to keep and bear arms

   (B) The right of accused person to a speedy trial

   (C) Freedom from unreasonable searches and seizures

   (D) Freedom of religion, speech, press, assembly, and petition

GO ON TO THE NEXT PAGE

54. Fifty years after the execution of Sacco and Vanzetti, then Massachusetts governor Michael Dukakis declared that the two men had not been given a fair trial. Given this fact, what conclusion can be drawn about the protest demonstration depicted in the photograph?

(A) Demonstrators hoped to be arrested to show solidarity with Sacco and Vanzetti.

(B) The demonstration was organized by people in the U.S., even though it took place in England.

(C) Demonstrators were justified in their concerns about Sacco and Vanzetti.

(D) The demonstration led to changes in the way evidence is gathered.

55. The ideas expressed in the photograph above most directly reflect which of the following continuities in United States history?

(A) Debates about the judicial system

(B) Debates about immigration

(C) Debates about labor practices

(D) Debates about states' rights

IF YOU FINISH BEFORE TIME IS CALLED, YOU MAY CHECK YOUR WORK ON THIS SECTION ONLY. DO NOT TURN TO ANY OTHER SECTION IN THE TEST. **STOP**

Part B: Short-Answer Questions

Time: 50 Minutes
4 Questions

1. **Quote 1:**

    "A statute which implies merely a legal distinction between the white and colored races—a distinction which is founded in the color of the two races and which must always exist so long as white men are distinguished from the other race by color—has no tendency to destroy the legal equality of the two races, or reestablish a state of involuntary servitude. Indeed, we do not understand that the Thirteenth Amendment is strenuously relied upon by the plaintiff in error in this connection."

    —From *Plessy v. Ferguson* majority decision, May 18, 1896

    Quote 2:

    "Segregation of white and Negro children in the public schools of a State solely on the basis of race, pursuant to state laws permitting or requiring such segregation, denies to Negro children the equal protection of the laws guaranteed by the Fourteenth Amendment—even though the physical facilities and other 'tangible' factors of white and Negro schools may be equal."

    —From *Brown v. Board of Education of Topeka, Kansas* decision, May 17, 1954

    Using the excerpts, answer parts A, B, and C:

    (A) Briefly describe the major premise behind the case relevant to the first quote.
    (B) Briefly describe the major premise behind the case relevant to the second quote.
    (C) Briefly describe events between 1896 and 1954 that led to the dramatic change in interpretation of the law, citing at least one specific event to support your claim.

GO ON TO THE NEXT PAGE

2.

Members of the National Women's Party outside of the White House, 1917

Use the picture to answer parts A, B, and C.

(A) Cite and briefly describe one historical event from the 19th century that expressed similar sentiment to that in the above picture.

(B) Cite and briefly describe one historical event from the early 20th century that is reflected in the above picture.

(C) Briefly describe how the women's movement was active in the second half of the 20th century and cite one specific example to support your answer.

GO ON TO THE NEXT PAGE

3. **Quote 1:**

"On September the 11th, enemies of freedom committed an act of war against our country. Americans have known wars—but for the past 136 years, they have been wars on foreign soil, except for one Sunday in 1941. Americans have known the casualties of war—but not at the center of a great city on a peaceful morning. Americans have known surprise attacks—but never before on thousands of civilians. All of this was brought upon us in a single day—and night fell on a different world where freedom itself was under attack."

—President George W. Bush, address to the nation on September 20, 2001

Quote 2:

"In the last decade [1990s], I have seen firsthand the consequences of armed conflict in Bosnia, Congo, Georgia, Rwanda, Sudan, and Uganda. As a professional in the field of conflict resolution, I have met with government and rebel leaders who argued eloquently, in the words of Bob Dylan's famous sixties song, that 'God was on their side.'

While each conflict may be different in its history and causes, each conflict is the same in causing deaths of innocents. Of the several million people who have been killed in wars in the last decade [1990s], estimates are that 80 percent to 90 percent of these are civilians. No matter how just the cause, these people did not deserve to die."

—Joyce Neu, executive director of the Joan B. Kroc Institute for Peace and Justice on September 27, 2001

Answer parts A, B, and C:

(A) Briefly describe the main idea behind George W. Bush's quote.

(B) Briefly describe the main idea behind Joyce Neu's quote.

(C) Briefly explain the ultimate policy adopted by the United States in dealing with the issues discussed in the two quotes. Provide one specific piece of factual evidence to support your explanation.

GO ON TO THE NEXT PAGE

4. **Political Cartoon 1:**

WELL, I HARDLY KNOW WHICH TO TAKE FIRST!

Boz, Boston Globe, May 28, 1898

Political Cartoon 2:

Source: J.S. Pugh, Puck, September 5, 1900 (adapted)

GO ON TO THE NEXT PAGE

Answer all three parts of the question.

(A) Briefly describe the main point of political cartoon 1 in relation to American overseas expansion at the turn of the 20th century.

(B) Briefly describe the main point of political cartoon 2 in relation to American overseas expansion at the turn of the 20th century.

(C) Briefly explain the action of the United States between the years 1890 and 1914 in reference to expansion policy of the government. Give one specific example to support your answer.

IF YOU FINISH BEFORE TIME IS CALLED, YOU MAY CHECK YOUR WORK ON THIS SECTION ONLY. DO NOT TURN TO ANY OTHER SECTION IN THE TEST.

STOP

Section II

Part A: Document-Based Question

Time: 55 Minutes
1 Question

Directions: Question 1 is based on the accompanying documents. The documents have been edited for the purpose of this exercise. You are advised to spend 15 minutes planning and 40 minutes writing your answer. Write your responses on the lined pages that follow the questions.

1. Analyze the impact of World War II on American national identity and the impact of the constitution on actions undertaken by the federal government.

DOCUMENT 1

"We believe in national unity which recognizes equal opportunity of black and white citizens to jobs in national defense and the armed forces and in all other institutions and endeavors in America. We condemn all dictatorships, Fascist, Nazi and Communist. We are loyal, patriotic Americans, all. But if American democracy will not defend its defenders; if American democracy will not protect its protectors; if American democracy will not insure equality of opportunity, freedom and justice to its citizens, black and white, it is a hollow mockery and belies the principles for which it is supposed to stand. Only power can affect the enforcement and adoption of a given policy. Power is the active principle of only the organized masses, the masses united for a definite purpose. We loyal Negro-American citizens demand the right to work and fight for our country."

Asa Philip Randolph, January 1941, "The Call to March," from *The Black Worker,* May 1941

DOCUMENT 2

"Now therefore, by virtue of the authority vested in me as President of the United States, and Commander in Chief of the Army and Navy, I hereby authorize and direct the Secretary of War, and the Military Commanders whom he may from time to time designate, whenever he or any designated Commander deems such action to be necessary or desirable, to prescribe military areas in such places and of such extent as he or the appropriate Military Commander may determine, from which any or all persons may be excluded, and with respect to which, the right of any persons to enter, remain in, or leave shall be subject to whatever restriction the Secretary of War or the appropriate Military Commander may impose in his discretion."

Executive Order 9066 signed by President Franklin Delano Roosevelt, February 19, 1942

GO ON TO THE NEXT PAGE

DOCUMENT 3

"Rosie the Riveter—We Can Do It" poster, 1942

GO ON TO THE NEXT PAGE ⟶

DOCUMENT 4

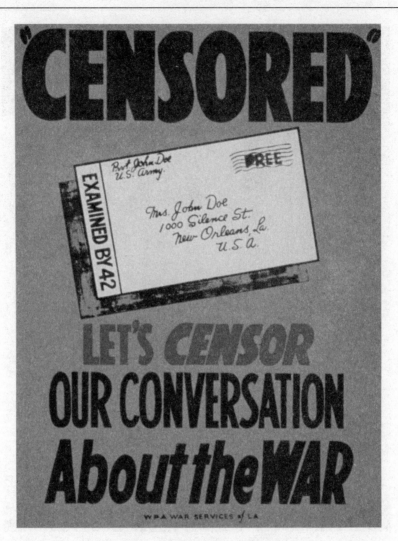

Propaganda supporting censorship during
World War II

GO ON TO THE NEXT PAGE ⇨

DOCUMENT 5

Tuskegee Airmen with white commanding officer, 1944

DOCUMENT 6

"1. Civilian Exclusion Order No. 34 which, during a state of war with Japan and as a protection against espionage and sabotage, was promulgated by the Commanding General of the Western Defense Command under authority of Executive Order No. 9066 and the Act of March 21, 1942, and which directed the exclusion after May 9, 1942, from a described West Coast military area of all persons of Japanese ancestry, held constitutional as of the time it was made and when the petitioner—an American citizen of Japanese descent whose home was in the described area—violated it."

– Supreme Court decision *Korematsu v. U.S.*

GO ON TO THE NEXT PAGE

DOCUMENT 7

Rationing propaganda poster, 1943

IF YOU FINISH BEFORE TIME IS CALLED, YOU MAY CHECK YOUR WORK ON
THIS SECTION ONLY. DO NOT TURN TO ANY OTHER SECTION IN THE TEST.

STOP

Part B: Long Essay Question

Time: 35 Minutes
1 Question

Directions: Choose ONE question from this part. You are advised to spend five minutes planning and 30 minutes writing your answer.

1. Analyze the motives for and the results of U.S. expansion on the North American continent and the impact of this expansion on American economics and politics. Limit your answer to the time period 1803–1865.

2. Analyze the motivations of American expansion at the end of the 19th century and the impact of this expansion on American economics and politics. Limit your answer to the time period 1865–1910.

PRACTICE TEST 4 ANSWER KEY

1.	D	15.	D	29.	B	43.	A
2.	C	16.	B	30.	D	44.	A
3.	A	17.	D	31.	B	45.	D
4.	D	18.	C	32.	B	46.	C
5.	C	19.	A	33.	C	47.	C
6.	C	20.	A	34.	D	48.	D
7.	A	21.	B	35.	A	49.	A
8.	C	22.	B	36.	B	50.	D
9.	B	23.	D	37.	C	51.	B
10.	B	24.	C	38.	B	52.	C
11.	C	25.	B	39.	B	53.	D
12.	D	26.	C	40.	D	54.	C
13.	B	27.	D	41.	C	55.	A
14.	C	28.	A	42.	C		

ANSWERS AND EXPLANATIONS

SECTION I

PART A: MULTIPLE-CHOICE ANSWERS

1. D
The Plains Indians became far more efficient in hunting the bison on the open plains and therefore became more nomadic as they followed the bison herds. The Plains Indians became more competitive and claimed larger tracts of land for their tribal nation. Though the horse did compete with the bison for grassland, it did not cause bison to become almost extinct.

2. C
After the Pueblo Revolt, the Spanish selected 300 men and 200 women (randomly) and killed them. They then cut off the right foot of the remaining surviving men, enslaved the remainder of the adult population, and separated the children from their people and educated them to live in the Spanish culture.

3. A
The *Pennsylvania Charter of Privileges* established the freedom of religion in Penn's colony of Pennsylvania, as long as the individual professed to believe in God, though it did not require Pennsylvanians to attend church services. Maryland was the first British North American colony to tolerate a faith other than the established faith of the colony, which was Catholicism. Although Puritans had banished many Quakers from the New England colonies (in the early 17th century), the Quakers allowed persons of all faiths to live in Pennsylvania.

4. D
The Maryland Act of Toleration is one of the documents that is the foundation of religious freedom in the United States. The document granted equal rights to all residents of Maryland, be they Catholic (the established faith) or Protestant.

5. C
The Bill of Rights guaranteed several freedoms for the American people. One of those freedoms is the freedom of religion. The Declaration of Independence was a justification for America to withdraw from the British Empire, and The South Carolina Exposition and Protest was a statement against the Tariff of 1828. The Alien and Sedition Acts were written to stop criticism against some of the policies of the John Adams administration.

6. C
A political and economic wedge developed between the North and South as the North began to develop industrially, eventually creating the first industrial revolution in the United States. The South's economy and politics were based upon the plantation system, which depended upon the growth of slavery.

7. A
The assembly line revolutionized American industry as it markedly increased production in factories, allowing industrialization to develop more quickly. As a result, human work became less specialized and more unskilled. The development of the assembly line propelled the United States to become the most productive industrial power at the time of World War I.

8. C
The Lowell factory system was developed in the early 1820s as a response to the rapid growth of the cotton industry in the South. Factories in the North were needed to produce textiles. Francis Cabot Lowell built a new type of factory in New England with a dormitory and provided a "cultured life" near the city, a life that the young women would not have experienced if they continued to live in the rural areas of New England.

9. B

The "West," as it was known in the late 18th century, was to be divided, according to Jefferson's plan, into states that would be on an equal par with the original 13. There was no delineation on which territories would be free and which would be slave, and though some land was sold to pay off the debt and to fill the treasury, that was not the purpose of this map. The United States tried to made diplomatic moves toward Spain to be able to use New Orleans, but could not until the signing of Pinckney's Treaty in 1795.

10. B

The English (with American assistance) defeat of the French and Indians in the Seven Years' War (The French and Indian War) gave Americans confidence that the French and Indian "menace" west of the Appalachian Mountains was gone and, despite the issuance of the Proclamation of 1763, many Americans moved west to take advantage of the new territory.

11. C

The Western settlers needed a way to get their produce to market. The Mississippi River system provided the best way to accomplish this but the port of New Orleans was under Spanish control and America needed to make a deal with Spain. This "deal" did not come to pass until 1795 with the signing of Pinckney's Treaty. As the territories were developed (east of the Mississippi) there was little controversy over which would be slave and which would be free. Industrialization was not an issue at the time, and the Land Ordinance of 1785 clearly stated that all new states would be equal with the original 13.

12. D

The Dawes Severalty Act of 1887 proposed that American Indians give up their tribal allegiance and culture in return for an allotment of land and American citizenship. This was a veiled attempt of the American government to dismantle the American Indian nations in order to gain land from them that was currently held in the Indian

Reservations. American Indians rejected this offer. This was a departure from previous government policy as the United States did not force the American Indians to accept this proposal, nor was violence used against the Indians to force them to take the offer.

13. B

The United States would interpret an attempt by any European nation to interfere in the newly independent nations of the Western hemisphere as interference in the affairs of the United States, thus violating American security.

14. C

In his Farewell Address, George Washington expressed that the United States should avoid entangling political alliances, especially with the European powers, as America was not able to get involved in a European war. The Monroe Doctrine extended, to an extent, this concept, warning European powers to not become re-involved in their former colonies in the Western hemisphere, nor should the Europeans consider claiming any new territory in the Western hemisphere.

15. D

The United States remained out of direct involvement in European affairs until the spring of 1917, when the United States declared war on Germany and the Central Powers. This was the first time in American history that the United States became directly involved in what was, at the time, considered a European conflict.

16. B

President James Monroe and his secretary of state John Quincy Adams became proactive in preventing the attempt of the "Holy Alliance" (Russian, Spain, Austria, France) to reclaim Spain's lost colonies in the Western hemisphere as the Europeans believed that the successful independence movements could inspire other peoples within the European sphere to fight for independence.

17. D

Thomas Jefferson's famous "Firebell in the Night" letter was a reaction to the passage of the Missouri Compromise in 1820, as he feared that the slavery issue would further divide the nation.

18. C

Bleeding Kansas was an event that illustrated Jefferson's fear that "every new irritation will mark it deeper and deeper," as Bleeding Kansas was a mini-Civil War fought over the issue of slavery. The South Carolina Exposition and Protest was a reaction to the tariff issue, not slavery. The Indian Removal Act met with very little opposition from most Americans and was not divisive. The destruction of the bank was not the issue covered in Jefferson's letter.

19. A

The Missouri Compromise was an effort to maintain a balance between free and slave states. The addition of Missouri and Maine meant that there were 12 free states and 12 slave states. The Panic of 1819 did not affect westward expansion. The tariff did not become a major issue until 1828, and Mexico was not yet fully independent from Spain. (Note: Mexico declared independence in 1810 but was not fully independent from Spain until 1821.)

20. A

According to Mr. O'Sullivan, part of America's Manifest Destiny was to not only expand across the North American continent but also expand with the purpose of spreading "individual freedom, etc." across the hemisphere; however, he fails to mention that this would be exclusive, mainly for white males.

21. B

The "universal suffrage" and equal rights that O'Sullivan refers to in the quote means "white male suffrage" but in the context of the time period, all white men having the right to vote (regardless of socioeconomic standing) was "universal suffrage." Irish immigrants to the United States in the 1830s and 1840s were discriminated against, especially on the east coast. Women did not enjoy any type of political equality in the United States at the time

of the publication of the excerpt, and plantation owners were of the privileged class and did not believe in equality of all persons (even all whites) and, although they supported Manifest Destiny, they did not support the sentiment of the excerpt.

22. B

The motivation for taking the Philippines after the Spanish-American War was to democratize the "little brown brothers" (according to President William McKinley) and share the superior ideals of the United States with the native population.

23. D

The United States acquired not only all of the claimed territory of Texas but also the vast southwest region of the modern United States through the acquisition of the Mexican Cession, which included California.

24. C

The Mexican Cession was predominantly south of the 36°30′ parallel, causing the South to claim that this region should be open to slavery. The North did not believe the region to be conducive to slavery as it was an arid and mountainous region. A compromise was made in 1850 and the new territories of New Mexico and Utah were open to popular sovereignty.

25. B

After a series of failed compromises (Compromise of 1850, the Kansas–Nebraska Act), the North and South had several differences that continued to create a split between the two regions, a split based on economics, slavery, and states' rights.

26. C

The purpose of the Constitutional Union Party was to focus on the ideals expressed by the founding fathers in the Constitution of the United States and to promote adherence to the laws expressed in the Constitution. (Note: The Constitution Union Party wanted to avoid a civil war at all costs and was made up of politicians who were predominantly from the border states, as they feared a civil war would bring destruction to their states. They were correct.)

27. D

President Woodrow Wilson used similar themes in his justification for declaring war on the Central Powers in World War I. The ideals of "union of the states" was extended to democracy-loving nations and the "enforcement of the laws" referred to the enforcement of international law, as Wilson wanted to see the establishment of a League of Nations to maintain world peace, just as the Constitution Union Party wanted to maintain peace in the United States.

28. A

The South's entire infrastructure was destroyed both physically and economically; the South had no way to maintain a wartime economy toward the end of 1864.

29. B

The Union navy was able to maintain an effective blockade on Southern ports throughout much of the Civil War. The Confederacy's economy suffered greatly and was unable to support the Confederate army or the infrastructure of the South.

30. D

By 1886, two of the most violent events in the United States after the Civil War were the Great Railroad Strike and the Haymarket Affair. Both events hurt the support of labor unions by the American people, as the union movement was looked upon as a radical movement led by anarchists and socialists.

31. B

Grover Cleveland believed that unions were harmful and sent troops in to help break up the Pullman Palace Car railroad strike as it was disrupting American mail service. Samuel Gompers was a founder of the American Federation of Labor and a strong supporter of labor unions; Terence V. Powderly was the president of the Knights of Labor at the time of the Haymarket Affair; and Mother Jones was a radical labor supporter, an early member of the Industrial Workers of the World.

32. B

The Taft-Hartley Act was passed to strip power from labor unions by basically reversing a lot of the autonomy and power they were granted by the Wagner Labor Relations Act from 1935. The War Labor Board was created to create a cooperative relationship between government policy and labor unions during World War I, and President Harry Truman's Fair Deal proposals attempted to give labor more bargaining power.

33. C

Based on the excerpt, an owner in the late 19th century paid his workers "as little as he could." Workers made very little—there was no minimum wage in the 19th century—and industrialists made huge profits.

34. D

Bellamy was criticizing the unrestricted capitalism in which workers were paid very little and wound up living in poverty, despite working 14-hour days. Bellamy proposed a world based on equality of all workers, considered to be Marxist by social intellectuals of the 19th century.

35. A

Many social utopian communities were established on the ideals of a classless society based upon the equality of all. Examples would be New Harmony in Indiana, the Amana Community in Iowa, and the Oneida Community in New York. Abolitionists supported the end of slavery but not necessarily the equality of all, nor, in general, did advocates of Indian Removal. Transcendentalists may have held some of the same philosophic beliefs as Bellamy, but for the most part were not as radical in their ideals.

36. B

The Agricultural Adjustment Act and the National Industrial Recovery Act were both declared unconstitutional by the U.S. Supreme Court, causing President Roosevelt to request legislation that would allow him to appoint one Supreme Court Justice for each one aged 70 years and six months or older. There were six justices that FDR deemed as "too old," and therefore he wanted to appoint six more. This idea brought a lot of criticism to FDR, because even some of his strongest allies in the Democratic Party saw this as an attempt to control the judicial branch of government.

37. C

Union Democrats were the demographic most loyal to the New Deal, based on those listed, largely due to the passage of the Wagner Labor Relations Act in 1935. Liberal Republicans believed that President Roosevelt was taking too much authority upon himself and the executive branch; Southern farmers tended to be more conservative and resented government interference in what they could and could not grow; and, although Southern Democrats supported most of Roosevelt's laws, they believed he was trying to exercise too much control over the federal government.

38. B

Andrew Jackson was outraged at the Supreme Court's decision (especially that of Chief Justice John Marshall) that expressed the opinion that the Georgia Cherokee Indians had a right to their land.

39. B

The development of the steel industry in the late 19th century, led by Andrew Carnegie, made the United States one of the largest exporting nations in the world.

40. D

Vertical and horizontal integration were two types of monopolies that developed legally during the late 19th century. An example of vertical integration is Andrew Carnegie's control of the steel industry: He owned steel production and the source for raw materials to make steel. An example of horizontal integration is John D. Rockefeller's Standard Oil in which one company owns all of the means of distribution of a product.

41. C

The Clayton Antitrust Act, passed in 1914, added substance to the antitrust legislation established with the Sherman Antitrust act, which had very little in the way of enforcement written into the law. The Sherman Act was not effective.

42. C

John Steinbeck described the plight of the Okies in his book *The Grapes of Wrath*, focusing on the trek made on Route 66 from Oklahoma City to California by the Joad family. The passage does not explain the Great Migration of African Americans, as they generally headed toward northern cities, where many found low-paying jobs. The *braceros* were invited into the United States; they settled in Texas and Arizona, taking low-wage jobs in some factories and also working as migrant farmers. The passage is not a metaphor of the trip made by European immigrants. Steinbeck wrote about the "American experience."

43. A

Many of the migrants were "Okies" from the Dust Bowl region. They had been tenant farmers who lost their jobs/land because they could not pay off their debts. Many fled to California with the false hope that jobs were plentiful and paid well. Many of these people shared similar experiences and huddled together to (paraphrasing Steinbeck) share their misery.

44. A

The modern (late 20th and early 21st century) immigrants were very similar to those who came to the United States one century before: many had skills, while many did not, and they came for an opportunity they could not get in their home countries. Many took the only jobs they could get, to begin a better life.

45. D

The Irish were fleeing starvation in their homeland as the potato famine raged on. Many Irish were unskilled workers but found menial jobs in the United States. Old immigrants were usually skilled workers or were farmers and moved toward the Midwest when they arrived in the United States. French immigrants arrived, many with skills, and assimilated into the rural agricultural community. The Chinese came to make their fortune but were not welcomed by the California settlers.

46. C

As a reaction to modern immigration, some political segments of society want to severely restrict immigration of all groups, as many Americans believe them to be a threat to their way of life. The Adams administration passed the Alien and Sedition Acts to end criticism of President John Adams's policies, which violated the freedom of speech and press, and to prevent French immigrants from obtaining citizenship and being able to vote. The Know-Nothings formed in response to the influx of Irish and German Catholics based upon the fear of a "papal plot to overrun the U.S. with European Catholics." A significant segment of American society wish to limit immigration to the United States and wish to build a wall to prevent people from coming to the United States illegally; they do not want to accept any immigrant group who would like to enter the United States.

47. C

Stokely Carmichael was a founding member of the Black Panthers, who were frustrated with what they perceived as the lack of success on the part of the civil rights movement in the 1960s. The NAACP, CORE, and the SCLC were all part of the "Negro Establishment" that Carmichael and Hamilton were writing about in their book.

48. D

Eldridge Cleaver, at least at the publication of the above excerpt, was a member of the Black Panthers (later in life Mr. Cleaver became a businessman, a Mormon, and a conservative Republican). John Lewis (SNCC) was a civil rights leader who marched with Martin Luther King, Jr.—he was part of the "Negro Establishment" Carmichael was complaining about. Martin Luther King, Jr. was the epitome of the "Negro Establishment" in the 1960s. Ralph Abernathy was also a member of the "Negro Establishment."

49. A

Despite the passage of the Civil Rights Act of 1964 and the Civil (Voting) Rights Act of 1965, Carmichael and Hamilton believed that economic inequality and social injustice were prominent in the African American community and that not much progress had been made.

50. D

Malcolm X was vocal about his frustration with mainstream civil rights leadership and expressed the idea that the civil rights movement needed to be more demanding and, to an extent, forceful than it was. The remaining groups were, for the most part, not too radical.

51. B

Answer B is the best answer. This photograph, taken in England, depicts the worldwide attention that the trial drew.

52. C

Answer C is the best answer. Many felt at the time that the atmosphere in this country caused people to be suspicious of foreigners like Sacco and Vanzetti, and that these suspicions were often unfounded. Therefore, U.S. immigrants would have been the group to most likely support the sentiments shown in the photograph.

53. D

Answer D is the best answer. Though the demonstration shown in the photograph relates to Sacco and Vanzetti and their rights as accused persons, the photograph more directly supports freedom of religion, speech, press, assembly, and petition.

54. C

Answer C is the best answer. Based on Governor Dukakis's declaration, as well as objections that evidence in the trial was circumstantial, one can conclude that the demonstrators shown in the photograph were justified in expressing their concerns about Sacco and Vanzetti.

55. A

Answer A is the best answer. The Sacco and Vanzetti trial most directly reflects the continuing debate about the effectiveness of our judicial system to guarantee a fair trial based on reasonable evidence.

PART B: SHORT-QUESTION RESPONSES

1. (A) The 1896 Supreme Court case *Plessy* v. *Ferguson* established the idea that the "separate but equal" facilities for whites and African Americans were constitutional. This granted the right to states, many in the South, to build separate school systems for white and African American children and it legalized the idea of separate waiting areas at train stations and other public accommodations.

    (B) The 1954 *Brown* v. *Board of Education of Topeka, Kansas* Supreme Court case overturned the "separate but equal" clause of *Plessy* v. *Ferguson*, as the Warren Court determined that "separate but equal" was inherently unequal and, therefore, unconstitutional. The result of this case was the integration of public schools. This legal victory inspired other civil rights events like the Montgomery Bus Boycott to take place.

    (C) African Americans had been working toward civil rights and equality since the time of Reconstruction. Without much success, African Americans began to develop and celebrate their own identity through the Harlem Renaissance, where the idea of racial pride was expressed through art, music, and literature. This racial pride gave African Americans confidence to begin fighting for their constitutional equality.

2. (A) In 1848, several women gathered in Seneca Falls, New York, to hold a convention to discuss more civil rights for women. The group produced the Declaration of Sentiments, borrowing the ideas of the Declaration of Independence in their defense of equality for women.

    (B) Alice Paul and other suffragists protested outside of the White House during World War I and immediately afterward to draw attention to the idea that women were still considered second-class citizens. At this time, some states had granted women the right to vote, and the state of Montana had even elected Jeanette Rankin to the U.S. House of Representatives in 1916, but suffrage was still not universal.

    (C) After the passage of the Nineteenth Amendment, which gave women the right to vote, Alice Paul immediately began demanding that an "equal rights" amendment be added to the Constitution in which no right can be denied to a person on account of her sex. Although the amendment did not pass a Congressional vote until the 1960s, it did not become part of the Constitution, as the minimum required number of states to ratify the amendment was never reached.

3. (A) President George W. Bush addressed the nation about the terrorist attacks made against the United States on September 11, 2001. Bush's main argument was that American freedom was under attack, and he was preparing the nation for the possibility of going to war to protect the freedoms Americans expect to enjoy in a democratic nation.

    (B) During the time of the September 11, 2001, attacks, many American politicians were in agreement with President Bush that Americans might need to prepare for war. However,

Joyce Neu, a respected conflict negotiator, crafted the argument that war was senseless, like in the conflicts she had witnessed, and too many innocents were killed. Therefore, Ms. Neu was trying to reverse the call for military intervention.

(C) The United States went to war, a multilateral war working with other NATO nations in their invasion of Afghanistan whose government was controlled by the Taliban, which was harboring training camps for terrorist organizations like al-Qaeda. The United States and some allies also invaded Iraq to bring down a terrorist regime that was also aiding various terror organizations and was thought to be holding "weapons of mass destruction" that would be used against Americans or their allies.

4. (A) The political cartoon expresses the opinion that an American empire was there for the taking by the United States (symbolized by the Uncle Sam character). President McKinley was in a position to offer the United States many new colonies based on the mood of the nation and the American success in their war with Spain. In the late 19th century, the United States gained its empire and was a source of pride for all Americans as, in that time, it was believed the United States could teach the people of these colonies how to "properly govern" themselves.

(B) The political cartoon "Declined with Thanks" expresses the idea that as a civilized nation the United States should not be taking on an empire. Members of the anti-imperialist side of the debate are offering Uncle Sam an opportunity to slim down, not take on any extra "weight" of colonies. However, Uncle Sam is politely declining the offer and wishes to remain "heavy."

(C) At the turn of the 20th century, the United States gained an empire mainly as a result of the Spanish-American War. The Philippines, Puerto Rico, and Guam were all added to Alaska and Midway Island. In 1898, the United States also annexed Hawaii. America's overseas policy became more aggressive as the United States made protectorates of various nations, hoping to maintain an agreeable relationship between the United States and those nations.

SECTION II

PART A: DBQ SAMPLE RESPONSES

The need for more laborers, soldiers, and support for the American cause during World War II dramatically altered American identity. However, at the time society was seemingly becoming more inclusive, some constitutionally questionable decisions were made that also altered the United States. Overall, World War II changed the face of the United States and set into motion movements that would transform what it meant to be an American in the decades to come.

As war seemed inevitable, Americans were called to factories to begin the process of rebuilding American military power and to also bolster America's only free ally, Great Britain. Most factories employed white men exclusively as most unionized jobs were held by whites. As America seemed to be preparing for war A. Philip Randolph, president of the Brotherhood of Sleeping Car Porters, started a movement to allow African Americans to gain access to jobs preparing for the war effort. Mr. Randolph threatened a "March on Washington" if "loyal Negro citizens" were not granted the right to work in the common effort to defeat Nazi Germany (Doc. 1). President Franklin Roosevelt responded with an executive order to require that all industries with government contracts hire African Americans. As the United States entered the war, the call for soldiers increased, and millions of men volunteered to fight to defeat Germany and Japan, including African Americans. While still having to serve in segregated units that had white officers, thousands of African American men served proudly. An example of their ability to fight well was demonstrated by the all-black Tuskegee Airmen who flew many missions with distinction (Doc. 5). Although inequality lasted for the duration of the war, the foundations for a modern civil rights movement were being created as acceptance of African Americans into traditional roles in the military began to extend to other aspects of American life.

Women began to change their role in American society to one in which they would be looked upon as more of an equal to men. As the war progressed and more men went off to serve in the military, more women were required to take their place in factories. "Rosie the Riveter" became an American icon during the war, where she demonstrated her devotion to the cause to defeat the Axis Powers (Doc. 3). African American women made great strides in society as they left their traditional service jobs as maids and washer-women and also took the role of Rosie. Women also joined the military in the WACS, WAVES, and WASPS, and although they usually served in clerical positions, they were able to free more men to fight in the war effort. After the war ended, many women remained on the job as their husbands returned home and took advantage of the GI Bill and went to college. Women remaining on the job led to an evolution of a society with dual-income homes. Women's identity as Americans thus was changing, as they became breadwinners and also gained respect as equals.

While African Americans and women were becoming more identified as equals and as "Americans," Japanese Americans were forced to lose what little American identity they had gained. Executive order 9066, signed by FDR after the Japanese attack on Pearl Harbor, forced thousands of *Nisei* and *Issei* to be sent to detention centers (Doc. 2). Families were forced to live in limited quarters with no freedoms. This action was declared constitutional by the Supreme Court in the 1944 decision *Korematsu v. U.S.* as the fear of espionage and sabotage seemed to be very real in places like California after America was attacked by Japan (Doc. 6). Therefore, although African Americans and women were beginning to take on the identity as full citizens, Americans of Japanese descent did not.

As the constitutionality of the detention of a group of Americans was determined, the constitutionality of censorship was not. During World War II, Americans gave up some of the freedoms that identified them as Americans; for example, the U.S. mail was censored to potentially protect the well-being of American troops overseas (Doc. 4). Americans also temporarily lost the freedom to buy as much of certain products through rationing.

For the duration of World War II, American identity changed. Groups traditionally not granted full rights as citizens were gaining more respect from those who had had rights and power since the inception of the United States. Within twenty years of the conclusion of the war, African Americans and women had made legal gains that led them to equality; even Japanese Americans had made headway to a semblance of equality. And as the war ended, Americans expected their freedoms to be restored. While Americans held proudly to their identity, it was clear that they were willing to give up some of the ideals they held as part of their identity and were also willing to expand the scope of who was considered an American during a time of national emergency.

Overall, this essay is very thorough and develops the analysis well. Considering there is a 45-minute suggested time limit for writing the DBQ essay, this essay is clear and well supported. It utilizes and analyzes all six documents very accurately. The narrative is complemented by outside information, which is also explained well.

This essay has a strong thesis, very clear and relevant and the context of the question is also very clear. This thesis would earn the one point possible for the thesis.

The use of factual information is exceptional, and the information is explained very well and is nicely linked to the analytic information. This essay would receive all 4 possible points for the analysis of historical evidence and support.

The context of the analysis is very clear; the reader can tell exactly when the events are taking place in American history. One point for the context out of 1 point available.

The evidence and analysis are all synthesized into a clear and well-developed narrative. One point of 1 for synthesis.

The total score for this essay would be a 7 out of 7 possible points.

PART B: LONG ESSAY SAMPLE RESPONSES

RESPONSE 1

From its inception in the United States, Americans were inspired by the West. The West had a fluid boundary and as the United States grew in population, the people looked to new opportunity that was possibly out there. Through the 19th century, the West had a profound impact on the development of the United States, both economically and politically, as the nation became wealthier and had more commercial potential, and this economic growth was aided by political developments of the second half of the century.

At the turn of the 19th century, President Thomas Jefferson was presented with an opportunity few world leaders had seen, the chance to double the size of the fledgling nation and remove the potential threat of one European power that claimed territory on the continent. Although there were some constitutional questions, President Jefferson purchased Louisiana from France, not only to gain complete control of the important port of New Orleans but also to increase America's legitimacy on the continent. Almost immediately "western farmers" in the Tennessee and Ohio River Valleys were able to ship their goods to international markets. The development of the cotton gin opened all of the river systems west of the Appalachian Mountains to the plantation system. In the North, small factories were built, eventually expanding into larger factories. These economic opportunities lay the groundwork for the development of differing regional political points of view that would eventually divide the nation.

During the second quarter of the 19th century, Manifest Destiny began to capture the imagination of Americans. After being able to successfully move American Indians off their tribal homeland in the Southeast and Ohio River Valley and occupy that land, Americans saw the territory west of the Mississippi River as the new area for development. The annexation of Texas and the beginning of the development of the Great Plains opened what would become America's heartland. This phase of westward growth continued to create friction between the developing industrial North and the plantation South. The motives for the Mexican War were hotly debated between North and South, and sectionalism and the desire for expansion grew in intensity. This split eventually led to the Civil War, a period of heightened political divide and also a time when expansion came to a temporary halt.

After the Civil War, Americans began to occupy the vast spaces between the Great Plains and California, which aided the further development of the American economy. With the war solving some of the political angst that had existed, America was able to develop in the East, and with the availability of precious metals in the West and the expansion of the railroad, the American economy ignited in the rapid growth of the industrial revolution. In the final quarter of the 19th century, the United States became one of the most industrialized nations in the world; politically, however, America became somewhat stagnant as neither major political party took a hard stance on any issue except to promote a *laissez-faire* attitude to allow big business to continue to grow, create jobs, and enrich the United States.

The United States was motivated to occupy a significant segment of North America for protection, national destiny, and economic development. During the 19th century, the U.S.-held territory from the Atlantic to the Pacific, and by the end of the century had one of the five most productive economies in the world. By the end of the century, American growth and development on the continent led to American interest in expanding overseas and the acquisition of colonies.

This essay clearly establishes the context of the time period and incorporates a strong thesis statement that is addressed throughout the essay. The chronological development is very clear, demonstrating a progression from the Louisiana Purchase to Manifest Destiny and the post–Civil War years. The essay also weaves the political changes and impact very neatly into the economic development of America.

There is sufficient factual support for the thesis, making the narrative very clear and easy to understand. The information also synthesizes the information with the thesis, clearly addressing all aspects of the question.

The conclusion is very clear and neatly ties the time period together. This essay would receive a 6 out of 6 possible points of the Long Essay Question rubric.

Sample 2

After the Civil War, the United States entered the industrial revolution, which brought America into the modern age as an equal competitor with Great Britain and France. Factories created thousands of jobs, output grew exponentially, and soon the United States was a leading industrialized power. However, America's prosperity met with some challenges. Through the late 19th century, the United States suffered through two major economic panics, creating unemployment and dire results such as a decrease in salary for many workers (resulting in violent strikes) and unemployment for others. These economic crises, coupled with ideals based on racial and social superiority, created a debate on whether the United States should take on a worldwide empire, much like those of America's two economic rivals—Britain and France. Ultimately by the turn of the 20th century, the United States had acquired an empire that greatly impacted the nation's politics and economy but not in an entirely positive manner.

During the industrial revolution, groups of Americans began to extol the superiority that the nation possessed. Individuals such as Josiah Strong praised the preeminence of the Anglo-Saxon race that populated the United States as he argued that God sent the best people of the European nations to create this great nation; in other words, the United States was the "best of the best," and it was America's duty to share its greatness and liberty with those not as blessed. This concept followed the ideas espoused in Rudyard Kipling's *White Man's Burden*. While Strong's opinion was more popular in the United States, not all Americans agreed with his idea, arguing that America becoming an empire would be counter to the values held by the nation as illustrated in the Constitution and the Declaration of Independence.

Coupled with America's dramatic economic growth and the desire to spread liberty worldwide, an argument developed that would encourage the building of a two-ocean American navy, led by naval captain Alfred Thayer Mahan. The argument focused on the fact that the United States was a two-ocean nation and that in order to protect the country, a two-ocean navy was needed. To supply a strong two-ocean navy, the United States needed refueling stations located around the world.

With the impact of the Panic of 1893 greatly felt around the nation, business leaders began supporting the idea that if the United States possessed an empire, American factories could sell more of its products overseas; more consumers equals a lesser chance of economic recession. With this philosophy added to the desire to spread liberty, many Americans began to support the idea of becoming more aggressive in taking an empire. First came a half-successful attempt at annexing Hawaii in 1893; President Grover Cleveland vetoed this idea. Later, in 1898, those who supported bringing Hawaii in as part of the United States were more successful, as President William McKinley was more than happy to sign to necessary legislation. Also, in 1898, the United States, in an effort to free Cubans of the "horrible human rights violations" of the Spanish government, went to war and not only gained Cuba's freedom but took the Philippines, Guam, and Puerto Rico from Spanish control.

Overall, a combination of spreading American liberty, gaining economic resources and new markets, plus having the ability to build naval bases around the globe motivated the United States to achieve, although not to the same level as Britain and France, an empire.

This analysis begins with a well-established context of the time period and a strong thesis statement that is addressed throughout the essay. The topical development is very clear, demonstrating a strong desire for overseas expansion and illustrating the impact it had in America.

There is above-average factual support for the thesis, making the narrative clear and easy to understand. The information also synthesizes the information with the thesis, clearly addressing all aspects of the question, although more development would have strengthened the argument.

The conclusion is clear. This essay would receive a 5 out of 6 possible points of the Long Essay Question rubric.

GLOSSARY

abolitionist
one who favors or works for the end of slavery

affirmative action
policies of the government aimed at increasing access to jobs, schooling, and opportunities to people previously discriminated against

agrarian
pertaining to farming or agriculture

anarchist
an individual who opposes of all forms of government

annexation
the act of incorporating a smaller territory into a larger one

antebellum
before the war; usually used to denote the time before the Civil War

anti-Semitic
having or showing prejudice against Jewish people

appeasement
a policy of giving into the demands of an enemy to avoid conflict

apportionment
the proportional distribution of the number of members of the U.S. House of Representatives on the basis of the population of each state

arbitration
the settlement of a dispute by a third, unbiased party

armistice
a suspension of fighting; a cease-fire

arsenal
a stockpile of weapons or a place for making and storing weapons

artisans
those considered skilled in certain occupations such as metalwork, carpentry, or printing

autocrat
a ruler having unlimited power; a despot

bandwagon
a political cause that draws increasing numbers of proponents because of its success

bicameral
political system based on two legislative chambers

blasphemy

a contemptuous or profane act, utterance, or writing concerning God or a sacred entity

blitzkrieg

Hitler's tactic of "lighting war," which involved swift action against the enemy

bond

an interest-bearing note issued by the government that guarantees repayment at a set date

boycott

to refrain from engaging, purchasing, or trading with another in an expression of protest

bracero

a Mexican farm worker brought to the United States to work during World War II

buying on margin

the act of purchasing stock on credit

capitalism

an economic system in which the means of production are controlled by individuals

caravel

any of several types of small, light sailing ships, especially one with two or three masts and lateen sails used by the Spanish and Portuguese in the 15th and 16th centuries

carpetbagger

a Northern Republican who moved South for financial and political gain after the civil war

ceded

given or surrendered to another, possibly by treaty

charter

a written document conferring the power of self-rule

closed shop

a workplace in which workers must join the labor union as a condition of employment

collective bargaining

the process by which organized workers and management negotiate wages, working conditions, and work hours

confederation

an alliance or body of countries, states, or groups loosely united for common purposes

conscription

compulsory enrollment of people in the armed forces

constituents

the voters or citizens of a particular region who are represented by an elected official

conquistador

a Spanish conqueror of the Americas

conversion experience

a rite of passage for Calvinists who publicly confessed all sins to become one of the "elect"

corollary

an inference that follows proof from a previous instance, often considered secondary

coup

the overthrow of a ruling party/person by a small group illegally and/or by force

de facto

"in fact"; usually used with regard to segregation

de jure

"in law"; usually used with regard to laws passed for segregation

demography

the study of the characteristics of human populations, such as size, growth, density, distribution, and vital statistics

depression

a prolonged period of declining economic activity characterized by rising unemployment and falling prices

détente

a period of relaxed tensions between countries

direct primary

an election in which registered members of a political party elect who their party nominees for office will be

dissenter

a protester or someone who has beliefs and opinions that differ from those of the majority

domestic policies

policies relating to a country's internal affairs

duty

a tax on imported goods

egalitarian

upholding the equality of all people

elect

according to Calvinists, those who have been chosen by God for salvation

elite

a group or class of persons or a member of such a group or class enjoying advanced intellectual, social, or economic status

emancipate

to free from slavery or bondage

embargo

a prohibition or ban, usually used with regard to trade or shipping

encomienda

the Spanish colonial labor system whereby Native Americans were bound to unpaid labor but were not legally owned by a master

enfranchise

to give the right to vote

entrepreneur

a person who who organizes and assumes the financial risks involved with a new business or enterprise

established church

a church that is officially recognized and protected by the government

excise tax

a fee collected on goods and services manufactured, bought, and sold within a country

executive privilege

the claim by a president that certain information is exempt from disclosure

expatriates

individuals who have chosen to leave their native country in favor of living abroad

fascism

a dictatorial form of government that glorifies militarism and nationalism

filibuster

the act of members of Congress of delaying a vote or action by refusing to release the floor during debate

Fire Eaters

term used by Northerners for extreme Southern slavery advocates

foreclosure

the repossession of a property by a lender after a borrower fails to repay the loan

fundamentalism

a religious movement or point of view characterized by a return to rigid adherence to fundamental principles

genocide

the systematic extermination of a race or ethnicity by another group

ghetto

an area where minority groups live, often due to social, legal, or economic pressure

graft

the use of public office to gain money or property illegally

greenback

paper currency that was not backed by gold or silver

gross national product (GNP)

the value of all goods and services produced within of a country in a given year

guerrilla warfare

irregular military tactics used to harass and surprise the enemy

headright system

a system in colonial times in which one received 50 acres of land for every indentured servant one sponsored

heresy

an opinion or a doctrine at variance with established religious beliefs

hierarchy

a system that places things in graduated order, from lowest to highest

homestead

a single-family home or farm

horizontal integration

the combining of businesses that are engaged in similar activities

ideology

a systematic body of ideas and beliefs that characterize an individual, culture, or large group

impeachment

charging a government official with a criminal offense

imperialism

a policy of extending a country's authority over a foreign country by domination

impress

to force into military service

incumbent

an individual running for an office he or she currently holds

indentured servant

a person who is bonded or contracted to work for another for a specified time in exchange for learning a trade or for travel expenses

indigenous

native to a particular region

inflation

an increase in the general price level, resulting in a decrease in the value of currency

infrastructure

the systems needed for the functioning of a society; usually transportation, sanitation, and communication

initiative

process by which voters can propose legislation and place that law on a ballot in a popular election

insurrection

the act or an instance of open revolt against civil authority or government

isolationist

an individual who advocated remaining uninvolved in world affairs

Jim Crow Laws

state and local laws enacted in the South after Reconstruction that discriminated against African Americans and supported segregation

jingoism

extreme nationalism coupled with a belligerent foreign policy

joint-stock company

a form of business organization in which investors can independently sell their shares of the company

laissez-faire

the doctrine that government should refrain from interfering in business and the economy

landslide

the winning of an election by a large margin

literacy test

an exam once given to individuals to prove they could read and write before they could vote

mandate

a command or instruction given by the electorate to its representative

martial law

military rule imposed upon an area when civilian agencies have failed or collapsed

martyr

an individual who makes a great sacrifice to further a cause; one who chooses death rather than renounce beliefs

materialism

a belief that the accumulation of possessions is more important than spiritual or intellectual pursuits

matrilineal

relating to, based on, or tracing ancestral descent through the maternal line

mercantilism

the theory that state power depends on wealth

mercenaries

foreign soldiers hired to serve in the military

mestizo

a person of European and Native American ancestry in a Spanish colony

mudslinging

unsubstantiated accusations and attacks on a political opponent

mulatto

an individual of African and European ancestry

nation-state

a political unit that has a defined territory and that is organized under a government, which has the power to make and enforce law

nationalism

devotion to the interests or culture of one's nation

nativism

the policy of favoring the rights of native citizens over those of immigrants

naturalization

the process of immigrants gaining citizenship

nullify

to declare a law void

oligarchy

rule by a few

omnibus bill

a potential law that includes a variety of measures under one bill

pacifist

an individual who is opposed to all war

pardon

the act of releasing an individual from responsibility for a crime

partisan

supporting a particular political party

patronage

the practice of rewarding political allies and supporters with jobs

peculiar institution

a name given to slavery by Southern apologists

political machine

an organization controlled through spoils and patronage

poll tax

a tax levied on individuals before they can vote

pool

an alliance of competing companies created to set prices and split profits by sharing customers

pork barrel

congressional appropriations made for political gain by a lawmaker for his or her particular constituency

precedent

a judicial decision that establishes a standard for later similar cases

predestination

the doctrine that God has foreordained all things, especially that God has chosen certain souls for eternal salvation

primogeniture

the right of the eldest child, especially the eldest son, to inherit the entire estate of one or both parents

proclamation

an official announcement

propaganda

information or materials provided by the proponents or opponents of an idea or cause to influence public thought

proprietary colony

territories granted by a king or queen to one or more proprietors who had full governing rights

proviso

a document or clause within a document that stipulates an exception or restriction

pump priming

an increase in government spending to stimulate the economy

puppet government

a government that is controlled by outsiders

quota

a proportional share of something to a group or members of a group; an allotment

ratification

the act of approving and giving formal sanction

recall

the act of removing a public official from office by a vote of citizens

referendum

the submission of a public measure directly to voters

reparations

payments made by a government for destruction and damage caused during a war

republic

a government whose power rests in a citizenry who vote for officials responsible to them

Rust Belt
states in the Northeast and Midwest that were once prosperous industrial centers

scabs
nonunion replacement workers during a strike

scalawag
a white Southerner who supported Radical Reconstruction

secession
the withdrawal from an alliance or association

sect
a group of people forming a distinct unit within a larger group by virtue of certain distinctions of belief or practice

secular
of worldly concern rather than religious in nature

sedition
actions or language inciting of rebellion against the government

segregation
the policy or practice of separating, usually regarding race and ethnicity

self-determination
the belief that people should have the opportunity to decide their own form of government

sharecropper
an individual who receives land on credit and pays back debt with a share of the crop yield

siege
the surrounding and blockading of a city, town, or fortress by an army attempting to capture it

socialist
an individual who believes that the means of production should be controlled by the community, not individuals

sovereignty
a nation-state's right to rule itself

speakeasies
illegal bars and clubs where liquor was sold during Prohibition

specie
coined (gold, silver, or other metal) currency

speculation
making risky business investments

sphere of influence
a region of a nation controlled by a foreign power

spoils system
the practice of the winning political party rewarding supporters with jobs, regardless of qualifications

stagflation
a combination of high unemployment and high inflation

stalwart
an individual who has unwavering support for a party or cause

strike
an action by organized labor to stop work in order to force management to negotiate

subversion
a systematic attempt to overthrow or undermine a government or political system by persons working from within

suffrage
the right to vote

Sun Belt

states in the southern and southwestern United States

tariffs

taxes placed on imported goods

temperance

the belief in moderation, particularly with regard to the use of alcohol

tenant farmer

a person who leases land from a landowner

tenement

an urban multifamily housing unit

theocracy

a government by religious rule

trust

an organization of corporations formed to gain control of an industry to reduce or eliminate competition

tycoon

a wealthy and powerful businessperson

urbanization

the growth of cities

utopian

seeking perfection in society

vertical integration

control of all aspects of manufacturing a good by a single company

Vietnamization

President Nixon's policy of turning over the Vietnam War to the South Vietnamese

virtual representation

the political practice of a small group of people being elected to speak for a larger group

wildcat banks

uncontrolled and unregulated western banks of the 1800s whose speculation and other risky practices helped spur the Panic of 1819

writ of habeas corpus

from the Latin "of the body," a formal order requiring the presentation of the accused before a judge to be charged with a crime or released from custody

yellow-dog contracts

agreements that forced employees to promise never to join a union in order to gain or maintain employment

yeomen

non-slave-owning farmers

PERMISSIONS